MEKHILTA DE-RABBI ISHMAEL

The publication of this book is made possible through these generous gifts:

In Loving Memory of Mayer and Basia Lauterbach and Jacob S. Lauterbach
by Ram and Ruth Lauterbach Gophna

Amy Lauterbach Kinkade

In Memory of Maks, Eugenia and Otto Lauterbach
by Ann and Alex Lauterbach, Robert and Cheri Lauterbach Family,
Jeanne and Eric Steinhauer Family, Debbie Lauterbach Abrams
and Paul Abrams Family

In Loving Memory of Clara and Samuel Lauterbach and Jacob Z. Lauterbach
by Mr. and Mrs. Bernard S. Lauterbach

In Memory of Henry Lauterbach
by Dr. Janina Lauterbach, Diana and Marvin Sugarman and Family,
Sandra and Alain Rogier and Family

Steve and Ann Lauterbach

Barbara Lauterbach Loeser

Deborah Lauterbach Robalin

Rachel Lauterbach Schulbaum

and also through gifts from:

Rabbi Eliot J. Baskin ♦ Batsheva and Dan Ben-Amos ♦ Rabbi Kenneth E. Berger ♦
Rabbi David Bockman, Raleigh, North Carolina ♦ Rabbi Scott M. Corngold ♦ Jeff and
Pat Feinberg ♦ Rabbi Ronne Friedman ♦ Rabbi Bernard H. Mehlman ♦ Rabbi Stephen
Fuchs ♦ Rabbi Albert E. Gabbai, Congregation Mikveh Israel ♦ The Gendler Family
Foundation ♦ Rabbi Neal and Heidi Gold ♦ Rabbi and Mrs. Harvey Goldscheider ♦
Rabbi Sherre Z. Hirsch ♦ Charles S. Houser ♦ Jewish Congregation at Graterford ♦
Harris and Eliza Kempner Fund ♦ Rabbi Jimmy Kessler ♦ Rabbi and Mrs. Barry S.
Kogan ♦ Rabbi Dr. Murray J. Kohn ♦ Rabbi Arthur Lavinsky ♦ Rabbi and Mrs. Robert
Layman ♦ Rabbi Shalom Lewis ♦ Rabbi Norman S. Lipson ♦ Morton J. and Arlene G.
Merowitz ♦ Patricia and Elliot Mininberg ♦ Barry and Carol Nove ♦ The Rabbi's Good
Works Fund of Temple Sholom of West Essex ♦ Rabbi Aaron M. Petuchowski ♦ Rabbi
Jonathan Stein ♦ Rabbi Ira F. Stone ♦ Temple Beth Torah, Westbury, NY ♦ Temple Mount
Sinai, El Paso ♦ Rabbi Lawrence Troster ♦ Eliana and Rabbi David Wolpe

MEKHILTA DE-RABBI ISHMAEL

A CRITICAL EDITION, BASED ON THE MANUSCRIPTS
AND EARLY EDITIONS, WITH AN ENGLISH
TRANSLATION, INTRODUCTION, AND NOTES

BY

JACOB Z. LAUTERBACH, Ph.D.

VOLUME TWO

New Introduction by David Stern

2004 • 5765

THE JEWISH PUBLICATION SOCIETY
PHILADELPHIA

The Jewish Publication Society
2100 Arch Street
Philadelphia, PA 19103

Composition by Varda Graphics
Manufactured in the United States of America

04 05 06 07 08 09 10   10 9 8 7 6 5 4 3 2

Library of Congress Cataloging-in-Publication Data

Mekhilta of Rabbi Ishmael. English.
  Mekhilta de-Rabbi Ishmael / translated by Jacob Z. Lauterbach. — New ed.
    p. cm.
  Originally published: Philadelphia: Jewish Publication Society of America, 1933–1935.
  Includes bibliographical references and index.
  ISBN 0-8276-0678-8
    1. Bible. O.T. Exodus—Commentaries—Early works to 1800. I. Lauterbach, Jacob
Zallel, 1873–1942. II. Title.

BM517.M4 E5 2001
296.1'4—dc21   00-055291

CONTENTS

VOLUME I

VOLUME II

INTRODUCTION TO THE 2004 EDITION

The *Mekhilta de-Rabbi Ishmael* is the classic anthology of early rabbinic interpretations of the Book of Exodus and one of our earliest sources for midrash, as the activity of biblical commentary that was practiced by the Rabbis is known. The sages whose opinions are recorded in the *Mekhilta* are all Tannaim—that is, early rabbis who lived in the first two centuries C.E., before the completion of the great law code of early Judaism, the Mishnah, in 220 C.E. It is therefore assumed that the *Mekhilta* was completed and edited in the Land of Israel by the second half of the fourth century C.E., at the latest. But whenever it reached its final state, there is little question that most of the traditions preserved in the anthology were originally composed and transmitted orally until they were set down in writing, generations later.

The title of the work, which is Aramaic, can be translated as "The Treatises According to Rabbi Ishmael." This Rabbi Ishmael, a famous second-century sage who reputedly founded one of the two main schools of early rabbinic exegesis, was probably not, however, the anthology's author or editor. He was merely the author of the first truly substantive attributed interpretation cited in the collection—a comment on Exodus 12:2 (I:11)—and for this reason, according to some scholars, the work as a whole was attributed to him. Other scholars believe the reason for the attribution is that many of the legal interpretations in the Mekhilta derive from Ishmael's school, rather than from that of his rival, Rabbi Akiba.[1]

---

1. For the most recent summary of scholarly views on the history of the Mekhilta, see H.L. Strack and Günter Stemberger, *Introduction to the Talmud and Midrash*, trans. and ed. by Markus Bockmühl, 2nd printing (Minneapolis: Fortress, 1996), 251–57.

Aside from these few facts, we know very little about the early history of the *Mekhilta*. But two points remain undisputed: its importance as a source for understanding how the Rabbis interpreted the Book of Exodus and its vivacity and originality as a work of the midrashic imagination.

As its name indicates, the *Mekhilta* is a collection of treatises, nine in all, each one devoted to a specific section of Exodus and its particular themes. These treatises are: (1) Pisḥa (Exod. 12:1–13:16), dealing with the injunctions concerning the original Passover sacrifice; (2) Beshallaḥ (Exod. 13:17–14:71), the Exodus from Egypt; (3) Shirta (Exod. 15:1–21), an extended commentary on the Song at the Sea sung by Moses and the Israelites; (4) Vayassaʻ (Exod. 15:22–17:7), dealing with the earliest period of the Israelites' wanderings in the desert; (5) Amalek (Exod. 17:8–18:27), the war with Amalek and subsequent events; (6) Baḥodesh (Exod. 19:1–20:23), on the Revelation at Mount Sinai; (7) Nezikin (Exod. 21:1–22:23), the longest treatise in the work, an extended explication of the many laws in this section of Exodus; (8) Kaspa (Exod. 22:24–23:19), still more legal exegesis; and (9) Shabbata (Exod. 31:12–17, 35:1–3), explanations of two passages concerning the Sabbath laws. Each treatise is divided into a number of chapters; within each chapter the midrash proceeds verse by verse, often phrase by phrase, offering whatever interpretations the editor chose to record and transmit to posterity. Not infrequently, several interpretations may be offered for a single item.

As this summary indicates, much of the second half of the *Mekhilta* is devoted to the explication of matters of halakhah, or law. In fact, the anthological commentary begins only with Exodus. 12:1, which is also the first extended section in the Book of Exodus—indeed, in the Pentateuch—to be devoted to legal injunctions. It seems, then, that the editor chose to begin his commentary at the same point that the Bible itself turns from strict narrative to legal treatise.

This decision to give first attention to matters of law may have allowed the *Mekhilta's* editor to justify his untraditional act of committing oral traditions to writing. Whether or not this was the editor's motive, the *Mekhilta*, like the other tannaitic midrashim, is often called a midrash halakhah, or legal midrash, because of its apparent predilection for legal matters. In actuality, though, the work contains as much aggadah (rabbinic legend and lore that is non-legal in substance and character) as it does halakhah, and the apparent editorial privileging of law over lore may simply have been evidence of the more practical need to record such legal matters. Hence, it is noteworthy that despite its apparent preference for halakhah, the *Mekhilta* entirely skips over the sections in the second half of Exodus dealing with the construction of the Tabernacle, its holy utensils, and the priestly garments—sections that had little practical application centuries after the destruction of the Temple in 70 C.E. Even if Jews had not ceased to hope and pray for the restoration of the Temple (whose biblical prototype they understood the Tabernacle to be), their minds, their imaginations, were set on other matters, and their dreams of redemption took other shapes than those of physical structures.

We do not know who the first readers of the *Mekhilta* were—whether it was intended for study in the academy or used for composing sermons. The anthological nature of the work and its elliptical form of recording interpretations suggests that it was not intended for a lay reader, but rather for a professional—a scholar or preacher who would have used the collection as either a kind of handbook of authoritative teachings or as a source for preparing sermons. Because it is an anthology of interpretations, and because its main rubric of organization is dictated by the biblical text upon which it offers its comments, it is also difficult to generalize about its contents or even to isolate continuous themes in it. Most strikingly consistent, however, is the work's interpretive energy, the freshness and vivaciousness with which it sees the biblical text, and its eye for the smallest detail and oddity.

Because midrash is more easily analyzed than talked about in the abstract, the best way to introduce a volume like this is to look briefly at one passage in the *Mekhilta* to observe the exegetical imagination at work. Consider its very first interpretation, a comment on the beginning of Exodus. 12:1: "And the Lord spoke unto Moses and Aaron in the land of Egypt, saying: . . ."

> From this I might understand that the divine word was addressed to both Moses and Aaron. When, however, it says: "And it came to pass on the day when the Lord spoke unto Moses in the land of Egypt" (Exod. 6:28), it shows that the divine word was addressed to Moses alone and not to Aaron. If so, what does Scripture mean to teach by saying here, "unto Moses and Aaron"? It merely teaches that just as Moses was perfectly fit to receive the divine words, so was Aaron perfectly fit to receive the divine words. And why then did He not speak to Aaron? It was in order to grant distinction to Moses. Thus you must say that Aaron was not directly addressed in any of the divine commandments of the Torah, with the exception of three, for in the case of these three [Lev. 10:8, Num. 18:1 and 18:8], it is impossible to say that they were not directly addressed to him.

To the novice or reader unfamiliar with midrash, this passage is likely to appear maddeningly circular and hair-splitting. But there is reason to the madness, an inspired logic even to the hair-splitting. The first thing necessary to understand about midrash is that every interpretation is based upon some feature in the biblical text, a "bump" on its surface, as it were, that the Rabbis saw as somehow noteworthy. The "bump" may be an unusual word or an odd grammatical or orthographic form, an atypical case of syntax, a nascent or obvious contradiction, or even an idea or deed that seemed to them exceptional. In this case, the Rabbis noted that the text says, "And the Lord spoke unto Moses and Aaron" rather than "And the Lord spoke unto Moses [alone]," as is more often the case when the subject of the divine speech is a law or injunction. So why does Scripture say that God spoke to Moses *and* Aaron? The answer the midrash gives is typically midrashic: it is not because God *actually* spoke to both persons, but to prove that Aaron was *in theory* as worthy of receiving the divine revelation as was Moses. But if he was sufficiently worthy in theory, the passage asks next, then why didn't God speak to him in actuality? To which the passage responds: so as not to diminish Moses' honor and distinctiveness in being the only person to whom God spoke alone. The midrash further concludes that one can safely assume that God *never* spoke directly to Aaron except in three cases, when the Torah specifically tells us that God spoke *only* to Aaron.

In this instance, the *Mekhilta* is using midrash to teach a lesson of proper conduct, the importance of upholding the honor of an elder such as Moses. To many readers, the argument behind this interpretation may seem convoluted and forced. Why go to such lengths to prove that God spoke only to Moses and not to Aaron? What difference does it really make? By doing so, the Rabbis infer two points: first, that Moses and Aaron were equally worthy of receiving the divine word; and second, that even though Aaron was sufficiently worthy of being addressed by the divine word, God still did not speak to him. Why not? In order not to sully the honor Moses deserved. Further, we may also discern here a slight jab at those priestly types— a social class still alive in the Rabbinic period even if they could no longer perform their cultic duties—who may have wished to contest the honor of scribes and teachers like the Rabbis. The figure of Moses may have represented for the Rabbis their typological ancestor, a biblical prototype for their own class, and in this seemingly trivial interpretation, they may have been using the biblical terrain as a field upon which to fight a somewhat more contemporary battle.

Whenever possible, the Rabbis always preferred to find several interpretations for a verse in Scripture rather than a single, original meaning. In fact, the preceding passage is only the first of three separate interpretations for the phrase "unto Moses and Aaron"! The subsequent interpretations, in contrast to the first one, all stress the exact equality of Moses and Aaron: both judged Pharaoh, both were identically fearless, and so on.

Following these interpretations, the *Mekhilta* then passes on to the next phrase in the verse, "In the land of Egypt" (I:3). Why does the Bible write "In the land of Egypt" when "In Egypt" would have been sufficient? (God never wastes words.) The midrash answers that the word "land" indicates that God spoke with Moses in the "countryside," outside the "city" in which Pharaoh reigned. Why? Because that "city" was "full of abominations and idols" and therefore unfit for God's presence. Next, the *Mekhilta* embarks upon a lengthy homiletical digression (lasting nearly eight pages in Lauterbach's edition!) beginning with the statement that before the Land of Israel was chosen, God had revealed Himself everywhere; but after Israel was chosen as God's promised land, all other lands were disqualified as sites of divine revelation.

What was the purpose of proving the superiority of the Land of Israel? Perhaps it was necessary, precisely at the time the midrash was being edited, to emphasize Israel's privileged position over such rising Diaspora communities as Babylonia. Perhaps this was intended to provide a reason for Jews living in Roman Palestine not to flee the onerous burdens of taxes and military service (which plagued the entire Roman empire) and to emigrate to the milder economic and political climes of Babylonia. Whatever its reason, the statement of Israel's superiority prompts a series of analogous examples to which the midrash typically responds with a number of counter-examples— cases that seem to prove that, even after He chose the Land of Israel, God still revealed Himself outside Israel. The last of these counter-examples is the case of the prophet Jonah, to whom God explicitly speaks outside of Israel, indeed even at the gates of the city of

Nineveh! Still, the lengthy digression concludes by re-affirming the truth of the original claim that God no longer revealed Himself outside the land. What about Jonah? The midrash replies that, even in Jonah's case, God refused to reveal himself to the derelict prophet outside the land "a third time."

This is not, however, the end of the passage. A final, dissenting opinion defends Jonah by saying that the prophet fled his mission only because he had the welfare of the nation of Israel in mind; he was even willing to give up his own life for Israel's sake (because he knew that God would capsize the ship if he tried to flee on it). And so, the section concludes, "you will find everywhere that the patriarchs and prophets," like Jonah, "offered [to give up] their lives on behalf of Israel." As proof, the midrash cites the examples of Moses and King David. Here, too, one may hear a contemporary ring: although the midrash never explicitly draws the connection, one cannot help but sense the pressure of a reality in which Jews did sacrifice their lives for Israel's sake. And what consolation could be more powerful than proof that such contemporary heroes were only emulating the heroic deeds of Moses, David, and Jonah!

This brief summary of the *Mekhilta's* opening passage should give you some sense of the powerful way in which the Rabbis used the biblical text as the prism through which they perceived the realities of their own time. My summary, however, has overlooked the most typically midrashic feature of the entire passage: the fact that this section, which takes up more than ten pages in Lauterbach's edition, is based upon a verse that we would most likely consider a throwaway line. In contrast to the subsequent verses in Exodus, which spell out in exquisite detail all the particulars of the Passover sacrifice and ritual, this opening verse tells us no more than the names of the persons to whom God spoke and the place in which he addressed them. The verse has little substantive content or information. Yet midrash loves nothing more than to rescue precisely such a verse from triviality or insignificance. And in this case it does so marvelously, making the verse an occasion for disquisitions about the relative importance of Moses and Aaron (and by implication, spelling out the protocol for honoring all such elders), the superiority of the Land of Israel over the Diaspora, and the altruistic devotion of Israel's ancestors to their nation. These separate disquisitions not only reveal a wealth of meaning in the specific words of the verse; they also make it certain that the reader will never again consider such a verse anywhere in Scripture as devoid of meaning or as essentially superfluous.

The sequence of the separate sections in the passage may seem to the reader largely associative—and, to some extent, it *is*—but the passage as a whole is far from chaotic or incoherent. The student familiar with midrash will recognize virtually every characteristic midrashic literary form and hermeneutical technique and will follow the leaps from one topic and section to another because its languages and linkages are deeply characteristic of much early Rabbinic literature. Its Hebrew, the Hebrew of the Tannaim, has the pristine lucidity of poetry. And sometimes the midrash actually becomes poetry itself! In Shirta, the treatise explicating the Song at the Sea, the midrash repeatedly breaks into its own song, inspired by the very text upon which it comments:

"*I Will Sing unto the Lord, for He Is Highly Exalted*" (Exod. 15:2):

To the Lord it is meet to ascribe greatness;

To the Lord it is meet to ascribe power;

To the Lord it is meet to ascribe the glory, and the victory, and the majesty.

And so David says, "Thine, O Lord, is the greatness and the power, and the glory, and the victory and the majesty." (I Chron. 29:11) (Lauterbach II:8)[2]

2. For further discussion of poetry in the *Mekhilta*, see Judah Goldin, *The Song at the Sea* (New Haven and London: Yale University Press, 1971), esp. 13–20.

Even if you're unfamiliar with midrash, you will sense the presence of an invisible hand leading the discussion, ordering the discourse, enlivening the commentary; even with the indulgence of yet another interpretation, the *Mekhilta* never completely strays from the bedrock presence of the biblical text.

THE LAUTERBACH EDITION

Since the early sixteenth century, shortly after the beginning of Hebrew printing, numerous editions of the *Mekhilta* have appeared, including a number with important commentaries. But the story behind the publication of the present edition, edited by J. Z. Lauterbach, deserves to be told in its own right because it represents a significant moment in the history not only of Jewish scholarship, but also of American Jewish culture.

Jacob Zallel Lauterbach (1873–1942) was born in Galicia, studied at the German universities of Berlin and Göttingen, and received rabbinical ordination at the Rabbinerseminar Judentum für das Orthodoxe.[3] In 1903 he emigrated to America, initially to work on the staff of the *Jewish Encylopaedia*; later, he took up pulpits in traditional synagogues in Peoria, Illinois, and Rochester, New York, and finally, in a Reform temple in Huntsville, Alabama. In 1911, he became professor of Talmud at the Hebrew Union College in Cincinnati; shortly thereafter, he began to publish a series of seminal articles on the history of Rabbinic literature and on Jewish customs and folklore. His essay on the history of the *Tashlikh* ceremony performed on Rosh Hashanah remains a classic study of its type. Lauterbach was also active in the Reform movement's law and responsa committees, writing on such important issues as birth control, the ordination of women rabbis, and the halakhic permissibility of autopsies. In all these decisions,

3. B. J. Bamberger, "Jacob Zallel Lauterbach," *Encylopaedia Judaica* (Jerusalem: Keter/Macmillan, 1971), vol. 10: 1473–74. See also J. Z. Lauterbach, *Rabbinic Essays* (Cincinnati: Hebrew Union College Press, 1951): vii–xv.

Lauterbach sought to show that the traditional halakhah, even if no longer binding and irrevocable, could still guide modern Jews in their religious commitments and acts.

Lauterbach's greatest work, however, remains his edition of the *Mekhilta*. In 1915, Lauterbach was approached by Solomon Schechter, the legendary chancellor of the Jewish Theological Seminary of America and the chairman of the Classics Committee of The Jewish Publication Society (JPS) to prepare an edition of the *Mekhilta* with English translation. The publication was to be included in a new series entitled *The Jewish Classics*, whose purpose was to reproduce "in the original and in the vernacular" the greatest and most important works of post-biblical Jewish literature.[4] The idea for the series was supposedly not Schechter's but that of Theresa Schiff, the wife of Jacob Schiff, the wealthy New York Jewish businessman and philanthropist who was perhaps the earliest and most powerful supporter of JPS.

How Theresa Schiff got the idea for the series is a story worth telling. In 1910, James Loeb, Mrs. Schiff's brother, undertook to publish new editions of all the Greek and Roman classics in their original languages, with facing-page English translations, a project that eventually came to be known as the Loeb Classical Library. One day, as the story goes, several of the volumes of the new Loeb Classics were lying on the table in the Schiff home. Admiring them, Mrs. Schiff turned to her husband and said, "Jack, why couldn't you do for the Jewish classics what Jimmie is doing for the Greek and Roman?"[5]

In fact, the idea for such a series had been under consideration for several years, but it was Schiff's $50,000 endowment that actually

4. Quoted in Jonathan Sarna, *JPS: The Americanization of Jewish Culture, 1888–1988* (Philadelphia: Jewish Publication Society, 1989): 120. My entire discussion is based upon Sarna's masterful treatment of the history of the Schiff Library of Jewish Classics, pp. 120–30.

5. This is the story as told by Cyrus Adler, quoted in Sarna, 120. Sarna disputes its veracity and traces the far more complicated, though less colorful, prehistory of the series.

made it possible. (After Schiff's death in 1920, his indispensable role in the creation of the library was recognized by JPS, which renamed the series the Schiff Library of Jewish Classics). The series was explicitly modeled upon the Loeb Library, whose purpose was to preserve and transmit to the modern reader the classical heritage of Western civilization. So, too, the volumes in the Schiff Library were intended to "awaken the interest and command the support of those who feel the obligation to see to it that the Jewish Classics which, with few exceptions have been unknown to English readers, shall come into their own, and take their rightful place among the classical literatures of all peoples."[6] According to the original plan, twenty-five volumes were to be published, covering "the entire range of Jewish literature . . . up to some [indefinite] point in modern times." The volumes would introduce "the Hebrew Classics into the world of general literature and scholarship" and "serve as an example and incentive to renew activity in this field by Jews."[7] Like the Loeb classics, the volumes were to be published in pocket-sized form, with an introduction, critically edited and annotated text, and facing English translation.

In the end, the Schiff Library fell somewhat short of its original ambitious goals. A number of the volumes never materialized, others were deemed unworthy of being published and, ultimately, the cost of the series proved to be too great. Nine volumes were published, among them Lauterbach's *Mekhilta*, which appeared in three volumes, the first two published in 1933, the third in 1935. The overall impact of the library was also less momentous than was originally hoped; commercially, it never rivaled the success of the Loeb Classical Library.

Nevertheless, the Schiff Library of Jewish Classics remains one of

6. From the advertisement to the first volume in the series, Israel Davidson's *Selected Religious Poems of Solomon Ibn Gabirol* (1924), quoted in Sarna, 126.

7. Quoted in Sarna, 123, 126.

the great monuments of American Jewish intellectual life in the first half of this century. The sheer undertaking of this enormous project was testimony to American Judaism's growing self-confidence in its intellectual energies and capabilities; it was also evidence of the existence of an audience of American Jews interested in preserving and transmitting the classical Jewish heritage in scholarly modern English. Nor did this project occur in a vacuum. Perhaps its closest equivalent was the project that Hayyim Nahman Bialik called *kinnus*, the "ingathering" of the classics of the Jewish literary heritage, either in the form of a book, like Bialik and Ravnitzky's own *Sefer Ha'Aggadah*, the Book of Legends, or in the form of an actual library, like the Jewish National and University Library in Jerusalem. The Schiff Library was, in its own way, the American version of this Zionist cultural ideal. It testified to the equivalent coming-of-age of American Judaism, and of American Jewish literary scholarship as a dynamic and creative presence in Jewish culture worldwide.

Of all the volumes in the Schiff Library, Jacob Z. Lauterbach's *Mekhilta* has proven to be perhaps the most durable and significant. This is not to diminish the other volumes that appeared in the series, but simply to give an accurate estimation of Lauterbach's achievement. The edition is widely recognized as a model of meticulous and thorough scholarship; its translation, though by no means elegant, is accurate, straightforward, and eminently usable by lay readers, students, and scholars. It is also, to the best of my knowledge, the first critical edition of a Rabbinic work produced on American soil. For all these reasons, then, its reissuing is a reason for our celebration.

David Stern

Ruth Meltzer Professor of Classical Hebrew Literature
University of Pennsylvania

INTRODUCTION TO ORIGINAL EDITION

With the very giving of the Torah to Israel there must have begun the activity of studying and interpreting it. For every code of law, if it is to regulate the life of a people, must be fully understood and correctly interpreted before the people can obey it and be guided by its precepts. This was even more necessary in the case of the Torah given to Israel and believed by them to be of divine origin and hence to contain or imply more than the plain, literal meaning of the words would convey. Tradition reports such an activity of studying and interpreting the Torah and of diligently searching out its full meaning and all its implications, even in pre-exilic times.[8] At any rate, it is historically well attested that such activity was carried on in the time of Ezra and his associates. Of "Ezra, the priest, the scribe, even the scribe of the words of the commandments of the Lord and of His statutes to Israel," (Ezra 7.11) it is said that he "had set his heart to seek, לדרוש, the Law of the Lord, and to do it and to teach in Israel statutes and ordinances"[9] (ibid. 7.10). And in the very solemn assem-

---

8. Thus, the prophet Samuel is supposed to have interpreted the passage in Lev. 1.3 as implying that the slaughtering of the sacrificial animals may be performed by a layman, i.e., a non-priest (Zeb. 32a; Ber. 31b). Likewise, the interpretation of the law in Deut. 23.4 as not applying to the women of Ammon and Moab is ascribed to Samuel and his school (Yeb. 77a). The high-priest Jehoiada is reported to have given an interpretation to the passage in Lev. 5.19, deriving from it an important principle, and his interpretation is characterized as a *Midrash,* כהן גדול זה מדרש דרש יהוידע (Shek. 6.8).

9. A better rendering of this verse would be perhaps: Had set his heart to interpret (לדרש) the Law of God and to labor and teach in Israel statutes and ordinances.

bly at which the Torah was presented and read to the people (Neh. 8.1–8) there went along with the reading of the Torah an interpretation of it and an explanation of its full or correct meaning. Ezra, assisted by his associates, "even the Levites, caused the people to understand the Law. And the people stood in their place. And they read in the book, in the Law of God, distinctly, and they gave the sense and caused them to understand the meaning"[10] (ibid. verses 7–8). This activity, begun by Ezra, the Scribe, *Sofer,* and his associates, who like him are designated by the epithet Scribes, *Soferim,*[11] was carried on and continued by their successors, the teachers of the subsequent generations. Such a study of the Torah, requiring a thorough investigation of its contents, a correct interpretation of the meaning of its words and a deeper penetration into the spirit and sense of its dicta with all their implications, is designated by the term *Midrash* or, in its fuller form, *Midrash Torah.*[12]

Since the entire Torah was believed to be the Law of God containing divine wisdom and ethical instruction in every one of its words, the study of the Torah, *Midrash,* was applied to the whole of the Torah, the narrative as well as the legal portions. The full meaning of the historic records of the nation, the ethical lessons to be derived

10. This passage certainly means that the reading was accompanied by interpretation. Comp. also Ned. 37b and Yer. Meg. 4.1 (74d) as to the meaning of this passage.

11. On the Soferim and their method of interpretation, *Midrash,* see N. Kroch-mal, *Moreh Nebuke ha-Zeman,* in *Nachman Krochmal's Werke,* ed. S. Rawidowicz (Berlin, 1924), p. 204 ff.; Z. Frankel, *Darke ha-Mishnah* (Leipzig, 1859), p. 3 ff. and Lauterbach, *Midrash and Mishnah* (New York, 1916), pp. 3 and 36 ff.

12. The term מדרש, from the root דרש, to search, to inquire, means research, inquiry. See Lauterbach, op. cit., p. 1, note 1, and comp. S. Horowitz, "Midrash," in *Jewish Encyclopedia* VIII, p. 548 f. The term occurs in II Chr. 13.22: הנביא עדו במדרש, and 24.27: מדרש ספר המלכים, where it probably means exposition, study, but not necessarily exegesis of the Law. Comp. Brown, Driver, Briggs, *Dictionary,* s. v. and Strack, *Einleitung in Talmud und Midrasch* (Munich, 1921), p. 4, note 1 (Eng. transl., p. 239, note 36). The term מדרש תורה occurs in a *Baraita,* Kid. 49b.

from the stories about the fathers, and the significance of the events of the past contained in the narrative portions of the Torah, were inquired into and searched out, just as were the full meaning and the correct application of the laws and commandments contained in the various codes of the legal portions of the Torah. Of course, the study of the latter may have been pursued more diligently because of the urge of practical needs for the guidance of the people.

Accordingly, *Midrash* is of two kinds, depending on the nature of the contents of the portion of the Torah with which it deals and the purpose had in view. The one deals chiefly with the legal portions of the Torah and seeks to define its laws, to discover the principles underlying them, to find in them new rules, decisions for new cases, and support or proof for all traditional practices and customs accepted by the people. This kind of Midrash is designated as *Midrash Halakah.* The other deals mainly with the narrative portions of the Torah, seeking to find out the significance of its stories, the ethical instruction and moral teachings that can be found or discovered in the events recorded. This is designated as *Midrash Haggadah.*[13]

The activity of studying and interpreting the Torah, *Midrash,* which was begun by Ezra and his associates and continued by their successors, the teachers of subsequent generations, resulted in an accumulation of a body of traditional explanations and comments supplementary to the written Torah, which were preserved by the teachers and handed down from generation to generation. Such bodies of comments and traditional interpretations are also designated by the term *Midrash,* in a concrete sense, meaning "a Study," "an Exposition." Since, as stated above, all the parts of the Torah were studied

13. See Horowitz, op. cit., l.c., Lauterbach, *Midrash Halakah,* ibid., p. 569 f. and J. Theodor, *Midrash Haggadah,* ibid., p. 550. Of course, there are instances when an halakic Midrash is given in connection with a passage in the narrative portions, and an haggadic comment made on a legal passage. But in the main, the *Midrash Halakah* deals with the legal portions and the *Midrash Haggadah* with the narrative portions of the Torah.

and interpreted by the teachers, there must have been already in very early times an accumulated body of comments and supplementary explanations, a *Midrash* in the concrete sense, to all the parts of the Torah.[14]

Yet it may be assumed that that part of the Torah which deals with the period preceding the beginning of Israel's peoplehood was not regarded as of equal interest and importance with that part of the Torah which deals with Israel and its experience as a people chosen by God. The latter, being of more direct concern and of greater interest to the people, would naturally be more favored by the teachers, more diligently studied and more thoroughly interpreted. The four books of the Torah, Exodus, Leviticus, Numbers and Deuteronomy, which deal with the history and the experiences of Israel as a people and contain laws given to them by God, and record their reactions to these laws—these four books were, as it seems, more diligently studied and more frequently commented upon. And it can be stated with safety that already in the early talmudic times there were accumulated bodies of comments and haggadic Midrashim to these four books of the Torah. These earlier collections of comments and interpretations formed the nucleus of those Midrashim to these four books of the Pentateuch which have been preserved to us and which even as literary compositions had their origin in tannaitic times, and which are therefore designated as *Tannaitic Midrashim*.

14. The talmudic-midrashic literature abounds in interpretations and comments to those parts of the Torah not covered by the extant tannaitic Midrashim. Some of these interpretations, no doubt, go back to earlier sources. Echoes of such old traditional interpretations and comments may be found also in the old Versions of the Bible and in the Apocrypha and Pseudepigrapha. Indeed, the Book of Jubilees is practically such a Midrash of both halakic and haggadic character, extending over the book of Genesis and part of the book of Exodus. Comp. J. Klausner, הבית השני בגדולתו (Tel Abib, 1930), p. 118, note 1, who would attach some significance to the fact that our *Mekilta* begins practically where the Book of Jubilees leaves off.

Among these Tannaitic Midrashim, the one to Exodus, now designated by the name *Mekilta*[15] (properly *Mekilata*) or *Mekilta de Rabbi Ishmael,* is one of the oldest Midrashim, although it is nowhere mentioned in the Talmud by its present name. It represents a tannaitic exposition of a large part of the book of Exodus,[16] and deals with practically all the laws contained in that book as well as with some of its most important narrative portions. The contents of this Midrash, accordingly, consist of both Halakah and Haggadah. In fact, they are more haggadic than halakic, even though the book is not infrequently referred to as an halakic Midrash. The biblical book of Exodus contains by far more narrative than law. Hence an exposition of it, such as our *Mekilta* is, naturally would be more haggadic than halakic. More specifically, only about two-fifths of its total contents is halakic in character, while about three-fifths is of an haggadic nature.

Both in its halakic and haggadic portions the *Mekilta* shows itself to be one of the older tannaitic works. It contains very old material and has preserved teachings of the early Tannaim. Its halakic teachings in many instances reflect the point of view of the older Halakah, which was different from that of the later or younger Halakah;[17] hence some of its interpretations of the law are not in agreement with the interpretation accepted in the Talmud.[18] Its Haggadah contains lofty teachings, frequently illustrated by beautiful parables. It voices a higher spiritual conception of God and is full of expressions of a broad universalism not so frequently found in the other Midrashim. It also contains many allusions to historical events, and has preserved

15. See Lauterbach, "The Name of the Mekilta," in *JQR*, N. S., XI (1920), pp. 169–195.

16. It covers the following portions of the Book of Exodus: chaps. 12.1–23.19; 31.12–17 and 35.1–3. See below, note 23.

17. See Geiger, *Urschrift,* pp. 184 ff. and pp. 435 ff.; also *Jüdische Zeitschrift,* IV, pp. 109 ff.

18. See Geiger, *Urschrift,* p. 447; Z. Frankel in *MGWJ* (1854), p. 153; and Lauterbach, **שבירת עצם בפסח**, in *Hazofeh,* IX (Budapest, 1925), pp. 235–241.

ancient legends and reports not found elsewhere in the haggadic literature.[19] In its exposition of the biblical text it follows for the most part older simple exegetical rules and logical hermeneutical principles.[20] And in many of its interpretations it is in accord with the ancient Bible versions.[21] The teachers mentioned in it by name are, with a very few doubtful exceptions, all Tannaim.[22]

All these features characteristic of the *Mekilta* stamp it as one of the oldest Midrashim, one which must have originated in tannaitic times and which as such must in the main have been well known to the Amoraim, even though they never refer to it as the *Mekilta,* the name by which it later came to be designated. The fact that our *Mekilta* is nowhere in the Talmud mentioned by name could, at most, only prove that in talmudic times it was not known under this name, or in other words—and this actually was the case—that the name *Mekilta* had not yet been given to it. The absence of the name *Mekilta* in the Talmud, however, cannot prove that the Midrash as such was unknown to the Amoraim.[23]

19. See I. H. Weiss, in the Introduction to his edition of the *Mekilta* (Vienna, 1865), pp. xx–xxii.

20. See Weiss, ibid., pp. xvi–xvii.

21. See Geiger, *Urschrift*, pp. 193–4 and p. 436; also Z. Frankel, op. cit. (1853), p. 398.

22. It is not quite correct to say positively, as Frankel (ibid. [1854], p. 156) does, that Amoraim are mentioned in the *Mekilta.* Aside from the fact that, as Frankel himself says (ibid., p. 152), the names have not always been preserved with absolute accuracy, it is not at all certain that the teachers cited by Frankel are Amoraim. Shela, Oshaya and Jose b. Zimra were all contemporaries of Judah ha-Nasi, and may be considered as still belonging to the tannaitic period. Besides, instead of Oshaya as in the editions, our text (*Vayassa'*, VII, 1. 19) has Joshua. R. Abba (*Vayassa'*, I, 1. 58) is not necessarily identical with Abba Areka, not to mention that some sources have Akiba instead. Hananiah ben Idi is not identical with the Amora Hanina or Hinnena b. Idi (comp. Weiss, Introd., p. xxxi). Neither is the R. Jeremiah mentioned in tractate *Pisḥa* II, 1. 76 identical with the Amora by that name.

23. Comp. Frankel, op. cit. (1853), p. 396 f.

In amoraic times the tannaitic exposition of Exodus formed a part of a larger collection of tannaitic Midrashim. This collection, comprising Midrashim to the three books of the Torah: Exodus, Numbers and Deuteronomy, was well known to the Amoraim, and is frequently referred to by them under the general title, *Shear Sifre Debe Rab,* or merely, *Sifre*.[24] Our Midrash to Exodus, therefore, may well have been, and in the main most likely was, known to the Amoraim, but known only as part of the collection of tannaitic Midrashim covering these three books of the Torah; and thus it may have been referred to in the Talmud under the name of *Sifre,* the designation given to the whole collection of which it was a part. Of course, this does not necessarily mean that our Midrash, in the form in which we have it now, was already known to the Amoraim as a part of their

24. The name *Sifre,* ספרי, is shortened from *Sifre debe Rab,* ספרי דבי רב, though the fuller form has been preserved only in geonic literature and does not occur in the Talmud. Originally it was the designation of the Midrashim to the four books of the Pentateuch: Exodus, Leviticus, Numbers and Deuteronomy, collections of which were used in the school, בי רב. And the original reading of an old report preserved in the *Halakot Gedolot* at the end of הלכות הספר (ed. Vienna (1810), p. 106a, ספרי ארבעה שהן וספרי) supports this (comp. Lauterbach, "The Name of the Mekilta," op. cit., p. 173). In the course of time, however, and this happened already in early amoraic times, the Midrash to the Book of Leviticus was singled out from among these four books of midrashic comments forming the original *Sifre,* and distinguished by being called separately by the name *Sifra,* "the Book," or ספרא דבי רב, "the Book of the Schoolhouse." The designation ספרי was thus left to comprise only the remaining three of the four original parts of the *Sifre,* i. e., Exodus, Numbers and Deuteronomy. Accordingly, it is sometimes referred to in the Talmud more specifically as שאר ספרי דבי רב, "the remaining three books of the schoolhouse," i. e., exclusive of the one to Leviticus (see Rashbam in his commentary to B. B. 124b, s. v., and comp. D. Hoffmann, *Zur Einleitung in die Mechilta de-Rabbi Simon ben Jochai* (Frankfort o. M., 1906), p. 2 and p. 5, especially note 1). It was only after the Midrash to Exodus in later geonic times came to be described as the Tractates or designated by the name *Mekilta* or *Mekilata,* that the designation Sifre, ספרי, was left to comprise only the *Midrash* to the two books, Numbers and Deuteronomy. See further Lauterbach, op. cit., p. 171 ff.

Sifre. There can, in fact, be no doubt that our Midrash, as we have it now, is not fully identical with that Midrash to Exodus which was known to the early Amoraim, and which formed a part of the *Sifre* mentioned by them. Like the other Midrashim of the same collection, referred to in the Talmud by the designation *Sifre*, or *Shear Sifre Debe Rab*, the Midrash to Exodus experienced considerable changes, both in form and content, in the various redactions which it must have gone through before it received its final redaction and was given its present form.[25] In the latter form the work, no doubt, is quite different from the one which was known to the Amoraim as a part of the *Sifre* of their times.

But there is no reason whatever to assume that the Midrash to Exodus which was known to the Amoraim and referred to by them under the general name *Sifre* was an altogether different work with no relation whatever to our *Mekilta*. It certainly cannot be assumed that at the time when the first redactors of our *Mekilta* and our *Sifre* set out to compile these works, the earlier amoraic collections containing Midrashim to the three books of the Torah, covered by our *Mekilta* and our *Sifre*, had already been entirely lost. And if those earlier collections had not been lost but were still known to the redactors of our *Sifre* and *Mekilta*, they certainly must have been made use of by the latter when arranging their works. It would be strange indeed if the redactors or compilers, to whom we owe our present Midrashim, had entirely neglected and ignored those earlier collec-

25. Comp. Geiger, *Urschrift*, p. 435, and Frankel, *MGWJ* (1854), p. 152. This would, in part at least, explain how some of the statements found in our *Mekilta* could have been unknown to the Amoraim. See also Frankel, ibid. (1853), p. 396 ff., and comp. Ch. Albeck, *Untersuchungen über die halakischen Midrashim* (Berlin, 1927), pp. 91–96. Albeck's conclusion, that the *Mekilta* collection, *das Mekiltabuch*, was unknown to the Talmud, might therefore hold good only as referring to the *Mekilta* in the form in which we have it now. It is not correct as referring to the *Mekilta* in the earlier stages of its redaction, in which it was known to the Amoraim.

tions of amoraic times and set out to compile and redact altogether new Midrashim from sources or collections, the existence of which is otherwise not known and nowhere indicated.

It is rather safe to assume, on the contrary, that the collections of amoraic times formed the nucleus of the Midrashim preserved to us, and are actually contained in them. As regards our *Mekilta,* then, we may safely assume that the part of the talmudic *Sifre* which dealt with portions of the book of Exodus, was used by the first redactor of our *Mekilta* and is embodied in it. The *Sifre* of the Talmud, that is, that part of it which covered the book of Exodus, then, constituted an early stage in the redaction of our *Mekilta,* if it was not, indeed, its original form.

This earlier work, or original draft of our *Mekilta,* most likely had its origin in the school of R. Ishmael, or at least was based for the greater part upon some collected teachings of his disciples.[26] The preponderance of R. Ishmael's teachings and the frequency with which his disciples are mentioned, which are characteristic features of the *Mekilta* in its present form, justify this supposition. But it would be unwarranted to assume that this earlier work known to the Amoraim was a work of the school of R. Ishmael exclusively, as contrasted with, or distinguished from, similar works of the school of R. Akiba. The Amoraim, even of the first generation, were not so strict as to maintain separately distinct collections containing exclusively the teachings of R. Akiba and other special collections containing exclusively the teachings of R. Ishmael. They would not hesitate to incor-

26. This may also have been partly the cause of assigning the work to R. Ishmael, or calling it the *Mekilta of R. Ishmael.* See, however, Lauterbach, "The name of the Mekilta," op. cit., p. 195. There can be no doubt, however, that the R. Ishmael to whom the later authorities ascribe the *Mekilta* was the Tanna, R. Ishmael, the colleague of R. Akiba, and not an Amora by the name of Ishmael, as Frankel in his *Einleitung in den Jerusalemischen Talmud* (Breslau, 1870), p. 108b–109a would assume. Comp. against him M. Friedmann in the Introduction to his edition of the *Mekilta* (Vienna, 1870), pp. LXXIV–LXXVII.

porate teachings originating in the one school in a collection consisting, in the main, of teachings from the other school,[27.] as long as these were, in the new collections, given in the names of their respective authors. Possibly, even in the collections of the younger Tannaim the separation between the schools of R. Akiba and R. Ishmael was not so strictly maintained. At any rate, the very first redactor of our *Mekilta* already embodied in it a considerable proportion of material drawn from sources coming from the school of R. Akiba.[28]

The Midrash underwent more than one revision and several subsequent redactions. One of these redactions, I have reason to believe, was made in the school of R. Johanan b. Nappaha. This would account for the fact that many sayings ascribed in the Palestinian or Babylonian Talmud to R. Johanan are found in the *Mekilta* as סתם, anonymous. This redaction in the school of R. Johanan was not the last one. There must have been another redaction or revision of the work of the school of R. Johanan. When and by whom this final redaction was made cannot be ascertained.

There is, however, no reason to assume that the work of the final redactor has not been preserved to us in its entirety. We have, on the contrary, sufficient evidence to prove that, with the exception of a few minor changes and a few omissions and additions, due in the main to mistakes by copyists, the *Mekilta* has been preserved to us completely in the extent and in the form given to it by its final redactor. From the earliest references to the *Mekilta* made by medieval rabbinic authorities it is evident that the *Mekilta* known to these men did not extend beyond the limits of its present compass.[29] Furthermore, the work, as we have it, shows in its arrangement the original plan of

27. Comp. Albeck, op. cit., pp. 140 ff.
28. Hence R. Johanan who in his comment on the *Sifre* (Sanhedrin 86a) includes also the *Mekilta* or the Midrash to Exodus (see Rashbam to B. B., 1. c.) could well have said that the anonymous sayings in the latter Midrash, as he knew it, follow the method, or come from the school, of R. Akiba.

its redactor, namely, to present a collection of tractates dealing with certain events or groups of laws found in the book of Exodus, but not to give a continuous or running commentary to the entire book. If by far the larger part of the book of Exodus is not commented upon or discussed in our *Mekilta,* it is not to be concluded that our *Mekilta* is defective or fragmentary. It rather proves that the compiler or final redactor of our *Mekilta* was not interested in collecting comments to the whole book of Exodus,[30] or that he considered such a thing beyond the scope of his work.

But if, as a whole, the work has been preserved to us in its entirety and in the form given to it by its final redactor, in details it suffered many changes and its original text did not remain absolutely intact. Not only was the original text in many instances corrupted by the negligence of copyists and printers, as well as by the misunderstanding of some would-be correctors, but it also suffered considerable alteration through insertions and omissions likewise made by copyists, editors and printers. There is, therefore, a need for a critical edition of the *Mekilta.* Such an edition based upon existing manuscripts, early editions, and an examination of extracts and quotations found in post-talmudic rabbinical works and compilations is presented in the present work.

In the preparation of the text for this edition I have made use of the following sources:

29. See Lauterbach, "The Arrangement and the Divisions of the Mekilta," in *Hebrew Union College Annual,* I (1924), p. 434. To the authorities cited there is to be added R. Hillel b. Eliakim, who in his commentary on the *Baraita de-Rabbi Ishmael* (ed. A. Freimann in *Livre d'Hommage à Mémoire du Dr. Samuel Poznanski* (Warsaw, 1927), Hebrew part, p. 179) describes the comment in our *Mekilta* on Ex. 35.3 as the end of the *Mekilta.*

30. See Lauterbach, op. cit., p. 433 and comp. Geiger, *Urschrift,* p. 435; and Frankel, *MGWJ* (1853), pp. 390–391; also מבוא ירושלמי, p. 27.

Manuscripts

1. Ms. Oxford No. 151 (n. 2).[31] According to A. Neubauer (*Catalogue of the Hebrew Manuscripts in the Bodleian Library,* part I, Oxford, 1886, p. 24), this Ms. dates from the year 1291. In the Apparatus Criticus it is designated by א.

2. Ms. Munich Codd. hebr. 117 (l).[32] This Ms. dates from about 1435. See M. Steinschneider, *Die hebräischen Handschriften der K. Hof- u. Staatsbibliothek in München* (Munich, 1895), p. 74. This Ms. is designated by מ.

3. Casanata Ms. H. 2736 (*Catalog* of G. Sacerdote, Florence, 1897, No. 67).[33] This Ms. contains part of the last chapter of the tractate *Beshallah,* beginning with ובני ישראל הלכו ביבשה והיו מלאכי השרת, line 50 of this edition (Friedmann, 33a, 1. 9), and the entire tractate *Shirata.* It is designated by ס.

4. Ms. Fragment Oxford No. 2657; comp. *Catalogue of the Hebrew Manuscripts in the Bodleian Library,* by A. Neubauer and Arthur Ernest Cowley, II (Oxford, 1906), p. 47. This fragment contains part of the Tractate *Vayassaʿ,* beginning with: לחם כפול והיה משנה, ch. III, 1. 39 of this edition (Friedmann, 47b, 1. 17), and closing with הבאיש ורמה ולא, ch. V, 1. 17 (Friedmann, 50a, 1. 3).

5. Ms. Fragment Oxford 2669 (n. 26); see *Catalogue,* Neubauer-Cowley, p. 70. This fragment covers part of ch. 5, the entire ch. 6 and part of ch. 7 of the tractate *Nezikin,* beginning with אומר בשם המפורש אתה, ch. V, line 98 of this edition (Friedmann, 82a, 1. 16), and closing with אעפ"י שקוטנה אמה, ch. VII, lines 16-17 of this edition

31. I am indebted to Dr. A. Marx for a copy of this Ms., which was made for him by Mr. Isaac Last.

32. My thanks are due to the authorities of the Library for their permission to have a photostatic copy of this Ms. made.

33. Dr. L. Finkelstein of the Jewish Theological Seminary of New York was kind enough to lend me the photostatic copy of this Ms., which he had secured from the Library for use in connection with his work on the *Sifre* to Deuteronomy.

(Friedmann, 83a, last line). Both of these fragments[34] are designated in the Apparatus by 2א.

6. Genizah Fragment in the Library of the Dropsie College;[35] comp. B. Halper, *Descriptive Catalogue of Genizah Fragments in Philadelphia* (Philadelphia, 1924, p. 24), no. 80. This fragment covers part of the tractate *Vayassaʿ* beginning with **עשיתם כן**, ch. V, 1. 20 of this edition (Friedmann, 50a, 1.4), and closing with **שמה תאמרו**, ch. VI, 1. 7 of this edition (Friedmann, 50b, 1. 9 from bottom). This fragment is designated by @@@.

7. Genizah Fragments in the Library of Columbia University, New York.[36] One of these fragments covers part of the tractate *Vayassaʿ*, beginning with **בפנים חשכות**, ch. III, 1. 54 of this edition (Friedmann, 48a, 1. 1), and closing with **יורד על**, ch. IV, 1. 69 of this edition (Friedmann 49a, 1. 12). The other covers part of the tractate *ʿAmaleḳ,* beginning with **מתחת השמים**, ch. II, 1. 144 of this edition (Friedmann, 56a, 1. 17), and closing with **שנאמר וילד**, ch. III, 1.38 of this edition (Friedmann 57a, 1. 5 from bottom). These fragments are designated in the Apparatus by **ג"ק**.

Printed Editions

8. The first edition of the *Mekilta,* Constantinople 1515, designated by **ק**.

9. The second edition, Venice 1545, designated by **נ**.

10. *Mekilta* edition with commentary *Shebut Yehudah,* **שבות יהודה**, by R. Judah Najar, Leghorn, 1801. This is the only later edition

34. Of these fragments, Nos. 4 and 5, I also had a copy made by Mr. Last for Dr. Marx.

35. Dr. Cyrus Adler, President of the Dropsie College, was kind enough to put this fragment at my disposal, for which my thanks are due to him.

36. My thanks are here expressed to the authorities of the Library of Columbia University in New York for permitting me the use of these fragments.

which contains readings not found in the first two editions.[37] The editor had some manuscript material at his disposal, and seems also to have seen the first edition. This edition is designated by ל.

Compendia Containing Parts of the Mekilta

11. *Yalkuṭ Shime'oni,* ילקוט שמעוני, editio princeps, part I on the Pentateuch (Salonica, 1526), and part II on the prophetical books and the Hagiographa (Salonica, 1521), designated in the Apparatus by ט. When other editions of the *Yalkuṭ* are referred to, it is expressly stated in the Apparatus that the reading is found in the later edition, בהוצאות מאוחרות, or the edition in which it is found is specified, as דפוס ווילנא or דפוס פראג.

12. Ms. of the *Yalkuṭ* to the Pentateuch, Oxford 2637; see *Catalogue,* Neubauer-Cowley, II, pp. 34–35 and the manuscript of the *Yalkuṭ* to the prophetical books, Cod. De Rossi 1172; see *Catalog,* I. B. de Rossi, III (Parma 1803), p. 89. These *Yalkuṭ* Mss.[38] are designated by ט״כ.

13. *Midrash Leḳaḥ Ṭob,* לקח טוב, by R. Tobiah b. Eliezer (11th cent.), ed. Solomon Buber (Wilna, 1884), designated by the abbreviation ל״ט.

14. *Midrash Sekel Ṭob,* שכל טוב, by R. Menaḥem b. Solomon (12th cent.), ed. Buber (Berlin, 1900), designated by the abbreviation ש״ט.

15. *Midrash Tanḥuma,* תנחומא, editio princeps (Constantinople, 1522), in which is embodied a whole section of the *Mekilta,* designated by the letter ת.

---

37. I could not make any use of the latest edition of the *Mekilta* by Horowitz-Rabin which appeared after the Hebrew text of my work had been printed and the second proof of it corrected. The publication of my work was delayed by the fact that the English translation was not finished till June 1930.

38. My thanks are here expressed to the authorities of the respective Libraries for their permission to have photostatic copies of these two manuscripts made.

16. *Yalḳuṭ ha-Makiri,* ילקוט המכירי, by R. Makir b. Abba Mari, designated by the letter כ.

17. *Sefer Vehizhir,* ספר והזהיר (10th cent.), edited by J. M. Freimann (part I to Exodus, Leipzig, 1873; part II to Leviticus and Numbers, Warsaw, 1880). This work contains extracts from the *Mekilta*. It is designated by the letter ה.

18. Ms. מדרש חכמים,[39] designated by מ״ח.

19. The Ms. work of *Yalḳuṭ Talmud Torah,*[40] ילקוט תלמוד תורה, by R. Jacob b. Hananel of Sicily (first half of the 14th cent.), designated by the abbreviation ת״ת.

20. *Mekilta de R. Simon b. Yoḥai,* מכילתא דרבי שמעון בן יוחאי, edited by D. Hoffmann (Frankfort-on-Main, 1905), designated by the letter ש.

*Commentaries and Other Works Containing Variant Readings
or Textual Corrections of the Text of the Mekilta*

21. Manuscript corrections on the margin of a copy of the *Mekilta,* Venice edition, in the possession of L. Ginzberg.[41] The author of these corrections had before him different Mss. from which he got variant readings and made his corrections. This Ms. is designated by ג.

22. *Ot Emet,* אות אמת, by Meier Benvenisti (Salonica, 1565), designated by the abbreviation א״א.

23. Corrections of the text given by R. Moses of Frankfort in his commentary to the *Mekilta,* זה ינחמנו (Amsterdam, 1712), designated by the abbreviation ז״י.

---

39. This manuscript, formerly in the possession of the late Abraham Epstein of Vienna, now belongs to Prof. Dr. V. Aptowitzer of Vienna, who was kind enough to permit me to make a photostatic copy of it, for which I am thankful to him.

40. This Ms. is found in the Library of the Jewish Theological Seminary and I am thankful to Dr. A. Marx for putting it at my disposal.

41. Dr. Ginzberg was kind enough to lend me this copy, for which I thank him.

24. Corrections of the text given in the commentary שבות יהודה, to the *Mekilta,* Leghorn edition. These corrections are not identical with the variant readings which the editor and author of that commentary has embodied in the text of his edition. They are, accordingly, separately designated by the abbreviation ש"י.

25. Corrections of the text of the *Mekilta* ascribed to R. Elijah of Wilna and printed under the title *Efat Zedek,* איפת צדק, in the *Mekilta* edition of Wilna 1884, designated by the abbreviation א"צ.

26. Quotations from the *Mekilta* found in works of medieval authors. These works are referred to in the Apparatus by their full title or by the abbreviations commonly used for them, as רמב"ן, רש"י, רא"ם, סמ"ג, סה"מ, with the exact reference to the chapter or page of the work where the quotation is found.

27. Commentaries to the *Mekilta* suggesting corrections or emendations not based on manuscripts or on quotations from early medieval authorities. These are: Commentary מרכבת המשנה by R. David Moses Abraham of Rohatyn (Lemberg, 1894), designated by the abbreviation מ"ה; Commentary בירורי המדות by R. Isaac Elijah Landau in the Wilna (1844) edition of the *Mekilta,* designated by the abbreviation בה"מ; Commentary to the *Mekilta* contained in the Pentateuch Commentary התורה והמצוה by M. L. Malbim (Warsaw, 1874–80), designated by the abbreviation הת"והם; Commentary מדות סופרים by I. H. Weiss in his edition of the *Mekilta* (Vienna, 1865), designated by the abbreviation מ"ס; Commentary מאיר עין by M. Friedmann in his edition of the *Mekilta* (Vienna, 1870), designated by the abbreviation מ"ע. Corrections put in by Weiss and Friedmann respectively in the texts of their editions are sometimes referred to under the abbreviations: (מאיר איש שלום =) מ"א"ש and (אייזיק הירש וויס =) אה"ו respectively.[42] To these may be added readings suggested in the

42. R. Abraham of Slonim the author of the commentary on the Mekilta באר אברהם, published in the reprinted edition of the *Mekilta* with commentary *Zeh Yenaḥamenu* (Warsaw, 1927), also makes some corrections in the *Mekilta* text

commentary on the *Yalḳuṭ* **זית רענן**, by R. Abraham Abali Gumbiner, designated by the abbreviation **ז"ר**.

Methods Followed in Deciding upon the Text Embodied in this Edition

Of the sources enumerated above only five contain the entire text of the *Mekilta* and are independent of one another, each of them having followed, in part at least, different original manuscripts. These are Nos. 1, 2, 8, 9, and 10. They are the main sources used in seeking to establish the correct text. The other sources are all, as regards the *Mekilta* text, fragmentary, and most of them are secondary in that they merely represent quotations or extracts from the *Mekilta.* First consideration, therefore, is given to the text as found in the five main sources, and in the fragmentary manuscripts.

The text adopted in this edition is eclectic. It is in the main based upon the readings as found in the five complete and independent sources mentioned above, viz., the two manuscripts of Oxford and Munich and the three editions of Constantinople, Venice and Leghorn, with special preference, however, given to the readings of the manuscripts.

In the majority of cases, therefore, when the two manuscripts agree in a reading as against the reading of the editions, the former has been embodied in the accepted text. In case of disagreement between the two manuscripts, the reading of the one supported by the editions has been accepted. In many cases, however, the reading of the editions has been retained, because in the opinion of the editor it seemed to be more correct than the one found in the manuscripts. Likewise, where the variant readings do not affect the real sense of

and sometimes suggests different readings. But I did not get this book before I had finished correcting the proof of my text, hence I could not make use of any of his suggested readings for it.

the passage, the editor deemed it advisable to retain in most instances the reading of the editions in preference to that of the manuscripts. This was done in order not to make the new text unnecessarily different from the text in the current editions to which students have been accustomed and from which quotations in scientific works have been made. All the more was this deemed advisable since, as will be stated below, where there is no real difference in the meaning of the passage, no variants are recorded in the Apparatus. If then the readings of the manuscripts had been embodied in the text, the student would have been disturbed and confused by finding a new and different text without being in a position to ascertain the sources of this new text, different from that to which he had been accustomed. In some cases the accepted text is based upon only one of the five main sources, as against the reading or readings found in the other four, because the reading of the one source appeared to the editor to be more correct. In most such cases, however, the editor did not decide in favor of the reading of the one main source unless support was given to it in one or more of the secondary sources.

In some instances the accepted text is based upon a corrected reading found only in one or more of the secondary sources, and not in any of the principal sources or fragmentary manuscripts. Such cases are pointed out in the Apparatus and the source or sources for the reading accepted are given, accompanied by the statement: פלוני וכן נראה מגירסת פלוני or וכן גרס פלוני, כן הגיה פלוני ,הגהתי ע"פ. The readings of the main sources in such cases are then cited in the Apparatus. In general, the principle has been followed not to embody in the text readings which are not supported by reliable authorities that can be supposed to have drawn their readings from original manuscripts.

In a few rare instances, however, corrections not based upon such authority, but nevertheless very plausible, have been embodied in the text. They have then been pointed out as such in the Apparatus. Still the rule has been rather to leave the text as found in the reliable sources unchanged, and to put the suggested corrections in the Apparatus, accompanied by the statement: נ"ל להגיה or אולי צ"ל, נראה לי שצ"ל.

Limitations of Apparatus

In accordance with the plan adopted for this series, the extent of the Apparatus is limited to what is necessary or helpful for a better understanding of the text. It is not meant to be a depository of all variae lectiones. Accordingly the following rules have been observed in the preparation of the Apparatus:

I. If the reading accepted in the text is found in all the principal sources, no variants from the secondary sources are recorded. There are only two exceptions to this rule: (1) If the passage presents some difficulty, then all the variants from all the sources available are recorded in the Apparatus, even though the accepted reading is based upon all the primary sources. For these variants may help to clear up the difficulty, and can therefore be considered as helpful for a better understanding of the text. (2) If a reading found in one of the secondary sources is very plausible and apparently better than the one accepted in the text on the basis of the five main sources, it is recorded in the Apparatus. For, while the editor thought that as long as the reading found in the five main sources makes good sense he had no right to exclude it from the text and to substitute for it a better and more plausible reading from a secondary source, he felt at the same time that the very plausible reading from another source should not be entirely ignored. Hence it is recorded in the Apparatus.

II. If the five sources disagree among themselves and the reading accepted in the text is based upon only some of them, then the Apparatus records not only the different readings from the other main sources but also the variants from the secondary sources. It is, therefore, understood that those sources not cited in the Apparatus as containing variants are those whose reading is accepted in the text. For example, if the text follows ק and מ, the Apparatus merely records the variants from א, נ, and ל. This means that the reading accepted in the text is the reading found in the remaining two main sources ק and מ, and there is no need of expressly stating this in the Apparatus. Of course, in the case of the secondary sources not containing the entire text of the *Mekilta,* the silence about them in the Apparatus would not always indicate their positive agreement with the accepted reading, since the entire section or passage in question may have been omitted or not quoted in that source. The silence in such cases, however, gives at least negative support to the accepted reading. For it means either that the secondary sources do not contain the passage in question, or that their readings agree with the one accepted in the text—otherwise the Apparatus would have recorded their variants. In either case, then, these sources are not against the accepted reading. It was not deemed necessary expressly to record the fact in the Apparatus when the secondary sources support the reading of the accepted text. For the latter, being based upon more than one of the five main sources, needs no such support. It is only where the accepted reading needs additional support, as when it is based upon only one of the five main sources as against the other four, or when though based on more than one it still may not seem preferable to the reading in the other main sources, that the secondary sources which support it are expressly cited. In such cases the sign =, followed by the secondary source, is put in the Apparatus before the variants from the other sources are recorded. Thus, for example, *Pisḥa* I, 1. 17 (= Friedmann, 1a, 1.4), the Apparatus records: כלל = א"א:מ. ד. כלול This indicates that the reading כלול, besides being found in א, i. e., the one main source not cited in the Apparatus as offering a variant, is also given by *Ot Emet,* thus explaining on what basis the editor decided in favor of א against the other four sources.

In keeping with the plan for limiting the scope of the Apparatus, variants are considered only in so far as they affect the meaning or have bearing upon the understanding of the text, or are otherwise of importance from a linguistic, theological or historical point of view. Variants which, though they may have the same meaning as the reading accepted in the text, also admit of another interpretation, are considered as affecting the meaning of the text and are, therefore, recorded. For example, to the reading יכול אף לעתיד לבא יהיה in *Pisḥa* ch. VII, 11. 17–19, there is a variant ואף לעתיד לבא יהיה. This variant is probably to be taken in a hypothetical sense and to be read in the tone of a question, בתמיה, in which case it has the same sense as the reading accepted in the text. But since it might also be read in the tone of a positive statement, בניחותא, in which case its sense would be the opposite of that of the reading accepted in the text, it is recorded in the Apparatus. Likewise ibid. ch. VII, 1. 18, the Apparatus records the variant תלמוד לומר to the accepted reading שנאמר, for the latter means to indicate that the preceding statement stands correct while the former implies that the preceding statement cannot be sustained.

Differences in phraseology which may be due to the differences between one school and another in the use of technical terms, such as, שומע אני and יכול or מגיד and מלמד, are recorded. For they may indicate or help to determine the origin of the Midrash in question— whether it goes back to the school of Akiba or of Ishmael. Differences in the spelling of certain names are recorded when the names may refer to different persons, such as חנניה and חנינא, אחאי and אחי, אליעזר and אלעזר. But where in spite of the differences of spelling there is no doubt that the same person is referred to, such as יוחאי and יוחי, יאשיה and יושיה, the differences are not recorded. Likewise, I have throughout the work adopted the spelling אלעזר for the name of Eleazar of Modiʻim, though in some instances I had only one source to rely on for this correct spelling, the other sources having אליעזר.

For since the appellative המודעי, following the name, leaves no doubt as to the identity of the teacher referred to, I thought it advisable to adopt the correct spelling אלעזר throughout and deemed it unnecessary even to record in the Apparatus that in some instances some of the sources have the wrong spelling אליעזר.

Additions and Omissions

The rules laid down for recording different readings are also observed with regard to the recording in the Apparatus of omissions and additions by the various sources. These are recorded only when they could possibly affect the meaning of the text. Hence they are recorded even when it may be apparent that the omission was due to a mistake on the part of a copyist, who skipped from one word or phrase to another similar one farther on, or that the addition was due to a mistaken repetition, by a similar error, on the part of the copyist. Of course, the editor relied on his own judgment in deciding whether a passage found in some of the sources and not in the others was to be recorded in the Apparatus as an addition, or was to be accepted into the text, the Apparatus recording that the other sources omit it.

Scriptural Quotations

In regard to the quotations from the Scriptures the following rules have been observed:

I. Bible quotations are sometimes extended by the editor if necessary for the understanding of the text, i.e., if the actual proof for the midrashic interpretation is based upon a word or part of the scriptural passage omitted in the quotation. Such extensions are indicated in the Apparatus by the word הוספתי. If, in extending the quotation, the editor followed a secondary source, that secondary source is given. Thus, e. g., in Tractate *Pisḥa,* ch. XVII, 1. 138, the Apparatus has: א"א = הוספתי [אביו יד ויתמוך, which means: I have added these words, following the reading in *Ot Emet.* If one or more of the main sources has the word וגו' after the shorter quotation, this is usually recorded in the Apparatus after the word הוספתי or after the sigla indicating the secondary source which the editor followed in making the extension. Thus, e. g., ibid., 1. 148, the Apparatus has: וגו' .מ הוספתי:א] עיניכם בין קרחה תשימו ולא, which means that the quotation was extended by the editor, and the manuscripts א and מ have וגו' instead of the extended passage. This statement also implies that in the other main source, i. e., ק and נ, the extended passage is missing and not even indicated by the word וגו'. But in some cases the Apparatus expressly mentions first the sources which omit the extended passage entirely, then cites those sources which have the word וגו', adding thereto the words הוספתי זה פי ועל, i. e. that on the basis of this וגו' the editor extended the quotation.

II. If one or more of the main sources give a shorter quotation with or without the word וגו', and others give an extended quotation but show in the extended portion of the scriptural text a reading different from the masoretic text, the editor simply retains the shorter quotation in the accepted text and records in the Apparatus the other sources with their variants from the masoretic text. Such an instance is found in Tractate *Beshallaḥ,* ch. III, 1. 100. If, however, the extended portion is necessary for the understanding of the text, the editor with but few exceptions has followed the sources giving the shorter quotations as far as they went and then extended the quotation in accordance with the masoretic text; the other sources he cites in the Apparatus with whatever variations from the masoretic text they may have. Thus, e. g., ibid., ch. IV, 11. 81–82, the Apparatus records: לפני .ט הימים כל מלפני .ד הוספתי: ועפ"ז 'וגו .הימים]א כל לפני יי נאום. This means that א has וגו', on the basis of which the editor extended the quotation, following however the masoretic text, and that the editions (=ד) as well as the Yalkuṭ (=ט) have readings which differ from the masoretic text. The editor is of the opinion that in such instances he is justified in assuming that the source giving only the shorter quotation but no doubt having in mind the longer or fuller quotation, whether referring to it by וגו' or not, had before it the correct reading of the masoretic text. Hence, when extending the quotation, the editor gives the rest of the verse according to the masoretic text. Thus the number of apparent differences between the masoretic text of the Bible and the scriptural text preserved in the *Mekilta* is reduced. This the editor considers very desirable. For on the one hand it makes it easier for the average student, who would otherwise be disturbed by what he might consider numerous mis-quotations. On the other hand, the student who is especially inter-ested in the scriptural text as presented in the *Mekilta* and its relation to the masoretic text will find all the available material in the Appara-tus. The importance of these variants and the need of recording them in the Apparatus cannot be doubted. In the first place, if we assume that the source containing the variant is correct and represents the original reading of the *Mekilta,* then, of course, it is of great impor-tance to record this difference from the masoretic text. But even if we assume that the variants in that source represent merely the mistakes made by copyists of that source and not the original readings of the redactor of the *Mekilta,* it is still important to record them. For such instances plainly prove that in many cases the changes from the masoretic text found in the *Mekilta* are due to the copyists and not to different readings in the Scripture which the author or redactor had before him. These cases should cause us to hesitate before we ascribe with certainty to the original author even such differences from the masoretic text as are reported in all the sources. For even then there is the possibility that the copyists made the mistake of not quoting accurately. We should be more cautious and less hasty in deciding questions dealing with the problem of the relation of the masoretic text to the scriptural text as preserved in the rabbinic works. There

must be other internal evidence either from the nature of the
midrashic proof or argument based upon the scriptural text, or from
the context of the passage to determine whether the authors or redactors of the ancient rabbinic works had before them another text than
the one preserved for us by the careful Masorites.

III. If a quotation as given in the text has a reading different from
the masoretic text, the latter is recorded in the Apparatus like any
other variant with its source, in this case the masoretic text, designated as במקרא or במקרא שלפנינו. Thus, e. g., in Tractate *Beshallaḥ,*
ch. V, 1. 95, the Apparatus has: ברוח] במקרא כתוב כרוח.

IV. If the extended part of a scriptural quotation, accepted in the
text or recorded in the Apparatus, contains the tetragrammaton, the
latter is indicated by the letter ה'. If, however, the extended part is
found in one of the sources, either in the text of the editions or in one
of the manuscripts, then the tetragrammaton contained in it is reproduced in the form in which it is found in that source, as יי or ד, or in
whatever form it may be.

V. The readings in all those sources which represent conscious
attempts to correct the scriptural quotation in order to make it agree
with the masoretic text are ignored. These are the readings found in
all later editions of the *Yalḳuṭ Shime'oni,* the readings given by Buber
and the other editors of the *Makiri* in their respective editions, or by
Freimann in the *Vehizhir;* also those found in the Leghorn edition of
the *Mekilta,* since the editor, Najar, expressly states in his introduction that he corrected the scriptural quotations according to the
masoretic text.

VI. If the variant consists of a quotation from another verse of
another part of the Scriptures, the Apparatus records it and gives the
reference to chapter and verse in parentheses. Thus in Tractate *Pisḥa,*
ch. I, 1. 33, to the words בלתי quoted from Num. 32.12, the Apparatus records: כי אם .ט (דברים א'. ל"ז) זולתי .מ .א (ל"א ד"י במדבר).

Methods of Indicating the Variants in the Apparatus Criticus

I. The lines of the text are numbered on the outer margin. The Apparatus Criticus is printed here on the lower part of each page under a horizontal line which sets it off from the rest of the page. In the Apparatus the number of the line which contains the word to which the variants belong is indicated.

The text word to which the variants belong is repeated in the Apparatus and put in a half bracket. Thus, e. g., Tractate *Beshallaḥ*, ch. II, 1. 26, the text on 1. 26 contains the word וכשיצאנו and the Apparatus gives the number of the line of the text, 26, and repeats the word in a half bracket before recording the variants: [וכשיצאנו26 ק. ל. וכשיצאנו נ. כשיצאו.

When, however, there could be no mistake as to which word in the line the variants refer to, the text word is not repeated in the Apparatus. Thus, e. g., ibid., 1. 25, where the Apparatus records the variants פרותנמה, פריתזמיה, to the text word פרותיזמיה, the latter need not be repeated in the Apparatus. Further, when the variant consists of a different arrangement or sequence of the words which occur in the text, the words in the order given in the text are not repeated in the Apparatus. For in such cases there can be no mistake as to which word or group of words the various readings refer to.

If the word to which the variant belongs occurs more than once in the same line in the text, the text word when repeated in the Apparatus is accompanied by a numeral 1, 2 or 3 before the half bracket; this is to indicate to which one of the words in the line the variant belongs. Thus, e. g., הגיד ק. [1 אמר, means that to the first אמר occurring in the line ק has the variant הגיד. Likewise, if the word occurs three times and the variant belongs only to the first and third, it is indicated thus: הגיד ק. [3 & 1 אמר. If no such number is added to the text word repeated in the Apparatus, it is to be understood that the variant belongs to this word wherever it occurs in the line.

Vertical lines are used to divide the variants to different words in the same line. For the end of the line the number of the next line is a sufficient division.

II. Readings are given in the Apparatus in the following order: First, readings from the Mss., then from the printed editions, then from the compendia and commentaries in their chronological order, and then from quotations in other sources, in the chronological order of their respective authors. Thus, to use the abbreviations employed for indicating them, the order reading from right to left is the follow-ing: ג. ק. נ. ל. ש. ה. ל״ט. ט. ט״כ. כ. א״א. ז״י. ש״י. א״צ. א. מ. ס. גג. סה״מ. רמב״ן. ג״ק.

In the case of the *Yalḳuṭim* reference to the biblical book—with the section רמז in case of the *Shime'oni,* or chapter and verse in case of *Makiri*—where the passage from the *Mekilta* containing the variant is found, is given in parentheses. Thus, e. g., כ. (ישעיה כ״ב׳ ח׳) means that *Makiri* to Isaiah 22.8 has this passage with such and such a variant. And ט. (יחזקאל קפ״ז) means that *Yalḳuṭ Shime'oni* to Ezekiel, section 187, has this passage with such and such a variant. If the variant is found in the *Yalḳuṭ Shime'oni* to Exodus on the very verse which is the basis of the *Mekilta* discussion, the Apparatus merely refers to ט. which stands for *Yalḳuṭ.*

III. Conjectures precede all other variants. They are introduced by נראה שצ״ל or אולי צ״ל if they be the editor's own conjectures, or by the phrase פלוני הניה if suggested by others. Likewise, if a suggested correction has been accepted in the text, it is indicated as such by the word הגהתי put in the Apparatus, before the other readings or variants are given. If more than one source or authority endorse the accepted correction, the Apparatus cites only the original source, or the first authority to suggest it, and the last source endorsing or quoting the correction, leaving unmentioned intermediary sources and authorities who likewise accepted the suggested correction. This is deemed justified on the ground that the latest source usually quotes

the preceding ones; hence there is no need of repeatedly citing them.
Thus, e. g., when it is stated in the Apparatus: עפ"י ט. ועיין גם מ"ע
הגהתי, it means: I have made this correction on the basis of the reading in *Yalḳuṭ*, see also *Meir 'Ayin*; the reference to Friedmann's *Meir
'Ayin* where א"א. ז"י. א"צ. are quoted saves the editor the citation of
these sources. When, however, there is another source endorsing the
correction which is not mentioned by Friedmann, e. g., ג. or ש"י., it is
cited. The editor deemed it necessary to cite all sources and authorities which give support to a reading accepted or corrected by him,
though it is against all the editions and Mss. The same is done with a
correction in the text made by omitting a reading found in the editions or Mss. This is likewise indicated in the Apparatus. After giving
the readings of the editions and Mss. with all their variants, it is
remarked: השמטתי ע"פ ט., I omitted it on the basis of ט., or: והסר בט.,
it is missing in ט, or ומוחקו ז"י, *Zeh Yenaḥamenu* also strikes it out.
Here too the Apparatus gives all the references to the authorities sup-
porting such an omission, but does not repeat authorities quoted in
the latest source. As in the above, it is recorded thus: ג. ועי"ג מ"ע
השמטתי ע"פי א"א ומוחקו, which means: I have omitted it on the basis
of *Ot Emet*. ג also strikes it out, and see also *Meir 'Ayin*.

The source of the variant always precedes the variant, thus: דבר
הגיד] ק. נ. אמר מ..

As stated above, the sources are designated by abbreviations. To
this may be added that where all the three editions, viz., of Constantinople, Venice and Leghorn, agree, they are collectively designated
by the letter ד (= דפוסים).

The abbreviations designating sources are indicated by large letters followed by a period. This is necessary to avoid misunderstanding. Without such a period, ל. ט. intended to designate Leghorn and
Yalḳuṭ respectively might be taken to indicate *Leḳaḥ Ṭob*.

Additions are indicated by the sign ~, omissions by the sign > put
after the source. Thus, when the Apparatus has: ניינו מ. ~ ושבחו it

means that the Munich Ms. adds the word ושבחו to נ"ינו, which has been accepted in the text. On the other hand, when the Apparatus has: > א. אמר it means that the Oxford Ms. omits the word אמר, which has been accepted in the text.

If two or more sources agree in a variant reading or omission or addition, they are all put together before the variant reading which they contain or before the sign ~ or >. Thus, e. g., *Shirata,* ch. I, 1. 8, the Apparatus has: [נ. ל. דבר אחר רבי אומר], which means, that both the editions, Venice (= נ) and Leghorn (= ל), have the variant דבר אחר instead of רבי אומר accepted in the text. Likewise ibid., 11. 54–55, the Apparatus has: >.ד .א [לאלהים הוא — שנאמר, which means that in the Oxford Ms. and in the editions the phrase שנאמר with the verse it introduces is missing, and on 1. 65 it has: א. ק. נ. ~ כי טוב [הודו ליי, which means that in the Oxford Ms. (= א) and in the editions of Constantinople (= ק) and Venice (= נ) the words כי טוב are added to the words הודו ליי given in the text. A colon is used to separate the source or sources indicating the basis for the reading accepted in the text from the other sources cited in the Apparatus as offering variants. Thus, if the reading accepted in the text is based upon one or two sources only or upon a suggested correction, the Apparatus first records the source or sources upon which the reading is based with the sign = preceding them, or cites the author of the suggested correction, and then puts a colon after this reference. The other sources giving the variant readings rejected by the editor then follow. Examples for this are *Shirata,* ch. I,1. 22, where the Apparatus has: > א. מ: ס. = [ליי, indicating that the reading ליי accepted in the text is found only in the Casanata Ms. (= ס) and in the Munich Ms. (= מ) but is missing in the Oxford Ms. (= א); and ibid. ch. II, 1. 105, the Apparatus has: אדם] הגהתי = א"צ: א. מ. ד. משל לאדם מ"ח. והלא, which means that the reading אדם accepted in the text is a correction by the editor following *Efat Zedek,* and that the Mss. and the editions have the variant reading משל לאדם, while *Midrash Ḥakamim* (= מ"ח) has the reading והלא. A source with a variant, or the sign ~ or > following it, is always to be understood as going with the text word repeated in the Apparatus, and not with what may precede from other sources giving variants to the text word. Thus in *Shirata,* ch. IV, 1. 6, the Apparatus has: **צדיק וישר נ. ל.~ כגבור וכובע] ק. ~ כגבור.** This is to be understood to mean that **נ** and **ל** add the word **כגבור** to the word **וכובע** of the text and not to **כגבור צדיק וישר,** the variant from **ק.**

When a source with its reading or sign for addition or omission is to be connected with what precedes it from another source and not with the text word, it is put in parentheses, which is to indicate that, excepting the difference as given in the parentheses, this source fully agrees with the source or sources preceding it. Thus *Kaspa,* ch. IV, 1. 76, the Apparatus has: **(ק. ~ ישפך זבחי] ד. זבחיך),** which means, that **ק.** while agreeing with the other editions in reading **זבחיך** instead of **זבחי** accepted in the text, yet differs from them by adding the word **ישפך** to the reading **זבחיך.**

In like manner parentheses are used to indicate slight differences between sources which otherwise agree in the variant from the reading accepted in the text. Thus *Beshallaḥ,* ch. VII, 1. 2, the Apparatus has: **(ל. ~ ולא ישנה בדבורך] ד. ~ מדבורך כנגדך).** This means that the printed editions (=**ד**) all add three words to the **כנגדך** of the text, but that **ל** differs from the others in that it has as the third word **מדבורך** while they have **בדבורך.**

Parentheses are also used sometimes to enclose readings suggested by the editor as possible corrections of the variant which precedes.

References to Sources and Parallels

References to the Bible as well as to all parallels found in the talmudic-midrashic literature are of great help for an understanding of the text. They enable the student to examine the basis for the comments of the *Mekilta,* to trace the origin of its ideas, and to compare them with similar ideas found elsewhere in the Talmud and the Midrashim. Such references, as complete as I could make them, are supplied in this edition. They are printed in smaller type on each page beneath the body of the text and above the horizontal line which marks off the space of the Apparatus Criticus. The manner of indicating to which part of the text the reference belongs is the same as the one used in the Apparatus to indicate to which passage a variant belongs, i. e., putting before the reference the number of the line or lines of the text to which the reference belongs.

Reference to the passages in Exodus which are the subject of the *Mekilta* discussion and form the basis of the Midrash are not given in this manner. However, to facilitate the finding of a *Mekilta* comment to a passage in Exodus, the verses covered by the *Mekilta* in each chapter are indicated at the beginning of that chapter. In the references to the Bible, chapter and verse of the respective biblical book are given. In the references to the Mishna, the name of the Tractate and chapter and paragraph are given. Thus the reference פחסים ג, ב׳ means, Tractate Pesaḥim of the Mishna, ch. 3, paragraph 2. In references to the *Tosefta,* the abbreviation תוס׳ for תוספתא is put before the name of the Tractate, thus: תוס פחסים ג, ב׳. The references to the Babylonian Talmud give the name of the Tractate with the number of the folio and side. Thus the reference שבת ל׳ ב׳ means, Tractate Sabbath, folio 30, side 2, or 30b. In references to the Palestinian Talmud the letter י׳, abbreviated from ירושלמי, is put before the name of the Tractate, then the chapter and halakah or paragraph in which the respective passage is found are given, and the folio and column of the Krotoshin edition is added in parentheses. Thus the reference י׳ סוטה ג, ד׳ (18d) means Tractate Sotah of the Palestinian Talmud, chapter 3, paragraph 4, folio 18, column d of the Krotoshin edition.

The names of some of the Tractates of the Talmud as well as of other works of talmudic-midrashic literature are indicated by abbreviations commonly used for them. Thus מ״ש indicates the Tractate

Ma'aser Sheni; ר"ה the Tractate Rosh Hashanah; מו"ק the Tractate
Mo'ed Ḳaton; ב"ק the Tractate Baba Ḳamma; ב"מ the Tractate Baba
Mezi'a; ב"ב the Tractate Baba Batra; and ע"ז the Tractate 'Abodah
Zarah. אדר"נ stands for Abot de Rabbi Nathan (ed. S. Schechter,
Vienna, 1887), א"ר for *Ekah Rabba,* אסת"ר for *Esther Rabba,* ב"ר for
Bereshit Rabba, במ"ר for *Bemidbar Rabba,* ד"ר for *Debarim Rabbah,* וי"ר
for *Vayyikra Rabbah,* מ"ת for *Midrash Tannaim* to Deuteronomy (ed. D.
Hoffman, Berlin, 1909), ס"ע for *Seder 'Olam Rabba* (ed. B. Ratner,
Wilna, 1897), סא"ר for *Seder Eliyahu Rabba* (ed. M. Friedmann,
Vienna, 1902), פסדר"כ for *Pesikta de Rab Kahana* (ed. S. Buber, Lyck,
1868), פס"ר for *Pesikta Rabbati* (ed. M. Friedmann, Vienna, 1880),
פדר"א for *Pirke de Rabbi Eliezer,* קה"ר for *Koheleth Rabba,* רו"ר for *Ruth
Rabba,* שהש"ר for *Shir ha-Shirim Rabba,* שמו"ר for *Shemot Rabba,* ת"כ for
Torat Kohanim or *Sifra* (ed. I. H. Weiss, Vienna, 1862), ת indicates
Midrash Tanḥuma; the other Midrash of the same name (edited by S.
Buber, Wilna 1885) is designated as ת. בובער. Reference to these
midrashic works is given according to chapter, as in the case of *Seder
'Olam Rabba* and *Seder Eliyahu Rabba;* according to chapter and para-
graph or subdivision, as in the case of the *Rabbot* to the Pentateuch
(following the divisions of the Romm edition of Wilna 1909); accord-
ing to the weekly section and paragraph, as in the case of the *Midrash
Tanḥuma;* or according to the respective chapter and verse of the
Bible, as in the case of the other Midrashim.

   In the case of those works of which there are modern editions,
reference to the folio or page of that edition is given in parentheses in
addition to the other reference. The references to the number of the
folio or page of a modern edition are given just as they are found in
that edition, whether in Hebrew letters or in Arabic numerals—
depending on how the pages in that edition are numbered. When the
edition has only Hebrew pagination the number of the folio is given
with a following א or ב to indicate the side or page. Thus the reference to the *Pesikta de Rab Kahana,* ed. Buber, 109, is indicated by ב'
פסדר"כ. קט',. If the edition has both Hebrew and Arabic pagination, as

is the case with Buber's edition of the Midrash to Proverbs, the Midrash to Psalms and others, it is quoted according to the actual numbering of the side on which the reference is found. Thus the reference to the Midrash on Proverbs 2.8 would, besides giving chapter and verse, also contain in parentheses the number of the page in the Buber edition given in Hebrew letters כ"ה like this: (כ"ה) ח' ,ב'; while the reference to the Midrash on the next verse of the same chapter in Proverbs, found on the next page of the Buber edition, would contain in parentheses the number of the page given in arabic numerals 50, like this: (50) ט' ב'. For the reverse side of page כ"ה is thus separately marked and numbered in the edition of Buber.

In the English Translation I have made an effort adequately to reproduce in English the exact meaning and the full sense of the Hebrew original. This was not an easy task. The nature of the contents of the *Mekilta* and its composite character made the difficulties which the translator of any ancient work into a modern language encounters even more numerous and more complicated. The nature of the work would not allow a loose and free translation. The halakic portions of the book, since they are on the order of a legal code, require a more literal translation, giving in precise language and in accurate terms the exact meaning of the laws. But the haggadic portions also would lose much of their original beauty and peculiar flavor if given in too free a translation or in a mere paraphrase. For the Haggadah in the *Mekilta* for the most part represents exegesis rather than free exposition of the biblical text. It derives its beautiful teachings and its high ethical ideas from the scriptural words by means of a special kind of interpretation. This interpretation is based upon a peculiar play on words, upon their position in the scriptural context, or upon the emphasis on certain words, or forms of words. All these interesting points would be lost in a paraphrase, or in too free a rendering of the original. And yet in both the halakic and haggadic portions a rendering too literal would in many instances fail to do justice to the original and in addition would make poor sense in English.

I have, therefore, tried throughout the work to avoid both extremes. I have endeavored to give not a mere paraphrase but an accurate and rather literal translation—not, however, at the expense of clearness. I have tried as far as is compatible with idiomatic English not only to give the sense but also to retain the spirit of the original. Wherever it could be achieved without doing violence to the English idiom, an effort has been made to reproduce the method of reasoning, the mode of argumentation, the forms of speech and the quaint expressions peculiar to the original. In many instances, however, this had to be abandoned for the sake of clarity. The chief consideration has been to give in the translation the correct sense and the accurate meaning of the original Hebrew.

This consideration accounts for the different renderings given to the same Hebrew phrase or expression in different places. For the same Hebrew expression or phrase very often has various meanings, depending on its position in the sentence, the purpose for which it is used, and the emphasis or the tone with which it is to be read. Accordingly, it cannot be rendered the same way in every instance. To give an illustration: the phrase *talmud lomar,* תלמוד לומר, which literally means: "There is a teaching for this in the scriptural saying,"[43] is never so translated. Depending on the nature of the proof sought from the scriptural passage, this introductory phrase is translated differently in different places. If it introduces a refutation, it is rendered: "But Scripture says," or: "It says, however." If it cites a direct proof, it is rendered: "Therefore Scripture says." If it introduces a simple answer to the question: מנין, "Whence do we know?" or "How do we know?" it is rendered respectively by: "From the scriptural passage," or: "Scripture says." Thus, by not aiming at uniformity in the render-

---

43. See Bacher, *Exegetische Terminologie,* I, p. 200, and comp. B. Arakin 146, where מה בא ללמוד is found instead of מה תלמוד לומר, though in הגהות הב״ח it is (incorrectly) corrected.

ing of the same phrases and expressions, and by not following slav-
ishly the structure of the Hebrew sentences, the translation, though
not attempting to be a commentary, does give a correct interpretation
of the text.

Of course there are many instances where a mere translation, no
matter how adequate, is not sufficient to convey the full meaning of
the passage. In such instances brief footnotes supply the necessary
help to a clearer understanding of the passage. The scope of these
notes is limited. They either give a brief explanation of the idea or the
principle underlying the passage, or merely refer to the commentaries and books of reference where the reader can find a fuller explanation or additional information. There are, however, quite a large
number of passages which require whole excursuses and long elabo-
rate notes to discuss and explain all the difficulties involved in them.
Such long notes could not be incorporated in this work. I reserve
these longer notes and discussions of very difficult *Mekilta* passages
for a separate work of *Mekilta Studies* which I hope to publish soon. I
do, however, call attention to all such difficult passages in the brief
footnotes. Wherever the footnote contains the reference: "See Introduction," it means to call attention to the difficulties requiring elabo-
rate discussions and long explanations which, as stated here in this
Introduction, the writer hopes to give elsewhere. Dashes are frequently used to indicate passages which in my opinion are of a parenthetical nature. In the majority of such cases attention is called to
this in the brief footnotes.

In the rendering of the scriptural passages cited in the text either
as basis or as proof for the interpretation, I allowed myself a certain
amount of freedom. It frequently occurs that the scriptural verse
cited is not given in full in the Hebrew text. The interpretation is
based upon or derived from that part of the verse which is omitted in
the Hebrew quotation and which is merely referred to by the expression וגו׳, "etc." There are also instances in which the real proof is

derived not from the cited passage itself but from the context of the
scriptural passage which makes it evident that the sense of the cited
passage is such as to furnish the proof required by the Midrash. In all
such instances the mere rendering into English of that part of the
verse cited in the Hebrew text would not be sufficient to make the
Mekilta passage intelligible. In most cases, of course, the student is
relied upon to follow the direction given him by the word וגו׳, "etc."
and to look up for himself the full scriptural passage and its context.
In many other cases, especially in those where not even the directing
word וגו׳, "etc.", is given in the Hebrew text, the scriptural quotation
in English has been extended beyond that cited in the Hebrew text so
as to include the crucial word as part of the verse upon which the
interpretation rests. In other instances a brief footnote points to the
part of the verse or to the context from which the proof is derived.

In rendering the scriptural verses into English I have usually followed the version of the Bible Translation issued by the Jewish Publication Society of America. But this could not be done consistently all
through the work. In many instances the biblical verses as rendered
by the J. P. S. Translation would be unsuitable for the purposes for
which they are cited in the *Mekilta*. In some instances the *Mekilta*
absolutely demands another rendering, as it assumes a meaning of the
scriptural passage different from the one given by the rendering of
the J. P. S. Translation. In such cases to cite the version of the J. P. S.,
which does not furnish the basis for the proof of the *Mekilta* or for its
interpretation, would make the *Mekilta* comment unintelligible. In
other instances the interpretations insisted upon by the *Mekilta* are
exactly like the interpretations implied in the version of the J. P. S.
And the whole comment of the *Mekilta* is merely an insisting against
taking the scriptural passage in another sense. To cite the passages
according to the J. P. S. version would be to anticipate the comment
of the *Mekilta* and thus make it superfluous. In all such cases, where
it was necessary to differ from the version of the J. P. S. Translation, I

have either followed the version of one of the other English Bible translations if it suited the *Mekilta* comment or given my own rendering of the verse in accordance with the sense required by the *Mekilta*. In the latter case it is always pointed out in a footnote that this special rendering of the verse is required by the *Mekilta*.

In many instances I did not succeed in finding an English rendering which would adequately reproduce the sense of the Hebrew verse as presupposed by the *Mekilta*. I have then either retained the version of the J. P. S. in the translation but have pointed out in a footnote that the *Mekilta* comment is based upon a different understanding of the meaning of the Hebrew verse, or have given the best English rendering I could find and added in brackets a transliteration of the crucial Hebrew word which furnishes the basis for the interpretation of the *Mekilta*. All these variations in the rendering of the verses were necessary in order to make the comment of the *Mekilta* intelligible by showing, as far as possible in a translation, how the Midrash arrives at its interpretation and on what basis it rests. Briefly then, in the interest of clarity and thoroughness I have not aimed at uniformity in the rendering of the biblical verses but have allowed myself whatever latitude I felt was necessary.

It is now my pleasant duty to acknowledge my indebtedness to my friends who have rendered me assistance in this work. Professors Ginzberg, Marx and Davidson of the Jewish Theological Seminary in New York, with whom I frequently discussed many problems in connection with this work, have greatly helped me with their advice. Prof. Davidson in addition was kind enough to read part of the proofs of the Hebrew text and Prof. Ginzberg also read the proofs of the English Translation. Prof. Marx read part of the proofs of the Hebrew text as well as part of the manuscript of the translation. He has made some valuable suggestions which in most cases I have followed. Dr. Samuel Schulman of New York, as a member of the Committee on Jewish Classics of the Jewish Publication Society, carefully and painstakingly read through the manuscript of the whole translation. He made some fine suggestions and offered many corrections which I have accepted and which are now embodied in the translation. Dr. Sol B. Finesinger of the Hebrew Union College was of great help to me in the work of revising the translation. Dr. Henry Englander and Dr. Sheldon Blank of the Hebrew Union College also read the proofs of the translation and of the notes. Dr. Isaac Husik of the University of Pennsylvania also read through the whole translation and suggested some corrections which I accepted. Dr. A. S. Oko, the Librarian of the Hebrew Union College Library, was very solicitous in providing me with all the books needed for my work. Books not found in the Hebrew Union College Library he borrowed for me from other libraries. He also borrowed for me the Genizah fragments (No. 7) from the Library of Columbia University in New York. Dr. Julius Grodinsky, the Secretary of the Jewish Publication Society, has obliged me by his readiness to help in the mechanical part of the work.

Last but not least, Dr. Cyrus Adler, the chairman of the Committee on Jewish Classics of the Jewish Publication Society, showed great interest in my work and furthered it in many ways. I benefited from his sage advice, and he was unsparing in his efforts to secure for me manuscripts and photostatic copies of manuscripts needed for my work. To all of them I here express my sincerest gratitude.

May 15, 1933.

SIGLA USED IN APPARATUS CRITICUS [1]

לוח סימנים בשנויי נוסחאות

א. =כתב יד אכספרד

2א. =דפים אחדים מכתב יד אחד באכספרד

א"א. =ספר אות אמת

אה"ו. =אייזיק הירש וייס

א"צ. =איפת צדק

בה"מ. =ברורי המדות

ג. =גירסאות כתב יד בגליון מכילתא דפוס וניציאה

ג"נ. =דפים אחדים מהגניזה שהובאו לפילאדלפיא

ג"ק. =דפים אחדים מהגניזה שהובאו לנוייארק

ד. =דפוסים

ה. =ספר והזהיר

ז"י. =זה ינחמנו

ט. =ילקוט שמעוני דפוס ראשון

ט"כ. =ילקוט שמעוני כתב יד

כ. =ילקוט מכירי (ישעיה הוצאת שפירא ברלין תרנ"ג;

תהלים הוצאת בובער ברדיטשוב תר"ס;

משלי הוצאת גרינהוט ירושלים תרס"ב;

תרי עשר הוצאות גראינוף)

ל. =מכילתא דפוס ליוורנו

ל"ט. =לקח טוב

מ. =כתב יד מינכן

מא"ש. =מאיר איש שלום

מ"ה. =מרכבת המשנה

1. For further explanation of these sigla and of other abbreviations used in the Apparatus Criticus, as well as in the references to parallels, see Introduction, pp. xxiii–xxix and xlii–xlv.

מ"ח. =מדרש חכמים

מ"ס. =מדות סופרים

מ"ע. =מאיר עין

מ"ת. =מדרש תנאים על ספר דברים הוצאת

ר' דוד צבי האפפמאנן ברלין תרס"ח

נ. =מכילתא דפוס וניציאה

ס. =כתב יד קאסאנאטא

ק. =מכילתא דפוס קושטא

ש. =מכילתא דרבי שמעון בן יוחאי

ש"ט. =שכל טוב

ש"י. =שבות יהודה

ת. =תנחומא

ת"ת. =ילקוט תלמוד תורה כתב יד

~ =נוסף

> =חסר

TRACTATE AMALEK

CHAPTER I
(Ex. 17.8–13)

Then Came Amalek. R. Joshua and R. Eleazar Ḥisma say: This verse is to be taken in an allegorical sense and explained in connection with the passage in Job where it is said: "Can the rush shoot up without mire? Can the reed-grass grow without water" (Job 8.11). Is it possible for the rush to grow without mire and without water, or is it possible for the reed-grass to exist without water? So also is it impossible for Israel to exist unless they busy themselves with the words of the Torah. And because they separated themselves from the Torah the enemy came upon them. For the enemy comes only because of sin and transgression. In this sense it is said: "Then came Amalek."[1] R. Eleazar of Modi'im says: *Then Came Amalek.* Because Amalek would come in under the very wings of the cloud and steal people of Israel and kill them, as it is said: "How he met thee by the way . . . and he feared not God" (Deut. 25.18). Others say: "And he feared not God," refers to Israel who had no meritorious deeds.

R. Eliezer says: *Then Came Amalek.* He came with defiance. Because all other times that he came, he came secretly,[2] as it is said: "How he met thee by the way," etc. This coming, however, was not

---

1. The rest of the verse reads: "And fought Israel in Rephidim." The last word in Hebrew, רפידים, is interpreted allegorically to mean רפיון ידים, "feebleness of hands in upholding the Torah" (see Lauterbach, "The Ancient Jewish Allegorists in Talmud and Midrash," op. cit., pp. 313–15).
2. I. e., unannounced, unexpected.

מסכת עמלק

פרשה א (שמות י״ז, ח׳—י״ג.)

ויבא עמלק רבי יהושע ורבי אלעזר חסמא
אומרים המקרא הזה רשום ומפורש על ידי איוב
שנאמר היגאה גומא בלא בצה ישגא אחו בלא מים
וכי איפשר לגומא זה להתגדל בלא ביצה ובלא מים
וכי אפשר לאחו זה להיות בלא מים כך אי איפשר
להן לישראל להיות אלא אם כן מתעסקין בדברי
תורה ולפי שפרשו מדברי תורה לכך בא שונא
עליהם שאין השונא בא אלא על החטא ועל
העבירה לכך נאמר ויבא עמלק רבי אלעזר
המודעי אומר ויבא עמלק לפי שהיה עמלק
נכנס תחת כנפי ענן וגונב נפשות מישראל והורגן
שנאמר אשר קרך בדרך וגו׳ ולא ירא אלהים
אחרים אומרים ולא ירא אלהים אלו ישראל שלא
היו בידם מצות רבי אליעזר אומר ויבא עמלק שבא
בגלוי פנים לפי שכל הביאות שבא לא בא אלא
במטמוניות שנאמר אשר קרך בדרך וגו׳ אבל ביאה

33—1 ש. 82—81.   3 איוב ח׳, י״א.   9—7 לעיל ויסע ז׳.   11—9 ספרי דברים
רצ״ו. פדר״א מ״ד.   12 דברים כ״ה, י״ח.

מסכת] הוספתי: / עמלק] א. ויבא עמלק.   1 יהושע] ש. יאשיה / אלעזר חסמא] ט.
חסמא. ט״ב. אליעזר א. ד. אלעזר בן חסמא.   2 רשום] ט. סתום מ״ח. ~ כאן.
4 ובלא מים] מ. ד. >.   5 אין] א. >.   6 להיות] מ״ח. לחיות ד. >.   7—6 להיות
אלא—בדברי תורה] ד. בלא תורה.   11 כנפי] ק. ענפי כנפי / ענן] מ״ח. השכינה.
12 ולא ירא אלהים] הוספתי=א״צ.

so, but was with defiance. In this sense it is said: "Then came Amalek"—he came with defiance.

R. Jose b. Ḥalafta says: *Then Came Amalek.* He came with a plan. Amalek had assembled all the nations and said to them: Come and help me against Israel. But they said to him: We will not be able to stand against them. Pharaoh could not stand against them, for God drowned him in the Red Sea, as it is said: "And He overthrew Pharaoh and his host in the Red Sea" (Ps. 136.15). How shall we be able to stand against them? Then he said to them: You come and act according to this plan which I give you: If they defeat me, you flee; if not, then you come and help me against Israel. In this sense it is said: "Then came Amalek"—he came with a plan. R. Judah the prince says: Amalek had to make his way through five nations to come and wage war against Israel. For it is said: "Amalek dwelleth in the land of the South" (Num. 13.29)—he was in the interior beyond all of them. R. Nathan says: Amalek came only from the mountains of Seir. He crossed four hundred parasangs to come and wage war against Israel. Others say: Let Amalek the ungrateful come and punish the people who were ungrateful. Similar to this: "And these are they that conspired against him: Zabad the son of Shimeath the Ammonitess, and Jehozabad the son of Shimrith the Moabitess" (II Chron. 24.26).—Let these ungrateful ones come and punish Joash the ungrateful one. For it is said: "Thus Joash the king remembered not the kindness which Jehoiada his father had done to him, but slew his son. And when he died, he said: 'The Lord look upon it, and require it' " (ibid. v. 22). And what was his punishment? "And it came to pass, when the year was come about, that the army of the Arameans came up against him" (ibid. v. 23). It is written: "And the Lord delivered a very great host into their hand"—because of what?—"because they had forsaken the Lord, the God of their fathers. So they executed judgment upon Joash" (ibid. v. 24). Read not: "judgments" (*Shefatim*) but "sports" (*shipputim*[3]). And

3. See R. Menahem de Lonzano in his *Ma'arik* (ed. Jellinek, Leipzig, 1853, p.

זו לא בא אלא בגלוי פנים לכך נאמר ויבא עמלק
שבא בגלוי פנים רבי יוסי בן חלפתא אומר ויבא
עמלק שבא בעצה שכינס עמלק את כל האומות
20 ואמר להם בואו וסייעוני על ישראל אמרו לו לא
נוכל לעמוד כנגדן פרעה לא עמד כנגדן שטבעו
הקב"ה בים סוף שנאמר וניער פרעה וחילו בים
סוף אנו היאך נוכל לעמוד כנגדן אמר להם בואו
ואתן לכם עצה מה תעשו אם ינצחוני ברחו לכם
25 ואם לאו בואו וסייעוני על ישראל לכך נאמר ויבא
עמלק שבא בעצה רבי יהודה הנשיא אומר חמשה
עמים פסע עמלק ובא ועשה מלחמה עם ישראל
שנאמר עמלק יושב בארץ הנגב שהיה לפנים מכולן
רבי נתן אומר לא בא עמלק אלא מהררי שעיר
30 ארבע מאות פרסה פסע עמלק ובא ועשה מלחמה
עם ישראל אחרים אומרים יבא עמלק כפוי טובה
ויפרע מן העם כפויי טובה כיוצא בו ואלה
המתקשרים עליו זבד בן שמעת העמונית ויהוזבד
בן שמרית המואבית יבאו אלו כפויי טובה ויפרעו
35 מן יואש כפוי טובה שנאמר ולא זכר יואש המלך
החסד אשר עשה יהוידע אביו עמו ויהרג את בנו
וכמותו אמר ירא יי וידרש ומהו ענשו ויהי לתקופת
השנה עלה עליו חיל ארם וגו' וכתיב ויי נתן בידם
חיל לרוב מאד מפני מה כי עזבו את יי אלהים ואת
40 יואש עשו שפטים אל תקרי שפטים אלא שפוטים

20—18 לעיל שירתא ט'. 23—22 תהלים קל"ו, ט"ו. 28 במדבר י"ג, כ"ט.
34—32 דהי"ב. כ"ד, כ"ו. 37—35 שם כ"ד, כ"ב. 38—37 שם כ"ד, כ"ג. 39—38 שם
כ"ד, כ"ד.

18 בגילוי פנים] מ. בשלשה פנים / יוסי] מ"ח. יוחנן. 19 בעצה] ד. ~ מלמד / האומות]
ד. ~ העולם א. ~ שבעולם. 21 לא עמד] א. מ"ח. שעמד / שטבעו] א. טבעו מ.
טובעו. 22 הקב"ה] א. ט. < > / אנו] מ. ד. אבל אנו. 26 הנשיא] ד. <. 27—26 חמשה
עמים] ק. חמשים פעמים. 28 הנגב] ק. נ. ~ החתי והחוי והיבוסי והאמורי יושב בהר
ש. ל. ~ והחתי והיבוסי והאמורי יושב בהר (ש. ~ והכנעני יושב על הים ועל יד הירדן).
/ שהיה] ד. לפי שהיה. 32 כיוצא בו]=מ"ח: א. מ. ד. שנאמר ט. כתיב ת. וכן הוא
אומר / ואלה] מ. אלה. 33 המתקשרים] א. המתקרשים / זבד בן שמעת העמונית] ד.
וגו' / העמונית] א. העמונים. 34—33 ויהוזבד בן שמרית] א. מ. ויוזבד בן שמרת.
36 החסד] ק. והחסד. 37 וכמותו] ק. נ. ובמותו / ירא—וידרש] א. וגו' / יי] מ. ד.
אלהים. 38 וגו'] מ. ויבאו אל יהודה וירושלים וישחיתו כל שדי העם וכל שלל שלחו
למלך דרמשק. 39—38 וכתיב—אלהים א. <. 39 אלהים] ט. אלהיהם, ובמקרא אלהי
אבותיהם.

what "sports" did they practice upon him? They say: They appointed over him cruel guards who had never in their life known a woman, and they tortured him with pederasty—just as when it is said: "And tortured the pride of Israel,"[4] etc. (Hos. 5.5)—and it is written: "And when they were departed from him—for they left him in great diseases—his own servants conspired against him for the blood of the sons of Jehoiada the priest, and slew him on his bed, and he died" (II Chron. 24.25).

And Fought with Israel in Rephidim. Said R. Ḥananiah: This thing I asked R. Eleazar when he was sitting in the great session: How is Rephidim to be understood? He said to me: "Literally." R. Ḥananiah also said: I asked R. Eleazar: Why is it that the Israelites redeem only the first-born of asses and not also the first-born of horses and camels? He said to me: It is a decree of the king. Furthermore the Israelites at the time of the exodus had only asses. There was not a single Israelite who did not bring up with him from Egypt ninety asses laden with gold and silver. Others say: Rephidim means only "feebleness of hands." Because they relaxed their hold on the words of the Torah the enemy came upon them. For the enemy comes only because of feebleness of hands in upholding the Torah, as it is said: "And it came to pass when the kingdom of Rehoboam was established and he was strong that he forsook the law of the Lord and Israel with him" (II Chron. 12.1). And what was the punishment for this thing? "And it came to pass in the fifth year of King Rehoboam that Shishak king of Egypt came up against Jerusalem; and he took away the treasures of the house of the Lord," etc. (I Kings 14.25–26). This is one of the three things that returned to their original place:

---

102) who, commenting on the word שפוטים, says: פירוש בעילות בלשון לעז; cf. also S. Krauss, *Lehnwörter,* II, pp. 582–83. Also J. Perles, "Miscellen Zur rabbinischen Sprach-u. Altertumskunde," in *Monatschrift,* 1872, p. 272, and Harkavy נדחים מאסף, No. 8 (Petersburg, 1879), p. 124 and No. 10, p. 161, note 5.

4. See Friedmann.

וכי מה שפוטים עשו בו אמרו העמידו עליו בריונות
קשים אשר לא ידעו אשה מימיהם וענו אותו במשכב
זכור כענין שנאמר וענה גאון ישראל וגו' וכתיב
ובלכתם ממנו כי עזבו אותו במחלאים רבים
התקשרו עליו עבדיו בדמי בני יהוידע הכהן
ויהרגהו על מטתו וימת.

וילחם עם ישראל ברפידים אמר רבי
חנניה הדבר הזה שאלתי את רבי אלעזר שהיה יושב
במותבא רבא רפידים מהו אמר לי כמשמעו ועוד
אמר רבי חנניה שאלתי את רבי אלעזר מה ראו
ישראל לפדות פטרי חמורים ולא פטרי סוסים
וגמלים אמר לי גזירת מלך היא ועוד שלא היה בידן
של ישראל אלא חמורים בלבד באותה שעה שאין
לך כל אחד ואחד מישראל שלא העלה עמו תשעים
חמורים טעונים כסף וזהב אחרים אומרים אין
רפידים אלא רפיון ידים לפי שרפו ישראל ידיהם
מדברי תורה לכך בא שונא עליהם לפי שאין
השונא בא אלא על רפיון ידים מן התורה שנאמר
ויהי במלכות רחבעם ובחזקתו עזב את תורת יי
וכל ישראל עמו ומה היה ענשו של דבר ויהי בשנה
החמשית למלך רחבעם עלה שישק מלך מצרים
על ירושלים ויקח את אוצרות בית יי וגו' וזה הוא אחד
משלשה דברים שחזרו למקומן גלות יהודה חזרה

45

50

55

60

---

43 הושע ה', ה'.   46 — 44 דהי"ב. שם, כ"ה.   57 — 47 בכורות ה', ב'.   67 — 47 ש. 82.
59 דהי"ב. י"ב, א'.   62 — 60 מלכים א. י"ד, כ"ה — כ"ו.   67 — 62 פסחים פ"ז, ב'.

---

41 אמרו] א. <.   42 קשים] מ. קשות.   43 וכתיב] מ. ד. <.   44 כי] א. ט. ט"כ. >
/ במחלאים] ד. בחלאים ובמקרא במחליים / רבים] מ. רעים.   45 עבדיו ט. ט"כ. >
א. ~ וימתהו / בני] ד. ט. ט"כ. <.   48 חנניה מ. חננא.   50 — 48 שהיה יושב—את
רבי אלעזר] א. <.   50 חנניה] ד. חנינא.   52 ועוד] הוספתי=א"א.   53 — 52 שלא היה
בידן—באותה שעה] מ"ח. א"צ. ז"י. ז"י. ועוד (ז"י ולא עוד אלא) שסייעו את ישראל
בשעת יציאת (ז"י בשעה שיצאו, מ"ח. ביציאת) מצרים (ז"י. ממצרים).   54 העלה
עמו] א. מ. עלו בידו.   59 ויהי במלכות] ל.=מקרא, ויהי כהכין מלכות / רחבעם] ד.
ירבעם / ובחזקתו] ט. < במקרא וכחזקתו.   61 החמישית] מ. השישית / למלך] ט.
ט"כ. למלכות.   63 יהודה] א. מ. ט. ט"כ. > מ"ח. ישראל.

The exiled community of Judea really returned to its original place. For it is said: "Your fathers dwelt of old time beyond the River" (Josh. 24.2). And it is written: "Who destroyed this house, and carried the people away into Babylon" (Ezra 5.12). The heavenly writing[5] returned to its original place, as it is said: "Wilt thou set thine eyes upon it? It is gone" (Prov. 23.5). The silver from Egypt returned to its original place, as it is said: "Shishak king of Egypt came up," etc. (I Kings 14.25–26).

And Moses Said unto Joshua: 'Choose Us out Men.' From this it is evident that Moses treated Joshua as his equal. Learn ye, all the world, proper conduct from Moses who did not say unto Joshua: "Choose me out men," but "Choose us out men"—he treated him as an equal. From this we learn that a teacher should hold his pupil as dear as he holds himself. And whence do we know that the respect for one's fellowman should be as dear to one as the reverence for one's teacher? It is said: "And Aaron said unto Moses: 'Oh my Lord' " (Num. 12.11). Was he not his older brother? What then does it mean by saying: "Oh my lord"? He treated him as though he were his master. And whence do we know that the respect for his teacher should be as dear to a man as the fear of heaven? It is said: "And Joshua the son of Nun, the minister of Moses from his youth up answered and said: 'My lord Moses, shut them in' " (ibid. 11.28). He said to him: My teacher Moses, just as God would shut them in, so you should shut them in. And you find it also in the case of Gehazi. At the time when Elisha said to Gehazi: "Gird up thy loins, and take my staff in thy hand," etc. (II Kings 4.29), Gehazi started to walk off, leaning on his staff. When people would say to him: "Whither are you going Gehazi?" he would answer them: "To revive a dead body." They would then say to him: "Are you able to revive a dead body, is it not God alone that can kill and bring back to life again, as it is said: 'The Lord killeth and

5. I. e., the writing upon the tables which Moses broke (Ex. 32.19; cf. Pes. 87b).

למקומה שנאמר בעבר הנהר ישבו אבותיכם וגו׳
וכתיב וביתא דנא סתריה ועמה הגלי לבבל כתב
שמים חזר למקומו שנאמר התעיף עיניך בו ואיננו
כסף מצרים חזר למקומו שנאמר עלה שישק וגו׳.
ויאמר   משה   אל   יהושע   בחר   לנו
אנשים מכאן שהיה משה עושה אותו כמותו למדו
כל העולם דרך ארץ ממשה שלא אמר ליהושע
בחר לי אנשים אלא בחר לנו אנשים עשאו כמותו
מכאן שיהא תלמיד חביב לפני רבו כמותו ומנין
שיהא כבוד חבירו של אדם חביב עליו כמורא
רבו שנאמר ויאמר אהרן אל משה בי אדני והלא
אחיו גדול היה ומה ת״ל בי אדני עשאו כרבו ומנין
שיהא כבוד רבו של אדם חביב עליו כמורא שמים
שנאמר ויען יהושע בן נון משרת משה מבחוריו
ויאמר אדני משה כלאם אמר לו רבי משה כשם
שהמקום כלאם כך אתה כלאם וכן אתה מוצא
בגחזי בשעה שאמר לו אלישע חגור מתניך וקח
משענתי בידך וגו׳ התחיל מסתמך על מקלו והולך
אמרו לו להיכן אתה הולך גחזי אמר להם להחיות
את המת אמרו לו וכי אתה יכול להחיות את המת
והלא הקב״ה ממית ומחיה שנאמר יי ממית ומחיה

---

64 יהושע כ״ד, ב׳.   65 עזרא ה׳, י״ב.   66 משלי כ״ג, ה׳.   72—70 ש. 82.   76—70 אבות
ד׳, י״ב.   79—70 אדר״נ כ״ז.   74 במדבר י״ב, י״א.   78—77 שם י״א, כ״ח.
80—81 מלכים ב. ד׳, כ״ט.   81—85 פדר״א ל״ג.   84 שמואל א. ב׳, ו׳.

64 הנהר] א. הירדן.   65 וביתא] מ. ד. ביתא.   67 כסף מצרים—וגו׳] הוספתי=ט.
א״א.   69 למדו] ט. ילמדו.   70 כל העולם ד. כל אדם.   71 עשאו כמותו] ד. מכאן
שהיה עושה אותו כמותו.   72 מכאן שיהא—רבו כמותו] א. מ. ט. מ״ח. <.
72—74 ומנין שיהא—כמורא רבו]=ט. מ״ח. א״א. ז״י. ש״י: ד. <.   73 חבירו] א.
מ. תלמידו.   73—74 כמורא רבו] א. מ. כמותו.   75 אחיו גדול היה] ד. אהרן היה
גדול ממנו ט. אחיו היה וגדול ממנו היה מ״ח. אחיו היה גדול ממנו.   76 שיהא
כבוד—חביב עליו] ד. שמורא רבו.   78 אמר לו] ד. < / רבי משה] ד. < א. ט. רבינו
משה.   84 שנאמר—ומחיה] א. ד. <.

maketh alive' " (I Sam. 2.6)? He then would say to them: "My master also can kill and bring back to life again."

Choose Us Out Men. R. Joshua says: "Choose us out," that is "heroes." "Men," that is "fearers of sin." R. Eleazar of Modi'im says: "Choose us out," that is "fearers of sin." "Men," that is "heroes."

And Go Out, Fight with Amalek. R. Joshua says: Moses said to him: Joshua, go out from under the protection of the cloud and fight with Amalek. R. Eleazar of Modi'im says: Moses said to him: Joshua, what do you wish to keep your head for? Is it not for a crown? Then go out from under the protection of the cloud and fight with Amalek.

Tomorrow I Will Stand. Tomorrow we shall be prepared to take our stand. *Upon the Top of the Hill,* to be taken literally—these are the words of R. Joshua. R. Eleazar of Modi'im says: Let us declare tomorrow a fast day and be ready, relying upon the deeds of the forefathers. For "the top" (*rosh*), refers to the deeds of the fathers; "the hill," refers to the deeds of the mothers.

With the Rod of God in My Hand. Said Moses before God: Lord of the universe, with this staff Thou didst bring Israel out of Egypt; with this staff Thou didst divide the sea for them; with this staff Thou didst perform for them miracles and mighty deeds. With this staff mayest Thou perform for them miracles and mighty deeds at this hour. Issi b. Judah says: These are the five expressions in the Torah whose syntactical construction is not certain: "Shall it not be lifted up," "cursed," "tomorrow," "made like almond blossoms," "and rise up." "Shall it not be lifted up," in the passage (Gen. 4.7), where it is said: "If thou doest well shall it not be lifted up," which, however, can also be construed to read: "Shall it not be lifted up, and even if thou doest not well." Likewise the passage where it is said: "Cursed be their anger for it was fierce" (ibid. 49.7), could also be construed to read: "For in their anger they slew men and in their self-will they houghed oxen cursed" (ibid. vv. 6–7). Likewise the passage where it is said: "Tomorrow I will stand upon the top of the hill," could also

85 אמר להם אף רבי ממית ומחיה.

בחר לנו אנשים רבי יהושע אומר בחר לנו
גבורים אנשים יראי חטא רבי אלעזר המודעי אומר
בחר לנו יראי חטא אנשים גבורים.

וצא הלחם בעמלק רבי יהושע אומר אמר
90 לו משה יהושע צא מתחת הענן והלחם בעמלק
רבי אלעזר המודעי אומר אמר לו משה יהושע
למה אתה משמר את ראשך לא לכתר צא מתחת
הענן והלחם בעמלק.

מחר אנכי נצב מחר נהיה מעותדים
95 ועומדים על ראש הגבעה כשמועו דברי רבי יהושע
רבי אלעזר המודעי אומר מחר נגזור תענית ונהיה
מעותדין על מעשה אבות ראש אלו מעשה אבות
הגבעה אלו מעשה אמהות.

ומטה האלהים בידי אמר משה לפני
100 המקום רבונו של עולם במטה הזה הוצאת את
ישראל ממצרים במטה הזה קרעת להם את הים
במטה הזה עשית להם נסים וגבורות במטה הזה תעשה
להם נסים וגבורות בשעה הזאת. איסי בן יהודה
אומר אלו חמשה דברים בתורה שאין להם הכרע
105 **שאת. ארור. מחר. משוקדים. וקם.** שאת
שנאמר הלא אם תיטיב שאת או שאת ואם לא
תיטיב. ארור אפם כי עז או כי באפם הרגו איש
וברצונם עקרו שור ארור. מחר אנכי נצב על ראש

---

90 — 86 שמו"ר כ"ו, ד'.   103 — 86 ש. 82.   113 — 103 ב"ר פ', ו'. יומא נ"ב. י' ע"ז ב',
ז' (41cd). שהש"ר א', ב'.   107 — 106 ב"ר כ"ב, ו'. ספרי דברים נ"ד.   106 בראשית ד',
ז'. 107 שם מ"ט, ז'.   108 — 107 שם מ"ט, ו'.

87 גבורים אנשים יראי חטא] ד. אנשים גבורים.   88 אנשים גבורים]=א. ט. ט"כ: מ.
ד. <.   91 אלעזר] ד. אליעזר.   93 — 91 רבי אלעזר—והלחם בעמלק] א. <.   92 לא]
מ. אלא.   94 מעותדים] ק. נ. עמכם מעתרים.   95 כשמועו] ד. <.   96 אלעזר] ד.
אליעזר.   97 מעותדין] ד. מעתרים.   104 אלו] א. ד. < / בתורה שאין להם] ד. יש
שאין להם בתורה.   106 ואם] א. מ. אם.

be construed to read: "Choose us out men and go out, fight with Amalek tomorrow." Likewise the passage where it is said: "Made like almond-blossoms the knops thereof and the flowers thereof" (Ex. 25.34), could also be construed to read: "And in the candlestick four cups made like almond-blossoms" (ibid.). Likewise the passage where it is said: "And this people will rise up and go astray" (Deut. 31.16), could also be construed to read: "Behold, thou art about to sleep with thy fathers and rise up." Thus, these five expressions in the Torah are in their syntactical construction uncertain.

So Joshua Did as Moses Had Said to Him. Just as he was commanded. He did not transgress the order of Moses.

And Moses, Aaron and Hur Went Up to the Top of the Hill. This bears upon what we have already said above—to make mention of the deeds of the fathers and of the deeds of the mothers, as it is said: "For from the top of the rocks I see him, and from the hills I behold him" (Num. 23.9).

And It Came to Pass, When Moses Held Up His Hand, etc. Now, could Moses' hands make Israel victorious or could his hands break Amalek? It merely means this: When Moses raised his hands towards heaven, the Israelites would look at him and believe in Him who commanded Moses to do so; then God would perform for them miracles and mighty deeds.

Similar to this: "And the Lord said unto Moses: 'Make thee a fiery serpent,' " etc. (Num. 21.8). Now, could that serpent kill or make alive? It merely means this: When Moses did so, the Israelites would look at him and believe in Him who commanded Moses to do so; then God would send them healing.

Similar to this: "And the blood shall be to you for a token," etc. (Ex. 12.13). Now, of what use could the blood be to the angel, or how could it help the Israelites? It merely means this: When the Israelites did so and put some of the blood upon their doors, the Holy One, blessed be He, had pity upon them, as it is said: "The Lord will pass over," etc. (ibid. v. 23).

הגבעה או צא הלחם בעמלק מחר. משוקדים
110 כפתוריה ופרחיה או ובמנורה ארבעה גביעים
משוקדים. וקם העם הזה וזנה או הנך שוכב עם
אבותיך וקם אלו חמשה דברים שבתורה שאין
להם הכרע.

ויעש יהושע כאשר אמר לו משה
115 מה שנתפקד לא עבר על גזירת משה.

ומשה ואהרן וחור עלו ראש הגבעה
לענין שאמרנו להזכיר מעשה אבות ומעשה אמהות
שנאמר כי מראש צורים אראנו ומגבעות אשורנו.

והיה כאשר ירים משה וגו' וכי ידיו של
120 משה מגברות את ישראל או ידיו שוברות את עמלק
אלא כל זמן שהיה משה מגביה את ידיו כלפי מעלה
היו ישראל מסתכלין בו ומאמינין במי שפיקד את
משה לעשות כן והמקום עושה להם נסים וגבורות.
כיוצא בו ויאמר יי אל משה עשה לך שרף וגו' וכי
125 הנחש ממית ומחיה אלא כל זמן שהיה משה עושה
כן היו ישראל מסתכלין בו ומאמינין במי שפקד את
משה לעשות כן והמקום שולח להם רפואות. כיוצא
בו והיה הדם לכם לאות וגו' וכי מה הדם מהנה
למלאך או מה מהנה להם לישראל אלא כל זמן
130 שהיו ישראל עושין כן ונותנין מן הדם על פתחיהם
הקב"ה חס עליהם שנאמר ופסח יי וגו' רבי אליעזר

110 — 109 שמות כ"ה, ל"ד.   111 דברים ל"א, ט"ז. סנהדרין צ', ב'.   115 — 114 ש. 82.
118 במדבר כ"ג, ט'.   127 — 119 ר"ה כ"ט, א'.   140 — 119 ש. 83 — 82.   124 במדבר
כ"א, ח'.   127 — 131 לעיל פסחא ז'.   128 שמות י"ב, י"ג.   131 שמות י"ב, כ"ג.

109 צא] במקרא רצא / הלחם] מ. א. והלחם.   110 ובמנורה] א. ק. נ. במנורה.
111 הנך] מ. והנך.   112 שבתורה] ד. יש בתורה.   113 הכרע] א. מכרע.   115 גזירת
משה] ד. ~ ואהרן.   116 ואהרן] במקרא אהרן / עלו ראש הגבעה] הוספתי: א. וגו' מ.
ד. <.   117 מעשה אבות ומעשה אמהות] ט"כ. זכות אבות ואמהות.   121 כלפין] מ.
כלפני.   122 במי] א. במפי.   125 משה] ד. <.   126 בו] ד. <.   127 כן] ד. < / שולח]
ד. עשה.   130 עושין כן ונותנים מן] א. מ. נותנים מן מ"ח. רואים.   131 הקב"ה חס]
א. מ. המקום נגלה וחס מ"ח. מאמינים במי שפיקדם לעשות והמקום חס.

R. Eleazar says: For what purpose does it say: "Israel prevailed," or what is the purpose of saying: "Amalek prevailed"? Merely to tell that when Moses raised his hands towards heaven, it meant that Israel would be strong in the words of the Torah, to be given through Moses' hands. And when he lowered his hands, it meant that Israel would lower their zeal for the words of the Torah to be given through his hands.

And Moses' Hands Were Heavy. From this we learn that one should not delay the carrying out of the commandments. Had he not said to Joshua: "Choose us out men," Moses would not have been troubled thus. They said: Moses' hands were heavy at that time, he felt like a man with two jugs full of water hanging on his hands.

And They Took a Stone, and Put It Under Him. And did they not have a bolster or a cushion or a pillow to put under Moses? But "Moses said,"[6] etc.

And Aaron and Hur Stayed Up His Hands. For else he would raise them and then have to lower them. "And his hands were steady until the going down of the sun." This tells that they were having a fast day[7]—these are the words of R. Joshua. R. Eleazar of Modi'im says: The sin weighed heavily upon the hands of Moses at that hour and he could not bear it. What did he do? He turned to the deeds of the forefathers. For it is said: "And they took a stone and put under him," which refers to the deeds of the fathers; "And he sat thereon," which refers to the deeds of the mothers. "And Aaron and Hur," etc. But why need Scripture say: "The one on the one side and the other on the other side"? Merely to tell that Aaron would make mention of the deeds of Judah, and Hur would make mention of the deeds of Levi.[8] On the basis of this the sages said: We should have no less

6. The rest of the Midrash may be found in Ta'an. 11a. It is omitted here and referred to by the expression וכו׳, "etc."

7. A fast day extends until the setting of the sun (see also Pseudo-Jonathan to this passage, ed. M. Ginsburger, p. 130).

8. See Commentaries. But there is no need of changing the text. Aaron and

אומר מה ת״ל וגבר ישראל או מה ת״ל וגבר עמלק
אלא כל זמן שהיה משה מגביה את ידיו כלפי מעלה
עתידין ישראל להגביר בדברי תורה שהם עתידין
להנתן על ידיו וכשהוא ממיך את ידיו עתידין
135 ישראל להמיך בדברי תורה שהן עתידין להנתן
על ידיו.

וידי משה כבדים מכאן שלא ישהה אדם
במצות אלולי שאמר משה ליהושע בחר לנו אנשים
140 לא היה מצטער כן. אמרו יקרו ידיו של משה
באותה שעה כאדם שתלויין בידיו שני כדים של
מים.

ויקחו אבן וישימו תחתיו וכי לא היה
להם כר אחד או כסת אחת או קלוקרון אחד שיניחו
145 תחתיו של משה אלא אמר משה וכו׳.

ואהרן וחור תמכו בידיו שהיה מעלן
ומורידן וידי ידיו אמונה עד בא השמש מגיד שהיו
בתענית דברי רבי יהושע רבי אלעזר המודעי
אומר יקר חטא על ידיו של משה באותה שעה ולא
150 היה יכול לעמוד בו מה עשה הפנה על מעשה אבות
שנאמר ויקחו אבן וישימו תחתיו אלו מעשה אבות
וישב עליה אלו מעשה אמהות ואהרן וחור וגו׳ ומה
ת״ל אחד אחד אלא שהיה אהרן מזכיר מעשה
יהודה וחור מזכיר מעשה לוי מכאן אמרו אין פוחתין

142 — 140 פס״ר זכור (ג׳, ב׳).   143 — 145 תענית י״א, א׳. פס״ר שם.   177 — 143 ש. 83.
156 — 152 פס״ר שם. פדר״א מ״ד.

─────────

133 מגביה] א. ט. מגביר.   134 עתידין ישראל] ט. א״א. הקב״ה זוכר את ישראל
שע=תידין / שהם] מ. שאין.   136 להמיך] מ. לתמוך.   140 כן] ד. בו.   141 בידיו] מ.
בו ד. לו / שני] ד. <.   142 — 141 כדים של מים] ל״ט. בדים שלמים.   144 להם] א.
לו ד. לו למשה / קלוקרון] מ. קלקלרון / אחד] מ. אחת ד. <. / שיניחו] ד. שינוח.
145 של משה] ד. < / אלא אמר משה] א. <.   146 ואהרן] ק. נ. אהרן.   147 שהיה]
ד. שהיה.   148 אלעזר] א. ד. אליעזר.   149 יקר] ק. יוקר / על] א. של / ולא] ד.
לא.   150 בו] ד. ~ משה.   154 יהודה] ט. ש. א״צ. לוי / לוי] ט. ש. א״צ. יהודה.

than three people passing to the front of the ark to read the prayers on a fast day.[9]

And His Hands Were Faithful. With one hand he pointed out that he had not received anything from Israel. And with a gesture of the other hand Moses said before the Holy One, blessed be He: Lord of the Universe, through my hand Thou didst bring Israel out of Egypt; through my hand Thou didst divide the Sea for them; through my hand Thou didst perform miracles and mighty deeds for them. And so also mayest Thou at this hour perform for them miracles and mighty deeds.

Until the Going Down of the Sun. Because we have learned about all other kingdoms that they engage in battle only during the first six hours of the day. This wicked kingdom, however, engaged in battle from morning to evening.

And Joshua Discomfited Amalek and His People. R. Joshua says: He went down and cut off the heads of the mighty men that were with Amalek, those who were standing at the head of the battle lines. R. Eliezer says of this word (*vayahalosh*) that it is an abbreviation of: He made them sick, he made them tremble and he crushed them. *Amalek.* Meaning Amalek himself, literally. The particle *et* means to include his wife and children. "His people," means the armies that were with him. And when it says "and" (*veet*), it includes the armies that were with his sons.

With the Edge of the Sword. R. Joshua says: He did not disfigure them, but treated them with some degree of mercy. R. Eliezer says: "With the edge of the sword." Why is this said? We can learn from this that this war was only by the order of the Almighty.[10] Others say:

Hur each mention the meritorious deeds of the tribe of the other. Hur came from the tribe of Judah.

9. This is connected with the statement above, "that they were having a fast day" (see note 7).

10. The phrase לפי חרב is interpreted to mean: "By the mouth of God was the sword of this war decreed."

משלשה בני אדם עוברין לפני התיבה בתענית
צבור ויהי ידיו אמונה בידו אחת שלא קבל בה
מישראל כלום ובידו אחת אמר משה לפני הקדוש
ברוך הוא רבונו של עולם על ידי הוצאת את
ישראל ממצרים ועל ידי קרעת להם את הים ועל
ידי עשית להם נסים וגבורות וכך על ידי תעשה
להם נסים וגבורות בשעה הזאת **עד בא השמש**
לפי שלמדנו על המלכיות כולן שאינן עושות
מלחמה אלא עד שש שעות אבל מלכות חייבת
זו עושה מלחמה משחרית לערבית.

ויחלוש יהושע את עמלק ואת עמו
רבי יהושע אומר ירד וחתך ראשי גבורים שעמו
העומדים בשורות המלחמה רבי אלעזר המודעי
אומר בו לשון נוטריקון ויחל ויזע וישבר **את**
עמלק כמשמעו את אלו אשתו ובניו **עמו** אלו
חיילים שעמו וכשהוא אומר ואת אלו חיילים שעם
בניו.

לפי חרב רבי יהושע אומר לא נוולם אלא
דנם ברחמים רבי אליעזר אומר לפי חרב למה
נאמר למדנו שהמלחמה הזאת לא היתה אלא על

---

156 צבור] מ. בצבור.   167 המודעי] ד. י.   168 בו] ד. בא.   169 — 168 את עמלק]
ט. ש. א"א. מא"ש. עמלק.   169 את] א. ט. ואת.   170 ואת] ק. נ. את.
171 — 170 וכשהוא אומר — שעם בניו] א. י.   172 נוולם] א. ניוולום מ. ניוולום.   173 דנם]
מ. ט. דנום.

The following verse was fulfilled with respect to them: "Therefore, as I live, saith the Lord God, I will prepare thee unto blood, and blood shall pursue thee; surely thou hast hated thine own blood, therefore blood shall pursue thee" (Ezek. 35.6).

CHAPTER II
(Ex. 17.14–16)

And the Lord Said Unto Moses: Write This for a Memorial in the Book. The former sages say: Such is the rule obtaining throughout all generations, the scourge with which Israel is smitten will in the end be smitten itself. Let all men learn proper conduct from the case of Amalek. He came to harm Israel but God made him lose the life of this world and the life of the world to come, as it is said: "For I will utterly blot out," etc. And so also was the case of Pharaoh. He came to harm Israel but God drowned him in the Red Sea, as it is said: "But overthrew Pharaoh and his host in the Red Sea" (Ps. 136.15). Likewise, every nation or kingdom that comes to harm Israel God always judges according to this rule. The sages said: With what measure a man metes it is meted unto him, as it is said: "Yea, for with the very thing with which they acted presumptuously against them" (Ex. 18.11).

Write This for a Memorial in the Book, etc. "This," refers to what is written in this book. "For a memorial," refers to what is written in prophets. "In the book," refers to what is written in the Scroll of Esther.[1]

---

1. Each word in this passage is interpreted as a reference to a record about Israel's fight with Amalek. Here in Exodus there is a record of the fight with Amalek. In the prophets, i. e., in I Samuel 15.8–32, there is a record of the fight with Agag the king of the Amalekites. And in the book of Esther there is a record of the fight against Haman who was an Agagite (Esth. 3.1), i. e., a descendant of Agag the king of the Amalekites (cf. Meg. 13a).

175 פי הגבורה אחרים אומרים נתקיים עליהם המקרא
הזה לכן חי אני נאם יי אלהים כי לדם אעשך ודם
ירדפך אם לא דם שנאת ודם ירדפך.

פרשה ב   (שמות י"ז, י"ד—ט"ז.)

ויאמר   יי   אל   משה   כתוב   זאת   זכרון
בספר זקנים הראשונים אומרים כך מדה מהלכת
על פני כל הדורות שוט שישראל לוקין בו סופו
ללקות ילמדו כל אדם דרך ארץ מעמלק שבא
5 להזיק את ישראל ואבדו המקום מחיי עולם הזה
ומחיי עולם הבא שנאמר כי מחה אמחה וגו' וכן
פרעה שבא להזיק את ישראל טבעו הקב"ה בים סוף
שנאמר ונער פרעה וחילו בים סוף וכן כל אומה
ומלכות שבאת להזיק את ישראל בו בדין דנן
10 לעולם אמרו במדה שאדם מודד בה מודדין לו
שנאמר כי בדבר אשר זדו עליהם.

כתוב   זאת   זכרון   בספר וגו'   זאת   מה
שכתוב בספר זה זכרון מה שכתוב בנביאים בספר
מה שכתוב במגלה.

177—176 יחזקאל ל"ה, ו'.

11—1 לעיל ויהי בשלח ו'—ז'. ש. 83.   8 תהלים קל"ו, ט"ו.   11 שמות י"ח, י"א.
14—12 מגלה ז', א'; י' שם א', ז' (70[d]).   22—12 ש. 84.

---

176 אלהים] א. מ. ט. צבאות.   177 ירדפך] מ. ארדפך ק. נ. יראת / אם לא—ירדפך]
א. וגו'.

2 בספר] א. וגו' ד. ~ ושים באזני יהושע מ. ~ בספר / זקנים] מ. הזקנים / אומרים]
מ. אומר ל. היו אומרים.   4 ארץ] מ. ט"כ. > / מעמלק] מ. עמלק.   7 שבא להזיק]
ד. הרשע ששעבד.   8 וכן כל] מ. >.   9 שבאת] ד. שבא.   11 עליהם] ד. ~ ונאמר.
12 זאת זכרון בספר וגו'] א. מ. >.

And Rehearse It in the Ears of Joshua. This tells that on that very day Joshua was anointed[2]—these are the words of R. Joshua. R. Eleazar of Modi'im says: This is one of the four cases of righteous men to whom a hint was given. Two of them apprehended and two did not. Moses was given a hint but he did not apprehend it. Likewise, Jacob was given a hint and he did not apprehend. David and Mordecai, however, apprehended the hint that was given to them. Whence do we know about Moses? It is said: "And rehearse it in the ears of Joshua." God, thereby, as much as told him: Joshua will lead Israel to inherit the land. And yet in the end, Moses was still standing and beseeching, as it is said: "And I besought the Lord," etc. (Deut. 3.23). To give a parable, this may be compared to the case of a king who decreed against his son that he should not come unto him into his palace. The son entered the first gate and the guards kept their peace. He entered the second gate and again the guards kept their peace. But at the third gate they rebuked him and said to him: It is enough for you to have come so far. So also was it when Moses conquered the lands of the two nations, the land of Sihon and the land of Og, and gave it to the tribe of Reuben and the tribe of Gad and to the half tribe of Manasseh. The people, then, said to him: It seems as if the decree against you was not unconditional. Maybe we likewise have not been sentenced unconditionally. Moses then said before the Holy One, blessed be He: Lord of the world, are Thy ways perhaps like the ways of human beings? When an administrator[3] issues a decree, only a prefect can make him revoke it. When a prefect issues a decree, only a commander can make him revoke it. When a commander issues a decree, only a general can make him revoke it. When a general issues a decree, only a governor can make him revoke it. When a governor issues a decree, only the viceroy can make him revoke it.

---

2. I. e., appointed to be the successor of Moses.

3. On the nomenclature of the various officers and their rank in the order mentioned here, see Frankel, *MGWJ*, 1854, pp. 192–193.

15 **ושים באזני יהושע** מגיד שבאותו היום
נמשח יהושע דברי רבי יהושע רבי אלעזר המודעי
אומר זה אחד מארבעה צדיקים שנתן להם רמז
שנים חשו ושנים לא חשו משה נתן לו רמז ולא חש
יעקב נתן לו רמז ולא חש דוד ומרדכי נתן להם

20 רמז וחשו משה מנין שנאמר ושים באזני יהושע אמר
לו יהושע מנחיל ישראל את הארץ ובסוף היה עומד
ומתחנן שנאמר ואתחנן אל יי וגו' משל למלך שגזר
על בנו שלא יכנס עמו לפלטין שלו נכנס פתח
הראשון ושתקו לו בשני ושתקו לו בשלישי ונזפו

25 בו אמרו לו דייך עד כאן כך כשכיבש משה ארץ
שני עממים ארץ סיחון ועוג ונתנה לראובני ולגדי
ולחצי שבט המנשי אמרו לו דומה שלא נגזרה גזרה
אלא על תנאי אף אנו אין אנו נידונין אלא על תנאי
אמר משה לפני הקב"ה רבונו של עולם שמא דרכיך

30 כדרכי בשר ודם אפוטרופוס גוזר גזירה כלירכוס
מבטל על ידו כלירכוס גוזר גזירה דיקוריון מבטל
על ידו דיקוריון גוזר גזירה היגמון מבטל על ידו
היגמון גוזר גזירה איפרכוס מבטל על ידו איפרכוס
גוזר גזירה איפיטיקוס מבטל על ידו איפיטיקוס

17—22 ת. בשלח כ"ח; אסת"ר ו', ה'.   20—28 מ"ת 15.   20—35 ספרי במדבר קל"ד,
דברים כ"ט ושנ"ג.   22 דברים ג', כ"ג.

---

16 אלעזר] ד. ט"כ. אליעזר.   20 שנאמר] א. ד. < / אמר] א. אמרו.   21 לו] הוספתי=
ט. / היה] ד. משה.   23 לפלטין] ד. לפלטרין.   27 לו] א. מ. < / דומה] מ. דוגמה.
31 כלירכוס] ד. קלידיקוס.   33—34 איפרכוס מבטל על ידו איפרכוס גזר גזירה] ד. <.
34 איפיטיקוס] א. איפיטקוס מ. אפיטיקוס.

When the viceroy issues a decree, the great ruler can come and make him revoke it. For they are all but appointees, one superior to the other, as it is said: "For one higher than the high watcheth," etc. (Eccl. 5.7). Are Thy ways like their ways? "For what God is there in heaven or on earth, that can do according to Thy works, and according to Thy mighty deeds?" (Deut. 3.24)—like Thy works in Egypt and like Thy mighty deeds at the sea, like Thy works at the sea and like Thy mighty deeds at the rivers of Arnon. *Let Me Go Over, I Pray Thee* (*na*). The word *na* is but an expression for prayer. *And See the Good Land* (ibid.), that is, the land of Israel. *That Goodly Hill,* that is the mountain of the King. *And Lebanon,* meaning the Temple, as in the passage: "Open thy doors, O Lebanon," etc. (Zech. 11.1). And it is also written: "And Lebanon shall fall by a mighty one[4]" (Isa. 10.34).

But the Lord Was Wroth with Me for Your Sakes. R. Eleazar the son of R. Simon says: With me He spoke harshly—this, however, a human being cannot say—you might say that it was because of myself, but— as it is said: "For your sakes"—it was because of you and not because of me. You caused it that I should not be permitted to enter the land of Israel.

And the Lord Said Unto Me: Let It Suffice Thee. He said to him: It is enough for you to have come so far. R. Joshua says: "Let it suffice thee," means it is enough for you to have the world to come. And still Moses was standing and making all these petitions. He said before Him: Lord of the world: Was there at all any decree made against my entering the land? "Therefore ye shall not bring this assembly," etc. (Num. 20.12), only means that in my position as a king I may not enter. Let me then enter as a private man. God said to him: A king cannot enter as a private man. Still Moses continued to pray and

4. Lebanon is one of the designations for the Temple. The Rabbis understood the passage in Zech. 11.1 (cf. Yoma 39b) and the passage in Isa. 10.34 (cf. Git. 56b) as referring to the Temple.

גוזר גזירה ובא המושל הגדול ומבטל על ידי כלם

מפני שהן ממונין זה למעלה מזה וזה למעלה מזה

שנאמר כי גבוה מעל גבוה שומר וגו' שמא דרכיך

כדרכיהם אשר מי אל בשמים ובארץ אשר יעשה

כמעשיך וכגבורותיך כמעשיך במצרים וכגבורותיך

על הים כמעשיך על הים וכגבורותיך על נחלי ארנון

אעברה נא אין נא אלא לשון בקשה **ואראה**

את הארץ הטובה זו ארץ ישראל **ההר**

הטוב הזה זה הר המלך **והלבנון** זה בית

המקדש שנאמר פתח לבנון דלתיך וגו' וכתיב

והלבנון באדיר יפול **ויתעבר יי בי למענכם**

רבי אלעזר ב"ר שמעון אומר בי דבר קשה מה שאי

איפשר לבשר ודם לומר כן שמא תאמרו בגיני ת"ל

למענכם בגינכם ולא בגיני אתם גרמתם לי שלא

אכנס לארץ ישראל **ויאמר יי אלי רב לך**

אמר לו דייך עד כאן רבי יהושע אומר רב לך

דייך העולם הבא עדיין היה עומד ומבקש כל

אותן הבקשות אמר משה לפניו רבונו של עולם

כלום נגזרה גזירה שלא אכנס לה לכן לא תביאו

את הקהל הזה וגו' במלכות לא אכנס כהדיוט

אמר לו אין המלך נכנס כהדיוט עדיין היה עומד

37 קהלת ה', ז'.   39—38 דברים ג', כ"ד.   40—38 ספרי במדבר שם ודברים כ"ז. ברכות
נ"ד, ב'.   45—41 ספרי במדבר שם ודברים כ"ח.   44 זכריה י"א, א'.   45 ישעיה י',
ל"ד.   46—63 ספרי במדבר קל"ה ודברים כ"ט ושמ"א.   67—50 מ"ת 19.   54—53 במדבר
כ', י"ב.

40—39 כמעשיך במצרים וכגבורותיך על הים] ד. >.   40 כמעשיך על הים] ד. >.
46 ב"ר שמעון] ד. בן שמעון / קשה] ד. בקשה הוא.   50 אמר] א. אמרו.   52 לפניו
רבונו של עולם] א. >.   54 וגו'] וגו' במלכות לא אכנס] א. / וגו' אמר לפניו רבש"ע הואיל
ונגזרה גזירה שלא אכנס במלכות ד. במלכות / אכנס] ד. ~ לה.   55 אמר לו—כהדיוט]
א. >.

make all these petitions. He said before Him: "Lord of the world, since the decree has been issued that I should enter it neither as a king nor as a private man, let me then enter it by the cave of Caesarion which is below Paneas."[5] He said to him: "But thou shalt not go over thither" (Deut. 34.4). Then Moses said before Him: Lord of the world, since the decree against me is that I should enter it neither as king, nor as a private man, and not even by the cave of Caesarion which is below Paneas, then let my bones at least go over the Jordan. But He said to him: "For thou shalt not go over this Jordan" (ibid. 3.27). R. Simon b. Johai says: There is no need of this. For has it not already been said: "But I must die in this land, I must not go over the Jordan" (ibid. 4.22). Now, would it be possible for a dead person to go over? It must, therefore, be that Moses had been told: Not even your bones shall go over the Jordan. R. Ḥananiah b. Iddi says: Moses was but bewailing for himself, as it is said: "But I must die in this land," etc. And it also says: "For ye are to pass over the Jordan," etc. (ibid. 11.31)—you are to pass over but I am not to pass over. Others say: Moses, bending over the feet of Eleazar, said to him: "Eleazar, son of my brother, pray for mercy on my behalf, just as I prayed for thy father Aaron." For it is said: "Moreover, the Lord was very angry with Aaron to have destroyed him; and I prayed for Aaron also" (ibid. 9.20).

Then he said before Him: "Ruler of the world, if so, then let me at least get a view of it." And regarding this He said to him: "Get thee up into the top of Pisgah" (ibid. 3.27). R. Ḥananiah b. Akabyah says: The view granted to our father Abraham was more favored than that granted to Moses. For Abraham was not put to any trouble, while Moses was. What does it say in the case of Abraham? "Lift up now thine eyes, and look from the place where thou art, northward and southward and eastward and westward" (Gen. 13.14). And what does it say in the case of Moses? "Get thee up into the top of Pisgah,

5. Cf. Isaac Goldhaar, *Admat Kodesh,* Jerusalem, 1913, pp. 275–80.

ומבקש כל אותן הבקשות אמר לפניו רבונו של
עולם הואיל ונגזרה גזירה שלא אכנס לה לא כמלך
ולא כהדיוט אכנס לה במחילה של קסריון שהיא
מתחת לפניס אמר לו ושמה לא תעבור אמר לפניו
רבונו של עולם הואיל ונגזרה גזירה שלא אכנס לה
לא מלך ולא הדיוט ולא במחילה של קסריון שהיא
מתחת לפניס מעתה עצמותי יעברו את הירדן
אמר לו כי לא תעבור את הירדן הזה רבי שמעון
בן יוחאי אומר אינו צריך והלא כבר נאמר כי אנכי
מת בארץ הזאת איניני עובר את הירדן וכי איך
איפשר למת לעבור אלא שאמרו לו למשה אף
עצמותיך אינן עוברין את הירדן רבי חנניה בן אידי
אומר היה משה בוכה על עצמו שנאמר כי אנכי
מת בארץ הזאת ואומר כי אתם עוברים את הירדן
וגו' אתם עוברים ואין אני עובר אחרים אומרים
היה משה מוטה על רגליו של אלעזר ואומר לו
אלעזר בן אחי בקש עלי רחמים כשם שבקשתי
על אהרן אביך שנאמר ובאהרן התאנף יי מאד
להשמידו ואתפלל גם בעד אהרן אמר לפניו רבונו
של עולם אם כן ראנה במראית העין ובדבר הזה
אמר לו עלה ראש הפסגה רבי חנניה בן עקביא
אומר חביבה היא ראייתו של אברהם אבינו יותר
מראייתו של משה שבאברהם לא לבטוהו ובמשה
לבטוהו באברהם מה הוא אומר שא נא עיניך וראה
מן המקום אשר אתה שם צפונה ונגבה וקדמה וימה
ובמשה מה הוא אומר עלה ראש הפסגה ושא עיניך

64 — 65 דברים ד', כ"ב.   68 — 69 שם י"א, ל"א.   73 — 74 שם ט', כ'.   83 — 74 ספרי
במדבר קל"ו.   76 דברים ג', כ"ז.   79 בראשית י"ג, י"ד.   81 דברים ג', כ"ז.

59 לפניס] א. לפנים ד. לפני לפנים ט. (ואתחנן תתי"ז לפמיס).   65 איננני] ק. ואיניני /
אין] ק. אי נ. ל. <.   66 אף] ק. אך.   67 אינן עוברין] ד. לא יעברו / אידי] א. אדו.
70 — 69 אתם עוברים את הירדן וגו'] ד. <.   72 אלעזר בן אחי] א. אלעזר אחי מ.
אלעזר אחי / שבקשתי] מ. שבקשת.   73 מאד] ק. נ. < א. וגו.   74 להשמידו — בעד
אהרן] א. מ. <.   75 אם כן] מ. < הוא.   76 אמר לו] ד. נאמר / חנניה] ק. חנניא נ.
ל. חנינא.   77 היא] ד. <.   78 לבטוהו] מ. ליבטוהו ק. בטוחו.   79 לבטוהו] מ.
ליבטוהו ק. בטוחו.

and lift up thine eyes westward, and northward, and southward, and eastward, and behold with thine eyes" (Deut. 3.27)—get thee up, look around and then you will see.

And whence do we know that whatever Moses requested to see the Holy One, blessed be He, showed him? It is said: "And the Lord showed him all the land" (ibid. 34.1), that is, the land of Israel. He desired to see the Temple and He showed it to him, as it is said: "Even Gilead" (ibid.), and Gilead here only means the Temple as in the passage: "Gilead, thou art unto Me the head of Lebanon"[6] (Jer. 22.6). And whence do we know that He showed him Samson the son of Manoah? It is said: "As far as Dan" (ibid.), and there it says: "And there was a man of Zorah, of the family of the Danites, whose name was Manoah" (Judg. 13.2).

Another Interpretation: *As Far as Dan*. As yet the tribes had not come into the land and the land of Israel had not been apportioned among the Israelites. Why then does it say: "As far as Dan"? Simply because God had said to Abraham our father: Twelve tribes are destined to come out of thy loins, and this will be the portion of one of them. Similarly: "And pursued as far as Dan" (Gen. 14.14). As yet the tribes had not come into the land and the land of Israel had not been apportioned among the Israelites. Why then does it say: "As far as Dan"? Simply because God had said to Abraham our father: In this place your children will in the future worship idols. Abraham's strength then failed him. And whence do we know that He showed him Barak the son of Abinoam? It is said: "And all Naphtali" (Deut. 34.2). And there it is said: "And she sent and called Barak the son of Abinoam out of Kedesh-naphtali" (Judg. 4.6). And whence do we know that He showed him Joshua in his kingship? It is said: "And the land of Ephraim" (Deut. 34.2). And there it is said: "Of the tribe of Ephraim, Hoshea the son of Nun" (Num. 13.8). And whence do we know that He showed him Gideon the son of Joash? It is said: "And

6. And Lebanon is but a designation for the Temple (see above, note 3).

ימה רצפונה ותימנה ומזרחה וראה בעיניך עלה
והביט וראה. ומנין לכל הבקשות שבקש משה
לראות הראהו הקב"ה שנאמר ויראהו יי את כל
הארץ זה ארץ ישראל בקש לראות בית המקדש
והראהו שנאמר את הגלעד ואין גלעד אלא בית
המקדש שנאמר גלעד אתה לי ראש הלבנון ומנין
שהראהו שמשון בן מנוח שנאמר עד דן ולהלן הוא
אומר ויהי איש אחד מצרעה ממשפחת הדני ושמו
מנוח. דבר אחר עד דן עדין לא באו השבטים
לארץ ולא נתחלקה ארץ ישראל לישראל ומה ת"ל
עד דן אלא שאמר לו לאברהם שנים עשר שבטים
עתידין לצאת מחלציך וזה חלקו של אחד מהם.
כיוצא בו וירדף עד דן לא באו השבטים לארץ
ולא נתחלקה ארץ ישראל לישראל ומה ת"ל עד
דן אלא שאמר לו הקב"ה לאברהם אבינו במקום
הזה עתידין בניך לעבוד עבודה זרה ותשש כחו
מעליו. ומנין שהראהו ברק בן אבינועם שנאמר
ואת כל נפתלי ולהלן הוא אומר ותשלח ותקרא
לברק בן אבינועם מקדש נפתלי ומנין שהראהו
יהושע במלכותו שנאמר ואת ארץ אפרים ולהלן
הוא אומר למטה אפרים הושע בן נון ומנין שהראהו

84 שם ל"ד, א'.   85 — 125   125 ספרי דברים שנ"ז.   87 ירמיה כ"ב, ו'.   89 שופטים י"ג, ב'.
94 בראשית י"ד, י"ד.   98 — 94 סנהדרין צ"ו, א'. ב"ר מ"ג, ב'. ת. לך לך י"ג.
100 — 99 שופטים ד', ו'.   102 במדבר י"ג, ח'.

84 לראות] ד. >.   85 זה] א. וגו' זה ק. נ. מן הגלעד עד דן ל. את הגלעד עד דן.
86 את הגלעד] א. את כל הגלעד ק. נ. ואת כל הגלעד.   88 שמשון] ד. אף שמשון
מ. אף לשמשון.   89 אחד] ק. נ. > / ממשפחת] א. משפחת.   96 — 92 לאברהם— שאמר
לו הקב"ה] א. >.   96 שאמר לו הקב"ה] ד. שאמרו לו.   101 במלכותו] מ. > / ואת]
א. את.   102 הושע] א. יהושע.

Manasseh" (Deut. 34.2), and there it is said: "Behold, my family is the poorest in Manasseh" (Judg. 6.15). And whence do we know that He showed him David in his kingdom? It is said: "And all the land of Judah" (Deut. 34.2). And there it is said: "Howbeit the Lord, the God of Israel, chose me out of all the house of my father to be king over Israel for ever; for He hath chosen Judah to be prince, and in the house of Judah, the house of my father, and among the sons of my father He took pleasure in me to make me king over all Israel" (I Chron. 28.4). And whence do we know that He showed him the entire West? It is said: "As far as the hinder sea" (Deut. 34.2). And whence do we know that He showed him the graves of the Patriarchs? It is said: "And the South" (ibid.). And whence do we learn that the graves of the Patriarchs are in the South? It is said: "And they went up into the South, and came unto Hebron" (Num. 13.22). And whence do we know that He showed him the ruins of Sodom and Gomorrah? It is said: "And the plain" (Deut. 34.2). And there it is said: "And He overthrew those cities, and all the plain" (Gen. 19.25). And whence do we know that He showed him Gog and all his multitude? It is said: "The valley of Jericho" (Deut. 34.2). And we have learned that Gog and his multitude are destined to come up and fall in the valley of Jericho.

Another Interpretation: *The Valley of Jericho*. But cannot any ordinary person see the valley of Jericho? It simply means this: Just as a valley is cultivated, a little plot covered with wheat, a little plot covered with barley, so He showed him the entire land of Israel cultivated, like the valley of Jericho. And whence do we know that He showed him Deborah? It is said: "The city of palm-trees" (Deut. 34.2). And there it is said: "And she sat under the palm-tree of Deborah" (Judg. 4.5). And whence do we know that He showed him Lot's wife? It is said: "As far as Zoar" (Deut. 34.2). And there it says: "The sun was risen upon the earth when Lot came unto Zoar" (Gen. 19.23).

גדעון בן יואש שנאמר ומנשה ולהלן הוא אומר הנה
אלפי הדל במנשה ומנין שהראהו דוד במלכותו
105 שנאמר ואת כל ארץ יהודה ולהלן הוא אומר ויבחר
יי אלהי ישראל בי מכל בית אבי להיות למלך
על ישראל לעולם כי ביהודה בחר לנגיד ובבית
יהודה בית אבי ובבני אבי בי רצה להמליך על
כל ישראל ומנין שהראהו את המערב כלו שנאמר
110 עד הים האחרון ומנין שהראהו קברי אבות שנאמר
ואת הנגב ומנין למדנו על קברי אבות שהם בנגב
שנאמר ויעלו בנגב ויבא עד חברון. ומנין שהראהו
מהפכת סדום ועמורה שנאמר ואת הככר ולהלן
הוא אומר ויהפך את הערים האל ואת כל הככר.
115 ומנין שהראהו גוג וכל המונו שנאמר בקעת יריחו
ולמדנו שעתידין גוג וכל המונו לעלות ולנפול
בבקעת יריחו. דבר אחר בקעת יריחו והלא
ההדיוט רואה את בקעת יריחו אלא מה בקעה זו
מיושבת שדה מלאה חטים כל שהוא שדה מלאה
120 שעורים כל שהוא כך הראהו את כל ארץ ישראל
כבקעת יריחו. ומנן שהראהו דבורה שנאמר עיר
התמרים ולהלן הוא אומר והיא יושבת תחת תומר
דבורה. ומנין שהראהו אשתו של לוט שנאמר עד
צער ולהלן אומר השמש יצא על הארץ ולוט בא

103—104 שופטים ו׳, ט״ו.   109—105 דהי״א כ״ח, ד׳.   112 במדבר י״ג, כ״ב.
114 בראשית י״ט, כ״ה.   123—122 שופטים ד׳, ה׳.   125—124 בראשית י״ט, כ״ג.

---

106 אלהי ישראל] מ. ד. <.   109—106 להיות למלך על ישראל—להמליך על כל
ישראל] א. וגו׳. ועפי״ז הוספתי.   107 ישראל] ק. נ. עמי ל. עמו. / לעולם] מ. ד. <
/ ובבית יהודה] מ. ובבני יהודה.   109—107 ובבית יהודה—להמליך על כל ישראל]
ד. <.   109 כל] מ. <.   110 הים] מ. היום. / שנאמר] ד. ת״ל.   111 ומנין] ד. <.
113 ואת הככר] ק. נ. ואת כל הככר.   114 הערים] ק. נ. כל הערים.

Jacob was given a hint but he did not apprehend. For it is said: "And, behold, I am with thee, and will keep thee," etc. (Gen. 28.15). And in the end he was afraid, as it is said: "Then Jacob was greatly afraid and was distressed" (ibid. 32.8). What! A man whom God had given assurance was still afraid and anxious? It is simply because Jacob thought, woe is me, perhaps sin will be the cause.[7] David was given a hint and he apprehended. For it is said: "Thy servant smote both the lion and the bear," etc. (I Sam. 17.36), which simply means that David said: Why was I so distinguished as to be able to kill these wild beasts? It must be that something is going to befall Israel and they will be saved through me. Mordecai was given a hint and he apprehended. For it is said: "And Mordecai walked every day," etc. (Esth. 2.11), which simply means that Mordecai said: Is it possible that this pious woman should be permitted to be married to this wicked one who is uncircumcised and unclean? It must be that something is going to befall Israel and they will be saved through her.

For Blot Out, Blot Out Will I. "Blot out," that is, in this world. "Blot out will I," that is, in the world to come; "the remembrance," that is Haman; "Amalek," that is, himself, taken literally.

Another Interpretation: "For blot out," that is him and all his descendants; "Blot out will I," that is him and all his family—these are the words of R. Joshua. R. Eleazar of Modi'im says: "The remembrance," that is, Agag; "Amalek," that is, himself, taken literally; "Blot out," that is, him and all his descendants; "Blot out will I," that is, him and all that generation.

From Under Heaven. That there shall be no offspring nor posterity of Amalek under the expanse of the entire heaven. Rabbi Joshua says: When Amalek came to harm Israel, removing them from under the wings of their kind Father in heaven, Moses said before the Holy One, blessed be He: Ruler of the world, this wicked one is coming to destroy Thy children from under Thy wings. Who then will read that

7. I. e., of God's withdrawing from him the promised protection.

צוערה. יעקב נתן לו רמז ולא חש שנאמר והנה 125
אנכי עמך ושמרתיך וגו' ובסוף היה ירא שנאמר
ויירא יעקב מאד וייצר לו אדם שהבטיחו הקב"ה
היה ירא ומפחד אלא שאמר יעקב אבינו אוי לי
שמא יגרום החטא. דוד נתן לו רמז וחש שנאמר
גם את הארי גם הדוב הכה עבדך וגו' אלא 130
אמר דוד וכי מה אני ספון שהכתי חיות רעות הללו
אלא שמא דבר עתיד לארע את ישראל והם עתידין
להינצל על ידי. מרדכי נתן לו רמז וחש שנאמר
ובכל יום ויום מרדכי מתהלך וגו' אלא אמר מרדכי
איפשר חסידה זו תנשא לרשע הזה ערל וטמא אלא 135
שמא דבר עתיד לארע לישראל והם עתידין
להנצל על ידיה.

כי מחה אמחה מחה בעולם הזה אמחה
לעולם הבא את זכר זה המן עמלק כמשמעו
דבר אחר כי מחה לו ולכל תולדותיו אמחה לו 140
ולכל משפחתו דברי רבי יהושע רבי אלעזר המודעי
אומר זכר זה אגג עמלק כשמועו מחה לו ולכל
דורותיו אמחה לו ולכל הדור ההוא.

מתחת השמים שלא יהא נין ונכד לעמלק
תחת מפרס כל השמים. רבי יהושע אומר כשבא 145
עמלק להזיק את ישראל מתחת כנפי אביהם
שבשמים אמר משה לפני הקב"ה רבונו של עולם
רשע זה בא לאבד את בניך מתחת כנפיך ספר
תורה שנתת להם מי יקרא בו רבי אלעזר המודעי
אומר כשבא עמלק להזיק לישראל מתחת כנפי 150
אביהם שבשמים אמר משה לפני הקב"ה רבונו של
עולם בניך שאתה עתיד לפזרן לארבע רוחות
השמים שנאמר כי בארבע רוחות השמים וגו' רשע
זה בא לאבד אותם מתחת כנפיך ספר תורה שנתת

125—126 שם כ"ח, ט"ו.   125—129 ברכות ד', א'.   125—137 אסת"ר
שם. ת. בשלחם.   127 בראשית ל"ב, ח'.   130 שמואל א. י"ז, ל"ו.   134 אסתר ב',
י"א.   153 זכריה ב', י'.

---

126 ובסוף היה] ד. והוא היה / ירא] מ. ~ ופחד ד. מפחד וייRA.   128 אוי לי] מ. אומר
ט. <.   130 גם הדוב] מ. וגם הדוב א. ד. גם את הדוב.   131—130 אלא אמר דוד]
ד. <.   131 ספון] ק. ספוק.   135 איפשר—תנשא] א. מ. ט. וכי איפשר לחסידה זו
תנשא (ט. שתנשא).   141 ולכל משפחתו] מ. ולכל משפחותיו ד. ולמשפחותיו.
143 דורותיו] ד. תולדותיו.   145 מפרס כל] ד. < ט. מפרש כל / השמים] ג"ק. ~ שלא
יהו אומרים גמל זה של עמלק דקל זה של עמלק רחל זו של עמלק ת"ל מתחת השמים

book of the law which Thou hast given to them? R. Eleazar of Modi'im says: When Amalek came to harm Israel, removing them from under the wings of their Father in heaven, Moses said before the Holy One, blessed be He: Ruler of the world, Thy children whom Thou wilt in the future scatter to the four winds of the heaven—as it is said: "For I have spread you abroad to the four winds of the heaven," etc. (Zech. 2.10)—this wicked one is coming to destroy them from under Thy wings. Who then will read that book of the law which Thou hast given to them? R. Eleazar says: When will the name of these people be blotted out? At the time when idolatry will be eradicated together with its worshipers, and God will be recognized throughout the world as the One, and His kingdom will be established for all eternity. For at that time, "shall the Lord go forth and fight," etc. (Zech. 14.3); "And the Lord shall be King," etc. (ibid. v. 9). And it also says: "Thou wilt pursue them in anger and destroy them," etc. (Lam. 3.66). R. Nathan says: Haman came but to serve as a reminder for all generations, as it is said: "And that these days of Purim should not fail from among the Jews, nor the memorial of them perish from their seed" (Esth. 9.28).

And Moses Built an Altar and Called the Name of It Adonai-nissi. R. Joshua says: Moses called its name Nissi—R. Eleazar of Modi'im says: God called its name Nissi, for it is said: "And He, Adonai, called its name Nissi."—Said Moses: This miracle which God has performed, He performed for His own sake. And so you find that whenever Israel benefits by a miracle the miracle is as it were, before[8] Him also, as it is said: "The Lord, my miracle." When Israel has trouble, it is as if the trouble were before Him also, as it is said: "In all their affliction He was afflicted" (Isa. 63.9). When joy comes to Israel, it is as if the joy were before Him also, as it is said: "Because I rejoice in Thy[9] salvation" (I Sam. 2.1).

8. "Before Him" is a euphemism for: "for Him" (cf. above *Pisha*, XIV, notes 4 and 8).

9. Probably the verse is interpreted as if God said this to Israel.

להם מי יקרא בו רבי אלעזר אומר אימתי יאבד 155

שמן של אלו בשעה שתעקר עבודה זרה היא

ועובדיה ויהיה המקום יחידי בעולם ותהי מלכותו

לעולם ולעולמי עולמים באותה שעה ויצא יי ונלחם

וגו׳ והיה יי למלך וגו׳ ואומר תרדף באף ותשמידם

וגו׳ רבי נתן אומר לא בא המן אלא זכר לדורות 160

שנאמר וימי הפורים האלה לא יעברו מתוך

היהודים וזכרם לא יסוף מזרעם.

ויבן   משה   מזבח   ויקרא   שמו   יי   נסי

רבי יהושע אומר משה קראו נסי רבי אלעזר המודעי

אומר המקום קראו נסי שנאמר ויקרא שמו יי נסי 165

אמר משה הנס הזה שעשה המקום בגינו עשאו וכן

אתה מוצא שכל זמן שישראל בנס כביכול הנס

לפניו שנאמר יי נסי צרה לישראל כאלו צרה לפניו

שנאמר בכל צרתם לו צר שמחה לישראל כאלו

שמחה לפניו שנאמר כי שמחתי בישועתך. 170

158 שם י״ד, ג׳.   159 שם י״ד, ט׳. / איכה ג׳, ס״ו.   162 — 161 אסתר ט׳, כ״ח.
180 — 163 ש. 84 — 85.   170 — 166 לעיל פסחא י״ד. י׳ סוכה ד׳, ג׳ (54c). וי״ר ט׳, ג׳.
מדרש תהלים צ״א, ח׳. מדרש שמואל ד׳. ת. בשלח שם.   169 ישעיה ס״ג, ט׳.   170 שמואל
א. ב׳, א׳.

155 אלעזר] ד. ג״ק. ~ המודעי.   156 בשעה] מ. אמר לו בשעה / שתעקר] א. שיאבד
ד. שנעקר.   159 ואומר] ד. >.   160 נתן] ד. יהושע.   161 וימי הפורים האלה לא
יעברו] מ. והימים האלה נזכרים ונעשים / האלה] ק. נ. >.   162 — 161 מתוך
היהודים — מזרעם] הוספת: א. ד. וגו׳.   164 רבי יהושע אומר משה קראו נסי] א. ד.
> ג״ק. ~ המקום.   165 — 164 רבי אלעזר—יי נסי] ד. >.   164 המודעי]
Pugio fidei צד 657 <.   165 ויקרא שמו] הוספת Pugio fidei=שם.   166 בגינו] הגהתי=א*א.
ט״ב. ג״ק: א. ד. ט. בגינו מ. בשבילי בגיניו / האלו] מ. / צרה לישראל
כאלו] ג״ק. <.   168 כאלו] א. מ. <.   169 — 168 צרה לפניו—לישראל כאלו] מ. <.   169 בכל צרתם לו]
ג״ק. לא / שמחה לישראל כאלו] ג״ק. <.

And He Said: 'The Hand Upon the Throne of the Lord, the Lord Will Have War,' etc. R. Joshua says: When the Holy One, blessed be He, will sit upon the throne of His kingdom and His reign will prevail, at that time, "the Lord will have war with Amalek." R. Eleazar of Modi'im says: The Holy One, blessed be He, swore by the throne of His glory: I will not leave any offspring or progeny of Amalek under the entire heaven, so that people will not be able to say: This camel belongs to Amalek, this ewe lamb belongs to Amalek. R. Eliezer says: God swore by the throne of His Glory that if a person of any of the nations should come desiring to be converted to Judaism, Israel shall receive him, but a person from the house of Amalek they shall not receive. For it is said: "And David said unto the young man that told him: 'Whence art thou?' And he answered: 'I am the son of an Amalekite stranger' " (II Sam. 1.13). At that moment David recalled what had been told to Moses our teacher—that if a person of any of the nations should come desiring to be converted to Judaism, Israel should receive him, but a person from the house of Amalek they should not receive. Immediately: "And David said unto him: 'Thy blood be upon thy head; for thy mouth hath testified against thee'" (ibid. v. 16). In this sense it is said, "From generation to generation."

Another Interpretation: *From Generation to Generation.* R. Joshua says: "From generation," that is, from the life of this world; "to generation," that is, from the life of the world to come. R. Eleazar of Modi'im says: From the generation of Moses and from the generation of Samuel. R. Eliezer says: From the generation of the Messiah which really consists of three generations. And whence do we know that the generation of the Messiah consists of three generations? It is said: "They shall fear Thee while the sun endureth and so long as the moon, a generation and two generations"[10] (Ps. 72.5).

10. This rendering of the verse is required by the Midrash, which interprets it as referring to the generation of the Messiah.

ויאמר כי יד על כס יה מלחמה ליי
וגו' רבי יהושע אומר לכשישב הקב"ה על כסא
מלכותו ותהי הממשלה שלו באותה שעה מלחמה
ליי בעמלק רבי אלעזר המודעי אומר נשבע הקב"ה

175 בכסא הכבוד שלו אם אניח נין ונכד של עמלק תחת
כל השמים שלא יהו אומרים גמל זה של עמלק
רחילה זו של עמלק רבי אליעזר אומר נשבע
המקום בכסא הכבוד שלו אם יבא אחד מכל אומות
העולם להתגייר שיקבלו אותו ישראל ומביתו של

180 עמלק לא יקבלו אותו שנאמר ויאמר דוד אל הנער
המגיד לו אי מזה אתה ויאמר בן איש גר עמלקי
אנכי נזכר דוד באותה שעה מה שנאמר למשה רבינו
אם יבא אחד מכל אומות העולם להתגייר שיקבלו
אותו ומביתו של עמלק אל יקבלו אותו מיד ויאמר

185 אליו דוד דמך על ראשך כי פיך ענה בך לכך
נאמר מדר דר. דבר אחר מדר דר רבי יהושע
אומר מדר אלו חיי העולם הזה דור אלו חיי העולם
הבא רבי אלעזר המודעי אומר מדורו של משה
ומדורו של שמואל רבי אליעזר אומר מדורו של

190 משיח שהם שלשה דורות ומנין לדורו של משיח
שהם שלשה דורות שנאמר ייראוך עם שמש ולפני
ירח דור דורים.

180 — 171 פסדר"כ זכור כ"ח, ב'. 182 — 180 שמואל ב. א', י"ג. 185 — 184 שם א',
ט"ז. 192 — 186 פסדר"כ שם, אי"ר ג'. ת. (בובער ג', ס"ז). 192 — 188 ספרי דברים ש"י.
סנהדרין צ"ט, א'. ש. שם. 192 — 191 תהלים ע"ב, ה'.

173 — 172 הקב"ה—הממשלה שלו] ג"ק. המלך על כסא על כסא של יה. 173 הממשלה
שלו] ד. ממלכתו. 175 הכבוד שלו] ג"ק. >. 175 — 178 הכבוד שלו—בכסא הכבוד
שלו] א. >. 176 כל השמים] מ. כנפי השמים ט. ט"כ. ג"ק. מפרס כל השמים /
עמלק] ג"ק. ~ דקל זה של עמלק. 177 רחילה זו של עמלק]=ט. א"א: מ. ~ אם
מניח אני נין ונכד תחת כנפי השמים ג"ק. ~ ת"ל מתחת השמים שלא יהיה נין ונכד
לעמלק תחת מפרס כל השמים ד. אם אניח נין ונכד לעמלק / אליעזר מ. אלעזר המודעי.
178 הכבוד שלו] ג"ק. >. 179 — 178 אם יבא—ישראל] ד. אם יבא מכל האומות
שיקבלוהו. 179 — 180 ומביתו של עמלק] ד. ולעמלק ולביתו. 183 אחד] ד. >. 184 של
עמלק] ד. / מיד] ג"ק. שנאמר. 185 דוד] א. > / בן] מ. ~ לאמור אנכי מותתי את
משיח יי. 192 — 186 דבר אחר—דור דורים] מ. >. 188 אלעזר] מ. ד. אליעזר.]
189 ומדורו] ט. לדורו. 190 משיח שהם] ג"ק. משה שהן / שהם] ט. >.
191 — 190 ומנין—שלשה דורות] ט. >.

CHAPTER III
(Ex. 18.1–12)

Now Jethro the Priest of Midian, Moses' Father-in-Law Heard. What tidings did he hear that he came? He heard of the war of Amalek, reported in the preceding passage, and came—these are the words of R. Joshua. R. Eleazar of Modi'im says: He heard of the giving of the Torah and came. For, at the time that the Torah was given to Israel all the kings of the world trembled in their palaces, as it is said: "And in his palace everyone says: 'Glory' "(Ps. 29.9). At that time all the kings of the nations of the world assembled and they came to Balaam the wicked. They said to him: "Balaam! Perhaps God is about to do unto us as He did to the generation of the Flood." For it is said: "The Lord sat enthroned at the flood" (ibid. v. 10).[1] He said to them: "Fools that ye are! Long ago the Holy One, blessed be He, swore that He would not bring a flood upon the world," as it is said: "For this is as the waters of Noah unto Me; for as I have sworn that the waters of Noah should no more go over the earth" (Isa. 54.9). They, then, said to him: "Perhaps He will not bring a flood of water, but He may bring a flood of fire."[2] But he said to them: "He is not going to bring a flood of water or a flood of fire. He is just going to give the Torah to His people." For it is said: "The Lord will give strength unto His people" (Ps. 29.11). As soon as they heard this from him, they all turned back and went each to his place. R. Eliezer says: He heard of the dividing of the Red Sea and came. For, when the Red Sea was divided for Israel, it was heard about from one end of the world to the other, as it is said: "And it came to pass, when all the kings of the Amorites . . . heard"[3]

1. VV. 9–11 of this Psalm are interpreted as being a dialogue between the kings of the world and Balaam. The kings tremble before God, and while saying: "Glory to Him," they are in fear lest He sit in judgment upon them and bring another flood.
2. On the idea of a "flood of fire" cf. L. Ginzberg in Horodetzky's *Hagoren*, VIII.
3. This verse actually refers to the dividing of the Jordan. It is probably assumed

פרשה ג   (שמות י״ח, א׳–י״ב.)

וישמע יתרו כהן מדין מה שמועה שמע
ובא מלחמת עמלק שמע ובא שהיא כתובה בצדו
דברי רבי יהושע רבי אלעזר המודעי אומר מתן
תורה שמע ובא שבשעה שנתנה תורה לישראל
זעו כל מלכי תבל בהיכליהם שנאמר ובהיכלו
כלו אומר כבוד באותה שעה נתכנסו כל מלכי
אומות העולם ובאו אצל בלעם הרשע אמרו לו
בלעם שמא המקום עושה לנו כמו שעשה לדור
המבול שנאמר יי למבול ישב אמר להם שוטים
שבעולם כבר נשבע הקב״ה לנח שאינו מביא מבול
לעולם שנאמר כי מי נח זאת לי אשר נשבעתי
מעבור מי נח עוד על הארץ אמרו לו שמא מבול
של מים אינו מביא אבל מבול של אש הוא מביא
אמר להם אינו מביא לא מבול של מים ולא מבול
של אש אלא תורה נותן לעמו שנאמר יי עוז לעמו
יתן כיון ששמעו מפיו הדבר הזה פנו כולם והלכו
להם איש איש למקומו רבי אליעזר אומר קריעת
ים סוף שמע ובא שבשעה שנקרע ים סוף לישראל
נשמע מסוף העולם ועד סופו שנאמר ויהי כשמוע

2 – 1 י׳ מגלה א׳, י״ג (72b).   30 – 1 זבחים קט״ז, א׳.   4 – 3 שהש״ר ד׳, ט״ז.
16 – 4 לקמן בחודש ה׳. ספרי דברים שמ״ג. פס״ר צ״ה, א׳.   6 – 5 תהלים כ״ט, ט׳.
9 שם כ״ט, י׳.   11 – 9 סוטה י״א, א׳.   12 – 11 ישעיה נ״ד, ט׳.   15 תהלים כ״ט, י״א.
19 – 17 י׳ מגלה שם.   20 – 19 יהושע ה׳, א׳.

2 – 4 מלחמת עמלק—שמע ובא] א. מ. <.   3 המודעי]=ט. ג״ק. ג. א״א: ד. <.
4 שבשעה] א. מ. רבי יהושע אומר שבשעה (מ. בשעה.   6 מלכי] א. ט. <.   7 הרשע]
א. ט. <.   8 המקום] ד. המעשה זה מ״ח. הוא.   12 שמא] א. <.   15 לעמו] ד. ~
ולידידיו. ג״ק. לבניו.   16 יתן] ג״ק. ~ שבח נותן לבניו שכר טוב משלם ליריאיו / וזה
פנו] ד. הזה ענו כולם ואמרו אחר כך יי יברך את עמו בשלום ופנו.   17 אליעזר] א.
מ. אלעזר המודעי.   23 – 19 ויהי כשמוע—מפניכם] א. ויהי כשמוע את אשר הוביש
וגו׳ ונשמע וימס וגו׳.

(Josh. 5.1). Likewise Rahab the harlot said to the messengers of Joshua: "For we have heard how the Lord dried up the water of the Red Sea before you, when ye came out of Egypt . . . And as soon as we had heard it, our hearts did melt, neither did there remain any more spirit in any man, because of you" (ibid. 2.10–11).

They say: Rahab was ten years old when Israel went out from Egypt. And during all the forty years that Israel was in the wilderness, she practiced harlotry. At the end of her fiftieth year, she became a proselyte, saying before the Holy One, blessed be He: "I have sinned in three things, forgive me because of three things, because of the cord, the window and the wall,"[4] as it is said: "Then she let them down by a cord through the window; for her house was upon the side of the wall, and she dwelt upon the wall" (ibid. v. 15).

Now Jethro . . . Heard. He was called by seven names: Jether, Jethro, Heber, Hobab, Ben Reuel, Putiel, Keni. Jether, because he caused an additional chapter to be put into the Torah. Jethro, because he abounded in good deeds. Heber, because he associated himself with God. Hobab, because he was beloved of God. Ben, because he was like a son unto God, and Reuel, because he was like a friend to God. Putiel, because he freed himself from idolatry. Keni, because he was zealous for God and also because he acquired the Torah for himself.[5]

Another Interpretation: *Now Jethro . . . Heard.* Originally they called him merely Jether, as it is said: "And Moses went and returned to Jether his father-in-law" (Ex. 4.18). After he had performed good deeds, they added one more letter to his name so that he was called Jethro.

---

that just as they heard of the dividing of the Jordan they also heard of the dividing of the Red Sea.

4. I. e., by means of which she saved the spies (cf. also Commentaries).

5. Each one of these names is interpreted as descriptive of a virtue in which Jethro excelled, or of a characteristic by which he was distinguished. Ben Reuel is counted as one name, describing him to be like a son and a friend to God.

כל מלכי האמורי וכן אמרה רחב הזונה לשלוחי
יהושע כי שמענו את אשר הוביש יי את מי ים סוף
מפניכם בצאתם ממצרים וגו' ונשמע וימס לבבנו
ולא קמה עוד רוח באיש מפניכם. אמרו בת עשר
שנים היתה רחב בשעה שיצאו ישראל ממצרים
וכל אותן ארבעים שנה שהיו ישראל במדבר זנתה
לסוף חמשים שנה נתגיירה והיא אומרת לפני הקב"ה
רבונו של עולם בשלשה דברים חטאתי בשלשה
דברים מחול לי בחבל בחלון ובחומה שנאמר
ותורידם בחבל בעד החלון כי ביתה בקיר החומה
ובחומה היא יושבת.

וישמע יתרו שבע שמות נקראו לו יתר יתרו
חבר חובב בן רעואל פוטיאל קיני יתר שהותיר
פרשה אחת בתורה יתרו שהותיר במעשים טובים
חבר שנתחבר למקום חובב שהיה חביב למקום
בן שהוא כבן למקום רעואל שהיה כריע למקום
פוטיאל שנפטר מעבודה זרה קיני שקנא לשמים
וקנה לו את התורה. דבר אחר וישמע יתרו
מתחלה לא היו קוראין אותו אלא יתר שנאמר וילך
משה וישב אל יתר חותנו וכשעשה מעשים טובים
הוסיפו לו אות אחת ונקרא יתרו וכן אתה

21 — 22 שם ב', י'—י"א.   98 — 24 ש. 85 — 86.   30 — 29 יהושע ב', ט"ו.   40 — 31 ספרי
במדבר ע"ח. שמו"ר כ"ז, ח'. ת. יתרו י"ג.   37 — 34 ב"ב ק"ט, ב'.   39 — 38 שמות ד',
י"ח.

27 חטאתי] ד. ~ נדה חלה הדלקה מ. אלו שחטאתי.   28 — 27 בשלשה דברים מחול
לי] מ. ובשלשה ימחול לי מ"ח. באלו ימחול לי.   28 בחבל בחלון ובחומה] רש"י זבחים
קט"ז, ב' בחבל ופשתים וחלון.   31 יתרו 2] מ"ח. <.   32 חבר] ק. ש. מ"ח. <. > בן
נ. ל. ט. <.   34 חבר שנתחבר למקום] מ. ק. ש. מ"ח. <. > נ. ל. חבר שנעשה כחבר
למקום.   35 בן שהוא כבן למקום] ד. <.   36 שנפטר מעבודה זרה] ש. שפט כל ע"ז
שבעולם.   37 — 36 קיני—התורה] ש. קני שקנה העולם הבא.   40 ונקרא יתרו] ד. <.

You find this also in the case of Abraham, whom they originally called merely Abram. And when he performed good deeds, they added one letter more, and he was called Abraham. You find this also in the case of Sarah. Originally they called her merely Sarai. But when she performed good deeds they added to her name by putting in a larger letter[6] so that she was called Sarah. And so you find it also in the case of Joshua, whom they originally called merely Hoshea. And when he performed good deeds, they added one more letter to his name so that he was called Joshua, as it is said: "And Moses called Hoshea the son of Nun Joshua" (Num. 13.16). And there are others from whose names they took off one letter. You can learn this from the case of Ephron, whom they originally called Ephrown. After he had taken the money from our father Abraham, they took off one letter from his name and he was called merely Ephron, as it is said: "And Abraham hearkened unto Ephrown and Abraham weighed to Ephron" (Gen. 23.16). And you see it also in the case of Jonadab whom they originally called Jehonadab.[7] But after he had come to act as he did, they took off one letter from his name so that he was called merely Jonadab. In this connection the sages said: Let a man never associate with a wicked person, not even for the purpose of bringing him near to the Torah.

The Priest of Midian. R. Joshua says: He was a priest of idolatry, just as when it is said: "And Jonathan, the son of Gershom, the son of Manasseh, he and his sons were priests" (*Kohanim*) (Jud. 18.30). R. Eleazar of Modi'im says: He was a chief, just as when it is said: "And David's sons were chiefs"[8] (*Kohanim*) (II Sam. 8.18).

Moses' Father-in-Law. Formerly Moses would give the honor to his father-in-law, as it is said: "And Moses went and returned to Jethro

6. The letter *He* is larger than the letter *Yod*.
7. This may refer to Jonadab the son of Shimah (II Sam. 13.3) or to Jehonadab the son of Rechab (II Kings 10.15) (see Introduction and cf. Commentaries).
8. See Introduction.

מוצא באברהם שמתחלה לא היו קוראין אותו
אלא אברם וכשעשה מעשים טובים הוסיפו לו אות
אחת ונקרא אברהם וכן אתה מוצא בשרה
שמתחלתה היו קוראין אותה שרי וכשעשתה מעשים
טובים הוסיפו לה אות אחת גדולה ונקראת שרה 45
וכן אתה מוצא ביהושע שמתחלה היו קוראין אותו
הושע וכשעשה מעשים טובים הוסיפו לו אות אחת
ונקרא יהושע שנאמר ויקרא משה להושע בן נון
יהושע ויש אחרים שפחתו מהן אות יש לך ללמד
מעפרון שמתחלה היו קוראין אותו עפרון וכשׁשׁקל 50
הכסף מיד אברהם אבינו פחתו אות אחת משמו
ונקרא עפרן שנאמר וישמע אברהם אל עפרון
וישׁקל אברהם לעפרן. וכן אתה מוצא ביונדב
שמתחלה היו קוראין אותו יהונדב וכשבא לאותו
מעשה פחתו לו אות אחת ונקרא יונדב מכאן אמרו 55
חכמים אל יתחבר אדם לרשע אפילו לקרבו
לתורה.

כהן מדין רבי יהושע אומר כומר היה כענין
שנאמר ויהונתן בן גרשם בן מנשה הוא ובניו היו
כהנים רבי אלעזר המודעי אומר שר היה כענין 60
שנאמר ובני דוד כהנים היו.

חותן משה מתחלה היה משה מכבד לחמיו

48 — במדבר י״ג, ט״ז.   53 — 49 ב״ר נ״ח, ז׳.   52 — 53 בראשית כ״ג, ט״ז.
57 — 53 אדר״נ ט׳.   58 — 59 שמו״ר א׳, ל״ב.   59 — 60 שופטים י״ח, ל׳.   61 שמואל
ב. ח׳, י״ח.   62 — 65 ספרי במדבר ע״ח.

44 — 45 וכשעשתה—גדולה] א. ט. < / גדולה מ. <.   46 — 48 שמתחלה—ונקרא יהושע]
א. שמתחלה וגו׳ ד. <.   49 אחרים] א. מ. < / שפחתו] א. מ. שמענו / אות] א. ט.
ד. < / ללמד] א. < מ. לומר.   51 — 50 וכשׁשׁקל—מיד] א. מ. ומשנשקל דמה של
ארץ ישראל מן. 51 משמו] א. מ. <.   52 ונקרא עפרן] ד. <.   54 — 55 וכשבא לאותו
מעשה] ש. וכין שנתחבר לרשע שהוא יהוא מ״ח. וכשנתחבר ליהוא.   55 פחתו לו]
א. מנעו ממנו מ. חסרו ממנו / יונדב] ד. ~ שנאמר בהתחברך לרשע.   56 אפילו] מ.
<.   59 בן מנשה הוא ובניו היו כהנים] א. וגו׳ ועפ״י הוספתו כמו במקרא: ד. בן מנשה
ובניו היו כהנים מ. בן מנשה היו כהנים.   62 מכבד לחמיו] נ. ל. מתכבד בחמיו.

his father-in-law" (Ex. 4.18). Now, however, his father-in-law would give the honor to him. If they asked him: "What is your distinction?" He would say to them: "I am the father-in-law of Moses."

Of All that God Had Done for Moses and for Israel His People. Moses was equal to all Israel, and Israel was equal to Moses. The master was equal to the pupil, and the pupil was equal to the master.

How that the Lord Had Brought Israel Out of Egypt. This tells that the exodus from Egypt was equal to all the other miracles and mighty deeds which the Holy One, blessed be He, did for Israel.

And Jethro, Moses' Father-in-Law, Took Zipporah, Moses' Wife, after He Had Sent Her Away. R. Joshua says: After she had been dismissed from him by a bill of divorce. Here the term "send" (*Shiluaḥ*) is used and there (Deut. 24.1) the term "send" (*Shiluaḥ*) is used. Just as the term "send" used there implies a bill of divorce, so also the term "send" used here implies a bill of divorce. R. Eleazar of Modi'im says: After she had been dismissed from him by a mere speech. For at the time when God said to Moses: "Go and bring out My people, the children of Israel, from Egypt," as it is said: "Come now therefore, and I will send thee unto Pharaoh," etc. (Ex. 3.10), Moses immediately took his wife and his two sons and led them to Egypt, as it is said: "And Moses took his wife and his sons, and set them upon an ass, and he returned to the land of Egypt" (ibid. 4.20). At the same time Aaron was told: "Go into the wilderness to meet Moses" (ibid. 4.27). Aaron then went to meet him. He threw his arms around him, embraced him and kissed him, and said to him: "Moses, my brother, where have you been all these years?" Moses said to him: "In Midian." Then Aaron said to him: "What about the children and women, that are with you?" Moses said to him: "My wife and my sons." "And whither are you taking them?" asked Aaron. "To Egypt," answered Moses. Then Aaron said to him: "We are worrying about those already there and now you bring upon us these newcomers." At that moment Moses said to Zipporah: "Go to your father's house." She

שנאמר וילך משה וישב אל יתר חתנו ועכשיו חמיו
מכבדו אמרו לו מה טיבך אמר להם אנכי חותן
משה.

65

אֵת כָּל אֲשֶׁר עָשָׂה אֱלֹהִים לְמֹשֶׁה
וּלְיִשְׂרָאֵל עַמּוֹ שקול משה כישראל וישראל
כמשה שקול הרב כתלמיד ושקול התלמיד כרב.

כִּי הוֹצִיא יְיָ אֶת יִשְׂרָאֵל מִמִּצְרַיִם מגיד

70 ששקולה יציאת מצרים כנגד כל הנסים וגבורות
שעשה הקב״ה לישראל.

וַיִּקַּח יִתְרוֹ חֹתֵן מֹשֶׁה אֶת צִפֹּרָה
אֵשֶׁת מֹשֶׁה אַחַר שִׁלּוּחֶיהָ רבי יהושע אומר
מאחר שנפטרה ממנו בגט נאמר כאן שלוח ונאמר

75 להלן שלוח מה שלוח האמור להלן גט אף שלוח
האמור כאן גט רבי אלעזר המודעי אומר מאחר
שנפטרה ממנו במאמר שבשעה שאמר לו המקום
למשה לך והוצא את עמי בני ישראל ממצרים
שנאמר ועתה לכה ואשלחך אל פרעה וגו׳ באותה

80 שעה נטל אשתו ושני בניו והיה מוליכם למצרים
שנאמר ויקח משה את אשתו ואת בניו וירכיבם על
החמור וישב ארצה מצרים באותה שעה נאמר
לאהרן לך לקראת משה המדברה וגו׳ יצא לקראתו
והיה מגפפו ומחבקו ומנשקו אמר לו משה אחי היכן

85 היית כל השנים הללו אמר לו במדין אמר לו מה
טף ונשים אלו עמך אמר לו אשתי ובניי אמר לו
ולהיכן אתה מוליכם אמר לו למצרים אמר לו
על הראשונים אנו מצטערים ועכשיו הבאת עלינו
את האחרונים באותה שעה אמר לה משה לצפורה

63 שמות ד׳, י״ח.　79 שמות ג׳, י׳.　82—81 שם ד׳, כ׳.　83 שם ד׳, כ״ז.

64 אמרו] ד. אומר / להם] ד. >.　68 כרב] מ. ש. כנגיד.　71 לישראל] מ. למשה.
76—75 שלוח האמור] ד. > / אלעזר] מ. אליעזר.　79 ועתה לכה] מ. מ. ג. ועתה
לך ק. נ. לכה נא.　79—80 באותה שעה נטל] א. בא ונטל.　84 מגפפו] ד. > / אחי]
ד. >.　86—87 אמר לו ולהיכן] ד. ולאן.　87 אמר לו] ד.　89—88 הבאת עלינו
את האחרונים] ד. נצטער גם באלו.　89 לה משה] ד. > / לצפורה] א. מ. >.

then took her two sons and went. Referring to this it is said: "After he had sent her away."

And Her Two Sons . . . in a Strange Land. R. Joshua says: It certainly was a land strange to him. R. Eleazar of Modi'im says: "In a strange land"—where God was like a stranger.[9] Moses said: Since the whole world is worshiping idols, whom shall I worship? Him by whose word the world came into being. For at the time when Moses said to Jethro: "Give me your daughter Zipporah to wife," Jethro said to him: "Accept one condition which I will state to you and I will give her to you for a wife." "What is it?" asked Moses. He then said to him: "The first son that you will have shall belong to the idol and the following may belong to God." Moses accepted. Jethro then said: "Swear unto me," and Moses swore, as it is said: "And he adjured (*vayoel*) Moses" (Ex. 2.21). For *Alah* is but an expression for swearing, as it is said: "But Saul adjured (*vayoel*) the people" (I Sam. 14.24). So also: "Be adjured[10] (*Hoel*) to take two talents" (II Kings 5.23). It was for this that the angel at first wished to kill Moses. Immediately: "Zipporah took a flint and cut off the foreskin of her son . . . So he let him alone" (Ex. 4.25–26). R. Eleazar b. Azariah says: Uncircumcision is detestable, for the wicked are reproached with it, as it is said: "For all the nations are uncircumcised" (Jer. 9.25). R. Ishmael says: Great is circumcision, for thirteen covenants[11] were made over it. R. Jose the Galilean says: Great is circumcision, for it sets aside the Sabbath, which is very important and the profanation of which is punishable by extinction. R. Joshua b. Karḥa says: Great is circumcision, for no

9. See Introduction.

10. The *Mekilta,* according to the reading accepted in our text, thus interprets the word הואל. See Arakin 16a and comp. שאלתות (Wilna, 1864) section מצורע, p. 38b (cf., however, the variant reading of this *Mekilta* passage as given in *Pugio Fidei,* and see Introduction).

11. I. e., the word ברית, "covenant," is used in the Torah thirteen times in connection with the rite of circumcision (cf. also commentary *Mirkebet ha-Mishneh,* ad loc.).

90 לכי לבית אביך נטלה שני בניה והלכה לה לכך
נאמר אחר שלוחיה.

ואת שני בניה וגו' **נכריה** רבי יהושע
אומר ארץ נכריה היתה לו ודאי רבי אלעזר
המודעי אומר בארץ נכריה נכר יה אמר משה
95 הואיל וכל העולם כולו עובדי עבודה זרה למי אני
אעבוד למי שאמר והיה העולם שבשעה שאמר
משה ליתרו תנה לי את צפורה בתך לאשה
אמר לו יתרו קבל עליך דבר אחד שאני אומר לך
ואני נותנה לך לאשה אמר לו מהו אמר לו בן שיהיה
100 לך תחלה יהיה לעבודה זרה ומכאן ואילך לשם
שמים וקבל עליו אמר לו השבע לי וישבע
שנאמר ויואל משה ואין אלה אלא לשון שבועה
שנאמר ויואל משה את העם וגו' וכן הואל וקח
ככרים וגו' לפיכך הקדים המלאך להרוג את משה
105 מיד ותקח צפורה צר ותכרות את ערלת בנה וגו'
וירף ממנו. רבי אלעזר בן עזריה אומר מאוסה
ערלה שנתגנו בה רשעים שנאמר כי כל הגוים
ערלים רבי ישמעאל אומר גדולה מילה ששלש
עשרה בריתות נכרתו עליה רבי יוסי הגלילי
110 אומר גדולה מילה שדוחה את השבת חמורה
שחייבין עליה כרת רבי יהושע בן קרחה אומר

---

102 שם ב/, כ״א.   103 שמואל א. י״ד, כ״ד.   104 — 103 מלכים ב. ה/, כ״ג. ערכין ט״ז,
א/ ובגליון שם. נדרים ס״ה, א/. שמו״ר א/, ל״ג. ת. שמות י״ב.   106 — 105 שמות ד/,
כ״ה — כ״ו.   126 — 106 נדרים ל״א, ב/, ל״ב, א/. י/ שם ג/, י״ג — י״ד ⁽b38⁾).   108 — 107 ירמיה
ט/, כ״ה.

---

90 נטלה שני בניה] ד. באותה שעה הלכה לבית אביה ונטלה שני בניה / והלכה לה ד.
 <.   93 ארץ] ד. <. / אלעזר] מ. אליעזר.   94 נכר יה] א. ד. <.   95 למי] ד. <.
96 למי שאמר] ד. לפני מי שאמר.   98 אחר] ד. זה.   104 — 103 וכן הואל וקח ככרים]
מ. וכת/ וקח נכריב ט. ד. וכתיב ויאמר נעמן הואל וקח ככרים מ״ח. וכתיב הואל וקח
ככרים. במקרא שלפנינו, הואל קח ככרים. Pugio fidei צד 597 וכן הוא לוקח בכורים.
108 ערלים] א. ~ וגו' ד. ~ וכל בית ישראל ערלי לב.   109 בריתות] מ. ק. כריתות.
110 חמורה] ד. החמורה.

merit of Moses could suspend the punishment for its neglect even for one hour. R. Nehemiah says: Great is circumcision, for it sets aside the laws concerning plagues. Rabbi says: Great is circumcision, for all the merits of Moses availed him not in the time of his trouble about it. He was going to bring out Israel from Egypt and yet because for one hour he was negligent about the performance of circumcision, the angel sought to kill him, as it is said: "And it came to pass on the way at the lodging place," etc. (Ex. 4.24). R. Jose says: God forbid! to think that this righteous man neglected the duty of circumcision even for one hour! But, should he perform the circumcision and immediately go on his journey—there is risk of life. Should he perform the circumcision and tarry a while—God had told him: "Go and bring out Israel from Egypt."[12] It was merely because he relaxed and thought of lodging before performing the circumcision, that the angel sought to kill him. For it is said: "And it came to pass on the way, at the lodging place," etc. R. Simon b. Gamaliel says: The angel sought to kill not Moses but the child. For it is said: "Surely a bridegroom of blood art thou to me" (ibid. v. 25). You must reason: Go and see who could have been designated bridegroom? Moses or the child? You must say: the child.[13]

And the Name of the Other Was Eliezer: 'For the God of My Father Was My Help, and Delivered Me from the Sword of Pharaoh.' R. Joshua says: When did God deliver him? At the time when Dathan[14] said to him: "Who made thee a ruler and a judge . . . Now when Pharaoh heard this thing" (Ex. 2.14–15). They[15] say: They seized Moses, brought him to the platform, bound him and put the sword to his throat. But then an angel came down and appeared to them in the

12. See Introduction and cf. *Shebut Yehudah,* ad loc.

13. Cf. Jastrow, *Dictionary,* p. 514, s. v. חתן.

14. According to the Rabbis, the "two men of the Hebrews striving together" (Ex. 2.13) were Dathan and Abiram (see *Midrash Abkir* quoted in *Yalkut* ad loc. (167); cf. also Ned. 64b).

15. See Introduction.

גדולה מילה שלא נתלה זכות למשה עליה מלא
שעה רבי נחמיה אומר גדולה מילה שדוחה את
הנגעים רבי אומר גדולה מילה שכל זכיותיו של
משה לא עמדו לו בשעת דחקו הלך להוציא את   115
ישראל ממצרים ועל שנתעצל במילה שעה אחת
בקש המלאך להרגו שנאמר ויהי בדרך במלון
וגו' רבי יוסי אומר חס ושלום לאותו צדיק שנתעצל
במילה שעה אחת אלא ימול ויצא הרי סכנת נפשות
ישהה וימול המקום אמר לו לך והוציא את ישראל   120
ממצרים אלא על שנתרשל בלינה קודם למילה לכך
בקש המלאך להרגו שנאמר ויהי בדרך במלון וגו'
רבן שמעון בן גמליאל אומר לא ביקש המלאך
להרוג למשה אלא לתינוק שנאמר כי חתן דמים
אתה לי אמרת צא וראה מי קרוי חתן משה או   125
התינוק הוי אומר התינוק.

ושם   האחד   אליעזר   כי   אלהי   אבי
בעזרי   ויצילני   מחרב   פרעה רבי יהושע
אומר אימתי הצילו המקום בשעה שאמר לו דתן
מי שמך לאיש שר ושופט וגו' וישמע פרעה את   130
הדבר הזה אמרו תפסו את משה והעלוהו לבימה
וכפתוהו והניחו את הסייף על צוארו באותה שעה
ירד מלאך ונדמה להם כדמותו של משה תפסו

---

113 — 126 שמו"ר ה', ח'.   117 שמות ד', כ"ד.   134 — 127 שמו"ר א', ל"א. ד"ר ב', כ"ח.
ש. 86 — 87.   131 — 130 שמות ב', י"ד—ט"ו.

---

112 — 114 שלא נתלה—גדולה מילה] מ. .>   114 גדולה מילה] א"צ. מא"ש. ~ שכל
המצות שעשה אברהם אבינו לא נקרא שלם עד שמל שנאמר התהלך לפני והיה תמים
(בראשית י"ז, א) אמר ר' יהושע בן קרחא בא וראה כמה גדולה מילה.   116 — 115 הלך
להוציא את ישראל ממצרים] ד. שאמר לו המקום לך להוציא את עמי בני ישראל
ממצרים.   119 אלא] מ"ח. ~ אמר ד. ~ דרש משה קל וחומר.   121 שנתרשל] ל.
מ"ח. שנתעסק.   122 המלאך] ד. המקום מ"ח. .>   125 קרוי חתן] מ. ~ דמים.
129 בשעה] ד. באותה שעה.   131 אמרו] ד. אמר.   132 באותה שעה] א. מ. .>

likeness of Moses, so that they got hold of the angel and let Moses escape. R. Eliezer says: God turned the people who set out to capture Moses into different groups. Some of them He made dumb, some He made deaf, and some He made blind. They asked the dumb ones: Where is Moses? And they could not answer. They asked the deaf ones, and they could not hear; the blind ones and they could not see, just as it is said: "And the Lord said unto him: 'Who hath made a man's mouth? or who maketh a man dumb,' " etc. (Ex. 4.11). Referring to this, it is said: "For the God of my father was my help."

And Jethro, Moses' Father-in-Law, Came with His Sons and His Wife. But has it not already been said: "And thy wife, and her two sons with her" (v. 6)? From this I might have understood that they were her sons from another marriage. Scripture, therefore, says here: "With his sons and his wife unto Moses"—they were also the sons of Moses and not Zipporah's sons from another marriage.

Into the Wilderness. Behold, Scripture expresses surprise at him. He was dwelling in the midst of the splendor of the world and yet was willing to go out to the desert, a place of desolation where nothing is to be had. In this sense it is said: "Into the wilderness."

And He Said unto Moses, etc. R. Joshua says: He wrote it to him in a letter. R. Eleazar of Modi'im says: Through a messenger he sent him the message, saying to him: Do[16] it for my sake. If you do not care to do it for my sake, do it for the sake of your wife. And if you do not care to do it for your wife's sake, then do it for the sake of your children. Therefore it is said: "And he said unto Moses." R. Eliezer says: This was said to Moses by God: "I, I who said the word by which the world came into being, I am One who welcomes, not One who repels." As it is said: "Behold, I am a God that brings near, saith the Lord, and not a God that repels"[17] (Jer. 23.23). "I am He that brought

---

16. I. e., come out to meet us.

17. The words מקרב and מרחק written defectively are interpreted as if they read מקרב and מרחק respectively.

את המלאך והניחו את משה רבי אליעזר אומר

135 בני אדם שתפסו את משה עשאן המקום כתים כתים
עשאן אלמים עשאן חרשים עשאן סומים והיו
אומרים לאלמים היכן משה ולא היו מדברים
ולחרשים ולא היו שומעים ולסומים ולא היו רואים
כענין שנאמר ויאמר יי אליו מי שם פה לאדם או

140 מי ישום אלם וגו' לכך נאמר כי אלהי אבי בעזרי.

ויבא יתרו חתן משה ובניו ואשתו
והלא כבר נאמר ואשתך ושני בניה עמה שומע אני
שהיו בניה ממקום אחר ת"ל ובניו ואשתו אל משה
בניו של משה היו ולא היו בניה ממקום אחר.

145 **אל המדבר** הרי הכתוב מתמיה עליו שהיה
שרוי בתוך כבודו של עולם ובקש לצאת אל
המדבר תוהו שאין בו כלום לכך נאמר אל
המדבר.

ויאמר אל משה וגו' רבי יהושע אומר

150 כתב לו באגרת רבי אלעזר המודעי אומר שלח
לו ביד שליח ואמר לו עשה בגיני ואם אין אתה
עושה בגיני עשה בגין אשתך ואם אין אתה עושה
בגין אשתך עשה בגין בניך לכך נאמר ויאמר אל
משה וגו' רבי אליעזר אומר נאמר למשה אני אני

155 הוא שאמרתי והיה העולם אני הוא המקרב ולא
המרחק שנאמר האלהי מקרב אני נאם יי ולא אלהי

140 — 135 שמו"ר שם. ד"ר שם. 246 — 136 ש. 87 — 88. 140 — 139 שמות ד', י"א.
164 — 149 שמו"ר כ"ז, ב'. ת. יתרו ו'. 157 — 156 ירמיה כ"ג, כ"ג.

135 — 134 רבי אליעזר אומר בני אדם שתפסו את משה] ד. ט. <. 135 כתים כתים]
א. <. 136 עשאן] ד. <. ג. מהם. 140 — 136 והיו אומרים—אלם וגו'] א. <. 142 ואשתך
ושני בניה עמה] ק. נ. ושני בניו עמו. 144 — 143 אל משה—ממקום אחר] א. <.
148 אל המדבר] מ"ח. ~ מקום ד. למדבר ציה ד/ אל] ק. נ. <. 152 עשה] ד. צא.
153 — 152 ואם אין—בגין אשתך] ד. ואם לאו. 153 בניך ד. בניה. 154 אליעזר] א.
אלעזר / נאמר למשה] א"א. ז"י. א"צ. ש"י. (א"א. ויאמר אל משה ~) הקב"ה אמר
למשה. 155 — 154 אני אני הוא] א"א. ז"י. א"צ. ש"י. ק. אני אני נ. ל. אני הוא.
156 האלהי מקרב אני]
ק. האלי מקרוב באו אני נ. האלי מקרוב אני / אלהי] ק. נ. אלי.

Jethro near, not keeping him at a distance. So also thou, when a man comes to you wishing to become a convert to Judaism, as long as he comes in the name of God for the sake of heaven, do thou, likewise, befriend him and do not repel him." From this you can learn that one should always be ready to bring near with the right hand even while repelling with the left—not as Elisha did unto Gehazi whom he pushed away forever.[18]

And Moses Went to Meet His Father-in-Law. They say: Moses went out and with him Aaron, Nadab and Abihu and seventy of the elders of Israel. Some say: The Shekinah also went with them.

And He Bowed Down and Kissed Him. From this I could not know who bowed down to whom and who kissed whom. It continues, however, to say: "And they inquired, each man of the other, about their welfare"—now, who is designated "man"[19] (*Ish*) is it not Moses, as it is said: "Now the *man* Moses was very meek" (Num. 12.3)? You must, therefore, say: It was Moses who bowed down and kissed his father-in-law. Hence we learn that a man should show respect to his father-in-law.

And They Came into the Tent. Meaning the house of study.

And Moses Told His Father-in-Law. In order to attract him and bring him near to the Torah.

All that the Lord Had Done, etc. That He had given the Torah to His people Israel.

All the Travail, while in Egypt; *that Had Come upon Them,* at the Red Sea; *by the Way,* that is, the war with Amalek; *and How the Lord Delivered Them,* from all these, God had delivered them.

And Jethro Rejoiced, etc. R. Joshua says: It is of the goodness of the manna that Scripture speaks. Moses said to Jethro: "In this manna which God has given to us, we can taste the taste of bread, the taste of meat, the taste of fish, the taste of locust, and the taste of all the

18. See Sanh. 107b.
19. Cf. Friedmann and *Shebut Yehudah* ad loc.

מרחק אני הוא שקירבתי את יתרו ולא ריחקתיו
ואף אתה כשיבא אדם אצלך להתגייר ואינו בא
אלא לשם שמים אף אתה קרבהו ולא תרחיקהו
160 מכאן אתה למד שיהא אדם דוחה בשמאל ומקרב
בימין ולא כשם שעשה אלישע לגחזי שדחפו לעולם.

ויצא משה לקראת חתנו אמרו יצא משה
ואהרן נדב ואביהוא ושבעים מזקני ישראל ויש
אומרים אף שכינה יצאת עמהם.

165 **וישתחו וישק לו** איני יודע מי השתחוה למי
או מי נשק למי כשהוא אומר וישאלו איש לרעהו
לשלום מי קרוי איש הלא משה שנאמר והאיש משה
ענו מאד הוי אומר לא השתחוה ולא נשק אלא משה
לחמיו מכאן למדנו שיהא אדם נוהג בכבוד חמיו.

170 **ויבאו האהלה** זה בית המדרש.

ויספר משה לחותנו למשכו ולקרבו
לתורה.

את כל אשר עשה יי וגו׳ שנתן תורה לעמו
ישראל. **את כל התלאה** במצרים **אשר** מצאתם
175 על הים **בדרך** זו מלחמת עמלק **ויצילם יי**
הצילם המקום מכולם.

ויחד יתרו וגו׳ רבי יהושע אומר בטובת המן
הכתוב מדבר אמר לו המן הזה שנתן לנו המקום
אנו טועמין בו טעם פת טעם בשר טעם דגים טעם

160—161 סוטה מ״ז, א׳. סנהדרין ק״ז, ב׳.   168—167 במדבר י״ב, ג׳.

---

158 אצלך] א. < / להתגייר] מ. < / ואינו] הגהתי עפ״י ט. וש״י: א. מ. ד. אינו.
159—158 ואינו בא—שמים] מ״ח. לשמים.   161 שדחפו]=א. ט: מ. ד. ודחפו /
לעולם] מ. מן העולם.   162—163 משה ואהרן] ד. אהרן.   163 ויש] מ. וישראל.
168 הוי אומר] א. הרי מ. הוי.   169 למדנו] ד. אמרו / נוהג] ד. מוכן / בכבוד] ד.
לכבוד.   173—174 את כל אשר עשה—ישראל] ט״ב. מ״ח. < / שנתן תורה לעמו
ישראל] מ. שתורה בעמך ישראל.   174 במצרים] ד. אשר מצאתם בדרך.   178 אמר
לו] ד. אמרו לו.

delicacies in the world." For, instead of saying merely "goodness," or "the goodness," or "all the goodness," it says: "Over all the goodness." R. Eleazar of Modi'im says: It is of the goodness of the well that Scripture speaks. Moses said to Jethro: "In the waters of this well which God has given us we can taste the taste of old wine, the taste of new wine, the taste of milk, the taste of honey, and the taste of all the sweet drinks in the world." For instead of saying merely "goodness," or "the goodness," or "all the goodness," it says: "Over all the goodness,"[20] R. Eliezer says: It is of the goodness of the land of Israel that Scripture speaks. Moses said to Jethro: "God is going to give us six good portions: the land of Israel, the future world, the new world, the kingdom of David, and the institutions of the priests and the Levites." Therefore, instead of merely "goodness," or "the goodness," or "all the goodness," it says: "Over all the goodness." Immediately Jethro began and said: "Blessed be the Lord."

And Jethro Said: 'Blessed Be the Lord.' Said R. Pappias: This passage expresses a reproach of the Israelites. For, behold there were six hundred thousand people and not one of them rose to bless God until Jethro came and blessed God, as it is said: "And Jethro said. 'Blessed be the Lord.' "

Who Hath Delivered You Out of the Hand of the Egyptians, and Out of the Hand of Pharaoh. From the hand of that great dragon, of whom it is said: "The great dragon that lieth in the midst of his rivers, that hath said: My river is mine own, and I have made it for myself" (Ezek. 29.3).

From under the Hand of the Egyptians. From the oppression by the Egyptians.

Now I Know. Up to now he had not admitted it.

That the Lord Is Great. They say: No slave had ever been able to run away from Egypt. And at this time the Holy One, blessed be He,

20. See Commentaries.

180 חגבים טעם כל המטעמים שבעולם שנאמר טובה
הטובה כל הטובה על כל הטובה רבי אלעזר
המודעי אומר בטובת הבאר הכתוב מדבר אמר
לו הבאר הזו שנתן לנו המקום אנו טועמין בו טעם
יין ישן טעם יין חדש טעם חלב טעם דבש טעם
185 כל המתוקים שבעולם שנאמר טובה הטובה כל
הטובה על כל הטובה רבי אליעזר אומר בטובת
ארץ ישראל הכתוב מדבר אמר לו עתיד המקום
ליתן לנו שש מדות טובות ארץ ישראל והעולם
הבא ועולם חדש ומלכות בית דוד וכהונה ולויה
190 לכך נאמר טובה הטובה כל הטובה על כל הטובה
מיד פתח ואמר ברוך יי.

ויאמר יתרו ברוך יי אמר רבי פפייס
בגנות ישראל הכתוב מדבר שהרי יש שם ששים
רבוא בני אדם ולא עמד אחד מהם ובירך למקום
195 עד שבא יתרו ובירך למקום שנאמר ויאמר יתרו
ברוך יי.

אשר הציל אתכם מיד מצרים ומיד
פרעה מיד התנין הגדול ההוא שנאמר בו התנין
הגדול הרובץ בתוך יאוריו אשר אמר לי יארי
200 ואני עשיתיני.

מתחת יד מצרים מתחת שעבוד ההוא של
מצרים.

עתה ידעתי עד עכשיו לא הודה בדבר.

כי גדול יי אמרו מתחלה לא היה עבד יכול
205 לברוח ממצרים ועכשיו הוציא הקב"ה ששים ריבוא

191 — 186 לעיל ויסע ד'.   194 — 192 סנהדרין צ"ד, א'.   200 — 198 יחזקאל כ"ט, ג'.

183 — 182 אמר לו] ד. אמרו לו.   183 הזו] ד. ~.   185 המתוקים] א. המתקים מ. נ.
ט. הממתקים.   187 אמר] ד. אמרו.   191 מיד פתח ואמר] ד. ואומר / ברוך יין=מ.
ט: א. ד. ~.   197 אשר הציל אתכם מיד מצרים] א. מ. / ומיד] א. מ. מיד.
198 פרעה] מ. ~ אלא ט. ~ לא מיד פרעה אלא / ההוא שנאמר בו] א. ק. נ. ל.
שנאמר.   200 — 198 התנין—עשיתיני] א. ~.   203 הודה] ד. ~ לו.   205 ממצרים] ד.
~ שהיתה סוגרת ומסוגרת.

brought out six hundred thousand people from Egypt. Referring to this it is said: "That the Lord is great."

Than All Gods. They say: There was not an idol in the world which Jethro failed to seek out and worship. For it is said: "Than all gods." Naaman, however, knew better than Jethro.[21] For it is said: "Behold now, I know that there is no God in all the earth, but in Israel" (II Kings 5.15). Likewise Rahab the harlot says: "For the Lord your God, He is God in heaven above, and on earth beneath" (Josh. 2.11).

Yea, for with the Very Thing with Which They Acted Presumptuously Against Them. I have acknowledged Him in the past, and now even more, for His name has become great in the world. For with the very thing with which the Egyptians planned to destroy Israel, God punished them, as it is said: "Yea, for with the very thing with which they acted presumptuously against them."

And Jethro, Moses' Father-in-Law, Took a Burnt-Offering and Sacrifices for God. Scripture expresses surprise at him. A man who has been a worshiper of idols; who would sacrifice, offer incense and libations and bow down to his idols, now brings a burnt-offering and sacrifices to God.

And Aaron Came, and All the Elders of Israel. and where did Moses go? Was it not he who first went out to meet him, as it is said: "And Moses went out to meet his father-in-law" (v. 7)? Where then was he now? Scripture thus teaches that Moses was standing and serving them. Whence did he learn this? From our father Abraham. They say: R. Isaac once mentioned this in a discourse. He said: When R. Gamaliel gave a banquet to the wise men, all of them sat reclining, while R. Gamaliel stood up and served them. They then said: "We are not right in letting R. Gamaliel wait upon us." But R. Joshua said to them: "Leave him alone, let him do the serving. We find that one greater than R. Gamaliel waited upon people." Said they to him:

21. Naaman knew that there was no other god. Jethro, however, implied that there were other gods, but that the Lord is greater than all of them.

בני אדם ממצרים לכך נאמר כי גדול יי.

מכל אלהים אמרו לא הניח יתרו עבודה
זרה בעולם שלא חזר עליה ועבדה שנאמר מכל
אלהים ונעמן יודע בדבר יותר ממנו שנאמר הנה
210 נא ידעתי כי אין אלהים בכל הארץ כי אם בישראל
וכן רחב הזונה אומרת כי יי אלהיכם הוא אלהים
בשמים ממעל ועל הארץ מתחת.

כי בדבר אשר זדו עליהם מכירו הייתי
לשעבר ועכשיו ביותר שנתגדל שמו בעולם
215 שבמחשבה שחשבו מצרים לאבד את ישראל בו
בדבר נפרע מהם המקום שנאמר כי בדבר אשר
זדו עליהם.

**ויקח יתרו חתן משה עולה וזבחים
לאלהים** הרי הכתוב מתמיה עליו אדם שהיה
220 עובד עבודה זרה ומזבח ומקטר ומנסך ומשתחוה
לעבודה זרה שלו עכשיו הוא מביא עולה וזבחים
ליי.

ויבא אהרן וכל זקני ישראל ומשה
להיכן הלך והלא מתחלה יצא לקראתו שנאמר
225 ויצא משה לקראת חותנו ועכשיו להיכן הלך מלמד
שהיה עומד ומשמש עליהם מהיכן למד מאברהם
אבינו. אמרו הדבר הזה דרש רבי יצחק ואמר
כשעשה רבן גמליאל סעודה לחכמים היו כל
החכמים יושבין מסובים אצלו עמד רבן גמליאל
230 ושמשן אמרו אין אנו בדין שישמשנו רבן גמליאל
אמר להן רבי יהושע הניחו לו וישמש מצינו גדול
מרבן גמליאל ששמש את הבריות אמרו לו איזה

209—207 ת. יתרו ז'.   212—207 ד"ר ב', כ"ז.   210—209 מלכים ב. ה', ט"ו.
212—211 יהושע ב', י"א.   243—227 ספרי דברים ל"ח. קידושין ל"ב, ב'.

---

207 מכל] א. ומה ת"ל מכל.   208 חזר] ד. עבר.   209 יודע] א. מ. נודע ש. ל"ט.
מ"ח. א"צ. הודה / בדבר יותר ממנו] א"צ. לו ביותר.   211 הוא אלהים] א. וגו' מ.
הוא יי האלהים ק. נ. הוא האלהים.   213 מכירו] מ"ח. אמר מכירו / הייתי ד. היה.
218 עולה] א. עולת.   219 הרי] ד. > / שהיה א. שהוא.   220 עובד ע"ז] מ. עומד
מ"ח. עובד.   221 שלו] מ. מ"ח. .>   225 הלך] ד. ~ אלא.   226 עליהם] א. מ. >
/ מהיכן] א. ומי מ. ממי אתה מ"ח. ממי ה. וממי.   227 יצחק] ג. א"צ. ש. צדוק
/ ואמר] א. מ. .>   229 החכמים] ד. חכמי ישראל.   230 אין אנו בדין] ק. נ. אין אנו
בדין ל. אין אנו כדאין ה. אינו בדין / רבן גמליאל] ד. .>

"Who was it?" Said he to them: "It was our father Abraham who waited upon the angels. And he believed them to be human beings, Arabs, worshipers of idols. All the more is it proper that R. Gamaliel should wait upon wise men, sons of the Torah." R. Zadok said to them: "Leave him alone, let him do the serving. We can find one greater than R. Gamaliel and even greater than our father Abraham who has waited upon people." Said they to him: "Who is it?" Said he to them: "It is the Holy One, blessed be He, who gives to every one his wants and to everybody according to his needs. And not to good people alone, but also to wicked people and even to people who are worshiping idols. All the more is it proper that R. Gamaliel should wait upon wise men, sons of the Torah."

And Aaron Came and All the Elders of Israel, etc. Why does it say: "Before God"? It is to teach that when one welcomes his fellow man, it is considered as if he had welcomed the Divine Presence.

CHAPTER IV
(Ex. 18.13–27)

And It Came to Pass on the Morrow. That is, on the morrow after the day of Atonement.

That Moses Sat to Judge the People from the Morning unto the Evening. And was Moses really sitting and judging Israel from morning to evening? Is it not the rule that judges hold court only until meal time? But this merely teaches that whosoever renders a true judgment is accounted as if he had been a co-worker of the Holy One, blessed be He, in the work of creation. Here it is written: "From the morning unto the evening," and there it says: "And there was evening and there was morning" (Gen. 1.5).

And When Moses' Father-in-Law Saw, etc. What did he see? He saw him behaving like a king who sits on his throne while all the people

הוא אמר להם זה אברהם אבינו ששימש את מלאכי
השרת והיה סבור שהם בני אדם ערביים עובדי
235　עבודה זרה על אחת כמה וכמה רבן גמליאל
ששימש חכמים בני תורה אמר להן רבי צדוק הניחו
לו שישימש מצינו גדול מרבן גמליאל ומאברהם
אבינו ששימש את הבריות אמרו לו אי זה הוא אמר
להם הקב״ה שהוא נותן לכל אחד ואחד צורכו
240　ולכל גוייה וגוייה כדי מחסורה ולא לבני אדם כשרים
בלבד אלא אף לבני אדם רשעים ולבני אדם עובדי
עבודה זרה על אחת כמה וכמה רבן גמליאל
ששימש חכמים בני תורה.

ויבא אהרן וכל זקני ישראל וגו׳ ומה
245　ת״ל לפני האלהים אלא מלמד שכל המקבל פני
חבירו כאלו מקבל פני שכינה.

פרשה ד　(שמות י״ח, י״ג—כ״ז.)

ויהי ממחרת ממחרת יום הכפורים.
וישב משה לשפוט את העם מן
הבוקר עד הערב וכי מן הבקר עד הערב
היה משה יושב ודן את ישראל והלא הדיינין אינן
5　דנין אלא עד זמן סעודה ומה ת״ל מן הבקר עד
הערב אלא מלמד שכל מי שמוציא את הדין לאמתו
מעלין עליו כאלו היה שותף עם הקב״ה במעשה
בראשית כתיב כאן מן הבקר עד הערב ולהלן
הוא אומר ויהי ערב ויהי בקר וגו׳.
10　**וירא חתן משה** וגו׳ מה ראה ראהו שהיה
כמלך יושב על כסאו והכל עומדין עליו אמר לו

---

182 — 1 ש. 88 — 93.　9 — 2 שבת י׳, א׳.　9 בראשית א׳, ה׳.

234 והיה] ד. שהיה / סבור] א. ~ בהן.　236 בני] ד. לומדי / צדוק] ד. יצחק.
237 — 236 הניחו לו שישמש] ד. >.　239 הקב״ה] מ. המקום שבשמים ד. שכינה.
240 — 239 שהוא נותן—כדי מחסורה] ד. שבכל שעה מספיק מזון לכל באי העולם כדי
צרכן ומשביע לכל חי רצון.　240 כשרים] ד. הכשרים והצדיקים.　243 בני] ד. ובני.
246 חבירו] ד. חכמים.

5 עד 2] מ. ועד.　6 את הדין] ד. דין אמת.　7 מעלין עליו] ד. מעלה עליו הכתוב
/ עם הקב״ה] א. מ. >.　9 — 8 ולהלן הוא אומר] ד. ובמעשה בראשית כתיב.　10 מה
ראה ראהו שהיה] א. מ. > ש. אמר לו.　12 — 11 אמר לו—עושה לעם] א. מ. ט.
ש. כך אתה עושה להן לישראל.

around him stand. He, therefore, said to him: "What is this thing that thou doest to the people? Why sittest thou thyself alone" (Ex. 18.14).

And Moses Said unto His Father-in-Law: 'Because the People Come unto Me to Inquire of God.' They say: The following question Judah of Kefar Akko asked R. Gamaliel: "Why did Moses see fit to say: 'Because the people come unto me'?" R. Gamaliel said to him: "If not thus, how should he have said?" Said Judah: "He should have said merely: 'Because the people come to inquire of God.' " Then R. Gamaliel said: "Inasmuch as he does say: 'To inquire of God,' he has spoken properly."

When They Have a Matter It Cometh to Me. That is, a matter in regard to uncleanness and cleanness. *And I Judge Between a Man,* that is, giving a decision of the law without compromise. *And His Neighbour,* that is, giving a decision based upon a compromise, for it speaks of the litigants parting from one another as friends. *And I Make Them Know the Statutes of God,* that is, the interpretations; *And His Laws,* that is, the decisions—these are the words of R. Joshua. R. Eleazar of Modi'im says: "Statutes" (*Ḥukkim*), means the laws against incestuous practices, as in the passage: "That ye do not any of these abominable customs (*meḥukkot*)" (Lev. 18.30). *And Laws,* means decisions.

And Moses' Father-in-Law Said unto Him . . . Thou Wilt Surely Wear Away. R. Joshua says: They will tire you out and cause you to drop down. R. Eleazar of Modi'im says: They will make you fade with their chiding—like a fig-tree whose leaves fade, as it is said: "As the leaf falleth off from the vine, and as a falling fig from the fig-tree" (Isa. 34.4).

Also[1] Thou. "Thou," that is Moses: "also," refers to Aaron; *And This People that is with Thee,* refers to the seventy elders—these are the words of R. Joshua. R. Eleazar of Modi'im says: "Thou," that is Moses; "also," refers to Aaron; and again "also," refers to Nadab and Abihu; *And this People that Is with Thee,* refers to the seventy elders.

1. The particle **גם**, "also," is regarded as having inclusive force (see Bacher, *Terminologie,* I, pp. 110 and 180).

מה הדבר הזה אשר אתה עושה לעם מדוע אתה
יושב לבדך.

ויאמר משה לחתנו כי יבא אלי העם
לדרוש אלהים אמרו הדבר הזה שאל יהודה
איש כפר עכו את רבן גמליאל מה ראה משה לומר
כי יבא אלי העם אמר לו אם לאו מה יאמר אמר
לו יאמר כי יבא העם לדרוש אלהים אמר לו
כשהוא אומר לדרוש אלהים יפה אמר.

כי יהיה להם דבר בא אלי בין טומאה
לטהרה ושפטתי בין איש זה הדין שאין בו פשרה
ובין רעהו זה הדין שיש בו פשרה מגיד ששניהם
נפטרין זה מזה כרעים והודעתי את חוקי אלהים
אלו המדרשות ותורותיו אלו ההוריות דברי רבי
יהושע רבי אלעזר המודעי אומר חקים אלו עריות
שנאמר לבלתי עשות מחקות התועבות והתורות
אלו ההוריות.

ויאמר חותן משה אליו וגו' **נבל תבל**
רבי יהושע אומר ילאו אותך וינשרו אותך רבי
אלעזר המודעי אומר ינבלו אותך ויקנתרו אותך
כתאנה זו שעליה נובלות שנאמר כנבל עלה מגפן
וכנבלת מתאנה.

גם אתה אתה זה משה גם זה אהרן העם הזה
אשר עמך אלו שבעים זקנים דברי רבי יהושע רבי
אלעזר המודעי אומר אתה זה משה גם זה אהרן
וגם זה נדב ואביהוא העם הזה אשר עמך אלו
שבעים זקנים.

20—27 ספרי דברים נ״ח—נ״ט וקנ״ב. ת״כ אחרי מות י״ג (86ᵈ). בחקותי ט' (112ᵈ).
25—27 לעיל ויסע א'. 26 ויקרא י״ח, ל'. 32—31 ישעיה ל״ד, ד'.

15—17 אמרו—אלי העם] מ. >. 18—17 אמר לו יאמר—לדרוש אלהים=מ. ט״כ.
ג: א. ד. >. 19—18 אמר לו כשהוא] ד. כשהוא] ק. נ. בין] 24 ותורותיו]
מ. והתורות. במקרא, ואת תורותיו. 27—24 דברי רבי יהושע—אלו ההוריות] א. >.
26 והתורות] ק. נ. והתורה. 31—29 רבי יהושע—שעליה] מ. >. 29 יהושע] ט.
יהודה / ילאו] הגהתי=ט. מ״ח. א״א. ש״י: א. יקללו ד. ט״כ. יחללו / וינשרו]
מ״ח. וינשאו. 30 אלעזר] ד. אליעזר / המודעי] ט. > / ויקנתרו] מ״ח. וינתרו.
31—32 כנבל עלה מגפן וכנבלת מתאנה] ד. כאלה נובלת עליה (ישעיה א', ל'). 34 אלו]
א. ד. זה. 36 וגם זה] הגהתי=ט״כ. וא״צ: מ. גם זה א. ד. / הזה] מ. / אשר
עמך] א. ד. >.

For the Thing Is Too Heavy for Thee, etc. He said to him: Observe, a beam when it is still fresh and moist, two or three people get under it and cannot support it. But four or five people get under it and they can support it, "for the thing is too heavy for thee; thou art not able to perform it thyself alone."

Hearken Now Unto My Voice. If you will listen to me, it will be well with you.

I Will Give Thee Counsel, and God Be with Thee. Go and consult with the Almighty.

Be Thou for the People, etc. Be for them like a vessel filled with divine revelations. *And Bring Thou the Causes.* The words which you hear, bring up and report about them.[2]

And Thou Shalt Teach Them the Statutes, that is the interpretations; *And the Laws,* that is the decisions—these are the words of R. Joshua. R. Eleazar of Modi'im says: "Statutes" (*Ḥukkim*) means the laws against incestuous practices, as in the passage: "That ye do not any of these abominable customs (*meḥukkot*)" (Lev. 18.30). *And Laws,* means decisions.

And Shalt Show Them the Way, etc., meaning the study of the Torah; *And the Work that They Must Do,* meaning good deeds—these are the words of R. Joshua. R. Eleazar of Modi'im says: *And Shalt Show Them,* means show them how to live; *The Way,* refers to visiting the sick; *They Must Walk,* refers to burying the dead; *In,* refers to bestowal of kindnesses; *And the Work,* meaning along the line of strict justice; *That They Must Do,* beyond the line of strict justice.

Moreover, Thou Shalt Provide Out of All the People. You shall look for them with your prophetic power. *Able Men,* that is, wealthy people, people of means. *Such as Fear God,* who, when sitting in judgment, fear only God. *Men of Truth,* that is, people of trust. *Hating Unjust Gain,* those who when sitting in judgment hate to accept money—

---

2. See Commentaries.

כי כבד ממך הדבר וגו' אמר לו הסתכל
בקורה זו כשהיא לחה שנים או שלשה נכנסין תחתיה

40 אינן יכולין לעמוד בה ארבעה חמשה נכנסין
תחתיה יכולין לעמוד בה כי כבד ממך הדבר לא
תוכל עשוהו לבדך.

ועתה שמע בקולי אם תשמעני ייטב לך.
איעצך ויהי אלהים עמך צא והמלך

45 בגבורה. היה אתה לעם וגו' היה להם ככלי מלא
דברות והבאת אתה את הדברים דברים שאתה
שומע תביא ותרצה בהם.

והזהרת אתהם את החוקים אלו מדרשות
והתורות אלו הוראות דברי רבי יהושע רבי אלעזר

50 המודעי אומר חוקים אלו עריות שנאמר לבלתי
עשות מחוקות התועבות והתורות אלו ההוראות.

והודעת להם את הדרך וגו' זה תלמוד
תורה ואת המעשה אשר יעשון זה מעשה הטוב
דברי רבי יהושע רבי אלעזר המודעי אומר והודעת

55 להם הודע להם חייהם את הדרך זה בקור חולים
אשר ילכו זו קבורת מתים בה זו גמילות חסדים
ואת המעשה זו שורת הדין אשר יעשון זה לפנים
משורת הדין.

ואתה תחזה מכל העם תחזה להם
60 בנבואה אנשי חיל אלו עשירים ובעלי ממון יראי
אלהים אלו שהם יריאים מן המקום בדין אנשי אמת
אלו בעלי הבטחה שונאי בצע אלו שהם שונאים

50—51 ויקרא י"ח, ל'.   52—58 ב"ק צ"ט א'; ק', א'. ב"מ ל', ב'.   59—70 ת. יתרו
ב'. ספרי דברים ט"ו.

38 וגו'] ד. > מ. לעשותו.   39 אם] מ. ד. >.   43 בקולין] ד. ~ ייטב לך] ק.
>.   47 תביא] ל"ט. > / ותרצה בהם] ט. תרצה ובין להם ש. תרצה להם מ"ח.
ותרצה אותן לפניו א"צ. ותרצה אותם.   50 המודעי] ד. >.   55 חייהם] ד. בית חייהם.

these are the words of R. Joshua. R. Eleazar of Modi'im says: *Moreover, Thou Shalt Provide Out of All the People.* You shall look for them with the *specularia,*[3] with the glass through which kings try to see. *Able Men,* people of trust. *Such as Fear God,* who seek to arbitrate litigations. *Men of Truth,* like R. Ḥanina b. Dosa and his companions. *Hating Unjust Gain,* those who disdain their own money. For if they disdain their own money, how much more will they disdain the money of others.

And Place Such over Them to Be Rulers of Thousands, Rulers of Hundreds, Rulers of Fifties, and Rulers of Tens. Rulers of thousands were six hundred; rulers of hundreds were six thousand; rulers of fifty were twelve thousand; rulers of ten were sixty thousand. Thus all the rulers in Israel were seventy-eight thousand and six hundred.

And Let Them Judge the People at All Seasons. R. Joshua says: People who are free from work shall judge the people at all times. R. Eleazar of Modi'im says: People who are free from work and busy themselves with the Torah,—they shall judge the people at all times.

And It Shall Be, that Every Great Matter They Shall Bring unto Thee. Matters that are important they shall bring unto thee. You interpret it so. Perhaps it is not so, but it means only matters of important people they shall bring unto thee, while matters of less important people they shall judge themselves? It says, however: "The hard causes they brought unto Moses" (v. 26)—hence, it is not of persons that the Scripture speaks but of matters.

So Shall They Make It Easier for Thee and Bear the Burden with Thee. If thou shalt do this thing. *And God Command Thee So.*[4] Go and consult with the Almighty.

And God Command Thee So, Then Thou Shalt Be Able to Endure. If He gives you His consent you will be able to endure, but if not, you will not be able to endure.

---

3. See Commentaries.
4. The *Mekilta* takes v. 23 to be a condition for the result promised in v. 22.

לקבל ממון בדין דברי רבי יהושע רבי אלעזר
המודעי אומר ואתה תחזה מכל העם אתה תחזה
להם באספקלריא במחזית זו שחוזין בה המלכים   65
אנשי חיל אלו בעלי הבטחה יראי אלהים אלו
שהן עושין פשרה בדין אנשי אמת כגון רבי
חנינא בן דוסא וחביריו שונאי בצע אלו שהן שונאין
ממון עצמם ואם ממון עצמם שונאין קל וחומר ממון
אחרים.   70

ושמת עליהם שרי אלפים שרי מאות
שרי חמשים שרי עשרות שרי אלפים שש
מאות שרי מאות ששת אלפים שרי חמשים שנים
עשר אלף שרי עשרות ששים אלף נמצאו כל שרי
ישראל שבע רבוא ושמונת אלפים ושש מאות.   75

ושפטו את העם בכל עת רבי יהושע
אומר בני העם בטלין ממלאכתן יהיו דנין את העם
בכל עת רבי אלעזר המודעי אומר בני אדם שהן
בטלין ממלאכתן ועוסקין בדברי תורה יהיו דנין
את העם בכל עת.   80

והיה כל הדבר הגדול יביאו אליך
דברים גדולים יביאו אליך אתה אומר כן או אינו
אלא דברים של בני אדם גדולים יביאו אליך
ודברים של בני אדם קטנים ישפטו הם כשהוא
אומר את הדבר הקשה יביאון אל משה הא אינו   85
מדבר בבני אדם אלא בדברים הכתוב מדבר.

והקל מעליך ונשאו אתך אם את הדבר
הזה תעשה.

וצוך אלהים צא המלך בגבורה. **וצוך**
אלהים ויכלת עמד אם מודה לך את יכול   90
לעמוד ואם לאו אין אתה יכול לעמוד. **וגם כל**

---

71 — 75 ספרי דברים שם. סנהדרין י״ח, א׳.   86 — 81 סנהדרין ט״ז, א׳. י״ח, ב׳.   85 שמות
י״ח, כ״ו.

63 לקבל] א. < / ממון] א. ~ עצמן.   65 — 64 אתה תחזה להם] ד. <.   70 אחרים]
א. מ. מ״ח. ט. חביריהם.   74 כל שרי] א. כל דייני.   77 העם 1] א. ד. אדם /
בטלין] ד. שהם בדלים / ממלאכתן] ד. ~ ועוסקים בתורה / יהוו] ק. נ. והיו.   80 — 78 רבי
אלעזר—בכל עת] ד. <.   85 את הדבר] ק. נ. והדבר.   86 בדברים] ד. ~ גדולים.
88 — 87 אם את הדבר הזה תעשה] א. וגו׳.   89 וצוך אלהים] א. < / וגו׳.   91 — 90 את
יכול—וגם] א. < / את יכול לעמוד] ד. ויכלת עמד.   92 — 91 כל העם] א. את כל
העם.

And All This People Also. That is, Aaron, Nadab and Abihu, and the seventy elders "shall go to their place in peace."

So Moses Hearkened to the Voice of His Father-in-Law—to be taken literally[5]—*And Did All that He Had Said.* That is, all that his father-in-law told him—these are the words of R. Joshua. R. Eleazar of Modi'im says: *So Moses Hearkened to the Voice of His Father-in-Law*—to be taken literally—*And Did All That He Had Said.* That is, what God had said.

And Moses Let His Father-in-Law Depart. R. Joshua says: He sent him off with all the honors in the world. R. Eleazar of Modi'im says: He gave him along many gifts. From the answer which he gave Moses you can learn all this.[6] It is said: "And he said: 'Leave us not, I pray thee' " (Num. 10.31). Moses said to him: You have given us good advice, fair advice. And God agreed with your words. "Leave us not, I pray thee." But Jethro said to him: Is a lamp of any use except in a dark place? Of what use could a lamp be with the sun and the moon? You are the sun and Aaron is the moon. What should a lamp be doing where there are the sun and the moon? No! I shall go to my land and tell everybody and convert all the people of my country, leading them to the study of the Torah and bringing them nigh under the wings of the Shekinah. One might think that he merely went back and did nothing, but Scripture says: "And the children of the Kenite, Moses' father-in-law, went up out of the city of palm-trees with the children of Judah into the wilderness of Judah, which is in the south of Arad; and they went and dwelt with the people" (Judg. 1.16). The term "people" here is but a designation for "wisdom," as in the passage: "No doubt but ye are the people and with you is the perfection of wisdom" (Job 12.2)—do not read *Tamut* "perfection," but *Tumat* "cessation." As long as the wise man is alive, his wisdom is kept alive with him. As soon as the wise man dies, his wisdom is lost

5. See Bacher, *Terminologie,* I, p. 48, s. v. ודאי.
6. See Introduction.

העם הזה אהרן נדב ואביהוא ושבעים איש
מזקני ישראל על מקומו יבא בשלום.

וישמע משה לקול חותנו ודאי ויעש כל
אשר אמר כל אשר אמר לו חותנו דברי רבי יהושע
רבי אלעזר המודעי אומר וישמע משה לקול חותנו
ודאי ויעש ככל אשר אמר לו אלהים.

וישלח משה את חותנו רבי יהושע אומר
שילחו בכבודו של עולם רבי אלעזר המודעי אומר
נתן לו מתנות רבות שמתוך תשובה שנתן לו אתה
למד שנאמר ויאמר אל נא תעזב אתנו אמר לו משה
אתה נתת לנו עצה טובה ועצה יפה והמקום הודה
לדבריך אל נא תעזוב אותנו אמר לו כלום הנר
מהנה אלא במקום חושך וכי מה הנר מהנה בין
חמה ללבנה אתה חמה ואהרן לבנה מה יעשה הנר
בין חמה ללבנה אלא הרי אני הולך לארצי ומגיד
לכל ומגייר כל בני מדינתי ואביאם לתלמוד תורה
ואקרבם תחת כנפי השכינה יכול שהלך ולא עשה
ת״ל ובני קני חותן משה עלו מעיר התמרים וגו'
וילך וישב את העם ואין עם אלא חכמה שנאמר
אמנם כי אתם עם ועמכם תמות חכמה אל תקרי
תמות אלא תומת חכמה כל זמן שהחכם קיים
חכמתו מתקיימת עמו מת החכם אבדה חכמתו

101 במדבר י', ל"א.   109 שופטים א', ט"ז.   111 איוב י"ב, ב'.

93 בשלום] ד. לשלום.   97—95 אשר אמר כל—ויעש ככל] א. מ. <.   97 ודאי]
הוספתי=ט. ש: ק. ויראה.   ש: ק. ויראה.   99 בכבודו] ט. מכבודו ק. כבודו ל"ט. לכבודו.
103—101 אמר לו משה—תעזוב אותנו] מ. <.   101 משה] ד. <.   104 מה הנר מהנה
בין] ד. מהנר נהנין.   104—105 בין חמה ללבנה] ד. ביניכם.   106—107 ומגיד לכל]
א. ד. <.   108 תחת] מ. לתחת / השכינה] א. השמים.   112 שהחכם קיים] ד. שהחכם
מתקיים.   113 מתקיימת] א. קיימת / עמו] א. ד. <.

with him. Thus we find that when R. Nathan died, his wisdom was
lost with him[7]—They went and sat with those sitting before Jabez[8]—
for were there inhabitants of Jabez? There were only disciples of
Jabez—as it is said: "And the families of scribes who sat before Jabez;
the Tirathites, the Shimeathites, the Sucathites. These are the Kenites
that came of Hammath, the father of the house of Rechab" (I Chr.
2.55). They were called Tirathites (*Tir'atim*) because when they
sounded the horn in supplication they were answered; Simeathites
(*Shim'atim*) because they heard the sound of the trumpet-blast at
Sinai; Sucathites (*Sukatim*) because they dwelt in tents, as it is said:
"But we have dwelt in tents, and have hearkened, and done according to all that Jonadab our father commanded us" (Jer. 35.10).

It happened once that one said [mockingly]:[9] "Today there is a
sacrifice of the sons of the water-drinkers!" And a heavenly voice
came forth from the Holy of Holies and called out: "He who received
their offerings in the desert, He will also receive their offerings now."

R. Nathan says: The covenant with Jonadab the son of Rechab
was greater than the one made with David. For the covenant made
with David was only conditional, as it is said: "If thy children keep
My covenant," etc. (Ps.132.12), and if not: "Then will I visit their
transgression with the rod" (Ps. 89.33). But the covenant with
Jonadab the son of Rechab was made without any condition. For it is
said: "Therefore thus saith the Lord of hosts, the God of Israel: There
shall not be cut off unto Jonadab the son of Rechab a man to stand
before Me for ever" (Jer. 35.19).

Three things were given conditionally: the land of Israel, the Temple, and the kingdom of David—thus excepting the book of the

7. The passage marked off by dashes is a sort of parenthetical remark, and
not of the original Midrash about the Kenites (see Introduction).

8. I. e., Jabez is not the name of a place but of a person (cf. S. Klein, "Die
Schreiberfamilien: I Chronik. 2.55," in *MGWJ*, 1926, pp. 410–416; also in ציון, II,
Jerusalem, 1927, pp. 8–9).

9. See Introduction, and comp. also Geiger, *Urschrift*, p.152.

עמו וכן מצינו משמת רבי נתן אבדה חכמתו עמו
הלכו וישבו להם אצל יושבי יעבץ וכי יושבי יעבץ
היו אלא תלמידי יעבץ היו שנאמר ומשפחות
סופרים יושבי יעבץ תרעתים שמעתים סוכתים המה
הקנים הבאים מחמת אבי בית רכב תרעתים שהיו
מתריעים ונענים שמעתים ששמעו קול תרועה בסיני
סוכתים על שם שהיו יושבין בסוכות שנאמר ונשב
באהלים ונשמע ונעש ככל אשר צונו יונדב אבינו.
מעשה באחד שאמר קרבן מבני שותי מים היום
ויצאה בת קול מבית קדשי הקדשים ואמרה מי
שקיבל את קרבנותיהם במדבר הוא יקבל את
קרבנותיהם בשעה הזאת. רבי נתן אומר גדול
הברית שנכרת עם יונדב בן רכב מהברית שנכרת
עם דוד שהברית שנכרת עם דוד לא נכרת עמו
אלא על תנאי שנאמר אם ישמרו בניך בריתי וגו'
ואם לאו ופקדתי בשבט פשעם אבל הברית שנכרת
עם יונדב בן רכב לא נכרת עמו על תנאי שנאמר
לכן כה אמר יי צבאות אלהי ישראל לא יכרת איש
ליונדב בן רכב עומד לפני כל הימים. שלשה
דברים נתנו על תנאי ארץ ישראל ובית המקדש
ומלכות בית דוד חוץ מספר תורה ובריתו של אהרן

114 — 121 ספרי במדבר ע״ח. ת. יתרו ד׳.   116 — 118 דהי״א. ב׳, נ״ה.   121 — 120 ירמיה
ל״ה, י׳.   128 תהלים קל״ב, י״ב.   129 שם פ״ט, ל״ג.   132 — 131 ירמיה ל״ה, י״ט.

116 אלא] א. ד. והלא / ומשפחות] ק. נ. ומשפחת מ. ממשפחות.   119 מתריעים] ש.
~ בבקשתן / קול] מ. כל / תרועה בסיני] ד. תרועת תורה ג. תורה תמימה ש. דברי
תורה.   121 ונעש] ק. נ. ונעשה.   122 שאמר]=ט. (ירמיה שכ״ג.) ג. ש : א. ד. שהקריב
/ קרבן] מ״ח. ~ עלי / מבני] ש. בית ג. שאני / שותי]=ט״כ. מ״ח. מ. ש״י : א. ד.
שותה מ. נשתה / היום] ד. מ״ח. > ג. שלי היום.   125 קרבנותיהם]=א. ד : מ.
קרבנותיכם ג. קרבנותיו מ״ח. קרבנכם / בשעה הזאת] ג. של זה / נתן] מ. ט. יונתן.
128 אם ישמרו בניך בריתי וגו'] מ. אם ישמרו בניך את דרכם.   131 אלהי ישראל] ד.
>.   134 חוץ מספר תורה] א״צ. אבל ספר תורה.

Torah and the covenant with Aaron, which were unconditional. How do we know about the Land of Israel? It is said: "Take heed of yourselves, lest your heart be deceived . . . and the anger of the Lord be kindled against you"[10] (Deut. 11.16–17). How do we know about the Temple? It is said: "As for this house which thou art building, if thou wilt walk in My statutes, and execute Mine ordinances, and keep all My commandments to walk in them; then will I establish My word with thee, which I spoke unto David thy father" (I Kings 6.12); and if not: "And this house which is so high [shall become desolate], and every man that passeth by it shall be astonished," etc. (ib. 9.8). How do we know about the kingdom of David? It is said: "If thy children keep My covenant," etc. (Ps. 132.12); and if not: "Then will I visit their transgression with the rod" (Ps. 89.33). And how do we know about the book of the Torah that it was given without any condition? It is said: "The Torah which Moses commanded us is an inheritance" (Deut. 33.4). And how do we know of the covenant with Aaron that it was made without any condition? It is said: "It is an everlasting covenant of salt," etc. (Num. 18.19). And it also says: "And it shall be unto him, and to his seed after him, the covenant of an everlasting priesthood" (ib. 25.13). And how do we know that the sons of Jonadab the son of Rechab were descendants of Jethro? It is said: "These are the Kenites that came of Hammath, the father of the house of Rechab" (I Chr. 2.55). They sought a teacher. And Jabez was seeking pupils, as it is said: "And Jabez called on the God of Israel, saying: 'Oh that Thou wouldest bless me indeed, and enlarge my border, and that Thy hand might be with me, and that Thou wouldest work deliverance from evil, that it may not pain me!' And God granted him that which he requested" (ib. 4.10). "Oh, that Thou wouldest bless me indeed," with the study of the Law; "and enlarge my border," with disciples; "and that Thy hand might be with me," so

10. And it goes on to say: "And ye perish quickly from off the good land which the Lord giveth you" (v. 17).

שלא נתנו על תנאי ארץ ישראל מנין שנאמר השמרו 135
לכם פן יפתה לבבכם וגו׳ וחרה אף יי בכם בית
המקדש מנין שנאמר והבית הזה אשר אתה בונה
אם תלך בחקותי ואת משפטי תעשה ושמרת את
כל מצותי ללכת בהם והקמתי את דברי אתך אשר
דברתי אל דוד אביך ואם לאו והבית הזה יהיה 140
עליון כל עבר עליו ישום וגו׳ מלכות בית דוד מנין
שנאמר אם ישמרו בניך בריתי וגו׳ ואם לאו ופקדתי
בשבט פשעם ומנין לספר תורה שלא ניתן על תנאי
שנאמר תורה צוה לנו משה מורשה ומנין לבריתו
של אהרן שלא נתנה על תנאי שנאמר ברית מלח 145
עולם וגו׳ ואומר והיתה לו ולזרעו אחריו ברית
כהונת עולם. ומנין לבני יונדב בן רכב שהם מבני בניו
של יתרו שנאמר המה הקינים הבאים מחמת אבי
בית רכב הם בקשו את הרב ויעבץ בקש תלמידים
שנאמר ויקרא יעבץ לאלהי ישראל לאמר אם ברך 150
תברכני והרבית את גבולי והיתה ידך עמי ועשית
מרעה לבלתי עצבי ויבא אלהים את אשר שאל אם
ברך תברכני בתלמוד תורה והרבית את גבולי
בתלמידים והיתה ידך עמי שלא אשכח את משנתי

135 — 136 דברים י״א, ט״ז — י״ז. 137 — 140 מלכים א. ו׳, י״ב. 141 — 140 מלכים א.
ט׳, ח׳. 142 תהלים קל״ב, י״ב. 143 — 142 שם פ״ט, ל״ג. 144 דברים ל״ג, ד׳.
145 — 146 במדבר י״ח, י״ט. 147 — 146 שם כ״ה, י״ג. 149 — 147 ספרי במדבר ע״ח.
152 — 150 דהי״א. ד׳, י׳. 177 — 150 תמורה ט״ז, א׳.

135 שלא] א״צ. לא / שנאמר] מ. ת״ל. 137 והבית הזה] במקרא הבית הזה ד. והבית.
141 — 137 והבית הזה — ישום וגו׳] ד. והיתה הארץ לשמה על יושביה (מיכה ז׳, י״ג).
147 שהם] מ. שהוא. 149 בית רכב] ד. רכב / הרב] מ. הדבר. 149 תלמידים=א״צ:
מ״ח. לתלמידים ג. לתלמידים (בשם ספרים אחרים, לחכמים) ק. ותלמידים חכמה א.
מ. נ. ל. חכמה. 150 לאלהי ישראל] מ״ח. אל יי. 151 ועשית] מ. ~ לי. 154 והיתה
ידך] מ״ח. והיתה חנך.

that the evil inclination should not cause me trouble to hinder me in the study of Thy Torah; "And God granted him that which he requested," this teaches that He gave to him what he asked for and to them He gave what they asked for. It is said: "The poor man and the man of means[11] meet together; the Lord giveth light to the eyes of both" (Prov. 29.13). And it also says: "The rich and the poor meet together—the Lord is the maker of them all" (ib. 22.2). How is this? If the disciple attends the master and the master is willing to let him learn, then "the Lord giveth light to the eyes of both"—the one acquires life eternal and so does the other. If the disciple attends the master and the master is unwilling to let him learn, then "the Lord is the maker of them all." He who had made the one wise will in the end make him ignorant, and He who had made the other ignorant will in the end make him wise. Something similar you find in the matter of giving charity. How so? If the poor man stretches out his hand towards the householder, and the householder gives willingly, then "the Lord giveth light to the eyes of both." If, however, the poor man stretches out his hand towards the householder, and the latter is unwilling to give, then "the Lord is the maker of them all"—He who had made the one poor will in the end make him rich, and He who had made the other rich will in the end make him poor. R. Judah ha-Nasi says: Behold, it says: "And Jabez called," etc. "Oh that Thou wouldest bless me indeed," with offspring; "and enlarge my border," with sons and daughters; "and that Thy hand might be with me," in business; "and that Thou wouldest work deliverance from evil," the life which Thou hast given me shall be free from any sickness of the stomach or of the eyes or of the head; "that it may not pain me," but if Thou wilt not do so for me, I shall go down with my grief to the grave; "And God granted him that which he requested"—He gave him what he asked for.

---

11. So the *Mekilta* understands the expression אִישׁ חֲכָכִים (cf. Rashi to Proverbs ad loc.).

ועשית מרעה שתעשה לי ריעים כמותי לבלתי עצבי 155
שלא יעציבני יצר הרע מלעסוק בתורתך ויבא
אלהים את אשר שאל מלמד שנתן לו מה ששאל ולהם
נתן מה ששאלו שנאמר רש ואיש תככים נפגשו
מאיר עיני שניהם יי ואומר עשיר ורש נפגשו עושה
כלם יי הא כיצד תלמיד ששימש את הרב והרב 160
רוצה להשנותו מאיר עיני שניהם יי זה קונה חיי
עולם וזה קונה חיי עולם אבל תלמיד ששימש את
הרב והרב אינו רוצה להשנותו עושה כולם יי מי
שעשה לזה חכם חפו לעשותו טיפש ומי שעשה לזה
טיפש חפו לעשותו חכם. כיוצא בדבר אתה 165
מוצא בנותני צדקה הא כיצד עני שפשט ידו לבעל
הבית ובעל הבית רוצה ליתן לו מאיר עיני שניהם
יי אבל עני שפשט ידו לבעל הבית ובעל הבית אינו
רוצה ליתן לו עושה כולם יי מי שעשה לזה עני
חפו לעשותו עשיר ומי שעשה לזה עשיר חפו 170
לעשותו עני רבי יהודה הנשיא אומר הרי הוא אומר
ויקרא יעבץ וגו' אם ברך תברכני בפריה ורביה
והרבית את גבולי בבנים ובבנות והיתה ידך עמי
במשא ומתן ועשית מרעה חיים שנתת לי לא יהיה
בהם לא חולי מיעים ולא מיחוש עינים ולא מיחוש 175
הראש לבלתי עצבי הא אם אתה עושה לי כן
הרי אני יורד בנסיסי לשאול ויבא אלהים את אשר

---

155 — 158 משלי כ"ט, י"ג.   160 — 159 שם כ"ב, ב'.

155 ועשית מרעה] מ. ק. נ. ועשית לי מרעה.   156 יעצביני יצה"ר מלעסוק] מ"ח.
ישבגני יצר הרע מלשנות.   157 — 156 ויבא אלהים את אשר] מ. ויאמר אלהים אשר.
157 מלמד] א. >.   158 — 157 ולהם נתן מה ששאלו] ד. ולמה נתן לו מה ששאל.
163 עושה כולם] ק. נ. עושה שניהם.   165 — 164 לזה טיפש] ד. תלמיד טיפש.
166 — 165 אתה מוצא] א. > מ. אתה אומר.   166 הא] ד. >.   167 — 166 לבעל הבית]
ד. ~ לקבל צדקה.   167 — 168 ובעל הבית רוצה—ידו לבעל הבית] ד.   169 ליתן
לו] ד. ~ כלום.   170 — 169 שעשה לזה—לעשותו עשיר] ד. שהשני זה סוף שיעשרנו.
171 — 170 שעשה לזה—לעשותו עני] ד. שהעשיר זה סוף שיעני אותו.   173 ידך] מ"ח.
חנך.   174 ועשית] מ. ~ לי/ לי לא] מ. לי שלא.   177 בנסיסי]=א"א. א"צ. ז"י.
ש"י: א. נ. ל. כבן סיסי מ"ח. ברסיסי ש. בנסיסות / אלהים] א. מ. יי/ את] ק. נ.
>.

R. Ḥananiah the son of Gamaliel says: Why are all these figures stated?[12] They were stated only in the second year when Moses was about to appoint magistrates' assistants over Israel, as it is said: "By their fathers' houses, every man with his own standard, according to the ensigns" (Num. 2.2).

12. See Introduction and cf. Commentaries.

שאל נתן לו מה ששאל. רבי חנניה בן גמליאל

אומר למה נאמרו כל השעורים הללו לא נאמרו

180 אלא בשנה השנייה בשעה שביקש משה להעמיד

מכסיוטינוס על ישראל שנאמר איש על דגלו

באותות לבית אבותם.

חסלת מסכתא דעמלק

182 — 181 במדבר ב׳, ב׳.

───────────────

178 חנניה] ד. חנינא.   179 למה] ד. לא / לא נאמרו] ד. >.   181 מכסיוטינוס] צ״ל טכסיוטינוס: מ. > א. מכסיוטנות א״א. טכסיוטנית מ״ח. מטכסונות ש. אכסלטיינות. 183 דעמלק] הוספתי=מא״ש ואה״ו: ק. דרפשת וישמע נ. ל. דוישמע.

TRACTATE BAHODESH

CHAPTER I
(Ex. 19.1–2)

In the Third Month after the Children of Israel Were Gone Forth Out of the Land of Egypt. This tells that months are counted from the one in which the exodus from Egypt took place. I know only about months. How about years? It says: "In the second year after they were come out of the land of Egypt" (Num. 1.1). Thus far I know only about that period. How about other periods? It says: "In the fortieth year after the children of Israel were come out of the land of Egypt" (ib. 33.38). All this was before the Israelites entered the land. How about the time after the Israelites entered the land? It says: "And it came to pass in the four hundred and eightieth year after the children of Israel were come out of the land of Egypt" (I Kings 6.1). All this was before the Temple was built. After the Temple was built they began counting from the time of its building, as it is said: "And it came to pass at the end of twenty years, wherein Solomon had built the two houses, the house of the Lord and the king's house" (ibid. 9.10).

They were not satisfied[1] to count from its building, so they had to count from its destruction, as it is said: "In the fourteenth year after the city was smitten" (Ezek. 40.1). They were not satisfied to count according to their own era—so they had to count according to the era of others, as it is said: "In the sixth month, in the second year of Darius the king" (Hag. 1.15). And thus it says: "If thou know not, O

---

1. I. e., they did not choose to conduct themselves so as to prevent the punishment of the destruction of the Temple.

מסכתא בחדש

פרשה א   (שמות י״ט, א׳–ב׳.)

בחדש השלישי לצאת בני ישראל
מארץ מצרים מגיד שמונים חדשים ליציאת
מצרים אין לי אלא חדשים שנים מנין ת״ל בשנה
השנית לצאתם מארץ מצרים אין לי אלא באותו
5 הפרק בפרק אחר מנין ת״ל בשנת הארבעים לצאת
בני ישראל מארץ מצרים כל אלו עד שלא נכנסו
ישראל לארץ משנכנסו ישראל לארץ מנין ת״ל
ויהי בשמונים שנה וארבע מאות שנה לצאת בני
ישראל מארץ מצרים כל אלו עד שלא נבנה
10 הבית משנבנה הבית התחילו מונין לבנינו שנאמר
ויהי מקץ עשרים שנה אשר בנה שלמה את שני
הבתים את בית יי ואת בית המלך לא רצו למנות
לבנינו ימנו לחורבנו שנאמר בארבע עשרה שנה
אחר אשר הוכתה העיר לא רצו למנות לעצמם
15 ימנו לאחרים שנאמר בששי בשנת שתים לדריוש
וכן הוא אומר אם לא תדעי לך היפה בנשים וגו׳

15—1 ספרי במדבר ס״ד. י׳ ר״ה א׳, א׳ (56ᵃᵇ). ש. 93.   4—3 במדבר א׳, א׳.   6—5 שם
ל״ג, ל״ח.   12—11 מלכים א. ט׳, י׳.   14—13 יחזקאל מ׳, א׳.   15 חגי א׳, ט״ו.
16 שה״ש א׳, ח׳.

מסכתא בחדש] הוספתי: ל. מא״ש. פרשת בחדש השלישי מ. דבירי. עיין מאמרי
The Arrangement and the Divisions of the Mekilta, Hebrew Union College Annual, I, p. 442
ff.   4 לצאתם מארץ מצרים] הוספתי: ד. > א. מ. לצאת מארץ מצרים.
10 התחילו—שנאמר] הגהתי=א״צ. ז״י. וש: א. מ. ד. מנין ת״ל מ״ח. מנין שמונין
לבנינו ת״ל.   11 מקץ] במקרא כתוב מקצה / עשרים] ד. ארבעים.   12—11 את שני
הבתים—בית המלך] מ. את הבית וגו׳ מ״ח. את הבית ד. בית יי.   14 אחר] ק. נ.
אחרי.   15 שנאמר] ד. שנאמר בשנת שתים למלכות נבוכדנצר חלם נבוכדנצר חלומות
(דניאל ב׳, א׳ ובמקרא כתוב ובשנת) ואמר.   16 וכן הוא אומר] ד. ואומר / אם] ק. נ.
ואם.

thou fairest among women,"[2] (Cant. 1.8), and it also says: "Because thou didst not serve . . . therefore shalt thou serve thine enemy" (Deut. 28.47–48). Once R. Joḥanan b. Zakkai was going up to Emmaus[3] in Judea and he saw a girl who was picking barley-corn out of the excrements of a horse. Said R. Joḥanan b. Zakkai to his disciples: "What is this girl?" They said to him: "She is a Jewish girl." "And to whom does this horse belong?" "To an Arabian horseman," the disciples answered him. Then said R. Joḥanan b. Zakkai to his disciples: All my life I have been reading this verse and I have not realized its full meaning: "If thou know not, O thou fairest among women," etc.—you were unwilling to be subject to God, behold now you are subjected to the most inferior of the nations, the Arabs. You were unwilling to pay the head-tax to God, "a beka a head" (Ex. 38.26); now you are paying a head-tax of fifteen shekels under a government of your enemies. You were unwilling to repair the roads and streets leading up to the Temple; now you have to keep in repair the posts and stations on the road to the royal cities. And thus it says: "Because thou didst not serve . . . therefore thou shalt serve thine enemy." Because thou didst not serve the Lord thy God with love, therefore shalt thou serve thine enemy with hatred; because thou didst not serve the Lord thy God when thou hadst plenty, therefore thou shalt serve thine enemy in hunger and thirst; because thou didst not serve the Lord thy God when thou wast well clothed, therefore thou shalt serve thine enemy in nakedness; because thou didst not serve the Lord thy God "by reason of the abundance of all things, therefore shalt thou serve thine enemy in want of all things." What is the

2. This verse has been understood as addressed to Israel (see interpretation of R. Joḥanan b. Zakkai immediately following; and cf. Rashi to Ket. 67a, s. v. לך אם לא תדעי).

3. Emmaus מאוס or אמאוס is the name of a place in Judea (see Rapoport, *'Erek Milin*, s. v., Warsaw, 1914, pp. 196–201; I. S. Horowitz, *Palestine*, Vienna, 1923, p. 51; and Isaac Goldhaar, *Admat Kodesh* (Jerusalem, 1913) p. 141 ff).

ואומר תחת אשר לא עבדת את יי אלהיך וגו'
ועבדת את אויביך. כבר היה רבי יוחנן בן זכאי
עולה למאוס דיהודה וראה ריבה אחת שהיא
מלקטת שעורים מתחת גללי הסוס אמר להם רבן
20   יוחנן בן זכאי לתלמידיו ריבו זו מה היא אמרו
לו עברית היא סוס זה של מי הוא אמרו לו של
פרש ערבי הוא אמר להם רבן יוחנן בן זכאי
לתלמידיו כל ימי הייתי קורא זה הפסוק ולא הייתי
יודע מה הוא אם לא תדעי לך היפה בנשים וגו'
25   לא רציתם להשתעבד לשמים הרי אתם משועבדים
לפגומי גוים ערביים לא רציתם לשקול שקלי שמים
בקע לגולגולת הרי אתם שוקלים חמשה עשר
שקלים במלכות אויביכם לא רציתם לתקן את
הדרכים ואת הרחובות העולים לבית הבחירה
30   הרי אתם מתקנין את הבורגסין ואת הבורגנין
העולים לכרכי המלכים וכן הוא אומר תחת אשר
לא עבדת וגו' ועבדת את אויביך תחת אשר לא
עבדת את יי אלהיך באהבה ועבדת את אויביך
בשנאה תחת אשר לא עבדת את יי אלהיך בשובע
35   ועבדת את אויביך ברעב ובצמא תחת אשר לא
עבדת את יי אלהיך בלבוש ועבדת את אויביך
בעירום תחת אשר לא עבדת את יי אלהיך מרוב
כל ועבדת את אויביך בחוסר כל מאי בחוסר כל

18—17 דברים כ"ח, מ"ז—מ"ח.   27—18 ספרי דברים ש"ח. כתובות ס"ו, ב'—ס"ז, א'.
תוס' שם ה'. י'. י' שם ה', י"ג (30°). אדר"נ י"ז. אי"ר א', מ"ה (בובער מ"ד). פס"ר ק"מ,
א'.

17 וגו'] הוספתי=ט.   19 למאוס] מ. למעוס (או למעוס?) ד. למעון.   20 הסוס] א. מ.
ג. הצאן.   21 ריבה] מ. תינוקת ד. ראיתם ריבה / מה] מ. מי.   22—23 של פרש
ערבי הוא] ד. פרש ערבי אחד.   24 הייתי קורא זה הפסוק] א. ד. הייתי מצטער על
הפסוק הזה (ד. ~ והייתי קורא אותו.   27 לפגומי גוים ערביים] ד. לפני גוים / שקלי
שמים] ד. לשמים.   30 העולים] א. לעולים ד. לעולי רגלים / לבית הבחירה] ד. ‹.
31 הבורגנין] ד. הבורגמין.   32 העולים לכרכי המלכים] ד. לעולי לכרמי (ל. כרמי
מלכים ט. העולים לשולחן מלכים ט. (מלכים קפ"א) העולים לצרכי מלכים.   34 באהבה]
מ. בשמחה.   36—35 תחת—ובצמא] א. ‹.   39—36 תחת אשר לא עבדת—בחוסר
כל] ד. בעירום ובחוסר כל.   37 בלבוש] א. מלובש.   39—38 מרוב כל] מ. ‹.

meaning of: "In want of all things"? They were out of their senses.[4] Another Interpretation: *In Want of All Things.* They were deficient in the study of the Torah.

The Same Day Came They into the Wilderness of Sinai. It was the day of the New Moon. In this sense it is said: "In the third moon after the children of Israel were gone forth out of the land of Egypt, the same day."[5]

And When They Were Departed from Rephidim, and Were Come to the Wilderness of Sinai. But has it not been specified in the section treating of the journeys: "And they journeyed from Rephidim, and pitched in the wilderness of Sinai" (Num. 33.15)? What need then is there of saying here: "And when they were departed from Rephidim, and were come to the wilderness of Sinai"?[6] It is to declare that their departing from Rephidim was like their coming into the wilderness of Sinai. Just as their coming into the wilderness of Sinai was with repentance, so also was their departing from Rephidim with repentance. Another Interpretation: It declares that their coming into the wilderness of Sinai was like their departing from Rephidim. Just as when they departed from Rephidim they provoked God, and yet when after a little while they repented they were again favorably received by Him, so also after they had come to the wilderness of Sinai they provoked God, and yet when after a little while they repented they were again favorably received by Him. R. Eliezer the son of R. Jose the Galilean says: Behold it says: "I answered thee in the secret place of thunder; I proved thee at the waters of Meribah" (Ps. 81.8)—from the time when I was answering you and protecting you and thundering at the whole world for your sake; even at that very time it was known to Me how you were going to act at the waters of Meribah. Abba Saul says: Behold it says: "I answered thee in

---

4. Cf. Lev. Rab., 1.6.
5. The Hebrew word חדש means "new moon" as well as "month."
6. See Introduction.

40 שניטלה הדעת מהן דבר אחר בחוסר כל שהן
חסרים בתלמוד תורה.

ביום הזה באו מדבר סיני ראש חדש
היה לכך נאמר בחדש השלישי לצאת בני ישראל
מארץ מצרים ביום הזה.

45 **ויסעו מרפידים ויבאו מדבר סיני**
והלא כבר מפורש בפרשת מסעות ויסעו מרפידים
ויחנו במדבר סיני ומה ת״ל ויסעו מרפידים ויבאו
מדבר סיני הקיש נסיעתם מרפידים לביאתם למדבר
סיני מה ביאתם למדבר סיני בתשובה אף נסיעתם
50 מרפידים בתשובה. דבר אחר הקיש ביאתם מדבר
סיני לנסיעתם מרפידים מה נסיעתם מרפידים
מכעיסין למקום ולשעה קלה עשו תשובה ונתקבלו
אף ביאתם מדבר סיני מכעיסין למקום ולשעה קלה
עשו תשובה ונתקבלו רבי אלעזר ב״ר יוסי הגלילי
55 אומר הרי הוא אומר אענך בסתר רעם אבחנך על מי
מריבה משעה שהייתי עונך ומגין עליך ומרעים עליך
את כל העולם מאותה שעה גלוי היה לפני מה שאתה
עתיד לעשות על מי מריבה אבא שאול אומר הרי

44—42 שבת פ״ו, ב׳.   52—42 ש. 93.   47—46 במדבר ל״ג, ט״ו.   56—55 תהלים
פ״א, ח׳.

40 בחוסר] ד. מאי / שהן] מ. שהן / שהיו ד. שיהיו.   41 בתלמוד] ד. מתלמוד.   42 ראש
חדש] מ״ח. ~ השלישי.   44 ביום הזה]=ג: א. וגו׳ ד. >.   46 מפורש] ד. נאמר.
46—48 בפרשת מסעות—ויבאו מדבר סיני] ט. ביום הזה באו מדבר סיני.   47 ויחנו]
א. ויבאו.   48—47 ומה ת״ל ויסעו—סיני] א. < / ד. ומה ת״ל באו מדבר סיני.   48 הקיש]
ט. אלא הקיש.   52 ולשעה] ד. לשעה.   53 מדבר] מ. מ״ח. למדבר. / מכעיסין] ד.
היו מכעיסין.   54 רבי אליעזר ב״ר יוסי הגלילי אומר] ד. אמר ר״א בר׳ יוסי הגלילי.
56 ומרעים] ד. ומרפס / היה] ד. >.

the secret place of thunder," etc. You call in secret and I answer you and thunder at the whole world for your sake. R. Judah b. Lakish says: Behold it says: "And God saw the children of Israel" (Ex. 2.25) —God saw in them that they were repenting though they themselves did not see it in one another. "And God took cognizance of them" (ibid.)—God knew of them that they had repented, but they themselves did not know it of one another. R. Eleazar the son of R. Jose says in the name of Abba Jose the son of the Damascene: Behold it says: "And God saw the children of Israel, that they would provoke Him in the future; "and God took cognizance of them," that they would in the future blaspheme. And with all that why?[7] Because of the power of repentance which is mighty. Similarly, R. Eleazar the son of Jose interpreted: Behold it says: "In all their afflictions He was afflicted," etc. (Isa. 63.9). And it also says: "For he said: 'Surely, they are My people, children that will not deal falsely' " (ibid. v. 8). And was it not revealed before Him that they would in the future deal falsely? Scripture says: "Surely!"[8] It was revealed before Him that they were going to deal falsely. Why then does it say: "So He was their Savior"[9] (ibid. v. 8)? It simply means that He helped them not as people who were going to provoke Him in the future, but as people who would never become faithless. And thus it says: "But they beguiled Him with their mouth, and lied unto Him with their tongues. For their heart was not steadfast with Him, neither were they faithful in His covenant" (Ps. 78.36–37). And yet: "He, being full of compassion, forgiveth iniquity" (ibid. v. 38). And it also says: "Make the heart of these people fat," etc. (Isa. 6.10) "lest they . . . return and"— repentance perforce achieving its task—"be healed" (ibid.).

They Encamped in the Wilderness. The Torah was given in public, openly in a free place. For had the Torah been given in the land of

7. I. e., why was so much leniency shown them?

8. The word אך here rendered by "surely" was regarded as having the force of a restriction or qualification (see Bacher, *Terminologie,* I, p. 110).

9. See *Shebut Yehudah* ad loc.

הוא אומר אענך בסתר רעם וגו' אתה קורא בסתר
ואני אענך בגלוי ומרעים עליך את כל העולם
רבי יהודה בן לקיש אומר הרי הוא אומר
וירא אלהים את בני ישראל ראה בהם
שעשו תשובה והם לא ראו זה את זה וידע אלהים
אלהים ידע בהם שעשו תשובה והם לא ידעו זה
בזה רבי אלעזר בר' יוסי אומר משום אבא יוסי
בן דורמסקית הרי הוא אומר וירא אלהים את בני
ישראל שהם עתידין להכעיס וידע אלהים שהם
עתידים לנאץ וכל כך למה מכח התשובה הקשה.
כיוצא בו דרש רבי אלעזר בן יוסי הרי הוא אומר
בכל צרתם לו צר וגו' ואומר ויאמר אך עמי המה
בנים לא ישקרו וכי לא היה גלוי לפניו שהן עתידין
לשקר ת"ל אך גלוי היה לפניו שהן עתידין לשקר
ומה ת"ל להם למושיע אלא אלא הושיען כבני
אדם שהם עתידין להכעיס אלא כבני אדם שאינם
עתידין לבגוד בו עולמית וכן הוא אומר ויפתוהו
בפיהם ובלשונם יכזבו לו ולבם לא נכון עמו ולא
נאמנו בבריתו ואף על פי כן והוא רחום יכפר עון
ואומר השמן לב העם הזה וגו' ושב אנכי לתשובה
לעשות שלה ורפא לו.

ויחנו במדבר נתנה תורה דימוס בפרהסיא
במקום הפקר שאלו נתנה תורה בארץ ישראל היו

61—64 שמו"ר א', ל"ו.   62 שמות ב', כ"ה.   63—64 שם.   70 ישעיה ס"ג, ט'.
71—70 שם ס"ג, ח'.   77—75 תהלים ע"ח, ל"ו-ל"ח.   78 ישעיה ו', י'.   83—80 ש.
93.

---

60 ומרעים] כ. (תהלים פ"א) ומרעיש.   61 בן לקיש] ד. <.   62 אלהים ראה] ד. ראה
מ. אלהים נראה.   63 ראו] מ. ג. ידעו.   65 בר' יוסי] ד. < מ. ~ הגלילי.   69—66 הרי
הוא אומר—דרש ר' אלעזר בן יוסי] מ. <.   67 וידע אלהים] ד. < מ"ח. ואעפ"י כן
וידע אלהים.   67—68 שהם עתידים לנאץ] מ"ח. < ג. < ואעפ"י כן וידע אלהים.
68 מכח התשובה] א"צ. מכח השבועה / הקשה]=א"א. ז"ר: א. נ. ל. בה הקשה ק.
בא הקשה מ"ח. ש"י. <.   70 ואומר] א. ד. <.   72 לפניו שהן עתידין לשקר] ד. <.
73 ומה ת"ל] א"צ. ואעפ"י כן / ויהי] ק. נ. ואהי / אלא] א"א. <.   75 לבגוד בו] כ.
(תהלים ע"ח) לבער.   76 יכזבו] מ. כזבו / ולבם] מ. ואומר לבם.   79—78 אנכי
לתשובה לעשות שלה] מ. אונקי (אינקי?) לתשובה לעשות שלה ט. אני לתשובה לעשות
ד. לתשובה לעשות ושב א"צ. ג. <.   80 דימוס] א. ג. <.

Israel, the Israelites could have said to the nations of the world: You have no share in it. But now that it was given in the wilderness publicly and openly in a place that is free for all, everyone wishing to accept it could come and accept it. One might suppose that it was given at night, but Scripture says: "And it came to pass on the third day when it was morning" (v. 16). One might suppose that it was given in silence, but Scripture says: "When there were thunders and lightning" (ibid.). One might suppose that they could not hear the voice,[10] but Scripture says: "The voice of the Lord is powerful, the voice of the Lord is full of majesty," etc. (Ps. 29.4). "The Lord sat enthroned at the flood," etc.[11] (ibid. v. 10). . . . . Balaam said to all the people who stood around him: "The Lord is giving strength unto His people" (ibid. v. 11). And they all opened their mouths and said: "The Lord will bless His people with peace" (ibid.). R. Jose says: Behold it says: "I have not spoken in secret," etc. (Isa. 45.19). When I gave the Torah from the very start, I gave it not in the place of a land of darkness, not in a secret place, not in an obscure place. "I said not: 'It is unto the seed of Jacob' " (ibid.), that is, to these only will I give it. "They sought Me in the desert" (ibid.). Did I not give it in broad daylight?[12] And thus it says: "I the Lord speak righteousness, I declare things that are right" (ibid.). Already before I gave them the commandments I advanced them the rewards for them, as it is said: "And it shall come to pass on the sixth day that they shall prepare that which they bring in, and it shall be twice as much" (Ex. 16.5). And it also says: "Then will I command My blessing upon you in the sixth year," etc. (Lev. 25.21). One might think that it was only in the case of these two commandments, but Scripture says: "And He gave them the lands of the nations," etc. (Ps. 105.44). What for? "That

10. I. e., of God.
11. The וגו', "etc.," refers to the rest of the midrashic comment which is omitted here (see above *Amalek*, III, note 1 and below V, note 7).
12. See Introduction.

אומרים להם לאומות העולם אין לכם חלק בה
אלא נתנה במדבר דימוס בפרהסיא במקום הפקר
כל הרוצה לקבל יבא ויקבל יכול נתנה בלילה
ת״ל ויהי ביום השלישי בהיות הבקר יכול   85
נתנה בשתיקה ת״ל ויהי קולות וברקים יכול
לא היו שומעין את הגול ת״ל קול יי בכח
קול יי בהדר וגו׳ יי למבול ישב וגו׳ אמר
בלעם לכל העומדים עליו יי עוז לעמו יתן ופתחו
כלם ואמרו יי יברך את עמו בשלום רבי יוסי אומר   90
הרי הוא אומר לא בסתר דברתי וגו׳ כשנתתיה
מתחילה לא נתתיה לא במקום ארץ חשך ולא
במקום הסתר ולא במקום אפלה לא אמרתי לזרע
יעקב לאלו אני נותנה תוהו בקשוני לא נתתיה פנגס
וכן הוא אומר אני יי דובר צדק מגיד מישרים כבר   95
עד שלא נתתי להם את המצות הקדמתי להם מתן
שכרן שנאמר והיה ביום הששי והכינו את אשר
יביאו והיה משנה וכתיב וצויתי את ברכתי לכם
בשנה הששית וגו׳ יכול אלו בלבד תלמוד לומר
ויתן להם ארצות גוים וגו׳ מפני מה בעבור ישמרו   100

---

85 שמות י״ט, ט״ז.   87 — 88 תהלים כ״ט, ד׳.   88 שם כ״ט, י׳.   90 — 89 שם כ״ט, י״א.
94 — 90 מ״ח.   209. ש. 93.   91 ישעיה מ״ה, י״ט.   98 — 97 שמות ט״ז, ה׳.   99 — 98 ויקרא
כ״ה, כ״א.   101 — 100 תהלים ק״ה, מ״ד – מ״ה.

---

82 להם לאומות העולם] א״צ. אומות העולם / לכם] ד. להם.   83 אלא] ד. לפיכך.
84 כל] ד. וכל.   87 הקול] ד. הקולות.   88 — 87 ת״ל קול—ישב וגו׳] ד. ת״ל וכל העם
רואים את הקולות ואומר קול יי בהדר וכו׳.   90 — 88 אמר בלעם—בשלום] Pugio, 429
fidei .>.   89 בלעם] ד. ~ הרשע.   90 — 89 ופתחו כולם] מ. שבחו / ופתחו—בשלום]
א. >.   91 כשנתתיה] ד. ~ אני.   94 לאלו] כ. (ישעיה מ״ה, כ״ט) לא לו / אני נותנה]
ט. (ישעיה תס״ג) < ולא לעו״א שנאמר יי מסיני בא וזרח משעיר וגו׳ לא אמרתי לזרע
יעקב / תהו בקשוני] ד. אלא תהו בקשוני כ. (שם) אלא בקשוני / פנגס] ד. כ. (תהלים
ק״ה) פנגס כ. (ישעיה שם) פדגוס.   96 להם] ד. לכם / להם] ד. לכם.   99 תלמוד
לומר] א. מ. והלא כבר נאמר.

they might keep His statutes and observe His laws" (ibid. v. 45). R. Eliezer the son of R. Jose the Galilean used to say: Behold it says: "He declareth His word unto Jacob . . . He hath not dealt so with any nation" (Ps. 147.19–20). But what had those wretched nations done that He would not give them the Torah? "His ordinances they have not known them" (ibid.)—they were unwilling to accept them,[13] as it is said: "God cometh from Teman . . . and a brightness appeareth as the light . . . before Him goeth the pestilence . . . He standeth, and shaketh the earth, He beholdeth, and maketh the nations to tremble," etc. (Hab. 3.3–6).[14]

And There Israel Encamped. (*vayyiḥan*). Wherever it says: "And they journeyed," "and they encamped," it indicates that they were journeying with dissension and that they were encamping with dissension. But here it says: "And there Israel encamped"[15] (*vayyiḥan*), indicating that they all agreed and were of one mind.

There. Telling, that He said to them: Too much time are you spending there. And so we do find that they stayed there twelve months less ten days.

Before the Mount. On the east side of the mount. Wherever you find the expression "before" (*neged*) it means on the side that is towards the east.

13. It was not a refusal on the part of God to give them the Torah, but a refusal on their part to accept it.
14. The וגו׳, "etc.," refers to the midrashic interpretation of the verses in Habakkuk to the effect that God offered the Torah to the other nations, which interpretation is omitted here (see ʿAb. Zarah 2b).
15. The singular form ויחן is contrasted with the plural form ויחנו used elsewhere.

חקיו ותורותיו ינצורו היה רבי אליעזר בנו של רבי

יוסי הגלילי אומר הרי הוא אומר מגיד דבריו

ליעקב וגו' לא עשה כן לכל גוי וכי מה עשו הגוים

דווים האלו שלא רצה ליתן להם את התורה

105 ומשפטים בל ידעום שלא רצו לקבל שנאמר אלוה

מתימן יבא וגו' ונגה כאור תהיה וגו' לפניו ילך דבר

וגו' עמד וימודד ארץ ראה ויתר גוים וגו'.

ויחן שם ישראל כל מקום שהוא אומר

ויסעו ויחנו נוסעים במחלוקת וחונים במחלוקת

110 אבל כאן הוא אומר ויחן שם ישראל השוו כלם

לב אחד.

שם מגיד שאמר להם זמן הרבה אתם עושים

שם וכן מצינו שהיו שם שנים עשר חדש פחות

עשרת ימים.

נגד ההר לצד מזרחו של הר כל מקום שאתה

115 מוצא נגד פנים למזרח.

101 — 107 לקמן ה'.   102 — 103 תהלים קמ"ז, י"ט—כ'.   105 — 107 חבקוק ג', ג'—ר'.
108 — 111 וי"ר ט', ט'. פדר"א מ"א. ש. 94.

___

103 — 104 הגוים דווים האלו שלא] א. מ. אילו דווים ולא.   105 ומשפטים] א. ד.
משפטים / שנאמר]=ט: א. ד. ר.   110 — 111 הוא אומר—לב אחד] ד. השוו לב אחד
לכך נאמר ויחן שם ישראל נגד ההר.   112 שם מגיד] ד. ר.   113 שם] ד. < / פחות]
א. מ. חסר.   115 של הר] מ. שלכל הר.

CHAPTER II
(Ex. 19.3–9)

And Moses Went Up unto God. That was on the second day.

And the Lord Called unto Him, etc. This tells that the call always preceded the address.

Thus. In the holy tongue. "Thus," in this order. "Thus," in this manner. "Thus," no more, no less.

Shalt Thou Say to the House of Jacob. That is, the women. *And Tell the Sons of Israel.* That is, the men. Another Interpretation: *Thus Shalt Thou Say to the House of Jacob*—because of the merit of Jacob. *And Tell the Sons of Israel*—because of the merit of Israel. Another Interpretation: *Thus Shalt Thou Say to the House of Jacob.* Tell the women the main things in a mild tone. *And Tell the Sons of Israel.* And be strict[1] with them.

Ye Have Seen. What I tell you is not received by tradition. I do not have to send documents to you.—I do not have to present witnesses to you, but you yourselves have seen what I have done to the Egyptians. Notice of how many offences—of idolatry, incestuous practices and murder—they had in the past been guilty before Me. Yet, I punished them only on your account.

And How I Bore You on Eagles' wings. R. Eliezer says: This refers to the day of Rameses. For they were all gathered and brought to Rameses within a little while. *And I Brought You unto Myself.* That is, before Mount Sinai. R. Akiba says: It refers to the day of the giving of the Law. For the Israelites were startled, and moved backward twelve miles and then again returning moved forward twelve miles—twenty-four miles at each commandment—. *And I Brought You unto Myself.* To the Temple. Another Interpretation: *And How I Bore You on Eagles' Wings.* How is the eagle distinguished from all other birds? All the other birds carry their young between their feet, being afraid of

1. Cf. Shab. 87a.

פרשה ב (שמות י"ט, ג'—ט'.)

ומשה עלה אל האלהים זה יום שני.

ויקרא אליו יי וגו' מגיד שהקריאה קדמה לדיבור.

כה בלשון הקדש כה כסדר הזה כה כענין הזה כה שלא תפחות ושלא תוסיף.

5 **תאמר לבית יעקב** אלו הנשים ותגד לבני ישראל אלו האנשים. דבר אחר כה תאמר לבית יעקב בזכות יעקב ותגיד לבני ישראל בזכות ישראל. דבר אחר כה תאמר לבית יעקב אמור בלשון רכה ראשי הדברים לנשים ותגד לבני

10 ישראל ותדקדק עמהם.

אתם ראיתם לא במסורת אני אומר לכם לא כתבים אני משגר לכם לא עדים אני מעמיד עליכם אלא אתם ראיתם אשר עשיתי למצרים ראו

15 על כמה הם חייבין לי על עבודה זרה ועל גילוי עריות ועל שפיכות דמים לשעבר ולא נפרעתי מהם אלא על ידיכם.

ואשא אתכם על כנפי נשרים רבי אליעזר אומר זה יום רעמסס לפי שנתקבצו כלם

20 ובאו לרעמסס לשעה קלה ואביא אתכם אלי לפני הר סיני רבי עקיבא אומר זה יום מתן תורה לפי שהיו ישראל נרתעין לאחוריהם שנים עשר מיל וחוזרין לפניהם שנים עשר מיל עשרים וארבעה מילין על כל דיבור ודיבור ואביא אתכם אלי

25 לבית הבחירה. דבר אחר ואשא אתכם על כנפי נשרים מה נשתנה הנשר הזה מכל העופות כלם שכל העופות כלן נותנין את בניהם בין רגליהם

---

1 שבת פ"ח, א'.   117—1 ש. 96—94.   3—2 ת"כ ויקרא א'. יומא ד', א'.   5—4 לקמן ט'. ספרי במדבר ל"ט.   7—6 פדר"א שם.   17—14 לעיל בשלח א'.   20—18 לעיל פסחא י"ד.   24—22 לקמן ט'.   31—25 ספרי דברים שי"ד.

---

6 תאמר] ד. כה תאמר.   9—7 דבר אחר—בזכות ישראל]=ג. ט. מ"ח: א. ד. >. 12 אתם ראיתם] ד. ואמרו להם אתם ראיתם.   13 לא כתבים] ד. לא כתובים הם לכם לא כתבים.   14 עליכם] ד. >.   15 לין] ד. >.   16 ולא] ד. לא.   17 מהם] ק. מכם / על ידיכם] ק. ידכם.   19 יום רעמסס] א"צ. יום יציאת מצרים.   20 אלי לפני] מ. אלי זה מתן תורה לפני.   23 לפניהם] ד. > / עשרים] ד. הרי עשרים. 27 בין] ד. תחת.   30 שמא] ד. שלא / אומר] מ. ד. >.

other birds flying higher above them. The eagle, however, is afraid only of men who might shoot at him. He, therefore, prefers that the arrows lodge in him rather than in his children. To give a parable: A man was going on the road with his son walking in front of him. If robbers, who might seek to capture the son, come from in front, he takes him from before himself and puts him behind himself. If a wolf comes from behind, he takes his son from behind and puts him in front. If robbers come from in front and wolves from behind, he takes the son and puts him upon his shoulders. As it is said: "And in the wilderness, where thou hast seen how that the Lord thy God bore thee, as a man doth bear his son" (Deut. 1.31).

Now Therefore If Ye Will Hearken. Take it upon yourselves now. For all beginnings are difficult.

If Ye Will Hearken. On the basis of this passage the sages said: If a man hearkens to one commandment, he is given the opportunity to hearken to many commandments. For, it really says: "If you begin to hearken you will continue to hearken."[2] If a man forgets but one commandment, he will be led to forget many commandments. For it says: "And it shall be, if you begin to forget that you will continue to forget" (Deut. 8.19).

And Keep My Covenant. R. Eliezer says: This refers to the covenant of the Sabbath. R. Akiba says: This refers to the covenant of circumcision and to the covenant against idolatry.

Then Ye Shall Be Mine. That is, you shall be turned to Me and be occupied with the words of the Torah and not with other matters.

Own Treasure. Just as a man's treasure is precious to him, so you will be precious to Me. R. Joshua the son of Karḥa says: This figure is used in order to penetrate the ear. One might suppose that, just as what a wife treasures is what her husband gives her, and what the son treasures is what his father gives him, and what the servant treasures is what his master gives him, and what the maid-servant treasures is

2. Cf. above *Vayassa'*, I, note 8.

מפני שהן מתייראין מעוף אחר שהוא פורח על
גביהם אבל הנשר הזה אינו מתירא אלא מאדם
30   בלבד שמא יזרוק בו חץ אומר מוטב שיכנס בו
ולא בבניו משל לאחד שהיה מהלך בדרך והיה
מנהג את בנו לפניו ובאו לסטים לשבותו נטלו
מלפניו ונתנו לאחוריו בא זאב לטרפו נטלו מאחריו
ונתנו לפניו ליסטים מלפניו וזאב מלאחריו נטלו
35   ונתנו על כתפיו שנאמר ובמדבר אשר ראית אשר
נשאך יי אלהיך כאשר ישא איש את בנו.

ועתה   **אם**   **שמוע**   **תשמעו**   עכשיו קבלו
עליכם שכל התחלות קשות.

אם   **שמוע**   **תשמעו**   מכאן אמרו שמע אדם
40   מצוה אחת משמיעין אותו מצות הרבה שנאמר
אם שמוע תשמעו שכח אדם מצוה אחת משכחין
אותו מצות הרבה שנאמר אם שכח תשכח.

ושמרתם   **את**   **בריתי**   רבי   אליעזר   אומר
זה ברית שבת רבי עקיבא אומר זה ברית מילה
45   ועבודה זרה.

והייתם   **לי**   שתהיו פנויין לי ועוסקין בדברי
תורה ולא תהיו עוסקין בדברים אחרים.

סגלה   מה סגולתו של אדם חביבה עליו כך
תהיו חביבין עלי רבי יהושע בן קרחה אומר כדי
50   שתבקע אוזן כשם שהאשה מסגלת מאחר בעלה
והבן מאחר אביו והעבד מאחר רבו והשפחה מאחר

31—36 לעיל בשלח ה'.   36—35 דברים א', ל"א.   42—39 לעיל ויסע א'.   42 דברים
ח', י"ט.

30—31 בו ולא בבניו] א. בי ולא בבני.   32 לשבותו] ד. ~ מלפניו.   33 לטרפו] א. מ.
מ"ח. ליטלו.   36 כאשר ישא איש את בנו] הוספתי: א. וגו'.   37 תשמעו] ק. נ. תשמע
/ עכשיו] ד. ועתה.   41 משכחין] א. משכיחין.   44 שבת] א"צ. תורה / ברית מילה]
ק. שבת מילה.   46 פנויין] ד. קנויין.   47—46 בדברי תורה] א. בדברי תורתי ד.
בתורה.   49 כדי] מ. הרי א"צ. >.   50 שתבקע] מ. ט. שתקבע / מאחר בעלה] מ.
ד. אחר בעלה.

what her mistress gives her, so you, treasured by Me, have been given to Me by others.[3] But Scripture says: "For all the earth is Mine."

And Ye Shall Be unto Me. I shall not appoint nor delegate any one else, so to speak, to rule over you, but I Myself will rule over you. And thus it says: "Behold, He that keepeth Israel doth neither slumber nor sleep" (Ps. 121.4).

A Kingdom. I will allow only one of your own to be king over you, but not one from the nations of the world. And thus it says: "My dove, my undefiled, is but one"[4] (Cant. 6.9). R. Eliezer the son of R. Jose the Galilean says: How can you prove that every Israelite is destined to have as many children as there were persons who came out of Egypt? It says: "Instead of thy fathers shall be thy sons" (Ps. 45.17). But "sons" might mean wretched and afflicted ones? It says, however: "Whom thou shalt make princes in all the land" (ibid.). But "princes" might mean merchant-princes? It says, however: "A kingdom." But "king" might mean one who goes around making conquests? It says, however: "And priests." But "priests" might mean non-functioning priests, as when it says: "And David's sons were (*Kohanim*) priests" (2 Sam. 8.18)? Therefore Scripture says: "And a holy nation." Hence, the sages said: The Israelites before they made the Golden Calf were eligible to eat of the holy things. But after they made the Golden Calf these holy things were taken from them and given to the priests exclusively.

It is said:[5] "Israel is a scattered sheep" (Jer. 50.17). The people of Israel are compared to a lamb. What is the nature of the lamb? If it is hurt in one limb, all its limbs feel the pain. So also are the people of Israel. One of them commits a sin and all of them suffer from the punishment. But the nations of the world are not so. One of them may be killed and yet all the others may rejoice at his downfall.

3. See Introduction.
4. I. e., homogeneous. Ruler and people are of one race and of one nationality.
5. See Introduction.

גבירתה יכול אף אתם מסוגלין לי מאחרים ת"ל
כי לי כל הארץ.

ואתם תהיו לי כביכול איני מעמיד ואיני
משליט עליכם אחרים אלא אני וכן הוא אומר הנה
לא ינום ולא יישן שומר ישראל.

ממלכת איני ממליך עליכם מאומות העולם
אלא מכם וכן הוא אומר אחת היא יונתי תמתי וגו'.
רבי אליעזר בנו של רבי יוסי הגלילי אומר מנין
אתה אומר שכל אחד ואחד מישראל עתיד להיות
לו בנים כיוצאי מצרים שנאמר תחת אבותיך יהיו
בניך אי בנים יכול דווים וסגופים ת"ל תשיתמו
לשרים בכל הארץ אי שרים יכול פרגמטיוטין
ת"ל ממלכת אי מלך יכול יהא חוזר ומכבש ת"ל
כהנים יכול כהנים בטלנים כענין שנאמר ובני דוד
כהנים היו ת"ל וגוי קדוש מכאן אמרו ראוין היו
ישראל לאכול בקדשים עד שלא עשו את העגל
משעשו את העגל ניטלו מהם וניתנו לכהנים שנאמר
שה פזורה ישראל וגו' משולין בשה מה דרכו של
שה לוקה על אחד מאיבריו וכולן מרגישין כך הן
ישראל אחד מהן חוטא וכולן נענשין אבל אומות
העולם אינן כן אלא אחד מהן נהרג וכולם שמחים
במפלתו.

56—55 תהלים קכ"א, ד'.   58 שה"ש ו', ט'.   62—59 מד' תהלים מ"ה, ז'.
62—61 תהלים מ"ה, ז'.   65—66 שמואל ב. ח', י"ח. לעיל עמלק ג'.   67—66 לעיל
פסחא א'.   69 ירמיה נ', י"ז.   73—69 וי"ר ד', ו'.   74—75 דהי"א. י"ז, כ"א.

---

52 מסוגלין] ק. מסגלין / לי מאחרים] הגהתי=ל"ט. ז"י: א. מ. לי מאחורי ד. לי
מאחרי ט. <.   57 עליכם] ד. >.   60 להיות] א. מ. לראות.   63 לשרים] ק. נ. שרים
/ פרגמטיוטין] ט. פרגמטיוטין מ"ח. פרקמטיוטין ד. פרגמיטיוטין מ. פרגמטיוסין.
64 ומכבש] ה. ומתכבש.   65 יכול כהנים] א. ט. ז"י. ש"י. < / בטלנים]=ט. א"א.
ה. ל"ט. ש. מ"ח: א. ד. מבטלים מ. מבטלנין ב. (תהלים מ"ה, ל"ד) בטלים.   66 ת"ל
וגוי קדוש] הגהתי=ה. ל"ט. ש.   67 ישראל] ד. המשילן / ד. המשילן.   69—70 דרכו של שה—וכולן
מרגישין] ד. שה זו כשהיא לוקה מאחת מאבריה כל איבריה מרגישין.   71 אחד מהן
חוטא וכולן נענשין] ד. אם נהרג אחד מהן כלן מרגישין ומצטערין.   72 אחד מהן נהרג
וכולם] ד. אם נהרג אחד מהם כולם.   74 קראן גוי] ד. ~ קדוש.

And a Nation. Scripture designates them as a nation,[6] as in the passage: "And who is like Thy people Israel, a nation one in the earth" (I Chron. 17.21).

Holy. Holy and sacred, separated from the nations of the world and from their abominations.

These Are the Words. No more no less. *Which Thou Shalt Speak unto the Children of Israel.* Exactly in this order.

And Moses Came and Called for the Elders of the People. This tells that Moses showed honor to the elders.

And Set Before Them. He enlightened their eyes. *All These Words.* The first first, and the last last.

Which the Lord Commanded Him. Also what was said for the women.

And All the People Answered Together. They did not give this answer with hypocrisy, nor did they get it one from the other, but all of them made up their mind alike and said: "All that the Lord hath spoken we will do."

And Moses Reported the Words of the People unto the Lord. And was there any need for Moses to report? Scripture merely wishes you to learn proper manners from Moses. He did not say: Since He who sent me knows anyhow there is no need for me to report back. Another Interpretation: It was to give Moses a reward for every going up and for every coming down.

And the Lord Said unto Moses: Lo, I come unto Thee in the Thickness of the Cloud. With a cloud that is thick. And which is this? It is the thick darkness, as it is said: "But Moses drew near unto the thick darkness [where God was]" (Ex. 20.21).

That the People May Hear When I Speak with Thee. R. Judah says: Whence can you prove that the Holy One, blessed be He, said to Moses: Behold, I will be saying something to you and you shall answer Me, and I will then agree with you, so that the Israelites

6. I.e., even though they are a kingdom of priests.

וגוי קראן גוי שנאמר ומי כעמך ישראל גוי
אחד בארץ.

75

קדוש קדושים ומקודשים פרושים מאומות
העולם ומשקוציהם.

אלה הדברים שלא תפחות ולא תוסיף אשר
תדבר אל בני שראל כסדר הזה.

ויבא משה ויקרא לזקני העם מגיד
שמשה חלק כבוד לזקנים.

80

וישם לפניהם האיר את עיניכם. את כל
הדברים ראשון ואחרון אחרון.

אשר צוהו יי אף לנשים אמור.

ויענו כל העם יחדו לא ענו בחנופה ולא
קבלו זה מזה אלא השוו כלם לב אחד ואמרו כל
אשר דבר יי נעשה.

85

וישב משה את דברי העם אל יי וכי
היה צריך משה להשיב אלא בא הכתוב ללמדך
דרך ארץ ממשה שלא אמר הואיל ויודע מי ששלחני
איני צריך להשיב. דבר אחר ליתן שכר למשה
על כל עלייה ועלייה ועל כל ירידה וירידה.

90

**ויאמר יי אל משה הנה אנכי בא
אליך בעב הענן** בענן עבה ואיזהו זה ערפל
שנאמר ומשה נגש אל הערפל.

95

בעבור ישמע העם בדברי עמך רבי
יהודה אומר מנין אתה אומר שאמר הקב"ה למשה
הריני אומר לך דבר ואתה מחזירני ואני מודה

76—77 ת"כ קדושים א' (86).   81—80 לעיל פסחא י"א.   91—90 לעיל פסחא א'.
93—95 לקמן ט'.   95 שמות כ'. כ"א.   100—96 לקמן ד'.

---

84 לנשים] מ"ח. לנערים לנשים.   89 בא הכתוב ללמדך] מ. נאמר הכתוב ללמדך ד.
למדה תורה.   91—90 ממשה—צריך להשיב] ד. בא משה והשיב תשובה לשלחו שכן
אמר משה אעפ"י שהוא יודע ועד אשיב תשובה לשולחני / אמר] א. נאמר / מי]=ש"ט.
מ"ח: א. מ. מה.   93 הנה אנכי] ק. נ. הנני.   95 שנאמר] א. ת"ל.   97 מנין אתה
אומר] מ"ח. >.

should say: Great is Moses, for even God agreed with him? From the passage: "And may also believe thee for ever." Rabbi says: We need not make Moses great if it is to be done only by making God change His mind and go back on His word. The passage merely teaches that God said to Moses: Behold, I am going to call you from the top of the mountain and you will come up. As it is said: "And the Lord called Moses to the top of the mount; and Moses went up" (v. 20).

And May Also Believe Thee for Ever, in thee and also in the prophets that are to arise after thee.

And Moses Told. But what had God told Moses to tell Israel, or what had the Israelites told Moses to tell God? R. Jose the Galilean says: It is in reference to what was said: "And thou shalt set bounds unto the people round about, saying" (v. 12). R. Eleazar b. Perata says: But what had God told Moses to tell Israel, or what had the Israelites told Moses to tell God? It is merely in reference to what was said: "And Moses came and told the people all the words of the Lord, and all the ordinances" (Ex. 24.3). He told them: If you will joyfully accept the stipulated penalties, you will receive a reward; but if not, you are going to get punishment. And they joyfully accepted the stipulated penalties. Rabbi says: But what had God told Moses to tell Israel, or what had the Israelites told Moses to tell God? It is simply this: They said: It is our wish to hear directly from the mouth of our King. To hear from the attendant is not like hearing from the mouth of the king. God then said: Give them what they ask for: "That the people may hear when I speak." Another Interpretation: They said: It is our wish to see our King. For hearing is not like seeing. God then said: Give them what they ask for: "For the third day the Lord will come down in the sight of all the people upon mount Sinai" (v. 11).

לך שיהיו ישראל אומרים גדול משה שהודה לו
המקום שנאמר וגם בך יאמינו לעולם רבי אומר
100 אין אנו צריכין לעשות למשה גדול אלא אם כן
עשינו להקב״ה שחזר בו ובדברו אלא מלמד שאמר
המקום למשה הריני קורא לך מראש ההר ואתה
עולה שנאמר ויקרא יי למשה לראש ההר ויעל
משה וגם בך יאמינו לעולם גם בך בנביאים
105 העתידים לעמוד אחריך.

ויגד משה וגו׳ וכי מה אמר המקום למשה לאמר
לישראל או מה אמרו לו ישראל לאמר למקום
רבי יוסי הגלילי אומר מתוך שנאמר והגבלת את
110 העם סביב לאמר רבי אלעזר בן פרטא אומר וכי
מה אמר המקום למשה לאמר לישראל או מה אמרו
ישראל למשה לאמר למקום אלא מתוך שנאמר
ויבא משה ויספר לעם את כל דברי יי ואת כל
המשפטים אמר להם אם מקבלים אתם עליכם
115 עונשים בשמחה הרי אתם מקבלים שכר ואם לאו
הרי אתם מקבלים פורענות וקבלו עליהן עונשין
בשמחה רבי אומר וכי מה אמר המקום למשה
לאמר לישראל או מה אמרו ישראל למשה לאמר
למקום אלא אמרו רצוננו לשמוע מפי מלכנו לא
120 דומה שומע מפי פרגוד לשומע מפי המלך אמר
המקום תן להם מה שבקשו בעבור ישמע העם. דבר
אחר אמרו רצוננו לראות את מלכנו לא דומה
שומע לרואה אמר המקום תן להם מה שבקשו כי
ביום השלישי ירד יי לעיני כל העם על הר סיני.

---

104 — 105 שמות י״ט, כ׳.   107 — 117 שבת פ״ז, א׳.   109 — 110 שמות י״ט, י״ב.   113 — 114 שם כ״ד, ג׳.   121 — 124 שמו״ר כ״ב, ד׳.   123 — 124 שמות י״ט, י״א.

---

100 שנאמר וגם בך יאמינו לעולם] הגהתי=מ״ח.   ז״י : א. שנאמר ט. א״א. וגם בך יאמינו לעולם מ. ד. >.   101 — 102 אא״כ עשינו] מ״ח. ונעשה.   102 שחזר מ״ח. שחזר / בו ובדברו מ״ח. בדברו.   104 לראש] במקרא שלפנינו אל ראש.   108 לאמר] ד. >.   109 מתוך] מ״ח. זו מצות הגבלה.   112 — 109 ר׳ יוסי — לאמר למקום] א. > / מתוך שנאמר—למקום אלא] ט. >.   113 ויבא משה ויספר לעם] מ. ויבא משה אל העם.   114 — 113 את כל דברי — כל המשפטים] מ. ד. >.   114 המשפטים הגהתי=ש : א. המעשה.   116 פורענות] ד. עליכם פורענות / עליהן] ד. >.   120 פרגוד] החכם י. ה. ש. בהחלוץ י״ב (1887 צד 80) הגיה פרגוד והוא לשון יוני ?????????? ה. פרג ש״ט. סרסור.   123 — 121 בעבור ישמע — שומע לרואה] א. >.   123 אמר המקום תן להם מה שבקשו] א. ד. >.

Chapter III
(Ex. 19.10–17)

And the Lord Said unto Moses: 'Go unto the People, and Sanctify Them To-day.' This was the fourth day of the week.

And Tomorrow. This was the fifth day of the week.

And Be Ready against the Third Day. This was the sixth day of the week on which day the Torah was given.

And what did Moses do on the fifth day? He got up early in the morning and built an altar at the foot of the mountain, as it is said: "And rose up early in the morning, and builded an altar under the mount" (Ex. 24.4). He put up twelve pillars corresponding to the twelve tribes of Israel—these are the words of R. Judah, but the other sages say twelve pillars for each tribe. Having built the altar he offered up on it a burnt-offering and a peace-offering. Of the blood of the burnt-offering he took one portion for God and one portion for the congregation—in two separate cups. And of the blood of the peace-offering he also took—in two cups—one portion for God and one portion for the people, as it is said: "And Moses took half of the blood," etc. (ibid. 24.6), that is, the portion of God. "And half of the blood he dashed against the altar" (ibid.), that is, the people's portion.[1] "And he took the book of the covenant and read in the hearing of the people" (ibid., v. 7). But we have not heard whence he read to them.[2] R. Jose the son of R. Judah says: From the beginning of Genesis up to here. Rabbi says: He read to them the laws commanded to Adam, the commandments given to the Israelites in Egypt and at Marah, and all other commandments which they had already been given.—R. Ishmael says: What does it say in the beginning of the section (Lev. 25.1 ff.)? "Then shall the land keep a sabbath unto the

1. The portion of God was sprinkled upon the people (v. 8) and the portion of the people was offered to God by being dashed against the altar (v. 6).

2. See Introduction and cf. Commentaries.

פרשה ג (שמות י״ט, י׳—י״ז.)

ויאמר יי אל משה לך אל העם
וקדשתם היום זה יום רביעי ומחר זה יום חמישי
והיו נכונים ליום השלישי זה יום ששי שבו נתנה תורה
ומה עשה משה בחמישי השכים בבקר ובנה מזבח

5 תחת ההר שנאמר וישכם בבקר ויבן מזבח תחת
ההר העמיד שתים עשר מצבות לשנים עשר שבטי
ישראל דברי רבי יהודה וחכמים אומרים שתים
עשרה מצבה לכל שבט ושבט בנה מזבח והקריב
עליו עולה ושלמים נטל מדם העולה בשני כוסות

10 חלק למקום וחלק לציבור ומדם השלמים בשני
כוסות חלק למקום וחלק לציבור שנאמר ויקח
משה חצי הדם וגו׳ זה חלק למקום וחצי הדם זרק
על המזבח זה חלק לציבור ויקח ספר הברית
ויקרא באזני העם אבל לא שמענו מהיכן קרא

15 באזניהם רבי יוסי ב״ר יהודה אומר מתחלת בראשית
ועד כאן רבי אומר מצוות שנצטווה אדם הראשון
ומצוות שנצטוו בני נח ומצוות שנצטוו במצרים
ובמרה ושאר כל המצוות כלן רבי ישמעאל אומר
בתחלת הענין מה הוא אומר ושבתה הארץ שבת

3—1 שבת פ״ו, ב׳.   9—1 ש׳. 96.   6—5 שמות כ״ד, ד׳.   14—8 וי״ר ו׳, ה׳.
27—8 מ״ת. 57—56.   12—11 שמות שם ו׳.   14—13 שם ז׳.   20—19 ויקרא כ״ה,
ב׳—ג׳.

8 לכל] א. ד. על כל.   10 חלק] מ. וחלק / וחלק] מ. וחצי.   15 ר׳ יוסי ב״ר יהודה]=ג.
מ״ח. ל״ט: מ. ר׳ יוסי ב״ר יוסי ד. ר׳ יוסי ברבי אסי ט. ר׳ ישמעאל בר׳ יוסי.

Lord. Six years shalt thou sow thy field," etc. (Lev. 25.2–3). He read to them the laws about the sabbatical years and the jubilees (ch. 25), the blessings and the curses (ch. 26). What does it say at the closing of the section? "These are the statutes and ordinances and laws," etc. (Lev. 26.46)—they said: We accept all these. When he saw that they accepted them, he took the blood and sprinkled it upon the people, as it is said: "And Moses took the blood, and sprinkled it on the people," etc. (Ex. 24.8). He said to them: Now you are bound, held and tied; tomorrow, come and receive all the commandments. R. Jose the son of R. Judah says: All these acts were performed on one and the same day.

And Let Them Wash Their Garments. And how do we know that they also required immersion? Behold, I reason thus: If even in cases where washing of garments is not required immersion is required, does it not follow that in this case where washing of the garments was required immersion was required? There is no case in the Torah where washing of the garments is prescribed without at the same time there being also a requirement of immersion.

And Be Ready against the Third Day. That was the sixth day of the week on which the Torah was given.

For the Third Day the Lord Will Come Down, etc. This is one of the ten descents[3] mentioned in the Torah.

In the Sight of All the People. This tells that there were no blind ones among them. Another Interpretation: *In the Sight of All the People.* This teaches that at that moment the people saw what Isaiah and Ezekiel never saw. For it is said: "And by the ministry of the prophets have I used similitudes"[4] (Hos. 12.11).

Another Interpretation: *In the Sight of All the People.* This teaches that if even only one of them had been missing they would not have

3. Cf. M. Friedmann, *Pseudo-Seder Elijahu Zuta*, Vienna, 1904, p. 50 ff.
4. I. e., the prophets did not see clear visions, while the people at Sinai did (cf. above *Shirata*, III).

20 ליי שש שנים תזרע שדך וגו' שמטים ויובלות ברכות
וקללות בסוף הענין מה הוא אומר אלה החוקים
והמשפטים והתורות וגו' אמרו מקבלין אנו עלינו
כיון שראה שקבלו עליהם נטל את הדם וזרק על
העם שנאמר ויקח משה את הדם ויזרוק על העם
25 וגו' אמר להם הרי אתם קשורין תפוסין וענובין
מחר בואו וקבלו עליכם את כל המצוות רבי יוסי
ברבי יהודה אומר בו ביום נעשו כל המעשים.

וכבסו שמלותם ומנין שיטענו טבילה הרי
אני דן ומה אם במקום שאין טעונין כבוס בגדים
30 טעונין טבילה וכאן שהן טעונין כבוס בגדים אינו
דין שיטענו טבילה אין כבוס בגדים בתורה שאינו
טעון טבילה.

והיו נכונים ליום השלישי זה יום ששי
שבו נתנה תורה.

35 **כי ביום השלישי ירד יי** וגו' זה אחד
מעשר ירידות שבתורה.

לעיני כל העם מגיד שלא היה בהם סומים.
דבר אחר לעיני כל העם מלמד שראו באותה שעה
מה שלא ראה ישעיה ויחזקאל שנאמר וביד הנביאים
40 אדמה. דבר אחר לעיני כל העם מלמד שאם היו

21 — 22 שם כ"ו, מ"ו.   24 שמות כ"ד, ח'.   28 — 32 יבמות מ"ו, ב'.   35 — 36 ש. 97.   36 ספרי
במדבר צ"ג. אדר"נ ל"ד. ב"ר ל"ח. ט'.   פדר"א י"ד ומ"א.   37 לקמן ט'.   38 — 40 לעיל
שירתא ג'.   39 — 40 הושע י"ב, י"ג.

25 קשורין תפוסין וענובין] ק. תפוסין.   31 בתורה] מ. מן התורה רמב"ן במה.   34 תורה]
ד. ט. ~ שנאמר.   36 שבתורה] ד. שכתובות בתורה.

been worthy of receiving the Torah. R. Jose says: Even if there had been only two and twenty thousand of them they would have been considered worthy of receiving the Torah. For it is said: "And when it rested, he said: 'Return, O Lord, unto the ten thousands[5] of the families of Israel' " (Num. 10.36).

And Thou Shalt Set Bounds unto the People. I might understand this to mean only on the east side, but it says: "Round about."

Saying. This teaches that they forewarned one another.[6]

Take Heed to Yourselves. Under the penalty of a prohibition.[7]

That Ye Go Not Up into the Mount. One might think that it was forbidden to go up but permitted to touch it. Therefore, it says: "Or touch the border of it." One might still think that while it was forbidden to go up or to touch it, one might be brought up in a litter, but it says: "That ye go not up into the mount or touch the border of it."[8]

Whosoever Toucheth the Mount Shall Be Surely Put to Death. This states the penalty.

No Hand Shall Touch It. Nor the sanctuary in Shiloh, nor the tent of meeting, nor the Temple in Jerusalem.[9]

But He Shall Surely Be Stoned. And how do we know that he was to be pushed down? It says: "To throw down (*Yaroh*)." And how do we know that if he died as a result of being thrown down the duty is done? It says: "Let him be thrown down (*yiyareh*)." And how do we know that it is the same with all those who are to be stoned. It says: "For he shall surely be stoned or thrown down."

Whether It Be Beast. I know only about domestic animals. How about wild animals? It says: "Whether it be beast."

5. The two words רבבות אלפי are taken as two separate numbers: רבבות as a plural form meaning at least two ten thousands, and אלפי as a plural form meaning at least two thousand, thus making a total of at least twenty-two thousand.

6. The word לאמור, "to say," is interpreted as meaning, to say it to one another by way of warning.

7. The expression השמר has the force of a prohibition לא תעשה (cf. ʿEr. 96a).

8. See Commentaries.

9. See *Shebut Yehudah* ad loc.

חסרים עד אחד אינן כדאי לקבל רבי יוסי אומר
אפילו יש שם שני אלפים ושני רבבות הם כדי לקבל
שנאמר ובנחה יאמר שובה יי רבבות אלפי ישראל.

והגבלת את העם שומע אני למזרחו ת"ל
45   סביב.

לאמר מלמד שהתרו זה בזה. **השמרו לכם**
בלא תעשה.

עלות בהר יכול לא יעלה אבל יגע ת"ל
ונגוע בקצהו יכול לא יעלה ולא יגע אבל יכנס
50   בלקטקא ת"ל עלות בהר ונגוע בקצהו.

כל הנוגע בהר מות יומת הרי זה עונש.

לא תגע בו יד ולא בשילה ולא באהל מועד
ולא בבית עולמים.

כי סקול יסקל ומנין שידחה ת"ל ירה ומנין
55   שאם מת בדחייה יצא ת"ל יירה ומנין לכל הנסקלין
כן ת"ל כי סקול יסקל או ירה יירה.

אם בהמה אין לי אלא בהם חיה מנין ת"ל

---

43 — 41 ספרי במדבר פ"ד. ב"ק פ"ג, א'. יבמות ס"ד, א'.   43 במדבר י', ל"ו.   106 — 44 ש.
97 — 99.   47 — 46 ספרי דברים קי"ז ורע"ד.   58 — 57 ב"ק נ"ד, ב'.

---

41 עד אחד] ג. מ"ח. אפילו אחד / אינן כדאי]=ל. ט: מ. נ. אינו כדאי ק. אינו יכול
מ"ח. אינו נראין.   46 מלמד] א. מ. < / שהתרו] א. מ. מ"ח. שהותרו.   49 יכנס]
ק. נ. יכניס.   50 בלקטקא] מ. בלקטנא בספר זכרון לר' אברהם בקראט (ליוורנו תר"ה)
בלקטתא מ"ח. בקטלקא ג. בקלמארקא ט. א"א. בגלונקא ש. בגלוגתא]ק ד. <.   51 כל
הנוגע בהר מות יומת] מ. ד. <.   55 בדחייה] מ. בדחיקה / ת"ל יירה] ד. וכו' הגירסא
בסנהדרין בפרק נגמר הדין תנו רבנן מנין שבדחייה ת"ל ירה מנין שבסקילה ת"ל סקול
ומנין שבסקילה ודחייה ת"ל או סקול יסקל או ירה יירה וגו'.   56 כן] א. מ. נתלין.
57 אם בהמה] מ. מ"ח. בהמה / אם בהמה—ת"ל] א. <.   58 — 57 ת"ל אם בהמה]
ד. ת"ל בהמה.

Or Man. I know only about men. How about women? It says: "Or man."

It Shall Not Live. R. Akiba says: Here it is said: "It shall not live," and there it is said: "Thou shalt not suffer a sorceress to live" (Ex. 22.17): just as here death by stoning is meant, so there also death by stoning is meant.

When the Ram's Horn Soundeth Long. After the ram's horn had given forth a prolonged sound everyone was permitted to go up to the mountain. R. Jose says: "That it is not the place which honors the man but the man who honors the place," was said by the sages in this connection. As long as the *Shekinah* was on the mount, "whosoever toucheth the mount shall be surely put to death." After the *Shekinah* removed itself, all people were permitted to go up to the mount.

And Moses Went Down from the Mount unto the People. This teaches that Moses did not turn to his business nor go down to his house, but went directly "from the mount unto the people." One might think it was so only in the case of this message. How do we know that it was so in the case of all the messages? It says: "And the Lord came down upon mount Sinai," etc. (v. 20), "so Moses went down unto the people and told them." Now this had already been said before (v. 14). What need then was there of saying again: "So Moses went down unto the people" (v. 25)? To teach us that Moses did not turn to his business nor go down to his house, but went directly "from the mount unto the people." Thus far I know it only of the commandments received at mount Sinai. How about the commandments received in the tent of meeting? It says: "And he came out, and spoke unto the children of Israel that which he was commanded" (Ex. 34.34). And how do we know that he made all his ascents in the morning? It says: "And be ready by the morning and come up in the morning . . . and no man shall come up with thee . . . and he hewed two tables of stone like unto the first; and Moses rose up early in the morning, and went up unto mount Sinai, as the Lord had com-

אם בהמה. אם איש אין לי אלא איש אשה מנין
ת״ל אם איש.

לא יחיה רבי עקיבא אומר נאמר כאן לא
יחיה ונאמר להלן מכשפה לא תחיה מה כאן
בסקילה אף להלן בסקילה.

במשוך היובל כשימשוך היובל את קולו
הכל רשאין לעלות בהר רבי יוסי אומר לא מקומו
של אדם מכבדו אלא הוא מכבד את מקומו מכאן
אמרו כל זמן שהשכינה בהר כל הנוגע בהר מות
יומת נסתלקה שכינה הכל רשאין לעלות בהר.

וירד משה מן ההר אל העם מלמד
שלא היה משה פונה לעסקיו ולא היה יורד לתוך
ביתו אלא מן ההר אל העם יכול לדיבור זה בלבד
ושאר כל הדברות מנין ת״ל וירד יי על הר סיני
וגו׳ וירד משה אל העם ויאמר אליהם כבר זה
אמור ומה ת״ל וירד משה אל העם מלמד שלא היה
משה פונה לעסקיו ולא יורד לתוך ביתו אלא מן
ההר אל העם אין לי אלא דברות הר סיני דברות
אהל מועד מנין ת״ל ויצא ודבר אל בני ישראל
את אשר יצוה ומנין לכל העליות שהיה עולה בבקר
היה עולה שנאמר והיה נכון לבקר ועלית בבקר
וגו׳ ואיש לא יעלה עמך וגו׳ ויפסול שני לוחות
אבנים כראשונים וישכם משה בבקר ויעל אל הר

61 שמות כ״ב, י״ז. 63 — 67 תענית כ״א, ב׳. 71 שמות י״ט, כ׳ — כ״ה. 76 — 75 לעיל
פסחא א׳. 76 — 77 שמות ל״ד, ל״ה. 81 — 78 שם ל״ד, ב׳, ד׳ — ד׳.

58 אם איש אין לי אלא איש] ד. איש מנין ת״ל אם איש. 63 כשימשוך]=ט. רש״י
ל: א. כימשוך ק. במאי שימשוך נ. בשימשוך / קולו] ק. ~ מלהשמע. 64 הכל] ד.
אתם ג. הם. 67 — 64 ר׳ יוסי אומר—רשאין לעלות בהר] א. <. 66 — 65 מכאן אמרו]
א״צ. מ״ח. <. 66 מות] א. ד. <. 67 נסתלקה שכינה] מ. נסתלק כבוד השכינה.
72 — 68 מלמד שלא—אל העם] א. ט. <. 71 וירד יי על הר סיני] א״צ. וירד משה
ויאמר אליהם ז״י. וירד משה וידבר אליהם ש״י. וירד משה אל העם. 72 וגו׳
וירד משה אל העם ויאמר אליהם] הוספתי=מ״ה. 73 — 72 כבר זה אמור] מ״ה. שאין
ת״ל. 75 — 72 כבר זה אמור—אלא מן ההר אל העם] א״צ. ז״י. <. 73 וירד משה
אל העם] הגהתי=ש״י: מ. ד. וירד משה מן ההר אל העם. 76 אל בני ישראל] ד.
אל משה. 77 את אשר יצוה] ד. <. 78 שנאמר] ד. ת״ל. 79 וגו׳] הוספתי.
81 — 80 אבנים כראשונים—הר סיני כאשר צוה יי אותו] הוספתי: א. ט. וגו׳ ד. אבנים.

manded him" (Ex. 34.2–4). There would be no need of saying: "As the Lord had commanded him," except to declare that it was the rule that every time he went up he went up in the morning.

And Sanctified the People. He summoned them and they washed their garments and purified themselves.

And He Said unto the People: 'Be Ready,' etc. But we have not heard that God expressly told Moses that they should keep away from women! But "be ready" (v. 15) and "and be ready" (v. 11) are the basis of an analogy, *Gezerah Shavah:* Just as the expression "be ready" used there (v. 15) means to refrain from coming near a woman, so also the expression "and be ready" used here (v. 11) means to refrain from coming near a woman. Rabbi says: It can be proved from its own context. God said to him: "Go unto the people and sanctify them today and tomorrow" (v. 10). For, if it meant only the requirement of immersion, it would have been enough for them to bathe on the fifth day and then be clean at about the time of the setting of the sun.[10] Why then does it say: "Go unto the people," etc.? Merely to indicate that God told Moses that they should keep away from women.

Come Not Near a Woman. Hence, the sages said: "That a woman discharging the virile semen on the third day does not thereby become unclean, can be proven from the precautions taken at Sinai." This is according to the opinion of R. Eleazar b. Azariah. R. Ishmael,

10. Sexual intercourse was regarded as defiling a person. After having sexual intercourse, one was therefore required to take a ritual bath in order to become clean again (Lev. 15.16–18). If the "sanctifying" commanded by God meant merely that they should purify themselves by immersion, i. e., by taking a ritual bath, then the words: "today and tomorrow," would not quite fit in. For the people could have had intercourse up to the fifth day and taken their ritual bath on the fifth day, i. e., on the day preceding the day of the giving of the Law and, with sunset, become clean and fit to receive the Torah the next morning. Evidently, then, "sanctify them today and tomorrow," must have meant that they should keep themselves away from any cause of defilement, i. e., not to have sexual intercourse.

סיני כאשר צוה יי אותו שאין ת״ל כאשר צוה יי

אותו אלא זה בנין אב כל זמן שהיה עולה בבקר

היה עולה.

ויקדש את העם זימנן וכבסו בגדיהם

והטהרו. 85

ויאמר אל העם היו נכונים וגו' אבל

לא שמענו שאמר המקום למשה לפרוש מן האשה

אלא היו נכונים והיו נכונים לגזירה שוה מה היו

נכונים האמור כאן לפרוש מן האשה אף והיו

נכונים האמור להלן לפרוש מן האשה רבי אומר 90

ממקומו הוא מוכרע לך אל העם וקדשתם היום

ומחר אם לענין טבילה יטבול בחמישי ויהי טהור

כמו הערב שמש ומה ת״ל לך אל העם וגו' אלא

שאמר המקום למשה לפרוש מן האשה.

אל תגשו אל אשה מכאן אמרו הפולטת 95

שכבת זרע ביום השלישי שהיא טהורה ראיה לדבר

מסיני דברי רבי אלעזר בן עזריה רבי ישמעאל

94 — 86 פדר״א מ״א.   99 — 86 שבת פ״ו, א'. י' שם ט', ג' (12a).

___

82 זה] ד. < .   עולה] ד. משה.   84 וכבסו] א. ויכבסו מ״ח. ויכבסו שמלותם.

85 — 84 בגדיהם והטהרו] ק. ט. ~ והחליפו שמלותיכם מ״ח. א״צ. <.   87 למשה] ד.

< / לפרוש] מ״ח. להפרישם.   89 כאן] מ״ח. להלן.   90 להלן] מ״ח. כאן. / רבי

אומר] ט. דבר אחר.   91 מוכרע] ד. מכריע.   92 לענין] ד. על ענין / ויהי] ק. והכי /

טהור] מ״ח. ט. מ״ח.   93 כמו הערב] מ. כמו ערב מ״ח. מוערב / ומה] ד.

<. 94 לפרוש] מ״ח. להפרישם.   97 ישמעאל] ד. אליעזר.

however, says: Sometimes this period[11] begins after four *onahs*,[12] some times after five, and sometimes after six. R. Akiba says: It always begins after five *onahs*.

And It Came to Pass on the Third Day, When It Was Morning. This teaches that God had come there before Moses. Thus is confirmed what has been said: "While the king sat at his table, my spikenard sent forth its fragrance"[13] (Cant. 1.12).

That There Were Thunders. Thunders upon thunders, all sorts of thunder.

And Lightnings. Lightnings upon lightnings, all sorts of lightning.

And a Thick Cloud upon the Mount. That is, the thick darkness, as it is said: "But Moses drew near unto the thick darkness" (Ex. 20.18).

And the Voice of a Horn Exceeding Loud. Ordinarily the more the sound of a voice is prolonged the weaker it becomes. But here the longer the voice lasted the stronger it became. And why was it softer at first? That the ear might get it in accordance with its capacity of hearing.

And All the People that Were in the Camp Trembled. This teaches that they were frightened.

And Moses Brought Forth the People Out of the Camp to Meet God. Said R. Jose: Judah used to expound: "The Lord came from Sinai" (Deut. 33.2). Do not read it thus, but read: "The Lord came to Sinai," to give the Torah to Israel. I, however, do not interpret it thus, but: "The Lord came from Sinai," to receive Israel as a bridegroom comes forth to meet the bride.

And They Stood. They were huddled together. This teaches that they were afraid of the winds, of the earthquakes, of the thunders and lightnings that came on.

---

11. I. e., the period during which the discharge does not make her unclean.

12. *'Onah* designates half of an astronomical day, either daytime or nighttime (cf. Jastrow, *Dictionary*, s. v. p. 1054).

13. See *Shebut Yehudah* ad loc.

אומר פעמים שהם ארבע עונות פעמים שהן חמש
פעמים שהן שש רבי עקיבא אומר לעולם חמש.

ויהי ביום השלישי בהיות הבקר 100
מלמד שהקדים המקום על ידיו לקיים מה שנאמר
עד שהמלך במסבו נרדי נתן ריחו.

ויהי קולות קולי קולות ומיני קולות משונים
זה מזה.

וברקים ברקי ברקים ומיני ברקים משונים 105
זה מזה.

וענן כבד על ההר זה ערפל שנאמר ומשה
נגש אל הערפל.

וקול שופר חזק מאד מנהג הדיוט כל
שהוא הולך קולו עמה אבל כאן כל שהוא הולך 110
קולו מגביר ולמה רך מבתחילה לשבר את האוזן
מה שהיא יכולה לשמוע.

ויחרד כל העם אשר במחנה מלמד
שנזדעזעו.

ויוצא משה את העם לקראת האלהים 115
אמר רבי יוסי יהודה היה דורש יי מסיני בא אל
תקרא כן אלא יי לסיני בא ליתן תורה לישראל ואני
איני אומר כן אלא יי מסיני בא לקבל את ישראל
כחתן זה שהוא יוצא לקראת כלה.

ויתיצבו ניצפפו מלמד שהיו מתיראין מפני 120
הזיקין ומפני הזוועות מפני הרעמים ומפני הברקים
הבאים.

---

101 — 102 שהש"ר א', י"ב.   102 שהש"ש א', י"ב.   108 — 107 לעיל ב'.   112 — 109 לקמן
ד'.   115 — 136 ש.   100 — 99.   116 דברים ל"ג, ב'.   119 פדר"א מ"א.

---

98 פעמים] ד. אף פעמים.   101 שהקדים] ד. שהסכים א"צ. שהשכים.   103 קולי
קולות] א. מ. ט. קול קולות מ"ח. / ומיני] ט. מ"ח. מיני ק. ומניין.   105 ברקי]
א. ט. ברק / ומיני] מ"ח. ט. א"א. ז"י. מיני.   110 — 109 כל שהוא] ד. כל זמן
שהוא.   110 עמה] ד. נמוך מ"ח. עמום.   111 רך] ד. ט. כך ג. לא היה כך / לשבר]
ד. לשכר.   116 א"ר יוסי יהודה] ט. א"ר יוסי ר' יוסי מ"ח. א"ר ר' אסי ש. ר' יוסי בר
יודן.   117 אל תקרא כן אלא] מ"ח. >.   118 — 117 ואני איני אומר כן] הגהתי=א"צ:
מ. ד. או אינו אומר (מ. אומר >) כן מ"ח. לא נאמר א. ט. >.   118 אלא יי מסיני
בא לקבל את ישראל] א. >.   120 ניצפפו] ד. נכפפו.   123 — 120 מלמד שהיו
מתיראין—בתחתית ההר] ד. >.

Below the Mount. Scripture indicates that the mount was pulled up from its place and the people came near and stood under it, as it is said: "And ye came near and stood under the mountain" (Deut. 4.11). Of them it is declared in the traditional sacred writings: "Oh my dove that art in the clefts of the rock," etc. (Cant. 2.14). "Let me see thy countenance," that is, the twelve pillars erected for the twelve tribes of Israel; "let me hear thy voice" (ibid.), that is, when responding to the Ten Commandments; "for sweet is thy voice" (ibid.), after having received the Ten Commandments; "and thy countenance is comely" (ibid.), when: "All the congregation drew near and stood before the Lord" (Lev. 9.5). R. Eliezer says: This may be interpreted as referring to the occasion at the Red Sea: "Let me see thy countenance," when told: "Stand still and see the salvation of the Lord" (Ex. 14.13); "let me hear thy voice," when: "They were sore afraid and the children of Israel cried out unto the Lord" (ibid., v. 10). "For sweet is thy voice," refers to: "And they cried and their cry came up" (Ex. 2.23); "and thy countenance is comely," refers to: "And did the signs in the sight of the people, and the people believed" (ibid. 4.30–31). Another Interpretation: "For sweet is thy voice," when saying at the Red Sea: "I will sing unto the Lord, for He is highly exalted" (ibid. 15.1); "and thy sight is comely," when: "Out of the mouth of babes and sucklings hast Thou founded strength"[14] (Ps. 8.3).

CHAPTER IV
(Ex. 19.18–20.1)

Now Mount Sinai Was Altogether on Smoke. One might think only that part of it where the Glory rested, but it says: "All of it."

14. See above *Shirata*, II and Midrash to Ps. 8.5; and cf. *Shebut Yehudah* ad loc.

בתחתית ההר מלמד שנתלש ההר ממקומו
וקרבו ועמדו תחתיו שנאמר ותקרבון ותעמדון
125 תחת ההר עליהם מפורש בקבלה יונתי בחגוי הסלע
וגו' הראיני את מראיך אלו שתים עשרה מצבה
לשנים עשר שבטי ישראל השמיעיני את קולך אלו
עשרת הדברות כי קולך ערך לאחר עשרת
הדברות ומראך נאוה ויקרבו כל העדה ויעמדו
130 לפני יי רבי אליעזר אומר על ים סוף הדבר
אמור הראיני את מראיך התיצבו וראו את ישועת
יי השמיעיני את קולך וייראו מאד ויצעקו בני ישראל
אל יי כי קולך ערב ויזעקו ותעל שועתם ומראך
נאוה ויעש האותות לעיני העם ויאמן העם. דבר
135 אחר כי קולך ערב על הים אשירה ליי כי גאה
גאה ומראך נאוה מפי עוללים ויונקים יסדת עוז.

פרשה ד   (שמות י"ט, י"ח—כ', א'.)

והר סיני עשן כלו יכול מקום הכבוד
ת"ל כולו.

125—124 דברים ד', י"א. שבת פ"ח, א'. שהש"ר ח', ב'.   126—125 שהש"ש ב', י"ד.
136—125 שהש"ר ב', י"ד.   130—129 ויקרא ט', ה'.   132—131 שמות י"ד, י"ג.
133—132 שם י"ד, י'.   133 שם ב', כ"ג.   134 שם ד', ל'—ל"א.   135 שם ט"ו, א'.
136 תהלים ח', ג'.
16—1 ת. יתרו י"ב, י"ג.

---

124 תחתיו] ד. תחת הר.   126 וגו'] מ. > ק. נ. ל. בסתר המדרגה / הראיני את
מראיך[=ט. מ"ח: א. ק. ~ < נ. ל. ~ השמיעיני את קולך כי קולך ערב ומראך נאוה.
128 לאחר] א. אלו לאחר / עשרת] ד. >.   130 אליעזר] א. מ. אלעזר.   133 ויזעקו]
ד. >.   136 מפי] א. אילו מפי.

1 יכול מקום הכבוד] מ"ח. ~ בלבד ט. יכול במקום אחד.   2 כולו] א. מ. ~ מפני
מה ק. >.

Because the Lord Descended Upon It in Fire. This tells that the Torah is fire, was given from the midst of fire, and is comparable to fire. What is the nature of fire? If one comes too near to it, one gets burnt. If one keeps too far from it, one is cold. The only thing for man to do is to seek to warm himself against its flame.[1]

And the Smoke Thereof Ascended as the Smoke of a Furnace. One might think that it was like an ordinary smoke. Therefore it says: "Of a furnace." But if: "Of a furnace," one might still think it was just like that of a furnace. It says, however: "And the mountain burned with fire unto the heart of heaven" (Deut. 4.11). Why then does it say: "Of a furnace"? That the ear might get it in accordance with its capacity of hearing. Similarly: "The lion hath roared, who will not fear," etc. (Amos 3.8). And who gave strength and force to the lion? Was it not He? But it is merely that we describe Him by figures known to us from His creations so that the ear may get it, etc. Similarly: "And, behold, the glory of the God of Israel came from the way of the east; and His voice was like the sound of many waters" (Ezek. 43.2). And who gave strength and force to the waters? Was it not He? But it is merely that we describe Him by figures known to us from His creations, so that the ear may get it, etc.

And the Whole Mount Quaked. And was not Sinai in one class with all other mountains? For it is said: "The mountains quaked at the presence of the Lord, even yon Sinai" (Judg. 5.5). And it also says: "Why look ye askance, ye mountains of peaks" (Ps. 68.17), meaning: He said to them: All of you are but crook-backed (*Gibnim*), as when it says: "Or crook-backed (*Giben*) or a dwarf"[2] (Lev. 21.20).—And why did the *Shekinah* rest in the portion of Benjamin? Because the heads of all the other tribes[3] were partners in the selling of Joseph, but Ben-

---

1. Cf. *Sifre*, Deut. 343 and Ḥag. 13a and 14b.
2. See Introduction.
3. Here it is assumed that Reuben participated in the selling of Joseph, though from Gen. 37.29 one would conclude that Reuben was not present when Joseph was sold by his brethren (cf. also Gen. Rab. 84.18).

מפני **אשר** **ירד** **עליו** **יי** **באש** מגיד
שהתורה אש ומאש נתנה ובאש נמשלה מה דרכה
של אש אם קרב אדם אצלה נכוה רחק ממנה צנן
אין לו לאדם אלא להתחמם כנגד אורה.

ויעל **עשנו** **כעשן** **הכבשן** יכול כעשן
זה בלבד ת״ל כבשן אי כבשן יכול ככבשן זה בלבד
ת״ל וההר בוער באש עד לב השמים ומה ת״ל כבשן
לשבר את האוזן מה שהיא יכולה לשמוע. כיוצא
בו אריה שאג מי לא יירא וגו׳ וכי מי נתן כח וגבורה
בארי לא הוא אלא הרי אנו מכנין אותו מבריותיו
לשבר את האוזן וגו׳ כיוצא בו והנה כבוד אלהי
ישראל בא מדרך הקדים וקולו כקול מים רבים
וכי מי נתן כח וגבורה במים לא הוא אלא הרי אנו
מכנין אותו מבריותיו לשבר את האוזן וכו׳.

ויחרד **כל** **ההר** והלא בכלל כל ההרים
היה שנאמר הרים נזלו מפני יי זה סיני ואומר למה
תרצדון הרים גבנונים אמר להם כלכם גבנים אתם
כמה דאת אמר או גבן או דק ומפני מה שרתה
שכינה בחלקו של בנימין שכל השבטים היו שותפים

---

115 — 7 ש. 100 — 105.   9 דברים ד׳, י״א.   11 עמוס ג׳, ח׳.   14 — 13 יחזקאל מ״ג, ב׳.
20 — 17 מגלה כ״ט, א׳. סוטה ה׳, א׳.   25 — 17 ב״ר צ״ט, א׳.   18 שופטים ה׳, ה׳.
19 — 18 תהלים ס״ח, י״ז.   20 ויקרא כ״א, כ׳.

7 יכול] ד. < כעשן] ק. <.   10 לשבר] ד. לשכך.   11 וגו׳ וכי] ד. <.   12 מבריותיו]
ד. <.   13 לשבר] ד. לשכך.   15 וכי] ד. <.   16 לשבר] ד. לשכך.   17 ויחרד] ק. ג.
כיוצא בו ויחרד.   19 גבנים]=ט״כ. א״א: מ. ד. גבנונים.   20 ומפני] א. מ. מפני.
21 שותפים] ד. <.   23 — 21 היו שותפים—וכל השבטים] ק. <.

jamin was not a partner with them. And furthermore, the heads of all the other tribes were born outside of the land, and only Benjamin was born in the land of Israel.—But even though this be so, it (Sinai) was: "The mountain which God hath desired for His abode" (Ps. 68.17).

And There Was the Voice of the Horn. Behold, this was a good omen. In the sacred writings wherever the horn is mentioned it augurs well for Israel, as when it says: "God is gone up amidst shouting, the Lord amidst the sound of the horn" (Ps. 47.6). And it also says: "And it shall come to pass in that day, that a great horn shall be blown" (Isa. 27.13). And it also says: "And the Lord God will blow the horn, and will go with whirlwinds of the south" (Zech. 9.14).

Waxing Louder and Louder. Ordinarily the more the sound of a voice is prolonged the weaker it becomes. But here the longer the voice lasted the stronger it became. And why was it softer at first? That the ear might get it in accordance with its capacity of hearing.

Moses Spoke and God Answered Him by a Voice. R. Eliezer says: How can you prove that God spoke only after Moses had told Him: Speak, for Thy children have already accepted? It is in this sense that it is said: "Moses spoke." Said to him R. Akiba: It surely was so. Why then does it say: "Moses spoke and God answered him by a voice"? It merely teaches that Moses was endowed with strength and force, and that God was helping him with His voice so that Moses could let Israel hear the same tone which he himself heard. In this sense it is said: "Moses spoke and God answered him by a voice."

And the Lord Came Down upon Mount Sinai. I might understand this to mean upon the entire mountain, but it says: "To the top of the mount." One might think that the Glory actually descended from heaven and was transferred to mount Sinai, but Scripture says: "That I have talked with you from heaven" (Ex. 20.19). Scripture thus teaches that the Holy One, blessed be He, bent down the lower heavens and the upper heavens of heaven, lowering them to the top of the mountain, and thus the Glory descended. He spread them upon

במכירתו של יוסף ובנימין לא היה שותף עמהם
וכל השבטים נולדו בחוץ לארץ ובנימין נולד
בארץ ישראל ואף על פי כן ההר חמד אלהים
לשבתו וגו׳.

25

ויהי קול השופר הרי זה סימן יפה
בכתובים כל מקום שנאמר שופר זה סימן יפה
לישראל שנאמר עלה אלהים בתרועה יי בקול
שופר ואומר והיה ביום ההוא יתקע בשופר גדול
ואומר ויי אלהים בשופר יתקע והלך בסערות
תימן.

30

הולך וחזק מאד מנהג הדיוט כל שהוא
הולך קולו עמה אבל כאן כל שהוא הולך קולו
מגביר ולמה רך מתחלה לשבר את האוזן מה שהיא
יכולה לשמוע.

35

משה ידבר והאלהים יעננו בקול
רבי אליעזר אומר מנין אתה אומר שאין המקום
מדבר עד שמשה אמר לו דבר שכבר קבלו עליהם
בניך לכך נאמר משה ידבר אמר לו רבי עקיבא
בודאי כן הוא הדבר ומה ת״ל משה ידבר והאלהים
יעננו בקול אלא מלמד שניתן כח וגבורה במשה
והיה הקב״ה מסייעו בקולו ובנעימה שהיה משה
שומע בו היה משמיע את ישראל לכך נאמר משה
ידבר והאלהים יעננו בקול.

40

וירד יי על הר סיני שומע אני על כלו
ת״ל אל ראש ההר יכול ממש שירד הכבוד והוצען
על הר סיני ת״ל כי מן השמים דברתי עמכם מלמד
שהרכין הקב״ה שמים התחתונים ושמי שמים
העליונים על ראש ההר וירד הכבוד והוצען על

45

25—20 ספרי דברים שנ״ב.   28 תהלים מ״ז, ו׳.   29 ישעיה כ״ז, י״ג.   31—30 זכריה
ט׳, י״ד.   35—32 לעיל ג׳. ת. שם.   39—44 לעיל פסחא א׳; ספרי במדבר קט״ז. ערכין
י״א, א׳. ברכות מ״ה, א׳.   45—53 פדר״א מ״א.   47 שמות כ׳, כ״ב.

22 שותף] ד. <.   25 לשבתו] מ. לשבטו.   27—26 סימן יפה—שנאמר שופר] מ. <.
32 כל שהוא] ד. כל זמן שהוא.   33 קולו עמה] ד. מחליש ומעכה ג. מחליש ומנמיך
א״צ. מחליש וממיך.   34 רך] מ. ד. כך ג. לא היה כך.   39 משה ידבר] א. מ. מ״ח.
~ והאלהים יעננו בקול.   40 כן] ד. כי.   41—40 והאלהים יעננו בקול] הוספתי: ש״י.
מ״ע. וגו׳.   41 שניתן] ד. שנתן הקב״ה.   46 אל ראש] ק. נ. על ראש / והוצען ד.
והציעו מ״ח. והוצע.   47—46 ת״ל אל ראש ההר—על הר סיני] א. <.   49 והציען]
מ. ט״כ. והוצען מ״ח. והוצע.

mount Sinai as a man who spreads the mattress upon the bed and speaks from the mattress. For it is said: "As when fire kindleth the brushwood, and the fire causeth the waters to boil," etc. (Isa. 64.1). Likewise it says: "When Thou didst tremendous things" (ibid., v. 2). R. Jose says: Behold, it says: "The heavens are the heavens of the Lord, but the earth hath He given to the children of men" (Ps. 115.16). Neither Moses nor Elijah ever went up to heaven, nor did the Glory ever come down to earth. Scripture merely teaches that God said to Moses: Behold, I am going to call you through[4] the top of the mount and you will come up, as it is said: "And the Lord called Moses to the top of the mount" (v. 20).

And the Lord Said unto Moses: 'Go Down, Charge the People.' Give them warning.

Lest They Break Through unto the Lord. Lest they force themselves through to gaze. *And Many of Them Perish.* This teaches that permission was given the agents to destroy.[5] Another Interpretation: If only one of them should fall it would be to Me as though all of them fell. This teaches that even one individual can impair the whole group. Another Interpretation: Every one of them that might be taken away is to Me as valuable as the whole work of creation, as it is said: "For the Lord's is the eye of man and all the tribes of Israel"[6] (Zech. 9.1).

And Let the Priests Also, that Come Near to the Lord, Sanctify Themselves. One would think that the priests are in the same class as the people, but Scripture has already said: "Go unto the people and sanctify them"[7] (v. 10). Hence, the priests are not in the same class as the people. Just as when it is said: "And he shall make atonement for the

4. I. e., you will hear the call as if it came from the top of the mountain.

5. Cf. above *Pisha*, XI.

6. To God one Israelite is as valuable as all the tribes of Israel. The work of creation was for the sake of Israel (Lev. Rab. 36.4). One Israelite, being equal to all the tribes of Israel, is, therefore, also as valuable as the whole work of creation.

7. If the priests were in the same class as the people, Scripture would not need to specify here that the priests also should sanctify themselves.

50 גבי הר סיני כאדם שהוא מציע את הכר על גבי
המטה וכאדם שהוא מדבר מעל גבי הכר שנאמר
כקדוח אש המסים מים תבעה אש וכו' וכן הוא אומר
בעשותך נוראות וגו' רבי יוסי אומר הרי הוא אומר
השמים שמים ליי והארץ נתן לבני אדם לא עלה
55 משה ואליהו למעלה ולא ירד הכבוד למטה אלא
מלמד שאמר לו המקום למשה הריני קורא לך
מראש ההר ואתה עולה שנאמר ויקרא יי למשה
וגו'.

ויאמר יי אל משה רד העד בעם הסהד
60 בהם. פן יהרגו אל יי שמא ידחקו לראות ונפל
ממנו רב מלמד שנתנה רשות לשלוחים לחבל דבר
אחר יחידי שיפול מהם הרי הוא עלי ככלם מלמד
שאף אחד ממעט על ידי כולן. דבר אחר יחידי
שיוטל מהם הרי הוא עלי כנגד כל מעשה בראשית
65 שנאמר כי ליי עין אדם וכל שבטי ישראל.

וגם הכהנים הנגשים אל יי יתקדשו
יכול הכהנים בכלל העם ת"ל לך אל העם וקדשתם
אין הכהנים בכלל העם שנאמר ועל הכהנים ועל

51—52 ב"ר ד', ב'.   52—53 ישעיה ס"ד, א'—ב'.   53—58 סוכה ה', א'.   54 תהלים
קט"ו, ט"ז.   65 זכריה ט', א'.   67 שמות י"ט, י'.   69—68 ויקרא ט"ז, ל"ג.

---

53 הרי הוא אומר] ד'. <.   55 משה ואליהו] א. ד. אליהו מ"ח. משה.   60—59 הסהד
בהם] ד. <.   60 פן יהרסו אל יי] ד. <.   61—60 שמא ידחקו—ממנו רב] א. <.
61 לשלוחים] מ"ח. למחבלין.   62—61 דבר אחר] הגהתי=א"א. ט. ט"ב: א"צ.
מ"ח. רב.   62 יחידי] ט. אפילו רב אחד ט"כ. אפילו אחד / עלי] ק. <.   63 ממעט]
ט. מ"ח. א"א. מעכב / דבר אחר] ד. <.   65 עין אדם] א. עין האדם ק. אדם.
67 יכול] א"צ. מלמד שאין.   67—68 ת"ל לך אל העם—בכלל העם] א. ד. <.
68 שנאמר] ז"י. ש"י. ת"ל א"צ. וכן הייתי אומר.   69—68 שנאמר ועל הכהנים—אין
הכהנים בכלל העם] א. <.

priests and for all the people of the assembly" (Lev. 16.33), the priests are not in the same class as the people. And also when it says: "And this shall be the priests' due from the people" (Deut. 18.3), the priests are not in the same class as the people.—And who were these priests? R. Joshua the son of Karḥa says: They were Nadab and Abihu. For it does not say here just "the priests," but "the priests that come near to the Lord."[8] And when it says: "And. . . also," it includes the elders with them.

And Moses Said unto the Lord, etc. I have already warned them and I have fixed the boundary lines for them.

And the Lord Said unto Him: 'Go, Get Thee Down.' You have spoken well. In connection with this it was that R. Judah said: Whence can you prove that the Holy One, blessed be He, said to Moses: Behold, I will be saying something to you and you shall answer Me, and I will then agree with you, so that the Israelites should say: Great is Moses, for even God agreed with him? From the passage: "And may also believe thee for ever." Rabbi says: We need not make Moses great if it is to be done only by making God change His mind and go back on His word. But one should warn a man when giving him instructions and again warn him when he is about to execute the instructions.

And Thou Shalt Come Up, Thou, and Aaron with Thee, and the Priests and the People. One might think then that all were to come up. But it says: "And the people shall not break through to come up." Then one might interpret it to mean: The priests shall also come up with thee. But it says: "And thou shalt come up, thou." Now you must interpret it to mean: Just as you are to be in a separate division by yourself, so also are they, the priests, to be in a separate division by themselves. The people, however, are not at all to "break through to come up unto the Lord, lest He break forth upon them"—lest they have to sound the alarm.[9]

8. Cf. the comment of R. Jose the Galilean on Lev. 16.1 in *Sifra, Aḥare,* I, Weiss, 79c.

כל עם הקהל יכפר אין הכהנים בכלל העם ואומר

70 וזה יהיה משפט הכהנים מאת העם אין הכהנים
בכלל העם ואיזה הם הכהנים רבי יהושע בן קרחה
אומר זה נדב ואביהוא אינו אומר הכהנים אלא
הכהנים הנגשים אל יי וכשהוא אומר וגם אף הזקנים
עמהם.

75 **ויאמר משה אל יי** וגו' כבר העידותי בהם
וקבעתי להם תחומין.

ויאמר אליו יי לך רד יפה אמרת זהו
שהיה רבי יהודה אומר מנין אתה אומר שאמר
המקום למשה הריני אומר לך דבר ואתה מחזירני

80 ואני מודה לך שידעו ישראל אומרים גדול משה
שהודה לו המקום רבי אומר אין אנו צריכין לעשות
למשה גדול אלא אם כן עשינו להקב"ה שחזר בו
ובדברו אבל מזרזין את האדם בשעת תלמוד
ומזרזין אותו בשעת מעשה.

85 **ועלית אתה ואהרן עמך והכהנים**
והעם יכול הכל יעלו ת"ל והעם אל יהרסו
לעלות יכול אף הכהנים יעלו עמך ת"ל ועלית
אתה אמור מעתה מה אתה מחיצה לעצמך אף
הן מחיצה לעצמן והעם כל עיקר אל יהרסו לעלות

90 אל יי פן יפרץ בם שמא יתריעו.

---

70 דברים י"ח, ג'.   74—70 זבחים קט"ו, ב'.

69 הקהל] מ. הקב"ה.   71—69 ואומר וזה יהיה—בכלל העם]=ט. מ"ח: א. ד. <.
70 משפט] מ. מעשה.   71 ואיזה הם] הגהתי=ט. ג. א"א: א. מ. ד. ואילו הן.
73—72 אלא הכהנים הנגשים אל יי] ק. הכהנים א. והכהנים הנגשים אל יי.   73 וכשהוא
אומר] נ. ל. < ק. כשהוא אומר / וגם] ק. ואף / אף] ד. <.   81 רבי אומר] א. דבר
אחר.   88 מה] ד. < / אתה] ד. ~ עושה.   89—88 אף הן מחיצה לעצמן] הגהתי=ט.
א"א. ש"י: ג. אף הכהנים מחיצה לעצמן.   89 לעלות] ד. לראות.   90 אל יי פן
יפרץ בם] ד. <.

So Moses Went Down unto the People, and Told Them. He told them immediately and without delay. Another Interpretation: *And Told Them.* He said to them: Be ready to accept the reign of heaven joyfully. Another Interpretation: *And Told Them.* He said to them: Respond "yes" to a positive commandment and "no" to a negative commandment.

And God Spoke. God (*Elohim*) designates the judge[10] who is just in exacting punishment and faithful in giving reward. Since there are many sections in the Law for the carrying out of which a man receives reward but for the neglect of which he does not receive punishment, I might think that the Ten Commandments are also such. Therefore, it says: "And God (*Elohim*) spoke." *Elohim* designates the judge who is just in exacting punishment and faithful in giving reward.

All These Words. Scripture hereby teaches that God spoke the Ten Commandments with one utterance—something impossible for creatures of flesh and blood—for it says: "And God spoke all these words, saying,"[11] If so, why then is it said: "I am the Lord thy God, thou shalt have no other gods before Me"?[12] It simply teaches that the Holy One, blessed be He, after having said all the Ten Commandments at one utterance, repeated them, saying each commandment

9. The passage may possibly mean: "Lest they be shattered" (cf. Commentaries and Jastrow, *Dictionary,* p. 1700).

10. Cf. above *Pisḥa* I, note 2.

11. I. e., in one saying, with one utterance.

12. I. e., why are the first two commandments spoken in the first person, while in the remaining commandments God is referred to in the third person? This change in person would suggest that God spoke the Ten Commandments in ten utterances, one after the other. The first two the people heard directly from God (cf. Mak. 24a). Then they got frightened "and they said unto Moses: 'Speak thou with us, and we will hear; but let not God speak with us, lest we die' " (Ex. 20.16). Moses then repeated to them the other eight commandments and the people did not hear them directly from God. And Moses, in repeating these commandments, referred to God in the third person (see Introduction and cf. Commentaries, esp. *Shebut Yehudah*).

וירד משה אל העם ויאמר אליהם אמר להם
מיד ולא עיכב. דבר אחר ויאמר אליהם אמר להם
היו עתידין לקבל מלכות שמים בשמחה. דבר
אחר ויאמר אליהם אמר להם היו אומרין על הן
95   הן ועל לאו לאו.

וידבר אלהים אין אלהים אלא דיין דיין
להפרע ונאמן לשלם שכר לפי שיש פרשיות בתורה
שאם עשאן אדם מקבל שכר ואם לאו אין מקבל
עליהן פורענות שומע אני אף עשרת הדברות כן
100   ת״ל וידבר אלהים אין אלהים אלא דיין דיין
להפרע ונאמן לשלם שכר.

את כל הדברים האלה מלמד שאמר
המקום עשרת הדברות בדיבור אחד מה שאי
איפשר לבשר ודם לומר כן שנאמר וידבר אלהים
105   את כל הדברים האלה לאמר אם כן מה ת״ל אנכי
יי אלהיך לא יהיה לך אלא שאמר הקב״ה
עשרת הדברות בדיבור אחד וחזר ופרטן דיבור

92—93 לקמן ו׳.   102—108 לעיל שירתא ח׳. לקמן ז׳. שבועות כ׳, ב׳. ספרי דברים
רל״ג. ת. שם י״א.

91 ויאמר אליהם] ד. ~ וידבר אלהים ויאמר אליהם.   92—93 דבר אחר—בשמחה] ד.
>.   92 דבר אחר ויאמר אליהם] מ. >.   93 מלכות שמים] מ. מלכות אלהים מ״ח.
מלכות.   96 דיין דיין] א. דיין להם ד. דיין.   97 לשלם] ד. לקבל.   97—101 לפי
שיש—לשלם שכר] ד. >.   98 אין] מ. >.   99 אף] א. אך.   103—102 הדברים האלה
מלמד שאמר המקום עשרת הדברות] ד. >.   106 אלא] ד. >.   107 ופרטן] ד. ופירשן.

separately. I might understand then that the other commandments of the Torah were likewise spoken all with one utterance. But it says: "All these words." These words only were spoken in one utterance, but all the rest of the commandments of the Torah were spoken separately, each one by itself.

Saying. This teaches that they answered 'yes' to a positive commandment and 'no' to a negative commandment—these are the words of R. Ishmael. R. Akiba says: They answered 'yes' to a positive commandment and also 'yes'[13] to a negative commandment. Another Interpretation: *Saying.* Go and tell them and bring back to Me their words. And how do we know that Moses did report back the words of the people before the Almighty? It is said: "And Moses reported the words of the people unto the Lord" (Ex. 19.8). And what were the words of the people? "All that the Lord hath spoken will we do and obey" (Ex. 24.7). And how do we know that God approved of their words? It is said: "And the Lord said unto me . . . they have well said all that they have spoken" (Deut. 5.25).

CHAPTER V
(Ex. 20.2)

I Am the Lord Thy God. Why were the Ten Commandments not said at the beginning of the Torah? They give a parable. To what may this be compared? To the following: A king who entered a province said to the people: May I be your king? But the people said to him: Have you done anything good for us that you should rule over us? What did he do then? He built the city wall for them, he brought in the water supply for them, and he fought their battles. Then when he said to them: May I be your king? They said to him: Yes, yes. Likewise, God. He brought the Israelites out of Egypt, divided the sea for

13. Their answer was: "Yes, we agree not to do it."

דיבור בפני עצמו שומע אני אף שאר כל הדברות
שבתורה נאמרו כולם בדיבור אחד ת"ל את כל
הדברים האלה הדברים האלה נאמרו בדיבור אחד
ושאר כל הדברות שבתורה נאמרו דיבור דיבור
בפני עצמו.

לאמר מלמד שהיו אומרים על הן הן ועל לאו
לאו דברי רבי ישמעאל רבי עקיבא אומר על הן
הן ועל לאו הן. דבר אחר לאמר צא ואמור להם
והשיבני את דבריהם ומנין שהיה משה משיב דברים
לפני הגבורה שנאמר וישב משה את דברי העם
אל יי ומה היו דברי העם כל אשר דבר יי נעשה
ונשמע ומנין שהמקום הודה לדבריהם שנאמר ויאמר
יי אלי וגו' היטיבו כל אשר דברו.

פרשה ה   (שמות כ', ב'.)

אנכי יי אלהיך מפני מה לא נאמרו עשרת
הדברות מתחלת התורה משלו משל למה הדבר
דומה למלך שנכנס למדינה אמר להם אמלוך
עליכם אמרו לו כלום עשית לנו טובה שתמלוך
עלינו מה עשה בנה להם את החומה הכניס להם
את המים ועשה להם מלחמות אמר להם אמלוך
עליכם אמרו לו הן והן כך המקום הוציא את
ישראל ממצרים קרע להם את הים הוריד להם

120—115 לעיל פסחא א'.   119—118 שמות כ"ד, ז'.   120—119 דברים ה', כ"ח.

111—109 נאמרו כולם—שבתורה נאמרו] א' <.   110 הדברים האלה נאמרו] ד. נאמרו.
113 מלמד] ד. <.   116 את דבריהם] א. מ. <.   120 וגו'] הוספתי=מא"ש / כל אשר]
א. ק. נ. את אשר ט. מ"ח. אשר.
4 טובה] הוספתי=ט. ש"י.

them, sent down the manna for them, brought up the well for them, brought the quails for them. He fought for them the battle with Amalek. Then He said to them: I am to be your king. And they said to Him: Yes, yes. Rabbi says: This proclaims the excellence of Israel. For when they all stood before mount Sinai to receive the Torah they all made up their mind alike[1] to accept the reign of God joyfully. Furthermore, they pledged themselves for one another. And it was not only concerning overt acts that God, revealing Himself to them, wished to make His covenant with them but also concerning secret acts, as it is said: "The secret things belong to the Lord our God[2] and the things that are revealed," etc. (Deut. 29.28). But they said to Him: Concerning overt acts we are ready to make a covenant with Thee, but we will not make a covenant with Thee in regard to secret acts lest one of us commit a sin secretly and the entire community be held responsible for it.

I Am the Lord Thy God. Why is this said? For this reason. At the sea He appeared to them as a mighty hero doing battle, as it is said: "The Lord is a man of war" (Ex. 15.3). At Sinai He appeared to them as an old man full of mercy. It is said: "And they saw the God of Israel," etc. (Ex. 24.10). And of the time after they had been redeemed what does it say? "And the like of the very heaven for clearness."[3] (ibid.) Again it says: "I beheld till thrones were placed" (Dan. 7.9). And it also says: "A fiery stream issued and came forth from before him," etc. (ibid., v. 10). Scripture, therefore, would not let the nations of the world have an excuse for saying that there are two Powers, but declares: "I am the Lord thy God." I am He who was in Egypt and I am He who was at the sea. I am He who was at Sinai. I am He who was in the past and I am He who will be in the future. I am He who is in this world

---

1. The use of the singular form אלהיך instead of אלהיכם suggests that they were all of one mind.

2. This is interpreted to refer to what God had wished to include in the covenant.

3. See above, *Shirata,* IV, note 1 and Introduction.

את המן העלה להם את הבאר הגיז להם את השליו
עשה להם מלחמת עמלק אמר להם אמלוך עליכם
אמרו לו הן והן רבי אומר להודיע שבחן של ישראל
שכשעמדו כולן לפני הר סיני לקבל את התורה
השוו כלם לב אחד לקבל מלכות אלהים בשמחה
ולא עוד אלא שהיו ממשכנין זה על זה ולא על
הנגלות בלבד נגלה הקב״ה עליהם לכרות עמהם
ברית אלא אף על הסתרים שנאמר הנסתרות ליי
אלהינו והנגלות וגו׳ אמרו לו על הגלויים אנו כורתין
עמך ברית ואין אנו כורתין עמך ברית על הסתרים
שלא יהא אחד ממנו חוטא בסתר ויהא הצבור
מתמשכן. אנכי יי אלהיך למה נאמר לפי שנגלה
על הים כגבור עושה מלחמות שנאמר יי איש
מלחמה ונגלה על הר סיני כזקן מלא רחמים שנאמר
ויראו את אלהי ישראל וגו׳ וכשנגאלו מה הוא אומר
וכעצם השמים לטהר ואומר חזה הוית עד די
כרסוון רמיו ואומר נהר די נור ונפק מן קדמוהי
וגו׳ שלא ליתן פתחון פה לאומות העולם לומר
שתי רשויות הן אלא אנכי יי אלהיך אני במצרים
אני על הים אני בסיני לשעבר אני לעתיד לבא

20 — 11 ת. יתרו י״ג.   20 — 14 סנהדרין מ״ג, ב׳.   17 — 16 דברים כ״ט, כ״ח.
33 — 20 לעיל שירתא ד׳.   22 — 21 שמות ט״ו, ג׳.   23 שם כ״ד, י׳.   25 — 24 דניאל ז׳,
ט׳ - י׳.

12 לפני[ן ד. על.   13 — 12 לקבל—לב אחד] א. >.   13 אלהים] ד. שמים.   14 ממשכנין]
ט. משתעשעין ת. מ״ח. ~ עצמן / על זה] א. מ. על ידי זה.   15 — 14 ולא על הנגלות
בלבד נגלה] א. ולא של כך אלא שנגלה מ. ולא עוד אלא שנגלה מ״ח. ולא על כך
אלא שנגלה ט. כשנגלה.   16 אלא] מ״ח. א. מ. ט. > / אף] א. מ. ט. >.   17 והנגלות
וגו׳] מ. ט. מ״ח. >.   19 ממנו מ. מ״ח. >.   20 מתמשכן] א. נתפס מ. נתמשכן
ט. מסתכן בו מ״ח. מ״ח. א״צ. מא״ש. ~ שנאמר הנסתרות ליי אלהינו והנגלות לנו ולבנינו
/ אנכי] מ. דבר אחר אנכי.   21 על הים] מ. עליהן.   23 — 22 וגו׳ וכשנגאלו—ואומר]
מ״ח. וכעצם השמים לטהר וכשנגאלים מהו אומר.   26 — 25 ואומר נהר די נור — קדמוהי
וגו׳] מ״ח. >.   27 אני במצרים ד. ט״כ. > ט. אני הוא במרה.   28 אני בסיני] ד. אני
על היבשה.

and I am He who will be in the world to come, as it is said: "See now that I, even I, am He," etc. (Deut. 32.39). And it says: "Even to old age I am the same" (Isa. 46.4). And it says: "Thus saith the Lord, the King of Israel, and his Redeemer the Lord of Hosts: I am the first, and I am the last" (ibid. 44.6). And it says: "Who hath wrought and done it? He that called the generations from the beginning. I, the Lord, who am the first," etc. (ibid. 41.4). Rabbi Nathan says: From this one can cite a refutation of the heretics who say: There are two Powers. For when the Holy One, blessed be He, stood up and exclaimed: "I am the Lord thy God," was there any one who stood up to protest against Him? If you should say that it was done in secret—but has it not been said: "I have not spoken in secret," etc. (Isa. 45.19)? "I said not unto the seed of Jacob" (ibid.), that is, to these only will I give it. "They sought me in the desert" (ibid.). Did I not give it in broad daylight? And thus it says: "I the Lord speak righteousness, I declare things that are right" (ibid.).

Another Interpretation: *I Am the Lord Thy God.* When the Holy One, blessed be He, stood up and said: "I am the Lord thy God," the mountains trembled and the hills wavered, Tabor was coming from Beth Elim and Carmel from Aspamea,[4] as it is said: "As I live, saith the king whose name is the Lord of hosts, surely as Tabor among the mountains and Carmel by the sea would come"[5] (Jer. 46.18). This one was saying: I have been called. And that one was saying: I have been called. But when they heard from His mouth: "Who brought thee out of the land of Egypt," each one of them remained standing in its place, and they said: "He is dealing only with those whom He brought out from Egypt."

Another Interpretation: *I Am the Lord Thy God.* When the Holy One, blessed be He, stood up and said: "I am the Lord thy God," the

4. On *Aspamea* and *Bet Elim* cf. I. S. Horowitz, *Palestine,* Vienna, 1923, p. 67, note 1 and p. 124.

5. This rendering of the passage in Jeremiah is required by the *Mekilta.*

אני בעולם הזה אני לעולם הבא שנאמר ראו עתה

30 כי אני אני הוא ואומר עד זקנה אני הוא ואומר כה
אמר יי מלך ישראל וגאלו יי צבאות אני ראשון
ואני אחרון ואומר מי פעל ועשה קורא הדורות
מראש אני יי אני ראשון וגו' רבי נתן אומר מכאן
תשובה למינין שהיו אומרים שתי רשויות הן

35 שכשעמד הקב"ה ואמר אנכי יי אלהיך מי עמד
ומיחה כנגדו אם תאמר במטמניות היה הדבר והלא
כבר נאמר לא בסתר דברתי וגו' לא אמרתי לזרע
יעקב לאלו אני נותנה אלא תהו בקשוני לא נתתיה
פנגס וכן הוא אומר יי דובר צדק מגיד מישרים.

40 דבר אחר אנכי יי אלהיך כשעמד הקב"ה ואמר
אנכי יי אלהיך היו ההרים מתרעשים והגבעות
מתמוטטות ובא תבור מבית אילים וכרמל
מאספמיא שנאמר חי אני נאם המלך יי צבאות שמו
כי כתבור בהרים וככרמל בים יבא זה אומר אני

45 נקראתי וזה אומר אני נקראתי וכיון ששמעו מפיו
אשר הוצאתיך מארץ מצרים עמד כל אחד ואחד
במקומו ואמרו לא עסק אלא עם מי שהוציא
ממצרים. דבר אחר אנכי יי אלהיך כשעמד הקב"ה

29—30 דברים ל"ב, ל"ט.   30 ישעיה מ"ו, ד'.   31—30 שם מ"ד, ו'.   33—32 שם
מ"א, ד'.   39—37 לעיל א'.   40—48 ב"ר צ"ט, א'.   מגלה כ"ט, א'.   43—44 ירמיה
מ"ו, י"ח.   63—48 לעיל עמלק ג'.   זבחים קט"ז, א'.   83—48 ספרי דברים שמ"ג.

30 ואומר] ד. / ואומר] ד. <.   33—32 ואני אחרון—אני ראשון וגו'] א. וגו' ואומר
אני אחרון ואת אחרונים אני הוא מ. ואני אחרון אני הוא אני יי ראשון אני יי ואת אחרונים
אני הוא.   34 שהיו אומרים] ד. שאומרים.   35 שכשעמד הקב"ה ואמר] א. <.   37 וגו']
מ. <.   38—37 לא אמרתי לזרע יעקב] מ. ד. <.   38 לאלו] מ. לא לו מ"ח. לא
לאלו / אלא] מ"ח. ולא ד. ~ לא אמרתי להם / לא] מ. ד. ולא.   39 פנגס] מ. פאנס
מ"ח. פנייס (פניים?).   40 הקב"ה] מ. ~ על הר סיני.   42 מבית אילים] מ. מ"ח.
מבית אלים ג. מבאר אלים ד. מבית אלהים.

earth trembled, as it is said: "Lord, when Thou didst go forth out of
Seir, when Thou didst march out of the field of Edom, the earth
trembled"[6] (Judg. 5.4). And it goes on to say: "The mountains
quaked at the presence of the Lord," (ibid., v. 5). And it also says:
"The voice of the Lord is powerful; the voice of the Lord is full of
majesty," etc. (Ps. 29.4) up to: "And in his palace every one says:
'Glory!' "[7] (ibid., v. 9). And their houses even were filled with the
splendor of the *Shekinah*. At that time all the kings of the nations of
the world assembled and came to Balaam the son of Beor. They said
to him: Perhaps God is about to destroy His world by a flood. He said
to them: Fools that ye are! Long ago God swore to Noah that He
would not bring a flood upon the world, as it is said: "For this is as
the waters of Noah unto Me; for as I have sworn that the waters of
Noah should no more go over the earth" (Isa. 54.9). They then said
to him: Perhaps He will not bring a flood of water, but He may bring
a flood of fire. But he said to them: He is not going to bring a flood of
water or a flood of fire. It is simply that the Holy One, blessed be He,
is going to give the Torah to His people. For it is said: "The Lord will
give strength unto His people," etc. (Ps. 29.11). As soon as they
heard this from him, they all turned back and went each to his place.

And it was for the following reason that the nations of the world
were asked to accept the Torah: In order that they should have no
excuse for saying: Had we been asked we would have accepted it.
For, behold, they were asked and they refused to accept it, for it is
said: "And he said: 'The Lord came from Sinai,' " etc. (Deut. 33.2). He
appeared to the children of Esau the wicked and said to them: Will
you accept the Torah? They said to Him: What is written in it? He
said to them: "Thou shalt not murder" (ibid. 5.17). They then said to
Him: The very heritage which our father left us was: "And by thy

6. This verse is interpreted as referring to the giving of the Law on Sinai (see
below, chap. IX; and cf. ʿAb. Zarah 2b).

7. See above, *Amalek*, III, note 1.

ואמר אנכי יי אלהיך היתה הארץ חלה שנאמר

50 יי בצאתך משעיר בצעדך משדה אדום ארץ רעשה

ואומר הרים נזלו מפני יי ואומר קול יי בכח קול

יי בהדר עד ובהיכלו כולו אומר כבוד עד

שנתמלאו בתיהם מזיו השכינה באותה שעה נתכנסו

כל מלכי אומות העולם ובאו אצל בלעם בן בעור

55 אמרו לו שמא המקום מחריב עולמו במבול אמר

להם שוטים שבעולם כבר נשבע המקום לנח שאינו

מביא מבול לעולם שנאמר כי מי נח זאת לי

אשר נשבעתי מעבר מי נח עוד על הארץ אמרו

לו מבול של מים אינו מביא אבל מביא הוא מבול

60 של אש אמר להם אינו מביא לא מבול של מים ולא

מבול של אש אלא הקב״ה נותן תורה לעמו ישראל

שנאמר יי עוז לעמו יתן וגו׳ כיון ששמעו מפיו הדבר

הזה פנו כלם והלכו להם איש למקומו ולפיכך

נתבעו אומות העולם כדי שלא יהא להם פתחון

65 פה לומר אלו נתבענו כבר קיבלנו עלינו והרי

שנתבעו ולא קבלו עליהם שנאמר ויאמר יי מסיני

בא וגו׳ נגלה על בני עשו הרשע ואמר להם מקבלים

אתם עליכם את התורה אמרו לו מה כתיב בה

אמר להם לא תרצח אמרו לו זו היא ירושה שהוריש

50—51 שופטים ה׳, ד׳—ה׳.   51—52 תהלים כ״ט, ד׳—ט׳.   62 שם כ״ט, י״א.
63—67 ע״ז ב׳, ב׳.   66—67 דברים ל״ג, ב׳.   81—67 פדר״א מ״א.

51 נזלו] א. נזולו.   54 מלכי] א. מ. / בן בעור] א. > אמרו לו
שמא—עוז לעמו יתן וגו׳] מ. ד. וכו׳ ג. וכו׳ עד.   64 יהא] מ. ד. ליתן.   65 לומר]
ד. כלפי שכינה לומר.   78—67 ואמר להם—מארץ העברים] מ. וכו׳.

sword shalt thou live" (Gen. 27.40). He then appeared to the children of Amon and Moab. He said to them: Will you accept the Torah? They said to Him: What is written in it? He said to them: "Thou shalt not commit adultery" (Deut. 5.17). They, however, said to Him that they were all of them children of adulterers,[8] as it is said: "Thus were both the daughters of Lot with child by their father" (Gen. 19.36). Then He appeared to the children of Ishmael. He said to them: Will you accept the Torah? They said to Him: What is written in it? He said to them: "Thou shalt not steal" (Deut. 5.17). They then said to Him: The very blessing that had been pronounced upon our father was: "And he shall be as a wild ass of a man: his hand shall be upon everything" (Gen. 16.12). And it is written: "For, indeed, I was stolen away out of the land of the Hebrews"[9] (ibid. 40.15). But when He came to the Israelites and: "At His right hand was a fiery law unto them" (Deut. 33.2), they all opened their mouths and said: "All that the Lord hath spoken will we do and obey" (Ex. 24.7). And thus it says: "He stood and measured the earth; He beheld and drove asunder the nations"[10] (Hab. 3.6). R. Simon b. Eleazar says: If the sons of Noah could not endure the seven commandments enjoined upon them, how much less could they have endured all the commandments of the Torah! To give a parable. A king had appointed two administrators. One was appointed over the store of straw and the other was appointed over the treasure of silver and gold. The one appointed over the store of straw was held in suspicion. But he used

8. Amon and Moab were born of incest but not in adultery, since Lot's daughters were not married. Perhaps the *Mekilta* here has in mind the midrashic legend (cf. Gen. Rab. 50) that Lot's daughters were betrothed.

9. And the Ishmaelites were those who brought Joseph from Palestine to Egypt (Gen. 37.28).

10. I. e., after they refused to accept the Torah. Perhaps the rendering: "Abandoned the nations," i. e., gave up hope of their accepting the Torah, would more adequately express the sense in which the *Mekilta* understood the phrase ויתר גוים (cf. above ch. I, note 14).

לנו אבינו על חרבך תחיה נגלה על בני עמון ומואב 70

אמר להם מקבלים אתם את התורה אמרו לו מה

כתוב בה אמר להם לא תנאף אמרו לו כולם בני

מנאפין הן שנאמר ותהרין שתי בנות לוט מאביהן

נגלה על בני ישמעאל אמר להם מקבלין אתם

עליכם את התורה אמרו לו מה כתוב בה אמר להם 75

לא תגנוב אמרו לו זו היא ברכה שנאמרה לאבינו

והוא יהיה פרא אדם ידו בכל וכתיב כי גנב גנבתי

מארץ העברים וכשבא אצל ישראל מימינו אש דת

למו פתחו כולם פיהם ואמרו כל אשר דבר יי

נעשה ונשמע וכן הוא אומר עמד וימודד ארץ ראה 80

ויתר גוים רבי שמעון בן אלעזר אומר אם בשבע

מצוות שנצטוו עליהן בני נח לא יכלו לעמוד בהן

על אחת כמה וכמה בכל המצות שבתורה משל

למלך שמנה לו שני אפיטרופין אחד ממונה על

אוצר של תבן ואחד ממונה על אוצר של כסף ושל 85

זהב נחשד זה שהיה ממונה על אוצר של תבן והיה

---

70 בראשית כ"ז, מ'.   73 שם י"ט, ל"ו.   77 שם ט"ז, י"ב.   78—77 שם מ', ט"ו. ב"ר פ"ד, כ"ב. פ"י, ג'. פ"ח, ה'.   79—78 דברים ל"ג, ב'.   80—79 שמות כ"ד, ז'. 81—80 חבקוק ג', ו'.

---

70 אבינו] ד. ~ שנאמר.   72—73 כולם—שנאמר] ד. כלנו מנואף דכתיב.   73 מאביהן] ד. ~ והיאך נקבלה.   76 זו היא ברכה שנאמרה לאבינו] ד. בזו הברכה נתברך אבינו דכתיב ט. זו ברכה שנתן לנו אבינו שנאמר ט"כ. זו ברכה שנאמרה בהן מ"ח. זהו שנאמר בהם.   78—77 וכתיב כי גנב גנבתי מארץ העברים] ג. כ. (חבקוק ג', ו') >. 81 שמעון] א. ט. ישמעאל.   82 בני נח] ד. ~ שקבלו עליהן / לא יכלו] ד. אינו יכולין. 83 על אחת—שבתורה] ד. קל וחומר למצות שבתורה.   84 אפיטרופין] ד. אפטרופסין.

to complain about the fact that they had not appointed him over the treasure of silver and gold. The people then said to him: "*Reka!*"[11] If you were under suspicion in connection with the store of straw how could they trust you with the treasure of silver and gold! Behold, it is a matter of reasoning by the method of *kal vaḥomer*: If the sons of Noah could not endure the seven commandments enjoined upon them, how much less could they have endured all the commandments of the Torah!

Why was the Torah not given in the land of Israel? In order that the nations of the world should not have the excuse for saying: Because it was given in Israel's land, therefore we have not accepted it. Another Reason: To avoid causing dissension among the tribes. Else one might have said: In my territory the Torah was given. And the other might have said: In my territory the Torah was given. Therefore, the Torah was given in the desert, publicly and openly, in a place belonging to no one. To three things the Torah is likened: To the desert,[12] to fire, and to water. This is to tell you that just as these three things are free to all who come into the world, so also are the words of the Torah free to all who come into the world.

Who Brought Thee Out of the Land of Egypt, Out of the House of Bondage. They were slaves to kings. You interpret it to mean that they were servants of kings. Perhaps it is not so, but means that they were slaves of servants? When it says: "And redeemed you out of the house of bondage, from the hand of Pharaoh king of Egypt" (Deut. 7.8), it indicates that they were servants of kings and not servants of slaves. Another Interpretation: *Out of the House of Servants.* Out of the house of worshipers, for they worshiped idols.

---

11. See Jastrow, *Dictionary,* p. 1476; and cf. Matth. 5.22, *Raca.*
12. See Commentaries.

מתרעם על שלא מנו אותו על אוצר של כסף ושל
זהב אמרו לו ריקה אם על אוצר של תבן נחשדת
היאך יאמינו אותך על אוצר של כסף ושל זהב
90 והרי דברים קל וחומר ומה אם בשבע מצוות
שנצטוו בני נח לא יכלו לעמוד בהן על אחת כמה
וכמה בכל המצוות שבתורה. מפני מה לא ניתנה
תורה בארץ ישראל שלא ליתן פתחון פה לאומות
העולם לומר לפי שנתנה תורה בארצו לפיכך
95 לא קבלנו עלינו. דבר אחר שלא להטיל מחלוקת
בין השבטים שלא יהא זה אומר בארצי נתנה תורה
וזה אומר בארצי נתנה תורה לפיכך ניתנה במדבר
דימוס פרהסיא במקום הפקר. בשלשה דברים
נמשלה תורה במדבר ובאש ובמים לומר לך מה
100 אלו חנם לכל באי העולם אף דברי תורה חנם
לכל באי העולם.

אשר הוצאתיך מארץ מצרים מבית
עבדים עבדים למלכים היו אתה אומר עבדים
למלכים היו או אינו אלא עבדים לעבדים היו
105 כשהוא אומר ויפדך מבית עבדים מיד פרעה מלך
מצרים עבדים למלכים היו ולא עבדים לעבדים.
דבר אחר מבית עבדים מבית העובדים שהיו
עובדים לעבודה זרה.

101 — 98 במ״ר א׳, ז׳. ת. במדבר ו׳.   106 — 105 דברים ז׳, ח׳.

88 אמרו לו] ד. כ. ג. וזה שהיה ממונה על הכסף ועל הזהב (ג. כ. ~ לא נחשד] אמר
לו.   89 — 88 אם על אוצר—ושל זהב] ד. בתבן כפרת בכסף וזהב על אחת כמה וכמה.
92 — 90 ומה אם—המצות שבתורה] ד. ומה בני נח בשבע מצות בלבד לא יכלו לעמוד
בהם בשש מאות ושלש עשרה מצות מצות על אחת כמה וכמה.   95 עלינו] ד. <. 99 נמשלה]
ד. נתנה.   100 אף דברי תורה] ד. אף אלו.   105 — 105 מיד פרעה מלך מצרים ד. >
א. ~ הוי.   107 העובדים] ד. ~ עבודה זרה.   108 — 107 שהיו—זרה] ד. <.

CHAPTER VI
(Ex. 20.3–6)

Thou Shalt Not Have Other Gods Before Me. Why is this said?
Because it says: "I am the Lord thy God." To give a parable: A king of
flesh and blood entered a province. His attendants said to him: Issue
some decrees upon the people. He, however, told them: No! When
they will have accepted my reign I shall issue decrees upon them. For
if they do not accept my reign how will they carry out my decrees?
Likewise, God said to Israel: "I am the Lord thy God, thou shalt not
have other gods—I am He whose reign you have taken upon yourselves in Egypt." And when they said to Him: "Yes, yes," He continued: "Now, just as you accepted My reign, you must also accept My
decrees: 'Thou shalt not have other gods before Me.' " R. Simon b.
Joḥai says: What is said further on: "I am the Lord your God," (Lev.
18.2) means: "I am He whose reign you have taken upon yourselves
at Sinai," and when they said: "Yes, yes," He continued: "Well, you
have accepted My reign, now accept My decrees: 'After the doings of
the land of Egypt,' etc." (ibid. v. 3). What is said here: "I am the Lord
thy God who brought thee out from the land of Egypt," means: "I am
He whose reign you have taken upon yourselves," and when they
said to Him: "Yes, yes," He continued: "You have accepted My reign,
now accept My decrees: 'Thou shalt not have other gods.' "

Thou Shalt Not Have. Why is this said? Because when it says:
"Thou shalt not make unto thee a graven image," etc. (v. 4), I know
only that it is forbidden to make any. But how do I know that it is forbidden to keep one that has already been made? Scripture says:
"Thou shalt not have other gods," etc.

Other Gods. But are they gods? Has it not been said: "And have
cast their gods into the fire; for they were no gods" (Isa. 37.19)?
What then does Scripture mean when it says: "Other gods"? Merely
those which others called gods.[1] Another interpretation is: Gods that

פרשה ו (שמות כ׳, ג׳—ו׳.)

לא יהיה לך אלהים אחרים על פני
למה נאמר לפי שהוא אומר אנכי יי אלהיך משל
למלך בשר ודם שנכנס למדינה אמרו לו עבדיו
גזור עליהם גזירות אמר להם לאו כשיקבלו את
5 מלכותי אגזור עליהם גזירות שאם אינן מקבלים
מלכותי היאך מקיימין גזירותי כך אמר המקום
לישראל אנכי יי אלהיך לא יהיה לך אלהים אחרים
אני הוא שקבלתם מלכותי עליכם במצרים אמרו
לו הן והן וכשם שקבלתם מלכותי עליכם קבלו
10 גזירותי לא יהיה לך אלהים אחרים על פני רבי
שמעון בן יוחאי אומר הוא שנאמר להלן אני יי
אליהכם הוא שקבלתם מלכותי עליכם בסיני
אמרו לו הן והן קבלתם מלכותי קבלו גזירותי
כמעשה ארץ מצרים וג׳ הוא שנאמר כאן אנכי יי
15 אלהיך אשר הוצאתיך מארץ מצרים אני הוא
שקבלתם עליכם מלכותי אמרו לו הן והן קבלתם
מלכותי קבלו גזירותי לא יהיה לך אלהים אחרים.

לא יהיה לך למה נאמר לפי שהוא אומר
לא תעשה לך פסל וג׳ אין לי אלא שלא יעשה
20 העשוי כבר מנין שלא יקיים ת״ל לא יהיה לך
אלהים אחרים וג׳.

אלהים אחרים וכי אלוהות המה והלא
כבר נאמר ונתן את אלהיהם באש כי לא אלהים
המה ומה ת״ל אלהים אחרים אלא שאחרים קוראין
25 אותם אלוהות. דבר אחר אלהים אחרים שהם

21—10 ת״כ אחרי מות י״ג (85°). 12—11 ויקרא י״ח, ב׳. 14 שם י״ח, ג׳.
21—18 מ״ת 20. 30—22 מ״ת 38. 51—22 ספרי דברים מ״ג. 24—23 ישעיה ל״ז,
י״ט. 26—25 לעיל בשלח ב׳. 28—25 ש. 104.

<hr>

4 עליהם] מ. ט. ט״כ. עלינו / לאו] ד. <. 5 עליהם] מ. ק. עליכם.
6—5 שאם—גזירותי] ד. שאם מלכותי לא יקבלו גזירותי לא יקבלו.
12—8 במצרים—מלכותי עליכם] מ. <. 8 במצרים] א״צ. < / הן והן] ד. כן.
12 אני הוא] ד. <. 16 מלכותי] א. ~ במצרים מ. ~ בסיני / אמרו לו הן] ד. <.
17 מלכותי] ד. ~ באהבה / גזירותי] מ. ~ לכך נאמר. 18 לא יהיה לך] הגהתי=מא״ש:
ט. ד״א לא יהיה לך. 22—21 וג׳ אלהים אחרים] ד. <. 24 אלהים אחרים] א. מ.
אחרים. 26—25 דבר אחר—מלבוא לעולם] א. <.

are backward (*Aḥarim*). For they hold back the coming of goodness into the world. Another Interpretation: *Other Gods*. Who turn those who worship them into others. Another Interpretation: *Other Gods*. Who act like strangers towards those who worship them. And thus it says: "Yea, though one cry unto him, he cannot answer, nor save him out of his trouble" (Isa. 46.7). R. Jose says: *Other Gods*. Why is this said? In order not to give the nations of the world an excuse for saying: "If the idols had been called by His name, they would have been worth while." Behold, then, they have been called by His name and they are not worth while anyhow. And when were they called by His name? In the days of Enosh the son of Seth. It is said: "Then began men to call upon the name of the Lord" (Gen. 4.26). At that time the ocean rose and flooded a third of the world. God said to them: "You have done something new by calling yourselves 'gods.' I also will do something new and will call Myself 'the Lord.' " And thus it says: "That calleth for the waters of the sea, and poureth them out upon the face of the earth; the Lord is His name"[2] (Amos 5.8). R. Eliezer says: *Other Gods*—For every day they make for themselves new gods. How so? If one has an idol of gold and then needs the gold, he makes the idol of silver. If he has one of silver and then needs the silver, he makes the idol of copper. If he has an idol of copper and needs the copper, he makes it of iron. And so also with one of tin and so also with one of lead, as it is said: "New gods that came newly up" (Deut. 32.17). R. Isaac says: If the name of every idol were to be specifically mentioned, all skins (parchments) in the world would not suffice. R. Ḥananiah b. Antigonos says: Come and consider the expression chosen by the Torah: "To Molek," "to a ruler" (Lev. 18.21)—that is, anything at all which you declare as ruling over you, even if it be a chip of wood or a piece of potsherd. Rabbi says: *Other Gods*.—Gods that are later than he who was last in the order of creation. And who is it

1. I.e., the gods of others.
2. See Introduction and cf. Commentaries.

מאחרים את הטובה מלבוא לעולם. דבר אחר
אלהים אחרים שהם עושין את עובדיהם אחרים.
דבר אחר אלהים אחרים שהם אחרים לעובדיהם
וכן הוא אומר יצעק אליו ולא יענה וממצרתו לא

30 יושיענו רבי יוסי אומר אלהים אחרים למה נאמר
שלא ליתן פתחון פה לאומות העולם לומר אלו
נקראו בשמו כבר היה בהם צורך והרי נקראו בשמו
ואין בהם צורך אימתי נקראו בשמו בימי אנוש בן
שת שנאמר אז הוחל לקרוא בשם יי באותה שעה

35 עלה אוקיאנוס והציף שלישו של עולם אמר להם
המקום אתה עשיתם מעשה חדש וקראתם עצמכם
אלוהות אף אני אעשה מעשה חדש ואקרא עצמי
יי וכן הוא אומר הקורא למי הים וישפכם על פני
הארץ יי שמו רבי אליעזר אומר אלהים אחרים

40 שהם מחדשים להם אלוהות בכל יום הא כיצד
היה לו של זהב וצריך לו עשאו של כסף היה לו
של כסף וצריך לו עשאו של נחשת היה לו של
נחשת ונצרך לו עשאו של ברזל וכן של בדיל וכן
של עופרת שנאמר חדשים מקרוב באו רבי יצחק

45 אומר אלו נפרט להם כל שם עבודה זרה לא היה
מספיק להם כל העורות שבעולם רבי חנניה בן
אנטיגנוס אומר בוא וראה לשון שתפסה תורה
למולך כל שתמליכנו עליך אפילו קיסם אחד או
חרס רבי אומר אלהים אחרים שהם אחרונים למי

50 שהוא אחרון במעשים ומי הוא אחרון שבמעשים

29—30 ישעיה מ״ו, ז׳.   33—39 מ״ת 195.   11—10 ב״ר כ״ג, ת. נח, י״ח.   34 בראשית
ד׳, כ״ו.   38—39 עמוס ה׳, ח׳.   44—39 מ״ת 20.   44 דברים ל״ב, י״ז.   49—44 סנהדרין
ס״ד, א׳.   יי׳ שם ז, י״ג (25°).

27 עובדיהם אחרים] הגהתי=ט.   מ״ח. א״א. ז״י. א״צ: א. מ. ד. אלהידהם אחרונים.
28 אחרים לעובדיהם] א. מ. ק. אחרונים לעובדיהם.   29 יצעק] ד. והן יצעק מ. מ״ח.
הן יצעק / וממצרתו] במקרא כתוב מצרתו.   32 כבר] א. ›.   36 עשיתם] ד. עושים.
36—37 עצמכם אלוהות] הגהתי=ט. ג. מ״ח. א״א. ש״י: א. מ. ד. עצמכם מ״ח.
שם לעעצמכם ז״י עצמכם בשמו א״צ. לחמנים בשמו.   38—37 עצמי יי=ט. א״א.
ש״י: מ״ח. שם לעצמי ג. שם עצמי ז״י. עצמי בשמו א״צ. למי הים א. מ. ד. עצמי.
38 וכן הוא אומר] ד. שנאמר.   39 אליעור] א. ט״כ. אלעזר ט. ~ המודעי.   40 להם
אלוהות] מ״ח. אותם.   44—43 וכן של בדיל—שנאמר] ד. או מעופרת וכן הוא אומר.
45 נפרט] ד. נפרש.   46 העורות] ג. היריעות / חנניה] ד. חנינא.   49—48 או חרס] א.
מ. ‹. ג. ~ או צרור.   49—51 שהם אחרונים—אלוהות] מ״ח. מי שהוא אחרון במעשים
קורא אותם אלוהות.   49 אחרונים] א. אחרות.

that was the last of the things created? The one who calls them "gods."

Before Me. Why is this said? In order not to give Israel an excuse for saying: Only those who came out from Egypt were commanded not to worship idols. Therefore, it is said: "Before Me," as much as to say: Just as I am living and enduring for ever and for all eternity, so also you and your son and your son's son to the end of generations shall not worship idols.

Thou Shalt Not Make unto Thee a Graven Image. He shall not make one that is engraven. But perhaps he may make one that is solid? Scripture says: "Nor any manner of likeness." He shall not make a solid one. But perhaps he may plant a plant as an idol for himself? Scripture says: "Thou shalt not plant thee an Asherah" (Deut. 16.21). He shall not plant a plant for an idol to himself. But perhaps he may make an idol of a tree? Scripture says: "Of any kind of tree" (ibid.). He shall not make an idol of a tree. But perhaps he may make one of stone? Scripture says: "Neither shall ye place any figured stone," etc. (Lev. 26.1). He shall not make an idol of stone. But perhaps he may make one of silver or of gold? Scripture says: "Gods of silver or gods of gold ye shall not make unto you" (Ex. 20.20). He shall not make an idol of silver or of gold. But perhaps he may make one of copper, iron, tin, or lead? Scripture says: "Nor make to yourselves molten gods" (Lev. 19.4). He shall not make for himself any of these images. But perhaps he may make an image of any figure? Scripture says: "Lest ye deal corruptly, and make you a graven image, even the form of any figure" (Deut. 4.16). He shall not make an image of any figure. But perhaps he may make an image of cattle, or fowl? Scripture says: "The likeness of any beast that is on the earth, the likeness of any winged fowl" (ibid. v. 17). He shall not make an image of any of these. But perhaps he may make an image of fish, locust, unclean animals, or reptiles? Scripture says: "The likeness of any thing that creepeth on the ground, the likeness of any fish that is in the water" (ibid., v. 18). He shall not make an image of any of these. But perhaps

זה הקורא אותם אלוהות.

על פני למה נאמר שלא ליתן פתחון פה
לישראל לומר לא נצטווה על עבודה זרה אלא
מי שיצא ממצרים לכך נאמר על פני לומר מה
אני חי וקיים לעולם ולעולמי עולמים אף אתה
ובנך ובן בנך לא תעבוד עבודה זרה עד סוף כל
הדורות.

לא תעשה לך פסל לא יעשה לו גלופה
אבל יעשה לו אטומה ת"ל כל תמונה לא יעשה
לו אטומה אבל יטע לו מטע ת"ל לא תטע לך
אשרה לא יטע לו מטע אבל יעשה לו של עץ ת"ל
כל עץ לא יעשה לו של עץ אבל יעשה לו של אבן
ת"ל ואבן משכית וגו' לא יעשה לו של אבן אבל
יעשה לו של כסף ושל זהב ת"ל אלהי כסף ואלהי
זהב לא תעשו לכם לא יעשה לו של כסף ושל זהב
אבל יעשה לו של נחשת ושל ברזל ושל בדיל ושל
עופרת ת"ל ואלהי מסכה לא תעשו לכם לא יעשה
לו דמות כל אלה אבל יעשה לו דמות כל סמל
ת"ל פן תשחיתון ועשיתם לכם פסל תמונת כל סמל
לא יעשה לו דמות כל סמל אבל יעשה לו דמות
בהמה חיה ועוף ת"ל תבנית כל בהמה אשר בארץ
תבנית כל צפור כנף לא יעשה לו דמות כל אלה
אבל יעשה לו דמות דגים וחגבים שקצים ורמשים
ת"ל תבנית כל רומש באדמה תבנית כל דגה אשר
במים לא יעשה לו דמות כל אלה אבל יעשה לו

---

57 — 52 מ"ת שם.   58 — 59 ע"ז מ"ג, ב'.   60 — 61 דברים ט"ז, כ"א.   62 שם.   63 ויקרא
כ"ו, א'.   64 — 65 שמות כ', כ"ג.   67 ויקרא י"ט, ד'.   69 דברים ד', ט"ז.   71 — 72 שם
ד', י"ז.

---

54 מי שיצא] ק. משיצאו / ממצרים] ק. נ. למצרים.   60 יטע] א. יעשה.   69 לכם]
א. <.   77 השמימה] ק. נ. השמים.

he may make an image of the sun, the moon, the stars, or the planets? Scripture says: "And lest thou lift up thine eyes unto heaven," etc. (ibid., v. 19). He shall not make an image of any of these. But perhaps he may make an image of the angels, the Cherubim or the *Ophannim?* Scripture says: "Of anything that is in heaven." As for "that is in heaven," one might think it refers only to sun, moon, stars, and planets? But it says: "Above," meaning, not the image of the angels, not the image of the Cherubim, and not the image of the *Ophannim.*[3] He shall not make an image of any of these. But perhaps he may make an image of the deeps and the darkness? Scripture says: "All that is in the water under the earth." This includes even the reflected image[4]—these are the words of R. Akiba. Some say: It includes the *Shabrire.*[5]—Scripture goes to such length in pursuit of the evil inclination to idolatry in order not to leave room for any pretext of permitting it.

Thou Shalt Not Bow Down unto Them nor Serve Them. Why is this said? Because it says: "And hath gone and served other gods" (Deut. 17.3), which means that one becomes guilty for the act of serving by itself and for the act of bowing down by itself. You interpret it thus. But may it not mean that one is guilty only if he both serves and bows down? Scripture however says here: "Thou shalt not bow down unto them nor serve them," declaring that one becomes guilty for the act of serving by itself and for the act of bowing down by itself.

Another Interpretation: *Thou Shalt Not Bow Down to Them.* Why is this said? Because it says: "He that sacrificeth unto the gods save unto

3. *Ophannim* literally means, wheels, but with reference to Ezek. 1.5 ff. is used as a designation for heavenly beings or angels. See Jastrow, *Dictionary,* p. 31, s. v.

4. The reflected image, בבואה, aram. בוביא, was believed by the ancient primitive people to be a counterpart of the real, and to have separate and independent existence (see Commentaries).

5. See Commentaries and Jastrow, *Dictionary,* p. 1518, and cf. Alexander Kohut, *Studies in Yemen-Hebrew Literaure,* II, New York, 1894, p. 125.

דמות חמה ולבנה כוכבים ומזלות ת״ל ופן תשא
עיניך השמימה וגו׳ לא יעשה לו דמות כל אלה
אבל יעשה לו דמות מלאכים וכרובים ואופנים
ת״ל אשר בשמים אי אשר בשמים יכול דמות חמה
ולבנה כוכבים ומזלות ת״ל ממעל לא דמות מלאכים

80

לא דמות כרובים ולא דמות אופנים לא יעשה לו
דמות כל אלה אבל יעשה לו דמות תהום וחשך
ת״ל ואשר במים מתחת לארץ להביא את הבוביא
דברי רבי עקיבא ויש אומרים להביא את השבריירים

85

כל כך רדף הכתוב אחר יצר הרע שלא ליתן
מקום למצא לו מתלת היתר.

לא   תשתחוה   להם   ולא   תעבדם למה
נאמר לפי שהוא אומר וילך ויעבוד אלהים אחרים
לחייב על העבודה בפני עצמה ועל ההשתחואה

90

בפני עצמה אתה אומר כן או לא יהיה חייב עד
שיעבוד וישתחוה ת״ל לא תשתחוה להם ולא תעבדם
לחייב על העבודה בפני עצמה ועל ההשתחויה
בפני עצמה. דבר אחר לא תשתחוה להם למה
נאמר לפי שהוא אומר זובח לאלהים יחרם בלתי

---

76 — 77 שם ד׳, י״ט.   87 — 93 ספרי דברים קמ״ח. סנהדרין ס״ב, א׳; ס״ג, א׳. י׳ שם ז׳,
י״א (25ל).   87 — 103 מ״ת 20.   88 דברים י״ז, ג׳.   93 — 96 לקמן נזיקין י״ז. סנהדרין
ס׳, ב׳.   94 שמות כ״ב, י״ט.

78 ואופנים] ד. ~ וחשמלים.   80 ומזלות] ד. < > / לא דמות מלאכים] ד. <.   82 וחשך]
מ. ~ ואפלה א. ט״כ. ~ והברה.   83 הבוביא] מ״ח. הבבואה. ט. הבובאה.
84 השבריירים] א. הסודיריוס (או הסורויירוס?) מ. הסורויריס ט״כ. הסורויירוס תוספות
יומא נ״ד ב׳ ד״ה צורתא, סורויירים. נתגאל בן ישעיה (A. Kohut, Studies in Yemen Hebrew
Literature (New York, 1894) II p. 125) סרסרויירין.   85 הכתוב] א. <. ד. הקדש ברוך
הוא / ליתן] ד. ~ פתחון פה.   86 מקום למצא לו] א. מ״ח. לו מקום למצא / מתלת]
ד. מתלא מ. מתלה.   92 — 93 על העבודה—בפני עצמה] ד. כל אחד בפני עצמו.

the Lord only shall be utterly destroyed" (Ex. 22.19), from which we have heard the penalty for it, but we have not heard the warning against it. Therefore it says here: "Thou shalt not bow down to them." And it also says: "Thou shalt bow down to no other god" (ibid. 34.14).

For I the Lord Thy God Am a Jealous God. Rabbi says: A God above jealousy. I rule over jealousy, but jealousy has no power over Me. I rule over slumber, but slumber has no power over Me. And thus it says: "Behold, He that keepeth Israel doth neither slumber nor sleep" (Ps. 121.4).

Another Interpretation: *For I the Lord Thy God Am a Jealous God.* Zealously do I exact punishment for idolatry, but in other matters I am merciful and gracious. A certain philosopher asked R. Gamaliel: It is written in your Torah: "For I the Lord thy God am a jealous God." But is there any power in the idol that it should arouse jealousy? A hero is jealous of another hero, a wise man is jealous of another wise man, a rich man is jealous of another rich man, but has the idol any power that one should be jealous of it? R. Gamaliel said to him: Suppose a man would call his dog by the name of his father, so that when taking a vow he would vow: "By the life of this dog." Against whom would the father be incensed? Against the son or the dog? Said the philosopher to him: Some idols are worth while. "What makes you think so?" asked R. Gamaliel. Said the philosopher: There raged a fire in a certain province but the temple of the idol in it was saved. Was it not because the idol could take care of itself? Said R. Gamaliel to him: I will give you a parable: To what is this comparable? To the conduct of a king of flesh and blood when he goes out to war. Against whom does he wage war, against the living or against the dead? The philosopher then said: "Indeed, only against the living." Then he said again: But if there is no usefulness in any of them, why does He not annihilate them? Said R. Gamaliel to him: But is it only one object that you worship? Behold, you worship the sun, the

95 ליי לבדו עונש שמענו אזהרה מנין ת״ל לא תשתחוה
להם וכן הוא אומר לא תשתחוה לאל אחר.

כי אנכי יי אלהיך אל קנא רבי אומר
אלוה של קנאה אני שליט בקנאה ואין קנאה שולטת
בי אני שליט בנומה ואין נומה שולטת בי וכן הוא
100 אומר הנה לא ינום ולא יישן שומר ישראל. דבר
אחר כי אנכי יי אלהיך אל קנא בקנאה אני נפרע
מהם מעבודה זרה אבל רחום וחנון אני בדברים
אחרים. שאל פלוסופוס אחד את רבן גמליאל
כתיב בתורתכם כי אנכי יי אלהיך אל קנא וכי
105 יש כח בעבודה זרה להתקנות בה גבור מתקנא
בגבור חכם מתקנא בחכם עשיר מתקנא בעשיר
וכי יש כח בעבודה זרה להתקנות בה אמר לו אלו
אדם קורא לכלבו בשם אביו וכשהוא נודר נודר
בחיי כלב זה במי האב מתקנא בבן או בכלב אמר
110 לו יש למקצתה צורך אמר לו מה ראית אמר לו
הרי שנפלה דליקה במדינה פלונית והוצל בית
עבודה זרה שלה לא שעמדה לעצמה אמר לו
אמשול לך משל למה הדבר דומה למלך בשר
ודם שיוצא למלחמה עם מי הוא נלחם עם החיים
115 או עם המתים אמר לו עם החיים אמר לו הואיל
ואין למקצתה צורך מפני מה אינו מבטלה אמר
לו וכי לדבר אחד אתם עובדין והרי אתם עובדין

96 — 95 שם ל״ד, י״ד.‏   100 תהלים קכ״א, ד׳.‏   124 — 103 ע״ז נ״ד, ב׳; נ״ה, א׳.‏

96 — 95 לא תשתחוה להם] ד. להם.‏   97 רבי אומר] מ. וכי אומר ט. וכי אני ד. ».
98 אלוה של קנאה] ד. ».‏   99 — 99 קנאה שולטת בי] ד. ~ שנאמר הנה לא ינום ולא
יישן שומר ישראל דבר אחר אני יי אלהיך אל קנא אני שליט בקנאה ואין קנאה שולטת
בי. וחסר בילקוט ומחוק בא״א. וז״י. וש״י. ומא״ש.‏   100 — 99 וכן הוא אומר] ד.
שנאמר.‏   101 כי אנכי] ד. אני.‏   102 מהם]=ט. מ״ח. ג: א. ד. ».‏   104 אנכי] מ.
ד. ».‏   105 גבור] מ. משל גבור.‏   107 — 105 גבור—להתקנות בה] א. ».‏   107 וכי יש]
ד. אלא יש.‏   110 יש] א. מ. וכי יש.‏   111 והוצל בית] ד. חוץ לבית.‏   112 שלה] ד.
שלהן.‏   115 אמר לו ו] ט. הוי אומר.

moon, the stars and the planets, the mountains and the hills, the springs and the glens, and even human beings. Shall he destroy His world because of fools? "Shall I utterly consume all things from off the face of the earth? Saith the Lord" (Zeph. 1.2).—The philosopher[6] also said to him: Since it causes the wicked to stumble, why does God not remove it from the world?—But R. Gamaliel continued saying: Because of fools? If so, then since they also worship human beings: "Shall I cut off man from off the face of the earth?" (ibid., v. 3).

Visiting the Iniquity of the Fathers upon the Children. When there is no skip, but not when there is a skip. How is this? The wicked son of a wicked father, who in turn also was the son of a wicked father. R. Nathan says: A destroyer the son of a destroyer, who in turn was the son of a destroyer. When Moses heard this word:[7] "And Moses made haste, and bowed his head toward the earth, and worshipped" (Ex. 34.8). For he said: God forbid! In Israel there is no case of a wicked son of a wicked father who in turn was also the son of a wicked father. One might think that just as the measure of punishment extends over four generations, so also the measure of rewarding the good extends only over four generations. But Scripture says: "Unto thousands." But: "Unto thousands" I might understand to mean the minimum of "thousands," that is, two thousand [people,][8] but it also says: "To a thousand generations" (Deut. 7.9)—generations unsearched and uncounted.

Of Them that Love Me and Keep My Commandments. "Of them that love Me," refers to our father Abraham and such as are like him. "And keep My commandments," refers to the prophets and the elders. R. Nathan says: "Of them that love Me and keep My commandments,"

6. The philosopher interrupted Gamaliel's quotation from Zephaniah by alluding to the words of the prophet: "And the stumbling-blocks with the wicked" (ibid. v. 3) (see Introduction).

7. This midrashic comment may have originally been made on Ex. 34.7, where it was followed by the comment on v. 8, also reproduced here.

8. See Introduction.

לחמה וללבנה ולכוכבים ולמזלות להרים ולגבעות
לאפיקים וגיאיות ואפילו לאדם יאבד עולמו מפני
120 השוטים אסף אסף כל מעל פני האדמה נאם יי.
אמר לו הואיל ונכשלו בה הרשעים מפני מה אינו
מעבירה מן העולם אמר לו מפני השוטין אם כן
אף לאדם עובדין והכרתי את האדם מעל פני
האדמה.

125 **פוקד עון אבות על בנים** בזמן שאינן
מסורגין ולא בזמן שהן מסורגין הא כיצד רשע בן
רשע בן רשע רבי נתן אומר קוצץ בן קוצץ בן קוצץ
כיון ששמע משה את הדבר הזה וימהר משה ויקד
ארצה וישתחו אמר חס ושלום אין בישראל רשע
130 בן רשע בן רשע יכול כשם שמידת הפורעניות
לארבעה דורות כך מדת הטוב לארבעה דורות
ת"ל לאלפים אי לאלפים שומע אני מיעוט אלפים
שנים ת"ל לאלף דור דורים לאין חקר ואין מספר.

לאוהבי ולשומרי מצותי לאוהבי זה
135 אברהם אבינו וכיוצא בו ולשומרי מצותי אלו
הנביאים והזקנים רבי נתן אומר לאוהבי ולשומרי

---

120 צפניה א', ב'.   124 — 123 שם א', ג'.   125 — 143 מ"ת 21.   129 — 128 שמות ל"ד,
ח'.   133 דברים ז', ט'.

---

120 אסף אסף כל] מ. שנאמר אסף אאסף כל.   122 אם כן] מ. ד. אמר לו אם כן.
126 — 125 בזמן שאינן מסורגין] ד. בזמן שהם אינן מסורגין ט. ג. ש"י. ז"י. בזמן שהם
מסורגין (ז"י. מסרגין).   126 ולא בזמן שהן מסורגין] הגהתי=ה. מא"ש: א. מ. מ. ד.
או בזמן שהן מסורגין ז"י. ולא בזמן שאינם מסרגין ט. ג. ש. א"צ. <. 127 נתן] מ.
יהושע.   129 אמר ח"ן] א. אמר המקום מ. אמר הקב"ה ח"ו.   130 יכול] הגהתי=ג.
א"א. ז"י: ט. א"צ. או א. מ. ד. <.   133 דורים] ד. <.   134 ולשומרי מצותי] מ.
<.

refers to those who dwell in the land of Israel and risk their lives for the sake of the commandments. "Why are you being led out to be decapitated?" "Because I circumcised my son to be an Israelite." "Why are you being led out to be burned?" "Because I read the Torah." "Why are you being led out to be crucified?" "Because I ate the unleavened bread." "Why are you getting a hundred lashes?" "Because I performed the ceremony of the Lulab." And it says: "Those with which I was wounded in the house of my friends"[9] (Zech. 13.6). These wounds caused me to be beloved of My father in heaven.

CHAPTER VII
(Ex. 20.7–11)

Thou Shalt Not Take the Name of the Lord Thy God in Vain. Swearing falsely was also included in the general statement which says: "Or if any one swear clearly with his lips" (Lev. 5.4). Behold, this passage here singles it out from the general statement, making the punishment for it severer but at the same time exempting it from carrying with it the obligation of bringing a sacrifice. One might think that just as it is exempt from the obligation of bringing a sacrifice it is also exempt from the punishment of stripes. But Scripture says: "Thou shalt not take the name of the Lord thy God," etc. It has been exempted only from carrying with it the obligation of bringing a sacrifice, but not from carrying with it the penalty of stripes.[1]

Thou Shalt Not Take. Why is this said? Because it says: "And ye shall not swear by My name falsely" (Lev. 19.12), from which I know only that one should not swear. But how would I know that one should not even take it upon himself to swear? Therefore Scripture

9. See Introduction.
1. Cf. saying of R. Joḥanan in the name of R. Jose the Galilean in Mak. 16a and see Introduction.

מצותי אלו שהם יושבין בארץ ישראל ונותנין נפשם
על המצות מה לך יוצא ליהרג על שמלתי את בני
ישראל מה לך יוצא לישרף על שקראתי בתורה
140 מה לך יוצא ליצלב על שאכלתי את המצה מה
לך לוקה מאה פרגל על שנטלתי את הלולב ואומר
אשר הכתי בית מאהבי מכות אלו גרמו לי ליאהב
לאבי שבשמים.

פרשה ז (שמות כ׳, ז׳—י״א.)

לא תשא את שם יי אלהיך לשוא אף
שבועת שוא היתה בכלל שנאמר או נפש כי תשבע
לבטא בשפתים · והרי הכתוב מוציאה מכללה
ומחמיר עליה ופוטרה מן הקרבן יכול כשם שהיא
5 פטורה מן הקרבן כך תהא פטורה מן המכות ת״ל
לא תשא את שם יי וגו׳ מכלל קרבן יצאת מכלל
מכות לא יצאת.

לא תשא למה נאמר לפי שהוא אומר לא
תשבעו בשמי לשקר אין לי אלא שלא ישבע ושלא

138—143 וי״ר ל״ב, א׳. מדרש תהלים י״ב, ה׳.   142 זכריה י״ג, ו׳.
7—1 שבועות כ״א, א׳.   17—1 מ״ת 21.   3—2 ויקרא ה׳, ד׳.   9—8 שם י״ט, י״ב.

137 אלו שהם יושבין] ד. אלו ישראל שהם יושבין ט. מ״ח. אלו שיושבין. 138 על
המצות] א. על כל המצות מ. בכל המצות.   139 ישראל] א. >.   141 מאה פרגל] ד.
מאפרגל מ״ח. מספרגל ה. מכף הרגל.   142 לי] א. > / ליאהב] ט. לאהוב מ״ח.
לאהב.   143 לאבי] א. לאביהם מ. לאבינו.
2 שנאמר] ד. >.   4 יכול] הגהתי=א״א. ג: א. מ. ד. > ט. אני אומר ט״ב. או /
כשם] מ״ח. וכשם.   6 לא תשא] ד. >.   7 לא יצאת] מ. יצאת.   8 לא תשא] מ.
דבר אחר לא תשא.   9—8 לא תשבעו] במקרא כתוב ולא תשבעו.

says: "Thou shalt not take the name of the Lord thy God." . . . Before you obligated yourself to take an oath I am a God to you. But after you have obligated yourself to take an oath I am a Judge over you. And thus it says: "For the Lord will not hold him guiltless that taketh His name in vain." R. Eleazar says: It is impossible to say:[2] "He will not clear," since it is also said: "And that will clear (ve-nakeh)" (Ex. 34.7). But it is just as impossible to say: "He will clear," since it is also said: "He will not clear" (lo yenakeh) (ibid.). You must therefore say: He clears those who repent but does not clear those who do not repent.

For four things did R. Matia b. Ḥeresh go to R. Eleazar ha-Kappar to Laodicea. He said to him: Master! Have you heard the four distinctions in atonement which R. Ishmael used to explain? He said to him: Yes. One scriptural passage says: "Return, O backsliding children" (Jer. 3.14), from which we learn that repentance brings forgiveness. And another scriptural passage says: "For on this day shall atonement be made for you" (Lev. 16.30), from which we learn that the Day of Atonement brings forgiveness. Still another scriptural passage says: "Surely this iniquity shall not be expiated by you till ye die" (Isa. 22.14), from which we learn that death brings forgiveness. And still another scriptural passage says: "Then will I visit their transgressions with the rod, and their iniquity with strokes" (Ps. 89.33), from which we learn that chastisements bring forgiveness. How are all these four passages to be maintained? If one has transgressed a positive commandment and repents of it, he is forgiven on the spot. Concerning this it is said: "Return, O backsliding children." If one has violated a negative commandment and repents, repentance alone has not the

---

2. It is impossible to take the phrase לא ינקה, "He will not clear," strictly and absolutely, since the preceding infinitive absolute, ונקה, may be interpreted independently of the finite verb and connected with the preceding phrase, in which case it means that God will clear the guilty. But it is also impossible to take the latter interpretation of the word ונקה absolutely, since the phrase that follows it, לא ינקה, espressly says: "He will not clear."

יקבל עליו לישבע מנין ת״ל לא תשא את שם יי
אלהיך עד שלא קבלת עליך להשבע הרי אני לך
לאלוה משקבלת עליך להשבע הרי אני לך לדיין
וכן הוא אומר כי לא ינקה יי את אשר ישא את שמו
לשוא ר׳ אלעזר אומר אי איפשר לומר לא ינקה
שכבר נאמר ונקה ואי איפשר לומר ינקה שכבר
נאמר לא ינקה אמור מעתה מנקה הוא לשבים ואינו
מנקה לשאינן שבים. מפני ארבעה דברים הלך
רבי מתיא בן חרש אצל רבי אלעזר הקפר
ללודקיא אמר לו רבי שמעת ארבעה חלוקי כפרה
שהיה רבי ישמעאל דורש אמר לו כתוב אחד אומר
שובו בנים שובבים וגו׳ הא למדנו שהתשובה
מכפרת וכתוב אחד אומר כי ביום הזה יכפר
עליכם הא למדנו שיום הכפורים מכפר וכתוב
אחד אומר אם יכופר העון הזה לכם עד תמותון
הא למדנו שהמיתה מכפרת וכתוב אחד אומר
ופקדתי בשבט פשעם ובנגעים עונם הא למדנו
שייסורין מכפרין כיצד יתקיימו ארבעה כתובים
אלו העובר על מצות עשה ועשה תשובה אינו זז
משם עד שמוחלין לו ועל זה נאמר שובו בנים
שובבים והעובר על מצות לא תעשה ועשה תשובה

12 לאלוה] ד. אלהים.   13 וכן הוא אומר] ד. שנאמר א״צ. <.   14 — 13 וכן הוא
אומר—שמו לשוא] ט. <.   14 ר׳ אלעזר אומר] הוספתי=מ״ח.   15 נאמר ונקה] ד.
נאמר ינקה.   16 אמור מעתה] מ״ח. הא כיצד / הוא] א. היא / ואינו] א. ואינה.
17 דברים] ד. ~ אלו.   18 רבי] ד. / אצל רבי אלעזר הקפר] א. מ. > מ״ח. אצל
ר׳ אלעזר.   19 ללודקיא] ד. ללודיא מ״ח. ללודיקיא ג. לרומי / ארבעה] ד. בארבע.
21 למדנו] ד. למדת.   25 למדנו] ד. למדת.   29 משם] א. מ״ח. ממקומו.

power of atonement. It merely leaves the matter pending and the Day of Atonement brings forgiveness. Concerning this it is said: "For on this day shall atonement be made for you." If one willfully commits transgressions punishable by extinction or by death at the hands of the court and repents, repentance cannot leave the matter pending nor can the Day of Atonement bring forgiveness. But both repentance and the Day of Atonement together bring him half a pardon. And chastisements secure him half a pardon. Concerning this it is said: "Then will I visit their transgressions with the rod, and their iniquity with strokes." However, if one has profaned the name of God and repents, his repentance cannot make the case pending, neither can the Day of Atonement bring him forgiveness, nor can sufferings cleanse him of his guilt. But repentance and the Day of Atonement both can merely make the matter pend. And the day of death with the suffering preceding it completes the atonement. To this applies: "Surely this iniquity shall not be expiated by you till ye die." And so also when it says: "That the iniquity of Eli's house shall not be expiated with sacrifice nor offering" (I Sam. 3.14) it means: With sacrifice and offering it cannot be expiated, but it will be expiated by the day of death. Rabbi says: I might have thought that the day of death does not bring forgiveness. But when it says: "When I have opened your graves," etc. (Ezek. 37.13), behold we learn that the day of death does bring atonement.

Rabbi says: For violations of laws, such as those preceding the commandment: "Thou shalt not take," repentance alone brings forgiveness. In cases of violations of laws, such as follow the commandment: "Thou shalt not take"—including the commandment: "Thou shalt not take" itself—repentance makes the matter pend and the Day of Atonement brings forgiveness.[3] What commandments are like those preceding the commandment: "Thou shalt not take"? Positive and negative commandments which carry no penalty with them—

3. See Introduction and cf. Commentaries.

אין כח בתשובה לכפר אלא התשובה תולה ויום
הכפורים מכפר על זה נאמר כי ביום הזה יכפר
עליכם והמזיד על כריתות ועל מיתות בית דין
ועשה תשובה אין כח בתשובה לתלות ולא ביום
הכפורים לכפר אלא התשובה ויום הכפורים   35
מכפרין מחצה וייסורין מכפרין מחצה ועל זה
נאמר ופקדתי בשבט פשעם ובנגעים עונם מי
שמחלל שם שמים ועשה תשובה אין כח בתשובה
לתלות ולא ביום הכפורים לכפר ולא בייסורין
למרק אלא התשובה ויום הכפורים תולין ויום   40
המיתה ממרק עם הייסורין ועל זה נאמר אם
יכופר העון הזה לכם עד תמותון וכן הוא אומר
אם יתכפר עון בית עלי בזבח ובמנחה בזבח
ובמנחה אינו מתכפר אבל ביום המיתה מתכפר
רבי אומר שומע אני שלא יכפר יום המיתה כשהוא   45
אומר בפתחי את קברותיכם וגו' הא למדנו שיום
המיתה מכפר רבי אומר כל שהוא מלא תשא
ולמעלה התשובה מכפרת מלא תשא ולמטה ולא
תשא עמהם התשובה תולה ויום הכפורים מכפר
ואיזה הוא מלא תשא ולמעלה עשה ולא תעשה   50

---

43 שמואל א. ג', י"ד.   46 יחזקאל ל"ז, י"ג.   54 — 47 יומא שם. תוספתא שם. 73 — 47 ש.
.107

---

31 התשובה] א. על התשובה.   33 ועל] א. והעובר על.   36 וייסורין מכפרין] ד. וייסורין
ממרקין ומכפרין.   40 — 39 בייסורין למרק] ד. ייסורין בלבד ממרקין.   42 וכן הוא אומר]
ד. ואומר.

thus excepting the commandment: "Thou shalt not take" itself. And which are like those following the commandment: "Thou shalt not take"? Matters subject to the penalty of death at the hands of the human court, death at the hand of heaven, excision by the hand of heaven, forty stripes, sin-offerings, and trespass-offerings. And the commandment: "Thou shalt not take" is classed with them.

Remember the Day of the Sabbath to Keep It Holy. "Remember" and "observe" (Deut. 5.12) were both spoken at one utterance. "Everyone that profaneth it shall surely be put to death" (Ex. 31.14) and: "And on the Sabbath day two he-lambs" (Num. 28.9) were both spoken at one utterance. "Thou shalt not uncover the nakedness of thy brother's wife" (Lev. 18.16) and: "Her husband's brother shall go in unto her" (Deut. 25.5) were both spoken at one utterance. "Thou shalt not wear a mingled stuff" (Deut. 22.11) and: "Thou shalt make thee twisted cords" (ibid., v. 12) were both spoken at one utterance.[4] This is a manner of speech impossible for creatures of flesh and blood. For it is said: "God has spoken one utterance which we have heard as two,"[5] etc. (Ps. 62.12). And it also says: "Is not My word like as fire? saith the Lord; and like a hammer that breaketh the rock in pieces?" (Jer. 23.29). *Remember* and *observe.* Remember it before it comes and observe it after it has gone.—Hence they said: We should always increase what is holy by adding to it some of the non-holy.—Thus it can be compared to a wolf moving backward and forward.[6] Eleazar b. Ḥananiah b. Hezekiah b. Garon says: "Remember the day of the Sabbath to keep it holy," keep it in mind from the first day of the week on, so that if something good happens to come your way fix it up for the Sabbath. R. Isaac says: You shall not count the days of

4. Each pair in the above group consists of two laws which contradict one another. Hence, it is explained that they were both given in the same utterance, the one being an exception to the general law contained in the other.

5. This rendering of the word שתים is required by the *Mekilta.*

6. See Commentaries.

חוץ מלא תשא מלא תשא ולמטה דברים שחייבין
עליהם מיתות בית דין מיתה בידי שמים כרת בידי
שמים ומלקות ארבעים חטאות ואשמות ולא תשא
עמהם.

55 **זכור את יום השבת לקדשו** זכור ושמור
שניהם בדבור אחד נאמרו מחלליה מות יומת וביום
השבת שני כבשים וג' שניהם בדבור אחד נאמרו
ערות אשת אחיך ויבמה יבא עליה שניהם בדבור
אחד נאמרו לא תלבש שעטנז וגדילים תעשה לך
60 שניהם בדבור אחד נאמרו מה שאי איפשר לבשר
ודם לומר כן שנאמר אחת דבר אלהים שתים זו
שמענו וג' ואומר הלא כה דברי כאש נאם יי
וכפטיש יפוצץ סלע זכור ושמור זכור מלפניו
ושמור מלאחריו מכאן אמרו מוסיפין מחול על
65 הקדש משל לזאב שהוא טורד מלפניו ומלאחריו.
אלעזר בן חנניה בן חזקיה בן גרון אומר זכור את
יום השבת לקדשו תהא זוכרו מאחד בשבת שאם
נתמנה לך חפץ יפה תהא מתקנו לשם שבת רבי

62—55 ספרי דברים רל"ג. י' שבועות ג', י' (34ᵈ).   65—55 מ"ת 21.   56 שמות ל"א,
י"ד.   57—56 במדבר כ"ח, ט'.   58 ויקרא י"ח, ט"ז. / דברים כ"ה, ה'.   59 שם כ"ב,
י"א—י"ב.   62—61 תהלים ס"ב, י"ב; לעיל ד'.   63—62 ירמיה כ"ג, כ"ט.   64—65 יומא
פ"א, ב'.   68—67 ביצה ט"ז, א'.

52 מיתה בידי שמים] א. מיתה בידי אדם.   55 זכור את יום השבת לקדשו] מ. ד. <.
62 כה דברי כאש נאם יין] מ. כה דברים א. כה דברי נאם יי כאש.   63 וכפטיש יפוצץ
סלע] הוספתי: א. מ. וגו'.   65 לזאב] ה. לואב ש. לארי / טורד] ט. טורף מ"ח. טוהר
ש. שם עורר ה. טרוד.   66 חזקיה] ד. ~ בן חנניה.   67 זוכרו] מ"ח. זוכה. חפץ] 68
ק. < נ. ל. מנה.

the week in the manner in which others count them. But you should count them with reference to the Sabbath.[7]

To Keep It Holy. To consecrate it with a benediction. On the basis of this passage the sages said: At the entrance of the Sabbath we consecrate it by reciting the sanctification of the day over wine. From this I know only about the "sanctification" for the day. Whence do we know that the night also requires a "sanctification"? It is said: "Ye shall keep the Sabbath," etc. (Ex. 31.14). So far I know only about the Sabbath. How about the holidays? Scripture says: "These are the appointed seasons of the Lord," etc. (Lev. 23.4).

Six Days Shalt Thou Labour and Do All Thy Work. But is it possible for a human being to do all his work in six days? It simply means: Rest on the Sabbath as if all your work were done. Another Interpretation: Rest even from the thought of labor. And it says: "If thou turn away thy foot because of the Sabbath," etc. (Isa. 58.13) and then it says: "Then shalt thou delight thyself in the Lord," etc. (ibid. v. 14).

But the Seventh Day Is a Sabbath unto the Lord Thy God. Why is this said? Because it says: "Whosoever doeth any work in the sabbath day, he shall surely be put to death" (Ex. 31.15). We have thus heard the penalty. But we have not heard the warning. Therefore it says here: "But the seventh day is a sabbath unto the Lord thy God, in it thou shalt not do any manner of work." I thus know only the penalty for and the warning against work on Sabbath during the daytime. How do I know that there is also a penalty for and a warning against work during the night time of the Sabbath? It says: "Everyone that profaneth it shall surely be put to death" (Ex. 31.14). From this however we only learn about the penalty. But we have not heard any warning. Scripture says: "But the seventh day is a sabbath unto the Lord thy

7. The weekdays are not designated by names, but are merely counted as the first, the second, etc. day of the week, or the first, the second, etc. day after the Sabbath.

יצחק אומר לא תהא מונה כדרך שאחרים מונין

70   אלא תהא מונה לשם שבת.

לקדשו לקדשו בברכה מכאן אמרו מקדשין

על היין בכניסתו אין לי אלא קדושה ליום קדושה

ללילה מנין ת״ל ושמרתם את השבת וגו׳ אין לי

אלא שבת ימים טובים מנין ת״ל אלה מועדי יי וגו׳.

75   **ששת ימים תעבוד ועשית כל מלאכתך**

ואי איפשר לבשר ודם לעשות כל מלאכתו בששת

ימים אלא שבות כאלו כל מלאכתך עשויה. דבר

אחר שבות ממחשבת עבודה ואומר אם תשיב

משבת רגליך וגו׳ ואומר אז תתענג על יי וגו׳.

80   **ויום השביעי שבת ליי אלהיך** למה

נאמר לפי שהוא אומר כל העושה מלאכה ביום

השבת מות יומת עונש שמענו אזהרה לא שמענו

ת״ל ויום השביעי שבת ליי אלהיך לא תעשה כל

מלאכה אין לי אלא עונש ואזהרה על מלאכת היום

85   עונש ואזהרה על מלאכת הלילה מנין ת״ל מחלליה

מות יומת עונש שמענו אזהרה לא שמענו ת״ל ויום

73 — 71 פסחים ק״ו, א׳.   74 — 71 מ״ת 22—21.   73 שמות ל״א, י״ד.   74 ויקרא כ״ג,
ד׳.   77 — 75 מ״ת 22.   99 — 75 ש. 108—100.   79 — 78 ישעיה נ״ח, י״ג—י״ד.
89 — 80 לקמן שבתא א׳.   82 — 81 שמות ל״א, ט״ו.   86 — 85 שמות ל״א, י״ד.

69 יצחק] מ. נתן.   70 לשם שבת] בפירוש הטור על התורה (הנובר תקצ״ט) דף מ׳. ליום
שבת.   73—72 אין לי אלא—ללילה מנין] מנו״ה פרק קנ״ה. מ״ח. א״צ. אין לי
אלא בלילה ביום (א״צ) מנין.   73 ושמרתם את השבת] מ״ח.
א״צ. זכור את יום.   76 כל מלאכתו] ד. מלאכתו.   77 כל] ד. >.   82 לא שמענו] ד.
מנין.   83 שבת ליי אלהיך] ד. >.

God." Now, there would be no purpose in saying "a sabbath"[8] except to include the nighttime in the warning.—These are the words of R. Ahai the son of Josiah.

Thou nor Thy Son nor Thy Daughter. That is, the minors. Perhaps it is not so but means the grown ups? You must reason: Have they not already been forewarned themselves? Hence what must be the meaning of: "Thou nor thy son nor thy daughter"? The minors.

Nor Thy Man-Servant nor Thy Maid-Servant. That is, children of the Covenant. You interpret it to mean children of the Covenant. Perhaps it is not so but refers to the uncircumcised slave? When it says: "And the son of thy handmaid and the stranger may be refreshed" (Ex. 23.12) behold, the uncircumcised slave is there spoken of. Hence whom does Scripture mean when it says here: "Nor thy man-servant nor thy maid-servant"? Those who are children of the Covenant.

Nor Thy Stranger. Meaning the righteous proselyte. Perhaps it is not so but means the resident alien?[9] When it says: "And the stranger" (Ex. 23.12), behold, it speaks there of the resident alien. Hence what does it mean by saying here: "Thy stranger"? The righteous proselyte.

For in Six Days the Lord Made Heaven and Earth, the Sea, and All that In Them Is. This tells that the sea[10] is equal to all the other works of creation.

And Rested on the Seventh Day. And is He subject to such a thing as weariness? Has it not been said: "The Creator of the ends of the earth fainteth not, neither is weary" (Isa. 40.28)? And it says: "He giveth power to the faint" (ibid. v. 29). And it also says: "By the word of the Lord were the heavens made," etc. (Ps. 33.6). How then can Scripture say: "And rested on the seventh day"? It is simply this: God allowed it to be written about Him that He created His world in six days and rested, as it were, on the seventh. Now by the method of *kal vahomer*

---

8. Instead of "a Sabbath day."
9. See above, *Pisha,* XV, note 4.
10. See Introduction.

השביעי שבת ליי אלהיך שאין ת"ל שבת אלא
להביא את הלילה בכלל אזהרה דברי רבי אחאי
בר יאשידו.

אתה ובנך ובתך אלו הקטנים או אינו אלא

90

הגדולים אמרת והלא כבר מוזהרים הם הא מה
ת"ל אתה ובנך ובתך אלו הקטנים.

עבדך ואמתך אלו בני ברית אתה אומר
אלו בני ברית או אינו אלא עבד ערל כשהוא אומר

95

וינפש בן אמתך והגר הרי עבד ערל אמור הא מה
ת"ל עבדך ואמתך אלו בני ברית.

וגרך זה גר צדק או אינו אלא גר תושב כשהוא
אומר והגר הרי גר תושב אמור הא מה ת"ל וגרך
זה גר צדק.

100

כי ששת ימים עשה יי את השמים
ואת הארץ את הים ואת כל אשר בם
מגיד שהים שקול כנגד כל מעשה בראשית.

וינח ביום השביעי וכי יש לפניו יגיעה
והלא כבר נאמר לא ייעף ולא ייגע ואומר נותן

105

ליעף כח וגו' ואומר בדבר יי שמים נעשו וגו' ומה
ת"ל וינח ביום השביעי אלא כביכול הכתיב על
עצמו שברא את עולמו בששה ימים ונח בשביעי

---

99 — 90 מ"ת 23 — 22.   96 — 93 לעיל פסחא ט"ו.   99 — 93 לקמן כספא ג'.   95 שמות
כ"ג, י"ב.   104 ישעיה מ', כ"ח.   105 — 104 שם מ', כ"ט.   105 תהלים ל"ג, ו'.

---

89 — 88 דברי ר' אחאי בר יאשידה]=ט. (כי תשא שצ"א) ג: מ. ד. מ"ח. ט. ה. ר'
אחאי בר יאשיה אומר.   90 הקטנים] מ. ~ אתה אומר אלו הקטנים / אינו אלא ד.
אלו.   98 והגר] ק. נ. הגר / תושב] א. ותושב.   101 — 100 עשה יי — אשר בם] הוספתי:
מ. ד. וגו'.   102 שהים] א. ט. ט"כ. ה. שהיום ט. שהיום ט. א"א. שהיה מ"ח. שהוא.

you must reason: If He, for whom there is no weariness, allowed it to be written that He created His world in six days and rested on the seventh, how much more should man, of whom it is written: "But man is born unto trouble" (Job 5.7), rest on the seventh day.

Wherefore the Lord Blessed the Sabbath Day and Hallowed It. He blessed it with the manna and hallowed it by the manna.—These are the words of R. Ishmael. R. Akiba says: He blessed it with the manna and hallowed it by prescribing a benediction for it. R. Isaac says: He blessed it with the manna and declared it holy by the verdict upon the wood-gatherer (Num. 15.35). R. Simon the son of Joḥai says: He blessed it with the manna and hallowed it by the lights. R. Simon the son of Judah of Kefar Akko says in the name of R. Simon: He blessed it with the manna and hallowed it by the shining countenance of man's face.[11] In this sense it is said: "Wherefore the Lord blessed the sabbath day and hallowed it."

CHAPTER VIII
(Ex. 20.12–14)

Honour Thy Father and Thy Mother. I might understand it to mean only with words but Scripture says: "Honour the Lord with thy substance," etc. (Prov. 3.9). Hence it must mean, with food and drink and with clean garments.

Another Interpretation: *Honour Thy Father.* Why is this said? Since it says: "For whatsoever man there be that curseth his father or his mother," etc. (Lev. 20.9), I know it only in regard to a man, but how about a woman, a *tumtum* or an hermaphrodite? It says here: "Honour thy father," etc.—in any case. And just as in regard to the honor due to parents no distinction is made between man and woman, so also in regard to the fear of parents no distinction is to be

11. See Commentaries and cf. Gen. Rab. 11.2.

והרי דברים קל וחומר ומה אם מי שאין לפניו
יגיעה הכתיב על עצמו שברא עולמו לששה ימים
110 ונח בשביעי על אחת כמה וכמה אדם שכתוב בו
כי אדם לעמל יולד.

על כן ברך יי את יום השבת ויקדשהו
ברכו במן וקדשו במן דברי רבי ישמעאל רבי
עקיבא אומר ברכו במן וקדשו בברכה רבי יצחק
115 אומר ברכו במן וקדשו במקוששש רבי שמעון בן
יוחאי אומר ברכו במן וקדשו במאורות רבי שמעון
בן יהודה איש כפר עכו אומר משום רבי שמעון
ברכו במן וקדשו במאור פניו של אדם לכך נאמר
על כן ברך יי את יום השבת ויקדשהו.

פרשה ח (שמות כ׳, י״ב—י״ד.)

כבד את אביך ואת אמך שומע אני
בדברים ת״ל כבד את יי מהונך וגו׳ במאכל
ובמשתה ובכסות נקייה. דבר אחר כבד את אביך
למה נאמר לפי שהוא אומר כי איש איש אשר יקלל
5 את אביו ואת אמו אין לי אלא איש אשה וטומטום
ואנדרוגינוס מנין ת״ל כבד את אביך וגו׳ מכל מקום
מה כבוד לא חלק בו בין איש לאשה אף מורא

119 — 109 ש. 109.   111 איוב ה׳, ז׳.   119 — 112 ב״ר י״א, ב׳.

3 — 1 לעיל פסחא ט׳. שבת קי״ט, א׳. קידושין ל״א, ב׳—ל״ב, א׳. ש. 110.   25 — 1 ת״כ
ריש קדושים (87ª — 86c). י׳ פאה א׳ (15cd).   2 משלי ג׳, ט׳.   12 — 3 לקמן נזיקין ה׳.
5 — 4 ויקרא כ׳, ט׳.

108 ומה אם] א. ד. <.   113 ישמעאל] א. ישהשע.   115 במקוששש] א״צ. במלאכה ה.
בקדושתו.   118 פניו] ה. עיניו / אדם] מ. ד. ~ הראשון / לכך נאמר] הוספתי=א״צ:
ג. שנאמר ועיין מ״ע.

4 למה נאמר] ד. <.   5 — 4 כי איש איש אשר יקלל את אביו ואת אמו] ק. נ. איש
איש כי יקלל אביו ואמו מ. ל. איש איש כי יקלל את אביו ואת אמו.   7 בו] ד. <.

made between man and woman.—These are the words of R. Ishmael. R. Judah b. Bathyra says: It is said: "Ye shall fear every man his mother and his father, and ye shall keep My sabbaths" (Lev. 19.3). Just as in regard to the Sabbath there is no distinction made between a man and a woman or a *tumtum* and a hermaphrodite so also in regard to the commandment to fear one's parents, no distinction is to be made between man and woman or a *tumtum* and a hermaphrodite. Rabbi says: The honoring of one's father and mother is very dear in the sight of Him by whose word the world came into being. For He declared honoring them to be equal to honoring Him, fearing them equal to fearing Him, and cursing them equal to cursing Him. It is written: "Honour thy father and thy mother," and correspondingly it is written: "Honour the Lord with thy substance" (Prov. 3.9). Scripture thus puts the honoring of one's parents on an equality with honoring God. It is written: "Ye shall fear every man his mother and his father" (Lev. 19.3), and correspondingly it is written: "Thou shalt fear the Lord thy God" (Deut. 6.13). Scripture thus puts the fear of one's father and mother on an equality with the fear of God. It is written: "And he that curseth his father or his mother shall surely be put to death" (Ex. 21.17), and correspondingly it is written: "Whosoever curseth his God," etc. (Lev. 24.15). Scripture thus puts the cursing of one's father and mother on an equality with the cursing of God. Come and see the rewards for obeying these two commandments. It is said: "Honour the Lord with thy substance . . . so shall thy barns be filled with plenty," etc. (Prov. 3.9–10). And it says: "Honour thy father and thy mother that thy days may be long." "Thou shalt fear the Lord thy God" (Deut. 6.13). And it promises in reward: "But unto you that fear My name shall the sun of righteousness arise with healing in its wings" (Mal. 3.20). It also says: "Ye shall fear every man his mother and his father, and ye shall keep My sabbaths" (Lev. 19.3). Now what is promised as a reward for keeping the Sabbath? "If thou turn away thy foot because of the sabbath . . . then shalt thou delight thyself in the Lord," etc. (Isa. 58.13–14).

לא תחלוק בו בין איש לאשה דברי רבי ישמעאל
רבי יהודה בן בתירה אומר נאמר איש אמו ואביו
תיראו ואת שבתותי תשמורו מה שבת לא חלק בו
בין איש לאשה טומטום ואנדרוגינוס אף מורא לא
תחלוק בו בין איש לאשה טומטום ואנדרוגינוס.
רבי אומר חביב כבוד אב ואם לפני מי שאמר
והיה העולם ששקל כבודן ככבודו ומוראן כמוראו
וקללתן כקללתו כתיב כבד את אביך ואת אמך
וכנגדו כתיב כבד את יי מהונך הקיש כבוד אב
ואם לכבוד המקום כתיב איש אמו ואביו תיראו
וכנגדו כתיב את יי אלהיך תירא הקיש מורא אב
ואם למורא המקום כתיב ומקלל אביו ואמו וגו׳
וכנגדו כתיב איש איש כי יקלל אלהיו וגו׳ הקיש
קללת אב ואם לקללת המקום בוא וראה מתן
שכרן נאמר כבד את יי מהונך וגו׳ וימלאו אסמך
שבע וגו׳ ואומר כבד את אביך ואת אמך למען
יאריכון ימיך את יי אלהיך תירא ואומר וזרחה
לכם יראי שמי שמש צדקה ומרפא בכנפיה ואומר
איש אמו ואביו תיראו ואת שבתותי תשמורו מה
אמו בשבת אם תשיב משבת רגליך וגו׳ את תתענג

9—10 ויקרא י"ט, ג׳.   21—13 ש. שם.   36—13 קידושין ל׳, ב׳—ל"א, א׳.   16 משלי
שם.   17 ויקרא שם.   18 דברים י׳, כ׳.   19 שמות כ"א, י"ז.   20 ויקרא כ"ד, ט"ו.
22 משלי שם.   23—22 שם ג׳, י׳.   24—23 דברים שם.   25—24 מלאכי ג׳, כ׳.
26 ויקרא י"ט, ג׳.   27 ישעיה נ"ח, י"ג.   28—27 שם נ"ח, י"ד.

8 תחלוק בו] ד. חלקו.   14 כבודן ככבודו ומוראן כמוראו] הגהתי עפ"י מ"ח. ה. ול"ט:
א. מ. כבודן ומוראן כמוראו ד. כבודן ומוראן לכבודו ג. כבודן ומוראן ככבודו וכמוראו.
15 וקללתן כקללתו] א. וקללתן כקיללתו.   19—18 מורא אב ואם] ד. מוראת אב.
22 נאמר] א. שנאמר מ. > / מהונך וגו׳] ד. מהונך וכנגדו כתיב.   23 אמן] ד. ~ וכנגדו.
24 ואומר] ד. <.   25 ומרפא בכנפיה] הוספתי: א. מ. וגו׳ / ואומר] א. ד. <.   27 משבת]
מ. בשבת / וגו׳ אז] א. וגו׳ וכתיב בתריה אז.

Rabbi says: It is revealed and known before Him by whose word the world came into being that a man honors his mother more than his father because she sways him with persuasive words. Therefore in the commandment to honor He mentions the father before the mother. And it is revealed and known before Him by whose word the world came into being that a man is more afraid of his father than of his mother because he teaches him the Torah. Therefore in the commandment to fear He mentions the mother before the father. Where something is imperfect Scripture seeks to make it complete. Perhaps, however, it means that the one preceding in this text should actually have precedence over the other, but there is a teaching against this in the passage: "Ye shall fear every man his mother and his father" (Lev. 19.3), where the mother precedes. Scripture thus declares that both are equal, the one as important as the other.

Honour Thy Father and Thy Mother that Thy Days May Be Long. If you honor them the result will be that your days will be long, and if not, the result will be that your days will be short. For the words of the Torah are *notarikon.*[1] The words of the Torah are to be interpreted so as to derive from the positive what applies to the negative and from the negative what applies to the positive.

Upon the Land which the Lord Thy God Giveth Thee. In connection with this passage the sages said: Every commandment the reward for which is mentioned along with it the courts here below are not under obligation to enforce.

Thou Shalt Not Murder. Why is this said? Because it says: "Whoso sheddeth man's blood," etc. (Gen. 9.6). We have thus heard the penalty for it but we have not heard the warning against it; therefore it says here: "Thou shalt not murder."

Thou Shalt Not Commit Adultery. Why is this said? Because it says: "Both the adulterer and the adulteress shall surely be put to death"

1. See Jastrow, *Dictionary,* p. 886; and cf. Bacher, *Terminologie,* I, p. 126 and *JE,* IX, 340.

על יי וגו'. רבי אומר גלוי וידוע לפני מי שאמר

והיה העולם שאדם מכבד את אמו יותר מאביו

30 מפני שהיא משדלתו בדברים לפיכך הקדים את

האב לאם בכיבוד וגלוי וידוע לפני מי שאמר והיה

העולם שאדם מתיירא מאביו יותר מאמו מפני

שהוא מלמדו תורה לפיכך הקדים את האם לאב

במורא מקום שחסר השלים או כל הקודם במקרא

35 קודם במעשה ת"ל איש אמו ואביו תיראו מגיד

ששניהם שקולין זה כזה.

כבד   את   אביך   ואת   אמך   למען

יאריכון ימיך אם כבדתן למען יאריכון ימיך

ואם לאו למען יקצרון ימיך שדברי תורה נוטריקון

40 שכן דברי תורה נדרשין מכלל הן לאו ומכלל לאו

הן.

על   האדמה   אשר   יי   אלהיך   נותן   לך

מכאן אמרו כל מצוה שמתן שכרה בצדה אין בית

דין שלמטה מוזהרין עליה.

45 **לא   תרצח** למה נאמר לפי שהוא אומר שופך

דם האדם וגו' עונש שמענו אזהרה לא שמענו ת"ל

לא תרצח.

לא   תנאף למה נאמר לפי שהוא אומר מות

36—34 לעיל פסחא א'. ת"כ שם.   60—37 מ"ת 23.   41—39 ספרי דברים מ"ו.   44—43 חולין ק"י, ב'.   46—45 בראשית ט', ו'.   49—48 ויקרא כ', י'.

---

28 רבי] ד. רבי אליעזר / וידוע] א. ~ היה מ. היה.   30 משדלתו] מ. ה. משתדלתו.
31 וידוע] א. מ. היה.   33 את האם לאב] ד. אב לאם.   38 כבדתן למען] Pugio fidei
צד 396 כבדתן.   39 למען] א. Pugio fidei   שם < / שדברי תורה נוטריקון] Pugio fidei
שם ג. >.   40—39 נוטריקון שכן דברי תורה נדרשין] מ"ח. <.

(Lev. 20.10). We have thus heard the penalty for it but we have not heard the warning against it; therefore it says here: "Thou shalt not commit adultery."

Thou Shalt Not Steal. Why is this said? Because it says: "And he that stealeth a man and selleth him" (Ex. 21.16). We have thus heard the penalty for it but we have not heard the warning against it; therefore it says here: "Thou shalt not steal." Behold then this is a warning against stealing persons. You interpret this to be a warning against stealing persons. Perhaps it is not so but it is a warning against stealing money? When it says: "Ye shall not steal" (Lev. 19.11) behold there you have the warning against stealing money. Hence what does the passage: "Thou shalt not steal" speak of? Of one who steals persons. But perhaps the passage here is a prohibition against stealing money and the passage there (Lev. 19.11) is a prohibition against stealing a person? You must reason: Go and learn it by one of the thirteen rules according to which the Torah is interpreted. What does scripture deal with here?[2] etc. And further you reason: There are three laws mentioned in this section. Two of them are explicit and one not explicit. Let us learn about the non-explicit from the explicit ones. Just as the explicit ones are laws for the violation of which one incurs the penalty of death at the hands of the court, so also the non-explicit one must be a law for the violation of which one incurs the penalty of death at the hands of the court. Hence it is impossible for you to argue as in the latter version but you must argue as in the former version: This one is a prohibition against stealing a person, and that one (Lev. 19.11) is a prohibition against stealing money.

Thou Shalt Not Bear False Witness against Thy Neighbour. Why is this said? Because it says: "Then shall ye do unto him as he purposed

---

2. The rest of the midrashic comment is to be found in Sanh. 86a. Here it is omitted and referred to by the expression גו׳, "etc." The rule cited is the seventh in the hermeneutic system of Hillel and the twelfth in that of R. Ishmael (cf. *JE*, X, 511–12).

יומת הנואף והנואפת עונש שמענו אזהרה לא
50 שמענו ת״ל לא תנאף.

לא תגנוב למה נאמר לפי שהוא אומר וגונב
איש ומכרו עונש שמענו אזהרה לא שמענו ת״ל לא
תגנוב והרי זה אזהרה לגונב נפש אתה אומר הרי
זה אזהרה לגונב נפש או אינו אלא אזהרה לגונב
55 ממון כשהוא אומר לא תגנובו הרי אזהרה לגונב
ממון הא מה ת״ל לא תגנוב בגונב נפשות הכתוב
מדבר או הרי זה אזהרה לגונב ממון והלה אזהרה
לגונב נפש אמרת צא ולמד משלש עשרה מדות
שהתורה נדרשת בהן במה הכתוב מדבר וגו' ועוד
60 אמרת שלש מצות נאמרו בענין זה שתים מפורשות
ואחת סתומה נלמד סתומה ממפורשות מה
מפורשות מצוות שחייבין עליהן מיתות בית דין
אף סתומה מצוה שחייבין עליה מיתת בית דין הא
אין עליך לומר כלשון אחרון אלא כלשון ראשון
65 הרי זה אזהרה לגונב נפש והלה אזהרה לגונב ממון.

לא תענה ברעך וגו' למה נאמר לפי שהוא
אומר ועשיתם לו כאשר זמם לעשות לאחיו עונש

51—52 שמות כ״א, ט״ז. / ש. 112.　51—65 לקמן נזיקין ה'. סנהדרין פ״ו, א'. מ״ת 157.
55 ויקרא י״ט, י״א.　66—124 ש. 113—112.　68—66 ספרי דברים ק״צ. מכות ד', ב'.
מ״ת 24.　67 דברים י״ט, י״ט.

52 לא שמענו] ד. מנין.　53 והרי] א. מ. הרי.　54—53 אתה אומר הרי זה אזהרה
לגונב] ד. אתה אומר לגונב.　54 אלא אזהרה] ד. אלא.　55 הרי אזהרה] א. הרי זה.
57 והלה]=מ״ח. ש״י. א״צ: מ. נ. ל. ולא ק. ה. והלא.　59 שהתורה נדרשת בהן
במה הכתוב מדבר וגו'] מ. ד. > א״צ. דבר הלמד מעניינו ג. במה הכתוב מדבר דבר
הלמד מעניינו.　59—60 ועוד אמרת] מ״ח. א״צ. ש״י. < ט. ועוד אמר רבי.　60 מצות]
מ״ח. ~ עשה / זה] א. ט. ה. >.　65 והלה] מ. נ. ל. והלא.

to do unto his brother" (Deut. 19.19). We have thus heard the penalty for it but we have not heard the warning against it; therefore it says here: "Thou shalt not bear false witness," etc.

How were the Ten Commandments arranged? Five on the one tablet and five on the other. On the one tablet was written: "I am the Lord thy God." And opposite it on the other tablet was written: "Thou shalt not murder." This tells that if one sheds blood it is accounted to him as though he diminished the divine image. To give a parable: A king of flesh and blood entered a province and the people set up portraits of him, made images of him, and struck coins in his honor. Later on they upset his portraits, broke his images, and defaced his coins, thus diminishing the likenesses of the king. So also if one sheds blood it is accounted to him as though he had diminished the divine image. For it is said: "Whoso sheddeth man's blood . . . for in the image of God made He man" (Gen. 9.6). On the one tablet was written: "Thou shalt have no other god." And opposite it on the other tablet was written: "Thou shalt not commit adultery." This tells that if one worships idols it is accounted to him as though he committed adultery, breaking his covenant with God. For it is said: "Thou wife that committest adultery, that takest strangers instead of thy husband" (Ezek. 16.32). And it is also written: "And the Lord said unto me: 'Go yet, love a woman beloved of her friend and an adulteress,' " etc. (Hos. 3.1). On the one tablet was written: "Thou shalt not take." And opposite it on the other tablet was written: "Thou shalt not steal." This tells that he who steals will in the end also swear falsely. For it is said: "Will ye steal, murder and commit adultery and swear falsely" (Jer. 7.9). And it is also written: "Swearing and lying, and killing, and stealing, and committing adultery" (Hos. 4.2). On the one tablet was written: "Remember the sabbath day to keep it holy." And opposite it on the other tablet was written: "Thou shalt not bear false witness." This tells that if one profanes the Sabbath it is as though he testified in the presence of Him by whose word the world came into

שמענו אזהרה לא שמענו ת"ל לא תענה ברעך וגו'.
כיצד נתנו עשרת הדברות חמשה על לוח זה
וחמשה על לוח זה כתיב אנכי יי אלהיך וכנגדו כתיב
לא תרצח מגיד הכתוב שכל מי שהוא שופך דמים
מעלין עליו כאלו ממעט בדמות משל למלך בשר
ודם שנכנס למדינה והעמידו לו איקונות ועשו לו
צלמים וטבעו לו מטבעות לאחר זמן כיפו איקונותיו
ושברו צלמיו ופסלו מטבעותיו ומיעטו בדמותו
של מלך כך כל מי שהוא שופך דמים מעלין עליו
כאלו ממעט בדמות שנאמר שופך דם האדם וגו'
כי בצלם אלהים עשה את האדם. כתיב לא יהיה
לך וגו' וכנגדו כתיב לא תנאף מגיד הכתוב שכל
מי שהוא עובד עבודה זרה מעלין עליו כאלו מנאף
מאחר המקום שנאמר האשה המנאפת תחת אישה
תקח את זרים וכתיב ויאמר יי אלי עוד לך אהב
אשה אהובת רע ומנאפת וגו'. כתיב לא תשא וכנגדו
כתיב לא תגנוב מגיד הכתוב שכל מי שהוא גונב
סופו לבוא לידי שבועת שוא שנאמר הגנוב רצוח
ונאוף והשבע לשקר וגו' וכתיב אלה וכחש ורצח
וגנוב ונאוף. כתיב זכור את יום השבת לקדשו
וכנגדו כתיב לא תענה מגיד הכתוב שכל מי שהוא
מחלל את השבת כאלו מעיד לפני מי שאמר והיה

69—102 י' שקלים ו', א' (49d). שהש"ר ה', י"ד.   76—77 סנהדרין נ"ח, ב'.
78—77 בראשית ט', ו'.   82—81 יחזקאל ט"ז, ל"ב.   83—82 הושע ג', א'.   86—85 ירמיה
ז', ט'.   87—86 הושע ד', ב'.

---

70 כתיב] א. מ. מגיד הכתוב.   72 מעלין עליו] ד. מעלה עליו הכתוב / בדמות] ד. ~
המלך.   73 והעמידו] הגהתי=כ. (הושע ג', א'): א. מ. ד. והעמיד / איקונות] א. כ.
מ"ח. איקוניות / ועשו] ד. ועשה.   74 וטבעו] ל. וטבע / כיפו] ט"כ. כיסו ד. לו.
75 ושברו] ד. ~ לו / צלמיו] א. מ. ט. צלמותיו / ופסלו] ד. ובטלו לו.   76 מעלין
עליו] ד. ~ המלך.   77—78 וגו'—האדם] ד. <.
80 מעלין עליו] ד. מעלה עליו הכתוב.   81 מאחר] ד. אחר.   82—81 תחת אשה תקח
את זרים] הוספתי: א. מ. וגו' ק. תקח את זרים נ. ל. תחת אשה תקח זרים.   82 אלי]
ד. ט. אליו.   85 הגנוב] נ. ל. גנוב.   87—86 ורצח וגנב ונאוף] מ. וגו' א. ד. רצוח
וגנוב ונאוף.   89 כאלו] מ. ד. <.

being that He did not create the world in six days and did not rest on the seventh day. But he who keeps the Sabbath does testify in the presence of Him by whose word the world came into being that He did create the world in six days and did rest on the seventh, as it is said: "Ye are my witnesses, saith the Lord" (Isa. 43.10). On the one tablet was written: "Honour thy father," etc. And opposite it on the other tablet was written: "Thou shalt not covet thy neighbour's wife." This tells that he who covets will in the end beget a son who may curse his real father while giving filial honor to one who is not his father. It was for this that the Ten Commandments were arranged five on one tablet and five on the other.—These are the words of R. Ḥananiah, the son of Gamaliel. But the other sages say: All the ten were written on each of the two tablets. For it is said: "These words ... and He wrote them upon two tablets of stone," etc. (Deut. 5.19). And it also says: "Thy two breasts are like two fawns that are twins of a gazelle" (Cant. 4.5). And it also says: "His hands are as rods of gold set with beryl" (ibid., 5.14).

Thou Shalt Not Covet. Rabbi says: One passage says: "Thou shalt not covet"[3] and one passage says: "Thou shalt not desire" (Deut. 5.18). How are both these passages to be maintained? Behold the latter one is a prohibition against seeking opportunity to benefit by encouraging the adulterer.[4]

Thou Shalt Not Covet Thy Neighbour's House. This is a general statement. *Nor His Man-Servant, nor His Maid-Servant, nor His Ox, nor His Ass,* are specific. Now a general statement followed by a specific statement cannot include more than the specific statement. When it says however: *Nor Anything that is Thy Neighbour's,* it again makes a general statement. But perhaps the second general statement is to be

3. "To covet" was understood by the Rabbis to mean, actually to seek to obtain (see comment at the end of this chapter), while "to desire" was understood by them to mean, merely to wish for without actually seeking to acquire.

4. See Commentaries.

90 העולם שלא ברא עולמו לששה ימים ולא נח
בשביעי וכל מי שהוא משמר את השבת מעיד
לפני מי שאמר והיה העולם שברא עולמו לששה
ימים ונח בשביעי שנאמר ואתם עדי נאם יי וגו׳.
כתיב כבד את אביך וגו׳ וכנגדו כתיב לא תחמוד

95 מגיד הכתוב שכל מי שהוא חומד סוף שהוא מוליד
בן שהוא מקלל לאביו ומכבד למי שאינו אביו לכך
נתנו עשרת הדברות חמשה על לוח זה וחמשה על
לוח זה דברי רבי חנניה בן גמליאל וחכמים אומרים
עשרה על לוח זה ועשרה על לוח זה שנאמר את

100 הדברים האלה וגו׳ ויכתבם על שני לוחות אבנים
וגו׳ ואומר שני שדיך כשני עפרים תאומי צביה
ואומר ידיו גלילי זהב ממולאים בתרשיש.

לא תחמוד רבי אומר כתוב אחד אומר לא
תחמוד וכתוב אחד אומר לא תתאוה כיצד יתקיימו

105 שני כתובים הללו הרי זה אזהרה לעוקף מאחר
המנאף.

לא תחמוד בית רעך כלל עבדו ואמתו
שורו וחמורו פרט כלל ופרט אין בכלל אלא מה
שבפרט וכשהוא אומר וכל אשר לרעך חזר וכלל

---

93 ישעיה מ״ג, י״ב.   99 — 100 דברים ה׳, י״ט.   101 שה״ש ד׳, ה׳.   102 שם ה׳, י״ד.
104 דברים ה׳, י״ח.   106 — 105 שבועות מ״ז, ב׳.

---

90 שלא ברא] מ. שברא.   96 לאביו] ד. את אביו ואת אמו.   98 חנניה] ד. חנינא.
106 — 103 עיין ש״י. ומ״ע.   105 מאחר] ד. אחר.   108 — 107 עבדו ואמתו שורו] ד.
ועבדו ואמתו ושורו.

considered identical with the first general statement? You must say: It is not so. For when it makes the second general statement, we have a general statement followed by a specific statement and by another general statement, all of which must be interpreted as including only things similar to those mentioned in the specific statement.[5] Now in this case, the specific statement specifies things that one can buy and sell. Hence all things which one can buy and sell are to be included in the general statement. Perhaps however: Just as the specific statement specifies movable property not possessing the quality of serving as permanent surety, so also I can include in the general statement only movable property not possessing the quality of serving as permanent surety? But in Deuteronomy (5.21) it mentions in the specific statement: "His field."—Just as the specific statement specifies things which one can buy and sell, so also all things which one can buy and sell are included in the general statement. And just as the specific statement specifies things that can come into your possession only with the consent of the owner, so also in the general statement I can include only such things as can come into your possession only with the consent of the owner. Thus the case of your wishing his daughter for your son, or his son for your daughter is excluded.[6] Perhaps even the mere expressing of one's desire for the neighbor's things in words is also meant? But it says: "Thou shalt not covet the silver or the gold that is on them so that thou take it unto thee" (Deut. 7.25). Just as there only the carrying out of one's desire into practice is forbidden, so also here it is forbidden only to carry out the desire into practice.

---

5. See "Talmud Hermeneutics," *JE*, XII, 33.

6. The grown-up son or daughter can marry without the consent of the father.

אי כלל כלל הראשון אמרת לאו אלא חזר וכלל

כלל ופרט וכלל אין אתה דן אלא כעין הפרט

מה הפרט מפורש בדבר שהוא קונה ומקנה אף כל

דבר שהוא קונה ומקנה אי מה הפרט מפורש

בנכסים המטלטלין שאין להם אחריות אף אין לי

אלא נכסים המטלטלין שאין להם אחריות וכשהוא

אומר במשנה תורה שדהו מה הפרט מפורש בדבר

שהוא קונה ומקנה אף כל דבר שהוא קונה ומקנה

ומה הפרט מפורש בדבר שאי איפשר לבא

ברשותך אלא לרצון הבעלים אף אין לי אלא דבר

שאי איפשר לו לבא ברשותך אלא לרצון הבעלים

יצא שאתה חומד בתו לבנך או בנו לבתך או אפילו

חומד בדבור ת״ל לא תחמוד כסף וזהב עליהם

ולקחת לך מה להלן עד שיעשה מעשה אף כאן

עד שיעשה מעשה.

122 דברים ז׳, כ״ה. מ״ת 24.

---

110 אין] ש״י. או / כלל כלל] א. ג. כלל ככלל / אמרת לאו]=ג. ש״י. ה: א. ק. הרי
אמרת לאו נ. ל. הרי אמרת / חזר וכלל] ד. ~ כלל ופרט אין בכלל אלא מה שבפרט.
111 ופרט וכלל] מ. ופרט.   113—112 אף כל דבר] ד. אף כלל מפורש בדבר.
116—115 וכשהוא אומר במשנה תורה] א. מ. וכשהוא אומר על כורחך כתוב במשנה
תורה ה. וכשהוא אומר על כורחך אתה מת במשנה תורה.   116 שדהו] מ״ח. ~ על
כרחך.   117 אף כל דבר]=ט. ג. א״צ: א. מ. ד. אף אין לי אלא בדבר שהוא.
118 ומה] הגהתי=א״צ. ז״י: א. ד. אי מ. או / ומה הפרט מפורש] ש״י. .>   120 שאי
איפשר] א. שאיפשר.   121 יצא] א. יצאת מ. מצא.   122 בדבור] ק. בדבר מ. בדברים.

CHAPTER IX
(Ex. 20.15–19)

And All the People Saw the Thunderings. They saw what was visible and heard what was audible.—These are the words of R. Ishmael. R. Akiba says: They saw and heard that which was visible.[1] They saw the fiery word coming out from the mouth of the Almighty as it was struck upon the tablets, as it is said: "The voice of the Lord hewed out flames of fire" (Ps. 29.7).

And All the People Saw the Thunderings and the Lightnings, the thundering of thunders upon thunders and the lightning of lightnings upon lightnings. But how many thunderings were there and how many lightnings were there? It is simply this: They were heard by each man according to his capacity, as it is said: "The voice of the Lord was heard according to the strength" (Ps. 29.4). Rabbi says: This is to proclaim the excellence of the Israelites. For when they all stood before mount Sinai to receive the Torah they interpreted the divine word as soon as they heard it. For it is said: "He compassed it, he understood it,[2] and he kept it as the apple of his eye" (Deut. 32.10), meaning: As soon as the word came out they interpreted it. Another Interpretation: This is to proclaim the excellence of the Israelites, for when they all stood before mount Sinai to receive the Torah there were—so Scripture tells us—no blind ones among them. For it is said: "And all the people saw." It also tells that there were no dumb ones among them. For it is said: "And all the people answered together" (Ex. 19.8). And it also teaches that there were no deaf ones among them. For it is said: "All that the Lord hath spoken will we do and listen to" (ibid., 24.7). And it also teaches that there were no lame ones among them. For it is said: "And they stood at the nether part of the mount" (ibid., 19.17). And it also teaches that there were

1. See Commentaries.
2. This rendering is required by the *Mekilta* (cf. also *Shebut Yehudah*).

פרשה ט   (שמות כ׳, ט״ו—י״ט.)

וכל העם רואים את הקולות רואין את
הנראה ושומעין את הנשמע דברי רבי ישמעאל
רבי עקיבא אומר רואין ושומעין את הנראה ראו
דבר של אש יוצא מפי הגבורה ונחצב על הלוחות
שנאמר קול יי חוצב להבות אש.
וכל העם רואים את הקולות ואת
הלפידים קול קולי קולות ולפיד לפידי לפידים
וכמה קולות היו וכמה לפידים היו אלא שהיו
משמיעים את האדם לפי כחו שנאמר קול יי בכח.
רבי אומר להודיע שבחן של ישראל שכשעמדו
כולן לפני הר סיני לקבל את התורה היו שומעין
את הדיבור והיו מפרשים אותו שנאמר יסובבנהו
יבוננהו יצרנהו כאישון עינו שמכיון שהיה הדיבור
יוצא היו מפרשין אותו דבר אחר להודיע שבחן
של ישראל שכשעמדו כולן לפני הר סיני לקבל
את התורה מגיד שלא היה בהם סומים שנאמר וכל
העם רואים מגיד שלא היה בהם אילמים שנאמר
ויענו כל העם יחדו ומלמד שלא היה בהם חרשין
שנאמר כל אשר דבר יי נעשה ונשמע ומלמד שלא
היה בהם חגרים שנאמר ויתיצבו בתחתית ההר

3—1 מדרש שמואל ט׳, ד׳ (74). פדר״א מ״א.   5—3 ספרי דברים שמ״ג.   5 תהים
כ״ט, ז׳.   7—6 לעיל ג׳.   9—8 שמו״ר ה׳, ט׳; כ״ט, א׳.   9 תהלים כ״ט, ד׳.   14—10 ספרי
דברים שי״ג.   13—12 דברים ל״ב, י׳.   22—14 במד״ר ז׳, א׳. פס״ר ז׳ (כ״ח, א׳).   18 שמות
י״ט, ח׳.   19 שם כ״ד, ז׳.   20 שם י״ט, י״ז.

---

3 ראן] הגהתי=ט. א״א. ג: ל״ט. רואין א. מ. ד. ואין.   4 של אש יוצא] נ. ל.
שלא יצא.   6 וכל העם] כ. (תהלים כ״ט, כ״ז) דבר אחר וכל העם.   7—6 את הקולות
ואת הלפידים] הוספתי: א. וגו׳.   7 קול] ד. > / ולפיד] ד. >.   9 את האדם] ד. > אל
כל אדם.   10 רבי אומר] ט. < מ. מ״ח. ר׳ אומר ד. ר׳ אליעזר אומר / להודיע]
ט. ולהודיע.   16 מגיד שלא] נ. ל. ט. לא.   17 רואים מגיד] א״צ. מ״ח. רואים ומנין.
18 ומלמד] א״צ. מ״ח. ומנין.   19 ומלמד] ד. ומנין.

no fools among them. For it is said: "Thou hast been shown to understand" (Deut. 4.35). R. Nathan says: Whence can you prove that God showed to our father Abraham Gehenna, the giving of the Law, and the division of the Red Sea? From the passage: "And it came to pass, that, when the sun went down, and there was thick darkness, behold a smoking furnace, and a flaming torch that passed between these pieces" (Gen. 15.17). "A smoking furnace" refers to Gehenna, as it is said: "And His furnace in Jerusalem"[3] (Isa. 31.9). "And a flaming torch," refers to the giving of the Law, as it is said: "And all the people saw the thunderings and the lightnings." "That passed between these pieces," refers to the division of the Red Sea, as it is said: "To Him who divided the Red Sea into parts" (Ps. 136.13). He also showed him the Temple with the order of the sacrifices. For it is said: "And He said unto him: 'Take Me a heifer of three years old,'" etc. (Gen. 15.9). He also showed him the four kingdoms that would in the future oppress his children. For it is said: "And it came to pass, that, when the sun was going down, a deep sleep fell upon Abram, and, lo, a dread, even a great darkness, was falling upon him" (Gen. 15.12). "A dread," refers to the Babylonian Empire. "Darkness," refers to the empire of Media. "Great," refers to the Greek Empire. "Was falling," refers to the fourth empire, wicked Rome. There are some who reverse the order by saying: "Was falling," refers to the Babylonian Empire, as it is said: "Fallen, fallen is Babylon" (Isa. 21.9). "Great," refers to the empire of Media, as it is said: "King Ahasuerus made great" (Esth. 3.1). "Darkness," refers to the Greek Empire which caused the eyes of Israel to become dark from fasting.[4] "A dread," refers to the fourth kingdom, as it is said: "Dreadful and terrible and strong exceedingly" (Dan. 7.7).

---

3. This passage was interpreted as referring to one of the three entrances to Gehenna (see 'Er. 19a).

4. See Introduction and cf. Commentaries.

ומלמד שלא היה בהם טיפשים שנאמר אתה הראת
לדעת רבי נתן אומר מנין אתה אומר שהראה
המקום לאברהם אבינו גיהנם ומתן תורה וקריעת
ים סוף שנאמר ויהי השמש באה ועלטה היה והנה
תנור עשן ולפיד אש אשר עבר בין הגזרים האלה 25
תנור עשן זה גיהנם שנאמר ותנור לו בירושלים ולפיד
אש זה מתן תורה שנאמר וכל העם רואים את
הקולות ואת הלפידים אשר עבר בין הגזרים האלה
זה קריעת ים סוף שנאמר לגוזר ים סוף לגזרים
הראהו בית המקדש וסדר קרבנות שנאמר ויאמר 30
אליו קחה לי עגלה משולשת וגו' הראהו ארבע
מלכיות שהן עתידין לשעבד את בניו שנאמר ויהי
השמש לבוא ותרדמה נפלה על אברם והנה אימה
חשכה גדולה נופלת עליו אימה זו מלכות בבל
חשכה זו מלכות מדי גדולה זו מלכות יון נופלת 35
זו מלכות רביעית רומי חייבתא. ויש מחליפין
בדבר נופלת זו מלכות בבל שנאמר נפלה נפלה
בבל גדולה זו מלכות מדי שנאמר גדל המלך
אחשורוש חשכה זו מלכות יון שהחשיכה את
עיניהם של ישראל בתענית אימה זו מלכות 40
רביעית שנאמר דחילא ואימתני ותקיפא יתירא.

21 — 22 דברים ד', ל"ה.   36 — 22 שמו"ר נ"א, ז'.   25 — 24 בראשית ט"ו, י"ז.   26 ישעיה
ל"א, ט'.   31 — 30 בראשית ט"ו, ט'.   41 — 31 ב"ר מ"ד, י"ז. וי"ר י"ג, ה'.   34 — 32 בראשית
ט"ו, י"ב.   38 — 37 ישעיה כ"א, ט'.   39 — 38 אסתר ג', א'.   41 דניאל ז', ז'.

21 ומלמד מ"ח. ומנין.   25 — 24 והנה תנור—הגזרים האלה] הוספתי: א. מ. וגו'.
32 את בניו] מ. מ"ח. בבניו.   38 — 35 גדולה זו—נפלה בבל] א. >.   36 רומי חייבתא]
מ. >.   40 בתענית] מ"ח. > א"צ. בצרות.

And When the People Saw It They Trembled. "Trembling" everywhere means only reeling to and fro, as it is said: "The earth reeleth to and fro," etc. (Isa. 24.20).

And Stood Afar Off. Beyond twelve miles. This tells that the Israelites were startled and moved backward twelve miles and then again, returning, moved forward twelve miles—twenty-four miles at each commandment, thus covering two hundred and forty miles on that day—. Then God said to the ministering angels: Go down and assist your brothers, as it is said: "The angels of Zebaot lead,[5] they lead" (Ps. 68.13)—they lead them when going, they lead them when returning. And not only the ministering angels assisted Israel, but the Holy One, blessed be He, Himself also, as it is said: "His left hand is under my head and His right hand embraces me" (Cant. 2.6). R. Judah b. Il'ai says: As the Israelites were scorched by the heat of the fire from above, the Holy One, blessed be He, said to the clouds of glory: Drop the dew of life[6] upon My children, as it is said: "Lord, when Thou didst go forth out of Seir, when thou didst march out of the field of Edom, the earth trembled, the heavens also dropped" (Judg. 5.4), and it also says: "A bounteous rain didst Thou pour down, O God" (Ps. 68.10). When was all this honor done her? When she was the most beautiful among the nations and showed appreciation of the Torah, as it is said: "And she that tarrieth at home taketh as her share the spoil"[7] (ibid., v. 13). For the "spoil" is nothing else

5. This rendering is required by the *Mekilta,* which interprets מלכי צבאות as if it read מלאכי צבאות.

6. I. e., the life–giving dew, the dew which will also be used in the future to revive the dead at the time of the resurrection (Shab. 88b). This dew is stored up in one of the heavens, *Arabot* (see Ḥag. 12b).

7. This rendering is required by the *Mekilta.* "She that tarrieth at home," is taken to refer to Israel. By a play on the word נות, deriving it from נאה, the *Mekilta* finds Israel described in this verse as the most beautiful in the family of the nations. The other nations refused to accept the Torah but Israel did accept the Torah as her share.

וירא **העם** **וינועו** אין נוע בכל מקום
אלא זיע שנאמר נוע תנוע הארץ וגו׳.

ויעמדו **מרחוק** חוץ לשנים עשר מיל מגיד
45 שהיו ישראל נרתעים לאחוריהם שנים עשר מיל
וחוזרין לפניהם שנים עשר מיל עשרים וארבעה
מיל על כל דיבור ודיבור נמצאו מהלכים באותו
היום מאתים וארבעים מיל באותה שעה אמר
הקב״ה למלאכי השרת רדו וסייעו את אחיכם
50 שנאמר מלכי צבאות ידודון ידודון ידודון בהליכה
וידודון בחזרה ולא מלאכי השרת בלבד אלא
אף הקב״ה שנאמר שמאלו תחת לראשי וימינו
תחבקני רבי יהודה ברבי אלעאי אומר לפי שהיו
ישראל משולהבין מחמת האש של מעלה אמר
55 הקב״ה לענני הכבוד הזילו טל חיים על בני שנאמר
יי בצאתך משעיר בצעדך משדה אדום ארץ רעשה
גם שמים נטפו ואומר גשם נדבות תניף אלהים אימתי
נעשה כל הכבוד הזה בשעה שהיתה נאה שבאומות
ומכבדת את התורה שנאמר ונות בית תחלק שלל

42—48 ש. 114—113. 46—42 לעיל ב׳. 43 ישעיה כ״ד, כ׳.
57—44 תוס׳ ערכין א׳, י׳. 51—48 שבת פ״ח, ב׳. 50 תהלים ס״ח, י״ג. 53—52 שה״ש
ב׳, ו׳. 57—56 שופטים ה׳, ד׳. 57 תהלים ס״ח, י. 59 תהלים שם י״ג.

42 בכל מקום] ד. >. 43 הארץ] במקרא כתוב ארץ. 46 עשרים] ד. הרי עשרים.
50 מלכי] מ. מלאכי. 51 ידודון] א. לראשי מ. ראשי. 54 מחמת האש] ד. מחמה.
56—55 שנאמר—משעיר] ק. נ. שנאמר ארץ רעשה גם שמים נטפו מפני אלהים וגו׳
(תהלים ס״ח, ט׳. במקרא שם כתוב אף שמים). 57—56 בצעדך—נטפו] הוספתי: א.
מ. וגו׳. 58 שבאומות] מ. > כ. (תהלים, ס״ח, י״ח) בין האומות. 59 ומכבדת] כ.
(שם) וקבלה.

but the Torah, as when it is said: "I rejoice at Thy word as one that findeth great spoil" (Ps. 119.162).

And They Said unto Moses: 'Speak Thou with Us and We Will Hear.' This tells that they did not have the strength to receive more than the Ten Commandments, as it is said: "If we hear the voice of the Lord our God any more, then we shall die" (Deut. 5.22). But: "Go thou near and hear" (ibid., v. 24). From that time on the Israelites merited that prophets should be raised among them, as it is said: "I will raise thee up a prophet" (Deut. 18.18).—I was going to raise up a prophet from among them in the future but by their merits they brought it about sooner. For it is said: "And the Lord said unto me: 'They have well said that which they have spoken' " (ibid., v. 17). Happy the people whose words God has approved! Likewise it says: "The daughters of Zelophehad speak right" (Num. 27.7). "The tribe of the sons of Joseph speaketh right" (ibid., 36.5). Happy the people whose words God has approved! Likewise it says: "I have pardoned according to thy word" (ibid. 14.20).—It is as you say. The nations of the world are bound to talk thus.—Happy the man whose words God has approved! *Oh that They Had Such a Heart as This Alway, to Fear Me, and Keep All My Commandments, that It Might Be Well with Them, and with Their Children for Ever* (Deut. 5.26). If it were possible to do away with the Angel of Death I would. But the decree has long ago been decreed. R. Jose says: It was upon this condition that the Israelites stood up before mount Sinai, on condition that the Angel of Death should have no power over them.[8] For it is said: "I said: Ye are godlike beings," etc. (Ps. 82.6). But you corrupted your conduct. "Surely ye shall die like men" (ibid., v. 7).

And Moses Said unto the People: 'Fear Not.' Behold! Moses is rallying them. This is to proclaim the wisdom of Moses, how he stood there pacifying all those thousands and myriads. Of him it is stated in

8. See Introduction.

60 ואין שלל אלא תורה שנאמר שש אנכי על אמרתך
כמוצא שלל רב. **ויאמרו אל משה דבר אתה עמנו
ונשמעה** מגיד שלא היה בהם כח לקבל יותר
מעשרת הדברות שנאמר אם יוספים אנחנו לשמוע
65 את יי אלהינו עוד ומתנו אלא קרב אתה ושמע וגו'
מאותה שעה זכו ישראל להעמיד מהם נביאים
שנאמר נביא אקים להם וגו' נביא עתיד אני להעמיד
מהם אלא שקדמו הם בזכות שנאמר ויאמר יי אלי
היטיבו אשר דברו אשרי בני אדם שהמקום הודה
70 לדבריהם וכן הוא אומר כן בנות צלפחד דוברות
כן מטה בני יוסף דוברים אשרי בני אדם שהמקום
הודה לדבריהם וכן הוא אומר סלחתי כדבריך
כדברך עתידין אומות העולם לומר אשרי אדם
שהמקום הודה לדבריו. **מי יתן והיה לבבם
75 זה להם** וגו' כל הימים וגו' אלו איפשר להעביר
מלאך המות הייתי מעבירו אלא שכבר נגזרה גזירה
רבי יוסי אומר על תנאי כך עמדו ישראל לפני
הר סיני על תנאי שלא ישלוט בהם מלאך המות
שנאמר אני אמרתי אלהים אתם וגו' חבלתם
80 מעשיכם אכן כאדם תמותון. **ויאמר משה אל העם אל תיראו** הרי
משה מזרזן להודיע חכמתו של משה היאך היה
עומד ומפייס כל אותם האלפים וכל אותן הרבבות

61 — 60 שם קי"ט, קס"ב. 62 — 64 לעיל ד'. שהש"ר א', ב'. 65 — 64 דברים ה', כ"ב. 65 שם ה', כ"ד. 66 — 74 מ"ת 111. 67 דברים י"ח, י"ח; ספרי דברים קע"ו. 74 — 67 ספרי במדבר קל"ד. 69 — 68 דברים י"ח, י"ז. 70 במדבר כ"ז, ז'. 71 שם ל"ז, ה'. 72 שם י"ד, כ'. 75 — 74 דברים ה', כ"ו. 80 — 75 ע"ז ה', א'. 79 — 80 תהלים פ"ב, ו' — ז'. 85 — 81 לעיל ויהי בשלח ג'.

63 — 64 יותר מעשרת] ט. אלא עשרת ז"י. (בשם ט.) עשרת. 65 — 64 לשמוע — ומתנו] א. מ. ט. וגו' לא אוסף לשמוע את קול יי וגו' (דברים י"ח, ט"ז). 66 להעמיד] מ"ח. שהעמיד א. ד. ~ המקום. 72 — 70 וכן הוא אומר — לדבריהם] מ. ~. 74 — 73 כדברך — לדבריו] נ. ל. ~. 73 כדברך] ק. מ"ח. < / עתידין] מ. ק. < / לומר] מ. ק. שואלים לומר. 76 — 75 אלו איפשר — היית מעבירו אלא] ק. אלו בני אדם שאי איפשר מלאך המות להיות מעבירו מ"ח. אלו איפשר להעביר מלאך המות שנאמר אני אמרתי אלקים אתם היית מעבירו אלא. 78 על תנאי שלא] נ. ל. על תנאי כך עמדו על הר סיני שלא מ"ח. ש"י. שלא. 79 — 80 חיבלתם מעשיכם] ד. <.

the traditional sacred writing: "Wisdom is a stronghold to the wise man more than ten rulers," etc. (Eccl. 7.19).

For God Is Come to Prove You. God has come in order to make you great among the nations.

And that His Fear May Be Before You. "His fear," that is, bashfulness. It is a good sign in a man if he is bashful.

That Ye Sin Not. This tells that bashfulness leads one to the fear of sin, as it is said: "They shall be put to shame because they have committed abomination; yea, they are not at all ashamed" (Jer. 6.15).

And the People Stood Afar Off. Those twelve miles.[9] This indicates that the camp of the Israelites extended over twelve miles. But how do we know that the camp of the Israelites extended over twelve miles? It says: "And they pitched by the Jordan, from Beth-jeshimoth even unto Abel-shittim" (Num. 33.49). And from Beth-jeshimoth to Abel-shittim is a distance of twelve miles.

But Moses Drew Near unto the Thick Darkness. What brought him this distinction? His meekness. For it is said: "Now the man Moses was very meek" (ibid., 12.3). Scripture tells that whosoever is meek will cause the Shekinah to dwell with man on earth, as it is said: "For thus saith the High and Lofty One that inhabiteth eternity, whose name is Holy: I dwell in the high and holy place, with him also that is of a contrite and humble spirit" (Isa. 57.15). And it also says: "The spirit of the Lord God is upon me; because the Lord hath anointed me to bring good tidings unto the humble" (ibid., 61.1). And it also says: "For all these things hath My hand made . . . but on this man will I look, even on him that is poor and of a contrite spirit" (ibid., 66.2). And it also says: "The sacrifices of God are a broken spirit; a broken and contrite heart, O God, Thou wilt not despise" (Ps. 51.19). But whosoever is proud of heart causes the land to be defiled and the Shekinah to withdraw, as it is said: "Whoso is haughty of eye and proud of heart, him will I not suffer" (ibid., 101.5). Furthermore,

---

9. This refers to the comment above on v. 15.

עליו מפורש בקבלה החכמה תעוז לחכם מעשרה
שליטים.

85

כי לבעבור נסות אתכם בשביל לגדל
אתכם בין האומות בא האלהים.
ובעבור תהיה יראתו על פניכם
יראתו זו בושה סימן טוב באדם שהוא ביישן.

לבלתי תחטאו מגיד שהבושה מביאה לידי

90

יראת חטא שנאמר הובישו כי תועבה עשו גם בוש
לא יבושו.

ויעמד העם מרחוק אלו שנים עשר מיל
מגיד שהיה מחנה של ישראל שנים עשר מיל ומנין
שהיה מחנה של ישראל שנים עשר מיל שנאמר

95

ויחנו על הירדן מבית הישימות עד אבל השטים
ומבית הישימות עד אבל השטים שנים עשר מיל.

ומשה נגש אל הערפל מי גרם לו ענותנותו
שנאמר והאיש משה ענו מאד מגיד הכתוב שכל
מי שהוא עניו סופו להשרות שכינה עם האדם בארץ

100

שנאמר כי כה אמר רם ונשא שוכן עד וקדוש שמו
מרום וקדוש אשכון ואת דכא ושפל רוח ואומר
רוח יי אלהים עלי יען משח יי אותי לבשר ענוים
ואומר ואת כל אלה ידי עשתה וגו' ואל זה אביט
אל עני ונכה רוח ואומר זבחי אלהים רוח נשברה

105

לב נשבר ונדכה אלהים לא תבזה וכל מי שהוא
גבה לב גורם לטמא את הארץ ולסלק את השכינה
שנאמר גבה עינים ורחב לבב אותו לא אוכל וכל

84 — 85 קהלת ז', י"ט.   88 — 92 נדרים כ', א'.   92 — 91 ירמיה ו', ט"ו.   96 במדבר
ל"ג, מ"ט.   97 — 96 יומא ע"ה, ב'.   99 במדבר י"ב, ג'.   102 — 101 ישעיה נ"ז, ט"ו.
103 שם ס"א, א'.   105 — 104 שם ס"ו, ב'.   106 — 105 תהלים נ"א, י"ט.   113 — 106 סוטה
ד', ב'—ה', א.   108 תהלים ק"א, ה'.

84 החכמה] א. ט. והחכמה.   87 בין האומות] ד. > מ. בין אומות העולם ט. ~ כנס
הזה של ספינה.   89 בושה] ד. בשת פנים.   93 ויעמד] ק. נ. ויעמדו.   94 מגיד שהיה]
מ"ח. ג. שהיה א"צ. כנגד.   95 — 94 ומנין—שנאמר] ט. וכן הוא אומר.   96 עד אבל
השטים] א. וגו' ד. >.   97 ומבית הישימות—עד אבל השטים] הוספתי=א"א.
99 — 98 ושמה—מגיד] א. <.   99 הכתוב] א. ~ מדבר.   100 מין] ד. < מ"ח. ומי /
סופו] מ. עתיד / האדם] מ. בני אדם.   101 אמר] ד. ~ יי.   102 מרום—ושפל רוח]
מ. ד. וגו' / ואת דכא] א. את מי את דכא.   103 אלהים] ק. נ. < / יי—ענוים] הוספתי:
א. וגו'.   104 ואת] מ. את.   105 — 104 ואל זה—ונכה רוח] הוספתי.   108 לבב] ק.
נ. לב.

one who is proud of heart is designated an abomination, as it is said: "Everyone that is proud in heart is an abomination of the Lord" (Prov. 16.5). Idols are also designated an abomination, as it is said: "And thou shalt not bring an abomination into thy house" (Deut. 7.26). Hence, just as idolatry defiles the land and causes the Shekinah to withdraw, so he who is proud of heart causes the earth to become defiled and the Shekinah to withdraw.

But Moses Drew Near unto the Thick Darkness. Past the three divisions: darkness, cloud and thick darkness. On the outside was darkness, inside of it cloud, and inside of the latter thick darkness. For it is said: "But Moses drew near unto the thick darkness," etc.

And the Lord Said unto Moses: Thus Thou Shalt Say unto the Children of Israel. In the language in which I speak to you you shall speak to My children, in the holy tongue. Wherever the expression "thus" (*ko*) "so" (*kakah*) or "answer and say" (*'Aniyyah ve-amirah*) is used, it means in the holy tongue.

Ye Yourselves Have Seen. There is a difference between that which a man sees and that about which others tell him. For about that which others tell him he may have doubts in his mind. Here, however, "Ye yourselves have seen." R. Nathan says: *Ye Yourselves Have Seen.* Why is this said? Since it says: "All the kings of the earth shall give Thee thanks, O Lord, for they have heard the words of Thy mouth" (Ps. 138.4), one might think that just as they heard they also saw; therefore it says: "Ye have seen"—but the nations of the world have not seen.

That I Have Talked with You from Heaven. One passage says: "That I have talked with you from heaven," and another passage says: "And the Lord came down upon mount Sinai" (Ex. 19.20). How can both these passages be maintained? The matter is decided by the third passage: "Out of heaven He made thee to hear His voice, that He might instruct thee; and upon earth He made thee to see His great fire" (Deut. 4.36).—These are the words of R. Ishmael. R. Akiba says:

גבה לבב קרוי תועבה שנאמר תועבת יי כל גבה
לב עבודה זרה קרויה תועבה שנאמר ולא תביא
תועבה אל ביתך כשם שעבודה זרה מטמאה את
הארץ ומסלקת את השכינה כך כל מי שהוא גבה
לב גורם לטמא את הארץ ולסלק את השכינה.
ומשה נגש אל הערפל לפנים משלשה
מחיצות חשך ענן וערפל חשך מבחוץ ענן מבפנים
וערפל מלפני ולפנים שנאמר ומשה נגש אל הערפל
וגו'.

**ויאמר יי אל משה כה תאמר אל בני
ישראל** בלשון שאני אומר לך בו תדבר אל בניי
בלשון הקודש כל מקום שנאמר כה ככה ענייה
ואמירה הרי זה בלשון הקודש.
אתם ראיתם יש הפרש בין מה שאדם רואה
בין מה שאחרים משיחין לו שכשאחרים משיחין
לו פעמים שלבו חלוק אבל כאן אתם ראיתם רבי
נתן אומר אתם ראיתם למה נאמר לפי שהוא אומר
יודוך יי כל מלכי ארץ כי שמעו אמרי פיך יכול
כשם ששמעו כך ראו ת"ל אתם ראיתם אבל לא
ראו אומות העולם.
כי מן השמים דברתי עמכם כתוב
אחד אומר כי מן השמים וגו' וכתוב אחר אומר וירד
יי על הר סיני וגו' כיצד יתקיימו שני מקראות הללו
הכריע השלישי מן השמים השמיעך את קולו ליסרך
ועל הארץ הראך את אשו הגדולה דברי רבי
ישמעאל רבי עקיבא אומר מלמד שהרכין הקב"ה

110 — 109 משלי ט"ז, ה'.	111 — 110 דברים ז', כ"ו.	117 — 114 לעיל ב'. ש. 114. מ"ת
158.	124 — 118 לעיל ב'.	120 — 119 ש. שם.	127 — 125 ספרי דברים שמ"ג.
126 תהלים קל"ח, ד'.	137 — 129 לעיל ד'. ש. שם, ברייתא דר"י ת"כ (a3).

110 עבודה זרה] ט. ט"ב. ועבודה זרה.	113 — 112 כך כל מי—ולסלק את השכינה] ד.
>.	119 לך בו תדבר אל בניי] ד. כה תאמר אל בני ישראל.	121 — 120 כל מקום—בלשון
הקודש] א. >.	122 יש]=ג. כ. (תהלים קל"ח, ג')=: א. ד. > / מה]=ג. כ. מ"ח. ל"ט:
א. מ. ד. >.	133 — 132 ליסרך ועל הארץ הראך את אשו הגדולה] מ. ד. ליסרך א.
וגו' ועפי"ז הוספתי.

Scripture teaches that the Holy One, blessed be He, lowered the upper heavens of heaven down to the top of the mountain and thus actually still spoke to them from the heavens. And thus it says: "He bowed the heavens also, and came down; and thick darkness was under His feet" (Ps. 18.10). Rabbi says: *And the Lord Came Down upon Mount Sinai,* etc. I might understand this literally, but you must reason: If the sun, one of the many servants of servants, remains in its place and yet is effective beyond its place, how much the more the glory of Him by whose word the world came into being.

CHAPTER X
(Ex. 20.20)

Ye Shall Not Make with Me. R. Ishmael says: Ye shall not make a likeness of My servants who serve before Me in heaven, not the likeness of angels, not the likeness of the cherubim, and not the likeness of the *ophannim.* R. Nathan says: *Ye Shall Not Make Me.* Lest you say: I am going to make some sort of a representation of God and thus worship Him, Scripture says: "Ye shall not make me."[1] And so it also says: "Take ye therefore good heed unto yourselves—for ye saw no manner of form" (Deut. 4.15). R. Akiba says: *Ye Shall Not Do with Me.* Ye shall not behave towards Me in the manner in which others behave toward their deities. When good comes to them they honor their gods, as it is said: "Therefore they sacrifice unto their net," etc. (Hab. 1.16). But when evil comes to them they curse their gods, as it is said: "And it shall come to pass that when they shall be hungry they shall fret themselves and curse their king and their god" (Isa. 8.21). But ye, if I bring good upon you, give ye thanks, and when I bring suffering upon you, give ye thanks. And thus David says: "I will

---

1. The word אתי is interpreted as if it read אותי @vowels@, "Me."

שמי השמים העליונים על ראש ההר ודבר עמהן 135
מן השמים וכן הוא אומר ויט שמים וירד וערפל
תחת רגליו רבי אומר וירד יי על הר סיני וגו׳ שומע
אני כשמועו אמרת ומה אם אחד משמשי שמשין
הרי הוא במקומו ושלא במקומו קל וחומר לכבודו
של מי שאמר והיה העולם. 140

פרשה י (שמות כ׳–כ׳.)

לא תעשון אתי רבי ישמעאל אומר לא
תעשון דמות שמשיי המשמשין לפני במרום לא
דמות מלאכים ולא דמות כרובים ולא דמות אופנים
רבי נתן אומר לא תעשון אתי שלא תאמר הרי אני
עושה כמין דמות ומשתחוה לו ת״ל לא תעשון אתי 5
וכן הוא אומר ונשמרתם מאד לנפשותיכם כי לא
ראיתם כל תמונה רבי עקיבא אומר לא תעשון אתי
שלא תנהגו בי כדרך שאחרים נוהגין ביראותיהן
כשהטובה באה עליהן הם מכבדין את אלהיהם
שנאמר על כן יזבח לחרמו וגו׳ וכשהפורענות באה 10
עליהן הם מקללין את אלהיהם שנאמר והיה כי
ירעב והתקצף וקלל במלכו ובאלהיו אבל אתם
אם הבאתי עליכם את הטובה תנו הודאה הבאתי
עליכם את הייסורין תנו הודאה וכן דוד אומר כוס

131–130 שמות י״ט, כ׳.   133–132 דברים ד׳, ל״ו.   137–136 תהלים י״ח, י׳.
3–1 לעיל ו׳. ע״ז מ״ג, א׳–ב׳. ש. 115.   5–4 ע״ז שם.   7–6 דברים ד׳, ט״ו.
10 חבקוק א׳, ט״ז.   12–11 ישעיה ח׳, כ״א.   17–13 ברכות ס׳, ב׳; י׳ שם ט׳, ז׳ (14b).
86–13 ספרי דברים ל״ב.   15–14 תהלים קט״ז, י״ג.

---

135 שמי] ד. >.   136 וכן הוא אומר] ד. שנאמר.   138 כשמועו] כתב תמים באוצר
נחמד חוברת שלישית צד 61, התחתונים והיו העליונים ריקנים.   139 במקומו]=ג. כתב
תמים שם. ל״ט] ד. או במקומו / ושלא במקומו ל״ט.
5 עושה] מ״ח. ~ לו / לו] א. ט. לה.   7–5 לא תעשון—כל תמונה] ד. לא תעשו
לכם ושמרתם מאד.   5 אתי] ט. ט״ב. ש״י. אותי.   8 שלא תנהגו בי] ד. < / נוהגין]
מ. ד. ונהגין / ביראותיהן] ד. במדינות ט. במדינות ג. באלהיהם ג. בו במדינות ראיתם.   9 כשהטובה]
א. מ. שכשהטובה.   12–11 כי ירעב] א. מ. כאשר ירעב.   12 אתם] ד. >.   13–14 אם
הבאתי—תנו הודאה] ד. אם אביא עליהם הטובה יתנו הודאה ואם אביא עליהם יסורין
יתנו הודאה.

lift up the cup of salvation, and call upon the name of the Lord" (Ps. 116.13). "I found trouble and sorrow, but I called upon the name of the Lord" (ibid., vv. 3–4). And so also Job says: "The Lord gave and the Lord hath taken away, blessed be the name of the Lord" (Job 1.21)—for the measure of goodness and also for the measure of trouble. What does his wife say to him? "Dost thou still hold fast thine integrity?" etc. (ibid., 2.9). And what does he say to her? "Thou speakest as one of the impious women speaketh" (ibid., v. 10). The people of the generation of the Flood acted unbecomingly when it was well with them. Yet when the punishment came upon them, they accepted it in spite of themselves. The people of Sodom acted unbecomingly when it was well with them. Yet when the punishment came upon them, they accepted it in spite of themselves. We who were decent when in prosperity, shall we not continue to be so even when we are in trouble? This is what he meant by saying to her: "Thou speakest as one of the impious women speaketh. What? shall we receive good at the hand of God, and shall we not receive evil?" (ibid.). Furthermore, a man should even rejoice when in adversity more than when in prosperity. For even if a man lives in prosperity all his life, it does not mean that his sins have been forgiven him. But what is it that does bring a man forgiveness? You must say, suffering. R. Eliezer the son of Jacob says: Behold it says: "My son, despise not the chastening of the Lord" (Prov. 3.11).—Why? "For whom the Lord loveth He correcteth," etc. (ibid., v. 12). You must reason: Go out and see what was it that made this son become a delight to his father? You must say, suffering. R. Meir says: "And thou shalt consider in thy heart, that, as a man chasteneth his son," etc. (Deut. 8.5). You should consider in your mind the deeds you have done as well as the sufferings I caused to come upon you. For the sufferings I brought upon you are not at all commensurate with the deeds you have done. R. Jose the son of R. Judah says: Precious are chastisements, for the name of God rests upon him to whom chastisements come, as it is

ישועות אשא ובשם יי אקרא צרה ויגון אמצא ובשם

יי אקרא וכן איוב אומר יי נתן ויי לקח יהי שם יי

מבורך על מדת הטוב ועל מדת הפורענות מה

אשתו אומרת לו עודך מחזיק בתומתך וגו' ומה

הוא אומר לה כדבר אחת הנבלות תדברי אנשי

דור המבול שהיו כעורין בטובה וכשבאה עליהם

הפורענות קבלו עליהן על כרחן אנשי סדום שהיו

כעורין בטובה וכשבאת עליהן הפורענות קבלו

אותה על כרחן ואנו שהיינו נאים בטובה לא נהא

נאים בפורענות זהו שאמר לה כדבר אחת הנבלות

תדברי גם את הטוב נקבל מאת האלהים ואת הרע

לא נקבל ועוד שיהא אדם שמח ביסורין יותר מן

הטובה שאפילו אדם בטובה כל ימיו אינו נמחל

לו מן העבירות שבידו ומי מוחל לו הוי אומר

היסורין רבי אליעזר בן יעקב אומר הרי הוא אומר

מוסר יי בני אל תמאס וגו' מפני מה כי את אשר

יאהב יי יוכיח וגו' אמרת צא וראה מי גרם לבן

זה לרצות את האב הוי אומר יסורין רבי מאיר

אומר וידעת עם לבבך כי כאשר ייסר איש את בנו

וגו' יהי לבך יודע מעשים שעשית ויסורין שהבאתי

עליך שלא לפי מעשיך הבאתי עליך את היסורין

רבי יוסי בן רבי יהודה אומר חביבין הן יסורין

ששמו של מקום חל על מי שהיסורין באין עליו

---

15 — שם קט"ז, ג'—ד'.   17 — 16 איוב א', כ"א.   18 שם ב', ט'.   19 שם ב', י'.

19 — ב"ר י"ט, י"ב.   30 משלי ג', י"א.   31—30 שם ג', י"ב.   33 דברים ח', ה'.

---

16 — צרה ויגון—אקרא]=ט. מ"ח. ג: א. וגו' ד. ›.   19 — 18 ומה הוא אומר לה]
ד. וכן הוא משיב.   19 אנשי] מ"ח. אמר אנשי ד. ואנשי.   20 כעורין] מ. כאורין נ.
ל. כעוררין.   23—21 אנשי סדום—על כרחן] ד. ›.   24—23 נהא נאים] ד. נהיה ט.
נאה ט"כ. נהא.   24 זהו שאמר לה] ד. לפיכך אמר.   26—25 גם את הטוב—הרע לא
נקבל] הוספתי: א. וגו'.   26 שיהא] ט. מ"ח. יהא.   27 שאפילו] מ"ח. שאם / אדם]
ד. ~ עומד.   28 מן] ד. ›.   29 אליעזר] מ"ח. אלעזר / בן יעקב] ד. מ"ח. ›.   32 מאיר]
ד. ›.   33 כי כאשר ייסר איש את בנו] א. ›.   34—38 יהי לבך—אלהיך מיסרך] ד.
›.   34 שהבאתי] מ"ח. שהבאת.   37 חל על מין] מ. חלכו, אולי צ"ל חל בו.

said: "The Lord thy God chasteneth thee"[2] (ibid.). R. Jonathan says: Precious are chastisements, for just as a covenant was established concerning the land so also a covenant is established by means of chastisements. For it is said: "The Lord thy God chasteneth thee" (ibid.). And it is also written: "For the Lord thy God bringeth thee into a good land" (ibid., v. 7). R. Simon b. Joḥai says: Precious are chastisements, for the three good gifts given to Israel which the nations of the world covet were all given only at the price of chastisements. And they are these: the Torah, the land of Israel, and the future world. How do we know it about the Torah? It is said: "To know wisdom and chastisement" (Prov. 1.2). And it says: "Happy is the man whom Thou chastenest, O Lord, and teachest out of Thy law" (Ps. 94.12). How do we know it about the land of Israel? It is said: "The Lord thy God chasteneth thee" (Deut. 8.5). And following it it says: "For the Lord thy God bringeth thee into a land" (ibid., v. 7). How do we know it about the future world? It is said: "For the commandment is a lamp and the teaching is light and reproofs by chastisement are the way to life" (Prov. 6.23). You interpret it thus: Go out and see which is the way that brings man to the life of the future world? You must say: Chastisements. R. Nehemiah says: Precious are chastisements. For just as sacrifices are the means of atonement, so also are chastisements. What does it say about sacrifices? "And it shall be accepted for him to make atonement" (Lev. 1.4). And what does it say in connection with chastisements? "And they shall be paid[3] the punishment of their iniquity" (ibid., 26.43). And not only this, but chastisements atone even more than sacrifices. For sacrifices affect only one's money, while chastisements affect the body. And thus it says: "Skin for skin, yea, all that a man hath will he give for his life" (Job. 2.4).

2. This verse suggests that God is called the God of him who is being chastened.

3. The root of the Hebrew word for "be accepted," ונרצה, is the same as that of the word for "shall be paid," ירצו.

שנאמר יי אלהיך מיסרך רבי יונתן אומר חביבין
הן יסורין שכשם שברית כרותה לארץ כך ברית
כרותה ליסורין שנאמר יי אלהיך מיסרך וכתיב
כי יי אלהיך מביאך אל ארץ טובה רבי שמעון
בן יוחאי אומר חביבין הן יסורין ששלש מתנות
טובות נתנו להן לישראל ואומות העולם מתאוין
להן ולא נתנו להם אלא ביסורין ואלו הן תורה
וארץ ישראל ועולם הבא תורה מנין שנאמר לדעת
חכמה ומוסר וגו' ואומר אשרי הגבר אשר תיסרנו
יה ומתורתך תלמדנו ארץ ישראל מנין שנאמר
יי אלהיך מיסרך ואומר כי יי אלהיך מביאך אל
ארץ טובה העולם הבא מנין שנאמר כי נר מצוה
ותורה אור ודרך חיים תוכחות מוסר אמרת צא
וראה איזה דרך שהיא מביאה את האדם לחיי
העולם הבא הוי אומר יסורין רבי נחמיה אומר
חביבין יסורין שכשם שהקרבנות מרצין כך היסורין
מרצין בקרבנות מהו אומר ונרצה לו לכפר עליו
בייסורין מה הוא אומר והם ירצו את עונם ולא עוד
אלא שהייסורין מרצין יותר מן הקרבנות מפני
שהקרבנות בממון והייסורין בגוף וכן הוא אומר
עור בעד עור וכל אשר לאיש יתן בעד נפשו. כבר

38 שם. 41 שם ח', ז'. 46—45 משלי א', ב'. 47—46 תהלים צ"ד, י"ב. 50—49 משלי
ו', כ"ג. 54 ויקרא א', ד'. 55 שם כ"ו, מ"ג. 58 איוב ב', ד'. 86—58 סנהדרין ק"א,
א'—ב'.

38 יונתן] מ. ~ בן יוסף. 44 אלא] ק. ל. 51 דרך] מ. ~ ארץ ט"כ. ~ טובה. 56 מפני]
א. ~ מה.

Some time ago R. Eliezer was sick and the four elders, R. Tarphon, R. Joshua, R. Eleazar b. Azariah, and R. Akiba, went in to visit him. R. Tarphon then began saying: Master, you are more precious to Israel than the globe of the sun, for the globe of the sun gives light only for this world, while you have given us light both for this world and for the world to come. Then R. Joshua began saying: Master, you are more precious to Israel than the days of rain, for rain gives life only for this world while you have given us life for this world and for the world to come. Then R. Eleazar the son of Azariah began saying: Master, you are more precious to Israel than father and mother. For father and mother bring a man into the life of this world, while you have brought us to the life of the world to come. Then R. Akiba began saying: Precious are chastisements.—R. Eliezer then said to his disciples: Help me up. R. Eliezer then sat up and said to him: Speak, Akiba.—Akiba then said to him: Behold it says: "Manasseh was twelve years old when he began to reign; and he reigned fifty and five years in Jerusalem. And he did that which was evil in the sight of the Lord," etc. (II Chron. 33.1–2). And it also says: "These also are proverbs of Solomon, which the men of Hezekiah king of Judah copied out" (Prov. 25.1). And could the thought enter your mind that Hezekiah king of Judah taught the Torah to all Israel, and to his son Manasseh he did not teach the Torah? You must therefore say that all the instruction which he gave him and all the trouble which he took with him did not affect Manasseh at all. And what did have effect upon him? You must say: chastisements. For it is said: "And the Lord spoke to Manasseh, and to his people; but they gave no heed. Wherefore the Lord brought upon them the captains of the host of the king of Assyria, who took Manasseh with hooks, and bound him with fetters, and carried him to Babylon. And when he was in distress, he besought the Lord his God, and humbled himself greatly before the God of his fathers. And he prayed unto Him; and He was entreated of him, and heard his supplication, and brought him back to Jerusalem

היה רבי אליעזר חולה ונכנסו ארבעה זקנים לבקרו
רבי טרפון ורבי יהושע ורבי אלעזר בן עזריה ורבי
עקיבא נענה רבי טרפון ואמר רבי חביב אתה
לישראל מגלגל חמה שגלגל חמה בעולם הזה מאיר
ואתה הארת לנו בעולם הזה ובעולם הבא נענה
רבי יהושע ואמר רבי חביב אתה לישראל מיום
הגשמים גשמים נותנין חיים בעולם הזה ואתה נתת
לנו חיים בעולם הזה ובעולם הבא נענה רבי אלעזר
בן עזריה ואמר רבי חביב אתה לישראל יותר מאב
ואם שאב ואם מביאין את האדם לחיי העולם הזה
אבל אתה הבאתנו לחיי העולם הבא נענה רבי
עקיבא ואמר רבי חביבין יסורין אמר להן רבי
אליעזר לתלמידיו סמכוני ישב לו רבי אליעזר אמר
לו אמור עקיבא אמר לו הרי הוא אומר בן שתים
עשרה שנה מנשה במלכו וחמשים וחמש שנה מלך
בירושלים ויעש הרע בעיני יי וגו' ואומר גם אלה
משלי שלמה אשר העתיקו אנשי חזקיה מלך יהודה
וכי תעלה על דעתך שחזקיה מלך יהודה למד
תורה לכל ישראל ולמנשה בנו לא לימד תורה
אלא אמור מעתה שכל תלמוד שלימדו וכל עמל
שעמל בו לא הועיל לו כלום ומה הועיל לו הוי
אומר ייסורין שנאמר וידבר יי אל מנשה ואל עמו
ולא הקשיבו ויבא יי עליהם את שרי הצבא אשר
למלך אשור וילכדו את מנשה בחוחים ויאסרוהו
בנחשתים ויוליכוהו בבלה וכהצר לו חלה את
פני יי אלהיו ויכנע מאד מלפני אלהי אבותיו
ויתפלל אליו ויעתר לו וישמע תחנתו וישיבהו

74 — 72 דה״ב. ל״ג, א׳—ב׳.   75 — 74 משלי כ״ה, א׳.   86 — 80 דהי״ב. ל״ג, י׳—י״ג.

61 טרפון] מ. יהושע / רבין[ד. <.   86 — 62 שגלגל חמה—ירושלים למלכותן[ד. <.
63 — 62 מאיר ואתה הארת לנו] מ. ורבי.   64 יהושע] מ. ורבי.   64 מיום הגשמים
גשמים נותנים חיים] מ. מטיפה של גשמים שכך יפה (צ״ל טיפה) של גשמים.   65 — 64 ואת
נתת לנו חיים] מ. ורבי.   67 רבי] מ. < / יותר] א. <.   69 — 65 שאב ואם—לחיי
העולם הבא] מ. שאב ואם בעוה״ז ורבי בעוה״ז ובעולם הבא.   72 — 71 סמכוני—אמור
עקיבא] מ. סמכוני באשישות ואשמע דברי עקיבא תלמידי שאמר חביבין ייסורין אמר
לו מנין לך.   72 אמר לו]=מ. ג: א. < / הרי הוא אומר] מ. כך למדתנו מקרא אני
דורש דכתיב.   73 עשרה] א. < / שנה] מ. <.   76 תעלה על דעתך] מ. < ט. עלתה
דעתו של. / שחזקיה] מ. ט. חזקיה.   77 — 76 למד תורה לכל ישראל] מ. על כל
העולם כולו לימד תורה.   77 לא] מ. <.   78 אמור מעתה] מ. <.   80 — 78 שכל
תלמוד—הוי אומר יסורין] מ. מכל טורח שטרח בו ומכל עמל שעמל בו לא העלוהו

into his kingdom" (II Chron. 33.10–13). Thus you learn that chastisements are very precious.

Gods of Silver or Gods of Gold. Why is this said? Since Scripture says: "And thou shalt make two cherubim of gold" (Ex. 25.18). And what if one should say: I am going to make four? By saying here "gods of gold," Scripture teaches that if you make more than two, they are like gods of gold.

Gods of Silver. Why is this said? Has it not already been said: "gods of gold"? And if we have forbidden even what is otherwise permitted, it is but logical that what has never been permitted should surely be forbidden. What need then is there of saying: "gods of silver"? Because we find in the case of all the vessels of the Temple that if there is no gold for them they may be made of silver, I might think that it is also so in the case of the two cherubim; therefore, it says: "gods of silver." Behold, if you change and do not make them of gold, they are like gods of silver.

Ye Shall Not Make unto You. Lest you say: Since the Torah has given permission to make the cherubim in the Temple, I am also going to make them in the synagogues and in the school-houses, Scripture says: "Ye shall not make unto you." Another Interpretation: *Ye Shall Not Make unto You Gods of Silver.* Lest you say: I am going to make them merely for adornment as others do in the various provinces, Scripture says: "Ye shall not make unto you."

CHAPTER XI
(Ex. 20.21–23)

An Altar of Earth Thou Shalt Make unto Me. An altar made especially for Me. You should not have first built it for the name of another. R. Ishmael says: An altar attached to the earth you shall make unto Me. You shall not build it upon stones or upon pillars. R.

ירושלם למלכותו הא למדת שחביבין ייסורין.

אלהי כסף ואלהי זהב למה נאמר לפי
שהוא אומר ועשית שנים כרובים זהב אמר הריני
עושה ארבעה מה תלמוד לומר אלהי זהב אם
90   הוספת על שנים הרי הם כאלהי זהב אלהי כסף
למה נאמר והלא כבר נאמר אלהי זהב ומה תלמוד
לומר אלהי כסף והלא מה שהתרנו בו אסרנו בו ומה
שאסרנו בו דין הוא שנאסר בו ומה ת״ל אלהי כסף
לפי שמצינו בכל כלי בית עולמים שאם אין להם
95   של זהב הן עושין אותן של כסף שומע אני אף שנים
כרובים כן ת״ל אלהי כסף הא אם שניתם משל
זהב הרי הם כאלהי כסף.

לא תעשו לכם שלא תאמר הואיל ונתנה
תורה רשות לעשות בבית המקדש הרי אני עושה
100   בבתי כנסיות ובבתי מדרשות ת״ל לא תעשו לכם.
דבר אחר לא תעשו לכם אלהי כסף שלא תאמר
הרי אני עושה לנוי כדרך שאחרים עושים במדינות
ת״ל לא תעשו לכם.

פרשה יא   (שמות כ׳, כ״א—כ״ג.)

מזבח אדמה תעשה לי מזבח מיוחד לי
שלא תבנהו מתחלה לשום אחר רבי ישמעאל אומר
מזבח מחובר באדמה תעשה לי שלא תבנהו על
גבי כיפים ולא על גבי עמודים רבי נתן אומר מזבח

---

88 שמות כ״ה, י״ח.   95—94 מנחות כ״ח, ב׳.   100—97 ש. 115.
4—2 זבחים נ״ח, א׳.

86 ירושלים] מ. לירושלים.   89 מזה] ק. ומה נ. ל. ט. < / זהב] ד. כסף מ״ח. כסף
ואלהי זהב.   91—93 ומה ת״ל—שנאסר בו] ד. <.   92 והלא[=ט: א. מ. אלא מ״ח.
וקל וחומר.   93 שאסרנו] מ. שאמרנו.   95 הן] ד. / שנים] ד. > מ״ח. שני.   96 שניתם]
ד. אינו נותן מ״ח. עשיתם.   97—96 משל זהב] ד. של זהב מ״ח. משל כסף.   97 כאלהי
כסף] מ״ח. כאלהי זהב.   102 אני עושין / לנוי] לנוי[=ל״ט. מ״ח. רמב״ם
בסה״מ. מצוה ד׳: ט. ~ או א. לנו אי (צ״ל לנואו) מ. לבנואי (?) ד. לנו.
3 מחובר] ד. <.

Nathan says: An altar hollowed[1] through to the earth shalt thou make for Me, as it is said: "Hollow with planks shalt thou make it" (Ex. 27.8). Issi b. Akiba says: An altar of copper filled in with earth thou shalt make unto Me, as it is said: "Because the brazen altar that was before the Lord was too little to receive,"[2] etc. (I Kings 8.64). And was it really too little? Has it not been said: "A thousand burnt-offerings did Solomon offer upon that altar" (ibid. 3.4)? What then does it mean by saying: "too little"? It merely teaches that on the day when the one was built the other was hidden away.[3]

And Shalt Slaughter on It. That is, near it. Perhaps "on it" literally? And the following reasoning would favor it: If the north side of the altar, which is not a fit place for the performance of atonement rites, is a fit place for the slaughtering, the top of the altar, which is a fit place even for the performance of atonement rites, should surely be a fit place for the slaughtering. But the case of the inner altar would disprove this. For the latter is a fit place for the performance of atonement rites and yet it is not a fit place for slaughtering. It would therefore prove concerning the outer altar that although it is a fit place for the performance of atonement rites, it should nevertheless not be a fit place for slaughtering. No! If you cite the case of the inner altar— [that is another matter], for it is not a place for any act which allows the meat to be eaten, or qualifies a person to partake of holy things, or completes the atonement. Therefore it is not a fit place for slaughtering. But will you say the same about the outer altar? It is a place for acts which allow the meat to be eaten, qualify a person to partake of holy things, and complete the atonement. It should therefore be a fit place for the slaughtering also. But Scripture says: "And thou shalt

---

1. See Introduction and cf. Commentaries.

2. See Introduction. It is assumed that the altar here referred to was the one made by Moses, presupposing in the parallel passage in II Chron. 7.7 the reading אשר עשה מהש as given in Zeb. 59a (cf., however, Rabbinovicz, *Dikduke Soferim* ad loc.) instead of אשר עשה שלמה, as found in our masoretic text.

3. See Introduction.

5 חלול באדמה תעשה לי שנאמר נבוב לוחות תעשה

אותו איסי בן עקיבא אומר מזבח מלא נחשת אדמה

תעשה לי שנאמר כי מזבח הנחשת אשר לפני יי

קטן מהכיל וגו׳ וכי קטן היה והלא כבר נאמר אלף

עולות יעלה שלמה על המזבח ההוא ומה ת״ל קטן

10 אלא מלמד שביום שנבנה זה נגנז זה.

וזבחת עליו עליו כנגדו או עליו כמשמעו

והדין נותן ומה אם צפון המזבח שאינו כשר לכפרה

כשר לשחיטה ראש המזבח שהוא כשר לכפרה דין

הוא שיוכשר לשחיטה והרי מזבח הפנימי יוכיח שהוא

15 כשר לכפרה ואינו כשר לשחיטה הוא יוכיח על

מזבח החיצון אף על פי שהוא כשר לכפרה לא

יוכשר לשחיטה לא אם אמרת במזבח הפנימי שאינו

לא מתיר ולא מכשיר ואינו גומר את הכפרה לפיכך

אינו כשר לשחיטה תאמר במזבח החיצון שהוא

20 מתיר ומכשיר וגומר את הכפרה לפיכך יהא כשר

6—5 שמות כ״ז, ח׳; זבחים ס״א, ב׳.   8—7 מלכים א. ח׳, ס״ד.   10—6 זבחים נ״ט,
א׳—ב׳; ס״א, ב׳.   9—8 מלכים א. ג׳, ד׳.   10—8 מ״ת 54.

---

5 חלול] מ״ח. מלא.   6 עקיבא] מ. עקביא.   10 מלמד] ד. < / נגנז] ק. נכנס.   11 או]
ד. ~ אינו אלא.   21—19 תאמר—כשר לשחיטה] ד. <.   20 יהא כשר] מ. לא יוכשר
(בתמיה?).

offer thy burnt-offerings, the flesh and the blood upon the altar of the Lord thy God" (Deut. 12.27)—the flesh and the blood shall be offered on the top of the altar, but the slaughtering shall not be performed on the top of the altar. R. Jose says that it is also permitted to slaughter on the top of the altar.[4] And this scriptural passage supports him: "An altar of earth thou shalt make unto Me and shalt slaughter on it," etc. (Ex. 20.21). One passage says: "Thy burnt-offerings and thy peace-offerings" (ibid.). And another passage says: "Thy burnt-offerings, the flesh and the blood" (Deut. 12.27). How are both these passages to be maintained? Said R. Jose the son of R. Judah: From the middle of the altar and northward is considered north. And from the middle of the altar and southward is considered south. I would know only that the northern part of the altar is a fit place for slaughtering. How about the entire northern part of the Temple court? Scripture says: "And he shall kill the he-lamb in the place where they kill the sin-offering and the burnt-offering in the place of the sanctuary" (Lev. 14.13). There can be no purpose in saying: "In the place of the sanctuary," except to declare its entire northern part a place fit for slaughtering.

And Thou Shalt Slaughter on It Thy Burnt-Offerings, etc. From this I know only about the burnt-offerings and the peace-offerings. How about other holy sacrifices? It says: "For as the sin-offering is the priest's so is the guilt-offering" (ibid.). There can be no purpose in continuing to say: "It is most holy" (ibid.), except to permit the slaughtering of all the sacrifices in the same place. Still I would know it only in regard to the sin-offering, burnt-offering and the peace-offering. How about all other sacrifices of the community? Scripture says: "Thy sheep and thine oxen." But this might be interpreted to include not only all the sacrifices but also ordinary animals. You must reason: What does the context deal with? With sacrifices only.

4. See above *Pisha*, II, note 1.

לשחיטה ת"ל ועשית עולותיך הבשר והדם על
מזבח יי אלהיך הבשר והדם בראש המזבח ואין
שחיטה בראש המזבח רבי יוסי אומר אף לשחוט
בראש המזבח והכתוב מסייעו שנאמר מזבח אדמה
תעשה לי וזבחת עליו וגו'. כתוב אחד אומר את
עולותיך ואת שלמך וכתוב אחד אומר ועשית
עולותיך הבשר והדם הא כיצד יתקיימו שני
כתובים הללו אמר רבי יוסי ברבי יהודה מחצי
המזבח לצפון כצפון מחצי המזבח לדרום כדרום
ואין לי אלא צפון המזבח שהוא כשר לשחיטה ושאר
כל צפון העזרה מנין ת"ל ושחט את הכבש במקום
אשר ישחט את החטאת ואת העולה במקום הקדש
שאין ת"ל במקום הקדש אלא להכשיר בו כל רוח
צפונית.

וזבחת עליו את עולותיך וגו' אין
לי אלא עולה ושלמים שאר כל הקדשים מנין ת"ל
כי כחטאת האשם הוא לכהן שאין ת"ל קדש קדשים
אלא להכשיר בו כל הקדשים אין לי אלא חטאת
ועולה ושלמים שאר כל קרבנות הצבור מנין ת"ל
את צאנך ואת בקרך משמע מביא את הקדשים
ואת החולין אמרת במי הענין מדבר בקדשים.

21—22 דברים י"ב, כ"ו. 23—34 זבחים נ"ח, א'. 31—32 ויקרא י"ד, י"ג. 41—33 ת"ב
מצורע ג' (71ᵈ). ש. שם.

───────────

23 יוסי] ד. אסי. 24 מסייעו] א. מ. מסייע. 27 הא] ד. >. 32 את החטאת ואת
העולה במקום הקדש] הוספתי: א. מ. וגו' ד. את העולה, וליתא במקרא. 33 אלא]
א. ומה ת"ל במקום הקדש אלא. 34—33 רוח צפונית] ד. הקדשים א"צ. הקדש.
38—35 וזבחת עליו—כל הקדשים] ד. >. 37 האשם] מ. כאשם. 39 הצבור] ד. >.

In Every Place, etc. Where I reveal Myself to you, that is, in the Temple. Hence they said: The tetragrammaton is not to be pronounced outside of the Temple.—R. Eliezer b. Jacob says: If you come to my house I will come to your house, but if you do not come to my house I will not come to your house. The place my heart loveth, thither my feet lead me.—In connection with this passage the sages said: Wherever ten persons assemble in a synagogue the Shekinah is with them, as it is said: "God standeth in the congregation of God" (Ps. 82.1). And how do we know that He is also with three people holding court? It says: "In the midst of the judges He judgeth" (ibid.). And how do we know that He is also with two? It is said: "Then they that feared the Lord spoke one with another," etc. (Mal. 3.16). And how do we know that He is even with one? It is said: "In every place where I cause My name to be mentioned I will come unto thee and bless thee."

And If Thou Make Me an Altar of Stone. R. Ishmael says: Every "if" in the Torah refers to a voluntary act with the exception of three.

"And if thou bring a meal-offering of first fruits" (Lev. 2.14) refers to an obligatory act. You interpret it to be obligatory. Perhaps it is not so, but is merely voluntary? Scripture however says: "Thou shalt bring for the meal-offering of thy first fruit" (ibid.)—it is obligatory and not voluntary. Similarly, "If thou lend money to any of My people," etc. (Ex. 22.24), refers to an obligatory act. You interpret it to be obligatory. Perhaps it is not so, but is merely voluntary? Scripture however says: "Thou shalt surely lend him" (Deut. 15.8)—it is obligatory and not voluntary. "And if thou make Me an altar of stone," refers to an obligatory act. You interpret it to be obligatory. Perhaps it is not so, but is merely voluntary? Scripture however says: "Thou shalt build . . . of unhewn stones" (ibid., 27.6). And what does Scripture teach by saying: "And if thou make Me an altar of stone"? Simply this: If one wishes to make an altar of stones one may do so, and if one wishes to make an altar of bricks one may do so. Now, by using the method of *kal vahomer,* one can reason: If in the case of the altar, a

בכל המקום וגו' שאני נגלה עליך בבית
הבחירה מכאן אמרו שם המפורש אסור להאמר
בגבולין רבי אליעזר בן יעקב אומר אם תבא לביתי
אבא לביתך ואם לא תבא לביתי אף אני לא אבא
לביתך מקום שלבי אוהב שם רגלי מוליכות אותי
מכאן אמרו כל עשרה בני אדם שנכנסין לבית
הכנסת שכינה עמהם שנאמר אלהים נצב בעדת
אל ומנין אפילו שלשה שדנין שנאמר בקרב אלהים
ישפוט ומנין אפילו שנים שנאמר אז נדברו יראי
יי איש אל רעהו ומנין אפילו אחד שנאמר בכל
המקום אשר אזכיר את שמי אבוא אליך.

ואם מזבח אבנים תעשה לי רבי
ישמעאל אומר כל אם ואם שבתורה רשות חוץ
משלשה ואם תקריב מנחת בכורים וגו' חובה אתה
אומר חובה או אינו אלא רשות ת"ל תקריב את
מנחת בכוריך חובה ולא רשות כיוצא בו אם כסף
תלוה את עמי וגו' חובה אתה אומר חובה או אינו
אלא רשות ת"ל העבט תעביטנו חובה ולא רשות
ואם מזבח אבנים תעשה לי חובה אתה אומר חובה
או אינו אלא רשות ת"ל אבנים שלמות תבנה חובה
ולא רשות ומה ת"ל ואם מזבח אבנים תעשה לי
אלא אם רצה לעשות של אבנים יעשה של לבנים
יעשה והרי דברים קל וחומר ומה אם מזבח החמור

44—46 סוכה נ"ג, ב'. אדר"נ י"ב.   52—47 אבות ג', ב'. ברכות ו', א'. ש. שם.   48 תהלים
פ"ב, א'.   50—49 תהלים שם.   51—50 מלאכי ג', ט"ז.   57—53 ת"כ ויקרא נדבה
י"ג (12°).   62—53 לקמן בספרא א'.   109—53 ש. 116.   55 ויקרא ב', י"ד.   58—57 שמות
כ"ב, כ"ד.   59 דברים ט"ו, ח'.   61 שם כ"ז, ו'.

42 בכל המקום] ט. ט"כ. ~ אמרת במי (ט. במה) הענין מדבר / שאני מ. ט. ט"כ.
שאינו / מ"ח. אינו ב. עליך / איני / עליך] ט. ט"כ. מ"ח. ~ אלא.   45 אף
אני] ד. <.   48 עמהם] מ. עליהן.   54 אם ואם] ד. אם.   55 ואם] א. אם.
57—56 תקריב—בכוריך] מ. תקריב מנחת בכורים.   60 ואם מזבח] ד. כיוצא בו ואם
מזבח.   62—61 חובה ולא רשות]=ג. ז". א"צ. ש"י: ט. ~ מזבח אדמה תעשה לי
רשות ולא חובה א. מ. ד. רשות אתה אומר רשות או אינו אלא חובה ת"ל מזבח
אבנים (מ. אדמה) תעשה לי רשות ולא חובה מ"ח. אבנים רשות או אינו אלא חובה.
62 ומה ת"ל] מ"ח. ת"ל / אבנים] א. אדמה.   64 קל וחומר] מ. ד. ~ לשאר כל הכלים.
64—65 ומה אם—כל הכלים] מ. <.

very important object, a change in the material is permitted if
desired, how much more should this be permitted in the case of all
the other Temple objects.

Thou Shalt Not Build It of Hewn Stones. "Hewn stones" means only
stones cut by lifting an iron tool upon them. R. Nathan says: Suppose
one has built into the altar two stones cut by lifting an iron tool upon
them, I might understand that the whole altar becomes unfit thereby.
But Scripture says: "Thou shalt not build with[5] hewn stones."—They
alone are unfit but the rest of the altar is still fit.

Thou Shalt Not Build It of Hewn Stones. It alone you are not allowed
to build of hewn stones, but you may build the Temple and even the
Holy of Holies of hewn stones. For the following argument might
have been advanced: If the altar, which is of lesser importance, is not
to be built of hewn stones, it is but logical that the Temple and the
Holy of Holies which are of greater importance should all the more
not be built of hewn stones. Therefore Scripture says: "Thou shalt not
build it of hewn stones."—It alone you are not to build of hewn
stones, but you may build the Temple and even the Holy of Holies of
hewn stones. And how am I to maintain the passage: "And there was
neither hammer nor axe nor any tool of iron heard in the house,
while it was in building" (I Kings 6.7)? "In the house" they were not
heard, but they had been heard outside of the house.

For If Thou Lift Up Thy Sword upon It, etc. In this connection R.
Simon b. Eleazar used to say: The altar is made to prolong the years of
man and iron is made to shorten the years of man. It is not right for
that which shortens life to be lifted up against that which prolongs
life, R. Johanan b. Zakkai says: Behold it says: "Thou shalt build . . .
of whole[6] stones" (Deut. 27.6). They are to be stones that establish

---

5. This rendering of the word אתהן is required by the *Mekilta,* which takes it
to be like עמהן, thus interpreting the passage to mean: Do not use hewn stones
with the other stones of which the altar is properly made.

6. This rendering of the word שלמות is required by the *Mekilta.*

65   אם רצה לשנות ישנה קל וחומר לשאר כל הכלים.

לא תבנה אתהן גזית אין גזית אלא גזוזות
שהונף עליהם ברזל רבי נתן אומר והרי שבנה בו
שתי אבנים גזוזות שהונף עליהם ברזל שומע אני
יהא המזבח כלו פסול ת״ל לא תבנה אתהן גזית
70   הן פסולות ושאר כל המזבח כשר.

לא תבנה אתהן גזית בו אין אתה בונה
גזית אבל אתה בונה בהיכל ובקדשי הקדשים שהיה
בדין ומה אם מזבח הקל אסור לבנות בו גזית
ההיכל וקדש הקדשים החמורים דין הוא שתהא
75   אסור לבנות בהן גזית ת״ל לא תבנה אתהן גזית
בו אין אתה בונה גזית אבל אתה בונה גזית בהיכל
ובקדש הקדשים ומה אני מקים ומקבות והגרזן
כל כלי ברזל לא נשמע בבית בהבנותו בבית אינו
נשמע אבל בחוץ נשמע.

80   **כי חרבך הנפת עליה** וגו׳ מכאן היה
רבי שמעון בן אלעזר אומר המזבח נברא להאריך
ימיו של אדם והברזל נברא לקצר שנותיו של אדם
אינו דין שיניף המקצר על המאריך רבן יוחנן בן
זכאי אומר הרי הוא אומר אבנים שלמות תבנה

70—66 מדות ג׳, ד׳.   79—71 סוטה מ״ח, ב׳. תמיד כ״ו, ב׳. מ״ת 180.   78—77 מלכים
א. ו׳, ז׳.   92—80 ת״כ קדושים י׳ (92ᵈ). תוס׳ ב״ק ז׳, ו׳—ז׳. ת. יתרו י״ח.   83—81 מדות
שם.

66 גזית 2] א. גזיו.   67 שהונף] מ. שהונח.   68 שהונף] מ. שהונה.   70 ושאר כל
המזבח כשר] ד. ולא המזבח כלו פסול.   71—72 בונה גזית] מ. ד. בונה.   74—75 שתהא
אסור לבנות בהן] ד. שלא יהו בונין בו.   78 כל כלי] א. ט. ט״כ. וכל כלי.   81 שמעון
בן] ג. < / נברא] א. נבנה.   82 נברא לקצר] ט. מקצר ד. לקצר.   83 דין שיניף] מ.
דין שיניח ד. רשאי להניף.

peace. Now, by using the method of *kal vahomer,* you reason: The stones for the altar do not see nor hear nor speak. Yet because they serve to establish peace between Israel and their Father in heaven the Holy One, blessed be He, said: "Thou shalt lift up no iron tool upon them" (ibid., v. 5). How much the more then should he who establishes peace between man and his fellow-man, between husband and wife, between city and city, between nation and nation, between family and family, between government and government, be protected so that no harm should come to him.

Neither Shalt Thou Go Up by Steps unto Mine Altar.—Hence they said: Make an inclined plane leading up to the altar.—From this passage I would know only about ascending. How about descending? Scripture says: "That thy nakedness be not uncovered thereon." Hence it matters not whether it is at going up or at coming down. What does matter is being covered. R. Ishmael says: This passage is not needed for this. For has it not already been said: "And thou shalt make them linen breeches to cover the flesh of their nakedness" (Ex. 28.42)? What then does Scripture teach by saying: "That thy nakedness be not uncovered thereon"? That one is not to take big steps on it but walk heel touching toe and toe touching heel.

That Thy Nakedness Be Not Uncovered On It. On it you are not allowed to take big steps but you may take big steps in the Temple and even in the Holy of Holies. For the following argument might have been advanced: If on the altar, which is of lesser importance, it is forbidden to take big steps, it is but logical that in the Temple and the Holy of Holies, which are of greater importance, it should be forbidden to take big steps. Therefore Scripture says: "That thy nakedness be not uncovered on it."—On it you are not allowed to take big steps, but you may take big steps in the Temple and even in the Holy of Holies. Behold now, using the method of *kal vahomer,* you reason: The stones of the altar have no sense of what is proper or improper. Yet God said that you should not treat them disrespectfully. It is

85 אבנים שמטילות שלום והרי דברים קל וחומר
ומה אם אבני המזבח שאינן לא רואות ולא שומעות
ולא מדברות על שהן מטילות שלום בין ישראל
לאביהן שבשמים אמר הקב"ה לא תניף עליהם
ברזל המטיל שלום בין איש לאשה בין איש לאשתו
90 בין עיר לעיר בין אומה לאומה בין משפחה
למשפחה בין ממשלה לממשלה על אחת כמה
וכמה שלא תבואהו פורענות.

ולא　תעלה　במעלות　על　מזבחי מכאן
אמרו עשה כבש למזבח אין לי אלא עלייה ירידה
95 מנין ת"ל אשר לא תגלה ערותך עליו הא לא
עלייה ולא ירידה גרמה אלא כסוי גורם רבי
ישמעאל אומר אינו צריך והלא כבר נאמר ועשה
להם מכנסי בד לכסות בשר ערוה ומה ת"ל אשר
לא תגלה ערותך עליו שלא יפסע בו פסיעה יתירה
100 אלא גודל בצד עקב ועקב בצד גודל.

אשר　לא　תגלה　ערותך　עליו עליו אין
אתה פוסע פסיעה יתירה אבל אתה פוסע פסיעה
יתירה בהיכל ובקדש הקדשים שהיה בדין ומה אם
מזבח הקל את אסור לפסוע בו פסיעה יתירה
105 ההיכל ובית קדש הקדשים החמורים דין הוא שתהא
אסור לפסוע בהן פסיעה יתירה ת"ל אשר לא
תגלה ערותך עליו בו אין אתה פוסע פסיעה יתירה
אבל אתה פוסע פסיעה יתירה בהיכל ובבית קדש
הקדשים והרי דברים קל וחומר ומה אם אבנים
110 שאין בהם דעת לא לרעה ולא לטובה אמר המקום

---

89 — 88 דברים כ"ז, ה'.　98 — 97 שמות כ"ח, מ"ב.　112 — 109 ת. שם.

---

88 לא תניף עליהם] מ. לא תניף עליו.　99 שלא יפסע—יתירה] ד. שלא ילך פסיעה
גסה.　100 אלא] מ. אבל.　101 אשר לא] ג. דבר אחר אשר לא.　102 יתירה] ד.
גסה.　103 יתירה] ד. גסה.　104 יתירה] ד. >.　105 ובית קדש] ד. וקדש.　106 לפסוע
בהן פסיעה יתירה] ד. לפסוע פסיעה גסה בהן לפי שהן חמורין.　108 ובין קדש] ד.
ובקדש.

therefore but logical that you must refrain from treating your fellow-man, who is made in the image of Him by whose word the world came into being, with disrespect.

That Thy Nakedness Be Not Uncovered on It. And These Are the Ordinances which Thou Shalt Set Before Them.[7] We can thus learn that the place for the Sanhedrin is alongside of the altar. Although there is no proof for it, there is a suggestion of it in the passage : "And Joab fled into the tent of the Lord and caught hold of the horns of the altar"[8] (I Kings 2.28).

7. The proximity of the laws about the altar and about justice suggests that the altar and the tribunal of justice, i. e., the *Sanhedrin*, should actually be adjacent.

8. See Commentaries.

לא תנהוג בהן בבזיון חברך שהוא בדמותו של מי
שאמר והיה העולם דין הוא שלא תנהוג בו בבזיון.

אשר לא תגלה ערותך עליו ואלה
המשפטים אשר תשים נמצינו למדין
שסנהדרין בצד המזבח ואף על פי שאין ראיה
לדבר זכר לדבר שנאמר וינס יואב אל אהל יי
ויחזק בקרנות המזבח.

¹¹⁵

חסלת מסכתא דבחודש השלישי

113–117 לקמן נזיקין ד׳.   116–117 מלכים א. ב׳, כ״ח.

111 בבזיון] ד.   מנהג בזיון / בדמותו] מ. בדמיונו.   112 בבזיון]
ד.   מנהג בזיון.   113 אשר לא תגלה ערותך עליו] ק. נ. ~ חסלת
פרשת יתרו.   115 בצד המזבח] ד. באין בצד המזבח מ. שמסר
דין (אולי צ״ל שמסדרין?) דידתו בצד המזבח ט״כ. שמצדדין
דירתן לצד המזבח.   118 חסלת מסכתא דבחודש השלישי] מ. ק.
נ. > ל.   חסלת פרשת יתרו.   עיין מאמרי The Arrangement and the
Divisions of the Mekilta, *Hebrew Union College Annual*, I. pp. 443–4.

TRACTATE NEZIKIN

CHAPTER I
(Ex. 21.1–3)

And These Are the Ordinances. R. Ishmael says: These are added to the preceding ones. Just as those preceding were given from Sinai, so also those following were given from Sinai. R. Akiba says: *And These Are the Ordinances,* etc. Why is this said? Since it says: "Speak unto the children of Israel and say unto them" (Lev. 1.2), I know only that he was to tell them once. How do we know that he was to repeat it to them a second, a third and a fourth time until they learned it? Scripture says: "And teach thou it the children of Israel" (Deut. 31.19). This might mean that they need only learn it but not repeat it. But Scripture says: "Put it in their mouths" (ibid.). Still this might mean that they need only repeat it but need not fully understand it. Therefore it says: "And these are the ordinances which thou shalt set before them." Arrange them in proper order before them like a set table, just as it is said: "Unto thee it was shown that thou mightest know" (ibid., 4.35).

R. Judah says: *And These Are the Ordinances.* These were commanded at Marah, as it is said: "There He made for them a statute and an ordinance" (Ex. 15.25). R. Eleazar the son of Azariah says: Now suppose the gentile courts judge according to the laws of Israel. I might understand that their decisions are valid. But Scripture says: "And these are the ordinances which thou shalt set before them." You may judge their cases but they are not to judge your cases.[1] On the basis of this interpretation the sages said: A bill of divorce given by

מסכת נזיקין

פרשתא קמייתא (שמות כ״א, א׳—ג׳.)

ואלה המשפטים רבי ישמעאל אומר אלו
מוסיפין על העליונים מה עליונים מסיני אף
תחתונים מסיני רבי עקיבא אומר ואלה המשפטים
וגו׳ למה נאמר לפי שהוא אומר דבר אל בני ישראל

5 ואמרת אליהם אין לי אלא פעם אחת מנין שנה
ושלש ורבע עד שילמדו ת״ל ולמדה את בני ישראל
יכול למדין ולא שונין ת״ל שימה בפיהם יכול שונים
ולא יודעין ת״ל ואלה המשפטים אשר תשים
לפניהם ערכם לפניהם כשלחן ערוך כעניין שנאמר

10 אתה הראית לדעת רבי יהודה אומר ואלה
המשפטים במרה נאמרו שנאמר שם שם לו חק
ומשפט רבי אלעזר בן עזריה אומר והרי הגוים
שדנו בדיני ישראל שומע אני יהיו דיניהם קיימים
ת״ל ואלה המשפטים אשר תשים לפניהם אתה דן

3 — 1 שמו״ר ל׳, ג׳; ת. משפטים ג׳. 10 — 3 ש. 117. 5 — 4 ויקרא א׳, ב׳.
9 — 5 עירובין נ״ד, ב׳. 6 דברים ל״א, י״ט. 7 שם. 10 שם ד׳, ל״ה. 12 — 11 שמות
ט״ו, כ״ה. 13 — 12 ת. שם. 15 — 14 ספרי דברים ט״ז. י׳ ב״ק ד׳, ג׳ (4^b).

5 אין לי אלא פעם אחת] א. מ. ט. הרא״ם בפרשה >. 6 ת״ל] ט. הרא״ם. צפנת
פענח להר׳ יוסף מטראני דף פ״א, שנאמר. 7 יכול] מ. < / יכול שונים] א. מ. ט. או
שונים. 9 — 8 אשר תשים לפניהם] הוספתי: א. ד. וגו׳. 11 נאמרו] הוספתי=א״א:
ג. נצטוו. 13 בדינין] ד. כדיני / דיניהם] ד. >. 14 אשר תשים לפניהם] הוספתי:
מא״ש. וגו׳.

force, if by Israelitish authority is valid, but if by gentile authority is not valid. It is, however, valid if the Gentiles merely bind the husband over[2] and say to him: "Do as the Israelites tell thee." R. Simon the son of Yoḥai says: What is the reason that the ordinances of law precede all the commandments of the Torah? Because as long as there is a law-suit between a man and his fellow-man, there is strife between them. But as soon as the case is decided for them, peace is established between them. And thus Jethro says to Moses: "And all this people also shall go to their place in peace" (Ex. 18.23).

If Thou Buy a Hebrew Slave.[3] Scripture here deals with one sold into servitude by the court for stealing. Such a one must serve not only the one who bought him, but also the latter's son after him. You say that Scripture here deals with one sold into servitude by the court for stealing, telling us that such a one must serve not only the one who bought him but also the latter's son after him. Perhaps however it deals only with one who sells himself? When it says: "And if thy brother be waxen poor with thee and sell himself unto thee" (Lev. 25.39), behold the one selling himself is there spoken of. Why then should Scripture say here: "If thou buy a Hebrew slave"? It must therefore deal with one sold into slavery by the court for stealing, telling that such a one must serve not only the one who bought him but also the latter's son after him.

1. In the Israelitish commonwealth only fully qualified citizens, priests, Levites and Israelites, could hold the office of judge. They could judge cases of non-Israelitish residents. But a non-Israelite, i. e., a foreigner who has not accepted the Jewish religion and hence was not a fully qualified citizen, could not function as judge in a Jewish state (see M. Sanh. 4.2; Sanh. 36b and Kid. 76b and cf. Commentaries).

2. I.e., use force against him.

3. The Jewish law does not allow an Israelite to become or to be made a slave in the real sense of the word. The term עבד, "slave," then, when applied to a Hebrew or an Israelite, can only mean one who has to serve for a certain definite period, either a number of years or up to the advent of the Jubilee or, in the case of a girl, till she becomes of age or attains puberty.

את שלהם והם אינם דנין את שלך מכאן אמרו גט

המעושה בישראל כשר ובגוים פסול אבל גוים

חובטין אותו ואומרים לו עשה מה שישראל אומרים

לך רבי שמעון בן יוחי אומר מה ראו דינין לקדם

לכל המצות שבתורה שכשהדין בין אדם לחבירו

תחרות ביניהם נתפסק להם הדין נעשה שלום

ביניהם וכן יתרו אומר למשה אם את הדבר הזה

תעשה וגו׳ וגם כל העם הזה על מקומו יבא בשלום.

כי תקנה עבד עברי בנמכר בבית דין

על גניבתו הכתוב מדבר שיהיה עובדו ועובד את

הבן אתה אומר בנמכר בבית דין על גניבתו הכתוב

מדבר שיהיה עובדו ועובד את הבן או אינו מדבר

אלא במוכר עצמו כשהוא אומר וכי ימוך אחיך עמך

ונמכר לך הרי מוכר עצמו אמור הא מה ת״ל כי

תקנה עבד עברי בנמכר בבית דין על גניבתו

15 — 18 גיטין פ״ח, ב׳. י׳ שם ט׳, י׳ (50a).   21 — 22 שמות י״ח, כ״ג.   23 — 30 ספרי
דברים קי״ח. קידושין י״ד, ב׳, וי״ז, ב׳. י׳ שם א׳, ב׳ (59c). ש. 119 — 118.   27 — 28 ויקרא
כ״ה, ל״ט.

16 המעושה] א. המעושה / אבל גוים] א. מ. ט. ובגוים א״א. אבל אם גוים. 17 חובטין]
מ. הגיטין. 18 — 17 אומרים לך] ד. ~ כשר. 20 נתפסק להם] ד. נפסק / נעשה] ק.
עושה. 21 למשה] ד. <. 22 וגם כל העם — יבא בשלום] הוספתי=ט. ול״ט. 24 על
גניבתו] ד. ט. על גניבות ט״כ. על גניבו. 26 — 25 אתה אומר — ועובד את הבן] ד. <.
25 גניבתו] א. מ. ט. ט״כ. גניבו. 27 עמך] ד. <. 28 הא מה] א. מ. ט. ומה.
29 גניבתו] א. מ. ט. ט״כ. גניבו.

If Thou Buy a Hebrew Slave. Scripture deals with a slave who is an Israelite. Perhaps however it deals only with the slave of an Israelite?[4] And to what am I to apply the passage: "And ye may make them an inheritance for your children after you," etc. (ibid., v. 46)? To those bought from a Gentile. Those of an Israelite however, so I might understand, should serve only six years and come out free in the seventh year. Scripture says: "If thy brother, a Hebrew man . . . be sold unto thee" (Deut. 15.12). Now, after having said: "Thy brother," there seems to be no purpose in saying: "A Hebrew man." Why then does Scripture say: "A Hebrew man"? Merely to furnish an expression free to be used in formulating the following *Gezerah shavah*: Here the expression "Hebrew" is used and there the expression "Hebrew" is used. Just as there when using the expression "Hebrew" Scripture deals with an Israelite, so also here when using the expression "Hebrew" Scripture deals with an Israelite. And even though there is no explicit scriptural proof for the matter, there is a suggestion[5] of it in the passages: "And they said: 'The God of the Hebrews hath met with us,' " etc. (Ex. 5.3); "And there came one that had escaped, and told Abram the Hebrew" (Gen. 14.13).

Slave. Perhaps he should not be called "slave" at all, it being a term of opprobrium?[6] But it says: "If thou buy a Hebrew slave." The Torah designates him a slave against his will.

If Thou Buy a Hebrew Slave. Why is this said? To include the proselyte.—These are the words of R. Eliezer. R. Ishmael says: This needs no scriptural proof. If an Israelite serves, shall a proselyte not serve? Perhaps, if an Israelite is to serve six years the proselyte should serve twelve? You must reason: It is enough for that which is derived by

4. I. e., the Canaanitish slave owned by an Israelite.

5. In the two passages cited the term עברי might mean a descendant of Eber the son of Shelah (Gen. 11.15) or one who came from beyond the River. Hence, there is no explicit proof that עברי means only an Israelite (see Commentaries. On the term זכר לדבר see Bacher, *Terminologie,* I, p. 51 ff.).

6. See above note 3, and cf. Friedmann.

30 הכתוב מדבר שיהיה עובדו ועובד את הבן.

כי תקנה עבד עברי בבן ישראל הכתוב
מדבר או אינו מדבר אלא בעבדו של עברי ומה
אני מקיים והתנחלתם אותם לבניכם אחריכם וגו'
בנלקח מן הגוי אבל בנלקח מישראל שומע אני
35 יהיה עובד שש ויצא בשביעית ת"ל כי ימכר לך
אחיך העברי שאין ת"ל העברי שכבר נאמר אחיך
ומה ת"ל העברי אלא מופנה להקיש ולדון גזירה
שוה נאמר כאן עברי ונאמר להלן עברי מה עברי
האמור להלן בבן ישראל הכתוב מדבר אף עבד
40 עברי האמור כאן בבן ישראל הכתוב מדבר ואף
על פי שאין ראיה לדבר זכר לדבר שנאמר ויאמרו
אלהי העברים נקרא עלינו וגו' ויבא הפליט ויגד
לאברם העברי.

עבד או אל תקראנו עבד לשום בזיון ת"ל כי
45 תקנה עבד עברי על כורחו התורה קראתו עבד.

כי תקנה עבד עברי למה נאמר להביא
הגר דברי רבי אליעזר רבי ישמעאל אומר אינו
צריך אם ישראל עובד הגר לא יעבוד אם ישראל

43—31 ש. שם.   33 שם כ"ה, מ"ו.   36—35 דברים ט"ו, י"ב.   42—41 שמות ה', ג'.
43—42 בראשית י"ד, י"ג.

37 אלא מופנה] א. מ. מפני / ולדון] ד. ~ ממנו.   40—39 עבד עברי] א. מ. ט. עברי.
42 ויבא הפליט ויגד] ד. <.   44 עבד] א. מ. ט. < / או אל תקראנו עבד] א. אל תקראנו
עבד ק. או אל תקראנו נ. ל. יכול תקראנו עבד ט. ט"כ. ר' אומר יכול (ט"כ. אל)
תקראנו עבד ה. או אינו אלא תקראנו עבד א"א. יכול תקראנו עבד או אל תקראנו
עבד. ועיין ז"י. ומ"ה. ומ"ע. / לשום] א"א. לשון / בזיון] א"צ. ~ ת"ל אחיך נהוג בו
אחוה יכול אף הוא ינהוג בעצמו אחוה.   45 על כורחו—עבד] ד. התורה קראתו עבד
בעל כרחו (נ. כרחה).   46 כי תקנה] ג. דבר אחר כי תקנה.   47 ר' אליעזר ר' ישמעאל]
ד. ר' ישמעאל ר' אליעזר סמ"ג עשין פ"ג ר' ישמעאל ר' עקיבא ה. ר' אלעזר ר' שמעון.
49—48 אם ישראל עובד שש] ג. א"צ. או (א"צ. ~ אינו אלא) ישראל עובד שש.

inference to be like that from which it is derived;[7] just as the Israelite serves six, so the proselyte should serve six.

Six Years He Shall Serve. Since it says: "If he have nothing then he shall be sold for his theft" (Ex. 22.2), I might understand that when it says: "Then he shall be sold for his theft," it means for ever, but it says here: "Six years he shall serve." Scripture thus tells you that he serves six years and goes out free in the seventh.

Six Years He Shall Serve. I might understand this to mean in any kind of service, but Scripture says: "Thou shalt not make him to serve as a bondservant" (Lev. 25.39). Hence the sages said: A Hebrew slave must not wash the feet of his master, nor put his shoes on him, nor carry his things before him when going to the bathhouse, nor support him by the hips when ascending steps, nor carry him in a litter or a chair or a sedan chair as slaves do. For it is said: "But over your brethren the children of Israel ye shall not rule, one over another, with rigour" (ibid., v. 46). But one's son or pupil may do so.

Six Years He Shall Serve. I might understand this to mean by doing any kind of work whether it is humiliating to him or not. Therefore it says: "As a hired man" (ibid., v. 40). Just as a hired man cannot be forced to do anything other than his trade, so also a Hebrew slave cannot be forced to do anything other than his trade. Hence the sages said: The master may not put him to work in a trade in which he has to attend upon the public, as being a well-master, a bathing-master, a barber, tailor, butcher, or baker. R. Jose says: If one of these was his trade, he must work at it for his master. But the master cannot make him change his trade to one of these. *As a Hired Man and as a Settler,* etc. (Lev. 25.40). Just as a hired man works only during the day and does not work during the night, so the Hebrew slave is to work only during the day and not during the night. R. Jose says: It all depends on what his trade is.

7. The result of any logical conclusion cannot go beyond the premises. On the principle of רין see "Talmud Hermeneutics" in *JE*, XII, 32.

עובד שש שנים הגר יעבוד שתים עשרה אמרת דיו
לבא מן הדין להיות כנדון מה ישראל עובד שש אף
הגר יעבוד שש.

שש שנים לפי שהוא אומר אם אין לו ונמכר
בגניבתו אי ונמכר בגניבתו שומע אני לעולם ת"ל
שש שנים יעבוד מגיד הכתוב שהוא עובד שש ויוצא
בשביעית.

שש שנים יעבוד שומע אני כל עבודה
במשמע ת"ל לא תעבוד בו עבודת עבד מכאן
אמרו לא ירחוץ לו רגליו ולא ינעול לו סנדליו
ולא יטול לפניו כלים לבית המרחץ ולא יסמוך
לו במתניו כיון שעולה במעלה ולא יטלנו לא
בפוריון ולא בכסא ולא בלקטקא כדרך שעבדים
עושין שנאמר ובאחיכם בני ישראל איש באחיו
לא תרדה בו בפרך אבל בבנו ובתלמידו רשאי.

שש שנים יעבוד שומע אני בין עבודה שיש
בה בזיון ובין עבודה שאין בה בזיון ת"ל כשכיר
מה שכיר אין אתה רשאי לשנותו מאומנותו אף עבד
עברי אין אתה רשאי לשנותו מאומנותו מכאן אמרו
לא יושיבנו רבו באומנות שהיא משמשת לרבים
כגון בייר בלן ספר חייט טבח נחתום רבי יוסי אומר
אם היתה אומנותו מיוחדת לכך יעשה אבל רבו
לא ישנה עליו. כשכיר כתושב וגו' מה שכיר עובד
ביום ואינו עובד בלילה אף עבד עברי עובד ביום

52—53 שמות כ"ב, ב'.   52—55 לקמן י"ג.   56—69 ת"כ בהר ה' (109cd).   מ"ת 85.
57 ויקרא כ"ה, ל"ט.   61 ספרי דברים ל"ז. לעיל בחודש ג'.   62—63 ויקרא כ"ה, מ"ו.
63 כתובות צ"ו, א'.   67—69 ש. 119.   71—73 ספרי דברים קכ"ג. קידושין ט"ו, א'. י'
שם א', ב' (59d).

49 הגר] א. מ. אף הגר.   52 שש שנים] הגהתי=ל"ט ומא"ש.   59 ולא יסמוך] א.
מ. לא יסמוך.   60 כיון שעולה] מ"ח. כשהוא עולה.   61 בפוריון] ה. באפריון /
בלקטקא] א. בקלסקא (בקלטקא?) ה. בקלקטליא.   62—63 איש באחיו—בפרך] הוספתי:
ד. וגומר.   65 כשכיר] ד. ~ כתושב.   69 בייר] ד. < / טבח] ק. <.   70 אומנותו] ד.
מלאכתו.

And in the Seventh. The seventh year counting from the date when
he was sold. You interpret it to mean the seventh year counting from
the date when he was sold. Perhaps it means the seventh calendar
year? It says: "Six years shall he serve." Hence it must be the seventh
year counting from the date when he was sold and not the seventh
calendar year.

He Shall Go Out Free. Why is this said? Because it says: "And when
thou sendest him out free from thee" (Deut. 15.13), which I might
understand to mean that the master must write him a writ of emancipation. It therefore says here: "He shall go out free." But perhaps he
must give his master money in order to go out free? It says: "Free for
nothing."

If He Come In by Himself He Shall Go Out by Himself. Why is this
said? Because of the following: It says: "If his master give him a wife."
This is to be interpreted as being optional. You interpret it to be
optional. Perhaps it is not so, but is obligatory? It says however: "If
he come in by himself he shall go out by himself." So it must be
optional and not obligatory.—These are the words of R. Ishmael. R.
Akiba says: *If He Come In by Himself He Shall Go Out by Himself,*
means, if he has come in with his chief external organs unimpaired,
he shall go out with his chief external organs unimpaired.[8] Since it
says: "And if a man sell his daughter to be a maid-servant she shall
not go out as the slaves do" (v. 7), it means she shall not go out free
because of the loss of any of the chief external organs, as Canaanitish
slaves do. You interpret: "She shall not go out as the slaves do," to
mean she shall not go out free because of the loss of any of the chief

---

8. The Hebrew word בגפו is interpreted as if it read בגופו, meaning "with his
body intact." If the master injures him so as to cause loss of limb, he must pay an
indemnity as he would pay a free man. A Canaanitish slave under similar circumstances goes out free but has no claim for indemnity. The master loses the slave
but pays nothing. See Ex. 21.26–27, which has been interpreted by the Rabbis to
mean, if the master causes the slave the loss of any limb or organ the use of which
could not be recovered (cf. below, ch. IX).

ואינו עובד בלילה רבי יוסי אומר הכל לפי
אומנותו.

75 **ובשביעית** שביעית למכירה אתה אומר
שביעית למכירה או שביעית לשנים ת״ל שש שנים
יעבוד שביעית למכירה ולא שביעית לשנים.

יצא לחפשי למה נאמר לפי שהוא אומר
וכי תשלחנו חפשי וגו׳ שומע אני שיכתוב לו גט
80 שחרור ת״ל יצא לחפשי או יתן לו מעות ויצא ת״ל
לחפשי חנם.

אם בגפו יבא בגפו יצא למה נאמר
לפי שהוא אומר אם אדוניו יתן לו אשה רשות אתה
אומר רשות או אינו אלא חובה ת״ל אם בגפו יבא
85 בגפו יצא רשות ולא חובה דברי רבי ישמעאל רבי
עקיבא אומר אם בגפו יבא בגפו יצא אם בראשי
איברים נכנס בראשי איברים יצא לפי שהוא אומר
וכי ימכור איש את בתו לאמה לא תצא כצאת
העבדים לא תצא בראשי איברים כדרך שהכנעניים

77—75 ערכין י״ח, ב׳. נדה מ״ח, א׳.   81—75 מ״ת 85.   79 דברים ט״ו, י״ג.
81—79 קידושין כ״ד, ב׳.   83—79 ש. 119.   85—82 לקמן ב׳.   87—82 קידושין כ׳,
א׳.   110—83 לקמן ג׳.   89—88 שמות כ״א, ז׳.

---

76 או שביעית] ד. או אינו אומר אלא.   80 יצא לחפשי] א. מ. לחפשי.   86 אם
בגפו—יצא] א. או בגפו יבא בגפו יצא.   87 לפי שהוא אומר] א״צ. ר׳ ישמעאל אומר
אינו צריך לפי שהוא אומר.   89—88 כצאת העבדים] הוספתי=ט..   89 לא תצא] א.
מ. >.

external organs. Perhaps it means she shall not go out after the six years nor in the jubilee year, as the Hebrew men-servants do? But Scripture says: "If thy brother, a Hebrew man, or a Hebrew woman, be sold unto thee, he shall serve six years" (Deut. 15.12). It expressly tells that she does go out free after six years. And how about the jubilee year? It says: "For they are My servants" (Lev. 25.42)—whatever they may be. Hence it is impossible for you to reason as in the latter version but you must reason as in the former version, that is, she shall not go out free because of the loss of any of the chief external organs, as Canaanitish slaves do. I thus know only of the Hebrew maid-servant that she does not go out free because of the loss of any of the chief external organs. How about a Hebrew man-servant? Scripture says: "A Hebrew man or a Hebrew woman" (Deut. l.c.), thus declaring the Hebrew man to be like the Hebrew woman. Just as the Hebrew woman does not go out free because of the loss of any of the chief external organs, so also the Hebrew man is not to go out free because of the loss of any of the chief external organs. Furthermore, one could reason by the method of *kal vaḥomer:* The Hebrew woman although she goes out free by showing the signs of puberty, does not go out free because of the loss of any of the chief external organs. It is therefore but logical that the Hebrew man who does not go out free by showing the signs of puberty should surely not go out free because of the loss of any of the chief external organs. Not necessarily! If you cite the case of the Hebrew woman—that is a different matter, because she cannot be sold into slavery for stealing. Therefore she is not to go out free because of the loss of any of the chief external organs. But how can you argue the same about the Hebrew man? He can be sold into slavery for stealing and therefore should go out free because of the loss of any of the chief external organs. But Scripture says: "A Hebrew man or a Hebrew woman" (ibid.), which declares the Hebrew man to be like the Hebrew woman. Just as the Hebrew woman does not go out free because of the loss of any of the

יוצאים אתה אומר לא תצא כצאת העבדים לא תצא

בראשי איברים כדרך שהכנענים יוצאים או לא

תצא בשנים וביובל כדרך שהעברים יוצאים ת״ל

כי ימכר לך אחיך העברי או העבריה ועבדך

שש שנים מגיד שהיא יוצאה בשש וביובל מנין ת״ל

כי עבדי הם מכל מקום הא אין עליך לדון בלשון

אחרון אלא בלשון ראשון לא תצא כצאן העבדים

לא תצא בראשי איברים כדרך שהכנענים יוצאים

אין לי אלא עבריה שאינה יוצאה בראשי איברים

עברי מנין ת״ל העברי או העבריה הקיש עברי

לעבריה מה עבריה אינה יוצאה בראשי איברים

אף עברי אינו יוצא בראשי איברים ועוד קל וחומר

ומה אם עבריה שהיא יוצאת בסימנין אינה יוצאה

בראשי איברים עברי שאינו יוצא בסימנין דין הוא

שלא יצא בראשי איברים לא אם אמרת בעבריה

שאינה נמכרת על הגנבה לפיכך אינה יוצאה

בראשי איברים תאמר בעברי שהוא נמכר על

גנבתו לפיכך יוצא בראשי איברים ת״ל העברי

93 — 94 דברים ט״ו, י״ב.   95 ויקרא כ״ה, מ״ב.

92 שהעברים]=ק. ל.: ט״כ. שעברים א. מ. נ. שהעברים] 93 — 94 ועבדך שש שנים]
הוספתי: ט. וגו'. 94 שהיא יוצאה] א. מ. שהוא יוצא. 95 לדון] ד. לומר. 98 — 97 כדרך
שהכנענים — בראשי איברים] מ. >.   100 — 99 עברי מנין — יוצאה בראשי איברים] א.
>.

chief external organs, so also the Hebrew man is not to go out free because of the loss of any of the chief external organs.

If He Has a Wife. This passage speaks of a wife who is an Israelitish woman. You say it refers to an Israelitish woman. Perhaps it is not so, but means a Canaanitish woman? When it says: "If his master give him a wife" (v. 4), behold, there the Canaanitish woman is spoken of. Hence what does the passage: "If he has a wife" refer to? To a wife who is an Israelitish woman.

Then His Wife Shall Go Out with Him. R. Isaac says: But was she ever brought in with him that Scripture should say she shall go out with him? Why then does Scripture say: "Then his wife shall go out with him?" To tell us that the master is obliged to provide food for the wife of his slave. He must also provide food for the slave's children. For it is said: "Then shall he go out from thee, he and his children with him" (Lev. 25.41). From the law about the going out you learn about the coming in. One might think that the master should also be obliged to provide food for the betrothed of the slave and for the widowed sister-in-law who is waiting for him to marry her? But Scripture says: "His wife," which excludes the sister-in-law waiting for him, who is not yet his wife; "with him," which excludes his betrothed, who is not yet with him.

CHAPTER II
(Ex. 21.4–6)

If His Master Give Him a Wife. This means that it is optional. You interpret it to mean that it is optional. Perhaps it is not so, but means that it is obligatory? But Scripture says: "If he come in by himself he shall go out by himself" (v. 3). Hence, it must be optional and not obligatory.

או העבריה הקיש עברי לעבריה מה עבריה אינה
יוצאה בראשי איברים אף עברי אינו יוצא בראשי
איברים.

אם בעל אשה הוא בבת ישראל הכתוב
מדבר אתה אומר בבת ישראל הכתוב מדבר או
אינו מדבר אלא בכנענית כשהוא אומר אם אדוניו
יתן לו אשה הרי אשה כנענית אמורה הא מה ת״ל אם
בעל אשה הוא בבת ישראל הכתוב מדבר.

ויצאה אשתו עמו רבי יצחק אומר מי
הביאה שהכתוב מוציאה מה ת״ל ויצאה אשתו
עמו מגיד שהוא חייב במזונותיה ובמזונות בניו
שנאמר ויצא מעמך הוא ובניו עמו מכלל יציאה
אתה למד על הכניסה יכול שיהא חייב במזונות
ארוסה ושומרת יבם ת״ל אשתו להוציא שומרת
יבם שאינה אשתו עמו להוציא ארוסה שאינה עמו.

פרשה ב (שמות כ״א, ד׳—ו׳.)

אם אדוניו יתן לו אשה רשות אתה אומר
רשות או אינו אלא חובה ת״ל אם בגפו יבא בגפו
יצא רשות ולא חובה דברי רבי ישמעאל.

120 — 116 קידושין כ״ב, א׳.   122 — 116 ש. 120. ת״כ בהר ה׳ (109d).   119 ויקרא כ״ה,
מ״א.
14 — 1 ש. 21 — 120.

108 עבריה] ד. היא.   109 עברי] ד. הוא.   115 — 114 אם בעל] מ. ואם בעל.   116 ר׳
יצחק אומר] א. <.   117 הביאה] א. מ. מביאה / מה] א. מ. <.
2 ת״ל] ד. כשהוא אומר.

If His Master Give Him a Wife. A wife to be exclusively his. She should not be like a common slave belonging to anybody.

If His Master Give Him a Wife. It is of a Canaanitish woman that this passage speaks. You interpret this passage as dealing with a Canaanitish woman. Perhaps it deals only with a Hebrew woman? It says: "The wife and her children shall be her master's." Hence, Scripture here must deal with a Canaanitish woman.

And She Bear Him Sons or Daughters. I know only about sons and daughters. How about a *tumtum* or a hermaphrodite? Scripture says: "The wife and her children shall be her master's"—whatever they may be. R. Nathan says: There would be no purpose in saying: "And she bear him," except to include the case of the master who had intercourse with his bondwoman. Her children from him are also slaves.

The Wife and Her Children. What purpose is there in saying this?[1] To declare that her children have her status. I thus know only about the bondwoman, that her children have her status. How about the case of a foreign woman?—R. Ishmael used to say: It could be argued by using the method of *kal vaḥomer.*[2]—Just as in the case of the Canaanitish slave, where marriage with an Israelite cannot take place, the children have the status of the mother, so also in any other case where marriage with an Israelite cannot take place the children have the status of the mother. And which are cases like this? The children of any bondwoman or of any foreign woman.[3]

And He Shall Go Out by Himself. This tells that the woman is not required to get a bill of divorce from him. I thus know only that a bondwoman is not required to get a bill of divorce from an Israelite.

1. I. e., "her children" instead of simply "the children."
2. Here it is merely stated that R. Ishmael used to say that by using the method of *kal vaḥomer* one could cite an argument to prove this matter. But his argument by *kal vaḥomer* is not presented. What follows is an argument by analogy, היקש (see Introduction).
3. I. e., if she has not accepted the Jewish religion. For in the latter case she is no longer considered a foreign woman.

אם אדוניו יתן לו אשה המיוחדת לו
שלא תהא כשפחת הפקר.

אם אדוניו יתן לו אשה בכנענית הכתוב
מדבר אתה אומר בכנענית הכתוב מדבר או אינו
מדבר אלא בעברית כשהוא אומר האשה וילדיה
תהיה לאדוניה הא בכנענית הכתוב מדבר.

וילדה לו בנים או בנות אין לי אלא
בנים או בנות טומטום ואנדרוגינוס מנין ת״ל האשה
וילדיה תהיה לאדוניה מכל מקום רבי נתן אומר
אין ת״ל וילדה לו אלא להביא את הרב שבא על
שפחתו שולדיה עבדים.

האשה וילדיה מה ת״ל מגיד שולדיה כמוה
אין לי אלא שפחה שולדיה כמוה נכרית מנין היה
רבי ישמעאל אומר קל וחומר הוא מה שפחה
כנענית שאין לה קידושין מכל אדם ולדיה כמוה
אף כל שאין לה קידושין מכל אדם ולדיה כמוה
ואיזה זה זה ולד שפחה ונכרית.

והוא יצא בגפו מגיד שאינה צריכה ממנו
גט אין לי אלא אמה שאינה צריכה מבן ישראל

14—12 ת״כ בהר ו׳ (109ᵈ).   15—20 קידושין ס״ח, א׳—ב׳, יבמות כ״ג, א׳.
20—19 קידושין ג׳, י״ב.

---

4 אם אדוניו] ד. ר׳ עקיבא אומר אם אדוניו.   7 אתה אומר—מדבר] ד. <.   8 מדבר]
ד. <.   10 או בנות] הוספתי: א. וגו׳.   13 אין ת״ל] מ״ח. <   / וילדה לו] ד. אלא
האשה וילדיה וילדה לו / אלא] ד. <.   15 מה ת״ל] מ״ח. <.   16 שפחה] ט. ט״ב.
> א. אשה.   17 קל וחומר הוא] ד. קל וחומר מ״ח. > ט. (הוצאות מאוחרות) בה״מ.
דין הוא.   20 שפחה ונכרית] ד. נכרית.   21 מגיד] ד. <.   22 מבן ישראל]=ט. ה.
מ״ח: א״צ. מישראל ד. מן העבד א. <.

How do I know that an Israelitish woman is not required to get a bill
of divorce from a slave? Scripture says: "Of them shall ye buy bondmen and bondmaidens" (Lev. 25.44), which declares the bondman to
be like the bondwoman and the bondwoman to be like the bondman: Just as the bondwoman needs no bill of divorce from an Israelite, so an Israelitish woman needs no bill of divorce from a bondman.
Another Interpretation: *And He Shall Go Out by Himself.* Why is this
said? Since it says: "Six years he shall serve" (v. 3), I know only that
the rule mentioned in this section applies to the slave who serves six
years. How about the slave who has been pierced through the ear?[4]
Scripture says: "and[5] he shall go out by himself," thereby including
even the slave who has been pierced through the ear. R. Isaac says:
There is no need of this scriptural proof: If the rule mentioned in this
section applies to the slave who serves six years, whose release takes
place, according to the law, after a comparatively short period, is it
not logical that the rule mentioned in this section should all the more
apply to the pierced slave whose release has been set by the law to
take place after a longer period. What purpose is there in saying: "Six
years he shall serve"? To include the case of the slave who was sick
during the six years. Might it not mean to include also the case of one
who had run away as well as of one who was sick? Scripture says:
"Six years he shall serve." You must reason: Whom does this section
deal with? With one who is in a position to do some service.[6]

But if the Servant Shall Plainly Say. This tells us that he is not to be
pierced through the ear unless he says it once and repeats[7] it.

I Love My Master, My Wife and My Children. I thus only know that
this applies when the slave has a wife and children and his master

4. Such a one must serve till the advent of the Jubilee year.

5. The *Vav* in the word והוא, meaning "and," has the force of including
another one.

6. The sick slave may render some service, the runaway slave none.

7. The infinitive absolute אמר is interpreted independently of the finite verb,
as pointing to a separate act.

גט בת ישראל שאינה צריכה מן העבד גט מנין ת״ל

מהם תקנו עבד ואמה הקיש עבד לאמה ואמה

25 לעבד מה אמה אינה צריכה מבן ישראל גט אף

בת ישראל אינה צריכה מן העבד גט. דבר אחר

והוא יצא בגפו למה נאמר לפי שהוא אומר שש

שנים יעבוד אין לי אלא עובד שש שנוהג בו מנהג

האמור בפרשה נרצע מנין ת״ל והוא יצא בגפו

30 להביא את הנרצע רבי יצחק אומר אינו צריך ומה

אם העובד שש שמיעט הכתוב יציאתו הרי הוא

נוהג בו מנהג האמור בפרשה נרצע שריבה הכתוב

יציאתו אינו דין שינהוג בו מנהג האמור בפרשה

מה ת״ל שש שנים יעבוד להביא את החולה משמע

35 מביא את החולה ואת הבורח ת״ל שש שנים יעבוד

אמרת במי העניין מדבר בראוי לעבוד.

ואם אמר יאמר העבד מגיד שאינו נרצע

עד שיאמר וישנה.

אהבתי את אדוני את אשתי ואת בני

40 אין לי אלא בזמן שיש לו אשה ובנים ולרבו אשה

---

24 ויקרא כ״ה, מ״ד.   26—25 ת״כ שם ז׳.   36—34 ספרי דברים קי״ח; קידושין ט״ז,
ב׳—י״ז, א׳; י׳ שם א׳, ב׳ (59^a).   46—37 י׳ שם (59^d).   50—37 ספרי דברים קכ״א.
קידושין כ״ב, א׳. מ״ת 86. ש. 121.

23 גט—שאינה צריכה] א. < / מן העבד] א. הימנו מן העבד.   25 מבן ישראל]=ט.
מ״ח. ג. א״א. ה.: ד. <.   29 ת״ל והוא יצא בגפו] הגהתי=ג. ט. א״א. א״צ. ז״י.
וש״י: א. מ. מ. ד. ת״ל שש שנים יעבוד.   34 מה ת״ל]=ק: נ. ל. < א. ה. ת״ל. ובענפי
יהודה שם הגיה ומה ת״ל.   35—34 מה ת״ל—ואת הבורח] מ. <.   35 ואת הבורח]=א.
ה: ד. בריא מנין / שש שנים יעבוד] מא״ש. ובענפי יהודה שם הגיהו. והוא בגפו יצא.
38 וישנה] א. שני פעמים.

also has a wife and children.[8] How do I know that it does not apply in case the master has no wife and children? It says: "And it shall be if he say unto thee: 'I will not go out from thee'; because he loveth thee and thy house"[9] (Deut. 15.16). In this connection the sages said: The slave is to be pierced through the ear only when he has a wife and children and his master has a wife and children, when he loves his master and his master loves him because his possessions were blessed through his labor.[10] In this sense it is said: "And it shall be when he say unto thee," etc. (ibid.).

Because He Fareth Well with Thee (ibid.). His well-being should be looked after like your own. In this connection the sages said: The master shall not treat the servant differently from himself in regard to food, drink or bed. In this sense it is said: "Because he fareth well with thee." Another Interpretation: *Because He Fareth Well with Thee.* This means, you both must be alike. But if he is lame or blind, he is not to be pierced through the ear.

Then His Master Shall Bring Him unto God. To the court. He is brought here merely that those who sold him may be consulted.— Rabbi says: Scripture here deals only with one who was sold by the court for theft.—He is, however, not to be pierced through the ear here[11] but privately.

And Shall Bring Him to the Door or unto the Doorpost, etc. This is merely to declare that the door must be like the doorpost. Just as the doorpost is in a standing position, so also must the door be in a standing position. You say the passage comes for this purpose. Perhaps it is to tell that the master may also pierce his ear while holding it against the doorpost? And the following reasoning would favor it: If it is proper to pierce the slave's ear against the door, which is not fit

8. See Commentaries.

9. The expression: "Thy house," here implies that the master has a wife (see M. Yoma 1.1).

10. I. e., the slave's labor.

11. I. e., publicly at the court (see Introduction and cf. Commentaries).

ובנים אין לרבו אשה ובנים מנין ת״ל והיה כי יאמר
אליך לא אצא מעמך כי אהבך ואת ביתך מכאן
אמרו לעולם אינו נרצע אלא אם כן יש לו אשה
ובנים ולרבו אשה ובנים אוהב את רבו ורבו אוהבו
45   שנתברכו נכסיו על ידו לכך נאמר והיה כי יאמר
אליך וגו׳. כי טוב לו עמך שתהא טובתו שוה לך
מכאן אמרו לא ישנה רבו עליו מאכלו ומשקהו
והסבו משלו לכך נאמר כי טוב לו עמך. דבר
אחר כי טוב לו עמך שתהיה שוה לו אם היה חגר
50   או סומא אינו נרצע.

והגישו   אדוניו   אל   האלהים   אצל
הדיינין שימלך במוכריו רבי אומר בנמכר בבית
דין על גניבתו הכתוב מדבר אבל כאן אינו נרצע
אלא בינו לבין עצמו.

55   **והגישו אל הדלת או אל המזוזה** וגו׳
מקיש דלת למזוזה מה מזוזה מעומד אף דלת
מעומד אתה אומר לכך בא או ירצענו במזוזה
והדין נותן מה אם הדלת שאינו כשר למצוה כשר

41—42 דברים ט״ו, ט״ז.   46—45 שם.   54—51 מ״ת שם. י׳ קידושין שם (59ᵃ).
65—55 ש. 121.

42 לא אצא מעמך כי אהבך ואת ביתך] הוספתי: ד. וגו׳.   44 ולרבו אשה ובנים] ד.
~ אהבתי את אדוני וגו׳ הוא.   45 ידו] ט. א״א. ~ מנין.   45—46 לכך נאמר והיה כי
יאמר אליך] מ״ח. שנאמר אשר ברכך יי אלהיך (דברים ט״ו, י״ד) ונאמר.   46 וגו׳] א.
מ. >.   48 והסבו] מ. ט. והסיבו מ״ח. והרכיבו / לכך נאמר] א. מ. מ. ת״ל.
49 שתהיה שוה לו] א. מ. מ. ט. מ״ח. א״צ. >.   52 רבי אומר] ג. מ״ח. ר׳ אליעזר
אומר א. ד״א.   53 כאן] ג. מ״ח. מוכר (מ״ח. מכר) עצמו.   57 לכך בא או] מ. לכך
נאמר.

for use in connection with any religious ceremony, is it not logical
that it should be proper to pierce the slave's ear against the doorpost,
which is fit for use in connection with a religious ceremony? But
Scripture says: "And thrust it through his ear and into the door"
(Deut. 15.17)—into the door you must thrust it, but you are not to
thrust it into the doorpost. But this may mean that he should thrust it
through the ear and through the door? It says however: "And his
master shall bore his ear through."—You are to bore through his ear
only, but you are not to bore through the door.[12] Hence it is impossible for you to argue as in the latter statement, but only as in the
former statement: This is to declare that the door must be like the
doorpost. Just as the doorpost is in a standing position, so also must
the door be in a standing position.

And His Master Shall Bore His Ear Through. Why is this said?
Because we find that everywhere else a man's agent is like himself.
But here it must be the master himself and not his agent.

His Ear. It is the right ear that Scripture speaks of. You say Scripture speaks of the right ear. But perhaps it speaks only of the left ear?
You must reason thus: Here it is said: "ear," and there (Lev. 14.17) it
is said: "ear."[13] Just as there the act is performed on the right ear, so
also here the act is performed on the right ear.

His Ear. Through the ear-lap.[14]—These are the words of R. Judah.
R. Meir says: Even through the cartilages. For R. Meir used to say: If
the slave is a priest, he is not to be pierced through the ear.—The
other sages, however, said: Even if he is a priest his ear is pierced
through.—A priest may not be sold into slavery.[15] But they said, he

12. He bores through the ear, which is held against the door, till he reaches
the surface of the door, but does not bore through the door itself.

13. The expression is not exactly the same, for here it is אזנו and there it is
אזן (see Kid. 15a).

14. In case the slave is a priest he would not thereby become disqualified for
the priesthood, since a hole in the ear-lap would not constitute a blemish.

15. This is an anonymous saying with which the other sages disagreed as
they disagreed with R. Meir's.

לרציעה מזוזה שהיא כשרה למצוה אינו דין

60 שתיכשר לרציעה ת״ל ונתת באזנו ובדלת בדלת
אתה נותן ואין אתה נותן במזוזה או יעבור באזנו
ובדלת ת״ל ורצע אדוניו את אזנו באזנו אתה מעביר
ואין אתה מעביר בדלת הא אין עליך לומר כלשון
אחרון אלא כלשון ראשון הקיש דלת למזוזה מה

65 מזוזה מעומד אף דלת מעומד.

ורצע אדוניו את אזנו למה נאמר לפי
שמצינו בכל מקום ששלוחו של אדם כמותו אבל
כאן הוא ולא שלוחו.

אזנו בשל ימין הכתוב מדבר אתה אומר בשל

70 ימין הכתוב מדבר או אינו מדבר אלא בשל שמאל
הרי אתה דן נאמר כאן אזנו ונאמר להלן אזנו מה
להלן בימין אף כאן בימין.

אזנו מן המילת דברי רבי יהודה רבי מאיר
אומר אף מן הסחוס שהיה רבי מאיר אומר אין

75 כהן נרצע והן אומרים נרצע אין כהן נמכר והן

---

60 דברים ט״ו, י״ז.   62—63 ספרי דברים קכ״ב.   66—67 י׳ קידושין ב׳, א׳ (62[a]).
72—69 קידושין ט״ו, א׳.   76—69 ספרי שם, ש. שם.   90—69 י׳ קידושין שם (59[d]).
76—73 קידושין כ״א, ב׳.

---

61 ואין] ד. אבל אי.   62 אדוניו] א. מ. ה. < / אזנו] ד. ~ במרצע.   71 הרי] ט. מדין.
73 המילת] נ. ל. הדלת.   74 אף] א״צ. ש״י.   < / הסחוס] א. הסכום.

may. And what is the reason that of all the organs the ear alone is to be pierced through? R. Johanan b. Zakkai interpreted it allegorically:[16] His ear had heard the commandment: "Thou shalt not steal" (Ex. 20.13). And yet he went and stole. Therefore it alone of all the organs shall be pierced through.

With an Awl. With any instrument. The Torah says: "And his master shall bore his ear through with an awl," but the Halakah says: It may be with any instrument. Rabbi says: I say, with a metal instrument of any kind.

And He Shall Serve Him for Ever. Until the jubilee year. For the following argument could be advanced: If money, which has greater powers, in that anything can be acquired by it, cannot in the case of the Hebrew slave acquire more than the right to six years of service, is it not logical that the act of perforation by which only slaves can be acquired should surely not have the power to acquire more than the right to six years of service?[17] Behold then, what does Scripture mean by saying: "And he shall serve him for ever?" Up to the jubilee. Well, "And he shall serve him for ever," could just as well be taken literally. But Scripture says: "And ye shall hallow the fiftieth year, and proclaim liberty throughout the land unto all the inhabitants thereof; it shall be a jubilee unto you; and ye shall return every man unto his possession," etc. (Lev. 25.10). Rabbi says: Come and see then that "for ever" here cannot mean more than fifty years.[18] It is said: "And he shall serve him for ever," that is, up to the jubilee year. How so?[19] When the jubilee arrives he goes out free. If his master dies sooner, he also goes out free.

16. See Lauterbach, "The Ancient Jewish Allegorists in Talmud and Midrash," in *JQR*, n. s., I (1911), 516 ff.

17. If there are more than six years till the jubilee, he should go out free after six years, before the jubilee.

18. See Introduction and cf. Commentaries.

19. I. e., how can you assume that they will both live to see the jubilee, which may happen to be forty-four years away?

אומרים נמכר ומה ראתה אוזן שתרצע מכל
איברים רבן יוחנן בן זכאי אומרה כמין חומר אזן
ששמעה לא תגנוב והלך וגנב היא תרצע מכל
אבריו.

במרצע בכל דבר התורה אמרה ורצע אדוניו
את אזנו במרצע והלכה אמרה בכל דבר רבי אומר
אומר אני במין מתכת בלבד.

ועבדו לעולם עד היובל שהיה בדין מה
אם הכסף שיפה כחו וקונה את הכל אינו קונה אלא
שש רציעה שאינה קונה אלא עבדים אינו דין שלא
תהא קונה אלא שש הא מה הוא ת״ל ועבדו לעולם עד
היובל או ועבדו לעולם כשמועו ת״ל ושבתם איש
אל אחוזתו רבי אומר בא וראה שאין עולם אלא
חמשים שנה שנאמר ועבדו לעולם עד שנת היובל
הא כיצד הגיע היובל יצא מת האדון יצא.

80

85

90

77—79 שם כ״ב, ב׳. תוס׳ ב״ק ז׳, ה׳.   82—80 קידושין כ״א, ב׳.   90—89 ספרי שם,
ש. שם.   90—83 מ״ת 87.   88—87 ויקרא כ״ה, י׳.   89 שם כ״ה, מ׳.

76 ראתה] ק. ראית.   77 רבן יוחנן] ד. היה רבן יוחנן / בן זכאי] ד. < / אומרה כמין
חומר] א. אומרה מן החמד ה. אמרה תורה מן החומר ט. אומר.   80 התורה]=ט.
ש״י: א. מ. ד. והתורה.   81 את אזנו] מ. אתה אומר / והלכה] ד. < / אמרה]=ט.
ש״י. א״א. ה: א. ד. ואמרה / רבי] א. רבי מאיר.   82 אומר אני] ד. < / במין] ק.
נ. כמין.   88 עולם] א. לעולם ד. העולם.   89 שנה] מ. ה. < / שנאמר] א. מ. ט.
ט״ב. <.   90—89 ועבדו לעולם—האדון יצא] ל״ט. א״צ. וישב שם עד עולם (שמואל
א. א׳, כ״ב).   89 עד שנת היובל]=א. ואולי צריך להוסיף, יעבד עמך (ויקרא כ״ה, מ׳)
מ. ד. עד היובל.

And He Shall Serve Him. Him only shall he serve, but not his son after him. For the following argument could be advanced: If the one who has to serve six years, whose release, according to the law, takes place after a comparatively shorter period, must serve his master and the master's son after him, is it not but logical that the pierced slave whose release has been set by law to take place after a longer period should surely serve his master and his master's son after him? Therefore Scripture says: "And he shall serve him"—him only shall he serve, but not his son after him. In this connection the sages said: A Hebrew slave is to serve the son of the master after the master's death, but not the daughter of the master. The pierced slave and the Hebrew female slave are to serve neither the son nor the daughter of the master after the master's death.

Chapter III
(Ex. 21.7–11)

And If a Man Sell His Daughter. This passage deals with a minor. You interpret it as dealing with a minor. Perhaps this is not so, but it deals with a grown up also? You must reason: Since the father has the right to invalidate his daughter's vows and he also has the right to sell her; just as the right to invalidate her vows is his only as long as she is a minor but not after she has grown up, so also the right to sell her is his only as long as she is a minor but not after she has grown up. But from the instance which you cite one could also argue: Just as in that case his right extends throughout the period of her maidenhood, so also his right to sell her should extend throughout the period of her maidenhood? You must reason however: Since the evidences of puberty, even if she has been sold, free her from the authority of her father, although he still has the right to betroth her, how much more should this be the case if she has never been sold.[1]

ועבדו אותו הוא עובד ואינו עובד את הבן
שהיה בדין מה אם העובד שש שמיעט הכתוב
יציאתו הרי הוא עובדו ועובד את הבן נרצע
שריבה הכתוב יציאתו אינו דין שיהא עובדו ועובד
את הבן ת״ל ועבדו אותו הוא עובד ואינו עובד
את הבן מכאן אמרו עבד עברי עובד את הבן ואינו
עובד את הבת נרצע והעבריה לא את הבן ולא
את הבת.

95

פרשה ג   (שמות כ״א, ז׳—י״א.)

וכי ימכור איש את בתו בקטנה הכתוב
מדבר אתה אומר בקטנה הכתוב מדבר או אינו
אלא אפילו בגדולה אמרת הואיל ורשאי בהפרת
נדריה ורשאי במכירתה מה הפרת נדריה קטנה
ולא גדולה אף מכירתה קטנה ולא גדולה ממקום
שבאת מה להלן כשהיא נערה אף כאן כשהיא
נערה אמרת הואיל ומוציאין אותה הסימנין מרשות
אביה שהוא רשאי בקידושיה כשהיא מכורה קל
וחומר עד שלא נמכרה.

5

91—98 ספרי שם. קידושין י״ז, ב׳. י׳ שם (59ᵃ).
5—1 כתובות מ״ג, ב׳.   33—1 ש.   122—123.   7—9 ערכין כ״ט, ב׳.

96—97 מכאן—את הבת] ט. ‹>.   98—97 נרצע—ולא את הבת] א. ‹>.
3 אפילו]=ט.   ג: מ. ד. ‹>.   4 ורשאין] הגהתי=ט. ז״י: א. מ. ד. רשאי.   6 אף
כאן] מ. אף כל.   7 אותה] ד. אותם / הסימנין] ט״כ. בסימנין.   8 כשהיא מכורה]=ק.
ורא״מ: א. מ. נ. ל. ט״כ. כשהיא נערה ט. ולא כשהיא נערה.

And If a Man Sell His Daughter. A man may sell his daughter, but a woman may not sell her daughter. For the following argument might be advanced: If the son who may not be sold by his father may nevertheless sell his own daughter, the daughter who may be sold by her father should surely have the right to sell her own daughter. Therefore it says: "And if a man sell his daughter"—a man only may sell his daughter, but a woman may not sell her daughter.

And If a Man Sell His Daughter. A man may sell his daughter, but he may not sell his son. For the following argument might be advanced: If in the case of the daughter, who may not be sold for theft, the father has the right to sell her, is it not logical that in the case of the son, who may be sold for theft, the father should have the right to sell him? Therefore it says: "And if a man sell his daughter"—his daughter a man may sell, but his son he may not.

And If a Man Sell. A man can sell himself, but a woman cannot sell herself. For the following argument might be advanced: If the son, whom his father has no right to sell, has the right to sell himself, it is but logical that the daughter, whom her father has a right to sell,

---

1. To understand the discussion in this chapter it is necessary to keep in mind the distinctions between minor קטנה, maiden נערה, and grown up woman בוגרת. Up to the age of twelve years, or before she shows signs of puberty, a girl is considered a minor, קטנה, and her father has the right according to biblical law to betroth her as well as to sell her. After the age of twelve, or after she shows signs of puberty, she is considered a maiden נערה. This period of maidenhood lasts six months. During this period her father has still the right to invalidate her vows (see Num. 30.4–6) as well as to betroth her (M. Kid. 2.1). He can also claim her earnings (M. Niddah 5.7). But he no longer has the right to sell her. And even if she had been sold when a minor, she becomes free from her master the moment she shows signs of puberty; her father then cannot sell her into slavery a second time. In this respect then the signs of puberty which free her from her master also free her from the authority of her father (see below, comment on "to be a maid-servant" and cf. Kid. 18a and 'Ar. 29b). Six months after she has shown the signs of puberty, or when she is twelve and a half years old, she is considered a grown up woman, בוגרת, and her father has no right whatever over her. He can no longer invalidate her vows, or even betroth her.

10 **וכי ימכור איש את בתו** האיש מוכר את

בתו ואין האשה מוכרת את בתה שהיה בדין מה

אם הבן שאין אביו רשאי למכרו הרי הוא מוכר

את בתו הבת שאביה רשאי למוכרה אינו דין

שתמכור את בתה ת״ל וכי ימכור איש האיש מוכר

15 את בתו ואין האשה מוכרת את בתה.

וכי ימכור איש את בתו האיש מוכר

את בתו ואינו מוכר את בנו שהיה בדין מה אם הבת

שאינה נמכרת על הגניבה אביה רשאי למוכרה

הבן שהוא נמכר על הגניבה אינו דין שיהא אביו

20 רשאי למוכרו ת״ל וכי ימכור איש את בתו האיש

מוכר את בתו ואינו מוכר את בנו. וכי ימכור איש

האיש מוכר את עצמו ואין האשה מוכרת את עצמה

שהיה בדין מה אם הבן שאין אביו רשאי למוכרו

הרי הוא מוכר את עצמו הבת שאביה רשאי למכרה

14 וכי] ק. נ. כי.   16 את בתו] הוספתי.   21 וכי ימכור איש] א. מ. ט. <.,   24 הבת]
א. מ. תאמר בבת.

should surely have the right to sell herself. No! If you cite the case of the son, that is another matter, for he may be sold for theft. Therefore he should have the right to sell himself. But will you argue the same in the case of the daughter? She cannot be sold for theft and therefore she should not have the right to sell herself. But let her be sold for theft! And the following argument would favor it: If the son, whom the father has no right to sell, is nevertheless sold for theft, it is but logical that the daughter, whom her father has the right to sell, should surely be sold for theft. No! If you cite the case of the son— that is another matter, for he is also subject to perforation of the ear. Therefore he may also be sold for theft. But will you argue the same about the daughter? She is not subject to perforation of the ear. Therefore she should not be sold for theft either. But let her be subject to perforation of the ear! And the following argument would favor it: If the son, whom the father has no right to sell, is nevertheless subject to perforation of the ear, it is but logical that the daughter, whom her father has a right to sell, should surely be subject to perforation of the ear. Therefore Scripture says: "And if a man sell"— a man can sell himself, but a woman cannot sell herself. Now, if Scripture makes an exception in her case in regard to "selling"—a weighty matter—all the more should an exception be made in her case in regard to "perforation of the ear"—a lighter matter.

And If a Man Sell. We thus learn that he has a right to sell his daughter. And how do we know that he has the right to betroth her? You must reason: If he has the right to bring her out of the state of potential betrothal[2] into a state of servitude, all the more should he have the right to bring her out of a state of potential betrothal into a

---

2. By selling her into servitude her father makes it impossible for her to become betrothed to any other man, and even makes her a servant. He thus reduces her from a higher state to a lower state. He should, therefore, all the more have the right to betroth her to one man and thus make it impossible for her to become betrothed to any other man.

25 דין הוא שתמכור את עצמה לא אם אמרת בבן

שהוא נמכר בגניבתו לפיכך הוא מוכר את עצמו

תאמר בבת שאינה נמכרת בגניבתה לפיכך לא

תמכור את עצמה ותמכר על גניבתה והדין נותן

ומה אם הבן שאין אביו רשאי למכרו הרי הוא נמכר

30 על גניבתו הבת שאביה רשאי למכרה דין הוא

שתמכר על גניבתה לא אם אמרת בבן שהוא נרצע

לפיכך הוא נמכר בגניבתו תאמר בבת שאינה

נרצעת לפיכך לא תמכר על גניבתה ותרצע והדין

נותן מה אם הבן שאין אביו רשאי למכרו הרי הוא

35 נרצע הבת שאביה רשאי למכרה דין הוא שתרצע

ת״ל כי ימכר איש איש מוכר עצמו ואין אשה מוכרת

עצמה אמרת אם מוציאה הכתוב מידי מכר החמור

קל וחומר מידי רציעה קלה.

וכי ימכור איש הא למדנו שהוא רשאי

40 במכירתה ומנין שהוא רשאי בקדושיה אמרת אם

מוציאה הוא מידי קדושיה לידי אמהות קל וחומר

27 תאמר בבת] ד. הבת.   30 דין הוא] ד. אינו דין.   37 — 36 ת״ל כי ימכר—מוכרת
עצמה] א. מ. ט. <.   ד. ל. ת״ל כי ימכר לך אחיך העברי או העבריה וגו׳ (דברים ט״ו,
י״ב). ועיין ש״י: א״צ. ת״ל וכי ימכר הוא מוכר אותה ואין היא מוכרת עצמה.
37 הכתוב] א. מ. ט. ה. הוא ט״ב. <.   39 הא] ד. <.

state of actual betrothal. And how do we know that she can be acquired as a wife with money? R. Ishmael used to say: Reason by using the method of *kal vaḥomer*: If a Canaanitish female slave, who cannot be acquired by coition, can nevertheless be acquired by money, it is but logical that an Israelitish woman, who can be acquired by coition, can surely be acquired by money. And how do we know that she can also be acquired as a wife by means of a document? Scripture says: "And goeth and becometh" (Deut. 24.2), which declares her "becoming" to be like her "going."[3] Just as a woman's going away from a husband is effected by a document, so also her becoming the wife of a man can be effected by a document. R. Akiba says: Behold it says: "If he take him another wife" (v. 10), thus declaring the latter to be like the former. Just as the former was acquired by money, so also the latter can be acquired by money.[4]

To Be a Maid-Servant. The father can sell his daughter once to be a maid-servant but he cannot sell her twice to be a maid-servant. R. Jose the Galilean says: We thus learn that he can give her into one betrothal after another and into betrothal after servitude; but not into servitude after a betrothal and, needless to say, not into one servitude after another.[5]

She Shall Not Go Out as the Slaves Do. This means she shall not go out free because of the loss of any of the chief external organs, as Canaanitish slaves do. You interpret it to mean, she shall not go out free because of the loss of any of the chief external organs. Perhaps it

---

3. The verse in Deut. refers to the woman's going out from her first husband's home, after receiving a bill of divorce. It could have said merely: "and she departeth out of his house and becometh another man's wife." The word "and goeth," before "and becometh," is to suggest that her becoming the wife of another man is effected by the same means by which her going away from the first husband's home is effected, i. e., by a written document.

4. "The former" refers to the servant bought for money, dealt with in vv. 7–9. "The latter" refers to any other woman whom he may wish to take as wife.

5. See above, note 1.

מידי קדושיה לידי קדושיה ומנין שתהא נקנית

בכסף היה רבי ישמעאל אומר קל וחומר ומה אם

שפחה כנענית שאינה נקנית בבעילה הרי היא נקנית

45 בכסף בת ישראל שהיא נקנית בבעילה דין הוא

שתקנה בכסף ומנין אף בשטר ת״ל והלכה והיתה

מקיש הויתה להליכתה מה הליכתה בשטר אף

הויתה בשטר רבי עקיבא אומר הרי הוא אומר

אם אחרת יקח לו אשה הקיש התחתונה לעליונה

50 מה העליונה בכסף אף התחתונה בכסף.

לאמה לאמה אחת הוא מוכרה ואינו מוכרה

לשתי אמהות רבי יוסי הגלילי אומר נמצינו למדין

שהוא מקדשה קידוש אחר קידוש וקידוש אחר

אמהות אבל לא אמהות אחר קידוש ואין צריך

55 לומר אמהות אחר אמהות.

לא תצא כצאת העבדים לא תצא

בראשי איברים כדרך שהכנענים יוצאים אתה

אומר לא תצא בראשי איברים כדרך שהכנענים

43—48 ספרי דברים רס״ח; קידושין ד׳, ב׳—ה׳, א׳; י׳ שם א׳, א׳ (58[b]).   46 דברים
כ״ד, ב׳.   46 דברים כ״ד, ב׳.   51—55 קידושין י״ח, א׳; י׳ שם א׳, ב׳ (59[c]).   56—77 לעיל
א׳.

---

42 לידי קידושיה] ק. י..   51 אחת] ד. י..   53—54 קידוש אחר קידוש וקידוש אחר
אמהות אבל לא] א. אחר קידוש קידוש ולא.

means she shall not go out after the six years nor in the jubilee year, as the Hebrew men-servants do? But Scripture says: "If thy brother, a Hebrew man, or a Hebrew woman, be sold unto thee, he shall serve six years" (Deut. 15.12), which expressly tells that she does go out free after six years. And how about the jubilee year? It says: "For they are My servants" (Lev. 25.42)—whatever they may be. Hence it is impossible for you to reason as in the latter version, but you must reason as in the former version, that is, she shall not go out free because of the loss of any of the chief external organs, as Canaanitish slaves do.[6] I thus know only of the Hebrew maid-servant that she does not go out free because of the loss of any of the chief external organs. How about a Hebrew man-servant? Scripture says: "A Hebrew man or a Hebrew woman" (Deut. l.c.), thus declaring the Hebrew man to be like the Hebrew woman. Just as the Hebrew woman does not go out free because of the loss of any of the chief external organs, so also the Hebrew man is not to go out free because of the loss of any of the chief external organs. Furthermore, one might argue by using the method of *kal vaḥomer*: The Hebrew woman although she goes out free by showing the signs of puberty, does not go out free because of the loss of any of the chief external organs. It is therefore but logical that the Hebrew man, who does not go out free by showing the signs of puberty, should surely not go out free because of the loss of any of the chief external organs. Not necessarily! If you cite the case of the Hebrew woman—that is different, for she cannot be sold into slavery for stealing. Therefore she is not to go out free because of the loss of any of the chief external organs. But how can you argue the same about the Hebrew man? He can be sold into slavery for stealing and therefore should go out free because of the loss of any of the chief external organs. But Scripture says: "A Hebrew man or a Hebrew woman" (ibid.), which declares the Hebrew man to be like the Hebrew woman. Just as the Hebrew

6. See vv. 26–27 and cf. above I, note 8.

יוצאים או לא תצא בשנים וביובל כדרך שהעברים

60 יוצאים ת״ל כי ימכר לך אחיך העברי או העבריה

ועבדך שש שנים מגיד שהיא יוצאה בשש וביובל

מנין ת״ל כי עבדיי הם מכל מקום הא אין עליך

לדון כלשון אחרון אלא כלשון ראשון לא תצא

כצאת העבדים לא תצא בראשי אברים כדרך

65 שהכנענים יוצאים אין לי אלא עבריה שאינה

יוצאה בראשי אברים עברי מנין ת״ל העברי או

העבריה הקיש עברי לעבריה מה עבריה אינה

יוצאה בראשי אברים אף עברי לא יצא בראשי

אברים ועוד קל וחומר הוא ומה אם עבריה שהיא

70 יוצאה בסימנין אינה יוצאה בראשי אברים עברי

שאינו יוצא בסימנין דין הוא שלא יצא בראשי

אברים לא אם אמרת בעבריה שאינה נמכרת על

גניבה לפיכך אינה יוצאה בראשי אברים תאמר

בעברי שהוא נמכר על גניבתו לפיכך יצא בראשי

75 אברים ת״ל העברי או העבריה הקיש עברי

לעבריה מה עבריה אינה יוצאה בראשי אברים

---

60 — 61 דברים ט״ו, י״ב.　62 ויקרא כ״ה, מ״ב.

---

60 — 61 או העבריה ועבדך שש שנים] הוספתי: א. ד. וגו׳.　61 שהיא יוצאה] א. מ.
ג. שהוא יוצא / בשש] א. ~ וגו׳. ד. בשנים / וביובל] א. >.　62 — 65 מנין ת״ל — כדרך
שהכנענים יוצאים] א. ד. > מא״ש. וכו׳.　66 בראשי אברים] א. ~ כדרך שהכנענים
יוצאים וגו׳.　69 — 66 עברי מנין — לא יצא בראשי אברים] א. > ד. וכו׳.　72 — 70 אינה
יוצאה — שלא יצא בראשי אברים] ד. > א. וגו׳.　77 — 73 תאמר בעברי — לא יצא בראשי
אברים] א. וגו׳ ד. וכו׳.

woman does not go out free because of the loss of any of the chief external organs, so also the Hebrew man is not to go out free because of the loss of any of the chief external organs.

If She Be Evil in the Eyes of Her Master. Being "evil" here only means that she finds no favor with him.

So That He Would Not Espouse Her, Then Shall He Let Her Be Redeemed. Hence the sages said: The duty to espouse her has precedence over the duty of allowing her to be redeemed. Another Interpretation: *So That He Would Not Espouse Her, Then Shall He Let Her Be Redeemed.* If the master does not espouse her, the father must redeem her. She may not be espoused to two at one time.[7] She may not be sold with the express condition that the master himself espouse[8] her.—These are the words of R. Jose the Galilean. R. Akiba says: The father only sells her, and if the master wishes to espouse her he may do so.

To Sell Her unto a Foreign People He Shall Have No Power. This is a warning to the court not to allow the father to sell her to a non-Jew.

Seeing He Hath Dealt Deceitfully with Her. Since he dealt treacherously with her, treated her contemptuously and not in the manner in which daughters should be treated, he[9] in turn shall not be permitted to have her under his authority.—These are the words of R. Jonathan b. Abtulemos. For "dealing deceitfully" here means dealing treacherously, as when it says: "Judah hath dealt treacherously" (Mal. 2.11); "For the house of Israel and the house of Judah have dealt very treacherously against Me" (Jer. 5.11). R. Ishmael says: This passage refers to the master who bought her with the understanding that he would espouse her, but did not espouse her. Therefore he is not per-

---

7. See Commentaries.

8. See Introduction and cf. Commentaries. Comp. also Geiger, *Urschrift,* p. 188.

9. I. e., her father. He did not treat her right by selling her into servitude. Hence, he no longer has authority over her. And once she is freed or redeemed he cannot sell her again into servitude. This is my interpretation of this passage (cf. however Commentaries).

אַף עֲבָרי לֹא יָצָא בְּרָאשֵׁי אֵבָרִים.

אִם רָעָה בְּעֵינֵי אֲדֹנֶיהָ אֵין רָעָה אֶלָּא שֶׁלֹּא נָגְמְלָה חֶסֶד לְפָנָיו.

80 **אֲשֶׁר לֹא יְעָדָהּ וְהֶפְדָּהּ** מִכָּאן אָמְרוּ מִצְוַת יִיעוּד קוֹדֶמֶת לְמִצְוַת פְּדִייָה. דָּבָר אַחֵר אֲשֶׁר לֹא יְעָדָהּ וְהֶפְדָּהּ אִם לֹא יְעָדָהּ אָדוֹן יִפְדֶּה אָב לֹא יִיעֵד לְשָׁנִים כְּאַחַת לֹא יִמְכּוֹר עַל מְנָת לִיעֵד דִּבְרֵי רַבִּי יוֹסֵי הַגְּלִילִי רַבִּי עֲקִיבָא אוֹמֵר מוֹכֵר וְאִם רָצָה 85 לִיעֵד מִיעֵד.

לְעַם נָכְרִי לֹא יִמְשֹׁל לְמָכְרָהּ הֲרֵי זֶה אַזְהָרָה לְבֵית דִּין שֶׁלֹּא יִמְכְּרֶנָּה לְגוֹי.

בְּבִגְדוֹ בָהּ מֵאַחַר שֶׁבָּגַד בָּהּ וְנָהַג בָּהּ בְּבִזָּיוֹן וְלֹא נָהַג בָּהּ כְּמִשְׁפַּט הַבָּנוֹת אַף הוּא אֵינוֹ רַשַּׁאי לְקַיְּימָהּ דִּבְרֵי רַבִּי יוֹנָתָן בֶּן אַבְטוֹלְמוֹס וְאֵין בְּגִידָה 90 אֶלָּא שִׁיקּוּר שֶׁנֶּאֱמַר בָּגְדָה יְהוּדָה וְאוֹמֵר כִּי בָגוֹד בָּגְדוּ בִי וְגוֹ' רַבִּי יִשְׁמָעֵאל אוֹמֵר בְּאָדוֹן הַכָּתוּב מְדַבֵּר שֶׁלְּקָחָהּ עַל מְנָת לִיעֵד וְלֹא יִיעֵד אַף הוּא

85—78 קידושין י"ט, א'.   124—78 ש.   124—123.   95—88 קידושין י"ח, ב'; י' שם
א', ב' (59°).   91 מלאכי ב', י"א.   92—91 ירמיה ה', י"א.

82 אדון] ד. ~ זה / יפדה] א. מ. יפדיה / אבן ט. יובל ט"ב. אבל.   83 ייעד] א. יעדה
/ כאחת] ט. כאחד/ על מנת ליעד] ג. אלא על מנת לייעד א"צ. ש"י. ז"י. ט. (הוראות
מאוחרות) על מנת שלא לייעד.   84 הגלילי] ד. >.   85—84 ואם רצה ליעד מ. ואם
לא רצה ליעד.   87 ימכרנה] כ. (מלאכי ב', י"א) ימכרוה.   88 בבזיון] ד. מנהג בזיין.
90 אבטולמוס] מ. אבוטלמס ד. אבטלמס כ. (שם) אבטליס (אבטלימוס) / ואין] ד. אומר
אין.   92 בי וגו'] א. בית וגו' ד. בית ישראל.   93 אף] א. מ. ואף.

mitted to retain her. R. Akiba says: *With His Garment on Her,*[10] means, after he spread his cloak upon her.[11]

And If He Espouse Her unto His Son. He may espouse her unto his son, but not unto his brother. For the following argument might be advanced: If he may espouse her to his son, who cannot substitute for him in case of a levirate,[12] it is but logical that he should be allowed to espouse her to his brother, who can substitute for him in case of a levirate. No! If you cite the instance of the son—that is another matter, for he takes the place of his father in connection with the inheritance.[13] Therefore he may espouse the father's maid-servant. But will you argue the same about the brother? He does not take his place in connection with the inheritance and therefore should not be allowed to espouse her. Scripture accordingly says: "And if he espouse her unto his son." Unto his son he may espouse her, but not unto his brother.

He Shall Deal with Her after the Manner of the Daughters. But have we learned anything as to the manner of the daughters? It is simply this: Behold this instance, cited to throw light, in reality receives light: Just as when espousing this one, "her food, her raiment and her conjugal rights he shall not diminish," so also when espousing any free Israelitish woman, "her food, her raiment and her conjugal rights he shall not diminish."—These are the words of R. Josiah. R. Jonathan says: This passage deals with the Hebrew maid-servant. You interpret it as dealing with the Hebrew maid-servant. Perhaps it is not so, but deals with a free Israelitish woman? When it says: "If he take him another wife" (v. 10), behold there Scripture deals with a free Israelitish woman. Why then should Scripture say here: "He

10. The word בבגדו is taken as being derived from בגד, "garment"; hence this rendering.

11. I. e., after she has been married (cf. Kid. 18ab).

12. I.e., when he has to marry his childless brother's widow.

13. The son inherits even if there are other relatives. The brother inherits only if no child or father survives the deceased (see B. B. 108b and 115a).

אינו רשאי לקיימה רבי עקיבא אומר בבגדו בה

מאחר שפירש בגדו עליה.

ואם לבנו ייעדנה לבנו ייעדנה ולא לאחיו

שהיה בדין ומה אם הבן שאינו בא תחתיו ליבום

הרי הוא ייעד אחיו שהוא בא תחתיו ליבום דין

הוא שייעד לא אם אמרת בבן שהוא נכנס תחתיו

לאחוזה לפיכך ייעד תאמר באחיו שאינו נכנס

תחתיו לאחוזה לפיכך לא ייעד ת״ל ואם לבנו

ייעדנה לבנו ייעד ולא לאחיו.

כמשפט הבנות יעשה לה וכי מה למדנו

על משפט הבנות אלא הרי זה בא ללמד ונמצא

למד מה זהו שארה כסותה ועונתה לא יגרע אף בת

ישראל שארה כסותה ועונתה לא יגרע דברי רבי

יאשיה רבי יונתן אומר בעבריה הכתוב מדבר

אתה אומר בעבריה הכתוב מדבר או אינו מדבר

אלא בבת ישראל כשהוא אומר אם אחרת יקח

לו אשה הרי בבת ישראל הכתוב מדבר ומה ת״ל

96—102 קידושין י״ז, ב׳; י׳ שם (59ª). י׳ יבמות י׳, י״ד (11ª).

---

95 שפירש] א. מ. שפרס. 97 בא] ד. נכנס. 99 שייעד] ק. ~ עליו. 100 לפיכך ייעד]
ד. <. 101 לפיכך לא ייעד] א. לפיכך ייעד. 104 על משפט] ט״ב. ממשפט.
108 בעבריה—או אינו מדבר] ד. כן או אינו. 110 בבת ישראל הכתוב מדבר] ד. בת
ישראל אמור / ומה] מ. ט. מה.

shall deal with her after the manner of the daughters"? It must refer to the Hebrew maid-servant.[14]

If He Takes Him Another Wife. In connection with this passage the sages said: A man is obliged to marry off his son. And in another passage what does it say? "But make them known unto thy children and thy children's children" (Deut. 4.9). When can you have the privilege of seeing your children's children? When you marry off your children while they are young.

Her Flesh.[15] This means, her food, as when it is said: "Who also eat the flesh of My people" (Micah 3.3). And it is written: "He caused flesh also to run upon them as the dust" (Ps. 78.27). *Her Raiment,* in its literal sense. *And Her Specific Time,* meaning cohabitation, as when it is said: "And lay with her and cohabited with her"[16] (Gen. 34.2).— These are the words of R. Josiah. R. Jonathan says: "Her body, her raiment," means raiment that is becoming to her. If she is young, he should not give her garments worn by older people. And if she is old, he should not give her garments worn by young people. *And Her Time,* meaning, he should not give her summer garments for the winter, nor winter garments for the summer. But he should give her each in its season. How about her food? You reason by the method of *kal vaḥomer:* If you cannot withhold from her things which are not necessary for sustaining life, it is but logical that you surely cannot withhold from her things that are necessary for sustaining life. How about sexual intercourse? You reason by the method of *kal vaḥomer:* If he cannot withhold from her those things for which she was not primarily married, it is but logical that he should not be allowed to withhold from her that for which she was primarily married. Rabbi says: "Her body," refers to sexual intercourse, as when it is said: "None of

14. See Introduction and cf. Commentaries.

15. This rendering is required by our Midrash, which deems it necessary to interpret it to mean merely "food," not her real flesh.

16. This rendering of the word ויענה is required by the *Mekilta.*

כמשפט הבנות יעשה לה בעבריה הכתוב מדבר.

אם אחרת יקח לו מכאן אמרו חייב אדם
להשיא את בנו ובמקום אחר מהו אומר והודעתם
לבניך ולבני בניך אימתי אתה זכאי לראות בני
בניך כשתשיא את בניך קטנים. 115

שארה אלו מזונותיה שנאמר ואשר אכלו שאר
עמי וכתיב וימטר עליהם כעפר שאר כסותה
כמשמעו ועונתה זו דרך ארץ שנאמר וישכב אותה
ויענה דברי רבי יאשיה רבי יונתן אומר שארה
כסותה כסות שהיא נופלת לשארה אם היתה ילדה 120
לא יתן לה של זקנה ואם היתה זקנה לא יתן לה
של ילדה ועונתה שלא יתן לה של ימות החמה
בימות הגשמים ולא של ימות הגשמים בימות החמה
אלא נותן לה כל אחד ואחד בעונתה מזונותיה מנין
אמרת קל וחומר ומה אם דברים שאינן קיום נפש 125
אין אתה רשאי למנוע הימנה דברים שהם קיום
נפש דין הוא שלא תהא רשאי למנוע הימנה דרך
ארץ מנין אמרת קל וחומר ומה אם דברים שלא
נשאת עליהם מתחלה אינו רשאי למנוע הימנה
דברים שנשאת עליהם מתחלה דין הוא שלא יהא 130
רשאי למנוע הימנה רבי שארה אומר זו דרך ארץ

112—113 לעיל פסחא י״ח; קידושין י״ט, א׳; ל׳, ב׳; ר׳ שם א׳, ב׳ (59); א׳, ז׳ (61ª);
יבמות ס״ב, ב׳.	113—114 דברים ד׳, ט׳.	134—114 כתובות מ״ז, ב׳—מ״ח, א׳.
116—117 מיכה ג׳, ג׳.	117 תהלים ע״ח, כ״ז.	118—119 בראשית ל״ד, ב׳.

113 בנו ובמקום אחר] ד. בנו קטן במקום אחר. ספר חסידים (הוצאת וויסטינעצקי) סי׳
תתשמ״ז, בנו במקום אחד / מהו] מ. הוא.	115 כשתשיא] מ. משתשיא ד. בזמן שאתה
משיא.	116 שנאמר] ד. וכן הוא אומר.	122 ועונתה] א. מ. ט. ט״כ. > / שלא] ט.
ט״כ. ושלא.

you shall approach to a body that is near of kin," etc. (Lev. 18.6). And it is also written: "She is thy father's near kinswoman" (ibid., v. 12). "For she is thy mother's near kinswoman" (ibid., v. 13). *Her Raiment,* in its literal sense. *Her Time,* refers to her food, as in the passage: "And he afflicted[17] thee and suffered thee to hunger" (Deut. 8.3).

Shall He Not Diminish. R. Josiah says: Why is this expression used? Because of this: It says: "If he take him another wife." I might understand that Scripture here refers to the free Israelitish woman. Therefore Scripture uses the expression: "Shall he not diminish"—from whom can one take away? From the one to whom it has been given.[18] R. Jonathan says: This passage refers to the free Israelitish woman. You interpret it as referring to the free Israelitish woman. Perhaps it is not so, but refers to the Hebrew maid-servant? When it says: "He shall deal with her after the manner of daughters" (v. 9), behold there the Hebrew maid-servant is spoken of. Hence when Scripture says here: "If he take himself another wife," it must refer to the free Israelitish woman.

And If He Do Not These Three unto Her. You must espouse her to yourself or to your son, or let her be redeemed. You interpret it to mean: You must espouse her to yourself or to your son, or let her be redeemed. Perhaps it is not so, but refers to "her food, her raiment and her conjugal rights"? You must reason: This passage is said only with reference to the Hebrew maid-servant. What then must Scripture mean by saying: "And if he do not these three unto her"? You must espouse her to yourself or to your son, or let her be redeemed.

Then She Shall Go Out for Nothing. I might understand "for nothing" to mean, without a bill of divorcement, and as for the passage:

17. The Hebrew equivalent for "He afflicted thee" is ויענך, *Piel* from ענה. In the context there, "He afflicted thee" means, "He caused thee to hunger." And if the *Piel,* which is taken to be privative, means, "to deprive of food," then the *Kal* from which the word עונתה here is formed must mean, "to provide with food."

18. I. e., from the maid-servant who even before she was espoused was given food and raiment (see above note 17, and see Introduction and cf. Commentaries).

שנאמר איש איש אל כל שאר בשרו וגו' וכתיב שאר

אביך היא שאר אמך היא כסותה כמשמעו עונתה

אלו מזונותיה שנאמר ויענך ויריבך וגו'.

135   **לא יגרע** רבי יאשיה אומר למה נאמר לפי

שהוא אומר אם אחרת יקח לו שומע אני בבת ישראל

הכתוב מדבר ת"ל לא יגרע ממי גורעים ממי שכבר

נתנו לו רבי יונתן אומר בבת ישראל הכתוב מדבר

אתה אומר בבת ישראל או אינו מדבר אלא

140   בעבריה כשהוא אומר כמשפט הבנות יעשה לה

הרי עבריה אמורה הא מה ת"ל אם אחרת יקח

לו בבת ישראל הכתוב מדבר.

ואם שלש אלה לא יעשה לה ייעד לך

או לבנך או פדה אתה אומר ייעד לך או לבנך

145   או פדה או אינו אלא שארה כסותה ועונתה אמרת

אין דבר אמור אלא בעבריה ומה ת"ל ואם שלש

אלה ייעד לך או לבנך או פדה.

ויצאה חנם שומע אני חנם מן הגט ומה אני

---

132 ויקרא י"ח, ו'.   133 — 132 שם י"ח, י"ב—י"ג.   134 דברים ח', ג'.   147 — 143 ש.
124.

---

132 אל כל] א. את כל.   137 מדבר] א. ~ או אינו מדבר אלא בעבריה.   138 יונתן]
ד. נתן.   141 מה ת"ל] ט"כ.   מה אני מקיים / אם] ק. נ. ואם.   145 ועונתה] א. מ.
~ לא יגרע.   146 ומה ת"ל] ד. <.   147 ייעד לך או לבנך או פדה]=ט. א"א. ג: א.
ד. וגו' מ. לא יגרע ייעד לך או לבנך או פדה אתה אומר או לבנך או פדה.
150 — 148 ויצאה חנם שומע אני—שלש אלה וגו'] א. <.   148 ויצאה חנם]=ט. מ"ח.
א"א. ג: מ. אם שלש אלה וגו' ד. <.

"That he writeth her a bill of divorcement" (Deut. 24.1), I would apply it to the case of all other women with the exception of the Hebrew maid-servant. And how about a Hebrew maid-servant then? Scripture says: "And if he do not these three unto her," etc. "For nothing" means, without paying money, but it does not mean without getting a bill of divorcement.[19]

Then Shall She Go Out for Nothing. That is, when she attains womanhood. *Without Money,* that is, when she attains maidenhood. It could have been inferred by the following reasoning: Since she goes out when attaining maidenhood, shall she not go out when attaining womanhood? But if there had been only one indication of a period, I would have said that it was that of womanhood. And the following argument would have favored it: Since by reaching a certain age she becomes free from the authority of the father, and by reaching a certain age she also becomes free from the authority of the master, it follows that just as from the father's authority she is freed only at the age when she changes from what she previously was, so also from the master's authority she is to be freed only at the age when she changes from what she previously was. And when does she change from what she previously was? At the time when she changes from maidenhood to womanhood. Therefore, in order that there be no room for an argument, both periods are indicated. "Then shall she go out for nothing," that is, when attaining womanhood.[20] "Without money," that is, when attaining maidenhood. R. Jonathan says: *Then Shall She Go Out for Nothing.* That is, when attaining womanhood. *Without Money.* That is, when attaining maidenhood. Abba Ḥanin says in the name of R. Eliezer: *Then Shall She Go Out for Nothing.* That is, when she attains womanhood. *Without Money.* That is, when showing the signs of puberty. This tells us that she can also go out free by repaying the purchase-money, proportionately reduced. R. Nathan says: The

19. Cf. Commentaries.
20. See Introduction and cf. Commentaries.

מקיים וכתב לה ספר כריתות בשאר הנשים חוץ

150 מן העבריה ובעבריה מנין ת"ל ואם שלש אלה וגו'

חנם מן הכסף ולא חנם מן הגט.

ויצאה חנם בבגר אין כסף בנעורים שהיה

בדין הואיל ויוצאה בימי הנעורים לא תצא בימי

בגרות שאלו לא נאמר אלא אחת הייתי אומר הן

155 הן ימי בגרות והדין נותן הואיל ויוצאה מרשות אב

ויוצאה מרשות אדון מה יוצאה מרשות אב שנשתנת

ממה שהייתה אף יוצאה מרשות אדון שנשתנת ממה

שהיית ואימתי נשתנת ממה שהיית בשעה שהיית

נערה ובגרה לכך נאמרו שתיהן שלא ליתן מקום

160 לבעל דין לחלוק ויצאה חנם בבגר אין כסף

בנעורים רבי יונתן אומר ויצאה חנם בבגר אין כסף

בנעורים אבא חנין אומר משום רבי אליעזר ויצאה

חנם בבגר אין כסף בסימנין מגיד שהיא יוצאה

בגרעון כסף רבי נתן אומר הואיל ואמרה תורה

149 דברים כ"ד, א'.   164 — 152 קידושין ד', א'; י' שם (59b).   162 — 161 ש. שם.

150 ובעבריה]=ט. ה: ד. או בעבריה מ"ח. או אף העבריה / מנין] הוספתי=ט.
153 ויוצאה] ד. ותצא.   154 לא נאמר] א. מ. נאמר.   157 אף]=ג. ד. ואף.
158 — 157 אף יוצאה—שנשתנת ממה שהיית] א. מ. ט. ◦.   158 ואימתי נשתנת ממה
שהיית] מ. ◦.   162 — 161 ר' יונתן—כסף בנעורים] א. ט. ◦.   162 חנין] ד. חנן.
163 שהיא יוצאה] ד. שהוא יוצא.

Torah said: "Give money," and also: "Do not give money." Just as "give money" applies only to the time before she showed the signs of puberty, so also "do not give money" applies only to the time after she has shown the signs of puberty.

CHAPTER IV
(Ex. 21.12–14)

One That Smiteth a Man So That He Dieth Shall Surely Be Put to Death. Why is this said? Because it says: "And he that smiteth any person shall surely be put to death" (Lev. 24.17), which I might understand to mean even if he merely slapped him. Therefore it says here: "He that smiteth a man so that he dieth," declaring that he is guilty only when he actually causes his life to depart.

One That Smiteth a Man. From this I know only about one who smites a man. How about one who smites a woman or a minor? Scripture says: "And if a man smiteth anybody he shall surely be put to death" (Lev. 1. c.). This includes even one who smites a woman or a minor. I still would know only about a man or a woman who kills a man, and also about a man who kills a woman or a minor. How about a woman that kills a minor or another woman? Scripture says: "He is a murderer" (Num. 35.16), which comes to teach us about this.[1]

One that Smiteth a Man. This could mean also a minor who smites. But Scripture says: "And if a man smiteth anybody" (Lev. 24.17). This excludes a minor.

And If a Man Smiteth Anybody. I might understand "anybody" to mean even a child born after only eight months of pregnancy.[2] But

1. See Commentaries.
2. Such a child was considered by the Rabbis as not viable (see Yer Yeb. 5cd and Bab. Niddah 38b).

165 תן כסף ובל תתן כסף מה תן כסף עד שלא באו
בה סימנין אף בל תתן כסף משבאו בה סימנין.

פרשה ד   (שמות כ״א, י״ב—י״ד.)

מכה איש ומת מות יומת למה נאמר
לפי שהוא אומר ואיש כי יכה כל נפש אדם מות
יומת שומעני אפילו סטרו סטירה ת״ל מכה איש
ומת מגיד שאינו חייב עד שתצא כל נפשו.

5 **מכה איש** אין לי אלא איש שהכה את איש
הכה את האשה ואת הקטן מנין ת״ל ואיש כי
יכה כל נפש אדם מות יומת להביא את שהכה את
האשה ואת הקטן אין לי אלא איש ואשה שהרגו
את האיש והאיש שהרג את האשה ואת הקטן האשה
10 שהרגה את הקטן ואת חברתה מנין ת״ל רוצח הוא
לתלמודו בא.

מכה איש אף הקטן במשמע ת״ל ואיש כי
יכה כל נפש אדם להוציא את הקטן ואיש כי יכה
כל נפש אדם שומעני אף בן שמונה במשמע ת״ל

4—1 סנהדרין ע״ח, א׳.   15—1 ת״כ. אמור י״ד (104[d]). סנהדרין פ״ד, ב׳. ש. 125—124.
3—2 ויקרא כ״ד, י״ז.   10 במדבר ל״ה, י״ז.

166 סימנין] א. מ. ק. ג. ~ ר׳ יוסי הגלילי אומר אין כסף (מ. ~ ומכה איש ומת מות
יומת ג. ~ וסמיך ליה מכה איש ומת מות יומת למדנו לחייבי מיתות שאינן בשילומין)
ועיין ל״ט. ובספר החינוך משפטים מ״ז.

1 מכה] א. מ. ומכה.   3 מכה] א. מ. ומכה.   4 כל] מ. ט. <.   5 אלא איש] ד.
אלא.   7 מות יומת] הוספתי: א. וגו׳.   9—8 אין לי אלא—ואת הקטן] א. ט. <.
11 לתלמודו בא] ד. ~ מכה איש שומעני להוציא את הקטן ת״ל ואיש כי יכה כל נפש
אדם להביא את הקטן שומע אני אף בן שמונה במשמע ת״ל מכה איש מגיד שאינו חייב
עד שיהרוג בן קיימא, וליתא בט. וה. ומחקוהו א״א. וא״צ.   12 אף הקטן] ה. שומעני
אף הקטן א״א. אף הקטן שהכה / במשמע] ט. או אינו אלא גדול כמשמעו.   13 להוציא
את הקטן] א. מ. ט. <.   14—13 ואיש כי יכה כל נפש אדם] הוספתי=ה. ג.
15—14 שומעני אף בן שמונה—בן קיימא] א״א. ש״י. ג. בשם ספרים אחרים, ומא״ש.
< / ת״ל מכה] א. מ. ת״ל ומכה.

Scripture says: "One that smiteth a man," telling us thereby that one is guilty only if he kills a viable child.

Shall Surely Be Put to Death. Provided there was a forewarning by the witnesses. You interpret it to mean only if there was a forewarning by the witnesses. Perhaps this is not so, but it means even if there was no forewarning by the witnesses? But Scripture says: "At the mouth of two witnesses," etc. (Deut. 17.6). Hence, when saying here: "Shall surely be put to death," Scripture must mean only if there was a forewarning by the witnesses.

Shall Surely Be Put to Death. That is, by order of the court. You interpret it to mean by order of the court. Perhaps this is not so, but it means even without the order of the court? Scripture however says: "That the manslayer die not until he stand before the congregation for judgment" (Num. 35.12). Hence, when saying here: "Shall surely be put to death," Scripture must mean, by order of the court.

Shall Surely Be Put to Death. By the sword. You say it means by the sword. Perhaps it is not so, but it means by strangulation? And you must reason thus: Here the expression: "Shall surely be put to death" is used, and there (Lev. 20.10) in the case of the adulterer the expression: "Shall surely be put to death" is used. Just as there it means by strangulation, so also here it means by strangulation. You compare the case of the murderer to the case of the adulterer. But I rather compare it to the case of the blasphemer: Here the expression: "Shall surely be put to death" is used, and there (Lev. 24.16) in the case of the blasphemer the expression: "Shall surely be put to death" is used. Just as there it means by stoning, so also here it means by stoning. Thus, if you would compare him to the adulterer, I could compare him to the blasphemer. And if you would compare him to the blasphemer, I could compare him to the adulterer. But Scripture says: "Whoso sheddeth man's blood," etc. (Gen. 9.6). Still I might say that he should be bled from any two organs so that he die thereby. But Scripture says: "And shall break the heifer's neck there in the valley"

15 מכה איש מגיד שאינו חייב עד שיהרוג בן קיימא.

מות **יומת** בהתראת עדים אתה אומר
בהתראת עדים או אינו אלא שלא בהתראת עדים
ת״ל על פי שנים עדים וגו' הא מה ת״ל מות יומת
בהתראת עדים.

20 **מות** **יומת** בבית דין אתה אומר בבית דין
או אינו אלא שלא בבית דין ת״ל ולא ימות הרוצח
עד עמדו לפני העדה למשפט הא מה ת״ל מות יומת
בבית דין.

מות **יומת** בסייף אתה אומר בסייף או אינו
25 אלא בחנק הרי אתה דן נאמר כאן מות יומת ונאמר
להלן בנואף מות יומת מה להלן בחנק אף כאן
בחנק אתה מקישו למנאף ואני מקישו למגדף נאמר
כאן מות יומת ונאמר במגדף מות יומת מה להלן
בסקילה אף כאן בסקילה אתה מקישו למנאף
30 ואני מקישו למגדף אתה מקישו למגדף ואני מקישו
למנאף ת״ל שופך דם האדם וגו' עדיין אני אומר
יקיז לו דם משני אברים וימות ת״ל וערפו שם את

15 נדה מ״ד, ב'.   16—23 ספרי במדבר קס״א.   18 דברים י״ז, ו'.   20—24 מכות י״ב,
א'.   21—22 במדבר ל״ה, י״ב.   24 ש. 125.   25 במדבר ל״ה, י״ג.   26 ויקרא כ', י'.
28 שם כ״ד, ט״ז.   31 בראשית ט', ו'.   32—33 דברים כ״א, ה' ט'.   36—32 סנהדרין
נ״ב, ב'. י' שם ז', ג' (24b). מ״ת. 126.

21 ולא ימות הרוצח=ש״י: א. מ. לא יומת הרוצח. ק. לא ימות הרוצח. נ.
ל. יומת הרוצח.   22 עד עמדו—למשפט] ד. < א. עד עמדו וגו'.   25 הרי ש״י. והרי.
28—25 ונאמר להלן—נאמר כאן מות יומת] מ. <   27—26 מה להלן בחנק אף כאן
בחנק] הגהתי=ט. ה. ז״י. א״צ. ש״י.: א. מ. ד. מה להלן בסייף אף כאן בסייף.
31—30 אתה מקישו למגדף ואני מקישו למנאף] נ. ל. <.   32 משני אברים] מ״ח. ג.
משאר אברים.

(Deut. 21.4); "So shalt thou put away the innocent blood from the midst of thee" (ibid., v. 9). This declares shedders of blood to be like the heifer whose neck is to be broken. Just as the latter is killed by cutting off its head, so all shedders of blood are to be killed by decapitation. We have heard the penalty for it but not the warning against it. But it says: "Thou shalt not murder" (Ex. 20.13).

And If a Man Lie Not in Wait, etc. If there be one who killed a person inadvertently and another who killed a person willfully, the latter comes and falls by the hand of the former. How so? The inadvertent slayer may have been leveling the roof with a roller and it fell upon the murderer and killed him. He may have been coming down a ladder and fell upon him and killed him. He may have been letting down a barrel and it fell upon the murderer and killed him.—In these cases the inadvertent slayer must leave for the city of refuge. If, however, he was pulling a roller up and it fell upon the other man and killed him, or if he was going up a ladder and fell down and killed him, or if he was drawing up a barrel and the rope broke so that the barrel fell upon the other man and killed him, the inadvertent slayer is not bound to flee to the city of refuge.—Thus the willful murderer came and fell by the hand of the inadvertent slayer. And thus it says: "As saith the proverb of the ancients," etc. (I Sam. 24.13). And where is such a proverb said? "And if a man lie not in wait, but God cause it to come to hand."[3]

Then I Will Appoint Thee a Place. But we have not heard where? You must reason thus: A refuge for the use of that period was ordered and a refuge to be used for future generations was ordered. Just as in the case of the refuge for the future generations it was the cities of the

3. In both cases the acts were committed in secret, so that the murderer was not brought to trial and the inadvertent slayer did not suffer the penalty of having to leave home to go to the city of refuge. God causes it to come to the hand of the inadvertent slayer to slay the murderer inadvertently but in the presence of witnesses. The murderer has thus suffered the penalty of death and the inadvertent slayer now has to flee to the city of refuge.

העגלה בנחל וגו' ואתה תבער הדם הנקי מקרבך

הקיש שופכי דמים לעגלה ערופה מה עגלה ערופה

35 בהתזת הראש אף כל שופכי דמים בהתזת הראש

עונש שמענו אזהרה לא שמענו ת"ל לא תרצח.

ואשר לא צדה וגו' אחד שהרג נפש בשוגג

ואחד שהרג נפש במזיד בא מזיד ונפל ביד שוגג

הא כיצד היה במעגלה ונפלה עליו והרגתהו

40 היה יורד בסולם ונפל עליו והרגו משלשל בחבית

ונפלה עליו והרגתו הרי זה גולה אבל היה מושך

במעגלה ונפלה עליו והרגתו היה עולה בסולם

ונפל עליו והרגו יהיה דולה בחבית ונפסק החבל

ונפלה עליו והרגתו הרי זה אינו גולה בא מזיד ונפל

45 ביד שוגג וכן הוא אומר כאשר יאמר משל הקדמוני

וגו' והיכן אמור ואשר לא צדה והאלהים אנה לידו.

ושמתי לך מקום אבל לא שמענו להיכן

הרי אתה דן נאמר מנוס לשעה ונאמר מנוס לדורות

מה מנוס האמור לדורות ערי הלוים קולטות אף

---

36 שמות כ', י"ג.   46—37 מכות ז', א'—ב'; י', ב'.   45 שמואל א. כ"ד, י"ג.
50—47 מכות י"ב, ב'.

33 וגו'] הוספתי.   35 בהתזת הראש] מ"ח. מן הצאור.   36 לא שמענו] א. מנין.
38 ביד] א. מ. על.   48 היה יורד—והרגנו] א. > / יורד] מ. ה. עולה ק. יורד עולה
ג. / ונפל] הגהתי=ה: מ. ד. ונפלה/ והרגנו] מ. והרגתהו.   41—43 הרי זה גולה—והרגנו]
א. >.   41—44 הרי זה גולה—הרי זה אינו גולה] א"צ. >.   42 עולה] מ. ה. יורד ק.
יורד עולה.   43 והרגנו] מ. והרגתהו / בחבית/ בחבית] א. ה. בחבל.   44 ונפלה] הגהתי=מא"ש:
א. מ. ד. ונפל / והרגתנו] ד. והרגו.   46] לידו] ד. וגו'.   47 ושמתי לך מקום] ד. >.
48—47 להיכן הרי] ד. היכן.

Levites that offered it (Num. 35.6 ff.), so also in the case of the refuge
for that period it was the camps of the Levites that offered it. Issi b.
Akabyah says: *Then I Will Appoint Thee a Place*. Why is this said?
Because of the following: It says: "Abide ye every man in his place, let
no man go out of his place," etc. (Ex. 16.29). This is to be interpreted
as referring to the limit of the 2,000 cubits. You interpret it as referring to the limit of the 2,000 cubits. Perhaps it is not so, but it refers
only to the limit of "four cubits"?[4] You must reason thus: Here
(Ex. 16.29) the expression "place" is used, and there (ibid., 21.13)
the expression "place" is used. Just as the "place" mentioned there
extends 2,000 cubits beyond its limits,[5] so also the "place" mentioned here extends 2,000 cubits beyond its limits. Therefore it says:
"Then I will appoint thee a place."

And If a Man Come Presumptuously, etc. Why is this said? Because
it says: "And he that killeth any man," etc. (Lev. 24.17), which might
be taken as including one who acts intentionally and one who acts
inadvertently, outsiders, a healer whose treatment results in death,
one administering stripes by authority of the court, and one chastis-
ing his son or his pupil, whose acts result in death. Therefore it says
here: "And if there come presumptuously," to exclude the one acting
inadvertently; "A man," to exclude the minor, "a man," to include
outsiders; "His neighbor," to include the minor, "his neighbor," to
exclude the outsiders.[6]—Issi b. Akabyah says: Before the giving of
the Torah we had been warned against shedding blood. After the giving of the Torah, whereby laws were made stricter, shall they be considered lighter? In truth, the sages said: He is free from judgment by
the human court but his judgment is left to heaven.—"To slay him
with guile," to exclude the deaf and dumb, the insane and the minor,
who cannot practice guile; "to slay him with guile," to exclude the

4. See above *Vayassa',* VI, note 1.
5. The place mentioned in Ex. 21.13 is a place of refuge which, according to
Num. 35.5 (cf. M. Sotah 5.3), includes 2000 cubits beyond its limits.
6. See Introduction and cf. Commentaries

מנוס האמור לשעה מחנות הלוים קולטות איסי
בן עקביה אומר ושמתי לך מקום למה נאמר לפי
שהוא אומר שבו איש תחתיו אל יצא איש ממקומו
וגו' אלו אלפים אמה אתה אומר אלו אלפים אמה
או אינו אלא ארבע אמות הרי אתה דן נאמר כאן
מקום ונאמר להלן מקום מה מקום האמור להלן
אלפים אמה אף מקום האמור כאן אלפים אמה
ושמתי לך מקום וגו'.

וכי יזיד איש וגו' למה נאמר לפי שהוא
אומר ואיש כי יכה כל נפש אדם וגו' יכול אף
המזיד והשוגג ואחרים והמרפא שהמית והמכה
ברשות בית דין והרודה בבנו ובתלמידו במשמע
ת"ל וכי יזיד להוציא את השוגג איש להוציא את
הקטן איש להביא את האחרים רעהו להביא את
הקטן רעהו להוציא את אחרים איסי בן עקביה
אומר קודם מתן תורה היינו מוזהרים על שפיכת
דמים לאחר מתן תורה שהוחמרו הוקלו באמת
אמרו פטור מדיני אדם ודינו מסור לשמים להרגו
בערמה להוציא חרש שוטה וקטן שאינן מערימין

57—50 עירובין נ"א, א'. ש. 125.   52 שמות ט"ז, כ"ט.   59 ויקרא כ"ד, י"ז.   71—64 ספרי
דברים קפ"א. מכות ח', א'. ש. 26—125.

51 עקביה] ק. נ. עקביא ט. יעקב.   52 אל יצא איש ממקומו] הוספתי.   56—55 האמור
להלן—כאן] א"צ. האמור כאן—להלן.   57 ושמתי לך מקום וגו'] אולי צ"ל לך נאמר
ושמתי לך מקום וגו' ט. > ומוחקו מא"ש.   58 למה נאמר] מ. ד. ~ פרשה זו.   59 יכול]
א. מ. ק. > / אף] א. מ. ק. ואף ט. ש"י. בין.   60 המזיד והשוגג] א"צ. ההורג
אחרים / ואחרים] א. והאחרים (אולי נשתבש מן החרש?) ג. והקטן א"צ. והחרש והשוטה
שהמיתו.   62 להוציא את השוגג] הגהתי=ט. א"א. ז"י. ש"י. ורש"י.   64—63 איש
להביא את האחרים רעהו להביא את הקטן] ט. א"א. >.   66 שהוחמרו] א. לאחר
שהוחמרו נ. ל. תחת שהוחמרו.   67—68 להרגו בערמה להוציא חרש שוטה וקטן שאינן
מערימין] מ. > א"צ. וכי יזיד להוציא חרש שוטה.   71 שהן] ד. שהיו / אבל] ד. >.

healer whose treatment results in death, the one who administers stripes by authority of the court, the one who chastises his son or his pupil, all of whom, though acting intentionally, do not practice guile.

Thou Shalt Take Him from Mine Altar, etc. This tells us that we interrupt him in his service and he is led out to be executed.

Thou Shalt Take Him from Mine Altar That He May Die. This passage comes to teach that the punishment of murder should set aside the Temple service. For the following argument might have been advanced: If the Sabbath, although it is set aside by the Temple service, is not set aside for the sake of punishing murder, is it not logical that the Temple service, which has precedence over the Sabbath, should surely not be set aside for the sake of punishing murder? Therefore it says: "Thou shalt take him from Mine altar that he may die." Scripture thus comes to teach that the punishing of murder should set aside the Temple service. The punishing of murder has precedence over the Temple service, but it is not to have precedence over the Sabbath. For the following argument might have been advanced: If the Temple service, which has precedence over the Sabbath, is set aside for the sake of punishing murder, it is but logical that the Sabbath, which is set aside by the Temple service, should surely be set aside for the sake of punishing murder. This is not conclusive! If you cite the instance of the Temple service—that is different, for the burial of the unclaimed dead has precedence over it. Therefore the punishing of murder should also have precedence over it. But will you argue the same about the Sabbath? The burial of the unclaimed dead has no precedence over it. Therefore, the punishing of murder shall not have precedence over it either.—Said one of the disciples of R. Ishmael: Behold, it says: "Ye shall kindle no fire in all your habitations on the sabbath day" (Ex. 35.3). Burning was included in the general category of prohibited works and it has been singled out for special mention to teach that just as in the case of "burning," specifically mentioned, which is one of the methods of

להרגו בערמה להוציא מרפא שהמית והמכה
70 ברשות בית דין והרודה בבנו ובתלמידו אף על
פי שהן מזידין אבל אינן מערימין.

מעם מזבחי וגו' מגיד שמבטלין עבודה מידו
ויוצא ליהרג.

מעם מזבחי תקחנו למות בא הכתוב
75 ללמד על רציחה שתתדחה את העבודה שהיה בדין
ומה אם שבת שעבודה דוחתה אין רציחה דוחתה
עבודה שהיא דוחה את השבת אינו דין שלא תהא
רציחה דוחתה ת"ל מעם מזבחי תקחנו למות בא
הכתוב ללמד על רציחה שתתדחה את העבודה.
80 רציחה שהיא דוחה את העבודה ואינה דוחה את
השבת שהיה בדין ומה אם עבודה שהיא דוחה
את השבת הרי רציחה דוחה אותה שבת שעבודה
דוחתה דין הוא שתהא רציחה דוחתה לא אם אמרת
בעבודה שקבורת מת מצוה דוחתה לפיכך רציחה
85 דוחתה תאמר בשבת שאין קבורת מת מצוה דוחתה
לפיכך לא תהא רציחה דוחתה אמר תלמיד אחד
מתלמידי רבי ישמעאל הרי הוא אומר לא תבערו
אש בכל מושבותיכם שריפה היתה בכלל ויצאה
ללמד מה שריפה מיוחדת שהיא אחת ממיתות

---

72 — 73 יומא פ"ה, א'. מכות י"ב, א'. י' שם ב', ז' (31^d). ש. 126.   105 — 74 סנהדרין
ל"ה, ב'.   92 — 86 לקמן שבתא ב'.   88 — 87 שמות ל"ה, ג'.

80 רציחה שהיא דוחה את העבודה] ד. > / ואינה] ד. אינו.   81 — 80 רציחה שהיא—שהיה
בדין] ט. ש"י. ותהא רציחה דוחה את השבת מקל וחומר.   86 לפיכך לא תהא] א.
מ. לפיכך תהא.   89 — 86 אמר תלמיד אחד—מה שריפה] מ"ח. משום ר' ישמעאל
אמרו הרי נאמר לא תבערו אש בכל מושבותיכם ולהלן הוא אומר והיו אלה לכם לחקת
משפט בכל מושבותיכם מה להלן בית דין אף מושבות האמור כאן בית דין ומה שריפה.
88 בכל מושבותיכם] ד. וגו'.   89 — 88 ויצאה ללמד] א. ג. ולמה יצאת ללמוד.

death decreed by the court, the Sabbath laws are not to be superseded, so also in the case of all the other modes of death decreed by
the court, the Sabbath laws are not to be superseded.—But let the
burial of the unclaimed dead set aside the Sabbath! And the following reasoning would favor it: If the Temple service, which supersedes
the Sabbath, is set aside by the burial of the unclaimed dead, it is logical that the Sabbath, which is set aside by the Temple service, should
surely be set aside by the burial of the unclaimed dead. But this is not
conclusive! If you cite the instance of the Temple service—that is different, for the punishing of murder sets it aside. Therefore, the burial
of the unclaimed dead also sets it aside. But will you argue the same
about the Sabbath? The punishing of murder does not set it aside.
Therefore, the burial of the unclaimed dead should likewise not set it
aside. It is said: "His body shall not remain all night upon the tree,
but thou shalt surely bury him the same day" (Deut. 21.23). Only on
a day on which he may be executed may he be buried. The punishing
of murder supersedes the Temple service. The saving of a life however is not to supersede the Temple service. For the following argument might have been advanced: If the Sabbath, which is not set
aside for the sake of punishing murder, is set aside for the sake of
saving life, is it not logical that the Temple service, which is set aside
for the sake of punishing murder, should surely be set aside for the
sake of saving life? But it says: "Thou shalt take him from Mine altar
that he may die." Scripture thus comes to teach in regard to the Temple service that it should not be set aside for the sake of saving a life.
R. Simon b. Menasya says: The duty of saving life should supersede
the Sabbath laws, and the following reasoning favors it: If the punishing of murder sets aside the Temple service, which has precedence
over the Sabbath, how much the more should the duty of saving life,
which likewise sets aside the Temple service, supersede the Sabbath
law.[7]

7. See Introduction and cf. Commentaries.

90 בית דין אינה דוחה את השבת אף כל שאר מיתות
בית דין לא ידחו את השבת ותהא קבורת מת מצוה
דוחה את השבת והדין נותן ומה אם עבודה שהיא
דוחה את השבת קבורת מצוה דוחתה שבת שעבודה
דוחתה דין הוא שתהא קבורת מצוה דוחתה לא
95 אם אמרת בעבודה שרציחה דוחתה לפיכך קבורת
מצוה דוחתה תאמר בשבת שאין רציחה דוחתה
לפיכך לא תהא קבורת מצוה דוחתה נאמר לא
תלין נבלתו על העץ כי קבור תקברנו ביום ההוא
ביום שנהרג בו ביום יקבר. רציחה דוחה את
100 העבודה ואין פקוח נפש דוחה את העבודה שהיה
בדין ומה אם שבת שאין רציחה דוחתה פקוח נפש
דוחה את השבת עבודה שרציחה דוחתה אינו דין
שיהא פקוח נפש דוחה את העבודה ת״ל מעם
מזבחי תקחנו למות בא הכתוב ללמד על עבודה
105 שאין פקוח נפש דוחה את העבודה רבי שמעון בן
מנסיא אומר ויהא פקוח נפש דוחה את השבת והדין
נותן אם דוחה רציחה את העבודה שהיא דוחה את
השבת פקוח נפש שהוא דוחה את העבודה לא כל
שכן.

97—98 דברים כ״א, כ״ג.   105—109 לקמן שבתא א׳. יומא פ״ה, ב׳.

90 אינה דוחה] מ״ח. אב מלאכה ואינה דוחה / אף] א. מ. ואף.   91 קבורת מת מצוה]
א. קבורת מצוה מ. מצות קבורת מצוה.   92 את השבת] מ. <.   97 לא תהא] א. מ.
תהא / נאמר] ד. לכך נאמר.   98 כי קבור תקברנו ביום ההוא] הוספת: מ. ד. וגו׳ /
ביום] ד. בו ביום.   100—101 ואין פקוח נפש דוחה את העבודה שהיה בדין] א״צ. קל
וחומר דוחה את העבודה ז״י. ופיקוח נפש דוחה את העבודה שהיה בדין. אה״ו הגיה
וכן פיקוח נפש דוחה את העבודה ודין הוא.   103—105 ת״ל מעם מזבחי—את העבודה]
מ. נ. ל. <.   105 שאין] הגהתי=ט: ט״כ. שלא תהא ג. שלא יהא א. ק. שיהא /
שמעון] ט. ישמעאל.   106 דוחה את השבת] ט״כ. דוחה את העבודה.   107—108 אם
דוחה רציחה את העבודה שהיא דוחה את השבת]=א. מ. ט״כ: ד. ט. אם רציחה
דוחה את העבודה שהיא <ט. עבודה] דוחה את השבת ש״י. אם רציחה את העבודה
שהיא דוחה את השבת לא ידחה את השבת את השבת ג. (בגליון למטה) אם דוחה רציחה שאינה דוחה
את השבת דוחה את העבודה פיקוח נפש שהוא דוחה דוחה את השבת דין הוא שידוחה
העבודה ת״ל תקחנו למות.   108—109 פקוח נפש שהוא דוחה דוחה את העבודה לא כל שכן]
הגהתי=ט. א״א. ג. (בגליון מן הצד). ומא״ש: א. ד. > מ. ת״ל ט״כ. וכי׳.

Thou Shalt Take Him from Mine Altar That He May Die. "That he may die," but not that he may be judged, nor that he be given the punishment of stripes, nor that he may leave for the city of refuge.

Thou Shalt Take Him from Mine Altar That He May Die. We can thus learn that the place for the Sanhedrin is alongside of the altar. Although there is no proof for it, there is a suggestion of it in the passage: "And Joab fled unto the tent of the Lord and caught hold of the horns of the altar"[8] (I Kings 2.28).

CHAPTER V
(Ex. 21.15–17)

And One That Smiteth His Father and His Mother Shall Be Surely Put to Death. Why is this said? Because it says: "Eye for eye," etc. (v. 24). Behold then, Scripture singles out this case from the general statement in order to declare it a graver offence punishable by death. For this purpose this section is set forth.

And One That Smiteth His Father and[1] His Mother. I thus know about the one who smites both his father and his mother. How about one who smites only his father or only his mother? You must reason thus: Since one becomes guilty by smiting his parents and one becomes guilty by cursing his parents, it follows that just as one becomes guilty by cursing either one of them, so also one should become guilty by smiting either one of them. But this is not conclusive! For if you cite the instance of the one who curses—that is different, for he becomes guilty by cursing them after they are dead as by cursing them when they are alive. Therefore he also becomes guilty

---

8. See above *Baḥodesh*, XI, note 8.

1. The Hebrew text can also be rendered by "his father or his mother" since the "ו" in ואמו may mean "or" as well as "and"; but such a translation would make the midrashic comment superfluous.

110 **מעם מזבחי תקחנו למות** למות ולא

לדון ולא ללקות ולא לגלות.

מעם מזבחי תקחנו למות נמצינו למדין

שסנהדרין בצד המזבח ואף על פי שאין ראיה

לדבר זכר לדבר וינס יואב אל אהל יי ויחזק

115 בקרנות המזבח.

פרשה ה   (שמות כ״א, ט״ו—י״ז.)

ומכה אביו ואמו מות יומת למה נאמר

לפי שהוא אומר עין תחת עין וג׳ והרי הכתוב

מוציאו מכללו להחמיר עליו שיהא במיתה לכך

נאמר פרשה זו.

5 **ומכה אביו ואמו** אין לי אלא אביו ואמו

אביו שלא אמו ואמו שלא אביו מנין הרי אתה דן

הואיל והמכה חייב והמקלל חייב מה המקלל

אחד אחד בפני עצמו אף המכה אחד אחד בפני

עצמו לא אם אמרת במקלל שהוא חייב על המתים

110—115 י׳ מכות שם.   112—115 לעיל בחודש י״א. ש. 126.   114—115 מלכים א.
ב׳, כ״ח.
1—24 ת״כ. אמור י״ד (105ª).

3 מכללו] א. מכלל מ. לכללו.

by cursing either one of them. But will you argue the same about the one who smites? He does not become guilty by smiting the dead as he does by smiting the living. Therefore he should not become guilty by smiting either one of them. But there would be no purpose in saying: "And he that smiteth his father and his mother," unless it meant, even one of them.[2]—These are the words of R. Josiah. R. Jonathan says: It can mean both of them together and it can also mean either of them, unless Scripture should expressly say: "together." R. Isaac says: And must it be that "his mother" comes to make it severer for him? May it not come to make it lighter for him? No! Once the law has been made stricter in this case should it be interpreted as being lighter?[3] Scripture says: "And he that smiteth his father and his mother shall be surely put to death."

And One That Smiteth His Father and His Mother. It must be a blow that results in a wound. You interpret it to mean a blow resulting in a wound. Perhaps this is not so, but it means even a blow which does not result in a wound? You must reason thus: If the rule in regard to damages, which is more comprehensive, is that one is obliged to pay damages only if one inflicts a wound, the rule in regard to punishment, being of lesser scope, surely should be that one should not be guilty unless he inflicts a wound. Hence, when it says: "And one that smiteth his father and his mother," it must mean, with a blow which results in a wound.

Shall Be Surely Put to Death. By strangulation. You interpret it to mean by strangulation. Perhaps this is not so, but means by any manner of death prescribed in the Torah? You must say: This is a rule of the Torah: Whenever a death penalty is mentioned in the Torah with the mode of execution undefined, you are not allowed to extend its meaning to include a severer mode, but you must confine it to the lightest mode.—These are the words of R. Josiah. R. Jonathan says:

2. See Commentaries.
3. See Introduction and cf. Commentaries.

כחיים לפיכך הוא חייב על כל אחד ואחד בפני
עצמו תאמר במכה שאינו חייב על המתים כחיים
לפיכך לא יהא חייב על כל אחד ואחד בפני
עצמו שאין ת״ל ומכה אביו ואמו אלא אפילו אחד
מהן דברי רבי יאשיה רבי יונתן אומר משמע שניהם
כאחת ומשמע אחד אחד בפני עצמו עד שיפרוט
לך הכתוב יחדו רבי יצחק אומר וכי לא באת אמו
אלא להחמיר עליו או להקל עליו לא מפני
שהוחמר בו הוקל בו ת״ל ומכה אביו ואמו.

ומכה אביו ואמו מכה שיש בה חבורה
אתה אומר מכה שיש בה חבורה או אינו אלא מכה
שאין בה חבורה אמרת ומה אם מדת נזיקין מרובה
אינו חייב עד שיעשה בהן חבורה מדת עונשין
מעוטה לא יהא חייב עד שיעשה בהם חבורה הא
מה ת״ל מכה אביו ואמו מכה שיש בה חבורה.

מות יומת בחנק אתה אומר בחנק או אינו אלא
באחת מכל המיתות האמורות בתורה אמרת זו
מדה בתורה כל מיתה האמורה בתורה סתם אין
אתה רשאי למושכה להחמיר עליה אלא להקל
עליה דברי רבי יאשיה רבי יונתן אומר לא מפני

24—19 סנהדרין פ״ד, ב׳. י׳ שם י״א, א׳ (30ᵃ) ש. שם.   31—25 י׳ סנהדרין ז׳, א׳ ד׳ (24ᵇ).

13 שאין ת״ל ומכה אביו ואמו] א״צ. ש״י. ג. ת״ל ומכה אדם יומת (ג. ~ שאין ת״ל שהרי כתוב ומכה אביו ואמו ואיש כי יכה כל נפש אדם אלא ללמד על אביו ואמו שחייב על כל אחד) / אלא] א״צ. ש״י. <.   15 שיפרוט] ט״כ. שיפטור.   16 יחדו] הגהתי=ט. ג. א״צ. ז״י: א. מ. ד. אחד. מא״ש כאחד / וכי לא באת אמו] ג. וכי למה באת אמו א״צ. וכי לא באת.   17 לא מפני] ג. הוי להחמיר עליו וכי מפני. 18 ת״ל ומכה אביו ואמו] ש״י. <.   19 ומכה אביו ואמו] ט. ט״כ. < מ. ד״א ומכה אביו ואמו.   21 שאין בה] ד. שאין עליה / נזיקין] מ. ניזוקין.   22 בהן] ד. בה. 27 סתם]=ט. ג. ה: מ. ד. <.

Not because it is the lighter manner of death but merely because the manner of death mentioned here is undefined, and whenever a death penalty is prescribed in the Torah with the mode of execution undefined it means death by strangulation. Rabbi says: It must be like the death penalty exacted by Heaven. Just as the death penalty exacted by Heaven is such as leaves no mark, so also the death penalty mentioned here should be exacted in a manner which leaves no mark. Hence they said: Death by strangulation is inflicted in the following manner: They place the criminal in dung up to his knees. Then they put a twisted scarf of coarse material within a soft one and wind it around his neck. The ends of the scarf are pulled on both sides until life is extinct. This is the manner of strangulation. We have heard the penalty for it, but we have not heard the warning against it. Scripture says: "Forty stripes he may give him, but shall not exceed" (Deut. 25.3). Behold then, by using the method of *kal vaḥomer,* you reason: If he whose duty it is to beat, is warned not to beat,[4] it is but logical that he whose duty is to refrain from beating is surely considered warned not to beat.

And One That Stealeth a Man and Selleth Him. Why is this said? Since it says: "If a man be found stealing any of his brethren," etc. (Deut. 24.7), I know only that there must be witnesses to the theft. But how do I know that there must be witnesses to the sale? It says here: "And one that stealeth a man and selleth him."[5]

And One That Stealeth a Man. I thus know only about one who steals a man. How about one who steals a woman or a minor? It says: "If a man be found stealing any of his brethren" (ibid.), thus including one who steals a woman or a minor. Still I know only about a man or a woman who steals a man, and also about a man who steals a woman or a minor. How about a woman who steals a minor or another woman? Scripture says: "Then that thief shall die" (ibid.)—in any case.

4. I. e., more than prescribed.
5. See Introduction and cf. Commentaries.

30 שהיא קלה אלא מפני שנאמרה סתם וכל מיתה
האמורה סתם הרי זו בחנק רבי אומר כמיתה
שנאמרה בידי שמים מה מיתה שנאמרה בידי שמים
מיתה שאין בה רושם אף מיתה שנאמרה כאן מיתה
שאין בה רושם מכאן אמרו מיתת חנק משקעין אותו
35 בזבל עד ארכובותיו ונותנין סודרין קשין בתוך
הרכין וכורך על צוארו זה מושך להלן וזה מושך
להלן עד שנפשו יוצאה זה סדר חנק עונש שמענו
אזהרה לא שמענו ת״ל ארבעים יכנו לא יוסיף והרי
דברים קל וחומר ומה אם מי שהוא מצוה להכותו
40 הרי הוא מוזהר שלא להכות מי שהוא מצוה שלא
להכות דין הוא שיהא מוזהר שלא להכות.

וגונב איש ומכרו למה נאמר לפי שהוא
אומר וכי ימצא איש גונב נפש מאחיו וג׳ אין לי
אלא עדים על גניבה עדים על מכירה מנין ת״ל
45 וגונב איש ומכרו.

וגונב איש אין לי אלא איש שגנב את האיש
גנב את האשה ואת הקטן מנין ת״ל וכי ימצא איש
גונב נפש להביא את שגנב את האשה ואת הקטן
אין לי אלא איש ואשה שגנבו את האיש והאשה שגנב
50 את האשה ואת הקטן האשה שגנבה את חברתה
ואת הקטן מנין ת״ל ומת הגנב ההוא מכל מקום.

37—25 סנהדרין נ״ב,ב׳. ת״כ. קדושים י׳ (92ª).   31—30 ספרי דברים קנ״ה. סנהדרין
פ״ט, א׳. ש. 126.   41—38 סנהדרין פ״ה, א׳. י׳ שם י״א, א׳ (30ª).   38 דברים כ״ה, ג׳.
41—39 מ״ת. 163.   51—42 שם 156.   51—46 סנהדרין פ״ה, ב׳.   48—47 דברים כ״ד,
ז׳. 51 שם.

34 מיתת] מ. ד. מצות / משקעין] ד. היו משקעין.   36—35 בתוך הרכין] ד. ברכין.
43 וכין] ל. כי, כמו במקרא שלפנינו.   46 וגונב איש] ג. ד״א וגונב איש.   47 וכין] ל.
כי.

And One That Stealeth a Man. This would mean even a minor who steals. But Scripture says: "If a man be found stealing any person" (ibid.), thus excluding a minor. *If a Man Be Found Stealing Any.* I might understand this to mean even a child born after only eight months of pregnancy. But it says: "And one that stealeth a man," telling us thereby that one is guilty only if he steals a viable child.

And Selleth Him. But not if he sells only half an interest in him. *Or if He Be Found.* Finding in every case means, ascertaining through witnesses. *In His Hand.* "In his hand" merely means in his possession. And although there is no explicit proof for it, there is a suggestion of it in the passage: "And taken all his land out of his hand" (Num. 21.26). And it also says: "Having all goodly things of his master's in his hand" (Gen. 24.10). Thus, "in his hand" everywhere only means in his possession.

Shall Be Surely Put to Death. By strangulation. You interpret it to mean by strangulation. Perhaps this is not so, but it means by any manner of death prescribed in the Torah? You must say: This is a rule of the Torah: Whenever a death penalty is mentioned in the Torah with the mode of execution undefined, you are not allowed to extend its meaning to include a severer mode, but you must confine it to the lighter mode.—These are the words of R. Josiah. R. Jonathan says: Not because it is the lighter manner of death, but merely because the manner of death mentioned here is undefined, and whenever a death penalty is prescribed in the Torah with the mode of execution undefined it means death by strangulation. Rabbi says: It must be like the death penalty exacted by Heaven. Just as the death penalty exacted by Heaven is such as leaves no mark, so also the death penalty mentioned here should be exacted in a manner which leaves no mark. Hence they said: Death by strangulation is inflicted in the following manner: They place the criminal in dung up to his knees. Then they put a twisted scarf of coarse material within a soft one and wind it around his neck. The ends of the scarf are pulled on both sides until

וגונב איש אף הקטן במשמע ת״ל וכי ימצא
איש גונב נפש להוציא את הקטן וכי ימצא איש גונב
נפש שומע אני אף בן שמונה במשמע ת״ל וגונב איש
מגיד שאינו חייב עד שיגנוב בן קיימא.

ומכרו ולא שמכר חציו. **ונמצא** אין מציאה
אלא בעדים.

בידו אין בידו אלא רשותו ואף על פי שאין
ראיה לדבר זכר לדבר ויקח את כל ארצו מידו
ואומר ויקח העבד עשרה גמלים מגמלי אדוניו
וילך וכל טוב אדוניו בידו הא אין ידו בכל מקום
אלא רשותו.

מות יומת בחנק אתה אומר בחנק או אינו
אלא באחת מכל מיתות האמורות בתורה אמרת
זו מדה בתורה כל מיתה האמורה בתורה סתם
אין אתה רשאי למושכה להחמיר עליה אלא להקל
עליה דברי רבי יאשיה רבי יונתן אומר לא מפני
שהיא קלה אלא מפני שנאמרה סתם וכל מיתה
שנאמרה סתם הרי זו בחנק רבי אומר כמיתה
שנאמרה בידי שמים מה מיתה שנאמרה בידי שמים
מיתה שאין בה רושם אף מיתה שנאמרה כאן מיתה

57 — 56 ספרי דברים קמ״ח, ורע״ג.   62 — 56 לקמן י״ג.   58 סנהדרין שם.   62 — 58 ספרי
במדבר קנ״ז. מ״ת. 154.   59 במדבר כ״א, כ״ו.   61 — 60 בראשית כ״ד, י׳.

52 וגונב איש] ד. מוסיפין עוד מאמר אחד לפני זה: וגונב איש להוציא את הקטן להביא
את הקטן מנין ת״ל כי ימצא איש גונב נפש להביא את הקטן משמע מביא את הקטן
ואת בן שמונה ת״ל וגונב איש (ק. ~ וכי יגונב איש) מגיד שאינו חייב עד שיגנוב בר
קיימא.   53 — 55 וכי ימצא איש—בן קיימא] ש״י. .>   54 ת״ל וגונב איש] א. מ. ת״ל
וגונב נפש וכי יגנוב איש.   55 שיגנוב] א. שיגרג.   58 שיהרג. א. שיהרג.   58 אין בידו] מ. ד. ~ בכל מקום.
61 אין ידו] ד. אין בידו.   71 רושם] א. דושנן.

life is extinct. This is the manner of strangulation. We have heard the penalty for it, but we have not heard the warning against it. Scripture says: "Thou shalt not steal" (Ex. 20.13).

Thou Shalt Not Steal. Behold, this is a warning against stealing persons. You interpret this to be a warning against stealing persons. Perhaps it is not so, but is a warning against stealing money? When it says: "Ye shall not steal" (Lev. 19.11), behold there you have the warning against stealing money. Hence, when it says here: "Thou shalt not steal," behold this is a warning against stealing persons. But perhaps the passage here is a prohibition against stealing money, and the passage there (ibid.) is a prohibition against stealing a person? You must reason: There are three laws mentioned in this section. Two of them are explicit and one not explicit. Let us learn about the non-explicit from the explicit ones. Just as the explicit ones are laws for the violation of which one incurs the penalty of death at the hands of the court, so also the non-explicit one must be a law for the violation of which one incurs the penalty of death at the hands of the court. Hence it is impossible for you to argue as in the latter version, but you must argue as in the former version. This one is a prohibition against stealing a person and that one (ibid.) is a prohibition against stealing money.

And One That Curseth His Father and His Mother, etc. Why is this said? Since it says: "For whatsoever man there be that curseth his father and his mother" (Lev. 20.9), I know only about a man that curses. But how do I know about a woman? It says here: "And one that curseth one's father and one's mother."

And One That Curseth His Father and His Mother. I thus know only about one who curses both his father and his mother. How about one who curses only his father or only his mother? It says: "His father and his mother hath he cursed" (ibid.)—in either case.—These are the words of R. Josiah. R. Jonathan says: It can mean both of them together and it also can mean either of them, unless Scripture should

שאין בה רושם מכאן אמרו מצות חנק וכו' עונש
שמענו אזהרה לא שמענו ת"ל לא תגנוב. **לא תגנוב**
הרי זה אזהרה לגונב נפש אתה אומר זה אזהרה
75 לגונב נפש או אינו אלא אזהרה לגונב ממון כשהוא
אומר לא תגנובו ולא תכחשו וגו' הרי זה אזהרה
לגונב ממון אמור הא מה ת"ל לא תגנוב הרי זה
אזהרה לגונב נפש או הרי זה אזהרה לגונב ממון
והלה אזהרה לגונב נפש אמרת שלש מצות נאמרו
80 בענין שתים מפורשות ואחת סתומה נלמד סתומה
מהמפורשות מה מפורשות מצות שחייבין עליהן
מיתות בית דין אף סתומה מצוה שחייבין עליה
מיתת בית דין הא אין עליך לומר כלשון אחרון
אלא כלשון ראשון זו אזהרה לגונב נפש והלה לגונב
85 ממון.

ומקלל אביו ואמו וגו' למה נאמר לפי
שהוא אומר כי איש איש אשר יקלל את אביו וגו'
אין לי אלא איש אשה מנין ת"ל ומקלל אביו ואמו.
ומקלל אביו ואמו אין לי אלא אביו ואמו
90 אביו שלא אמו ואמו שלא אביו מנין ת"ל אביו ואמו
קלל מכל מקום דברי רבי יאשיה רבי יונתן אומר
משמע שניהם כאחת ומשמע אחד אחד בפני עצמו

85—72 לעיל בחודש י"א. סנהדרין פ"ו, א'. מ"ת. 159.   73 שמות כ', י"ד.   76 ויקרא
י"ט, י"א.   109 — 86 ש. 127.   126 — 86 ת"כ קדושים י' (91d).   87 ויקרא כ', ט'.

72 רושם] א. דושנן.   79 והלה] ד. והלא.   81 עליהן] א. ד. עליה.   84 והלה] ד.
והלא.   90 — 88 ת"ל ומקלל—אביו מנין] א. >.   91 יאשיה] א. יושיה.

expressly say: "together." And why does it say: "And one that curseth his father and his mother"? Because it is said: "For whatsoever man" (ibid.), from which I know only about a man. How about a woman or a *tumtum* or a hermaphrodite? It says here: "And one that curseth his father and his mother." I thus know only about cursing them while they are alive. How about cursing them after they are dead? It says: "And one that curseth his father and his mother"—in any case.

And One That Curseth His Father and His Mother. With the tetragrammaton. You interpret it to mean cursing by using the tetragrammaton. Perhaps it is not so, but it means cursing even by using a substitute designation? Scripture says: "When he blasphemeth[6] the Name, shall be put to death" (Lev. 24.16). There would be no purpose in saying: "When he blasphemeth the Name," except to include the case of one cursing his father and his mother who is likewise not to be guilty unless he curses them with the tetragrammaton.—These are the words of R. Aḥai the son of Josiah. R. Ḥananiah the son of Idi says: Since the Torah says: "Swear" (Ex. 22.10) and: "Do not swear" (Lev. 19.12); "Curse" (Num. 5.21) and "Do not curse" (Lev. 19.14), it follows that just as when it says: "Swear" it means by the divine name, so also when it says "Do not swear" it means not to swear by the divine name. And just as when it says: "Curse" it means by using the divine name, so also when it says: "Do not curse" it means not to curse by using the divine name.

Shall Surely Be Put to Death. By stoning. Perhaps it is not so, but it means by any manner of death prescribed in the Torah? You must reason: In the case here the expression: "His blood shall be upon him" (Lev. 20.9) is used, and there (ibid. v. 27) the expression: "Their blood shall be upon them" is used. Just as there it means death by

---

6. The Mekilta understands the word בנקבו rendered in the Bible translations by "when he blasphemeth," to mean "when he pronounces." Cf. J. Morgenstern, "The Book of the Covenant," in *Hebrew Union College Annual,* VIII–IX, Cincinnati, 1931–32, p. 28.

עד שיפרוט לך הכתוב יחדיו ומה ת״ל ומקלל אביו

ואמו לפי שנאמר איש אין לי אלא איש אשה טומטום

95 ואנדרוגינוס מנין ת״ל ומקלל אביו ואמו אין לי אלא

בחיים במתים מנין ת״ל ומקלל אביו ואמו מכל

מקום.

ומקלל אביו ואמו בשם המפורש אתה

אומר בשם המפורש או אינו אלא בכינוי ת״ל בנקבו

100 שם יומת שאין ת״ל בנקבו שם אלא להביא את

המקלל אביו ואמו שלא יהא חייב עד שיקללם

בשם המפורש דברי רבי אחי בר יאשיה רבי חנניה

בן אידי אומר הואיל ואמרה תורה השבע ולא

תשבע קלל ולא תקלל מה השבע בשם אף לא

105 תשבע בשם מה קלל בשם אף לא תקלל בשם.

מות יומת בסקילה או אינו אלא באחת מכל

מיתות האמורות בתורה הרי אתה דן נאמר כאן

דמיו בו ונאמר להלן דמיהם בם מה להלן בסקילה

100 שם כ״ד, ט״ז.   105 — 102 לקמן ט״ז. ספרי במדבר י״ד. שבועות ל״ה, ב׳.   108 ויקרא
כ׳, ט׳ / שם כ׳, י״א.

---

93 יחדיו] הגהתי=א״צ. ש״י: מ. ד. אחד א. באחד מא״ש. כאחד.   95 ואמו] א.
חי.   96 בחיים במתים] מ. במתים בחיים.   100 — 99 ת״ל בנקבו שם] הגהתי=ט. (הוצאה
מאוחרת) ועיין מ״ה: א״א. ת״ל ונוקב שם יי וגו׳.   100 אלא] ד. <.   102 אחי] ד.
אחאי אי. מ. יוחי / בר יאשיה] ד. < א. מ. בר׳ יושיה / חנניה] ד. חנינא.   103 בן
אידי] א. בן אחי אי. בר׳ אדי מ. בר׳ אידי.

stoning so also here it means death by stoning. We have heard the penalty for it, but we have not heard the warning against it. Scripture says: "Judges thou shalt not curse" (Ex. 22.27). Now, if your father is a judge, then he is included in the warning: "Judges thou shalt not curse." If he is a ruler, then he is included in the warning: "Nor curse a ruler of thy people" (ibid.). But suppose he is neither a judge nor a ruler, but an ordinary person? Behold, you reason and establish a general rule on the basis of what is common to both of them. The peculiar aspect of the case of a judge is not the same as the peculiar aspect of the case of a ruler, and the peculiar aspect of the case of a ruler is not the same as the peculiar aspect of the case of a judge. But their common feature is that they are "of thy people," and therefore you are warned against cursing them, so also in the case of your father; since he is "of thy people," you are warned against cursing him. Well, then one could argue thus: What is the common feature of both of them? They are great and "of thy people." And because of their greatness you are warned against cursing them. So also you are warned against cursing your father, if he is great and "of thy people"—but only because he is great—otherwise you are not warned against cursing him. But Scripture says: "Thou shalt not curse the deaf" (Lev. 19.14). Here Scripture speaks of the lowest of people. Now you can establish a general rule on the basis of what is common to all three of them. The peculiar aspect of the case of a judge is not the same as the peculiar aspect of the case of a ruler, and the peculiar aspect of the case of a ruler is not the same as the peculiar aspect of the case of a judge. Neither is the peculiar aspect of both of them the same as the peculiar aspect of the deaf, nor is the peculiar aspect of the deaf the same as the peculiar aspect of the two others. The common feature of all three of them is that they are "of thy people" and, therefore, you are warned against cursing them. And so also it is with your father. He is "of thy people," and therefore you are warned against cursing him.

אף כאן בסקילה עונש שמענו אזהרה לא שמענו

110 ת״ל אלהים אל תקלל אם דיין הוא אביך הרי הוא

בכלל אלהים לא תקלל ואם נשיא הוא אביך הרי

הוא בכלל ונשיא בעמך לא תאור אינו לא דיין

ולא נשיא אלא בור הרי אתה דן בנין אב מבין

שניהם לא הרי דיין כהרי נשיא ולא הרי נשיא כהרי

115 דיין הצד השוה שבהן שהם בעמך ואתה מוזהר על

קללתם אף אביך שהוא בעמך אתה מוזהר על

קללתו אי מה הצד השוה שבהן שהם גדולים ובעמך

וגדולתן גרמה להן אתה מוזהר על קללתם ואביך

שהוא גדול ובעמך וגדולתו גרמה לו לא תהא

120 מוזהר על קללתו ת״ל לא תקלל חרש דבר

הכתוב באמללים שבאדם הרי אתה דן בנין אב

מבין שלשתן לא הרי דיין כהרי נשיא ולא הרי נשיא

כהרי דיין ולא הרי זה וזה כהרי חרש ולא הרי

חרש כהרי זה וזה הצד השוה שבהן שהם בעמך

125 ואתה מוזהר על קללתם אף אביך שבעמך אתה

מוזהר על קללתו.

111 שמות כ״ב, כ״ז. 112 שם. 120 ויקרא י״ט, י״ד.

─────────────

109 לא שמענו] ד. מנין. 112—111 בכלל אלהים—הרי הוא] א. >. 118 וגדולתן] נ.
ל. וגדולתך / אתה מוזהר] ד. לפיכך אתה מוזהר. 120—118 ואביך שהוא גדול—על
קללתו] ד. ג. תאמר באביך (ג. ~ שאינו גדול בעמך ואין גדולתו גרמה לו אין אתה
מוזהר על קללתו). 119 לו לא]=מ. א. א״י: ואולי צ״ל לו תאמר באביך שאינו גדול
בעמך ואין גדולתו גרמה לו לא. 123 הרי זה וזה]=ל: א. מ. זה וזה ק. נ. כהרי זה
וזה.

CHAPTER VI
(Ex. 21.18–19)

And if Men Contend. Why is this section set forth? Because it says
only: "Eye for eye"; but we have not heard about the indemnity for
the loss of time and for the expenses of healing. Therefore it says
here: "And if men contend . . . if he rise again and walk abroad . . .
and shall cause him to be thoroughly healed," etc. (vv. 18–19). Scripture thus comes to teach about this subject those regulations that
were missing.

And if Men Contend. I thus know only about men. How about
women? R. Ishmael used to say: All the laws about damages found in
the Torah are not explicit on this point. But since in the case of one of
them Scripture explicitly states (Num. 5.6) that women are to be
regarded like men, it has thus made it explicit in regard to all the
laws about damages found in the Torah that women are to be
regarded like men. R. Josiah says: "A man or a woman" (Num., ibid.).
Why is this said? Because it says: "And if a man shall open a pit" (v.
33), from which I know only about a man. But how about a woman?
Therefore it says: "A man or a woman." Scripture thus comes to
declare man and woman alike in regard to all the laws about damages
found in the Torah. R. Jonathan says: There is no need of this scriptural proof. Has it not been said: "The owner of the pit shall make it
good" (v. 34); "The one that kindled the fire shall surely make restitution" (Ex. 22.5)? Hence, what purpose is there in saying: "A man or a
woman"? It comes for a special teaching of its own.[1]

And One Smite the Other with a Stone or with His Fist. This is to
declare that one is guilty if he smites with either one of them. *With a
Stone or with His Fist.* This is to tell that a stone and the fist are merely
types of instruments capable of producing death. You say it comes to
teach this. Perhaps however it only comes to teach that if he smite him

1. See Commentaries.

פרשה ו ‏(שמות כ"א, י"ח — י"ט.)

וכי יריבון אנשים למה נאמרה פרשה זו
לפי שהוא אומר עין תחת עין אבל שבת ורפוי לא
שמענו ת"ל וכי יריבון אנשים וגו' אם יקום והתהלך
בחוץ וגו' ורפא ירפא וגו' בא הכתוב ללמד בו
דברים המחוסרים בו.

וכי יריבון אנשים אין לי אלא אנשים
נשים מנין היה רבי ישמעאל אומר הואיל וכל
הניזקין שבתורה סתם ופרט הכתוב באחד מהם
עשה בו נשים כאנשים פרט לכל הניזקים שבתורה
לעשות בהם נשים כאנשים רבי יאשיה אומר איש
ואשה למה נאמר לפי שהוא אומר וכי יפתח איש
בור אין לי אלא איש אשה מנין ת"ל איש ואשה בא
הכתוב והשוה אשה לאיש לכל הניזקין שבתורה
רבי יונתן אומר אינו צריך והלא כבר נאמר בעל
הבור ישלם שלם ישלם המבעיר את הבערה הא
מה ת"ל איש ואשה לתלמודו הוא בא.

והכה איש את רעהו באבן או באגרוף
לחייב על זה בפני עצמו ועל זה בפני עצמו.

באבן או באגרוף מגיד שאבן ואגרוף סימני
מיתה הן אתה אומר לכך בא או או לא בא אלא ללמד

---

2 שמות כ"א, כ"ד; ויקרא כ"ד, כ'. ‏ 10—6 ב"ק ט"ז, א'. ‏ 16—6 לקמן ז', ח', ט'.
14—10 ספרי במדבר ב'. ‏ 12—11 שמות כ"א, ל"ג. ‏ 15—14 שמות כ"א, ל"ד. לקמן
י"ד. ‏ 15 שם כ"ב, ה'. ‏ 27—19 לקמן ז'. ספרי במדבר ק"ס. סנהדרין ע"ח, ב'—ע"ט,
א'.

---

1 פרשה ו‎] א. ‎<. ‏ 2 לפי‎] מ. לפרש. ‏ 4—3 והתהלך—ירפא וגו'‎]א‎2=‎: א. מ. ד.
‎<. ‏ 4 ללמד בו‎] ד. ללמד. ‏ 7 אומר‎] ד. דורש אומר. ‏ 9 פרט לכל‎] א. פורט אני לכל
ד. אף פורט אני. ‏ 10—11 איש ואשה‎] ק. נ. והמית איש ואשה ל. אה"ו. והמית איש
או אשה מא"ש. איש או אשה (במדבר ה', ו'). ‏ 11 לפי‎] ד. אלא לפי / וכי‎] ד. כי.
17 באבן או באגרוף‎] הוספתי‎=ג. א"צ. ט. וגו'. ‏ 21—19 מגיד—או באגרוף‎] ד. ‎<.

with a stone or with his fist he is guilty,[2] but if he smite him with any other thing he is not guilty?[3] It says however: "And if he smote him with a stone in the hand, whereby a man may die, and he died, he is a murderer," etc. (Num. 35.17). This expressly tells that he is not guilty unless he struck him with a thing that is capable of producing death. And how do we know that he is not guilty unless he struck him on a part of the body where such a blow could produce death? It says: "And lie in wait for him and rise up against him, and smite him mortally that he die" (Deut. 19.11). This tells that he is not guilty unless he struck him with a thing that is capable of producing death and on a part of the body where such a blow could produce death. R. Nathan says: This is to declare that a stone must be like the fist, and the fist must be like a stone. Just as the stone is something that can produce death, so also the fist must be such as to be capable of producing death. And just as the fist is something that can be identified, so also the stone must be such as can be identified. Thus, if the stone with which he struck him became mixed with other stones, the assailant is free.

And He Die Not but Keep His Bed. This intimates that bad temper may lead to death.

And He Die Not but Keep His Bed. But if he struck a blow strong enough to produce death, he is free from paying indemnity for the loss of time and for the expenses of healing.[4]

If He Rise Again and Walk. I might understand this to mean within the house, but it says: "Abroad." But even when it says: "Abroad," I might still understand it to mean even if he is falling away. Therefore it says: "If he rise again, and walk abroad upon his support," that means, restored to his health. This is one of the three expressions in

2. I. e., even though ordinarily the blow would not be capable of producing death.

3. I. e., even though the thing is capable of producing death.

4. Because in this case he suffers the severer penalty in that he is punished by death. And one who incurs the penalty of death is exempt from making monetary compensation (see below, ch. VIII, saying of Rabbi).

שאם הכהו באבן או באגרוף יהא חייב ובשאר כל
דבר יהא פטור ת"ל ואם באבן יד אשר ימות בה
הכהו וימות רוצח הוא וגו' מגיד שאינו חייב עד
שיכה בדבר שיהיה בו כדי להמית ומנין במקום
25   שיהיה בו כדי להמית ת"ל וארב לו וקם עליו והכהו
נפש ומת מגיד שאינו חייב עד שיכהו בדבר שיהיה
בו כדי להמית ואל מקום שהוא כדי להמית רבי
נתן אומר הקיש אבן לאגרוף ואגרוף לאבן מה
האבן שיש בו כדי להמית אף אגרוף שיש בו כדי
30   להמית ומה אגרוף בידוע אף אבן בידוע הא אם
נתערבה באבנים אחרות פטור.

ולא ימות ונפל למשכב מגיד שהצהיבה
מביאה לידי מיתה.

ולא ימות ונפל למשכב הא אם הכהו
35   מכה שיש בה כדי להמית הרי זה פטור מן השבת
ומן הריפוי.

אם יקום והתהלך שומע אני בתוך הבית
ת"ל בחוץ אי בחוץ שומע אני אפילו מתנוונה ת"ל
אם יקום והתהלך בחוץ על משענתו על בוריו.

22—23 במדבר ל"ה, י"ז.   25—26 דברים י"ט, י"א.   32—33 סנהדרין ע"ח, ב'; י' שם
ט', ג' (27ª).   37—39 ש. 128.   46—37 לקמן י"ג.

22 ואם באבן]=א²: א. מ. ד. אם באבן.   23—22 אשר ימות—רוצח הוא וגו']=א²:
א. מ. ד. <.   24 שיהיה] ד. שיש.   27—24 ומנין—ואל מקום שהוא כדי להמית] א.
<.   24—25 במקום שיהיה] ד. במקום שיש.   26—25 והכהו נפש ומת]=א²: א. מ.
ד. <.   30 ומה] א. אי. מ. או מה.   32 שהצהיבה] מ. שהשנאה ט. שהציהבה.
38 אי בחוץ] ד. < / אפילו מתנוונה] ק. נ. בשוקים ל. בשווקים.   39 אם יקום והתהלך
בחוץ] ד. <.

the Torah which R. Ishmael used to interpret as being figurative. Similarly: "If the sun be risen upon him" (Ex. 22.2). But does the sun rise upon him alone? Does it not rise upon the whole world? It simply means this: What does the sun signify to the world?—Peace. So, then, if it is known that this burglar would have left the owner in peace,[5] and yet the latter killed him, he is guilty of murder. Similarly: "They shall spread the sheet" (Deut. 22.17). They should make the matter clear as a white sheet. Also here you interpret "Upon his support" to mean, restored to his health.

Then Shall He That Smote Be Quit. I might understand that he can offer surety and in the meantime walk around in the streets free. But Scripture says: "If he rise again and walk abroad." This tells that they keep the assailant imprisoned until the victim is restored to health. *Then Shall He That Smote Be Quit.* Of the death penalty. I might understand it to mean also free from paying indemnities for the loss of time and for curing expenses. But Scripture says: "Only he shall pay for the loss of his time and shall cause him to be thoroughly healed." Aside from compensation for injury to limb, he is paid for his loss of time and the expenses of his cure.

Only He Shall Pay for the Loss of His Time. I might understand this to mean, for an unlimited time. But it also says: "And shall cause him to be thoroughly healed." Just as in regard to the curing expenses he pays only for the cure of ailments resulting from the injury, so also in regard to the loss of time he is to pay only for such loss of time as resulted from the injury. Perhaps just as no distinctions are made as regards the curing expenses, so also no distinctions should be made as regards indemnity for the loss of time? Now, as regards healing, he is obliged to pay for the cure in case of a recurrence just as he is obliged to pay for it the first time. Perhaps then he should pay indemnity for every subsequent loss of time just as he pays for the

5. I. e., if the owner had merely offered resistance the burglar would not have used violence against him.

40 זה אחד משלשה דברים שהיה רבי ישמעאל דורש
בתורה כמין משל כיוצא בו אם זרחה השמש עליו
וכי עליו החמה זורחת בלבד והלא על כל העולם
כלו זורחת היא אלא מה השמש שלום בעולם אף
זה אם ידוע שבשלום הלך הימנו והרגו הרי זה חייב.

45 כיוצא בו ופרשו השמלה וגו' מחוורין את הדברים
כשמלה אף כאן אתה אומר על משענתו על בוריו.

ונקה המכה שומע אני יתן ערבים ויטייל
בשוק ת"ל אם יקום והתהלך בחוץ מגיד שחובשין
אותו עד שנתרפא.

50 **ונקה המכה** מן המיתה שומע אני מן השבת
ומן הריפוי ת"ל רק שבתו יתן ורפא ירפא חוץ ממה
שנותנין לו דמי איבריו נותנין לו דמי שבתו וריפויו.

רק שבתו יתן שומע אני לעולם ת"ל ורפא
ירפא מה ריפוי מחמת מכה אף שבת מחמת מכה
55 או כשם שלא חלק מכלל ריפוי כך לא נחלוק
מכלל השבת כשם שהוא זקוק לרפאת את זה כך
הוא זקוק לרפאת את זה כשם שנותנין שבת לזה

---

41 שמות כ"ב, ב'.   45 דברים כ"ב, י"ז.   46—45 כתובות ל"ג, ב'.   52—50 תוס' ב"ק
ט', ב'.   67—50 ב"ק פ"ה, א'; ש. 128.

---

40 דורש] מ. ד. יושב ודורש.   41 אם] א. מ. ואם.   42 וכי—בלבד] ד. וכי השמש
בלבד עליו זרחה מ"ח. וכי חמה עליו בלבד זורחת.   43 כלן] מ. ד. < / זורחת] ד.
זרחה / היא] א. ד. < / השמש] ד. שמש זה.   44 ידוע שבשלום—והרגו] מ. ידוע
שבשלום הימנו והרגו ד. ידוע בו שבשלום נהרג מ"ח. ידוע שבשלום עמו והרגו.
46—45 וגו' מחוורין את הדברים כשמלה] נ. ל. דברים מחוורין כשמלה.   48 והתהלך
בחוץ מ"ח. ונקה.   52 נותנין] ד. ונותנין] א. מ. <.   55 או כשם שלא חלק חלק]
הגהתי=ט. ג. א"א: א. אילו חלק מ. אלא חלק ק. או כשיש לו חלק נ. ל. או לא
חלק.   56 כשם] ד. שכשם.   57 שנותנין] ד. ~ לו.

first time? Scripture says: "Only for the loss of time he shall pay," thereby telling us that distinctions are made as regards the rule about indemnity for the loss of time.[6]

And Shall Cause Him to Be Thoroughly Healed. If it gets healed and then gets sore again, gets healed and gets sore again, and even if this happens four or five times, he is still obliged to pay for curing it. It is to teach us this that Scripture says: "And shall cause him to be thoroughly healed." Suppose ulcers grow on his body around the wound. If they are results of the wound he is obliged to pay for curing them, but if they are not results of the wound he is not obliged to pay for curing them. For, when the Torah says: "Only he shall pay for the loss of his time, and shall cause him to be thoroughly healed," it indicates that just as he pays for the loss of time only when it is the result of the injury, so also when he is to pay for the healing he is to pay only for the healing of ailments resulting from the injury.

Another Interpretation: This passage suggests that you can learn proper conduct[7] from the Torah. "Only he shall pay for the loss of his time, and shall cause him to be thoroughly healed."

CHAPTER VII
(Ex. 21.20–21)

And If a Man Smites His Bondman, etc. His bondman and his bondwoman were also included in the general statement, which says: "He that smiteth a man so that he dieth," etc. (v. 12). Behold, this passage here singles them out from the general statement, making it lighter for

---

6. The word "only," רק, is to exclude indemnity for the loss of time, even if caused by a recurrence of the sickness. Only once he shall pay for the loss of time.

7. The proper conduct for a man who takes sick is to rest from work and seek to get thoroughly cured (see Commentaries).

כך נותנין שבת לזה ת"ל רק שבתו יתן מגיד שחלק
מכלל השבת.

60 **ורפא ירפא** נתרפא וחזר נתרפא וחזר אפילו
ארבעה וחמשה פעמים חייב לרפאתו ת"ל ורפא
ירפא עלו בו צמחים סביבות המכה אם מחמת
המכה חייב לרפאתו שלא מחמת המכה פטור
וכשאמרה תורה שבתו יתן ורפא ירפא מה שבת
65 מחמת המכה אף רפואה מחמת מכה. דבר אחר
בא הכתוב ללמדך דרך ארץ מן התורה רק שבתו
יתן ורפא ירפא.

פרשה ז (שמות כ"א, כ'—כ"א.)

וכי יכה איש את עבדו וגו' אף עבדו
ואמתו היו בכלל שנאמר מכה איש ומת והרי הכתוב

63—62 תוס' ב"ק ט', ד'.
2 שמות כ"א, י"ב.

───────────────

58 שחלק] ד. שחלוק.   60 ירפא] ד. ~   61 ת"ל] ג. שנאמר.   62 עלו] מ. ד.
ועלו.   63—62 סביבות—מחמת המכה] ד. מחמת מכה סביבות מכה.   63 לרפאתו]
א. מ. / שלא מחמת] א². שלא סביבות.
2—1 וגו' אף—היו בכלל] ק. נ. אף את עבדו ושפחתו בכלל.   2 מכה איש ומת]
הגהתי=מ"ח. ומא"ש. ואולי צ"ל ומכה אדם יומת (ויקרא כ"ד, כ"א): ט"כ. ז"י. א"צ.
ש"י. ומכה איש ומת א. מ. ד. והמית איש או אשה (שמות כ"א, כ"ט) ט. והכה איש
ומת.

the master in that he is to be judged under the rule: "If he continue a day or two." For this purpose this section is set forth.

And If a Man Smite. I thus know it only about a man. How about a woman? R. Ishmael used to say: All the laws about damages found in the Torah are not explicit on this point, etc. R. Josiah says: "A man or a woman" (Num. 5.6). Why are these mentioned, etc.? R. Jonathan says: There is no need, etc.

His Bondman or His Bondwoman. This is to declare one guilty for smiting either of them. R. Eliezer says: Scripture here deals with a Canaanitish slave. You say this passage deals with a Canaanitish slave. Perhaps this is not so, but it deals only with a Hebrew slave? Scripture says: "And of them shall ye buy bondmen and bond-women" (Lev. 25.44), thereby declaring the bondman to be like the bondwoman and the bondwoman to be like the bondman. Just as by the "bondman" is meant one who can be a bondman after he is grown up as well as when he is still a minor, so also by the "bond-woman" is meant one who can be a bondwoman while still a minor as well as after she is grown up. The Hebrew slave is thus excluded, for although he can become a slave after he is grown up, he cannot be made a slave while a minor. The Hebrew maid-servant is also excluded, for although she can be made a maid-servant while still a minor, she cannot be made one after she is grown up.[1] R. Isaac says: I might understand that this means to include also a slave belonging to partners and one who is only half a slave and half free. But Scripture says: "His bondman or his bondwoman." Just as by "his bondman" is meant one who is entirely his, so also by "his bondwoman" is meant one who is entirely his. This excludes the slave belonging to partners and the one who is half a slave and half free. For neither of these belongs entirely to the one master. R. Ishmael says: Scripture here

1. Hence the "bondman or bondwoman" mentioned here must also mean those who are alike as regards the age in which they can be made bondman or bondwoman (cf. *Shebut Yehudah*).

מוציאו מכללו להקל עליו שיהא נדון ביום או יומים

לכך נאמרה פרשה זו.

וכי יכה איש אין לי אלא איש אשה מנין   5

היה רבי ישמעאל אומר הואיל ונאמרו כל הנזקין

שבתורה סתם וכו׳ רבי יאשיה אומר איש ואשה

למה נאמרו וכו׳ רבי יונתן אומר אינו צריך וכו׳.

את עבדו או את אמתו לחייב על זה

בפני עצמו ועל זה בפני עצמו רבי אליעזר אומר   10

בכנעני הכתוב מדבר אתה אומר בכנעני הכתוב

מדבר או אינו מדבר אלא בעברי ת״ל מהם תקנו

עבד ואמה הקיש עבד לאמה ואמה לעבד מה עבד

שגודלו וקוטנו עבד אף אמה שגודלה וקוטנה אמה

יצא עבד עברי שאף על פי שגודלו עבד אבל אין   15

קוטנו עבד יצאת אמה העבריה שאף על פי שקוטנה

אמה אבל אין גודלה אמה אמר רבי יצחק שומע

אני עבד של שותפין ועבד שחציו עבד וחציו בן

חורין במשמע ת״ל עבדו ואמתו מה עבדו שכלו

שלו אף אמתו שכלה שלו יצא עבד של שותפין   20

ועבד שחציו עבד וחציו בן חורין שאין כלו שלו

8—5 לעיל ו׳.   13—12 ויקרא כ״ה, מ״ד.   30—17 ב״ק צ׳, א׳.

---

5 מנין] ק. נ. ~ ת״ל.   6 הנזקין] א. המזיקין.   8 יונתן] ד. נתן / וכו׳] ד. ~ כדכתיב
לעיל.   9 או את אמתו] ק. נ. ואת אמתו.   13—12 ת״ל מהם תקנו עבד ואמה] ג.
מ״ח. נאמר כאן עבדו ואמתו (ג. ~ ונאמר להלן עבדו ואמתו, ובגליון למטה שם נתקן=מ״ח.)
ונאמר להלן מהם תקנו עבד ואמה מה להלן בכנענים הכתוב מדבר אף כאן בכנענים
הכתוב מדבר (ג. ~ דבר אחר מהם תקנו עבד ואמה).   20 שכלה שלו] ק. נ. שכלה
שלה.

deals with a Canaanitish slave. You say it deals with a Canaanitish slave. Perhaps it is not so, but it deals only with a Hebrew slave? It says: "He shall not be avenged, for he is his money" (v. 21). Just as his money can be acquired by him as a lasting possession and, when acquired by inheritance, is completely his, so also the slave must be one who can be acquired as a lasting possession and who, when acquired by inheritance, is completely his. The Hebrew slave is thus excluded, for although when acquired by inheritance he is completely his, he cannot be acquired as a lasting possession. The slave belonging to partners and one who is half slave and half free are also excluded. For although they can be acquired as a lasting possession, they cannot be inherited so as to be the one heir's complete possession.

With a Rod. I might understand this to mean, such as is capable of producing death as well as such as is not capable of producing death. But Scripture says: "Or if he smote him with a weapon of wood in the hand, whereby a man may die, and he died, he is a murderer" (Num. 35.18). This expressly tells us that he is not guilty unless he struck him with a thing that is capable of producing death. And how do we know that he is not guilty unless he struck him on a part of the body where such a blow could produce death? It says: "And lie in wait for him and rise up against him, and smite him mortally that he die" (Deut. 19.11). This tells us that he is not guilty unless he struck him with a thing that is capable of producing death and on a part of the body where such a blow could produce death. But even if Scripture had not said this, I could have inferred it by reasoning: If in the case of smiting an Israelite, where the law is stricter, in that the rule: "If he continue a day or two" does not apply,[2] one is not guilty unless he struck him with a thing that is capable of producing death and on a part of the body where such a blow could produce death, is it not logical to assume that in the case of smiting a Canaanitish slave,

---

2. The slayer of a free man is punished even if the victim lingers on for a day or two.

רבי ישמעאל אומר בכנעני הכתוב מדבר אתה
אומר בכנעני הכתוב מדבר או אינו מדבר אלא
בעברי ת״ל לא יוקם כי כספו הוא מה כספו שקנינו
קנין עולם וירושתו גמורה לו כך כל שקניינו קנין
עולם וירושתו גמורה לו יצא עבד עברי אף על פי
שירושתו גמורה לו אבל אין קניינו קנין עולם יצא
עבד של שני שותפין ועבד שחציו עבד וחציו בן
חורין אף על פי שקניינו קנין עולם אבל אין ירושתו
גמורה לו.

בשבט שומע אני בין שיש בו כדי להמית בין
שאין בו כדי להמית ת״ל או בכלי עץ אשר ימות
בה הכהו וימות רוצח הוא מגיד שאינו חייב עד
שיכנו בדבר שיש בו כדי להמית ומנין אל מקום
שהוא כדי להמית ת״ל וארב לו וקם עליו והכהו
נפש ומת מגיד שאינו חייב עד שיכנו בדבר שיש בו
כדי להמית אל מקום שהוא כדי להמית עד שלא
יאמר יש לי בדין ומה אם ישראל שהוחמר בו שאינו
ביום או יומים אינו חייב עד שיכנו בדבר שיש בו
כדי להמית אל מקום שהוא כדי להמית כנעני

31—43 ספרי במדבר ק״ס.   32—33 במדבר ל״ה, י״ח.   35—36 דברים י״ט, י״א.

25 וירושתו] ד. ט. ורשותו.   25—26 כך כל שקנינו—גמורה לו] א. ד. <.   27 שירושתו]
ד. ט. שרשותו / גמורה] ד. קניה.   29 ירושתו] מ. ד. ט. רשותו.   32—33 אשר
ימות בה—רוצח הוא] הוספתי: א. מ. אשר ימות וגו׳.   34 שיכנו בדבר] ד. <.
37—34 ומנין—להמית] מ. <.   35—36 והכהו נפש ומת] הוספתי: א. וגו׳.

where the law is more lenient, in that the rule: "If he continue a day or two" applies, one should surely not be guilty unless he struck him with a thing that is capable of producing death and on a part of the body where such a blow could produce death? But if you say so, you would be decreeing punishment merely on the basis of a logical inference. Therefore, it is said: "With a rod," thus teaching you that punishment cannot be decreed on the basis of a mere logical inference.[3] Rabbi says: *With a Rod.* Why is this said? Even if it had not been said I could have inferred it by reasoning: If in the case of smiting an Israelite, where the law is stricter, in that the rule: "If he continue a day or two" does not apply, one is not guilty unless he struck him with a thing that is capable of producing death and on a part of the body where such a blow could produce death, is it not logical that in the case of smiting a Canaanitish slave, where the law is more lenient, in that the rule: "If he continue a day or two" applies, one should not be guilty unless he struck him with a thing that is capable of producing death and on a part of the body where such a blow could produce death? Why then does Scripture say: "With a rod"? Merely to furnish an expression free to be used in formulating the following *gezerah shavah*: Here the expression "with a rod" is used, and there (Lev. 27.32) the expression "the rod" is used. Just as there, where the expression "the rod" is used, any thing bought by partners is excluded, so also here, where the expression "with a rod" is used, the slave bought by partners is to be excluded.

And He Die under His Hand. That is, both the smiting and the death take place while the slave is still in his possession. But if he smote him and then sold him to another man and then the slave died, he is free.

He Shall Surely Be Avenged. That is, by the death of the master. You interpret it to mean by the death of the master. Perhaps this is not so, but it means by making the master pay money? R. Nathan used to

---

3. Cf. "Talmud Hermeneutics" in *JE,* XII, 32.

שהוקל בו שהוא ביום או ביומים אינו דין שלא יהא

חייב עד שיכנו בדבר שיש בו כדי להמית אל מקום

שהוא כדי להמית אלא אם אמרת כן ענשת מן הדין

לכך נאמר בשבט ללמדך שאין עונשין מן הדין

45   רבי אומר בשבט למה נאמר עד שלא יאמר יש לי

בדין אם ישראל שהוחמר בו שאינו ביום או ביומים

אינו חייב עד שיכנו בדבר שיש בו כדי להמית אל

מקום שהוא כדי להמית כנעני שהוקל בו שהוא

ביום או יומים אינו דין שלא יהא חייב עד שיכנו

50   בדבר שיש בו כדי להמית אל מקום שהוא כדי

להמית ומה ת״ל בשבט אלא מופנה להקיש לדון

גזירה שוה נאמר כאן בשבט ונאמר להלן השבט

מה השבט שנאמר להלן להוציא את הלקוח של

שותפין אף בשבט שנאמר כאן להוציא את הלקוח

55   של שותפין.

ומת תחת ידו שתהא מכתו ומיתתו ברשותו

הא אם הכהו ומכרו לאחר ומת הרי זה פטור.

נקם ינקם מיתה אתה אומר מיתה או אינו

52 ויקרא כ״ז, ל״ב.   53—54   — ב.   53—54 בכורות נ״ו, ב׳.   56 לעיל ה׳.   56—57 ב״ק צ׳, א׳. תוס׳
שם ט׳, כ״ב. י׳ קידושין ג׳, א׳ (63ᶜ). ש. 129.   58—61   ש. שם.

42 שיכנו בדבר] ד. >.   43 אלא] ד. < /   45 רבי אומר] ד.
דבר אחר.   46 שהוחמר בו] ד. < / שאינו ביום] ד. שאין בו יום.   47—48 אל מקום
שהוא כדי להמית] מ. ד. >.   48 שהוקל] ד. שהקל.   50—51 אל מקום שהוא כדי
להמית] א. < נ. ל. ~ לא אם אמרת כן ענשת מן הדין.   51 ומה ת״ל]=ט. ומא״ש:
א. מ. ד. לכך נאמר בשבט ומה ת״ל / בשבט] א. מ. ט. השבט / מופנה] א. מ. ט.
ט״כ. מפני.   52 להלן השבט] מ. ד. להלן בשבט.   53 השבט שנאמר] ד. >.   54 שותפין]
ד. שני שותפין / בשבט שנאמר] ד. >.

say: Here "vengeance" is spoken of, and there "vengeance" is spoken of: "And I will bring a sword upon you, that shall execute the vengeance of the covenant" (Lev. 26.25). Just as there it means by the sword, so also here it means by the sword. R. Akiba says: Here "vengeance" is spoken of, and there "vengeance" is spoken of: "Avenge the children of Israel" (Num. 31.2). Just as there it means by the sword,[4] so also here it means by the sword. And just as here it means at the order of the court, so also there it means at the order of the court.[5]

Notwithstanding if He Continue a Day. I might take this literally. But it says: "Or two." Well, then I would take "two" literally. It says, however, "Notwithstanding if he continue a day." How then can both these expressions be maintained? "A day" means one that is as long as two days,[6] and "two" means two days that are as long as one. How so? A twenty-four hour interval. R. Jose the Galilean says: *But if He Continue a Day.* I might take this literally. Scripture, however, says: "But," thereby suggesting that it is to be taken differently.

He Shall Not Be Avenged for He Is His Money. It is on the basis of this expression that R. Ishmael used to say that Scripture here deals with a Canaanitish slave. R. Simon b. Yoḥai says: Why is this said? Because if it had not been said I could have argued: His own ox is to be put to death for killing his bondman or his bondwoman, and so also is the ox of another to be put to death for killing his bondman or his bondwoman. Likewise, he himself is to be put to death for killing his bondman or his bondwoman, and any other man is also to be put to death for killing his bondman or his bondwoman. Now, since, as you have learned, no distinction is made between his own ox and the ox of another man in regard to the death penalty for killing his bondman or bondwoman, then no distinction should be made between himself and another man in regard to the death penalty for killing his

4. For it says there: "They slew with the sword" (v. 8).
5. Cf. saying of R. Nathan in *Sifre,* Numbers 157.
6. I. e., counting daytime only (see Introduction and cf. Commentaries).

אלא ממון היה רבי נתן אומר נאמר כאן נקימה

ונאמר להלן נקימה והבאתי עליכם חרב נוקמת

נקם ברית מה להלן בחרב אף כאן בחרב רבי

עקיבא אומר נאמר כאן נקימה ונאמר להלן נקם

נקמת בני ישראל מה להלן בחרב אף כאן בחרב

מה כאן בבית דין אף להלן בבית דין.

אך אם יום שומע אני כשמועו ת"ל יומים אי

יומים שומע אני כשמועו ת"ל אך אם יום כיצד

יתקיימו שני כתובים הללו יום שהוא כיומים ויומים

שהן כיום הא כיצד מעת לעת רבי יוסי הגלילי

אומר אך אם יום שומע אני כשמועו ת"ל אך חלק.

לא יוקם כי כספו הוא זה הוא שהיה

רבי ישמעאל אומר בכנעני הכתוב מדבר רבי

שמעון בן יוחאי אומר למה נאמר עד שלא יאמר

יש לי בדין הואיל ושורו במיתה על עבדו ועל

אמתו ושור אחר במיתה על עבדו ועל אמתו והוא

במיתה על עבדו ועל אמתו ואחר במיתה על עבדו

ועל אמתו אם למדת שלא חלק בין שורו לשור אחר

במיתה על עבדו ועל אמתו לא נחלק בינו לבין

---

60 ויקרא כ"ו, כ"ה.   62—63 במדבר ל"א, ב'.   64 ספרי במדבר קנ"ז.

59 היה] ד. <.   61—63 ר' עקיבא אומר—אף כאן בחרב] ד. <.   64 מה כאן] א. מה
אם כאן מ"ח. ומה להלן / אף להלן] מ"ח. אף כאן.   65 אם יום] ד. ~ או יומים.
66—65 ת"ל יומים—כשמועו] מ. ד. ט. <.   70 כי כספו הוא] הוספתי: א. וגו' ד. וכו'
/ זה] מ. ד. < / הוא] ד. והוא.   73 הואיל ושורו] א. הוא ושורו.   74—76 ושור
אחר—על עבדו ועל אמתו] <. א.   74 ושור אחר] נ. ל. ~ א'.

bondman or his bondwoman.[7] By saying however: "He shall not be avenged for he is his money," Scripture tells us that although no distinction is made between his ox and another man's ox in regard to the death penalty for killing his bondman or his bondwoman, we should make a distinction between himself and any other man in regard to the death penalty for killing his bondman or his bondwoman. It is for this purpose that Scripture says: "he shall not be avenged for he is his money."

CHAPTER VIII
(Ex. 21.22–25)

And if Men Strive Together, etc. Why is this section set forth? Because of this. It says: "And if a man come presumptuously upon his neighbour," etc. (v. 14). From this we have heard only that one who aims to kill his enemy and actually kills him is to be punished by death. But we have not heard about one who, aiming to kill his enemy, kills his friend. Therefore it says here: "And if men strive together . . . But if any harm follow," etc. (vv. 22–23). Scripture thus comes to teach you about one who, aiming to kill his enemy, kills his friend. Such a one is likewise to be punished by death. For this purpose this section is set forth. Rabbi says: If one who aims to kill an enemy of his but kills another person who is likewise his enemy is free, it is but logical that one who aims to kill his enemy but kills his friend should surely be free. Scripture here merely comes to teach you that the compensation for injuries to a wife is to be paid to her husband, and compensation for causing a miscarriage also belongs to the husband; and that one who incurs the penalty of death is exempt

7. The rule: "If he continue a day or two," then, should apply also in the case of the stranger killing a bondman or a bondwoman (Cf. Commentaries, esp. *Mirkebet ha-Mishneh*).

אחר במיתה על עבדו ועל אמתו ת"ל לא יוקם
כי כספו הוא מגיד הכתוב אף על פי שלא חלק
בין שורו לשור אחר במיתה על עבדו ועל אמתו
80 נחלק בינו לבין אחר במיתה על עבדו ועל אמתו
לכך נאמר לא יוקם כי כספו הוא.

פרשה ח   (שמות כ"א, כ"ב–כ"ה.)

וכי ינצו אנשים וגו' למה נאמרה פרשה
זו לפי שהוא אומר וכי יזיד איש על רעהו וגו' לא
שמענו אלא על המתכוין להכות את שונאו והכהו
שהוא במיתה אבל המתכוין להכות את שונאו והכה
את אוהבו לא שמענו ת"ל וכי ינצו אנשים וגו' ואם
5 אסון יהיה וגו' בא הכתוב ללמדך על המתכוין
להכות את שונאו והכה את אוהבו שהוא במיתה
לכך נאמרה פרשה זו רבי אומר אם נתכוון להכות
שונאו זה והכה אחר שהוא שונאו פטור המתכוין
10 להכות שונאו והכה אוהבו דין הוא שיהא פטור
אבל בא הכתוב ללמדך שחבל אשה לבעל ודמי
וולדות לבעל וכל המתחייב מיתה פטור מן

18 — 1 סנהדרין ע"ט, א'. י' שם ט', ג'–ו'. (27[ab]).   13 — 11 ב"ק מ"ב, ב'.

82 לכך נאמר] הגהתי=ג. א"צ. ול"ט. ועיין ז"י: א. מ. ד. הא מה ת"ל. ועיין מא"ש.
10 — 8 אם נתכוין—שהוא פטור] א. ט. אף המתכוין שלא להכות והכה דין הוא
שיהא פטור מ. המתכוין להכות והכה פטור אבל המתכוין שלא להכות והכה דין הוא
שיהא פטור.   8 נתכוון] ג. המתכוין.   9 פטור] ד. ~ אבל. ומחקתיהו א"צ. ז"י. ג. ש"י.
10 להכות] ד. שלא להכות. והגהתי=א"צ. ש"י. וז"ר.

from making monetary compensation. R. Isaac says: Even if one aims to kill and kills he is free, unless he has expressly said: I am going to kill this man.[1] For it is said: "And lie in wait for him, and rise up against him and smite him mortally" (Deut. 19.11). What then is the purpose of saying: "And if men strive together"? Because it says: "And he that smiteth anybody mortally" (Lev. 24.17), which I might understand to mean even if he kills a child born after only eight months of pregnancy. Therefore it says: "And if men strive together," thereby telling us that one is not guilty of death unless he kills a viable child.

And if Men Strive Together. I thus know only about men. How about women? R. Ishmael used to say, etc. R. Josiah says: "A man or a woman" (Num. 5.6). Why is this said, etc.? R. Jonathan says: There is no need of this scriptural proof. Has it not been said: "The owner of the pit shall make it good"[2] (v. 34), etc.?

And Hurt a Woman with Child so That Her Young Come Out. Abba Ḥanin says in the name of R. Eliezer: "And hurt a woman with child." What need is there of saying this? Since it says: "So that her young come out," we learn that she is with child. What then is the need of saying: "With child"? Simply this: Suppose he hit her upon the head or upon any other part of her body, I might understand that he should nevertheless be guilty. Therefore it says: "With child," thereby telling us that he is not guilty unless he hit her upon that part of the body in which the child is carried. Another Interpretation: *And Hurt a Woman with Child.* What need is there of saying this? Because it is said: "According as the woman's husband shall lay upon him," I might understand it to mean, the woman's husband even if he be not the natural father of the child. Therefore it says here: "With child," declaring thereby that payment is to be made only to the natural father of the child.

1. See Commentaries.
2. See above, ch. VI.

התשלומין רבי יצחק אומר אף המתכוין להכות
והכה פטור עד שיאמר לאיש פלוני אני מכה שנאמר
וארב לו וקם עליו והכהו נפש ומה ת״ל וכי ינצו
אנשים לפי שהוא אומר ואיש כי יכה כל נפש אדם
שומע אני אף בן שמונה במשמע ת״ל וכי ינצו אנשים
מגיד שאינו חייב עד שיהרג בן קיימא.

וכי ינצו אנשים אין לי אלא אנשים נשים
מנין היה רבי ישמעאל אומר וגו׳ רבי יאשיה אומר
איש ואשה למה נאמר וגו׳ רבי יונתן אומר אינו צריך
והלא כבר נאמר בעל הבור וגו׳.

ונגפו אשה הרה ויצאו ילדיה אבא
חנין אומר משום רבי אליעזר ונגפו אשה הרה מה
תלמוד לומר לפי שנאמר ויצאו ילדיה הא למדנו
שהיא הרה ומה ת״ל הרה אלא אם הכה על ראשה
או על אחד מאיבריה שומע אני יהא חייב ת״ל הרה
מגיד שאינו חייב עד שיכנה במקום עוברה. דבר
אחר ונגפו אשה הרה מה ת״ל לפי שנאמר כאשר
ישית עליו בעל האשה שומע אני אף על פי שאין
ההריון שלו ת״ל הרה מגיד שאינו משלם אלא לבעל
ההריון.

15 דברים י״ט, י״א.   16 וקירא כ״ד, י״ז.   22—19 לעיל ר׳.   28—23 ב״ק מ״ט, א׳; ר׳
שם ה׳, ו׳ (5ᵃ).   32—28 ר׳ ב״ק שם. תוס׳ שם ט׳, כ׳.

14 שנאמר] הגהתי=ג. א״צ. ול״ט: א. מ. ד. ת״ל.   16 אנשים] ד. שומע / ואיש כי
יכה כל נפש אדם] ד. וכי יכה נפש אדם.   18 בן קיימא] ד. בן של קיימא.   20 אומר
וגו׳] ד. וכו׳ כדלעיל.   21 איש ואשה] ד. איש איש.   22 וגו׳] ק. < נ. ל. וכו׳ כדלעיל.
26—23 אבא חנין—למדנו שהיא הרה] מ״ח. ר׳ אליעזר אומר ממשמע שנאמר ויצאו
ילדיה שומע אני שהיא הרה.   24 חנין] מ. חנן / אומר] ד. > / אליעזר] ק. אלעזר.
25—24 מה תלמוד לומר] ט. ט״ב. מה תלמוד ד. למה נאמר.   25 לפי שנאמר] א.
ט. לפי שהוא אומר א״צ.   והלא כבר נאמר ג. ממשמע שנאמר.   26 אלא] ד. <.
27—26 על ראשה או] מ. <.   30 שומע אני] ד. <.   31 ת״ל הרה] א. < / משלם] ד.
חייב.

So That Her Children[3] Come Out. The expression: "Her children," suggests at least two. And how do we know that the law applies even when there is only one? Scripture says: "With child"—in any case.

And Yet No Harm Follow. That is, to the woman. *He Shall Surely Be Fined.* For the young. You interpret it to mean "no harm follow" to the woman. Perhaps it is not so, but means "no harm follow" to the young, "he shall surely be fined" for the woman? But it says: "But if any harm follow, then thou shalt give life for life" (v. 23). Hence when it says: "And yet no harm follow," it must mean, to the woman; "He shall surely be fined," for the young. But may it not mean, No harm follow to the woman nor to the children? If you should interpret it thus—then the husband would even have to pay for the services of a midwife. Hence, when it says: "No harm follow," it must mean, to the woman only; "He shall surely be fined," for the children.

He Shall Surely Be Punished. By paying money. You interpret it to mean by paying money. Perhaps it is not so, but it means to be punished by death? You must reason: Here punishment is mentioned and there it is said: "And they shall punish him," etc. (Deut. 22.19). Just as there it means a fine of money, so also here it means a fine of money.

According as the Woman's Husband Shall Lay upon Him. This passage comes to teach that the compensation for injuries to a wife is to be paid to her husband, and compensation for causing a miscarriage also belongs to the husband; and that one who incurs the penalty of death is exempt from making monetary compensation. Another Interpretation: *According as the Woman's Husband Shall Lay upon Him.* I might understand this to mean, the woman's husband, even if he is not the natural father of the child. It says, however: "With child," declaring thereby that payment is to be made only to the natural father of the child. Another Interpretation: *According as the Woman's Husband Shall Lay upon Him.* I might understand this to mean, what-

3. The literal rendering is required by the *Mekilta*.

ויצאו ילדיה מיעוט וולדות שנים ומנין
אפילו אחד ת"ל הרה מכל מקום.

35 **ולא יהיה אסון** באשה ענוש יענש בוולדות
אתה אומר לא יהיה אסון באשה ענוש יענש בוולדות
או אינו אלא לא יהיה אסון בוולדות ענוש יענש
באשה ת"ל ואם אסון יהיה ונתת נפש תחת נפש הא
מה ת"ל לא יהיה אסון באשה ענוש יענש בוולדות או
40 לא יהיה אסון לא באשה ולא בוולדות אם אמרת
כן אף הוא צריך ליתן דמי שכר דמי חיה הא מה ת"ל
לא יהיה אסון באשה ענוש יענש בוולדות.

ענוש יענש ממון אתה אומר ממון או אינו
אלא מיתה הרי אתה דן נאמר כאן עונש ונאמר
45 להלן וענשו אותו מה להלן ממון אף כאן ממון.

כאשר ישית עליו בעל האשה בא
הכתוב ללמדך שחבל אשה לבעלה ודמי וולדות
לבעל וכל המתחייב מיתה פטור מן התשלומין.
דבר אחר כאשר ישית עליו בעל האשה שומע אני
50 אף על פי שאין ההריון שלו ת"ל הרה מגיד שאינו
משלם אלא לבעל ההריון. דבר אחר כאשר
ישית עליו בעל האשה שומע אני כל שירצה ת"ל

34—33 ש. שם.   45 דברים כ"ב, י"ט.   48—46 ב"ק מ"ב, ב'.   53—51 ש. 130.

37—38 אלא לא יהיה—יענש באשה] ד. אלא אסון בוולדות וענוש באשה א. לא יהיה
אסון לא באשה ולא בוולדות.   40—38 ת"ל ואם—ולא בוולדות] א. <.   38 ונתת נפש
תחת נפש] הוספתי=ז"י: מא"ש. וגו'.   40—39 ענוש יענש—לא באשה] ק. <.   40 אם
אמרת] מ. נ. ל. אלא אם אמרת.   41 הוא] ד. / דמי] א. <.   45 וענשו אותו] א.
מ. עונש.   51—49 דבר אחר—לבעל ההריון] ד. < ונמצא בג. בשם ס"א. ובט. קטיע.

ever he pleases. But it says: "And he shall pay according to *pelilim*."
This tells us that he pays only what the judges say. For it is said: "And
he shall pay according to *pelilim*." And "*pelilim*" only means judges, as
in the passage: "Even our enemies themselves being judges (*pelilim*)"
(Deut. 32.31). And it also says: "If one man sin against another, God
shall judge him"[4] (I Sam. 2.25).

And if Any Harm Follow. "Harm" here means only death. And
although there is no proof for this, there is a suggestion of it in the
passage: "If harm befall him by the way" (Gen. 42.38).

Then Thou Shalt Give Life for Life. It is with life that he must pay for
life. He cannot pay for life with money. Another Interpretation: *Then
Thou Shalt Give Life,* etc. With life only shall he pay, but he is not to
pay for a life with life and with money. Rabbi says: *Then Thou Shalt
Give Life for Life.* This means, monetary compensation. You interpret
it to mean monetary compensation. Perhaps this is not so, but it means
death? Behold, you reason thus: Here the expression "laying upon" is
used and there (v. 30) the expression "laying upon" is used. Just as
the expression "laying upon" used there implies only monetary compensation, so also here it implies only monetary compensation.

Eye for Eye. This means, monetary compensation for an eye. You
interpret it to mean money for an eye. Perhaps this is not so, but it
means an eye literally? R. Ishmael used to say: Behold it says: "And
he that killeth a beast shall make it good and he that killeth a man
shall be put to death" (Lev. 24.21). Scripture thus declares cases of
injuries inflicted upon man to be like cases of injury inflicted upon
beasts, and vice versa. Just as cases of injuries inflicted upon beasts
are subject only to payment of indemnity so also cases of injuries
inflicted upon man are subject only to payment of indemnity. R. Isaac
says: Behold it says: "If there be laid on him a ransom," etc. (v. 30).
Now then, by using the method of *kal vaḥomer,* you reason thus: If

4. The Hebrew word for "shall judge him," ופללו, is from the same root as
‏פלילים.

ונתן בפלילים מגיד שאינו משלם אלא על פי דיינין
שנאמר ונתן בפלילים ואין פלילים אלא דיינין
שנאמר ואויבינו פלילים ואומר אם יחטא איש לאיש
ופללו אלהים.

ואם אסון יהיה אין אסון אלא מיתה ואף
על פי שאין ראיה לדבר זכר לדבר וקראהו אסון
בדרך.

ונתת נפש תחת נפש נפש תחת נפש הוא
משלם ואינו משלם ממון תחת נפש. דבר אחר
ונתת נפש וגו' נפש הוא משלם ואינו משלם נפש
וממון תחת נפש רבי אומר ונתת נפש תחת נפש ממון
אתה אומר ממון או אינו אלא מיתה הרי אתה דן
נאמר כאן השתה ונאמר להלן השתה מה השתה
האמור להלן ממון אף כאן ממון.

עין תחת עין ממון אתה אומר ממון או אינו
אלא עין ממש היה רבי ישמעאל אומר הרי הוא
אומר מכה בהמה ישלמנה ומכה אדם יומת הקיש
הכתוב נזקי אדם לנזקי בהמה ונזקי בהמה לנזקי
אדם ומה נזקי בהמה בתשלומין אף נזקי אדם
בתשלומין רבי יצחק אומר הרי הוא אומר אם
כופר יושת עליו וגו' והרי דברים קל וחומר מה

---

55 דברים ל"ב, ל"א.   56—55 שמואל א. ב', כ"ה.   59—58 בראשית מ"ב, ל"ח.
62—66 סנהדרין ע"ט, א'.   72—68 ת"כ אמור י"ד (104ᵈ). מגלת תענית פ"ד. ב"ק פ"ג,
ב'—פ"ד, א'.   69 ויקרא כ"ד, כ"א.   73—72 שמות כ"א, ל'.

53—54 מגיד שאינו—שנאמר ונתן בפלילים] א. רמב"ן בפרשה <.   55 אם יחטא] ד.
כי יחטא.   60—61 נפש תחת נפש הוא משלם] ד. נפש הוא משלם.   61 ואינו משלם
ממון] מ. נפשו ממון (אולי צ"ל נפש וממון).   61—63 דבר אחר—תחת נפש]=א. ט.
ג: מ. ד. <.   62—63 נפש וממון] ט. ט"כ. נפשו בממון.   63 רבי אומר] מ. דבר
אחר.   65 השתה] ד. השיתה.   68 ישמעאל] ד. אלעזר.   69—68 הרי הוא אומר] ד.
<.

even in a case where the penalty of death is imposed only a monetary compensation is exacted, it is but logical that in this case, where no death penalty is imposed, surely no more than a monetary compensation should be exacted. R. Eliezer says: *Eye for Eye,* etc. I might understand that whether one injures intentionally or unintentionally one is to pay only an indemnity. But behold Scripture singles out the one who inflicts an injury intentionally, declaring that he is not to pay money but is actually to suffer a similar injury. It is said: "And if a man maim his neighbour, as he hath done so shall it be done to him" (Lev. 24.19). This is a general statement. "Eye for eye" (ibid. v. 20) is a specific statement. Now, a general statement followed by a specific statement cannot include more than the specific statement. When it says however: "As he hath maimed a man," etc. (ibid.), it again makes a general statement. But perhaps the second general statement is to be considered identical with the first general statement? You must say: No! This is a general statement followed by a specific statement and by another general statement, all of which must be interpreted as including only things similar to those mentioned in the specific statement.[5] Now, in this case the specific statement specifies that for injuries resulting in a permanent defect and affecting chief organs and visible, though inflicted intentionally, one is subject only to payment of indemnity. Hence, for any injuries resulting in a permanent defect and affecting chief organs and visible, though inflicted intentionally, one is subject only to payment of indemnity. Thus Scripture says: "As he hath maimed a man"—that is, if he has intentionally inflicted an injury.[6]

Burning for Burning. If you interpret it to mean that he wounded him thereby and drew blood from him—has it not already been said: "Wound for wound"? And if you should say it means that he thereby produced a visible mark upon him—has it not already been said:

5. See "Talmud Heremeneutics," *JE,* XII, 33.
6. See Introduction and cf. Commentaries.

אם במקום שענש מיתה לא ענש אלא ממון וכאן

75 שלא ענש מיתה דין הוא שלא יענש אלא ממון רבי

אליעזר אומר עין תחת עין וגו' שומע אני בין מתכוין

בין שאינו מתכוין אינו משלם אלא ממון והרי הכתוב

מוציא את המתכוין לעשות בו מום שאינו משלם אלא

ממש שנאמר ואיש כי יתן מום בעמיתו כאשר עשה

80 כן יעשה לו כלל עין תחת עין פרט כלל ופרט אין

בכלל אלא מה שבפרט וכשהוא אומר כאשר יתן

מום באדם חזר וכלל אי כלל ככלל הראשון אמרת

לאו אלא כלל ופרט וכלל אין אתה דן אלא כעין

הפרט מה הפרט מפורש מומין קבועין וראשי

85 איברים בגלוי ובמתכוין שאינו משלם אלא ממון

אף אין לי אלא מומין קבועין וראשי איברים ובגלוי

ובמתכוין משלם ממון תלמוד לומר כאשר יתן

מום באדם עד שיתכוין לעשות בו מום.

כויה תחת כויה אם תאמר שפצעו והוציא

90 את דמו והלא כבר נאמר פצע תחת פצע ואם

תאמר שעשה בו חבורה והלא כבר נאמר חבורה

---

75 — 78 ב״ק פ״ד, א'.   79 — 80 ויקרא כ״ד, י״ט.   89 — 95 ש. 130.   96 — 95 ב״ק פ״ד, ב'. י' שם ח', א' (6b).

74 שענש] ד. ~ הכתוב.   76 אליעזר] ד. יצחק / וגו'] מ״ח. ממש עין תחת עין שן
תחת שן כויה תחת כויה.   79 ממש] ד. ט. ממון.   80 — 79 כאשר עשה כן יעשה לו]
הוספתי: א. וגו'.   80 כלל ופרט] א. פרט וכלל וכלל מ. ט. פרט וכלל.   82 ככלל] ד.
כלל ט. בכלל.   84 מה הפרט] מ. לומר מה הפרט / קבועין] ד. הקבועין בו.   86 — 87 אף
אין לי—משלם ממון] מ. >.   86 אין לי אלא] ד. כל.   87 משלם ממון] א. שאינו
משלם אלא ממון.   89 שפצעו] מ״ח.   89 שכואו.   90 דמו] ד. מוחו.

"Stripe for stripe"? What need then is there of saying: "Burning for burning"? Simply this: Suppose he burned him on the sole of his foot without producing a visible mark, or he put a load of stones upon him, thereby causing him pain, or put snow upon his head and made him suffer from cold; behold, in such cases he has to pay him indemnity for the pain. But suppose he was tender and delicate and reared with indulgence so that his pain is double? This sort of pain too is referred to in the Torah when it says: "Burning for burning."

CHAPTER IX
(Ex. 21.26–27)

And if a Man Smite the Eye of His Bondman, etc. Why is this section set forth? Since it says: "And ye may make them an inheritance for your children," etc. (Lev. 25.46), I might understand it to mean, even if he struck out his tooth or blinded his eye. Therefore it says here: "And if a man smite the eye of his bondman," etc.; "and if he smite out his bondman's tooth," etc. Behold then this passage makes an exception to the general rule about the Canaanitish slave, being stricter with the master in that the slave goes out free by the loss of any of his chief external organs. For this purpose this section is set forth.

And if a Man Smite. I thus know it only about men. How about women? R. Ishmael used to say, etc. R. Josiah used to say: "A man or a woman" (Num. 5.6). Why is this said? Because it says: "And if a man shall open a pit" (v. 33), etc. R. Jonathan says: There is no need of this scriptural proof. Has it not been said: "The owner of the pit shall make it good" (v. 34), etc?[1]

The Eye of His Bondman or the Eye of His Bondwoman. This is to declare the master guilty in either case. R. Eliezer says: Scripture here

1. See above, ch. VI.

תחת חבורה ומה ת"ל כויה תחת כויה אלא כוואו
על כף רגלו ולא רשם בו טענו אבנים וציערו הטיל
שלג על ראשו וצננו הרי זה נותן לו דמי צערו אבל
95 אם היה מרוכך ומעודן ומפונק כל שכן צערו
מכופל זהו הצער האמור בתורה כויה תחת כויה.

פרשה ט (שמות כ"א, כ"ו–כ"ז.)

וכי יכה איש את עין עבדו וגו' למה
נאמרה פרשה זו לפי שהוא אומר והתנחלתם אותם
לבניכם וגו' שומע אני אפילו הפיל את שנו וסימא
את עינו ת"ל וכי יכה איש את עין עבדו וגו' ואם
5 שן עבדו וגו' והרי הכתוב מוציא עבד כנעני מכללו
להחמיר עליו שיהא יוצא בראשי איברים לכך
נאמרה פרשה זו.

וכי יכה איש אין לי אלא איש אשה מנין
היה רבי ישמעאל אומר וגו' רבי יאשיה אומר איש
10 ואשה למה נאמר לפי שהוא אומר וכי יפתח איש
בור וגו' רבי יונתן אומר אינו צריך והלא כבר נאמר
בעל הבור ישלם וגו'.

את עין עבדו או את עין אמתו לחייב
על זה בפני עצמו ועל זה בפני עצמו רבי אליעזר

2–3 ויקרא כ"ה, מ"ו.   20–14 ש. 131.

93 כף רגלו] ד. ציפרנו ועל רגלו.   94 שלג] א. ~ רצונין.   96–95 צערו מכופל] ד.
שכפול בו צערו.

5–4 וגו' ואם שן עבדו] ק. נ. ואת שן אמתו ל. א"צ. או את עין אמתו.   5 עבד]
ד. עבדו / כנעני] מ. עברי.   6 להחמיר] ט. להקל.

deals with a Canaanitish slave. You say this passage deals with a Canaanitish slave. Perhaps it is not so, but it deals only with a Hebrew slave? Scripture says: "And of them shall ye buy bondmen and bondwomen"[2] (Lev. 25.44).

The Eye of His Bondman. I might understand this to mean even if it only shows white spots. But it says: "And destroy it." I can therefore interpret it to mean only such a blow as can destroy it. In this connection the sages said: If he struck his slave on the eye, thereby blinding it, or on the ear, thereby making him deaf, the slave goes out a free man. But if he struck the slave alongside the eye so that he cannot see, or alongside the ear so that he cannot hear, he is not to go out a free man.[3]—These are the words of R. Ḥananiah b. Gamaliel. For it is said: "And if a man smite," that is, if the effect is the direct result of his act. If the master knocked out two of the slave's teeth at one stroke or blinded both his eyes at one stroke, the slave goes out a free man and gets nothing else. Scripture teaches this by saying: "Eye for eye, tooth for tooth" (v. 24). If however the master first blinds the one eye of the slave and then the other, or knocks out one tooth of the slave and then another, the slave goes out free because of the loss of the first, and therefore receives indemnity for the loss of the second. Scripture teaches this by saying: "For his eye's sake, for his tooth's sake."[4]

He Shall Send Him Out Free. I might understand this to mean that the master must write him a writ of emancipation. But it says: "For his eye's sake." R. Eliezer says: Here "sending out" is spoken of and there (Deut. 24.1) "sending out" is spoken of. Just as the "sending out" spoken of there means by a writ, so also the "sending out" spoken of here means by a writ. I thus know this only about one who is

2. See above, ch. VII.
3. See Introduction and cf. Commentaries.
4. See Commentaries. The moment the master destroys the one eye of the slave the latter becomes a free man. And when his second eye is destroyed he is to be paid indemnity for it as any other free man would.

15 אומר בכנעני הכתוב מדבר אתה אומר בכנעני

הכתוב מדבר או אינו אלא בעברי ת״ל מהם תקנו

עבד ואמה.

את עין עבדו שומע אני אפילו העלת חרור

ת״ל ושחתה לא אמרתי אלא מכה שיש בה כדי

20 השחתה מכאן אמרו טפח על עינו וסימא אותו על

אזנו וחרשו הרי זה יוצא בן חורין כנגד עינו ואינו

רואה כנגד אזנו ואינו שומע הרי זה אינו יוצא בן

חורין דברי רבי חנניה בן גמליאל שנאמר וכי יכה

איש עד שיעשה מעשה הפיל שתי שניו כאחת וסימא

25 שתי עיניו כאחת הרי זה יוצא בן חורין ואינו נוטל

כלום ת״ל עין תחת עין שן תחת שן זו אחר זו יוצא

על הראשונה ונוטל נזקי שנייה ת״ל תחת עינו תחת

שנו.

לחפשי ישלחנו שומע אני יכתוב לו גט

30 שחרור ת״ל תחת עינו רבי אליעזר אומר נאמר כאן

שילוח ונאמר להלן שילוח מה שילוח האמור להלן

גט אף שילוח האמור כאן גט אין לי אלא שהוא

23 — 20 ב״ק צ״א, א׳. תוס׳ שם ט׳, כ״ו.   30 — 26 גיטין מ״ב, ב׳.   34 — 30 י׳ גיטין ד׳,
ד׳ (45d).   39 — 32 ספרי במדבר א׳.

18 חורין] ט. חוורור ד. ירוד.   19 כדי] ד. >.   23 חנניה] ד. חנינא.   26 ת״ל עין תחת
עין שן תחת שן] א. מ. ת״ל עין עין שן שן א״צ. ז״י. >.

qualified[5] to be set free. How about one who is not qualified to be set free? Scripture says: "He shall send him out free for his eye's sake"—in any case. R. Ishmael says: The Torah speaks of one who sets free and of one who is set free. Since in regard to the one who sets free we have learned that only one who is grown up can do so, I might think that as regards the one who is set free it should also be only one who is grown up that can be set free. But Scripture says: "He shall send him out free for his eye's sake"—in any case.

And if He Smite Out His Bondman's Tooth. I might understand this to mean even if it is only a milk tooth that he knocked out. But it also says: "Eye"—just as the eye is such as cannot grow back again, so also the tooth must be such as cannot grow back again. Thus far I know only about the tooth and the eye which are specifically mentioned. How about other chief organs? Behold, you reason and establish a general rule on the basis of what is common to both of these: The peculiar aspect of the case of the tooth is not the same as the peculiar aspect of the case of the eye. Neither is the peculiar aspect of the case of the eye the same as the peculiar aspect of the case of the tooth. But what is common to both of them is that their loss constitutes a permanent defect, they are chief organs, they are visible. And if the master intentionally destroys them, the slave goes out free for their sake. Perhaps then even if he cut off flesh from his body? But Scripture mentions the tooth and the eye. Their peculiar characteristic is that their loss constitutes a permanent defect, they are chief organs, and they are visible. And if the master intentionally destroys them, since they cannot be restored, the slave goes out free for their sake. Hence, I can include only such parts of the body the loss of which constitutes a permanent defect, which are chief organs, and which are visible. And if intentionally injured by the master the slave goes out free for their sake.

5. I. e., a grown up slave.

יכול להשתלח שאינו יכול להשתלח מנין ת"ל
לחפשי ישלחנו תחת עינו מכל מקום רבי ישמעאל
35　אומר הואיל ואמרה תורה במשלח ואמרה
במשתלח אם למדת על המשלח שאינו משלח אלא
מי שהוא גדול יכול אף המשתלח לא יהא משתלח
אלא מי שהוא גדול ת"ל לחפשי ישלחנו תחת עינו
מכל מקום.

40　**אם שן עבדו** וגו' שומע אני אפילו הפיל
שן של חלב ת"ל עין מה עין שאינה יכולה לחזור
אף שן שאינה יכולה לחזור אין לי אלא השן והעין
מיוחדות ושאר כל ראשי איברים מנין הרי אתה
דן בנין אב מבין שתיהן לא הרי השן כהרי העין
45　ולא הרי העין כהרי השן הצד השוה שבהן שהם
מומין קבועין וראשי איברים בגלוי ובמתכוין יוצא
עליהם בן חורין או אפילו חתך הימנו בשר ת"ל
השן והעין מיוחדות מומין קבועין ראשי איברים
בגלוי ובמתכוין שאין יכולין לחזור יוצא עליהן
50　בן חורין אף אין לי אלא מומין קבועין ראשי
איברים בגלוי ובמתכוין שאינן יכולין לחזור יוצא
עליהן בן חורין.

41—42　ש. 131.　52—48　קידושין כ"ד, ב'. ש. שם.

40 אם] במקרא ואם / אם שן עבדו וגו'] ד. <.　43 ראשי] ד. <.　44 דן] ד. אומר ודן
/ אבן] ק. <.　46 ובמתכוין] א"צ. ש"י.　< ד. ~ שאינן יכולין לחזור.　50—47 או
אפילו—יוצא עליהם בן חורין] ד. <.　52—50 אף אין לי—יוצא עליהם בן חורין] ק. >
נ.ל. אף כל ראשי איברים שאינן יכולין לחזור יוצא עליהם בן חורין.

He Shall Send Him Out Free. I might understand this to mean that the master must write him a writ of emancipation. But it says: "For his eye's sake." R. Eliezer says: Here "sending out" is spoken of and there (Deut. 24.1) "sending out" is spoken of. Just as the "sending out" spoken of there means by a writ, so also the "sending out" spoken of here means by a writ. I thus know it only about one who is qualified to be set free. How about one who is not qualified to be set free? Scripture says: "He shall send him out free for his eye's sake"— in any case. R. Ishmael says: A Canaanitish slave can have no redemption, he can go out free only at the pleasure of his master. For it is said: "And ye may make them an inheritance for your children after you, to hold for a possession" (Lev. 25.46). And by our method we learn from this that the Canaanitish slave is a permanent possession like inherited land. Yet, if the master in punishing him knocks out his tooth or blinds his eye or injures any other of his chief external organs, the slave obtains his release at the price of these sufferings. Now, by using the method of *kal vaḥomer,* you reason: If a person can at the price of suffering obtain his release from the hands of flesh and blood, all the more should it be that he thus[6] can obtain his pardon from Heaven. And thus it says: "The Lord hath chastened me sore: but He hath not given me over unto death" (Ps. 118.18).

CHAPTER X
(Ex. 21.28–30)

And If an Ox Gore. The ox was also included in the general statement which says: "One that smiteth a man so that he dieth" (v. 12). Behold Scripture here singles it out from the general statement, making its punishment severer in that it is to be stoned. For this purpose this section is set forth.

6. I. e., at the price of suffering.

לחפשי ישלחנו שומע אני יכתוב לו גט
שחרור ת"ל לחפשי ישלחנו תחת שינו רבי אליעזר
אומר נאמר כאן שילוח ונאמר להלן שילוח מה
שילוח האמור להלן גט אף שילוח האמור כאן גט
ואין לי אלא שיכול להשתלח שאינו יכול להשתלח
מנין ת"ל לחפשי ישלחנו תחת שינו מכל מקום רבי
ישמעאל אומר עבד כנעני אין לו פדיון לעולם
ואינו יוצא אלא לרצון רבו שנאמר והתנחלתם אותם
לבניכם אחריכם לרשת אחוזה לפי דרכנו למדנו
שעבד כנעני כשדה אחוזה לעולם אבל אם היה
רבו רודהו והפיל את שינו וסמא את עינו או אחד
מכל ראשי איברים גלוים בו הרי זה קונה עצמו
ביסורין והרי דברים קל וחומר אם מידי בשר ודם
אדם קונה את עצמו ביסורין קל וחומר מידי שמים
וכן הוא אומר יסור יסרני יה ולמות לא נתנני.

פרשה י   (שמות כ״א, כ״ח—ל׳.)

וכי יגח שור אף השור היה בכלל שנאמר
מכה איש ומת והרי הכתוב מוציאו מכללו להחמיר
עליו שיהא בסקילה לכך נאמרה פרשה זו.

60—61 ויקרא כ״ה, מ״ו. קידושין כ״ב.   65—67 ברכות ה', א'.   67 תהלים קי״ח, י״ח.

53 שומע אני] ד. >.   54 ת"ל לחפשי ישלחנו תחת שינו] הגהתי=ג: א. ד. ת"ל ישלחנו
מ. >.   54—55 רבי אליעזר אומר] הגהתי=ג.   55—56 מה שילוח—אף שילוח האמור
כאן גט] הוספתי: א. מ. וגו'.   58 תחת שינו] א. ד. >.   60 רבו] ד. >.   61 לבניכם
אחריכם לרשת אחוזה] הוספתי: א. ג. וגו'.   64 מכל ראשי איברים גלוים בו] ד.
מאיבריו שהם ראשין וגלויים.   66 אדם קונה את עצמו] ד. קנה עצמו.

2 מכה איש ומת] הגהתי=א"צ. ז"י. ש"י. ועיין ז"ר: א. מ. ד. ט. והמית איש
או אשה.

And If an Ox Gore. I thus know only about the ox. How do I know
that any other animal is to be regarded like the ox? Behold, I reason
thus: Here the ox is mentioned and on Sinai the ox was mentioned
(Deut. 5.14). Just as when the ox was mentioned on Sinai the law
considered all other animals to be like the ox,[1] so also when the ox is
mentioned here, it is but logical that we should consider all animals
to be like the ox. And how do we know that any other manner of
killing by the ox is to be regarded like goring? You must reason thus:
A *mu'ad*[2] is subject to death by stoning[3] and a *tam* is likewise subject
to death by stoning.[4] Now, inasmuch as you have learned that in the
case of the *mu'ad* any manner of killing is regarded like goring,[5] it follows that in the case of the *tam* likewise we should regard any manner of killing like goring. No! If you cite the case of the *mu'ad*—that
is different, for there the owner has even to pay ransom. Therefore
the law regards any manner of killing like goring. But will you argue
the same about the *tam*? There the owner does not have to pay ransom. But there would be no purpose in saying: "But it hath killed a
man or a woman" (v. 29), except it be used as a basis for comparison
to formulate the following *gezerah shavah*: Here it is said: "A man or a
woman," and there (v. 29) it is said: "A man or a woman." It is therefore but logical that just as there the law regards any manner of killing like goring, so also here we should regard any manner of killing
like goring. And how do we know that the law is the same when
minors are killed as when grown-ups are killed? You must reason

1. For it says there: "Nor thine ox, nor thine ass nor any of thy cattle."
2. *Mu'ad* is an ox, or any other animal, that has done damage three times and
whose owner having been forwarned is liable to full indemnity. *Tam* designates
the innocuous animal that has not done damage three times, and whose owner
has not been forewarned (see *JE*, II, 392–3 and Jastrow, *Dictionary*, p. 745 and
1674–5).
3. I. e., for killing a man or a woman (see Ex. 21.29).
4. Ibid. v. 28.
5. In the case of the *Mu'ad* (v. 29) Scripture uses the expression: "It hath
killed a man or a woman," without specifying that it means by goring only.

וכי יגח שור אין לי אלא שור מנין

לעשות כל הבהמה כשור הרי אני דן נאמר כאן

שור ונאמר בסיני שור מה שור האמור בסיני

עשה בו כל הבהמה כשור אף שור האמור כאן

דין הוא שנעשה בו את כל בהמה כשור ומנין

לעשות כל המיתות כנגיחה הרי אתה דן הואיל

ומועד בסקילה ותם בסקילה אם למדת על המועד

שעשה בו כל המיתות כנגיחה אף התם נעשה בו

כל המיתות כנגיחה לא אם אמרת במועד שהוא

משלם את הכופר לפיכך עשה בו כל המיתות

כנגיחה תאמר בתם שאינו משלם את הכופר שאין

ת"ל והמית איש או אשה אלא להקיש לדון גזירה

שוה נאמר כאן איש או אשה ונאמר להלן איש או

אשה מה להלן עשה בהן כל המיתות כנגיחה אף

כאן דין הוא שנעשה בהן כל המיתות כנגיחה ומנין

לעשות הקטנים כגדולים הרי אתה דן הואיל ומועד

4—8 ב"ק נ"ד, ב'. תוס' שם ר', י"ח.   40—18 ב"ק מ"ג, ב'—מ"ד, א'.

6 בסיני] ד. ט. להלן.   8 בו את] ד. <.   12—11 אף התם—כנגיחה] א. <.   14—13 לפיכך
עשה—כנגיחה] ד. ט. <.   14 הכופר] א. מ. ג. ~ לפיכך נעשה בו כל המיתות כנגיחה.
15—14 שאין ת"ל והמית איש או אשה] א. איש או אשה והמית איש או אשה ט. ת"ל
איש או אשה שאין ת"ל א"צ. ת"ל והמית איש או אשה שאין ת"ל איש או אשה.
17 עשה] א. <. / בהן] א. ד. <. ט. בו.   18 דין הוא שנעשה] א. <. / בהן] א. ד. <.
19 הרי אתה] א. ד. הריני.

thus: A *mu'ad* is subject to death by stoning and a *tam* is likewise subject to death by stoning. Now, inasmuch as you have learned that in the case of the *mu'ad* no distinction is made between minors and grown-ups,[6] it follows that in the case of the *tam* likewise no distinction should be made between minors and grown-ups. No! If you cite the case of the *mu'ad*—that is different, for there the owner has even to pay ransom. Therefore the law regards the case of minors like the case of grown-ups. But will you argue the same about the *tam*? There the owner does not have to pay ransom and therefore the case of minors should not be regarded like the case of grown-ups. But there would be no purpose in saying: "Whether it have gored a son or have gored a daughter" (v. 31), except to furnish an expression free to be used in formulating the following *gezerah shavah:* Here the expression "gore" is used and there (v. 31) the expression "gore" is used. Just as there the case of minors is regarded like the case of grown-ups, so also here the case of minors is to be regarded like the case of grown-ups. R. Simon b. Yoḥai says: Why is this said? Even if it had not been said I could have reasoned thus: If in the case where with respect to those who kill, the law does not regard minors like grown-ups, nevertheless, with respect to those who are killed, it does regard minors like grown-ups,[7] is it not logical that here where with respect to those who kill, the law regards minors[8] like grown-ups we should, with respect to those who are killed, surely regard minors like grown-ups? No! If you cite that case—that is a different matter, for there the law regards the one acting unintentionally like the one acting intentionally as regards liability for damages. Therefore the law also regards minors like grown-ups with respect to those who are killed. But will you argue the same about this case? Here the one act-

6. See v. 31.

7. I. e., in the case of human beings. A minor is not liable for killing a grown-up, but a grown-up is liable for killing a minor.

8. No distinction is made by the law, whether the ox that killed was a young one or an old one.

20 בסקילה ותם בסקילה אם למדת על מועד שעשה

בו קטנים כגדולים אף התם נעשה בו קטנים

כגדולים לא אם אמרת במועד שהוא משלם את

הכופר לפיכך עשה בו קטנים כגדולים תאמר בתם

שאינו משלם את הכופר לפיכך לא נעשה בו קטנים

25 כגדולים שאין ת״ל או בן יגח וגו׳ אלא מופנה להקיש

לדון גזירה שוה נאמר כאן יגח ונאמר להלן

יגח מה להלן עשה בו קטנים כגדולים אף כאן עשה

בו קטנים כגדולים רבי שמעון בן יוחאי אומר למה

נאמר עד שלא יאמר יש לי בדין ומה אם במקום

30 שלא עשה בו קטנים כגדולים בהורגין עשה בו קטנים

כגדולים בנהרגין וכאן שעשה קטנים כגדולים

בהורגין אינו דין שנעשה קטנים כגדולים בנהרגין

לא אם אמרת להלן שעשה את שאינו מתכוין

כמתכוין בנזיקין לפיכך עשה קטנים כגדולים

35 בנהרגין תאמר כאן שלא עשה את שאינו מתכוין

---

20 שעשה] א. מ. שיעשה.   24 לפיכך לא נעשה] ד. שנעשה.   25 שאין] ד. ט. /
וגו׳] ט. שאין ת״ל א״צ. ~ שאין ת״ל. / מופנה] א. מ. ט. ט״כ. מפני.   27 אף כאן
עשה בו] א. מ. אף (מ. אם) יגח שנאמר כאן דין הוא שנעשה בו.   29 בדין] מ. בית
דין.   30 בהורגין] ק. ג. (בשם ס״א) אדם שהמית בהורגין.   31 וכאן] ד. מקום.
34 בנזיקין] ד. בנזוקיו.

ing unintentionally is not regarded like the one acting intentionally as regards liability for damages.[9] Therefore minors are not to be regarded like grown-ups with respect to those who are killed. But there would be no purpose in saying: "Whether it have gored a son or have gored a daughter" (v. 31), except to furnish an expression free to be used in formulating the following *gezerah shavah:* Here the expression "gore" is used and there (v. 31) the expression "gore" is used. Just as there the law regards the case of minors like the case of grown-ups with respect to those who are killed, so also here it is but logical that we should regard the case of minors like the case of grown-ups with respect to those who are killed.

The Ox Shall Be Surely Stoned and Its Flesh Shall Not Be Eaten. Why is this said? From the literal meaning of: "Shall be surely stoned" we can learn that the flesh is forbidden to be eaten.[10] What need then is there of saying: "And its flesh shall not be eaten"? Simply this: If the owners of an ox that is being led out to be stoned, anticipating its stoning, slaughter it ritually, its flesh is nevertheless forbidden to be eaten. In this sense it is said: "And its flesh shall not be eaten." I thus know that it is forbidden to be eaten. How do I know that it is also forbidden to have any benefit from it? You reason by using the method of *kal vaḥomer:* If the heifer whose neck is broken, which atones for the shedding of blood, is forbidden to be made use of, it is but logical that the ox which is stoned, being a shedder of blood, should surely be forbidden to be made use of. Perhaps just the reverse! If the stoned ox, though being a shedder of blood, is permitted to be made use of, is it not but logical that the heifer whose neck is broken, which atones for the shedding of blood, should surely be permitted to be made use of? But it says: "And shall break the heifer's

9. In the one case, i. e., of the *tam*, the liability is only for half the damage, while in the other, that of the *mu'ad*, the liability is for the full damage.

10. If it is killed by stoning and not ritually slaughtered, its flesh cannot be eaten.

כמתכוין בנזקין לפיכך לא עשה קטנים כגדולים
בנהרגין שאין ת"ל או בן יגח או בת יגח אלא מופנה
להקיש לדון גזירה שוה נאמר כאן יגח ונאמר להלן
יגח מה להלן עשה בו קטנים כגדולים בנהרגין אף

40 כאן דין הוא שנעשה בו קטנים כגדולים בנהרגין.

סקול **יסקל** **השור** **ולא** **יאכל** **את**
בשרו למה נאמר ממשמע שנאמר סקול יסקל
השור הא למדנו שבשרו אסור באכילה ומה ת"ל
לא יאכל את בשרו אלא שור שהוא יוצא ליסקל

45 וקדמו בעלים ושחטוהו בשרו אסור באכילה לכך
נאמר לא יאכל את בשרו אין לי אלא שהוא אסור
באכילה מנין שהוא אסור בהנאה אמרת קל וחומר
ומה אם עגלה ערופה שהיא מכפרת על שפיכות
דמים הרי היא אסורה בהנאה שור הנסקל שהוא

50 שופך דמים דין הוא שיהא אסור בהנאה או חילוף
אם שור הנסקל שהוא שופך דמים הרי הוא
מותר בהנאה עגלה ערופה שהיא מכפרת על
שפיכות דמים אינו דין שתהא מותרת בהנאה ת"ל

41—47 ב"ק מ"א. פסחים כ"ב, ב'. ש. 131.   65—47 מ"ת 25—124.   49—48 ספרי
דברים ר"ז.

36 בנזקין] ד. < / לפיכך לא עשה] ט. ~ בו ד. שנעשה בו.   37 שאין] ד. ט. < / בת
יגח] מ. ג. ~ ומה ת"ל או בן יגח או בת יגח / אלא] ד. < / מופנה] א. מ. מפני.
49—39 מה להלן—כגדולים בנהרגין] ד. כדכתיב לעיל.   42—41 ולא יאכל את בשרו]
הוספתי=ג. ז"י: א"צ. וגו'.   43 הא למדנו] ד. איני יודע.   46 שהוא אסור] ד. <.
47 שהוא אסור בהנאה] ד. שאף בהנאה אסור.   49 הרי היא אסורה בהנאה] מ. אינו
דין שתהא מותרת בהנאה.   51 אם] ד. ומה.

neck there in the valley"[11] (Deut. 21.4). Thus, I have advanced an argument and tried to argue the reverse. The reverse, however, has been proved invalid. Hence, I was right in my first argument: If the heifer whose neck is broken, which atones for the shedding of blood, is forbidden to be made use of, it is but logical that the ox which is stoned, being a shedder of blood, should surely be forbidden to be made use of. R. Isaac says: There is no need of this. If the heifer whose neck is broken, which does not defile the land nor cause the Shekinah to remove, is nevertheless forbidden to be made use of, it is but logical that the stoned ox, which does defile the land and does cause the Shekinah to remove, should surely be forbidden to be made use of.[12]

Rabbi says: If the bullocks and he-goat sacrifices—required by law to be wholly burned—which serve as an atonement for the world are forbidden to be made use of, it is but logical that the stoned ox which does not serve as an atonement for the world, should surely be forbidden to be made use of. I thus far know only about its flesh. How about its skin? R. Ishmael used to say: You reason by using the method of *kal vaḥomer:* If in the case of the sin-offering where ritual slaughter makes the flesh permissible,[13] the skin is forbidden to be made use of if the animal dies a natural death,[14] it is but logical that in the case of the stoned ox where ritual slaughter cannot make the flesh permissible, its skin should surely be forbidden to be made use of after it is dead. But the case of a *nebelah*[15] disproves this, for its

11. This verse was understood to imply that the heifer must be buried in the valley and no use whatever was permitted to be made of it (see Commentaries here, especially *Zeh Yenaḥamenu,* and cf. *Sifre,* Deut. 207).

12. Cf. Friedmann.

13. See M. Zeb. 5.3.

14. See ibid. 8.1 and M. Tem. 4.1.

15. *Nebelah,* נבלה, literally, an animal that has died a natural death, or carrion, also designates an animal still living, but so injured or diseased as to make it forbidden as food even though it be ritually slaughtered. These are designated as

וערפו שם את העגלה בנחל דנתי וחלפתי בטל

החלוף וזכיתי בדין מתחלה מה אם עגלה ערופה

שהיא מכפרת על שפיכות דמים הרי היא אסורה

בהנאה שור הנסקל שהוא שופך דמים דין הוא שיהא

אסור בהנאה רבי יצחק אומר אינו צריך ומה אם

עגלה ערופה שאינה מטמאה את הארץ ולא מסלקת

את השכינה הרי היא אסורה בהנאה שור הנסקל

שהוא מטמא את הארץ ומסלק את השכינה דין

הוא שיהא אסור בהנאה רבי אומר ומה אם פרים

הנשרפים ושעירים הנשרפים שהן באין לכפרה

לעולם אסורין בהנאה שור הנסקל שאינו בא כפרה

לעולם דין הוא שיהא אסור בהנאה אין לי אלא

בשרו עורו מנין היה רבי ישמעאל אומר אמרת

קל וחומר ומה אם חטאת שבשרה מותר בשחיטתה

עורה אסור במיתתה שור הנסקל שבשרו אסור

בשחיטתו דין הוא שיהא עורו אסור במיתתו הרי

---

54 דברים כ"א, ד'.   58—60 ספרי במדבר קס"א.   65—79 ב"ק שם. פסחים שם.

55 בדין מתחלה] א. מ. ט. לדין בתחלה.   58—62 ר' יצחק אומר—דין הוא שיהא
אסור בהנאה] א"צ. <.   59 שאינה מטמאה] א. מ. שאינה לא לטמא.   64 אסורין]
א. מ. לפיכך אסורין.   66 היה] ק. נ. הרי היה / אמרת] ד. <.

flesh remains forbidden even if it is ritually slaughtered, yet its skin is permitted to be made use of after it is dead. This should prove about the stoned ox that although its flesh would remain forbidden even if it were ritually slaughtered, nevertheless its skin should be permitted after it is dead. Said one of the disciples of R. Ishmael: No! If you cite the case of the *nebelah*—that is different, for it is altogether permitted to be made use of. Therefore its skin, after its death, remains permitted. But will you argue the same about the stoned ox? It is forbidden to be made use of, and therefore its skin, after its death, should still be forbidden to be made use of.

The Ox Shall Be Surely Stoned and Its Flesh Shall Not Be Eaten. Why is the particle *et*[16] used? To include the blood, the fat and the skin.

But the Owner of the Ox Shall Be Quit. R. Judah b. Bathyra says: Quit from punishment by Heaven. For the following argument could have been advanced: The *mu'ad* is subject to death by stoning and the *tam* likewise is subject to death by stoning. Now, inasmuch as you have learned in the case of the *mu'ad* that although its owners are free from punishment at the hands of the human court, they are not free from punishment by the heavenly court, it follows that in the case of the *tam* likewise although its owners are free from punishment at the hands of the human court they should not be free from punishment by the heavenly court. Behold then, what does Scripture mean by saying: "But the owner of the ox shall be quit"? Quit from punishment by Heaven. Simon the son of Azzai says: *But the Owner of the Ox Shall Be Quit.* Free from the payment of half damage.[17] For the following argument might have been advanced: In the case of an ox

---

carcasses though still alive, **נבלות מחיים** (see Ḥul. 20b–21a and cf. Joseph Caro in *Bet Yosef* to *Tur Yoreh De'ah,* 27 end).

16. The particle **את** like **גם** and **אף** was regarded as having inclusive force (see Bacher, op. cit., p. 180).

17. It probably means: Free from payment of half the ransom **חצי כופר** (see Commentaries).

70 נבלה תוכיח אף על פי שבשרה אסור בשחיטתה
עורה מותר במיתתה היא תוכיח על שור הנסקל
שאף על פי שבשרו אסור בשחיטתו דין הוא שיהא
עורו מותר במיתתו אמר אחד מתלמידי רבי
ישמעאל לא אם אמרת בנבלה שהיא מותרת בהנאה
75 לפיכך עורה מותר במיתתה תאמר בשור הנסקל
שהוא אסור בהנאה לפיכך יהא עורו אסור בהנאה.

סקול יסקל השור ולא יאכל את
בשרו את בשרו למה נאמר להביא דמו וחלבו
ועורו.

80 **ובעל השור נקי** רבי יהודה בן בתירה
אומר נקי מידי שמים שהיה בדין הואיל ומועד
בסקילה ותם בסקילה אם למדת על מועד אף
על פי שיצאו בעליו מידי בית דין של בשר ודם
לא יצאו מידי בית דין של שמים אף התם אף על
85 פי שיצאו בעליו מידי בית דין של בשר ודם לא
יצאו מידי בית דין של שמים הא מה ת"ל ובעל
השור נקי נקי מידי שמים שמעון בן עזאי אומר ובעל
השור נקי נקי מחצי נזק שהיה בדין הואיל ושור

87 — 104 ב"ק מ"א, ב'—מ"ב, ב'. י' שם ד', ו' (4^{bc}).

76 בהנאה 2] ד. במיתתו.   77 ולא] ד. לא.   78 את בשרו למה נאמר] הגהתי=ג: א.
למה נאמר מ. את למה נאמר ד. בשרו למה.   80 בן בתירה] ד. >.   82 — 83 אף על
פי] ד. >.   86 ובעל] א. בעל.   88 מחצי נזק] ד. מחצי כופר.

which kills another ox payment is to be made, and likewise in the case of an ox which kills a man[18] payment is to be made. Now, just as in the former case one makes full payment for the act of a *mu'ad* and a half payment for the act of a *tam*, so also in the latter case where full payment is made for the act of a *mu'ad*,[19] half payment should be made for the act of a *tam*. Behold then, what does Scripture mean by saying: "But the owner of the ox shall be quit"? Free from making a half payment.

R. Gamaliel says: *But the Owner of the Ox Shall Be Quit.* Free from paying the price of the slave. For the following argument might have been advanced: The *mu'ad* is subject to death by stoning and the *tam* is subject to death by stoning. Now, inasmuch as you have learned that in the case of the *mu'ad* the owner also must pay the price of the slave (v. 32), I might think that in the case of the *tam* likewise he should also have to pay the price of the slave. But it says: "But the owner of the ox shall be quit."

R. Akiba says: *But the Owner of the Ox Shall Be Quit.* Free from paying damages for causing a miscarriage. For the following argument might have been advanced. The law declares a man guilty in case he himself kills, and also declares a man guilty in case his ox kills. Now, inasmuch as you have learned that when a man aims at another man but instead hits a woman so that her young come out, he must pay damages for causing a miscarriage, it follows that when an ox aims at another ox but instead hits a woman so that her young come out, the owner should also have to pay damages for causing a miscarriage. But it says: "But the owner of the ox shall be quit."

But if the Ox Was Wont to Gore. This passage comes to distinguish between an ox that is a *tam* and one that is a *mu'ad*. There are five differences between the *tam* and the *mu'ad*: In the case of the *mu'ad* wit-

18. I. e., a slave (see v. 32).

19. In case the *mu'ad* kills a free man it is put to death and its owner must in addition to losing his ox also pay a ransom (v. 30).

שהמית את השור בתשלומין ושור שהמית את האדם

90 בתשלומין מה להלן מועד משלם נזק שלם ותם

משלם חצי נזק אף כאן מועד משלם נזק שלם ותם

משלם חצי נזק הא מה ת"ל ובעל השור נקי נקי

מחצי נזק רבן גמליאל אומר ובעל השור נקי נקי

מדמי העבד שהיה בדין הואיל ומועד בסקילה

95 ותם בסקילה אם למדת על מועד שהוא משלם

דמי העבד יכול אף התם משלם דמי העבד הא

מה ת"ל ובעל השור נקי נקי מדמי העבד רבי

עקיבא אומר ובעל השור נקי נקי מדמי ולדות

שהיה בדין הואיל וחייב באדם וחייב בשור אם

100 למדת על אדם שהיה מתכוין לחבירו והכה את

האשה ויצאו ילדיה משלם דמי ולדות אף השור

שהיה מתכוין לחבירו והכה אשה ויצאו ילדיה

משלם דמי ולדות הא מה ת"ל ובעל השור נקי

נקי מדמי ולדות.

105 **ואם שור נגח הוא** בא הכתוב לחלוק בין

שור תם למועד חמשה דברים בין שור תם למועד

nesses[20] are required but in the case of the *tam* they are not. In the case of the *mu'ad* the owner must also pay a ransom but in the case of the *tam* he does not have to pay a ransom. In the case of the *mu'ad* the owner has to pay thirty *selas* when the victim is a slave (v. 32), but in the case of the *tam* he does not have to pay thirty *selas*. In the case of the *mu'ad* the owner has to pay the full damage but in the case of the *tam* he pays only half the damage. For the damage done by the *mu'ad* the owner makes full payment from whatever property[21] he may have. For the damage done by the *tam* the owner makes payment only to the extent of the value of the *tam* itself.

In Time Past. One day and another day preceding it and still another day preceding the latter. What is a *tam*-ox and what is a *mu'ad*-ox? A *mu'ad* is one about which the owner has been warned three times. Such a one is considered a *tam* again if a child can safely play with its horns.—These are the words of R. Meir. R. Judah says: A *mu'ad* is the one about which the owner has been warned for three days; and it is again considered a *tam* if for three successive days it refrained from goring. R. Jose says: Even if the owner has been warned about it three times in one day he is fully responsible for a *mu'ad*. And what does Scripture mean by saying: "In time past"? Merely that if the owner has been warned about it for three days but not consecutively, the ox is still considered a *tam*.[22]

And Warning Hath Been Given to Its Owner. This tells us that he is not responsible unless he has been forewarned.

And He Hath Not Guarded It. This includes the gratuitous bailee. *And He Hath Not Guarded It.* Adequately. In this connection the sages

20. I. e., witnesses who saw the previous acts of the ox and who forewarned the owner.

21. In the case of the *mu'ad* the owner must pay for the full damage, even if it amounts to more than the value of the ox.

22. According to R. Jose, if there was an interval of more than one day between one act and the following one, the ox does not become a *mu'ad* after three acts.

מועד צריך עדים ותם אינו צריך עדים מועד משלם

את הכופר ותם אינו משלם את הכופר מועד נותן

שלשים סלע ותם אינו נותן שלשים סלע מועד משלם

110 נזק שלם ותם משלם חצי נזק מועד משלם מן

העלייה ותם משלם מגופו.

מתמול שלשום יום ואמש ושלפניו איזהו

שור תם ואי זה הוא מועד מועד שהעידו בו

שלשה פעמים ותם כדי שיהא התינוק ממשמש

115 בקרניו דברי רבי מאיר רבי יהודה אומר מועד

שהעידו בו שלשה ימים ותם שיחזור בו שלשה ימים

זה אחר זה רבי יוסי אומר אפילו העידו בו שלשה

פעמים ביום אחד הרי זה חייב ומה ת״ל מתמול

שלשום אלא אם התרה בו שלשה ימים שלא בזה

120 אחר זה אינו נידון אלא כתם.

והועד בבעליו מגיד שאינו חייב על שהתרו

בו.

ולא ישמרנו להביא שומר חנם. ולא ישמרנו

109—111 ב״ק ט״ו, א׳.   112—120 שם כ״ג, ב׳—כ״ד, א׳. תוס׳ שם ב׳, ב׳. י׳ שם ב׳,
ו׳ (3ª). ש. 132.   121 ב״ק שם. תוס׳ שם.   123—130 ב״ק מ״ה, ו׳; תוס׳ שם ה׳, ו׳.

107 אינו צריך] ד. צריך.   112 איזהו] ד. זהו.   114—116 ותם כדי שיהא—שהעידו בו
שלשה ימים] ד. <.   116 שלשה ימים] א. שלשה פעמים.   117 יוסי] א״צ. ש״י.
מאיר.   118 הרי זה] ד. זה אחר זה.   119—120 אם התרה—בזה אחר זה] א. מ. אם
כן חזר בו שלשה ימים זה אחר זה / התרה] ק. הקרה.

said: If he guarded it adequately he is free, but if he guarded it inadequately he is liable. Suppose he tied it up with a rope and yet it went
out and did damage. If it is a *tam* he is free. But if it is a *mu'ad* he is
liable, for it is said: "And he hath not guarded it." And in this case it
was not well guarded.—These are the words of R. Meir. R. Judah
says: If it is a *tam* the owner is liable. But if it is a *mu'ad* he is free, for
it is said: "And he hath not guarded it." And in this case it was
guarded.[23] R. Eliezer says: The only adequate guard it can have is the
knife.[24] R. Eliezer b. Jacob frees the owner in either case.

And He Hath Killed a Man or a Woman. This expression is free to be
used as a basis for comparison and to formulate a *gezerah shavah.*

The Ox Shall Be Stoned. Why is this said? Even if it had not been
said, I could have inferred it by the following reasoning: If the *tam* is
subject to death by stoning, shall the *mu'ad* not be stoned? No! If you
cite the instance of the *tam*—that is different, for there the owner
does not have to pay a ransom. Therefore it should be stoned. But
will you argue the same about a *mu'ad*? There the owner pays a ransom and therefore, so I might think, it should not be stoned. Therefore it says here: "The ox shall be stoned."

Another Interpretation: It had been included in the general statement. But then it has been singled out[25] by having a new regulation
applied to it. Scripture therefore here declares it still to be included
in the general statement.[26]

R. Akiba says: *The Ox Shall Be Stoned and Its Owner Also Shall Be
Put to Death.* This compares the death of the ox to the death of its
owner. Just as the death of the owner can be decided only by a tribunal of twenty-three judges, so also the death of the ox is to be
decided by a tribunal of twenty-three judges.

23. Cf. B. K. 45b.
24. I. e., it should be slaughtered.
25. See above, beginning of this chapter.
26. See Commentaries.

כראוי לו מכאן אמרו שמרו כראוי פטור שלא

125 כראוי חייב קשרו במוסרה ויצא והזיק תם פטור

מועד חייב שנאמר ולא ישמרנו בעליו ולא שמור

הוא זה דברי רבי מאיר רבי יהודה אומר תם חייב

ומועד פטור שנאמר ולא ישמרנו בעליו ושמור הוא

זה רבי אליעזר אומר אין לו שמירה אלא סכין

130 רבי אליעזר בן יעקב פוטר בזה וזה.

והמית איש או אשה מופנה להקיש לדון

גזרה שוה.

השור יסקל למה נאמר עד שלא יאמר יש

לי בדין אם התם בסקילה מועד לא יהא בסקילה

135 לא אם אמרת בתם שאינו משלם את הכופר לפיכך

הוא בסקילה תאמר במועד שהוא משלם את הכופר

לפיכך לא יהא בסקילה ת״ל השור יסקל. דבר

אחר היה בכלל ויצא לידון בדבר חדש והחזירו

הכתוב לכללו רבי עקיבא אומר השור יסקל וגם

140 בעליו הקיש מיתת השור למיתת בעלים מה מיתת

הבעלים בעשרים ושלשה אף מיתת השור בעשרים

ושלשה.

142 — 140 סנהדרין ב׳, א׳. ר׳ שם א׳, ב׳ (19[b]). ש. 132.

125 — 126 תם פטור מועד חייב] ג. א״צ. אחד תם ואחד מועד חייב.   128 — 129 ושמרנו הוא זה] ד. ~ דברי ר׳ מאיר.   131 מופנה] א. מופני.   138 בדבר חדש] א. מ. בחדש. 140 הקיש—בעלים] ד. הקיש מיתת בעלים למיתת השור.

And Its Owner Also Shall Be Put to Death. By the hand of Heaven. You interpret it to mean by the hand of Heaven. Perhaps this is not so, but it means by the hand of man? When it says however: "If there be laid upon him a ransom," then, since ransom can be offered for those that are to be put to death by the hand of Heaven I can still interpret "Shall be put to death" to mean, by the hand of Heaven. You can interpret it to mean by the hand of Heaven. Perhaps however it simply means by the hand of man? When it says: "Moreover ye shall take no ransom for the life of a murderer that is guilty of death" (Num. 35.31), behold then, ransom cannot be offered for those that are to be put to death by the hand of man, but ransom may be offered for those who are to be put to death by the hand of Heaven.[27]

If There Be Laid on Him a Ransom Then He Shall Give for the Redemption of His Life. "Redemption of his life"—that is, the life of the one who was killed.—These are the words of R. Ishmael. R. Akiba says: "Redemption of his life"—that is, the life of the one who caused the death. And thus we find that in no case do we allow ransom to be given for those who are to be put to death by the human court. Those who incur the penalty of death by the human court cannot be ransomed. For it is said: "None devoted,[28] that may be devoted of men, shall be ransomed; he shall surely be put to death" (Lev. 27.29). But here: "Then he shall give for the redemption of his life."

R. Ishmael says: Come and see how merciful He by whose word the world came into being is to flesh and blood. For a man can redeem himself from the Heavenly judgment by paying money, as it is said: "When thou takest the sum of the children of Israel, according to their number," etc. (Ex. 30.12), and it says: "The money of the persons for whom each man is rated" (II Kings 12.5), and it says: "The ransom of a man's life are his riches" (Prov. 13.8), and it says: "Therefore, O king, let my counsel be acceptable to thee, and break

27. See Introduction and cf. Commentaries. Also Geiger, op. cit., p. 488 ff.
28. I. e., devoted to death, sentenced to death by a human court.

וגם בעליו יומת בידי שמים אתה אומר
בידי שמים או אינו אלא בידי אדם כשהוא אומר
אם כופר יושת עליו ונתן פדיון נפשו הא נותנין
פדיון למומתין בידי שמים עדיין אני אומר יומת
בידי שמים אתה אומר בידי שמים או אינו אלא
בידי אדם כשהוא אומר לא תקחו כופר לנפש
רוצח אשר הוא רשע למות הא אין נותנין פדיון
למומתין בידי אדם אבל נותנין פדיון למומתים
בידי שמים.

אם כופר יושת עליו ונתן פדיון נפשו
פדיון נפשו של מומת דברי רבי ישמעאל רבי
עקיבא אומר פדיון נפשו של ממית וכן מצינו שאין
נותנין פדיון למומתים בידי אדם בכל מקום חייבי
מיתות בית דין אין להם פדיון שנאמר כל חרם
אשר יחרם מן האדם לא יפדה מות יומת אבל כאן
ונתן פדיון נפשו רבי ישמעאל אומר בא וראה רחמיו
של מי שאמר והיה העולם על בשר ודם שאדם
קונה את עצמו בממון מידי שמים שנאמר כי תשא
את ראש בני ישראל לפקודיהם וגו' ואומר איש
כסף נפשות ערכו ואומר כופר נפש איש עשרו
ואומר להן מלכא מלכי ישפר עלך וחטאך בצדקה

143 — 147 סנהדרין ט״ו, ב׳. ש. שם.   145 ערכין ו׳, ב׳.   149 — 148 במדבר ל״ה, ל״א.
151 — 148 ספרי במדבר קס״א. כתובות ל״ז, ב׳.   154 — 152 ב״ק מ׳, א׳. תוס׳ שם ד׳, ז׳.
י׳ שם ד׳, ז׳ (4c). י׳ כתובות ג׳, י׳ (28a).   156 — 157 ויקרא כ״ז, כ״ט.
161 — 160 שמות ל׳, י״ב.   162 — 161 מלכים ב. י״ב, ה׳.   162 משלי י״ג, ח׳.
164 — 163 דניאל ד׳, כ״ד.

145 הא] ט. הוי.   146 — 145 נותנין — בידי שמים] נ. ל.   ~ ומה ת״ל מות יומת המכה
רוצח הוא ק. רא״ם. ש״י. נותנין פדיון למומתין בידי אדם] (ק. ~ ומה תלמוד לומר
מות יומת המכה רוצח הוא רא״ם. ש״י. ~ והתורה אמרה ולא תקחו כופר לנפש רוצח).
מ״ח. אין נותנין פדיון למומתין בידי אדם שנאמר לא תקחו כופר לנפש רוצח.
146 — 149 עדיין אני אומר — אשר הוא רשע למות] רא״ם. ש״י. >.   149 — 148 לא
תקחו כופר — רשע למות] במקרא שלפנינו. ולא, וגו' מ״ח. מות יומת המכה רוצח הוא.
150 למומתין בידי אדם אבל נותנין פדיון] מ. >.   153 — 152 אם כופר — של מומת] ג.
>.   155 בכל מקום] ט. ~ שהן.   157 — 158 אבל כאן ונתן פדיון נפשו] א. מ. >.

off thy sins by almsgiving" (Dan. 4.24), and it says: "If there be for him an angel, an intercessor, one among a thousand, to vouch for man's uprightness; then He is gracious unto him, and saith: 'Deliver him from going down to the pit, I have found a ransom' " (Job 33.23–24). We thus can learn: There are sacrifices that can be redeemed and there are sacrifices that cannot be redeemed, there are things forbidden to be eaten which can be redeemed, and there are things forbidden to be eaten which cannot be redeemed. There are things forbidden for any use which can be redeemed, and there are things forbidden for any use which cannot be redeemed. There are fields and vineyards which can be redeemed and there are fields and vineyards which cannot be redeemed. There are bondmen and bondwomen that can be redeemed and there are bondmen and bondwomen that cannot be redeemed. There are those declared by court guilty of death that can be redeemed and there are those sentenced by court to death that cannot be redeemed.[29] So also in the future world there will be some for whom there will be redemption and there will be some for whom there will be no redemption. For the heathen nations there will be no redemption, as it is said: "No man can by any means redeem his brother,[30] nor give to God a ransom for him—for too costly is the redemption of their soul" (Ps. 49.8–9). Beloved are the Israelites, for the Holy One, blessed be He, has given the heathen nations of the world as ransom for their souls, as it is said: "I have given Egypt as thy ransom." Why? "Since thou art precious in My sight and honourable and I have loved thee; therefore will I give men for thee, and peoples for thy life" (Isa. 43.3–4).

29. See Commentaries.
30. "Brother" here is interpreted to mean other nations, the brothers of Israel (see Commentaries).

פרוק ואומר אם יש עליך מלאך מליץ אחד מני

165 אלף להגיד לאדם ישרו ויחוננו ויאמר פדעהו מרדת

שחת מצאתי כופר נמצינו למדין קדשים יש להם

פדיון קדשים אין להם פדיון אסורים באכילה

יש להם פדיון אסורין באכילה אין להם פדיון

אסורין בהנאה יש להם פדיון אסורין בהנאה אין

170 להם פדיון שדות וכרמים יש להם פדיון שדות

וכרמים אין להם פדיון עבדים ושפחות יש להם

פדיון עבדים ושפחות אין להם פדיון חייבי מיתות

בית דין יש להם פדיון חייבי מיתות בית דין אין

להם פדיון אף לעתיד לבא יש שיש להם פדיון ויש

175 שאין להם פדיון אומות העולם אין להם פדיון

שנאמר אח לא פדה יפדה איש ולא יתן לאלהים

כפרו ויקר פדיון נפשם חביבין ישראל שנתן

הקב"ה אומות העולם כפרה תחת נפשותיהם שנאמר

נתתי כפרך מצרים וגו' מפני מה מאשר יקרת

180 בעיני נכבדת ואני אהבתיך ואתן אדם תחתיך

ולאמים תחת נפשך.

---

164 — 166 איוב ל"ג, כ"ג — כ"ד.   177 — 176 תהלים מ"ט, ח' — ט'.   181 — 179 ישעיה
מ"ג, ג' — ד'.

---

165 ויחוננו] ד. ואומר ויחוננו.   169 — 168 אסורין באכילה אין להם פדיון אסורין בהנאה
יש להם פדיון] ד. >.   170 — 174 שדות וכרמים אין להם — חייבי מיתות בי"ד אין להם
פדיון] ד. >.   174 אף לעתיד לבא יש]=מ"ח. כ. (ישעיה מ"ג, ג') ד. ויש.   174 — 175 שיש
להם — אומות העולם אין להם פדיון]=מ"ח. כ. (שם): א. מ. להן פדיון.   176 שנאמר]
הגהתי=מ"ח. כ.: א. מ. ד. ת"ל / אח] מ. אך. / ולא] במקרא שלפנינו. לא.   178 אומות
העולם] ד. ~ תחתיהן.

CHAPTER XI
(Ex. 21.31–34)

Whether It Have Gored a Son or Have Gored a Daughter. Why is this said? Since it says: "But it hath killed a man or a woman" (v. 29), I know only about grown-ups. How about minors? It says here: "Whether it have gored a son or have gored a daughter." I thus know only about a real boy and a real girl. How about a *tumtum* and a her-maphrodite? It says: "Whether it have gored a son or have gored a daughter." I still would know only about the son and the daughter of somebody else. How about the owner's own son or his own daugh-ter? It says: "Whether it have gored a son or have gored a daughter." I still would know only about Israelites. How about proselytes? It says: "According to this judgment[1] shall it be done unto him."

If the Ox Gore a Bondman or a Bondwoman. The bondman and the bondwoman were included in the general statement which says: "But it hath killed a man or a woman" (v. 39). Behold this passage here singles out their case from the general statement, making it both severer and lighter. It makes it lighter in that even if the slave was worth a hundred *mana* the owner of the ox is to pay only thirty *selas*.[2] It makes it severer in that even if the slave was worth only one gold *dinar* he must still pay thirty *selas*.

If the Ox Gore a Bondman or a Bondwoman. This is to declare the owner of the ox responsible for either one.

Another Interpretation: *If the Ox Gore a Bondman.* It is a Canaanit-ish slave that Scripture here speaks of. Perhaps however this is not so, but it deals only with a Hebrew slave? When it says: "He shall give unto their master thirty shekels of silver," behold then, it must be a Canaanitish slave that Scripture here speaks of.

1. And "judgment" משפט according to Lev. 24.22 makes no distinction between the home-born and the stranger.
2. A *sela'* or a *shekel* is like four silver *dinars*. One gold *dinar* is twenty-four silver *dinars*. A *mana* is one hundred silver *dinars*.

פרשה יא　(שמות כ״א, ל״א—ל״ד.)

או בן יגח או בת יגח למה נאמר לפי
שהוא אומר והמית איש או אשה אין לי אלא גדולים
קטנים מנין ת״ל או בן יגח או בת יגח אין לי אלא
בן גמור או בת גמורה טומטום ואנדרוגינוס מנין
ת״ל או בן יגח או בת יגח אין לי אלא בנו ובתו
של אחר בנו ובתו שלו מנין ת״ל או בן יגח או בת
יגח מכל מקום אין לי אלא ישראל גרים מנין ת״ל
כמשפט הזה יעשה לו.

אם עבד יגח השור או אמה אף עבד
ואמה היו בכלל שנאמר והמית איש או אשה והרי
הכתוב מוציאו מכללו להקל ולהחמיר עליו להקל
עליו שאם היה יפה מאה מנה נותן לו שלשים סלעים
להחמיר עליו שאם יפה אינו אלא דינר. זהב נותן
לו שלשים סלעים.

אם עבד יגח השור או אמה לחייב על
זה בפני עצמו ועל זה בפני עצמו. דבר אחר אם

עבד יגח השור בכנעני הכתוב מדבר או אינו
מדבר אלא בעברי כשהוא אומר כסף שלשים
שקלים יתן לאדוניו הרי בכנעני הכתוב מדבר.

3—1 לעיל י׳. ב״ק מ״ג, ב׳. ש. 133.　9—14 ב״ק מ״א, א׳. ש. שם.

6—5 ת״ל או בן יגח—בנו ובתו שלו מנין] א. ‹.　7—6 ת״ל או בן יגח—מכל מקום]
א. מ. ת״ל כמשפט הבנות יעשה לה ט. ט״כ. מ״ח. ת״ל כמשפט הזה יעשה לו.
7 אין לי] ד. כמשפט הזה יעשה לו אין לי.　8 כמשפט הזה יעשה לו] אין ‹.　11 מכללו]
ד. ‹.　13 להחמיר עליו] ד. להחמיר עליהם / אינו יפה] ד. לא שוה / זהב] ד. ‹.
15 אם עבד] ד. דבר אחר אם עבד.　16 דבר אחר] ט. ז״י. א״צ. ש״י. ‹.　19 הרי]
ד. הוי מ. ט. הא.

He Shall Give Thirty Shekels of Silver unto Their Master. Whether their master be a man or a woman.

The Ox Shall Be Stoned. Why is this said? Because if it had not been said I could have argued thus: He himself is to be put to death for killing his bondman or his bondwoman. And any other man is also to be put to death for killing his bondman or his bondwoman. Likewise his own ox is to be put to death for killing his bondman or his bondwoman. And so also is the ox of any other man to be put to death for killing his bondman or his bondwoman. Now, since, as you have learned, a distinction is made between himself and another man in regard to the death penalty for killing his bondman or his bondwoman, then we should also make a distinction between his own ox and the ox of another in regard to the death penalty for killing his bondman or his bondwoman. By saying: "The ox shall be stoned," Scripture tells us that although a distinction is made between himself and another man with regard to the death penalty for killing his bondman or his bondwoman, we should make no distinction between his own ox and the ox of another with regard to the death penalty for killing his bondman or his bondwoman.

Another Interpretation: It had been included in the general statement. But then it has been singled out by having a new regulation applied to it. Scripture therefore here declares it still to be included in the general statement.

And If a Man Shall Open a Pit. Why is this said? Even if it had not been said I could have reasoned thus: The ox is his property and the pit likewise is his property. Now, inasmuch as you have learned that he is responsible for the damage done by his ox, shall he not be responsible for the damage done by his pit? No! If you cite the instance of the ox—that is a different matter, for its characteristic is to go about doing damage. But will you argue the same about the pit? Its characteristic is not to go about doing damage. Therefore it says: "And if a man shall open a pit or if a man shall dig a pit." Behold

כסף שלשים יתן לאדוניו אחד איש
ואחד אשה.

השור יסקל למה נאמר עד שלא יאמר יש
לי בדין הואיל והוא במיתה על עבדו ועל אמתו
ואחר במיתה על עבדו ועל אמתו ושורו במיתה
על עבדו ועל אמתו ושור אחר במיתה על עבדו
ועל אמתו אם למדת שחלק בינו לבין אחר במיתה
על עבדו ועל אמתו כך נחלוק בין שורו לשור אחר
במיתה על עבדו ועל אמתו ת״ל השור יסקל מגיד
הכתוב אף על פי שחלק בינו לבין אחר במיתה
על עבדו ועל אמתו לא נחלוק בין שורו לשור אחר
במיתה על עבדו ועל אמתו. דבר אחר היה בכלל
ויצא לידון בדבר החדש והחזירו הכתוב בכללו.

וכי יפתח איש בור למה נאמר עד שלא
יאמר יש לי בדין הואיל והשור ממונו והבור ממונו
אם למדת שהוא חייב על ידי שורו לא יהיה חייב
על ידי בורו לא אם אמרת בשור שדרכו לילך
ולהזיק תאמר בבור שאין דרכו לילך ולהזיק ת״ל
וכי יפתח איש בור או כי יכרה איש הא לפי שלא

32—22 לעיל ז׳.   79—33 ש. 135—134.   39—33 ב״ק ט׳, ב׳—י׳, א׳.

22 השור יסקל למה נאמר] א. מ. ד. גורסין כאן המאמר, דבר אחר היה בכלל ויצא
לידון בדבר החדש והחזירו הכתוב לכללו, דלקמן שורה 31 ולאחריו המאמר השור יסקל
למה נאמר ג. ז״י. והשור יסקל היה (ז״י למה נאמר לפי שהיה) בכלל ויצא לידון בדבר
החדש והחזירו הכתוב לכללו, דבר אחר השור יסקל למה נאמר ש״י. דבר אחר היה
בכללו וכי׳ השור יסקל למה נאמר.   26—27 אם למדת—ועל אמתו] מ. >.   27 כך]
א. מ. >.   28 ת״ל השור יסקל] ד. ת״ל שלשים שקלים והשור יסקל.   31—28 מגיד
הכתוב—ועל אמתו]—ט.: ד. >. א. מ. ~ ת״ל כסף שלשים שקלים.   32—31 דבר
אחר היה בכלל—לכללו] הצגתיו כאן=א״צ. ש״י. ומא״ש: מ״ח. והשור יסקל למה
נאמר היה בכלל—לכללו.   37—36 לא אם אמרת—שאין דרכו לילך ולהזיק] א. מ.
ט. >.   38—37 ת״ל וכי יפתח—יכרה איש] א. ת״ל כי יכרה איש בור מ. ת״ל איש
כי יכרה איש.   38 הא] ד. > מ. ~ ת״ל.

then, since I could not succeed in inferring it by reasoning, Scripture has to cite it.

Another Interpretation: *And If a Man Shall Open,* etc. I thus know only about one who opens a pit. How about one who digs a pit? It says: "Or if a man shall dig." But even if it had not been said I could have reasoned: If the one who opens a pit is responsible, shall the one who digs a pit not be responsible? But if you say so, you would be decreeing punishment merely on the basis of a logical inference. Therefore it is said: "Or if a man shall dig," thus teaching you that punishment cannot be decreed on the basis of a mere logical inference. Another Interpretation: It compares the one who opens a pit to the one who digs one, and vice versa. Just as one who opens a pit, having the right to do so, is free, so also one who digs a pit, having the right to do so, is free. And just as one who digs a pit is liable only when digging a certain measure, so also one who opens a pit is liable only when making an opening of a certain measure. R. Judah b. Bathyra says: The peculiar aspect of the one who opens a pit is not like that of the one who digs a pit, neither is the peculiar aspect of one who digs a pit like that of the one who opens a pit. The feature common to both of them, however, is that the owner is obliged to guard them, and therefore he is responsible for any damage done by them. So also one is responsible for any damage done by anything which he is obliged to guard. I thus far know only about one who opens or digs a pit. How about one who paints it, cements it, or plasters it, or does any other work on it? it says: "And not cover it." Hence, it is not the opening nor the digging which matters. What does matter is its being uncovered.

And Not Cover It. This includes the gratuitous bailee. *And Not Cover It,* meaning that he did not cover it adequately. Hence the sages said: If he covered it adequately, he is free; if inadequately, he is liable. If he covered it and some one else uncovered it, the one that uncovered it is liable. If two partners owning a pit covered it and

זכיתי מן הדין צריך הכתוב להביאו. דבר אחר וכי
40 יפתח איש בור או כי יכרה וגו׳ לחייב על זה בפני
עצמו ועל זה בפני עצמו. דבר אחר וכי יפתח וגו׳
אין לי אלא פותח כורה מנין ת״ל או כי יכרה איש
עד שלא יאמר יש לי בדין אם הפותח חייב הכורה
לא יהיה חייב הא אם אמרת כן ענשת מן הדין לכך
45 נאמר או כי יכרה ללמדך שאין עונשין מן הדין.
דבר אחר הקיש פותח לכורה וכורה לפותח מה
פותח ברשות פטור אף כורה ברשות פטור ומה
הכורה בשיעור אף הפותח בשיעור רבי יהודה
בן בתירה אומר לא הרי פותח כהרי כורה ולא
50 הרי כורה כהרי פותח הצד השוה שבהן שהוא חייב
בשמורו חייב בנזקו אף כל שהוא חייב בשמורו
חייב בנזקו אין לי אלא פותח וכורה צײרו וכײרו
וסײדו ועשה בו מעשה מנין ת״ל ולא יכסנו הא לא
פתיחה גורם ולא כרײה גורם אלא כיסוי גורם.

55 **ולא יכסנו** להביא שומר חנם ולא יכסנו
שלא כיסה כראוי לו מכאן אמרו כסהו כראוי פטור
שלא כראוי כיסהו חייב כיסהו וגילהו אחר המגלה חייב

39 להביאו] ד. ~ בפני עצמו / וכי] ד. כי.   44 יהיה חייב] ד. כל שכן.   45 עונשין]
א״א. עפ״י תוספתא ב״ק ב׳, א׳ ד״ה ולא ~ ממון.   46 דבר אחר] מ. הא ד. ~ כי יפתח
איש בור.   47 פטור] א. מ. ›.   50 שהוא חייב] ד. כל שהוא חייב.   51 בשמורו] נ.
ל. א. מ. בשמרו א״א. בשמירתו.   53 ולא] א. לא.   55 ולא] ק. נ. לא / ולא יכסנו]
ד. דבר אחר לא יכסנו.   56 שלא כיסה] מ. ›.

then one of them uncovered it, the one that uncovered it is liable. If after they had covered it, it was uncovered and only one of them knew about it, the one that knew about it is liable and the one that did not know about it is free.

And an Ox or an Ass Fall Therein. One is liable in either case. *An Ox,* and not an ox and its equipment. *An Ass,* and not an ass and its equipment. For the following argument might have been advanced: If in the case where one is not liable for the beast one is liable for the equipment,[3] here where one is liable for the beast, is it not logical that one should be liable for the equipment? Therefore it says: "And an ox or an ass fall therein"—an ox and not an ox and its equipment, an ass and not an ass and its equipment.

And . . . Fall Therein. In the direction in which it is going. In this connection the sages said: If the animal falls forward, frightened by the sound of the digging, the digger is liable. If it falls backward, frightened by the sound of the digging, he is not liable.[4] But if it falls into the pit, no matter whether it falls forward or backward, he is liable.

The Owner of the Pit Shall Make It Good. Whoever it may be.[5]

He Shall Give Money unto the Owner of Them. I thus know only that one can pay with money. How about paying with cattle? You must reason thus: Here it is said: "And the dead beast shall be his" and there (v. 36) it is said: "And the dead beast shall be his." Just as there one can pay with cattle[6] so also here one can pay with cattle. And just as here one can pay with money so also there one can pay with money.

And the Dead Beast Shall Belong to Him. To the one who suffered the damage. You interpret it to mean to him who suffered the dam-

---

3. See Commentaries.
4. See *Shebut Yehudah* ad loc.
5. See Friedmann.
6. For it says there: "He shall surely pay ox for ox."

השותפין שכסו את הבור אם גלה אחד מהן המגלה

חייב נתגלה וידע בו אחד מהם זה שידע בו חייב

וזה שלא ידע בו פטור. 60

ונפל שמה שור או חמור חייב על זה

בפני עצמו ועל זה בפני עצמו. שור ולא שור וכליו

חמור ולא חמור וכליו שהיה בדין ומה אם במקום

שלא חייב על הבהמה חייב על הכלים וכאן

שחייב על הבהמה אינו דין לחייב על הכלים ת"ל 65

ונפל שמה שור או חמור שור ולא שור וכליו

חמור ולא חמור וכליו.

ונפל שמה בדרך הילוכו מכאן אמרו נפל

לפניו מקול הכרייה חייב לאחריו מקול הכרייה

פטור אבל בבור בין מלפניו בין מאחריו חייב. 70

בעל הבור ישלם מכל מקום.

כסף ישיב לבעליו אין לי אלא כסף

בהמה מנין הרי אתה דן נאמר כאן והמת יהיה לו

ונאמר להלן והמת יהיה לו מה להלן בהמה אף

כאן בהמה מה כאן כסף אף להלן כסף. 75

והמת יהיה לו לניזק אתה אומר לניזק או

61 — 67 שם נ"ה, א'. י' שם ה', ז' (5ª).   70 — 68 ב"ק נ"ג, א'. י' שם, שם. תוס' שם ו',
י"ג.   75 — 72 לקמן י"ב.   79 — 76 ב"ק י', ב'.

75 ט. מה להלן כסף אף כאן כסף.   77 אלו כן היה מה] א"צ. והלא כן היה ומה.

age. Perhaps this is not so, but it means that it belongs to the one who caused the damage? You must reason however: If this were so, what need would there be for Scripture to say it?[7] "And the dead beast shall belong to him" therefore means, to the one who suffered damage. And Scripture merely tells us that we appraise the value of the carcass and reduce thereby the amount which he has to receive for the damage.

CHAPTER XII

(Ex. 21.35–37)

And If the Ox of a Man Hurt. Hurting includes goring, pushing, lying down upon, kicking, and biting.—These are the words of R. Josiah. Abba Ḥanin in the name of R. Eliezer says: Hurting includes goring, pushing, lying down upon, and kicking. And how about biting? It says: "And its owner hath not kept it in" (v. 36). Behold by using the method of *kal vaḥomer* you can reason: If when he kept it in he is responsible, how much more should he be responsible when he did not keep it in? What need then is there for Scripture to say: "And its owner hath not kept it in"? Simply this: Scripture adds one thing more from which the owner must keep it. And what is it? Biting.

The Ox of a Man. This excludes the ox of a minor. *The Ox of a Man.* This includes the ox of outsiders.

The Ox of His Neighbour. This includes the ox of a minor. *Of His Neighbour.* This excludes the ox of a Samaritan, the ox of a foreigner, and the ox of a resident alien.[1]

Then They Shall Sell the Live Ox and Divide. One might argue: You say Scripture here deals with a case where the two oxen are equal in

7. It would be obvious that if the owner of the ox that caused the damage pays the full price for the killed ox, the carcass should belong to him.

1. See above *Baḥodesh*, VII, note 10.

אינו אלא למזיק אמרת אלו כן היה מה ת"ל והמת
יהיה לו לניזק אלא מגיד הכתוב ששמין לו דמי
נבלתו ומנכה לו דמי נזקו.

פרשה יב   (שמות כ"א, ל"ה—ל"ז.)

וכי יגוף בכלל נגיפה נגיחה דחייה רביצה
בעיטה נשיכה דברי רבי יאשיה אבא חנין אומר
משום רבי אליעזר בכלל נגיפה נגיחה דחייה רביצה
ובעיטה ונשיכה מנין ת"ל ולא ישמרנו בעליו והרי
דברים קל וחומר אם כשישמרו ויצא והזיק חייב
5 קל וחומר עד שלא ישמרנו ומה ת"ל ולא ישמרנו
בעליו אלא שהוסיף לו הכתוב עוד שמירה אחרת
ואיזו זו זו נשיכה.

שור איש להוציא שור של קטן שור איש
10 להביא שור של אחרים.

את שור רעהו להביא שור של קטן רעהו
להוציא שור של כותי שור נכרי שור של תושב גר.
ומכרו את השור **החי** **וחצו** וגו' יכול
אתה אומר בשוים הכתוב מדבר או אינו אלא בשום

8—1 ב"ק ב', ב'. י' שם א', א' (2ª). תוס' שם א', ט'. ש. 135.   6—4 לעיל י'.
12—11 ב"ק ל"ז, ב'—ל"ח, א'. תוס' שם ד', ב'—ג'. י' שם ד', ג' (4ᵇ).   31—13 ב"ק
ל"ד, א'—ב'. י' שם ג', י"א (3ᵈ). תוס' שם ג', ג'. ש. 136—135.

---

78 לניזק] ט. <.

1 נגיפה נגיחה] ד. נגיחה נגיפה.   2 נשיכה] ט. < ~ מנין ת"ל כי יגח / חנין] ט.
ט"ב. <.   3 בכלל נגיפה נגיחה] ד. נגיחה נגיפה.   5—6 אם כשישמרו—עד שלא ישמרנו]
ד. אם כשלא שמרו חייב כשהזיק לא כל שכן עד שלא ישמרנו בעליו.   7 אלא] ד. <
/ שהוסיף] ד. הוסיף.   10 של אחרים] א. של נכרי שור כותי שור גר.   13—11 את
שור רעהו—וחצו וגו'] א. <.   11 את שור] מ. ט. < / להביא] מ. להוציא / קטן] ט.
ט"ב. ~ רעהו להביא שור של אחרים מ. ~ רעהו להוציא שור של אחרים.
13 ומכרו—וגו'] מ. ט. ט"ב. <. או / יכול] ק. אי אתה יכול ג. א"צ. ז"י. ש"י. <.
14 אתה אומר] ד. < / בשוים] מ. בשוורים / בשוים] מ. בשוורים.

value. Perhaps this is not so, but it deals both with the case where both oxen are equal in value and with the case where they are not? But you must reason thus: What is the rule for those who cause damage? Are they to gain or to lose? Of course you must admit they are to lose. Likewise what is the rule for those who suffer damage? Are they to receive the amount of the damage suffered or more than the amount of the damage suffered? Of course you must admit that they should receive the amount of the damage suffered and not more than the amount of the damage suffered. R. Akiba says: "Dividing in halves" is mentioned in connection with the living ox, and likewise "dividing in halves" is mentioned in connection with the dead ox. Hence Scripture must deal with a case where both are equal in value.[2]

And the Dead Also They Shall Divide. In this connection the sages said: If an ox worth one hundred shekels gores another ox worth one hundred shekels, or if an ox worth two hundred gores one worth two hundred, the claimant gets half of the living ox. If an ox worth one hundred gores one worth two hundred, the claimant gets the whole of the living ox. If an ox worth two hundred gores one worth only one hundred, the claimant receives one fourth of the living ox. Of the case where an ox worth two hundred gores another ox worth two hundred R. Meir said: It is to such a case that the passage: "And they shall sell the living ox," etc. applies. Said to him R. Akiba: Read this whole verse to its end: "And the dead also they shall divide." To which case then does it apply? To the case where an ox worth two hundred gores another ox worth two hundred, whose carcass is worth one hundred. In this case they sell both the living ox and the dead one, and they divide equally the sum realized for both. And the

2. Akiba's statement sums up the preceding argument. Since Scripture says in both cases that the ox be divided into halves and that the owner of the one causing the damage as well as the owner of the one damaged receive half of each, and since neither one of them is to profit by the accident, it follows that Scripture must deal with a case where both oxen are equal in value.

15 ובשאינן שוים אמרת מה דרך המזיקין נשכרים או

מפסידים הוי אומר מפסידין אף דרך הניזקין

נוטלין נזקן או יתר על נזקן הוי אומר נזקן ולא יותר

על נזקן רבי עקיבא אומר נאמרה חצייה בחי

ונאמרה חצייה במת הא בשוין הכתוב מדבר.

20 **וגם את המת יחצון** מכאן אמרו שור שוה

מנה שנגח שור שוה מנה או שוה מאתים שנגח שור

שוה מאתים נוטל חציו שור שוה מנה שנגח שור שוה

מאתים נוטל כולו שור שוה מאתים שנגח שור שוה

מנה נוטל רבעו שור שוה מאתים שנגח שור שוה

25 מאתים אמר רבי מאיר על זה נאמר ומכרו את

השור החי וגו' אמר לו רבי עקיבא קרא את כל

המקרא הזה וגם את המת יחצון ואיזה זה שור

שוה מאתים שנגח שור שוה מאתים והנבלה שוה

מנה מוכרין את החי ואת המת וחולקין בשוה ובעל

owner of the carcass is to attend to its disposal. In this sense it is said: "And the dead also they shall divide."

Or If It Be Known, etc. This passage comes to distinguish between an ox that is a *tam* and one that is a *mu'ad*. There are five differences between the *tam* and the *mu'ad*, etc.[3]

In Time Past. One day and another day preceding it and still another day preceding the latter, etc.

And He Hath Not Guarded It. This includes the gratuitous bailee. *He Shall Surely Pay Ox for Ox.* I thus know only that one can pay with cattle. How about paying with money? You must reason thus: Here it is said: "And the dead beast shall be his," and there (v. 36) it is said: "And the dead beast shall be his." Just as here one can pay with cattle, so also there one can pay with cattle. And just as there one can pay with money, so also here one can pay with money.

And the Dead Beast Shall Belong to Him. To the one who suffered the damage. You interpret it to mean to him who suffered the damage. Perhaps this is not so, but it means that it belongs to the one who caused the damage? etc.

And If a Man Steal, etc. The case of one who after stealing an animal kills it or sells it was also included in the general statement which says: "If the thief be found he shall pay double" (Ex. 22.6). Behold then, this passage singles it out from the general statement to make it severer in that he must pay indemnity fourfold or fivefold. It is for this purpose that this section is set forth.

And If a Man Steal an Ox or a Sheep. This is to declare one liable for stealing either one.

And Kill It. From this I would know only about one who kills it. How about one who sells it? It says: "Or sell it." But even if it had not been said I could have reasoned thus: If one who slaughters it is liable, shall the one who sells it not be liable? But if you say so, you would be decreeing punishment on the basis of a logical inference.

3. See above, ch. X.

30 הנבלה מטפל בנבלתו לכך נאמר וגם את המת
יחצון.

או נודע וגו' בא הכתוב לחלק בין שור תם
למועד חמשה דברים בין שור תם למועד וגו'.

מתמול שלשם יום ואמש ושלפניו וגו'.

35 **ולא ישמרנו** להביא שומר חנם וגו'.

שלם ישלם שור אין לי אלא בהמה כסף
מנין הרי אתה דן נאמר כאן והמת יהיה לו ונאמר
להלן והמת יהיה לו מה כאן בהמה אף להלן
בהמה מה להלן כסף אף כאן כסף.

40 **והמת יהיה לו** לניזק אתה אומר לניזק או
אינו אלא למזיק וגו'.

וכי יגנוב איש וגו' אף הטובח והמוכר היו
בכלל שנאמר אם ימצא הגנב ישלם שנים והרי
הכתוב מוציאו מכללו להחמיר עליו שישלם
45 תשלומי ארבעה וחמשה לכך נאמרה פרשה זו.

וכי יגנוב איש שור או שה לחייב על
זה בפני עצמו ועל זה בפני עצמו.

וטבחו אין לי אלא טובח מוכר מנין ת"ל או
מכרו עד שלא יאמר יש לי בדין אם הטובח חייב
50 מוכר לא יהא חייב אלא אם אמרת כן ענשת מן

36—39 לעיל י"א.   43 שמות כ"ב, ו'.

---

33 חמשה דברים—למועד וגו'] ד. .>   34 יום] ד. .>   / ואמש] מ. .>   38 כאן] ד. להלן
/ להלן] ד. כאן.   41—40 או אינו אלא] נ. ל. או אתה אומר.   41 וגו'] נ. ל. וכי
כדלעיל.   42 וכי] במקרא, כי.   45—42 וכי יגנוב—פרשה זו] מ. .>   46 וכי יגנוב] ד.
> במקרא, כי יגנוב / שור או שה] א. .>   49—48 או מכרו] מ. ומכרו.   50 אלא] ד.
.>.

Therefore it says: "Or sell it," thus teaching you that punishment cannot be decreed on the basis of a mere logical inference. Another Interpretation: This compares the one who kills to the one who sells, and vice versa: Just as the selling can take place only after it had been taken out of the owner's territory, so also the slaughtering must be such as takes place after it had been taken out of the owner's territory. Just as the selling leaves the animal still permitted to be eaten, so also the slaughtering must be such as to leave the animal permitted to be eaten. Just as the selling leaves the animal permitted to be made use of, so also the slaughtering must leave the animal permitted to be made use of. And just as the slaughtering cannot be undone, so also the selling must be such as cannot be undone. And just as the slaughtering affects the whole animal, so also the selling must be such as affects the whole animal. Another Interpretation: *If a Man Steal.* The animals for sacrifices were also included in this rule, so that for stealing them and for slaughtering them outside of the Temple one would have to pay fourfold or fivefold. But Scripture (Lev. 17.2ff.) excepts them from the general rule, making their case severer in subjecting the offender to the penalty of extinction. One might think that in their case payments also should be made. And the following argument would favor this: If one incurs in their case the penalty of extinction, which is a severer penalty, shall one not incur the penalty of making payment, which is a lighter penalty? Scripture however says: "This is the thing which the Lord hath commanded" (Lev. 17.2). Their case has been singled out to subject the offender to the penalty of extinction and has not been singled out so as to subject the offender to the additional penalty of making payments.[4]

He Shall Pay Five Oxen. That is, four in addition to the one stolen. *And Four Sheep.* That is, three in addition to the one stolen. R. Meir

4. According to R. Neḥunyah the son of Hakaneh, the penalty of extinction is like the death penalty with respect to payments, i. e., that one who incurs it is not to pay any monetary indemnity (Pes. 29a et passim). As regards this rule, Scripture has made no exception in the case of stealing sacrificial animals.

הדין לכך נאמר או מכרו ללמדך שאין עונשין מן
הדין. דבר אחר הקיש טובח למוכר ומוכר לטובח
מה מכירה חוץ לרשותו אף טביחה חוץ לרשותו
מה מכירה מותרת באכילה אף טביחה מותרת
55 באכילה מה מכירה מותרת בהנאה אף טביחה
מותרת בהנאה מה טביחה שאינה יכולה לחזור
אף מכירה שאינה יכולה לחזור מה טביחה כולה
אף מכירה כולה. דבר אחר וכי יגנוב איש אף
המוקדשין היו בכלל שאם גנבן ושחטן בחוץ משלם
60 תשלומי ארבעה וחמשה והרי הכתוב מוציאן מכלל
להחמיר עליהם לזוקקן להכרת יכול שיהו חייבין
בתשלומין והדין נותן אם חייבין על כרת החמור
לא יהו חייבין בתשלומין הקלים ת"ל זה הדבר
אשר צוה יי לכלל כרת יצאו ולא יצאו לכלל
65 תשלומין.

חמשה בקר ישלם ארבעה והוא וארבע

52—58 תוס' ב"ק ז', י"ח—כ'.   53 ב"ק ע"ט, א'.   55—54 ב"ק ע"א, א'.   58—56 שם
ס"ח, א'; ע"ח, ב'.   58—65 גיטין נ"ה, ב'. כתובות ל"ג, ב'—ל"ד.   64—63 ויקרא י"ז,
ב'. ב"ק ע"ט, ב'. תוס' שם ז', י'.

51 או מכרו] א. ומכרו.   58 דבר אחר] א. מ. ט. ט"כ. >.   61 יכול] א. מ. ט. ט"כ.
> / שיהו] א. מ. ט. ט"כ. שהיו.   62 על כרת] ט"כ. בכרת מ"ח. עליהם בכרת.
63 יהו] א. ד. יהא.   64 לכלל כרת] הגהתי=מ"ח. א"צ. מא"ש: א. מ. ד. ט.
מכלל כרת. ואולי צ"ל מכלל לכרת, ועיין ז"י.   64—65 יצאו לכלל תשלומין]
הגהתי=מ"ח. ומא"ש: א. מ. ד. ט"כ. יצאו מכלל תשלומי א"צ. לתשלומין.
67—66 וארבע צאן] א. מ. <.

says: Come and see how highly regarded labor is by Him who by His word caused the world to come into being. For an ox, which has to perform labor, one must pay fivefold. For a sheep, which does not perform labor, one pays only fourfold. R. Johanan b. Zakkai says: God has consideration for the dignity of human beings. For an ox, since it walked with its legs, the thief pays fivefold. For the lamb, since he had to carry it on his shoulders, he pays only fourfold. R. Akiba says: "For an ox. For a sheep." This is to exclude the beast of chase.[5] For the following argument might have been advanced: Since payment is to be made for a domestic animal and payment is also to be made for a beast of chase, it would follow that, inasmuch as you have learned that for a domestic animal one must pay fourfold or fivefold, one should likewise pay fourfold or fivefold for the beast of chase. No! If you cite the instance of the domestic animal—that is a different matter, for it can be offered on the altar, and therefore one should pay for it fourfold or fivefold. But will you argue the same for the beast of chase? It cannot be offered on the altar and therefore one should not pay for it fourfold or fivefold. But the case of an animal with a blemish disproves this. For it likewise cannot be offered on the altar and yet one must pay for it fourfold or fivefold. This should prove that for the beast of chase, although it cannot be offered on the altar, one should pay fourfold or fivefold. No! If you cite the case of the animal with a blemish—that is different, for its species can be offered on the altar and therefore one must pay for it fourfold or fivefold. But will you argue the same for the beast of chase? None of its species can be offered on the altar and therefore one should not pay for it fourford or fivefold. Hence, what must Scripture mean by saying: "For an ox. For a sheep"? To exclude the beast of chase.

5. I. e., like the gazelle and the hart which are permitted to be eaten.

צאן שלשה והוא. רבי מאיר אומר בא וראה כמה
חביבה מלאכה לפני מי שאמר והיה העולם שור
לפי שיש לו מלאכה ישלם חמשה ושה שאין לו
מלאכה ישלם ארבעה רבי יוחנן בן זכאי אומר
חס המקום על כבודן של בריות שור לפי שהולך
ברגליו ישלם חמשה שה לפי שהוא טוענו על כתפו
ישלם ארבעה רבי עקיבא אומר תחת שור תחת
שה להוציא את החיה שהיה בדין הואיל ובהמה
בתשלומין וחיה בתשלומין אם למדת על בהמה
שהוא משלם תשלומי ארבעה וחמשה אף החיה
ישלם תשלומי ארבעה וחמשה לא אם אמרת
בבהמה שהיא קריבה על גבי המזבח לפיכך משלם
תשלומי ארבעה וחמשה תאמר בחיה שאינה קריבה
על גבי המזבח לפיכך לא ישלם תשלומי ארבעה
וחמשה והרי בעלת מומין תוכיח שאינה קריבה על
גבי המזבח ומשלם תשלומי ארבעה וחמשה היא
תוכיח על החיה שאף על פי שאינה קריבה על גבי
המזבח ישלם תשלומי ארבעה וחמשה לא אם אמרת
בבעלת מום שכן במינה קריבה על גבי המזבח
לפיכך ישלם תשלומי ארבעה וחמשה תאמר בחיה
שאין במינה קרב על גבי המזבח לפיכך לא ישלם
תשלומי ארבעה וחמשה הא מה ת״ל תחת שור תחת
שה להוציא את החיה.

70, 75, 80, 85

---

73 — 74 ב״ק ס״ז, ב׳.　　81 — 82 שם ע״ח, ב׳.

67 ר׳ מאיר אומר] ט. היה ר׳ מאיר אומר ד. אמר ר׳ מאיר.　69 לפי] ד. <.
72 שהוא — כתפו] א. מ. שטענו.　78 שהיא] ד. לפי שהיא.　78 — 79 לפיכך — וחמשה]
ד. <.　80 לפיכך לא] ד. לפיכך אינו מ. < / ישלם] ד. משלם מ. ומשלם.　82 ומשלם
תשלומי ארבעה וחמשה] ד. וחייבין עליה תשלומין.　85 שכן במינה] הגהתי=ל: מ.
ד. שמין במינה א״צ. שיש במינה ט. ט״כ. שאינה ט. (הוצאת מאוחרות) שמינה.
86 — 85 שכן במינה — תאמר בחיה] א. <.　87 שאין במינה] א. ט. שאין מינה ד. שאין
מין במינה.　88 — 87 לפיכך — וחמשה] ד. <.

CHAPTER XIII
(Ex. 22.1–3)

If a Thief Be Found Breaking In, etc. With what case does this law deal? With a case where there is doubt whether the burglar came merely to steal or to kill as well. You interpret it as dealing with a case where there is doubt whether the burglar came merely to steal or to kill as well. Perhaps this is not so, but it deals with a case where there is doubt whether he came to steal or not? You must reason: If even in the case where he actually steals the owner of the house is guilty of murder if he kills him, all the more so should the owner be guilty if he kills him in the case where there is doubt whether he came to steal or not.—From this you can draw a conclusion with regard to the saving of life. Since even shedding of blood, which defiles the land and causes the Shekinah to remove, is permitted in disregard of the doubt, all the more should saving of life be done in disregard of any doubt.[1]—Hence it is impossible for you to interpret it as in the latter version, but you must interpret it as in the former version—it deals with a case where there is doubt whether the burglar came merely to steal or to kill as well.

If the Sun Be Risen upon Him. R. Ishmael says: But does the sun rise upon him alone? Does it not rise upon the whole world? It simply means this: What does the sun signify to the world? Peace. So, then, if it is known that this burglar had peaceful intentions toward the owner and yet the latter kills him, he is guilty of murder. Similarly: "They shall spread the sheet" (Deut. 22.17) is to be interpreted as

---

1. This passage marked off by dashes is a sort of parenthetical remark and interrupts the argument. It assumes that the law here deals with a case where there is doubt whether the burglar came with the intention to kill. Although there the owner is in doubt whether his life would be endangered, he may, nevertheless, as a measure of self-protection, kill the burglar. All the more should the work of saving life, even when involving the violation of a ritual law like the Sabbath, be permitted, although there be doubts as to its success in actually saving life.

פרשה יג (שמות כ״ב, א׳—ג׳.)

אם במחתרת ימצא הגנב וגו׳ ומה זה
ספק שהוא בא לגנוב ספק שהוא בא להרוג אתה
אומר ספק שהוא בא לגנוב ספק שהוא בא להרוג
או אינו אלא ספק שהוא בא לגנוב ספק שאינו בא
5 לגנוב אמרת אם כשיגנוב ודאי והרגו הרי זה חייב
קל וחומר זה שספק בא לגנוב ספק לא בא לגנוב
מכאן אתה דן על פקוח נפש ששפיכות דמים
שמטמאה את הארץ ומסלקת את השכינה היא
דוחה את הספק קל וחומר לפקוח נפש שידחה
10 את הספק הא אין עליך לומר בלשון האחרון אלא
בלשון הראשון ספק שהוא בא לגנוב ספק שהוא
בא להרוג.

אם זרחה השמש עליו וגו׳ רבי ישמעאל
אומר וכי חמה עליו בלבד זורחת והלא על כל
15 העולם היא זורחת אלא מה שמש שלום בעולם
אף זה אם ידוע הוא שבשלום עמו והרגו הרי זה
חייב כיוצא בו ופרשו השמלה וגו׳ מחוורין הדברים

12—1 לקמן שבתא א׳; יומא פ״ה, א׳. י׳ סנהדרין ח׳, ח׳ (26c). תוספתא שם י״א, ט׳.
17—1 ש. 138.   12—17 סנהדרין ע״ב, א׳. תוס׳ שם. י׳ סנהדרין שם.   12—19 לעיל
ר׳. ספרי דברים רל״ז.   17 דברים כ״ב, י״ז.

---

1 ומה] ט. א״צ. ‹. א״א. ~ אם.   3—2 אתה אומר] ט. או אינו אלא.   4—3 ספק
שהוא בא להרוג או אינו אלא ספק שהוא בא לגנוב] א. ט. ‹.   5 ודאי] א. ודיו.
6 ספק לא בא לגנוב] א. מ. ק. ספק (א. מ. ~ שהוא) בא להרוג.   10—7 דן על פקוח
נפש—שדחה את הספק] ק. בא דן על פקוח נפש שספיקו דוחה את השבת ומה שפיכות
דמים שמטמא את הארץ חמור ומסלקת את השכינה ספקו דוחה את השבת הקל דין
הוא שתהא ספק דוחה אותו ק״ו לפיקוח נפש שדוחה ספקו את השבת.   8 היא] נ. ל.
היה.   10—9 קל וחומר לפקוח נפש שדחה את הספק] נ. ל. ‹.   13—14 ר׳ ישמעאל
אומר] ד. ‹.

meaning, they should make the matter clear as a white sheet. Similarly: "Upon his support" (Ex. 21.19) is to be interpreted as meaning, restored to his health. And so also here: "If the sun be risen upon him," R. Ishmael says, etc. You say it comes for this purpose. Perhaps this is not so, but it comes to make a distinction in this case between daytime and nighttime, telling you that if the owner kills the burglar in the daytime he is guilty, but if he kills him in the nighttime he is free? It says: "But unto the damsel thou shalt do nothing,"[2] etc. (Deut. 22.26). Now, what have we learned in regard to the murderer? As a matter of fact, the case of the murderer, cited to throw light, also receives light. Just as there (Deut. 22.26) the law makes no distinction between daytime and nighttime, so also here (Ex. 22.1) no distinction is to be made between daytime and nighttime. And just as here if the owner anticipates the attack of the burglar and kills him, he is free, so also there, if the girl, anticipating the attack of the pursuer, kills him, she is free. And just as there if the girl has some one to protect her from the attack of the pursuer and she nevertheless kills him, she is guilty of murder,[3] so also here if the owner of the house had someone to protect him from an attack by the burglar and the owner nevertheless kills him, he is guilty.

There Shall Be Bloodguiltiness for Him—He Shall Make Restitution. R. Eliezer b. Jacob says: Suppose there were jugs of wine or jugs of oil lying in the way of the burglar and he broke them while he was breaking in. As long as it is known that he had peaceful intentions towards the owner, even though the owner killed him, the burglar is liable for the damage.[4] In this sense it is said: "There shall be bloodguiltiness for him—he shall make restitution."[5]

---

2. The rest of the verse reads: "There is in the damsel no sin worthy of death; for as when a man riseth against his neighbour, and slayeth him, even so is this matter."

3. See *Shebut Yehudah* ad loc.

4. And the owner is to be indemnified for the damage from the estate of the burglar.

כשמלה כיוצא בו על משענתו על בוריו ואף כאן

אם זרחה השמש רבי ישמעאל אומר וגו' אתה אומר

20 לכך בא או לא בא אלא לחלק בין יום ללילה

לומר לך אם הרגו ביום יהיה חייב ובלילה יהיה

פטור ת״ל ולנערה לא תעשה דבר וכי מה למדנו

לרוצח מעתה אלא הרי זה בא ללמד ונמצא למד

מה להלן לא חלק בו בין יום ללילה אף כאן לא

25 נחלוק בו בין יום ללילה ומה כאן אם קדמו והרגו

פטור אף להלן אם קדמתו והרגתו פטורה מה להלן

היו לה מושיעין הימנו והרגתו חייבת אף כאן היו

לו מושיעין הימנו והרגו חייב.

דמים לו שלם ישלם רבי אליעזר בן יעקב

30 אומר הרי שהיו לפניו כדי יין וכדי שמן ושברן

כשהוא חותר כל זמן שהוא בידוע שבשלום עמו

והרגו הרי זה חייב לכך נאמר דמים לו שלם ישלם.

---

22 שם כ״ב, כ״ו.   22—28 סנהדרין ע״ג, א'; ע״ד, א'. מ״ת. 143.   32—24 תוספתא

שם. י' שם.   28—26 ספרי דברים רמ״ג.

---

18 ואף כאן] א. ד. ~ אתה אומר כן.   19 וגו'] א. ד. <.   20 או לא בא אלא] ד. <.

28 לו] א. מ. ק. לה.   31 כשהוא חותר] נ. ל. < / כל זמן א. ט. וכל זמן / בידוע]

ד. יודע ט. ידוע.

If He Have Nothing, Then He Shall Be Sold for His Theft. As for: "If he have nothing then he shall be sold for his theft," I might understand it to mean, for ever. But it says: "Six years shall he serve," etc. (Ex. 21.2), thereby telling us that he serves six years and goes out free in the seventh.

Then Shall He Be Sold for His Theft. Not for less nor for more. R. Judah says: If what he stole is worth less than he is, he is not to be sold. If what he stole is worth more than he is, the one from whom he stole has the choice of either selling him or receiving from him a note of indebtedness. R. Eliezer says: If what he stole is worth less than he is, he is not to be sold. If what he stole is worth more than he is, it is enough for the owner to regain half and to lose half.[6]

If the [Theft] Be Found. Finding simply means ascertaining by witnesses.

In His Hand. "In his hand" merely means in his possession. And although there is no explicit proof for it, there is a suggestion of it in the passage: "And taken all his land out of his hand" (Num. 21.26). And it is written: "Having all goodly things of his master's in his hand" (Gen. 24.10). Thus, "in his hand" everywhere only means in his possession.

Whether It Be Ox or Ass. R. Akiba says: There would be no purpose in saying: "Living ones,"[7] except to include also the wild animals.

Living Ones He Shall Pay Double. But not dead ones.

5. I. e., if his life is protected by the law which would hold the one who kills him guilty of murder, then the burglar or his estate must make restitution for any damage which he may cause. But in the case where the law declares his life free, so that the owner may kill him without incurring bloodguiltiness, then he is not liable for any damage he may cause. For he has as much as received a sentence of death, in which case one is exempted from making any monetary compensation (see above, ch. VI, note 11).

6. See Commentaries, esp. *Shebut Yehudah.*

7. Thus is the word חיים interpreted by R. Akiba, and not "alive" as rendered by the Bible translations.

ואם אין לו ונמכר בגניבתו אי ונמכר

בגניבתו שומע אני לעולם ת"ל שש שנים יעבוד וג'

35 מגיד שהוא עובד שש שנים ויוצא בשביעית.

ונמכר בגניבתו לא פחות ולא יותר רבי

יהודה אומר גנב פחות ממה ששוה אינו נמכר יותר

על מה ששוה הרשות ביד בעל הגניבה אם רצה

למכור מוכר ואם לאו כותב לו שטר רבי אליעזר

40 אומר גנב פחות ממה ששוה אינו נמכר יותר על מה

ששוה דיו להשתכר מחצה ולהפסיד מחצה.

אם המצא תמצא אין מציאה אלא בעדים.

בידו אין בידו בכל מקום אלא רשותו אף על

פי שאין ראיה לדבר זכר לדבר שנאמר ויקח את

45 כל ארצו מידו וכתיב ויקח העבד עשרה גמלים

וגו' הא אין ידו בכל מקום אלא רשותו.

משור ועד חמור רבי עקיבא אומר שאין

ת"ל חיים אלא להביא את החיה.

חיים שנים ישלם ולא מתים.

35—33 לעיל א'.   41—36 קידושין י"ח, א'.   42 לעיל ה'. ב"ק ס"ד, ב'. ש. שם.
46—43 לעיל שם.   45—44 במדבר כ"א, כ"ו.   45 בראשית כ"ד, י'.   58—47 לעיל
י"ב. ב"ק ס"ד, א'. י' שם ז', א'. א' (5ᵈ).   49 י' שם א', א' (2ᶜ).

34—33 אי ונמכר בגניבתו] ד. <.   37 גנב] ק. גר נ. ל. אם גנב.   41 דיו] מ. דין.
43 בכל מקום] ד. <.   46—43 אף על פי—אלא רשותו] א. <.   44 זכר לדבר] מ. זכר
הוא.   47 ר' עקיבא אומר]=ט. מ"ח: א. ד. <.   48 חיים] מ. ~ ומה ת"ל חיים.

He Shall Pay Double. You find that you must say: There are seven kinds of thieves.[8] First, there are those who steal the hearts of people: He who urges his neighbor to be his guest when in his heart he does not mean to invite him; he who frequently offers gifts to his neighbor knowing well that they will not be accepted; and he who makes his guest believe that he is opening a barrel of wine especially for him when in reality it had been sold to the retailer. Also one who cheats in measuring and swindles in weighing; one who mixes seed of St. John's bread among seeds of fenugreek, or sand among beans, or puts vinegar into oil;—for they say oil does not admit of adulteration, and for this reason it is used for anointing kings.—And furthermore he is accounted as one who, if he could, would deceive the Most High. For thus we find that Absalom committed three thefts: Stealing the heart of his father, the heart of the court and the hearts of the men of Israel, as it is said: "So Absalom stole the hearts of the men of Israel" (II Sam. 15.6). And who is greater, the thief or the one from whom he steals? You must say: The one from whom he steals who, though knowing that it has been stolen from him, keeps his peace. And thus we find that our forefathers at the time when they stood before Mount Sinai to receive the Torah, sought to deceive the Most High, as it is said: "All that the Lord hath spoken will we do, and obey" (Ex. 24.7), and—as though such a thing were conceivable—they almost succeeded. For it is said: "O that they had such a heart as this alway" (Deut. 5.26). You might say then that not all things are revealed and known before Him. But has it not already been said: "But they beguiled Him . . . For their heart was not stedfast with Him" (Ps. 78.36–7). And yet: "He, being full of compassion, forgiveth iniquity," etc. (ibid., v. 38)? And it also says: "Burning lips and a wicked heart are like an earthen vessel overlaid with silver dross" (Prov. 26.23).

8. The seven thieves are graded according to the severity of the penalty to which they are liable (see Commentaries).

שנים ישלם נמצאת אומר שבעה גנבין הם 50
הראשון שבגנבים גונב דעת בני אדם והמסרב
בחבירו לארחו ואין בלבו לקראתו והמרבה לו
בתקרובת ויודע בו שאינו מקבל והמפתח חביותיו
והן מכורות לחנוני והמעול במדות והמשקר
במשקלות והמערב את הגירה בתלתן ואת החול 55
בפול ואת החומץ בשמן מפני שאמרו השמן אינו
מקבל מכל לפיכך מושחין בו מלכים ולא עוד
אלא שמעלין עליו שאם היה יכול לגנוב דעת
העליונה היה גונבה וכן מצינו באבשלום שגנב שלש
גניבות לב אביו ולב בית דין ולב אנשי ישראל 60
שנאמר ויגנוב אבשלום את לב אנשי ישראל וכי
מי גדול הגונב או הנגנב הוי אומר הנגנב שהוא יודע
שהוא נגנב ומחריש וכן מצינו באבותינו בשעה
שעמדו לפני הר סיני לקבל את התורה בקשו לגנוב
דעת העליונה שנאמר כל אשר דבר יי נעשה ונשמע 65
כביכול נגנבה בידן שנאמר מי יתן והיה לבבם זה
להם ואם תאמר שאין הכל גלוי וידוע לפניו והלא
כבר נאמר ויפתוהו בפיהם וגו׳ ולבם לא נכון עמו
ואף על פי כן והוא רחום יכפר עון וגו׳ ואומר כסף
סגים מצופה על חרס שפתים דולקים ולב רע. 70

94—50 תוס׳ ב״ק ז׳, ח׳—י״ג.   56—51 חולין צ״ד, א׳. דרך ארץ ח׳.   54—56 תוס׳
ב״ב ה׳, ה׳—ו׳.   61—59 לעיל שירתא ר׳.   61 שמואל ב. ט״ו, ו׳.   65 שמות כ״ד, ז׳.
66 דברים ה׳, כ״ו.   69—68 תהלים ע״ח, ל״ז—ל״ח.   70—69 משלי כ״ו, כ״ג.

51 הראשון שבגנבים] א. והראשון שבהם / בני אדם] ד. הבריות.   52 לקראתו] ד.
לקרותו / לו] ד. <.   53 בו] ד. < / והפותח] א. מ. והמפתח.   54 לחנוני] א. מ. ט.
<.   55 והמערב] א. מ. והמערה / הגירה] ק. ל. הגררה נ. הגרה בה״מ. הגרדן.
56—55 ואת החול בפול ואת החומץ בשמן] מ. הנותן משקלותיו בחול המערב את
החומץ בשמן.   56 מפני] א״צ. ג. אף על פי.   57—56 אינו מקבל מכל] א. אינו נוכל
ט״כ. אינו מקבל מנבל ט. אינו מקבל מעל ל״ט. אינו מקבל נבל.   59 וכן מצינו] א״צ.
שכן מצינו שכל הגונב דעת הבריות נקרא גנב.   60 ולב אנשי ישראל] מ. ולב אנשי
ירושלים ד. ולב בית ישראל.   62 מי] ד. מה.   64—63 בשעה שעמדו—סיני] ד. כשעמדו
על הר סיני.   66 כביכול נגנבה] ק. כביכול ונגנבה בית דין נ. ל. כביכול ונגנב לב בית
דין.   67—68 והלא כבר נאמר] ד. ת״ל.   70 שפתים דולקים ולב רע] ד. וגו׳ מ. ד׳
(=דולקים) ולא רע.

Ranking above these are: One who steals things forbidden to be used. Such a one is not obliged to make restitution. One who steals garments, fruit, vessels, domestic animals, wild animals, or birds. Such a one has to pay double. One who steals male or female slaves, documents, lands, or consecrated property only pays the principal. One who steals the firstling of an ox must pay double; for although for the present it is not permitted to be used, it can become permissible later on.[9] For an ox one sometimes has to pay fivefold. For a lamb one sometimes has to pay fourfold, as it is said: "He shall pay five oxen," etc.

Ranking above these is he who steals a human being, for he forfeits his life. R. Simon b. Yoḥai says: Behold it says: "Whoso is partner with a thief hateth his own soul: He heareth the adjuration and uttereth nothing" (Prov. 29.24). They illustrate this by the following parable: One comes out from another man's house carrying away a load of things. A friend of his meets him and says to him: "What are you doing?" He answers: "Take your share and do not tell on me." After a while the owner of the stolen articles comes and says to the friend of the thief: "I adjure you, tell me, have you not seen so-and-so coming out from my house and carrying away a load of things?" He answers: "I swear that I do not know what you are talking about." Behold, such a one forfeits his life and to him applies the verse: "Whoso is partner with a thief hateth his own soul" (ibid.).

But he who steals away from his friend and goes and studies the words of the Torah, although he might be called a thief, acquires merit for himself. To him applies the verse: "Men do not despise a thief, if he steal," etc.[10] (ibid. 6.30). He will in the end be appointed a leader of the community, as it is said: "He will be found out and will

9. I. e., after it is redeemed from the priest.
10. The rest of the verse reading: "to satisfy his soul," is interpreted as meaning, to satisfy his spiritual needs, or his hunger for knowledge.

למעלה מהן גנב אסורי הנאה פטור מלשלם כסות
ופירות וכלים בהמה חיה ועוף משלם תשלומי
כפל עבדים ושפחות שטרות וקרקעות והקדשות
אינו משלם אלא קרן הגונב פטר חמור משלם
תשלומי כפל אף על פי שהוא אסור עכשיו יש לו
היתר לאחר זמן תחת השור ישלם חמשה תחת השה
ישלם ארבעה שנאמר חמשה בקר ישלם וגו'.
למעלה מהם גונב נפש בני אדם שהוא מתחייב
בנפשו רבי שמעון בן יוחאי אומר הרי הוא אומר
חולק עם גנב שונא נפשו אלה ישמע ולא יגיד משלו
משל למה הדבר דומה לאחד שהיה יוצא מביתו
של חבירו טעון כלים מצאו חבירו ואמר לו מה
אתה עושה אמר לו טול חלקך ואל תגיד לאחר
זמן בא בעל הגניבה ואמר לו משביע אני עליך לא
ראית לפלוני יוצא מתוך ביתי טעון כלים ואמר
לו שבועה שאיני יודע מה אתה מדבר הרי זה
מתחייב בנפשו ועליו הוא אומר חולק עם גנב שונא
נפשו וגו' אבל המתגנב מאחר חבירו והלך ושנה
בדברי תורה אף על פי שהוא נקרא גנב הרי
זה זוכה לעצמו ועליו הוא אומר לא יבוזו לגנב כי
יגנוב לסוף נמצא מתמנה על הצבור שנאמר ונמצא

75

80

85

90

80 משלי כ"ט, כ"ד.   91—90 שם ו', ל'.

72 ופירות] ד. >.   73—72 תשלומי כפל] הגהתי=מ"ח. ג. א"צ. ש"י: א. מ. ד.
ט. ט"כ. תשלומי ארבעה וחמשה.   73 והקדשות] א. מ. ט. >.   74 הגונב] א. מ.
> מ"ח. החמישי הגונב.   76—77 תחת השור—ישלם ארבעה] מ"ח. הששי הגונב את
השור וטבחו או מכרו משלם חמשה שה משלם ארבעה.   78 למעלה מהם] מ"ח.
השביעי למעלה מכולן.   78—79 גונב נפש בני אדם שהוא מתחייב בנפשו] מ"ח. ק.
הגונב את (ק. >) בן חורין שנידון בנפשו (ק. ~ גונב נפש בני אדם שהוא מתחייב בנפשו.)
79—80 הרי הוא אומר—שונא נפשו] א. מ. ט. >.   80 אלה ישמע ולא יגיד] הוספתי.
82 כלים] כ. (משלי כ"ט, כ"ד) כלום.   83 תגיד] ד. ~ לאדם.   84 לא] ד. שלא ט. אם
לא.   85 מתוך ביתי] ד. מביתו / כלים] כ. כלום.   86 מה אתה מדבר] ד. >.   88 ושנה]
ד. לשנות.   91 לסוף] א. מ. ט. >.   92—91 שנאמר ונמצא ישלם שבעתים] הגהתי=א"צ.
ש"י. ומא"ש: א. מ. ט. ד. ישלם (ד. וישלם) שבעתים שנאמר.

pay sevenfold.[11] He will give all the wealth of his house" (ibid., v. 31). "Sevenfold" is but a designation for the words of the Torah, as it is said: "The words of the Lord are pure words, as silver tried in a crucible on the earth, refined seven times" (Ps. 12.7).

CHAPTER XIV
(Ex. 22.4–5)

If a Man Cause . . . to Be Eaten. Why is this said? Even if it had not been said I could have reasoned: The pit is his property and the grazing animal is his property. Now, then, since you have learned that he is responsible for the damage caused by his pit, shall he not be responsible for the damage caused by his grazing animal? If, then, I succeed in proving this by logical reasoning, what need is there of saying: "If a man cause. . . to be eaten"? Simply this: Scripture comes to teach you thereby that the tooth of an animal is considered a *mu'ad* as regards eating what is fit to be eaten by it, and that the animal is considered a *mu'ad* as regards breaking things which are in its way as it walks along—in this connection the sages said: The owner is responsible only when the animal causing the damage goes outside of his own territory and does the damage—also that in appraising the damage we estimate it as damage done to the choicest field.[1] All the more does this rule apply in the case of Temple property.[2]

If a Man Cause a Field or a Vineyard to Be Eaten. This is to declare one liable in either case.

---

11. This rendering is required by the Midrash which interprets the verse as referring to one who studied secretly but is found out, recognized and made a teacher who gives of the wealth of his knowledge to others.

1. See Commentaries.

2. If, e. g., one promise or donate one acre of his fields to the Temple, he must give an acre of his choicest fields.

ישלם שבעתים את כל הון ביתו יתן ואין שבעתים

אלא דברי תורה שנאמר אמרות יי אמרות טהורות

כסף צרוף בעליל לארץ מזוקק שבעתים.

פרשה יד   (שמות כ״ב, ד׳—ה׳.)

כי יבער איש למה נאמר עד שלא יאמר יש

לי בדין הואיל והבור והבער ממונו והבער ממונו אם

למדת שהוא חייב על ידי בורו לא יהא חייב על

ידי הבערו אם זכיתי מן הדין מה ת״ל כי יבער איש

5   אלא בא הכתוב ללמדך שהשן מועדת לאכול את

הראוי לה והבהמה מועדת לשבור בדרך הילוכה

מכאן אמרו לעולם אינו חייב עד שיצא המזיק

מרשותו והזיק ששמין נזקין בעדית וקל וחומר

להקדש.

10   **כי יבער איש שדה או כרם** לחייב על

זה בפני עצמו ועל זה בפני עצמו.

91—92 שם ו׳, ל״א.   93—94 תהלים י״ב, ז׳.
   4—6 ב״ק י״ט, ב׳.

2 והבור] ד. והבאר / והבער] ד. וההבער מ״ח. והבהמה ט. והבערה.   3 שהוא חייב
על ידי בורו] ד. על הבאר שהוא חייב.   3—4 על ידי הבערו] א. על ידי הבערה מ״ח.
על ידי בהמתו.   5 שהשן] א. מ. שהיא ט. ט״כ. שהוא.   6 והבהמה] מ״ח. והרגל.
7 עד] ק. >.   8 מרשותו] ק. ברשותו / בעדית] א. בעדיות.   10 כי יבער] ד. דבר אחר
כי יבער.

A Field or a Vineyard. Just as a vineyard yields fruit, so also the field must be such as yields fruit.

And Shall Let His Beast Loose. Hence the sages said: If he turned over his sheep to his son, his servant or his agent, he is not liable. But if he turned them over to a deaf and dumb person, to an insane person or to a minor, he is liable.

And It Feed in Another Man's Field. R. Nathan says: Suppose one piles up stacks of grain in the field of his neighbor without permission, and the animal of the owner of the field comes out and does damage to the stacks, I might apply to him: "And shall let his beast loose." Therefore it is said: "And it feed in another man's field"—but this is not another man's field.

Of the Best of His Field and of the Best of His Vineyard. Of the best field of the one causing the damage and of the best vineyard of the one causing the damage.—These are the words of R. Ishmael. R. Akiba says: Scripture comes to teach you that in appraising the damage we estimate it as damage done to the choicest field. All the more does this rule apply in the case of Temple property.

If Fire Break Out, etc. Why is this said? Even if it had not been said I could have reasoned: Since he is liable for damage done by what is owned by him, shall he not be liable for damage done by himself?[3] If, then, I succeed in proving it by logical reasoning, what need is there of saying: "If fire break out"? Simply this: Scripture comes to declare that in all cases of liability for damage mentioned in the Torah one acting under duress is regarded as one acting of his own free will, one acting unintentionally is regarded as one acting intentionally, and the woman is regarded like the man.

And Catch in Thorns. Behold, "thorns" are mentioned only with regard to fixing the distance within which one is liable. If there are

3. See Friedmann. From the end of the verse: "He that kindled the fire shall surely make restitution," it is evident that it deals with a fire made by a person, not with one breaking out by itself.

שדה או כרם מה כרם יש בו פירות אף שדה
שיש בה פירות.

ושלח את בעירה מכאן אמרו מסר צאנו
לבנו לעבדו ולשלוחו פטור לחרש שוטה וקטן
חייב.

ובער בשדה אחר רבי נתן אומר והרי
המגדיש בתוך שדה חברו שלא ברשות ויצאת
בהמתו של בעל הבית והזיקה קורא אני עליו ושלח
את בעירה לכך נאמר ובער בשדה אחר ולא אחר
הוא זה.

מיטב שדהו ומיטב כרמו מיטב שדהו
ומיטב כרמו של מזיק דברי רבי ישמעאל רבי
עקיבא אומר בא הכתוב ללמדך ששמין נזקין
בעדית קל וחומר להקדש.

כי תצא אש וגו׳ למה נאמר עד שלא יאמר
יש לי בדין הואיל וחייב על ידי קנוי לו לא יהא
חייב על ידי עצמו אם זכיתי מן הדין מה ת״ל כי
תצא אש וגו׳ אלא בא הכתוב לעשות את האונס
כרצון ואת שאינו מתכוין כמתכוין ואת האשה כאיש
לכל הנזקין שבתורה.

ומצאה קוצים הא לא באו קוצים אלא

13 — 12 ש. 140.   16 — 14 ב״ק ג׳, א׳; נ״ה, ב׳. י׳ שם ו׳, ב׳ (5).   21 — 17 ב״ק נ״ט, ב׳.
25 — 22 שם ו׳, ב׳.   31 — 28 ש. 141.   44 — 32 שם ס״א, א׳–ב׳.

13 שיש בה] א. ד. יש בו.   21 — 20 לכך נאמר ובער בשדה אחר ולא אחר הוא זה]
הגהתי=א״צ. ש״י: א. מ. וגו׳ בשדה (מ. כשדה?) אחר הוא זה ד. לכך נאמר בשדה
אלא אחר הוא זה ט. ת״ל בשדה אחר.   22 שדהו 2] ד. ~ של מזיק ז״י. ש״י. ~ של
ניזק.   23 של מזיק] ד. ל״ט. של ניזק.   27 קנוי לו] ק. כינוי נ. ל. קוצים.

thorns around, there is a certain distance within which one is liable. If there are no thorns around, there is no such distance.[4]—Hence the sages said: If the fire gets across a river, or a road, or a stone fence higher than ten handbreadths and causes damage, he is not liable.— How do we determine the matter? We regard him as standing in the center of a field, requiring a *kor* of seed, and lighting the fire.—These are the words of R. Eleazar b. Azariah. R. Eliezer says: The distance within which he is liable is 16 cubits, the usual width of a public road. R. Akiba says: The distance is fifty cubits. R. Simon says: "He that kindled the fire shall surely make restitution"—it all depends on the size of the fire. It happened once that a fire spread across the Jordan and did damage there, since it was a big fire. When does this obtain? When the fire jumps. But if it keeps close to the ground and spreads that way, even though it go a distance of a mile, he is liable.

So That the Stack . . . Be Consumed. This means any kind of a pile. It also includes a row of reeds or of beams, and likewise a heap of stones or of pebbles prepared to be used for plastering.

Or the Standing Corn. Trees are also included.

Or the Field. That is, even if it just dried up the ground. May it not mean, even if there were implements hidden in the stacks and they were burnt? It says: "Or the standing corn or the field." Just as the field is open, so also what stands in it must be open.

The One That Kindled the Fire Shall Surely Make Restitution. Why is this said? Because it says: "A man" (v. 4), from which I know only about a man. But how about a woman, a *tumtum* or a hermaphrodite? It says: "The one that kindled the fire shall surely make restitution"— whoever it may be. I thus far know only about damage caused by

---

4. A man has a right to build a fire on his territory if there is nothing inflammable lying around which might carry the fire beyond his territory. But if there are inflammable things lying around which are likely to carry the fire beyond his territory, he is liable for the damage done up to a certain distance beyond his territory, but only up to a certain distance.

ליתן שיעור אם יש קוצים יש שיעור ואם אין קוצים
אין שיעור מכאן אמרו עברה את הנהר ואת הדרך
ואת הגדר שהוא גבוה מעשרה טפחים והזיקה פטור
מלשלם כיצד עומדין על הדבר רואין אותו כאלו
הוא עומד באמצע בית כור ומדליק דברי רבי
אלעזר בן עזריה רבי אליעזר אומר שש עשרה
אמה כדרך הרבים רבי עקיבא אומר חמשים אמה
רבי שמעון אומר שלם ישלם המבעיר את הבערה
הכל לפי הדליקה מעשה שעברה דליקה את
הירדן והזיקה כשהיא מרובה אימתי בזמן שקפצה
אבל אם היתה מצפצפת ומהלכת אפילו עד מיל
הרי זה חייב.

ונאכל גדיש הכל במשמע וכן סדר של
קנים ושל קורות וכן מדבך של אבנים ושל צרורות
שהתקינן לסיד.

או הקמה אף האילן במשמע.

או השדה אפילו ליחכה את העפר או אפילו
היו לו כלים מוטמנין בגדיש והדליקן ת״ל או הקמה
או השדה מה השדה בגלוי אף הקמה בגלוי.

שלם ישלם המבעיר את הבערה למה
נאמר לפי שנאמר איש אין לי אלא איש אשה
טומטום ואנדרוגינוס מנין ת״ל שלם ישלם המבעיר
את הבערה מכל מקום אין לי אלא המבעה

34—36 ש. שם.   44—34 תוס' ב״ק ו', כ״ב—כ״ג. י' שם ו', ז' (5⁹).   51—45 ב״ק ס',
א'; ס״א, ב'. י' שם ו', ה' וז' (5⁹).   54—52 לעיל ו'.

33—34 אם יש קוצים יש—אין שיעור] ז״ר. א״צ. ש״י. הגיהו אם אין קוצים יש שיעור
ואם יש קוצים אין שיעור.   34 הנהר] ט. ט״צ. הניר.   35 מעשרה טפחים] ד. עשרה
טפחים מ״ח. מארבע אמות.   38 אלעזר בן עזריה] ק. נ. אליעזר בן עזריה / אליעזר]
א. אלעזר.   42 כשהיא] ד. מפני שהיא מ״ח. מפני שהיתה.   43 מצפצפת] מ״ח.
מסוכסכת.   45 סדר] ד. סואר.   47 שהתקינן] מ. ד. שהתקינו.   48 או הקמה] א. מ.
ט״כ. שנאמר או הקמה / האילן] א. האלון.   50 והדליקן] ד. והדליקו.   55—56 המבעה
וההבער] מ. מ״ח. הבעה וההבער ט. הבער וההבערה ט״כ. הבער והבעה.

grazing or by burning. How about all other kinds of damage mentioned in the Torah? Behold, you reason and establish a general rule on the basis of what is common to these two: The peculiar aspect of damage by grazing is not like the peculiar aspect of damage by burning, nor is the peculiar aspect of damage by burning like the peculiar aspect of damage by grazing. What is common to both of them is: that it is their characteristic to do damage, they are your property, and it is incumbent upon you to guard them. And when damage is done, the one causing the damage is liable to pay for the damage from the best of his land.

R. Simon the son of Eleazar used to state in the name of R. Meir four general rules in regard to liability for damage: If the damage is done in a place to which the one causing the damage had the right of access but the one suffering the damage had not, the one causing the damage is not liable. If it happened in a place to which the one suffering the damage had the right of access but the one causing the damage had not, the latter is liable. If it happened in a place to which, although it is private, both had the right of access, like a yard belonging to partners or an inn, or if it happened in a place to which neither the one causing the damage nor the one suffering damage had the right of access, like private territory of other people, then the owner is liable for any damage done by the tooth or foot of his animal. And in the case of his ox goring he must pay full damage if it is a *mu'ad* and half damage if it is a *tam*. If it happened in any place to which both had the right of access, like a valley or a public place and the like, then the owner is not liable for any damage done by the tooth or foot of his animal. But in the case of his ox goring he must pay the full damage if it is a *mu'ad* and half damage if it is a *tam*.[5]

5. See Commentaries, and cf. Z. Karl in the Hebrew Monthly המשפט, II, 3, Jerusalem, 1927, pp. 115 ff.

וההבער שאר כל המזיקין שבתורה מנין הרי אתה

דן בנין אב מבין שניהן לא הרי המבעה כהרי

הבער ולא הרי הבער כהרי המבעה הצד השוה שבהן

שדרכן להזיק וממונך ושמירתן עליך וכשהזיק חב

המזיק לשלם תשלומי נזק במיטב הארץ. ארבע

כללות היה רבי שמעון בן אלעזר אומר משום רבי

מאיר בנזקין כל מקום שיש רשות למזיק ולא לניזק

פטור לניזק ולא למזיק חייב לניזק ולמזיק אפילו

מיוחדת כגון חצר של שותפין והפונדקי לא לניזק

ולא למזיק כגון רשות אחרת על השן ועל הרגל

חייב ועל השור מועד משלם נזק שלם ותם משלם

חצי נזק בכל מקום שיש רשות לניזק ולמזיק

והבקעה ורשות הרבים וכיוצא בהן על השן ועל

הרגל פטור ועל השור מועד משלם נזק שלם ותם

משלם חצי נזק.

60 — 56 ב״ק ד׳, א׳; ו׳, א׳.   70 — 60 ב״ק י״ד, א׳. תוס׳ א׳, ט׳. י׳ שם א׳, ב׳ (2°).

59 וממונך]=ל: א. ט. < מ. ד. וממונן / ושמירתן] מ. שבירתן / חב] נ. ל. <.
60 לשלם] א. מ. משלם.   61 שמעון בן אלעזר] ד. ישמעאל.   63 חייב] ד. ~ בכל.
65 אחרת] א. מ. אחת.   66 חייב]=מ: א. ד. ט. ט״כ. השאר.   67 שיש]
מ. ~ בו.   69 השור]=א. מ. ט: ד. ט״כ. השאר.

CHAPTER XV
(Ex. 22.6–8)

If a Man Deliver unto His Neighbour Money or Vessels to Keep. R. Ishmael says: Only if when depositing it with him he says to him: Here,
take this and keep it for me. But if he has merely said to him: Keep
your eye on it, the one to whom he said this is not liable.

Money or Vessels. Just as it is a characteristic of money that it can
be counted, so also must it be a characteristic of the vessels that they
can be counted. On the basis of this interpretation the sages said: A
claim not definite as to measure, weight or number is not a valid
claim. R. Nathan says: "Money" is to include money with which the
tithe has been redeemed: "vessels" is to include any kind of imple-
ment. I thus far know only about money and vessels. How about all
other things? It says: "To keep," thus including anything that needs
guarding.

And It Be Stolen Out of the Man's House. This is to declare that one
who steals from the thief is not liable. You interpret "and it be stolen
out of the man's house" to mean that one who steals from the thief is
not liable. Perhaps "and it be stolen out of the man's house," then, "if
the thief be found he shall pay double" means, only when it is found
outside of the keeper's premises; but if it is found in the possession of
the keeper, I might understand that, even though he swore falsely
that it had been stolen from him, he still is not liable to pay double.
But behold what does Scripture mean by saying: "If the theft be
found in his hand" (v. 3)? In any case. Then it is impossible for you to
interpret as in the latter version, but you must interpret as in the
former version: "And it be stolen out of the man's house," means to
declare that one who steals from the thief is not liable.

If the Thief Be Found He Shall Pay Double. The thief pays double
but the robber pays back only the principal. And what is the reason
that the Torah made it severer for the thief than for the robber?

פרשה טו (שמות כ"ב, ו'—ח'.)

וכי יתן איש אל רעהו כסף או כלים לשמור
רבי ישמעאל אומר עד שיפקיד אצלו ויאמר לו
הילך שמור לי זה אבל אם אמר לו עיניך בו הרי
זה פטור.

5   **כסף או כלים** מה כסף שדרכו להמנות
אף כלים שדרכן להמנות מכאן אמרו כל טענה
שאינה במדה במשקל ובמנין אינה טענה רבי נתן
אומר כסף להביא כסף מעשר כלים להביא כלים
אין לי אלא כסף וכלים שאר כל דבר מנין ת"ל
10   לשמור להביא כל דבר שצריך שמירה.

וגונב מבית האיש לפטור הגונב מאחר
הגנב אתה אומר וגונב מבית האיש לפטור הגונב
מאחר הגנב או וגונב מבית האיש אם ימצא הגנב
ישלם שנים אימתי בזמן שלא נמצא ברשותו אבל
15   אם ימצא ברשותו שומע אני ישבע ויהא פטור הא
מה ת"ל אם המצא תמצא בידו הגניבה מכל מקום
הא אין עליך לומר כלשון אחרון אלא כלשון ראשון
וגונב מבית האיש לפטור הגונב מאחר הגנב.

אם ימצא הגנב ישלם שנים הגנב משלם
20   תשלומי כפל והגזלן אינו משלם אלא קרן ומה
ראתה התורה להחמיר על הגנב יותר מן הגזלן

4—1 לקמן ט"ז. ב"מ פ"א, ב'. י' שבועות ח', א' ([38b]).   10—5 שבועות מ"ב, ב'—מ"ג,
א'. ב"ק ס"ג, א'. ב"מ נ"ז, ב'.   9—7 י' שבועות ו', א' ([36d]). י' קידושין א', ([58c]).
12—11 ב"ק ס"ט, ב'.   16—14 שם ס"ג, ב'; ק"ז, ב'.   29—19 שם ע"ט, ב'. תוס' שם
ז', ב'.

1 וכי יתן] במקרא שלפנינו כי יתן.   7 במשקל] מ. במשך / ובמנין] ט. ובמשורה.
8 להביא כלים] א"צ. ~ כל שהוא ועיין ש"י.   12 אתה אומר וגונב מבית האיש] ד.
>.   13—12 לפטור הגונב מאחר הגנב] הוספתי.   13 או] נ. ל. > / או וגונב מבית
האיש] א. > ק. או נגנב מבית האיש / אם] א. מ. ואם.   15 אם ימצא] ד. נמצא.
16—15 הא מה] נ. ל. >.   20 אלא קרן] ד. תשלומי כפל.

R. Johanan b. Zakkai says: The robber regarded the servant like the Master.[1] The thief honored the servant more than the Master. The thief, as though such a thing were possible, regarded the Eye above as if it could not see, and the Ear as if it could not hear—just as when it is said: "Woe unto them that seek deep to hide their counsel from the Lord, and their works are in the dark, and they say: 'Who seeth us? and who knoweth us?' " (Isa. 29.15). And it says: "And they say: 'The Lord will not see,' " etc. (Ps. 94.7). And it also says: "For they say: 'The Lord hath forsaken the land, and the Lord seeth not' " (Ezek. 9.9).

If the Thief Be Not Found. Why is this said? From the literal meaning of the passage: "If the thief be found he shall pay double," we can learn that only if the thief be found is the master of the house[2] free from any liability. Why then does Scripture need to say: "If the thief be not found," etc.? I must understand this to mean that if the thief be found but is unable to pay, the owner of the stolen article cannot say to the keeper: Come and swear to me that you did not have in mind to sell it. It is just for this that it is said: "If the thief be not found"—that is, as long as the thief is found the master of the house is free in any case.

Then the Master of the House Shall Come Near unto Elohim. I might understand this to mean, to consult the Urim and Thummim.[3] But it says: "He whom *Elohim* shall condemn" (v. 8). I can therefore interpret it to mean only judges who can condemn.

Then the Master of the House Shall Come Near unto Elohim. For the purpose of taking an oath. You interpret it to mean, for the purpose of taking an oath. Perhaps this is not so but it means, for the purpose

1. The master is God, the servant is man. The robber commits his act in the open and does not mind being seen by God and man. The thief is careful not to be seen by man, but does not mind being seen by God.
2. "The master of the house" is the keeper from whose house the article was stolen.
3. I. e., the oracle (see *JE*, XII, 384–86, s. v. Urim and Thummim).

רבי יוחנן בן זכאי אומר הגזלן השוה את העבד
לקונו והגנב חלק כבוד לעבד יותר מקונו כביכול
עשה הגנב את העין של מעלה כאלו אינה רואה
ואת האוזן כאלו אינה שומעת כענין שנאמר הוי
25   המעמיקים מיי לסתיר עצה והיה במחשך מעשיהם
ויאמרו מי ראנו ומי יודענו ואומר ויאמרו לא יראה
יה וגו' ואומר כי אמרו עזב יי את הארץ ואין יי
ראה.

30   **ואם לא ימצא הגנב** וגו' למה נאמר
ממשמע שנאמר אם ימצא הגנב ישלם שנים למדנו
אם נמצא הגנב בעל הבית פטור מכל דבר ומה
ת"ל ואם לא ימצא הגנב וגו' שומע אני שאם נמצא
הגנב ואין לו לשלם לא יאמר לו בעל הגנבה בא
35   והשבע לי שלא היה בלבך למוכרו לכך נאמר אם
לא ימצא הגנב שאם נמצא הגנב בעל הבית פטור
מכל מקום.

ונקרב בעל הבית אל האלהים שומע
אני לשאול באורים ותומים ת"ל אשר ירשיעון
40   אלהים לא אמרתי אלא אלהים שהם מרשיעין.
ונקרב בעל הבית אל האלהים לשבועה
אתה אומר לשבועה או אינו אלא בשבועה ושלא

---

27 — 25 ישעיה כ"ט, ט"ו.   28 — 27 תהלים צ"ד, ז'.   29 — 28 יחזקאל ט', ט'.   37 — 30 י'
שבועות ז', א', (38b).   39 — 38 יומא ע"ג, ב'.   41 — 43 ב"מ מ"א ב'.   48 — 41 לקמן
ט"ז.

---

22 את העבד] ד. כבוד העבד.   23 לקונו] א. מ. לקוניו / מקונו] א. מ. מקוניו.   24 של
מעלה] א. מ. < ק. של מטה.   26 מיי] מ. ק. נ. ביי.   27 מי ראנו ומי יודענו]
הוספתי=ל: א. וגו'מ. ק. נ. מי ראוהו ומי יודיעגו.   28 כי אמרו] ד. כי יאמרו / עזב]
ד. כי עזב.   29 — 28 ואין יי ראה] הוספתי כמו במקרא: א. מ. וגו' ד. אין לי רואה.
31 למדנו] ד. שומע אני.   32 הגנב] ד. ~ ויש לו.   33 ואם] ד. אם.   35 בלבך] ט. כל
כך.   36 שאם נמצא הגנב] ק. שאם לא מצא הגנב.   37 מכל מקום] א. מ. ט. מכל
דבר.   41 לשבועה] מ. ט. בשבועה.

of making a declaration, whether with an oath or without an oath? Behold, you must reason: Here the expression "putting the hand" is used and there (v. 10) the expression "putting the hand" is used. Just as there the declaration is made under oath, so also here the declaration must be made under oath. Just as there the oath is by the tetragrammaton,[4] so also here the oath is by the tetragrammaton. And just as here the oath is taken in court, so also there it is to be taken in court. And just as here "putting the hand" means appropriating it for his private use, so also there. Just as here the oath is taken "for every matter of trespass," so also there it is to be taken "for every matter of trespass."

Whether He Have Not Put His Hand unto His Neighbour's Goods. For his private use. You interpret it to mean for his private use. Perhaps it is not so, but it means whether it be for his private use or not for his private use? But it says: "For every matter of trespass" (v. 8).—For the school of Shammai declares one liable for the mere intention to "put his hand," since it is said: "For every thought of trespass." And the school of Hillel declares one liable only from the moment when he actually did "put his hand."[5]—Accordingly, when it is said: "Whether he have not put his hand unto his neighbour's goods," it must mean, for his private use.

For Every Matter of Trespass. This is a general statement. *Whether It Be for Ox, for Ass, for Sheep, for Raiment,* is a specific statement. Now, a general statement followed by a specific statement cannot include more than the specific statement. When it says however: "Or for any manner of lost thing," it again makes a general statement. But per-

---

4. Literally, by *Yod He*. But *Yod He* is a designation for the tetragrammaton (see Lauterbach, "Substitutes for the Tetragrammaton," *Proc. Amer. Acad. for Jewish Research*, 1931, p.43 ff).

5. The section set off by dashes is a sort of parenthetical remark, declaring that no matter what difference there may be between the two schools as to whether he is liable even for intention, they both agree that trespass only means, for his private use.

בשבועה הרי אתה דן נאמר כאן שליחות יד ונאמר
להלן שליחות יד מה להלן שבועה אף כאן שבועה
מה להלן ביו״ד ה״א אף כאן ביו״ד ה״א מה כאן
בבית דין אף להלן בבית דין מה כאן לצרכיו אף
להלן לצרכיו מה כאן על כל דבר פשע אף להלן
על כל דבר פשע.

אם   לא   שלח   ידו   במלאכת   רעהו

לצרכו אתה אומר לצרכו או אינו אלא לצרכו
ושלא לצרכו ת״ל על כל דבר פשע שבית שמאי
מחייבין על מחשבת הלב בשליחות יד שנאמר על
כל דבר פשע ובית הלל אין מחייבין אלא משעה
ששלח בה יד לכך נאמר אם לא שלח ידו במלאכת
רעהו לצרכו.

על   כל   דבר   פשע כלל על שור ועל חמור
על שה ועל שלמה פרט כלל ופרט אין בכלל אלא
מה שבפרט וכשהוא אומר על כל אבדה חזר וכלל

54—49 ב״מ מ״ד, א׳. ש. 144.   51 ויקרא ה׳, כ״ד.   62—56 ב״ק ס״ב, ב׳. ב״מ נ״ז, ב׳.
שבועות מ״ב, ב׳.

45 ביו״ד ה״א] א. מ. ט. ט״כ. ביד / מה כאן] א. מ. או מה כאן.   47—46 מה כאן
לצרכיו אף להלן לצרכיו] ד. מה להלן לצרכה אף כאן לצרכה.   51—47 אף להלן על
כל דבר פשע—ת״ל על כל דבר פשע] א. >.   50 לצרכו אתה אומר לצרכו] מ. ט.
לצרכה אתה אומר לצרכה.   51—50 לצרכו ושלא לצרכו] הגהתי=א״צ. ש״י. ג.
וא״א: מ. ד. לצרכה ושלא לצרכה.   52 מחייבין] ד. אומרין מחייבין / הלב] א. > /
יד] א. >.   53 אין מחייבין]=ט: א. מ. מחייבין] ד. אומרין אין מחייבין.   55 לצרכו]
הגהתי=א״א. ש״י. ומא״ש: א. מ. ד. לצרכה.   57 ועל שלמה] במקרא שלפנינו על
שלמה / פרט 1] א. ~ או מ. ~ אי.

haps the second general statement is to be considered identical with
the first general statement? You must say: It is not so, but it is a case
of a general statement followed by a specific statement and by
another general statement, all of which must be interpreted as
including only things similar to those mentioned in the specific statement.[6] Now, since the specific statement specifies movable property,
not possessing the quality of serving as permanent surety, I can
include only movable property not possessing the quality of serving
as permanent surety.

For Every Matter of Trespass. Scripture here speaks with regard to
the difference between one kind of a bailee and another. You say it
speaks with regard to the difference between one kind of bailee and
another. Perhaps however it comes to make a distinction between silver and vessels (v. 6), and cattle? But it says: "For raiment." Now, "raiment" has been included in the general statement (v. 6). And it has
been singled out for special mention merely to teach that just as
when "raiment" is specifically mentioned Scripture speaks with
regard to the difference between the one kind of bailee and the other,
so also with all the others mentioned with it Scripture speaks with
regard to the difference between one kind of bailee and the other.
Behold, then, Scripture does not come to make a distinction between
silver and vessels on the one hand and cattle on the other.[7]

Whereof One Saith: 'This Is It.' That is, the one says: This is it; and
the other says: This is not it. On the basis of this interpretation the
sages said: The admission must be homogeneous with the claim.[8]

Then the Master of the House Shall Come Near unto Elohim, behold
this is one. *The Cause of Both Parties Shall Come Before Elohim* (v. 8),
behold this makes two. *He Whom Elohim Shall Condemn,* behold this
makes three. Hence, the sages said: Civil cases must be tried by a tri-

6. See "Talmud Hermeneutics," *JE,* XII, 33.
7. See Introduction and cf. Commentaries.
8. See Introduction and cf. Commentaries.

או כלל הראשון אמרת לאו אלא כלל ופרט

60 וכלל אי אתה דן אלא כעין הפרט מה הפרט
מפורש בנכסים מטלטלין שאין להם אחריות אף
אין לי אלא נכסים מטלטלין שאין להם אחריות.

על כל דבר פשע בין שומר לשומר הכתוב
מדבר אתה אומר בין שומר לשומר הכתוב מדבר

65 או לא בא אלא לחלוק בין כסף וכלים לבהמה
ת״ל שלמה ושלמה הייתה בכלל ויצאת מן הכלל
ללמד אלא מה שלמה מיוחדת בין שומר לשומר
הכתוב מדבר אף כל בין שומר לשומר הכתוב
מדבר הא לא בא הכתוב לחלוק בין כסף לכלים

70 ובהמה.

אשר יאמר כי הוא זה שזה אומר זה הוא
וזה אומר אינו הוא מכאן אמרו עד שתהא הודאה
ממין הטענה. ונקרב בעל הבית אל האלהים
הרי אחד עד האלהים יבא דבר שניהם הרי שנים

75 אשר ירשיעון אלהים הרי שלשה מכאן אמרו דיני

70—63 ב״ק נ״ט, א׳; ק״ו, ב׳.   71—73 ב״ק ק״ז, א׳—ב׳.   שבועות ל״ט, ב׳.
88—73 סנהדרין ג׳, ב׳; ד׳, א׳. י׳ שם א׳. א׳ (18ª).

59 ככלל] A. בכלל.   62—61 אף אין לי אלא] ד. ~ הכלל מפורש.   63 על כל דבר
פשע] ד. >.   64—63 בין שומר—אתה אומר] A. ד. >.   65 בין כסף וכלים לבהמה]
הגהתי=A״צ. ש״י. וז״י: A. מ. ד. ט. בין כסף לכלים לבהמה (ט. ולבהמה).
66 שלמה ושלמה] ד. שמלה ושמלה.   69—68 אף כל—מדבר] A. מ. ט. >.   68 הכתוב]
A. מ. > ד. ~ אלא.   70 ובהמה] A. לבהמה ט. ולבהמה.   71 שזה אומר] מ״ח. ולא
שזה אומר.   73 ממין] ד. במקצת.   79—75 מכאן אמרו—הרי שנים] A. >.

bunal of three.—These are the words of R. Josiah. R. Jonathan says: As regards the first of these passages—that is the very first statement of the subject. And first statements cannot be employed for any special interpretation. Hence, in the passage: "The cause of both parties shall come before *Elohim*," we have one. "He whom *Elohim* shall condemn," behold this makes two. And since the tribunal must not be evenly balanced, we must add one more, thus making three. Rabbi says: "The cause of both parties shall come before *Elohim*." Scripture here speaks of two judges. You say Scripture speaks of two. Perhaps however it speaks of only one? When it says: "He whom *Elohim* condemn"—notice, it is not written here: "He whom *Elohim* condemns," but: "He whom *Elohim* condemn"[9]—behold, then, Scripture must be speaking of two. And since a tribunal must not be evenly balanced, we must add one more, thus making it three. Hence the sages said: Civil cases are to be tried by a tribunal of three. Rabbi says: By a tribunal of five, so that the final judgment be decided by three.[10]

Shall Pay Double unto His Neighbour. R. Ishmael says: Here I read about him: "Shall pay double unto his neighbour," and there I read about him: "He shall even restore it in full, and shall add the fifth part more thereto" (Lev. 5.24). How can both these passages be maintained? One who pays the mere principal must also pay an additional fifth. But one who does not pay the mere principal does not have to add an additional fifth.

Shall Pay Double unto His Neighbour. But not unto the sanctuary. *Unto His Neighbour.* But not unto others.

9. See Introduction and cf. Commentaries.

10. I. e., the majority of the tribunal according to which the decision will be rendered will consist of at least three.

ממונות בשלשה דברי רבי יאשיה רבי יונתן אומר
הראשון תחלה נאמר ואין דורשין תחלות עד
האלהים יבא דבר שניהם הרי אחד אשר ירשיעון
אלהים הרי שנים ואין בית דין שקול מוסיפין עליהם
עוד אחד הרי שלשה רבי אומר עד האלהים יבא
דבר שניהם בשנים הכתוב מדבר אתה אומר בשנים
הכתוב מדבר או אינו מדבר אלא באחד כשהוא
אומר אשר ירשיעון אלהים אשר ירשיע אלהים אין
כתיב כאן אלא אשר ירשיעון אלהים הא בשנים
הכתוב מדבר ואין בית דין שקול מוסיפין עליהם
עוד אחד הרי שלשה מכאן אמרו דיני ממונות
בשלשה רבי אומר בחמשה כדי שיגמור הדין
בשלשה.

ישלם שנים לרעהו רבי ישמעאל אומר
קורא אני עליו כאן ישלם שנים לרעהו וקורא אני
עליו להלן ושלם אותו בראשו וחמשיתו יוסף עליו
כיצד יתקיימו שני כתובים הללו כל המשלם את
הקרן חייב לשלם את החומש וכל שאינו משלם את
הקרן פטור מן החומש.

ישלם שנים לרעהו ולא להקדש לרעהו
ולא לאחרים.

79—89 ב״ק ס״ה, א׳—ב׳. ת״כ ויקרא חובה י״ג (28ᶜ). ש. 145.   91 ויקרא ה׳, כ״ד.
97—96 ב״מ נ״ז, ב׳.

---

79 שנים] מ. שלשה.   80 הרי שלשה] א. מ. <.   83 אשר ירשיע אלהים] הגהתי=
מ״ח. ש״י: א. מ. ד. < א״צ. ז״י. אשר ירשיען אלהים.   84 ירשיען אלהים] א.
ד. ירשען.   87 רבי] ד. ~ מאיר.   89 ישמעאל] ד. שמען.   90 עלין] מ״ח. <.   91 עלין]
ד. <.   95—94 וכל שאינו משלם את הקרן] מ״ח. וכל המשלם יותר מקרן.   96 ישלם
שנים] ד. <.

Chapter XVI
(Ex. 22.9–14)

If a Man Deliver unto His Neighbour an Ass, or an Ox, or a Sheep, etc.
R. Ishmael says: Only if while depositing it with him he says to him:
Here, take this and keep it for me. But if he has merely said to him:
Keep your eye on it, the one to whom he said this is not liable. *An
Ass, or an Ox, or a Sheep.* I thus know only about an ass, an ox, and a
sheep. How about any other beast? It says: "And all beasts to keep." It
could have read merely: "All beasts." What need then is there of saying: "An ass, or an ox, or a sheep"? Because if it had read only: "All
beasts," I might have understood that the keeper is liable only if all
beasts have been put into his care. Therefore it says: "An ass, or an
ox, or a sheep," to declare him liable for each one by itself. And what
does Scripture mean to teach by saying: "All beasts"? It merely comes
to teach you that a general statement which is added to a specific
statement includes everything.

And It Die. That is, its death occurs by the hand of Heaven. *Or Be
Hurt.* That is, a wild beast injures it. *Or Driven Away.* That is, robbers
capture it. I still might say that for injury and capture he should be
liable whether he could have saved it or not. Therefore it says: "And
it die." Just as for death, peculiar in that it is impossible for him to
prevent it, he is not liable to pay, so also for any other accident which
it is impossible for him to prevent he is not liable to pay.—These are
the words of R. Eliezer. Said to him R. Akiba: Master, you are judging
cases where prevention may be possible on the basis of a case where
prevention is impossible. For from death, protection is impossible
except by Heaven. But from injury and capture protection is possible
both by Heaven as well as by man.[1] R. Eliezer then retracted and
judged these cases on the basis of the case of theft.[2] R. Ishmael says:

1. See Introduction and cf. Commentaries.
2. Just as he is liable in the case of theft because he could have prevented it by

פרשה טז   (שמות כ״ב, ט׳—י״ד.)

**וכי יתן איש אל רעהו חמור או שור
או שה** וגו׳ רבי ישמעאל אומר עד שיפקיד אצלו
ויאמר לו הילך שמור לי אבל אם אמר לו עיניך
בו הרי זה פטור.

חמור או שור או שה אין לי אלא חמור
ושור ושה שאר כל בהמה מנין ת״ל וכל בהמה
לשמור אני אקרא כל בהמה ומה ת״ל חמור או שור
או שה שאם אני קורא כל בהמה שומע אני לא יהיה
חייב עד שיפקיד אצלו כל בהמה ת״ל חמור או שור
או שה לחייב על כל אחד ואחד בפני עצמו ומה
ת״ל וכל בהמה אלא בא הכתוב ללמדך שכל
הכלל שהוא מוסיף על הפרט הכל בכלל.

ומת שתהא מיתתו בידי שמים או נשבר ששברתו
חיה או נשבה ששבוהו לסטים עדיין אני אומר השבר
והשבי בין שהוא יכול להציל בין שאינו יכול להציל
ת״ל ומת מה מיתה מיוחדת שאי אפשר לו להצילה
פטור מלשלם אף כל דבר שאי אפשר לו להצילה
פטור מלשלם דברי רבי אליעזר אמר לו רבי
עקיבא רבי אתה דן איפשר משאי איפשר שאי
איפשר למיתה להיות אלא בידי שמים אבל השבר
והשבי איפשר להיות בין בידי שמים בין בידי אדם
חזר ודנן כמו גנבה רבי ישמעאל אומר הטרפה

1 וכי יתן] במקרא שלפנינו כי יתן.   2 עד] ד. <.   3 אם] א. <.   7 כל בהמה] א.
מ. וכל בהמה.   8 שאם—כל בהמה] ד. אם נאמר כך.   11 וכל] מ. ד. כל.   12 הפרט]
הגהתי=ט. ג. א״א. ז״י. וש״י: א. מ. ד. הכלל.   13 או נשבר] א. מ. ונשבר.
17 להצילן] א. מ. ~ יהיה.   19—18 אמר לו רבי עקיבא רבי] ד. רבי עקיבא אומר
הרי.   20—19 משאי איפשר שאי איפשר] ד. מי שאין איפשר.   20 אבל] מ. אף.
22 ודנן] א. ודנו / כמו] מ. ד. ט. כמין א״צ. מן / ישמעאל] מ. ד. שמעון.

"He shall not make good that which is torn," implies that there are cases where he must pay for that which is torn[3] and cases where he does not have to pay for that which is torn.[4]

No Man Seeing It. It is of witnesses that Scripture speaks. *No Man Seeing It, the Oath of the Lord Shall Be Between Them Both.* But if there be one who saw it, the master of the house is not liable for anything.

The Oath of the Lord Shall Be Between Them Both. An oath by the tetragrammaton. From this you can draw a conclusion with regard to all the oaths prescribed in the Torah. Since all the oaths prescribed in the Torah are not explicit as to how they are to be taken and the Torah explicitly states in the case of one of them that it must be taken only by the tetragrammaton, it has thus made it explicit with regard to all the oaths prescribed in the Torah that they must be taken only by the tetragrammaton.

Between Them Both. This is to exclude their heirs. *Between Them Both.* This excludes the case where the party[5] is suspected of swearing falsely. *Between Them Both.* The judge cannot make him swear against his will. R. Nathan says: "The oath of the Lord shall be between them both." This tells us that the oath affects both of them. *Whether He Have Not Put His Hand unto His Neighbour's Goods.* To make use of it. You interpret it to mean to make use of it. Perhaps it is not so, but it means whether to make use of it or not? Behold, I am reasoning: Here the expression "putting the hand" is used and there (v. 7) the expression "putting the hand" is used. Just as here the declaration must be made under oath, so also there the declaration must be made under oath. Just as here the oath is by the tetragrammaton, so also there the oath must be by the tetragrammaton. Just as there

---

watching, so also for any other loss he is liable only in case he could have prevented it.

3. I. e., when he could have prevented it.
4. I. e., when it was impossible for him to prevent it.
5. See Introduction and cf. Commentaries.

לא ישלם יש טרפה שהוא משלם ויש טרפה שאינו
משלם.

אין רואה בעדים הכתוב מדבר. אין רואה
שבועת יי תהיה בין שניהם הא יש רואה בעל הבית
פטור מכל דבר.

שבועת יי תהיה בין שניהם ביו"ד ה"א
מכאן אתה דן כל השבועות שבתורה הואיל ונאמרו
כל השבועות שבתורה סתם ופרט לך הכתוב
באחת מהם שאינה אלא ביו"ד ה"א פורט אני כל
השבועות שבתורה שאינן אלא ביו"ד ה"א.

בין שניהם להוציא את היורשין בין שניהם
להוציא את שכנגדו חשוד על השבועה בין שניהם
שלא ישביענו הדיין על כרחו רבי נתן אומר שבועת
יי תהיה בין שניהם מגיד שהשבועה חלה על שניהם.

אם לא שלח ידו במלאכת רעהו לצרכה אתה
אומר לצרכה או אינו אלא לצרכה ושלא לצרכה
הריני דן נאמר כאן שליחות יד ונאמר להלן שליחות
יד מה כאן שבועה אף להלן שבועה מה כאן ביו"ד

27—25 ב"מ פ"ג, א'. ש. 146.   28—32 ספרי במדבר י"ד.   34—33 שבועות מ"ז, א'.
47—33 ש. שם.   36—35 שבועות ל"ט, ב'.   44—37 לעיל ט"ו.

────────────

28—26 בין שניהם—שניהם ביו"ד ה"א] א. וגו' כיון הא.   30—29 הואיל—שבתורה]
א. ‹.   30 לך הכתוב] א. מ. ‹.   32—31 פורט אני כל השבועות שבתורה] ק. פרט
לך אף פורט שבועות לכולן שבתורה נ. ל. מכאן לכל שבועות שבתורה.   34 שכנגדו]
א. מ. בן שכנגדו.   35 שלא ישביענו הדיין] ד. להוציא את הדיין שלא ישביעו.   36 על
שניהם] א. מ. על יד שניהם.   38—37 לצרכה אתה אומר לצרכה] ד. לצרכו אתה
אומר לצרכו.

"putting the hand" means, to make use of it, so also here. Just as there the oath is taken "for every matter of trespass," so also here the oath is taken "for every matter of trespass."

And the Owner Thereof Shall Accept It and He Shall Not Make Restitution. Hence the sages said: All those who are bound to swear, swear and are free from payment. *And the Owner Thereof Shall Accept It.* Hence the sages said: The owner of the carcass has to attend to its disposal.

But If It Be Stolen from Him. This section deals with the bailee for hire and the section above deals with the gratuitous bailee. You say this deals with the bailee for hire and the above deals with the gratuitous bailee. Perhaps however this deals with the gratuitous bailee and the above with the bailee for hire? Behold you must reason thus: Since the hirer is liable and the bailee here mentioned is liable, it follows that just as the hirer is one who derives some benefit, also the bailee here mentioned must be one who derives some benefit. Hence it is impossible for you to argue as in the latter version, but you must argue as in the former version: This one deals with the bailee for hire and the above deals with the gratuitous bailee.

And If It Be Stolen. I thus know only about theft. How about loss? You must reason thus: Since theft is due to insufficient care, and loss also is due to insufficient care, it follows that inasmuch as you have learned that he is liable to pay in case of theft, he should also be liable to pay in case of loss. *And If It Be Stolen.* R. Jose the Galilean says: This is to include loss.

From Him. This excludes the shepherd's boy. *From Him.* This includes the shepherd.

If It Be Torn in Pieces, Let Him Bring It for Witness. That is, the skin.[6]—These are the words of R. Josiah. And although there is no explicit proof for this, there is a suggestion of it in the passage: "Thus saith the Lord: As the shepherd rescueth out of the mouth of the lion

6. See Kohut, *Aruk Completum,* I, pp. 38–39.

ה"א אף להלן ביו"ד ה"א מה להלן בבית דין אף
כאן בבית דין מה להלן לצרכה אף כאן לצרכה
מה להלן על כל דבר פשע אף כאן על כל דבר
פשע.

ולקח בעליו ולא ישלם מכאן אמרו
כל הנשבעין נשבעין ולא משלמין. ולקח בעליו
מכאן אמרו בעל הנבלה מטפל בנבלתו.

ואם גנב יגנב מעמו זה שומר שכר
והעליון שומר חנם אתה אומר זה שומר שכר
והעליון שומר חנם או שזה שומר חנם והעליון שומר
שכר הרי אתה דן הואיל והשוכר והשומר חייב
חייב מה שוכר שהוא נהנה אף שומר שהוא נהנה
יצא שומר חנם שאינו נהנה הא אין עליך לומר
בלשון אחרון אלא בלשון ראשון זה שומר שכר
והעליון שומר חנם.

ואם גנב יגנב אין לי אלא גנבה אבדה
מנין הרי אתה דן הואיל וגנבה חסרון שמירה ואבדה
חסרון שמירה אם למדת על הגניבה שהוא חייב
לשלם אף אבדה יהא חייב לשלם. אם גנב יגנב
רבי יוסי הגלילי אומר להביא את האבידה.

מעמו להוציא את הצוער מעמו להביא את
הנוקד.

אם טרוף יטרף יביאהו עד זה עדר
דברי רבי יאשיה אף על פי שאין ראיה לדבר זכר
לדבר שנאמר כה אמר יי כאשר יציל הרועה מפי

46—45 שבועות מ"ה, א'. י' שם ז', א' (37c).   47 ב"ק י', ב'.   60—48 ב"מ צ"ד, ב'.
שבועות מ"ט, ב'. י' שם ז', א' (38bc).   62—61 ב"ק נ"ז, ב'. ב"מ ל"ו, א'.   68—63 ב"ק
י', ב'—י"א, א'. ש. 147.   66—65 עמוס ג', י"ב.

46—45 ולקח בעליו—ולא משלמין] א. מ. <. ~ 47 הנבילה] א. הגניבה.   50—49 אתה
אומר—והעליון שומר חנם] א. < ד. אתה אומר כן. ~ 50 או שזה] ד. או אינו אומר
אלא זה.   51—52 הואיל והשוכר—שומר שהוא נהנה] מ"ח. הואיל והשואל חייב
והשומר חייב מה שואל שהוא נהנה אף שומר שהוא נהנה א"צ. הואיל והשומר חייב
מה שואל שהוא נהנה אף שומר שכר שהוא נהנה.   51 והשוכר] א. מ. ט. והשכיר.
52 שוכר] א. שכיר מ. שכר שכיר ט. שכיר שכור / אף שומר] ד. ~ שכר מ. או שומר
שומר.   60 הגלילי] ד. < / להביא את האבידה] הגהתי=ט. ז"ר. א"צ: ט"כ. < א.
מ. ד. להביא את הגנבה.   61 להוציא] ד. להביא.   62—61 להביא את הנוקד] ד.
ולהוציא את הצוער] מ. זה עדר (או ערך או עדר או עדר?) ט. ט"כ. זה ערך מ"ח. זה ארי א"צ. מביא
העורה לב"ד.   65—64 ראיה לדבר זכר לדבר] מ. ראיה דבר הוא.   66—65 שנאמר
כה אמר—בדל אזן] מ"ח. שנאמר כאשר יציל הרועה עדרו ובא ארי וטרף (ולא נמצא

two legs, or a piece of an ear" (Amos 3.12). R. Aḥai the son of Josiah says: *If It Be Torn in Pieces, Let Him Bring Witness for It,* that is, let him bring witnesses that it was torn in pieces and then he will be free from payment. R. Jonathan says: *Let Him Bring Him to*[7] *the Torn Animal,* that is, he shall conduct the owner to the torn animal; and be free from payment, or he may even then be liable to pay. And the following argument favors this: Since loss of the animal is due to insufficient care and the animal's being torn is also due to insufficient care, it follows that inasmuch as you have learned that one is liable to pay for its loss, one should also be liable to pay for its being torn. Does it not follow from the meaning of the passage: "He shall not make good that which was torn," that there are cases where he has to make it good and there are cases where he does not have to make it good? And in what case would he be liable to pay even if it be torn? In case it has been torn by a cat or a fox. And how can one prove that the Torah says so? It says: "If it be torn in pieces."—Just as in the case of the animal being torn, peculiar in that it would have been possible for him to prevent it, he is liable to pay, so also for any other accident which he could have prevented he is liable to pay.—And in what case would he not be liable to pay for that which is torn in pieces? In case it has been torn by a wolf, a lion, a bear, a tiger, a leopard, or a serpent. And who tells you that the Torah says so? It says: "And it die" (v. 9). Just as for death, peculiar in that it is impossible for him to prevent it, he is not liable to pay, so also for any other accident which it is impossible for him to prevent he is not liable to pay—and thus: "He shall not make good that which was torn."[8]

And If a Man Borrow Aught of His Neighbour. Scripture removes the borrower from the category of the bailee, treating his case as a subject by itself.

7. R. Jonathan interprets the word עד as if it read עד instead of עד. Comp. also Geiger, op. cit., p. 194.

8. See Introduction and cf. Commentaries.

האָרי שתי כרעים או בדל אוזן רבי אחי בר יאשיה

אומר אם טרוף יטרף יביאהו עד יביא עדים

שנטרפה ויהא פטור מלשלם רבי יונתן אומר

יביאהו עד הטרפה יוליך את הבעלים אצל

70 הטרפה ויהא פטור מלשלם או אף על פי כן יהא

חייב והדין נותן הואיל ואבדה חסרון שמירה וטרפה

חסרון שמירה אם למדת על אבדה שהוא חייב

לשלם אף טרפה חייב לשלם לא ממשמע שנאמר

הטרפה לא ישלם יש טרפה שהוא משלם ויש טרפה

75 שאינו משלם ואי זה טרפה שהוא חייב לשלם כגון

טרפת חתול ושועל ומנין שאמרה תורה ת"ל אם טרוף

יטרף מה טרפה מיוחדת שאפשר לו להצילה חייב

לשלם אף כל דבר שאפשר לו להצילה חייב לשלם

ואיזו היא טרפה שהוא פטור מלשלם כגון טרפת הזאב

80 והאָרי והדוב והנמר והברדלס והנחש ומי לחשך

שאמרה תורה ת"ל ומת מה מיתה מיוחדת שאי אפשר

לו להצילה פטור מלשלם אף כל דבר שאי אפשר

להצילה פטור מלשלם והטרפה לא ישלם.

וכי ישאל איש מעם רעהו נתק הכתוב

85 השואל מכלל השומר ואמרו ענין בפני עצמו.

75 — 68 ב"ק י', ב'.   83 — 75 ב"מ צ"ג, ב'.   95 — 84 ש. שם.

66 אחי] מ. יוחי ד. יוחנ.   67 אם] ק. נ. אף / יביאהו עד] א. מ. ט. > מ"ח. ~
הטרפה.   68 שנטרפה] מ"ח. ~ באוס.   70 או] מ. מ. ט. ט"ב. ק. > / אף] ק. ט. ואף.
73 לא ממשמע] א. לא מי משמע ד. לא אמרת ממשמע.   74 הטרפה] ק. נ. והטרפה.
76 ושועל] ק. מ"ח. ~ בגדיים נ. ל. ~ ונמיה א. ~ ומרים (ומריס?) / ומנין] א. ק. >
נ. ל. ומתוך / שאמרה תורה] ט. ט"ב. שנאמרה (ט. שנאמר) בתורה / ת"ל] ז"י.
ומא"ש. >.   78 — 77 שאפשר לו להצילה חייב לשלם אף — חייב לשלם] ק. שאי אפשר
לו להצילה פטור מלשלם חייב לשלם אף כל דבר שאי אפשר להצילו פטור חייב לשלם.   80 ומי
לחשך] הגהתי=א"צ: א. מ. ומלחשך ט"ב. מלחשך ט. ק. ~ נ. ל. מלחשך.   81 שאמרה
תורה] ט. <. / ת"ל] נ. ל. <.   83 והטרפה לא ישלם] ט. א"צ. ז"י. ומא"ש. <.

Of His Neighbour. This tells us that the borrower is not liable unless he takes it out of the owner's territory.

And It Be Hurt or Die. I thus know only about that which is injured or dies. How about that which is captured? Behold you must reason thus: Here "dying" is mentioned and there (v. 9) "dying" is mentioned. Just as there when "dying" is mentioned the law regards being injured or captured like dying, so also here when "dying" is mentioned we should regard being injured or captured like dying. How about theft and loss? You can reason by using the method of *kal vaḥomer:* If where one is not liable for death one is liable for theft and loss,[9] is it not logical that here where one is liable for death one should surely be liable for loss and theft?

The Owner Thereof Not Being with It, He Shall Surely Make Restitution. If the Owner Thereof Be with It, He Shall Not Make It Good. Scripture here tells us that if when it went out from the territory of the lender into the territory of the borrower, the owner was with it, even if only for a little while, the borrower is not liable. But if the owner was not with it the borrower is liable.

If It Be a Hired Thing, It Came to Him for His Hire. I might understand that the hirer should take an oath and be free. Behold, however, you must reason: Since the bailee for hire benefits the owner and the hirer likewise benefits the owner, it follows that inasmuch as you have learned that the bailee for hire takes an oath concerning unavoidable accidents but pays for theft and loss, so also the hirer should take an oath concerning unavoidable accidents and pay for theft and loss. But the case of the gratuitous bailee disproves this. For the latter likewise benefits the owner and yet he is not liable to pay for loss and theft. This should prove concerning the hirer that even though he benefits the owner he should nevertheless be free from liability for theft and loss. You must however admit that there is a difference. The bailee for hire benefits himself as well as the owner, and so

9. In the case of a bailee for hire.

מעם רעהו מגיד שאינו חייב עד שיוציאנו
חוץ לרשותו.

ונשבר או מת אין לי אלא שבורה ומתה
שבויה מנין הרי אתה דן נאמר כאן מיתה ונאמר
להלן מיתה מה מיתה האמורה להלן עשה שבורה

90 ושבויה כמיתה אף מיתה האמורה כאן נעשה שבויה
ושבורה כמיתה גנבה ואבדה מנין אמרת קל וחומר
מה אם במקום שלא חייב על המיתה חייב על
האבדה ועל הגנבה וכאן שחייב על המיתה דין
הוא שנחייב על האבדה ועל הגנבה.

95 **בעליו אין עמו שלם ישלם אם בעליו**
עמו לא ישלם מגיד הכתוב שמכיון שיצאת
מרשות הנשאל לרשות השואל אפילו שעה אחת
בבעלים פטור שלא בבעלים חייב.

100 **אם שכיר הוא בא בשכרו** שומע אני
ישבע ויהא פטור הרי אתה דן דן הואיל ונושא שכר
מהנה והשוכר מהנה אם למדת על נושא שכר שהוא
נשבע על האונסין ומשלם את הגנבה ואת האבדה
אף שוכר נשבע על האונסין ומשלם את הגנבה ואת

105 האבדה והרי שומר חנם יוכיח שהוא מהנה ופטור
מלשלם הוא יוכיח על שוכר אף על פי שהוא מהנה
יהיה פטור מלשלם אמרת הפרש נושא שכר נהנה
ומהנה והשכיר נהנה ומהנה ואל תביא שומר חנם

---

87 — 86 ב״מ צ״ט, א׳.   95 — 88 שם צ״ד, ב׳ — צ״ה, א׳. י׳ שבועות שם.   99 — 96 ב״מ
צ״ה, ב׳. י׳ שם ח׳, א׳ (11cd).   114 — 100 ב״מ צ״ג, א׳. ש. 148.

---

92 — 90 מה מיתה האמורה—נעשה שבויה ושבורה כמיתה] ד. מה מיתה האמורה להלן
שבויה בכלל אף כאן כך.   95 שנחייב] מ. ד. שנתחייב.   96 אם] מ. ואם.   98 הנשאל]
מ״ח. המשאיל.   102 מהנה] ט. מא״ש. נהנה / והנה.   98 אם] מ. ואם.   ט. והשכיר /
מהנה] ט. ט״כ. ומא״ש. נהנה / אם למדת] ד. הא למדת מ״ח. ולמדנו.   105 יוכיח]
מ. וכאן.   106 שוכר] א. מ. שכיר.   107 הפרש] ד. ~ הפרש נושא.   הואיל / נושא] ד. ונושא.
110 — 108 ואל תביא—והשכיר נהנה ומהנה] ד. <.

also the hirer benefits himself as well as the owner. So you cannot cite in argument the case of the gratuitous bailee where the owner derives benefit but does not give any benefit. My argument then is simply this: The bailee for hire receives and gives benefit and the hirer also both receives and gives benefit. Now, inasmuch as you have learned that the bailee for hire takes an oath concerning unavoidable accidents, but pays for theft and loss, so also the hirer should take an oath concerning unavoidable accidents but pay for theft and loss. It is in this sense that it is said: "If it be a hired thing, it came to him for his hire."[10]

CHAPTER XVII
(Ex. 22.15–19)

And If a Man Entice a Virgin, etc. This passage comes to teach concerning the seduced girl that in her case also he must pay the fine. But mere logical reasoning would prove this: Since the law of rape applied only to a girl under the jurisdiction of her father and the law of seduction applies only to a girl under the jurisdiction of her father, it follows that inasmuch as you have learned that in the case of rape he has to pay a fine,[1] he should likewise pay a fine in case of seduction. No! If you cite the case of rape—that is different, for there he sinned against her own wish and against her father's wish. Therefore he should pay the fine for raping her. But will you argue the same in the case of seduction? There he only sinned against her father's wish and therefore in her case he should not pay the fine. Thus, since I could not succeed in proving it by logical inference, Scripture has to cite it.

---

10. See Introduction and cf. Commentaries. The *Mekilta* requires this rendering of the verse, not: "If it be a hireling he loseth his hire," as given by the Bible translations. The whole passage in the *Mekilta*, however, admits also of a different interpretation. Comp. also Geiger, op cit., p. 191 ff.

1. See Deut. 22.28–29.

יוכיח שהוא מהנה אבל הוא אינו נהנה אלא נושא

110 שכר נהנה ומהנה והשכיר נהנה ומהנה אם למדת

על נושא שכר שהוא נשבע על האונסין ומשלם את

הגנבה ואת האבדה אף השכיר נשבע על האונסין

ומשלם את הגנבה ואת האבדה לכך נאמר אם

שכיר הוא בא בשכרו.

פרשה יז (שמות כ״ב, ט״ו—י״ט.)

וכי יפתה איש בתולה וגו׳ בא הכתוב

ללמד על המפותה שישלם עליה קנס והדין נותן

הואיל ותפוסה ברשות אביה ומפותה ברשות אביה

אם למדת על תפוסה שהוא משלם עליה קנס אף

5 המפותה ישלם עליה קנס לא אם אמרת בתפוסה

שעבר על דעתה ועל דעת אביה לפיכך הוא

משלם עליה קנס תאמר במפותה שלא עבר אלא

על דעת אביה לפיכך לא ישלם עליה קנס הא

לפי שלא זכיתי מן הדין צריך הכתוב להביאו.

.143 מ״ת 1—2

109 יוכיח] ט. ‹.   110 אם למדת] ק. אם למדת על נושא שכר שהוא נשבע על מהנה
אבל הוא אינו נהנה או לא נושא שכיר נהנה ומהנה והשכיר נהנה ומהנה אם למדת.
113 ואת האבדה] נ. ל. ~ ואל יוכיח שומר חנם שהוא מהנה אבל אינו נהנה והשכיר
נהנה ומהנה / לכך נאמר] א. מ. ט. ‹.
3 ותפוסה ברשות אביה] מ. ותפוסה ברשות אמה.   6 על דעתה] מ. עליה דעתה.

That Has Not Been Betrothed. This excludes one who after betrothal became widowed or was divorced.—These are the words of R. Jose the Galilean. R. Akiba says: How do we know that the law applies even in the case of the one who became widowed or was divorced? The following reasoning proves it: Since the father has the right to invalidate his daughter's vows and he also has the right to get the fine for her seduction,[2] it follows that just as with regard to the invalidating of her vows his right is valid even if she has been widowed or was divorced, so also with regard to his right to the monetary fine for her seduction, it is valid even if she has been widowed or was divorced. What need then is there of saying: "That has not been betrothed"? Simply to furnish an expression free to be used as a basis for comparison to formulate the following *gezerah shavah:* Here the expression "that has not been betrothed" is used and there (Deut. 22.28) the expression "that has not been betrothed" is used. Just as there the fine is fifty shekels of silver, so also here the fine is fifty shekels of silver.

He Shall Surely Pay a Dowry for Her to Be His Wife. Why is this said? Because it says: "Then the man that lay with her shall give," etc. (ibid., v. 29), one might think that just as in the case of rape he must pay the fine immediately, so also in the case of seduction he should have to pay the fine immediately. Therefore it says: "He shall surely pay a dowry for her to be his wife," thereby telling us that he takes it upon himself as part of the *mohar.* And *mohar* only means, the *ketubah,*[3] as it is said: "Ask me never so much dowry and gift, and I will give according as ye shall say unto me; but give me the damsel to wife" (Gen. 34.12).

He Shall Surely Pay a Dowry for Her to Be His Wife. Scripture deals with those cases where the girl is fit to be his wife. This excludes the

2. This is evident from v. 16 here.
3. On *Ketubah* see *JE,* VII, 472–474.

אשר לא אורסה להוציא את שנתאלמנה

ואת שנתגרשה מן האירוסין דברי רבי יוסי הגלילי

רבי עקיבא אומר מנין אפילו נתאלמנה אפילו

נתגרשה והדין נותן הואיל ורשאי בהפר נדריה

ורשאי בכסף קנסה מה בהפר נדריה אפילו

נתאלמנה או נתגרשה אף בכסף קנסה אפילו

נתאלמנה או נתגרשה ומה ת"ל אשר לא אורסה

אלא מופנה להקיש ולדון גזירה שוה נאמר כאן

אשר לא אורסה ונאמר להלן אשר לא אורסה מה

להלן חמשים כסף אף כאן חמשים כסף.

מהור ימהרנה לו לאשה למה נאמר

לפי שהוא אומר ונתן האיש השוכב עמה וגו' יכול

כשם שבתבוסה נותן מיד כך במפותה נותן מיד

ת"ל מהור ימהרנה לו לאשה מגיד שהוא עושה

עליו מוהר ואין מוהר אלא כתובה שנאמר הרבו

עלי מאד מוהר ומתן ואתנה כאשר תאמרו אלי

ותנו לי הנערה לאשה.

מהור ימהרנה לו לאשה בראויה לו

11—10 ש. שם.   19—10 כתובות ל"ח, א'; י' שם ג', ד' ([279]). ספרי דברים רמ"ד; מ"ת
143.   18 דברים כ"ג, כ"ח.   22 שם כ"ב, כ"ט.   26—21 כתובות ל"ט, ב'; י' שם ג',
ה' ([27d]).   24—26 בראשית ל"ד, י"ב.   30—27 כתובות כ"ט, ב'; ל"ט, א'. ספרי דברים
רמ"ה. ש. 149 — 148.

---

11 האירוסין] הגהתי=א"צ. ז"י. ש"י: א. מ. ד. הנישואין.   13 ורשאי בהפר] א.
ורשאי בהפר.   16 ומה] ד. אם כן מה.   17 מופנה] א. מפני / ולדון] ד. ~ ממנו.
19—18 מה להלן חמשים כסף אף כאן חמשים כסף] כנ"ל להגיה ועיין מ"ת. צד 143:
א. מ. מה להלן כסף אף כאן כסף ד. מה להלן חמשים אף כאן חמשים מה להלן
בכסף אף כאן בכסף.

case of a widow seduced by the high priest, a divorced woman or one
released from levirate[4] seduced by an ordinary priest, a bastard or a
nethinah seduced by an Israelite, or an Israelitish girl seduced by a
bastard or a *nathin*.[5]

He Shall Surely Pay a Dowry for Her to Be His Wife. I might understand this to mean, whether her father consents or not. Therefore it
says: "And[6] if her father utterly refuse," etc. (v. 16). Scripture thus
tells us that if the father wishes he can let him keep her as his wife,
but if the father wishes he may insist that he give her up. I thus far
know only that in the case of seduction if the father wishes he can let
him keep her as his wife and if the father wishes he may insist that he
give her up. How about the case of rape? You can reason thus: Since
the law of rape applies only to a girl under the jurisdiction of her
father and the law of seduction applies only to a girl under the jurisdiction of her father, it follows that inasmuch as you have learned
that in case of seduction if the father wishes he can let him keep her
as his wife but if the father wishes he may insist that he give her up,
in the case of rape likewise if the father wishes he can let him keep
her as his wife but if the father wishes he may insist that he give her
up. Furthermore, by using the method of *kal vaḥomer* you can reason
thus: If in the case of seduction, where he only sinned against her
father's wish, he can keep her only if her father so wishes, but if her
father wishes he must give her up, it is but logical that in the case of
rape, where he sinned against her own wish and her father's wish, he
should have to give her up if her father wishes it and keep her as his
wife only if her father consents to it.

And If Her Father Utterly Refuse, etc. I thus know only about the
case where she has a father. How about the case where she has no

4. Such a one may not be married to an (ordinary) priest.
5. On *Nathin* or *Nethinah* see M. Kid. 4; and *JE*, IX, 233, s. v. Nethinim.
6. The *Mekilta* had the reading ואם like the ספרים אחרים quoted by Ch. D.
Ginsburg in his edition of the Bible.

לאשה הכתוב מדבר להוציא אלמנה לכהן גדול
גרושה וחלוצה לכהן הדיוט ממזרת ונתינה לישראל
בת ישראל לנתין וממזר.

30

מהור ימהרנה לו לאשה שומע אני בין
שהאב רוצה ובין שאין האב רוצה ת"ל ואם מאן
ימאן אביה וגו' מגיד הכתוב שאם רוצה האב יקיים
ואם רוצה האב יוצא ואין לי אלא מפותה שאם
רוצה האב יקיים ואם רוצה האב יוציא תפוסה

35

מנין הרי אתה דן הואיל ותפוסה ברשות אביה
ומפותה ברשות אביה אם למדת על מפותה שאם
רצה האב יקיים ואם רצה האב יוציא אף תפוסה
אם רצה האב יקיים ואם רצה האב יוציא ועוד קל

40

וחומר ומה אם מפותה שלא עבר אלא על דעת
אביה רצה האב יוציא רצה האב יקיים תפוסה
שעבר על דעתה ועל דעת אביה דין הוא שאם רצה
האב יוציא רצה האב יקיים.

ואם מאן ימאן אביה וגו' אין לי אלא
בזמן שיש לה אב בזמן שאין לה אב מנין ת"ל ואם

45

43—31 כתובות ל"ט, ב'.   46—44 כתובות מ', א'; מ"ד, ב'. מ"ת 144.

___

24—23 עושה עליו מוהר ואין מוהר] ק. עליו עשהו מוהר ואין מהור.   34—33 שאם
רוצה האב יקיים ואם רוצה האב יוציא] ד. <.   39—38 אף תפוסה—יוציא] ד. אף
תפוסה כן. 40 אלא] ד. <.   42—43 שאם רצה האב] ד. שאם לא רצה האב.   44 ואם
מאן] לפנינו במקרא, אם מאן.

father? It says: "And if her father utterly refuse"—in any case.[7]— These are the words of R. Jose the Galilean.

He Shall Pay Silver. But we have not heard how much. Behold then, I must reason thus: Here a payment of silver is mentioned and there (Deut. 22.29) a payment of silver is mentioned. Just as there it means fifty shekels of silver, so also here it means fifty shekels of silver.

According to the Dowry of Virgins. And what have we learned as to the dowry of virgins? It is simply this: Behold this instance, cited to throw light, in reality receives light: Just as there (ibid.) the amount paid is fifty shekels of silver, so also is the dowry of virgins fifty shekels of silver.

Thou Shalt Not Suffer a Witch to Live, whether it be a man or a woman. R. Ishmael says: Here it is said: "Thou shalt not suffer . . . to live" and there (Deut. 20.16) it is said: "Thou shalt not suffer to live anything that breathes." Just as there it means killing by the sword, so also here it means killing by the sword. R. Akiba says: Here it is said: "Thou shalt not suffer . . . to live" and there (Ex. 19.13) it is said: "Whether it be beast or man it shall not live." Just as there it means killing by stoning, so also here it means killing by stoning. Said to him R. Ishmael: I prove the meaning of the expression "Thou shalt not suffer . . . to live" from the expression "Thou shalt not suffer to live" in another passage. And you cite against me the expression "It shall not live" to prove the meaning of the expression "Thou shalt not suffer . . . to live." R. Jose the Galilean says: It is said: "Thou shalt not suffer a witch to live" and it is also said: "Whosoever lieth with a beast shall surely be put to death" (v. 18). The former has been put close to the latter to indicate that just as in the latter stoning is the death penalty, so also in the former stoning is the death penalty. R. Judah b. Bathyra says: Behold it says: "A man also or a woman that divineth by a ghost or a familiar spirit shall surely be put to death; they shall stone them with stones" (Lev. 20.27). But were not the nec-

7. See Commentaries.

מאן ימאן מכל מקום דברי רבי יוסי הגלילי.

כסף ישקול אבל לא שמענו כמה הריני דן
נאמר כאן כסף ונאמר להלן כסף מה להלן חמשים
כסף אף כאן חמשים כסף.

כמוהר הבתולות וכי מה למדנו למוהר ⁵⁰
הבתולות אלא הרי זה בא ללמד ונמצא למד מה
להלן חמשים כסף אף מוהר הבתולות חמשים
כסף.

מכשפה לא תחיה אחד איש ואחד אשה
רבי ישמעאל אומר נאמר כאן לא תחיה ונאמר ⁵⁵
להלן לא תחיה מה נשמה כל להלן בסייף אף כאן
בסייף רבי עקיבא אומר נאמר כאן לא תחיה ונאמר
להלן אם בהמה אם איש לא יחיה מה להלן
בסקילה אף כאן בסקילה אמר לו רבי ישמעאל אני
דן לא תחיה מלא תחיה ואתה משיבני לא יחיה על ⁶⁰
לא תחיה רבי יוסי הגלילי אומר מכשפה לא
תחיה ונאמר כל שוכב עם בהמה מות יומת סמכו לו
מה זה בסקילה אף זה בסקילה רבי יהודה בן בתירה
אומר הרי הוא אומר ואיש או אשה כי יהיה בהם
אוב או ידעוני מות יומתו באבן ירגמו אותם והלא ⁶⁵

---

53 — 44 ש. 149.   53 — 50 כתובות י׳, א׳, ל״ח, ב׳.   57 — 54 מ״ת 121.   70 — 54 סנהדרין
ס״ט, א׳—ב׳. ר׳ שם ז׳, י״ט (25ᵈ).   77 — 54 ש. 149.   56 דברים כ׳, ט״ז. ספרי דברים
ר״א.   58 שמות י״ט, י״ג.   65 — 64 ויקרא כ׳, כ״ז.

---

50 למוהר] נ. ל. מן מוהר.   52 מוהר הבתולות] ד. כאן.   54 אשה] א״צ. ~ אלא
שדבר הכתוב בהווה.   58 אם בהמה] ד. לא תחיה אם בהמה.   59 אמר לו רבי ישמעאל]
מ. אמר רבי ישמעאל ד. ר׳ ישמעאל אומר.   61 רבי יוסי הגלילי] ל״ט. ר׳ אליעזר
א״צ. בן עזאי / נאמר] ד. ~ כאן / מכשפה] מ. במכשפה.   62 סמכו לו] ד. וסמכו
לומר.   63 בן בתירא] מ״ח. ^.   65 או ידעוני] ק. נ. וידעוני א. נ. מות יומתו
באבן ירגמו אותם] הוספתי:

romancer and the charmer included in the category of witches? Why then were they singled out for special mention? That we may compare the others to them, to tell you that just as these are to be killed by stoning, so also all others who practice witchcraft are to be killed by stoning. We have thus heard the penalty for it, but we have not heard the warning against it. It says: "There shall not be found among you any one that maketh his son or his daughter to pass through the fire, one that useth divination, a soothsayer, or an enchanter, or a witch" (Deut. 18.10).

Whosoever Lieth with a Beast Shall Surely Be Put to Death. Why is this said: Because of the following: It says: "And if a man lie with a beast he shall surely be put to death" (Lev. 20.15)—by stoning. You interpret it to mean by stoning. Perhaps however it means by any manner of death prescribed in the Torah? It says however: "And ye shall kill the beast" (ibid.). Now, here the expression "kill" is used and there (Deut. 13.10) the expression "kill" is used. Just as there it means by stoning, so also here it means by stoning. We have heard the penalty but we have not heard the warning. It says: "And thou shalt not lie with any beast" (Lev. 18.23). I thus far know only the penalty and the warning with respect to the person who lies[8] with the animal. But how would we know the penalty and the warning with respect to the person who is being lain with?[9] Therefore it says: "Whosoever lieth with a beast shall surely be put to death."—Here Scripture refers both to the person that is being lain with and to the one that is lying with the animal. Just as the latter is punishable by stoning, so also the former is punishable by stoning. We have thus heard the penalty but we have not heard the warning. It says: "There shall be no harlot of the daughters of Israel, neither shall

---

8. I. e., a man who lies with a beast. The active form of the participle designates the man.

9. I. e., a woman who lies down to a beast. The passive form of the participle designates the woman.

אוב וידעוני בכלל מכשפים היו ולמה יצאו להקיש

עליהם ולומר לך מה אלו בסקילה אף כל מכשפין

בסקילה עונש שמענו אזהרה לא שמענו ת״ל לא

ימצא בך מעביר בנו ובתו באש קוסם קסמים מעונן

70 ומנחש ומכשף.

כל שוכב עם בהמה מות יומת למה

נאמר לפי שהוא אומר ואיש אשר יתן שכבתו

בבהמה מות יומת בסקילה אתה אומר בסקילה

או באחת מכל מיתות האמורות בתורה ת״ל ואת

75 הבהמה תהרוגו נאמר כאן הריגה ונאמר להלן

הריגה מה להלן בסקילה אף הריגה האמורה כאן

בסקילה עונש שמענו אזהרה לא שמענו ת״ל ובכל

בהמה לא תתן שכבתך וגו׳ אין לי אלא עונש ואזהרה

לשוכב עונש ואזהרה לנשכב מנין ת״ל כל שוכב

80 עם בהמה מות יומת קרא הכתוב לנשכב כשוכב

מה זה בסקילה אף זה בסקילה עונש שמענו ואזהרה

לא שמענו ת״ל לא תהיה קדשה מבנות ישראל

70 — 67 מ״ת 110.   70 — 68 דברים י״ח, י׳.   84 — 71 סנהדרין נ״ד, ב׳. ת״כ קדושים י׳
(92°).   73 — 72 ויקרא כ׳, ט״ו.   78 — 77 ויקרא י״ח, כ״ג.   82 דברים כ״ג, י״ח.

65 — 67 והלא—אף כל מכשפין] א. מ. ‹.   68 לא שמענו] ד. מנין.   71 מות יומת]
הוספתא=מא״ש.   73 מות יומת] הוספתי: א. מ. וגו׳.   74 או] ד. ~ אינו אלא.
75 ונאמר להלן] א. ונאמר.   76 הריגה האמורה] ד. ‹.   79 ואזהרה לנשכב] ד. לנשכב.

there be a sodomite of the sons of Israel" (Deut. 23.18). And it also says: "And there were also sodomites in the land; they did according to all the abominations of the nations which the Lord drove out" (I Kings 14.24).

He That Sacrifices unto the Gods Shall Be Utterly Destroyed. We have thus heard the penalty for it, but we have not heard the warning against it. It says: "Thou shalt not bow down unto them nor serve them" (Ex. 20.5). Sacrificing was included in the category of worship and it has been singled out for special mention to teach you the following: Just as for the act of "sacrificing," peculiar in that it is also performed in the worship of God, one is guilty if he performs it for an idol, no matter whether the idol is customarily worshiped in that manner or not,[10] so also for any other act, the like of which is performed in the service of God, one is guilty for performing it for an idol, no matter whether the idol is customarily worshiped in that manner or not.[11] But for such acts as are not performed in the service of God one is guilty for performing them for an idol if the idol is customarily worshiped in that manner, but is not guilty if the idol is not customarily worshiped in that manner.

Save unto the Lord Alone. Because the others say: Had the Israelites not associated the. name of the Holy One, blessed be He, with their idol they would have perished from the world, for it is said: "He that sacrifices unto any god alone—save unto the Lord—shall be utterly destroyed."[12] R. Simon b. Yoḥai says: But is not one who associates the name of the Holy One, blessed be He, with an idol liable to destruction? It merely was like what is said in the passage: "They

10. For it says: "One who sacrifices to the gods," meaning to any god, even to those that are ordinarily not worshiped in that manner.

11. Literally, whether one would ordinarily worship it in that manner or not.

12. According to this interpretation of the others, one who, sacrificing to any other god, associates the Lord with it is not to be destroyed. Hence, the Israelites who associated God with the golden calf (see Sanh. 63a) were not destroyed.

ולא יהיה קדש מבני ישראל ואומר וגם קדש היה

בארץ עשו ככל התועבות הגוים אשר הוריש יי.

85   **זובח לאלהים יחרם** עונש שמענו ואזהרה

לא שמענו ת״ל לא תשתחוה להם ולא תעבדם

זביחה בכלל היתה ויצאת ללמד מה זביחה

מיוחדת שכיוצא בה עובדים לשמים וחייבין עליה

בין שהוא עובדה בכך בין שאינו עובדה בכך אף

90   כל כיוצא בהן עובדין לשמים יהו חייבין עליהם

בין שהוא עובדה בכך ובין שאינו עובדה בכך

אלא כל שאין כיוצא בהן עובדין לשמים לשום

עבודתו חייב שלא לשום עבודתו פטור.

בלתי ליי לבדו לפי שאחרים אומרים

95   אלולי ששתפו ישראל שמו של הקדוש ברוך הוא

בעבודה זרה כלים היו מן העולם שנאמר זובח

לאלהים יחרם בלתי ליי לבדו רבי שמעון בן יוחי

אומר והלא כל המשתף שמו של הקדוש ברוך הוא

בעבודה זרה חייב כלייה אלא כמה שנאמר את

84—83 מלכים א. י״ד, כ״ד.   85—83 לעיל בחדש ו׳. מ״ת 100—99. ש. שם.   86 שמות
כ׳, ה׳.   99—94 סנהדרין ס״ג, א׳.   100—99 מלכים ב. י״ז, ל״ג.

84 ככל התועבות] א. מ. וגו׳, ועפי״ז תקנתי כמו במקרא: ק. נ. מכל תועבות ל.
כתועבות.   86 ולא] ק. ואל.   88 בה] א. מ. בהן.   89 שהוא עובדה] א. מ. שהוא
עובדין / בכך] א. < / שאינו עובדה] א. מ. שאינו עובדין.   91—89 בכך אף כל—שאינו
עובדה בכך] א. מ. <.   92 אלא] א״צ. < / כל שאין] מ. <.   94 בלתי ליי לבדו] א.
מ. < / לפי] ז״י. ש״י. < א״צ. למה נאמר לפי / שאחרים] ז״י. ש״י. אחרים.   99 חייב
כלייה] ט״כ. נעקר מן העולם / אלא כמה]=ט״כ: ד. ט. כמה.

feared the Lord and served their own gods" (II Kings 17.33). Some say: The Torah was given with all its tittles.[13] Lest the Israelites say: Since we were commanded to destroy the idols, what about those hidden in pits, ditches and caves? Scripture says: "Upon the high mountains" (Deut. 12.2)—you are commanded only concerning such as are open, but not concerning such as are hidden.[14]

CHAPTER XVIII
(Ex. 22.20–23)

And a Stranger Shalt Thou Not Vex, Neither Shalt Thou Oppress Him; for Ye Were Strangers in the Land of Egypt. You shall not vex him—with words. Neither shall you oppress him—in money matters. You should not say unto him: But yesterday you were worshiping Bel, Kores,[1] Nebo, and until now swine's flesh was sticking out from between your teeth,[2] and now you dare to stand up and to speak against me! And how do we know that if you vex him he can also vex you? It is said: "And a stranger shalt thou not vex, neither shalt thou oppress him; for ye were strangers in the land of Egypt." In connection with this passage R. Nathan used to say: Do not reproach your fellow man with a fault which is also your own.

Beloved are the strangers.[3] For in ever so many passages Scripture warns about them: "And a stranger thou shalt not vex," etc.; "Love ye

---

13. The dots on the words לנו ולבנינו (Deut. 29.28) were taken to indicate that God would not punish them for such as are hidden (cf. Sanh. 43b).

14. This whole section admits of different interpretations (see Introduction and cf. Commentaries).

1. The word קורס (Isa. 46.1) seems to have been understood by the *Mekilta* as the name of an idol.

2. The reading in the text is rather difficult (see Introduction and cf. Commentaries).

3. By stranger, גר, here is meant a proselyte.

100 יי היו יראים ואת אליהם היו עובדים יש אומרים
באותיותיה נתנה תורה שלא יהיו ישראל אומרים
הואיל ואנו מצווין על עבודה זרה והן כבשין
בבורות בשיחין ובמערות ת״ל על ההרים הרמים
וגו' על הגלוים ולא על הסתרים.

פרשה יח   (שמות כ״ב, כ'—כ״ג.)

וגר לא תונה ולא תלחצנו כי גרים
הייתם בארץ מצרים לא תוננו בדברים
ולא תלחצנו בממון לא תאמר לו אמש היית עובד
לבל קורס נבו ועד עכשיו הרי חזירין נוצר מבין
5 שיניך ואתה עומד ומדבר כנגדי ומנין שאם הוניתו
אף הוא יכול להונתך שנאמר וגר לא תונה ולא
תלחצנו כי גרים הייתם בארץ מצרים מכאן היה
רבי נתן אומר מום שבך אל תאמרהו לחברך.
חביבין הגרים שבכל מקום הוא מזהיר עליהם

104—100 מ״ת 60.   103 דברים י״ב, ב'.

8—1 ת״כ קדושים ח' (91ᵃ). ב״מ נ״ח, ב'; נ״ט, ב'. תוס' שם ג', כ״ה. מס' גרים ד', א'.
12—9 ב״מ נ״ט, ב'. גרים ד', ב'.   48—9 במ״ר ח', ב'.

101 ט״כ. ש״י. באותויה.   102 הואיל ואנו] א״צ. שאין אנו / והן] א. מ. ט. ט״כ.
נהא.   104 ולא על הסתרים=מ. ק. ט. ש״י: א. נ. ל. ועל הסתרים.
4 ועד עכשיו] מ. Pugio fidei צד 457 ועכשיו ד. > / הרי] ד. והרי מ״ח. והיו / חזירין]
ט. בשר חזיר Pugio fidei בשר חזירים / נוצר] ד. ט. > Pugio fidei נוער מ״ח. מוסרים
/ מבין] ד. ט. בין.   5 עומד] ד. > מ. עתיד / ומדבר] ד. מדבר מילין א. ומוני (?
המעתיק תקן וכתב למעלה ומדבר).   6 אף הוא] ד. שהוא / להונתך] Pugio fidei להונותך
ד. להונך / שנאמר]=ט: Pugio fidei א. ד. ש״י. ה. ת״ל.   6—7 ולא תלחצנו—בארץ
מצרים] הוספתי: א. מ. וגו' ד. >.   8 תאמרהו] א. Pugio fidei תאמרו ד. תאמר.
9 מזהיר] ק. נ. מחזיר Pugio fidei מוזהר.

therefore the stranger," etc. (Deut. 10.19); "For ye know the heart of
a stranger," etc. (Ex. 23.9). R. Eliezer says: It is because there is a bad
streak in the stranger that Scripture warns about him in so many passages. R. Simon b. Yoḥai says: Behold, it says: "But they that love Him
be as the sun when he goeth forth in his might" (Judg. 5.31). Now,
who is the greater, he who loves the king or he whom the king loves?
You must say: It is he whom the king loves. And it is written: "And
loveth the stranger," etc. (Deut. 10.18).

Beloved are the strangers. For in ever so many passages Scripture
applies to them the same designations as it does to the Israelites. The
Israelites are called "servants," as it is said: "For unto Me the children
of Israel are servants" (Lev. 25.55). And so also the strangers are
called "servants," as it is said: "And to love the name of the Lord, to
be His servants" (Isa. 56.6). The Israelites are referred to as "ministers," as it is said: "But ye shall be named the priests of the Lord, men
shall call you the ministers of our God" (ibid. 61.6). And so also the
strangers are referred to as "ministers," as it is said: "Also the aliens,
that join themselves to the Lord, to minister unto Him" (ibid. 56.6).
The Israelites are referred to as "friends," as it is said: "But thou,
Israel, My servant, Jacob whom I have chosen, the seed of Abraham
My friend" (ibid. 41.8). And the strangers are also referred to as
"friends," as it is said: "And loveth the stranger"[4] (Deut. 10.18). A
"covenant" is mentioned in connection with the Israelites, as it is
said: "And My covenant shall be in your flesh" (Gen. 17.13). And a
"covenant" is also mentioned in connection with the strangers, as it is
said: "And holdeth fast by My covenant" (Isa. 56.6). "Acceptance" is
mentioned in regard to the Israelites, as it is said: "That they may be
accepted before the Lord" (Ex. 28.38). And "acceptance" is also mentioned in regard to the strangers, as it is said: "Their burnt-offerings

---

4. "The stranger" is taken to be the subject of "loveth" and not the object.
Hence, it means the stranger is a lover, a friend, of God.

וגר לא תונה וגו' ואהבתם את הגר וגו' ואתם ידעתם
את נפש הגר וגו' רבי אליעזר אומר גר לפי שסיאורו
רע לפיכך מזהיר עליו הכתוב במקומות הרבה
רבי שמעון בן יוחאי אומר הרי הוא אומר ואוהביו
כצאן השמש בגבורתו וכי מי גדול מי שהוא אוהב
את המלך או מי שהמלך אוהבו הוי אומר מי שהמלך
אוהבו וכתוב ואוהב גר וגו'. חביבין הגרים שבכל
מקום הוא מכנן כישראל נקראו ישראל עבדים
שנאמר כי לי בני ישראל עבדים ונקראו הגרים
עבדים שנאמר לאהבה את שם יי ולהיות לו
לעבדים נקראו ישראל משרתים שנאמר ואתם כהני
יי תקראו משרתי אלהינו יאמר לכם ונקראו הגרים
משרתים שנאמר ובני הנכר הנלוים על יי לשרתו
נקראו ישראל אוהבים שנאמר ואתה ישראל עבדי
יעקב אשר בחרתיך זרע אברהם אוהבי ונקראו
הגרים אוהבים שנאמר ואוהב גר נאמר בישראל
ברית שנאמר והיתה בריתי בבשרכם ונאמר בגרים
ברית שנאמר ומחזיקים בבריתי נאמר בישראל
רצון שנאמר לרצון להם לפני יי ונאמר בגרים

10 דברים י', י"ט.   11—10 שמות כ"ג, ט'.   14—13 שופטים ה', ל"א.   48—14 גרים
ד', ג'.   16 דברים י', י"ח.   18 ויקרא כ"ה, נ"ה.   19—19 ישעיה נ"ו, ר'.   21—20 שם
ס"א, ר'.   22 שם נ"ו, ר'.   23—24 שם מ"א, ח'.   26 בראשית י"ז, י"ג.   27 ישעיה
נ"ו, ר'.   28 שמות כ"ח, ל"ח.

11 שסיאורו] א. ד. שסורו.   16 וכתוב] מ. ד. שנאמר.   17 הוא מכנן כישראל] ד.
שנקראו בישראל.   19 לאהבה] במקרא שלפנינו, ולאהבה / את שם יי] א. את יי /
ולהיות] במקרא שלפנינו, להיות.   21 אלהינו] א. מ"ח. אלוהכם ד. אלהים.   22 על
יי] ~ Pugio fidei   28 להם] ד. <.

and their sacrifices shall be acceptable upon Mine altar" (Isa. 56.7). "Guarding" is mentioned in regard to the Israelites, as it is said: "Behold, He that guardeth Israel doth neither slumber nor sleep" (Ps. 121.4). And "guarding" is also mentioned in regard to the strangers, as it is said: "The Lord guardeth the strangers" (ibid. 146.9). Abraham called himself a "stranger," as it is said: "I am a stranger and a sojourner with you" (Gen. 23.4). David called himself a "stranger," as it is said: "I am a stranger in the earth" (Ps. 119.19). And he also says: "For we are strangers before Thee, and sojourners, as all our fathers were: our days on the earth are as a shadow, and there is no abiding" (I Chr. 29.15). And it also says: "For I am a stranger with Thee, a sojourner, as all my fathers were" (Ps. 39.13).

Beloved are the strangers. It was for their sake that our father Abraham was not circumcised until he was ninety-nine years old. Had he been circumcised at twenty or at thirty years of age, only those under the age of thirty could have become proselytes to Judaism. Therefore, God bore with Abraham until he reached ninety-nine years of age,[5] so as not to close the door to future proselytes.—Also to determine the reward according to the days and years, thus increasing the reward of him who does His will. This is to confirm what has been said: "The Lord was pleased, for His righteousness' sake, to make the teaching great and glorious" (Isa. 42.21).—And you find them[6] also among the four groups who respond and speak before Him by whose word the world came into being: "One shall say: 'I am the Lord's'" (Isa. 44.5), that is: "All of me is the Lord's and there is no admixture of sin in me." "And another shall call himself by the name of Jacob" (ibid.), these are the righteous proselytes. "And another shall subscribe with his hand unto the Lord" (ibid.), these

5. God tolerated Abraham in an imperfect condition, i. e., uncircumcised, up to the age of 99, when He commanded him to become circumcised and be perfect (Gen. 17.1 ff).

6. I. e., the proselytes.

רצון שנאמר עולותיהם וזבחיהם לרצון על מזבחי

30 נאמר בישראל שמירה שנאמר הנה לא ינום ולא

יישן שומר ישראל ונאמר בגרים שמירה שנאמר יי

שומר את גרים אברהם קרא עצמו גר שנאמר גר

ותושב אנכי עמכם דוד קרא עצמו גר שנאמר גר

אנכי בארץ ואומר כי גרים אנחנו לפניך ותושבים

35 ככל אבותינו כצל ימינו על הארץ ואין מקוה ואומר

כי גר אנכי עמך תושב ככל אבותי. חביבין הגרים

שלא מל אבינו אברהם אלא בן תשעים ותשע שנים

שאלו מל בן עשרים או בן שלשים לא היה גר יכול

להתגייר אלא בפחות מבן שלשים לפיכך גלגל

40 המקום עמו עד שהוא מגיע לתשעים ותשע שנים

שלא לנעול דלת בפני הגרים הבאים וליתן שכר

ימים ושנים לרבות שכר עושה רצונו לקיים מה

שנאמר יי חפץ למען צדקו יגדיל תורה ויאדיר

וכן אתה מוצא בארבע כתות שהן עונות ואומרות

45 לפני מי שאמר והיה העולם זה יאמר ליי אני כולי

ליי ואל יתערב בי חטא וזה יקרא בשם יעקב אלו

---

29 ישעיה נ"ו, ז'. 31—30 תהלים קכ"א, ד'. 32—31 שם קמ"ו, ט'. 33—32 בראשית
כ"ג, ד'. 34—33 תהלים קי"ט, י"ט. 35—34 דהי"א. כ"ט, ט"ו. 36 תהלים ל"ט, י"ג.
41—36 ת. לך לך י"ב. 42—48 אדר"נ ל"ו. סא"ר י"ח (105). 43 ישעיה מ"ב, כ"א.
45 ישעיה מ"ד, ה'.

---

29 ק. נ. עולותיכם וזבחיכם. 33—34 גר אנכי בארץ ואומר] א. >. 34 לפניך] א. >.
35 כצל] נ. ל. כי צל / הארץ] ד. האדמה. 39 אלא בפחות מבן שלשים] א. מ. אלא
מבן שלשים שנה ומעלה א"צ. אלא בפחות מבן עשרים או שלשים / לפיכך] א. מ.
ט. אלא. 40 עמו] מ. ט. בו / לתשעים] א. מ. בן תשעים. 41 שלא לנעול דלת]
מ. נימל / וליתן] מ"ח. כ. (ישעיה נ"ד, ה') ולא עוד אלא ליתן. 42 לרבות] מ"ח.
כ. כדי לרבות / לקיים מה] ד. >. 44 כתות] Pugio fidei ~ של גרים. 45 זה יאמר]
ד. >. 46—45 כולי ליי] Pugio fidei כולו ליי ט. וגו' ליי ד. שנאמר זה יאמר ליי אני
וזה יקרא בשם יעקב וזה יכתוב ידו ליי ובשם ישראל יכנה ליי אני. 46 וזה יקרא] מ.
והוא יקרא.

are the repentant sinners. "And surname himself by the name of Israel" (ibid.), these are the God-fearing ones.[7]

Ye Shall Not Afflict Any Widow or Fatherless Child. From this I know only about the widow and the fatherless child. How about any other person? It says: "Ye shall not afflict them"—these are the words of R. Ishmael. R. Akiba says: "Any widow or fatherless child"—Scripture mentions them because they are likely to be afflicted.

If Thou Afflict in Any Wise, whether by a severe affliction or a light affliction. Another Interpretation: *If Thou Afflict in Any Wise.* This tells us that one becomes guilty of oppression only after he has repeated the act. At the time when R. Simon and R. Ishmael were led out to be killed, R. Simon said to R. Ishmael: Master, my heart fails me, for I do not know why I am to be killed. R. Ishmael said to him: Did it never happen in your life that a man came to you for a judgment or with a question and you let him wait until you had sipped your cup, or had tied your sandals, or had put on your cloak? And the Torah has said: "If thou afflict in any wise"—whether it be a severe affliction or a light affliction. Whereupon R. Simon said to him: "You have comforted me, master."

When R. Simon and R. Ishmael were killed, R. Akiba said to his disciples: Be prepared for trouble. For, if something good had been destined to come upon our generation, R. Simon and R. Ishmael—and none else—would have been the first ones to receive it. Now then, it must, therefore, be that these two men have been taken from our midst only because it is revealed before Him by whose word the world came into being that great suffering is destined to come upon our generation. This confirms what has been said: "The righteous perisheth, and no man layeth it to heart, and godly men are taken away, none considering that the righteous is taken away from the evil to come" (Isa. 57.1). And it also says: "He entereth into peace, they

7. I. e., among the Gentiles. On the distinction between "the righteous proselytes" and "the God-fearing Gentiles" see G. F. Moore, *Judaism,* I, p. 325 ff.

גרי צדק וזה יכתוב ידו ליי אלו בעלי תשובה ובשם
ישראל יכנה אלו יראי שמים.

כל אלמנה ויתום לא תענון אין לי אלא
אלמנה ויתום שאר כל אדם מנין ת״ל לא תענון
דברי רבי ישמעאל רבי עקיבא אומר כל אלמנה
ויתום שדרכן ליענות בהן דבר הכתוב.

אם ענה תענה אחד עינוי מרובה ואחד
עינוי מועט דבר אחר אם ענה תענה מגיד שאינו
חייב עד שיענה וישנה. כבר היה רבי שמעון ורבי
ישמעאל יוצאין ליהרג אמר לו רבי שמעון לרבי
ישמעאל רבי לבי יוצא שאין אני יודע על מה אני
נהרג אמר לו רבי ישמעאל מימיך לא בא אדם
אצלך לדין או לשאלה ושהיתו עד שתהא גומא
כוסך עד שתהא נועל סנדלך או עד שתהא עוטף
טליתך ואמרה תורה אם ענה תענה אחד עינוי
מרובה ואחד עינוי מועט ובדבר הזה אמר לו
ניחמתני רבי וכשנהרגו רבי שמעון ורבי ישמעאל
אמר להם רבי עקיבא לתלמידיו התקינו עצמכם
לפורענות שאלו טובה עתידה לבא בדורנו
מתחילה לא היו מקבלין אותה אלא רבי שמעון
ורבי ישמעאל ועכשיו גלוי היה לפני מי שאמר
והיה העולם שפורענות גדולה עתידה לבא בדורנו
ונסתלקו אלו מבינותינו לקיים מה שנאמר הצדיק
אבד ואין איש שם על לב ואנשי חסד נאספים באין
מבין כי מפני הרעה נאסף הצדיק ואומר יבא שלום

52 — 49 ש. 150.   63 — 56 אדר״נ ל״ח.   73 — 56 שמחות ח׳.   73 — 69 ישעיה נ״ז,
א׳ — ג׳.

---

54 דבר אחר] ד. ~ רבי אומר.   56 — 55 ר׳ שמעון ור׳ ישמעאל] ד. ר׳ ישמעאל ור׳
שמעון.   58 לא] א] ד. >.   59 ושהיתו] ד. ועכבתו / גומא] מ. גומא ט. גומר נ. ל. שותה.
60 עד שתהא] ד. כ. (ישעיה נ״ז, א׳) > ט. או שהיית / נועל] ד. ונוטל כ. (שם) ונועל
/ עד שתהא] ד. >.   62 ובדבר הזה] ד. > כ. וכדבר הזה.   66 מתחילה] ד. ט. >.
67 ועכשיו] ד. אלא / היה] ד. ט. וידוע ט״כ. וידוע היה.   69 ונסתלקו] ד. וסילק /
לקיים מה] ד. >.   71 — 70 ואין איש שם על לב—נאסף הצדיק] הוספתי: א. מ. וגו׳.
70 באין] ק. נ. ואין.

rest in their beds, each one that walketh in his uprightness" (ibid. v. 2). And then: "But draw near hither, ye sons of the sorceress, the seed of the adulterer and the harlot" (ibid. v. 3).

For If They Cry At All unto Me, I Will Surely Hear Their Cry. Does it mean only if he cries I will hear, and if he does not cry I will not hear? But Scripture says: "I will surely hear their cry!" Behold, then, what does Scripture mean by saying: "If they cry at all unto Me, I will surely hear"? Simply this: I will punish more quickly when there is one crying than when there is no one crying. Now it may be reasoned by using the method of *kal vaḥomer:* If God hears when an individual cries, how much more will He hear when many cry. And it is further to be reasoned, by using the method of *kal vaḥomer:* If with regard to meting out evil, which is of less importance, the rule is that when the individual cries against the group God hears his cry, how much more should this be the rule with regard to meting out good, which is of greater importance, and especially in the case when the group prays for the individual.

My Anger Shall Wax Hot. R. Ishmael says: Here God's anger is spoken of, and there (Deut. 11.17) God's anger is spoken of: Just as there it means drought and exile, as it is said: "And the anger of the Lord be kindled against you, and He shut up the heaven, so that there shall be no rain," etc. (ibid.), so here also it means drought and exile. And just as here it means punishment by means of the sword, so also there it means punishment by the sword.

And Your Wives Shall Be Widows and Your Children Fatherless. But do I not know from the very literal meaning of the passage: "And I will kill you" that your wives will be widows and your children fatherless? What need then is there of saying: "And your wives shall be widows and your children fatherless"? It is but to indicate that they will be widowed, and yet not widows, in the same sense as when it is said: "So they were shut up unto the day of their death, in widowhood, with their husband alive" (II Sam. 20.3). And your chil-

ינוחו על משכבותם הולך נכוחו ולבסוף ואתם
קרבו הנה בני עוננה זרע מנאף ותזנה.

כי אם צעק יצעק אלי שמוע אשמע
צעקתו כל זמן שהוא צועק אני שומע ואם אינו
צועק איני שומע ת"ל שמוע אשמע צעקתו מכל
מקום הא מה ת"ל כי אם צעק יצעק אלי שמוע
אשמע אלא ממהר אני להיפרע על ידי שהוא צועק
יותר ממי שאינו צועק והרי הדברים קל וחומר
אם כשהיחיד צועק המקום שומע צעקתו קל וחומר
כשהרבים צועקים והרי דברים קל וחומר ומה אם
מדת הפורענות מעוטה כשהיחיד צועק על הרבים
המקום שומע צעקתו קל וחומר מדת הטובה
מרובה כשיהיו הרבים מתפללים על היחיד.

וחרה אפי רבי ישמעאל אומר נאמר כאן
חרון אף ונאמר להלן חרון אף מה להלן עצירת
גשמים וגלות שנאמר וחרה אף יי בכם ועצר את
השמים ולא יהיה מטר וגו' אף כאן עצירת גשמים
וגלות ומה כאן בחרב אף להלן בחרב.

והיו נשיכם אלמנות ובניכם יתומים ממשמע
שנאמר והרגתי אתכם איני יודע שנשיכם אלמנות
ובניכם יתומים ומה ת"ל והיו נשיכם אלמנות ובניכם
יתומים אלא אלמנות ולא אלמנות כענין שנאמר
ותהיין צרורות עד יום מותן אלמנות חיות אלמנות ובניכם

89—85 ספרי דברים מ"ג. 96—85 ש. 150. 87—88 דברים י"א, י"ז. 96—90 ב"מ
ל"ח, ב'. אדר"נ ל"ח. 94 שמואל ב. כ', ג'.

72 ולבסוף] א. ט. < מ. ואומר. 75 כל זמן] ט. יכול כל זמן מ"ח. יכול בזמן. 76 ת"ל]
ד. מ. הא מה ת"ל. 76—77 צעקתו מכל מקום] א. ד. >. 77 הא מה ת"ל] מ"ח.
אם כן מה ת"ל / כי אם צעק יצעק אלי הוספתי=ט. ז"י. ש"י. מ"ח: 78 אלא] ק.
>. 80 צועק] ד. ~ על היחיד ט. ~ על הרבים / קל וחומר] ד. >. 81 צועקים] א.
ט. ~ על היחיד ד. על אחת כמה וכמה / והרי דברים קל וחומר] ד. >. 82 כשהיחיד]
א. מ. אם כשהיחיד. 83 המקום שומע צעקתן] ד. כך. 84—83 קל וחומר—הרבים]
ד. מדה טובה ורבים. 84 היחיד] ד. ~ על אחת כמה וכמה. 86 להלן חרון אף] ד.
~ וחרה אף יי בכם. 88—87 שנאמר—מטר וגו'] ד. >. 89 כאן] ד. להלן / להלן] ד.
כאן. 91 איני יודע] מ. ט. הא למדנו. 93 אלא אלמנות ולא אלמנות] ד. >.

dren will be fatherless, and yet not orphans, in that the court will not permit them to sell any of the property of their fathers on the presumption that the latter are still alive.[8] Now it is to be reasoned by using the method of *kal vaḥomer:* If for mere refraining from violating justice your reward will be that your wives will not become widows and your children will not be fatherless, how much more so when you actually execute justice. And thus it says: "Execute true judgment" (Zech. 7.9). And it also says: "Execute the judgment of truth and peace in your gates" (ibid. 8.16). And it also says: "Thus saith the Lord: Keep ye justice, and do righteousness; for My salvation is near to come" (Isa. 56.1). All the more is it to be expected that your wives will not become widows and your children will not become fatherless. And thus it says: "That thou mightest fear the Lord thy God, to keep all His statutes and His commandments, which I command thee, thou, and thy son, and thy son's son, all the days of thy life; and that thy days may be prolonged" (Deut. 6.2). And it says: "And ye shall teach them your children . . . that your days may be multiplied," etc. (ibid. 11.19–21). And it also says: "For as the days of a tree shall be the days of My people," etc. (Isa. 65.22). And it also says: "They shall not labour in vain, nor bring forth for terror; for they are the seed blessed of the Lord, and their offspring with them" (ibid. v. 23). And it also says: "Thy seed also would be as the sand," etc. (ibid. 48.19). And it also says: "Oh that they had such a heart as this alway . . . that it might be well with them and with their children for ever" (Deut. 5.26). And it also says: "For as the new heavens . . . so shall your seed and your name remain" (Isa. 66.22). And it also says: "And a redeemer will come to Zion . . ." and it continues to say: "And as for Me, this is My covenant with them, saith the Lord; My spirit that is upon thee,

8. The husbands and fathers will be killed or lost in war with no evidence as to their death. And as long as there is no official or sufficient evidence of their death the wives are not permitted to remarry and the sons cannot dispose of the estate.

יתומים ולא יתומים שאין בית דין מניחין אותן 95
למכור בנכסי אביהן בחזקת שהן קיימין והרי
דברים קל וחומר ומה אם כשלא תענון את הדין
לא יהיו נשיכם אלמנות ובניכם יתומים קל וחומר
לכשתעשון את הדין וכן הוא אומר משפט אמת
שפטו ואומר אמת ומשפט שלום שפטו בשעריכם 100
ואומר כה אמר יי שמרו משפט ועשו צדקה כי
קרובה ישועתי לבא על אחת כמה וכמה שלא
יהיו נשיכם אלמנות ובניכם יתומים וכן הוא אומר
למען תירא את יי אלהיך לשמור את כל חקותיו
ומצותיו אשר אנכי מצוך אתה ובנך ובן בנך כל 105
ימי חייך ולמען יאריכון ימיך ואומר ולמדתם אותם
את בניכם וגו׳ למען ירבו ימיכם וגו׳ ואומר כי כימי
העץ ימי עמי וגו׳ ואומר לא יגעו לריק ולא ילדו
לבהלה כי זרע ברוכי יי המה וצאצאיהם אתם
ואומר ויהי כחול זרעך וגו׳ ואומר מי יתן והיה 110
לבבם זה להם וגו׳ למען ייטב להם ולבניהם לעולם
ואומר כי כאשר השמים החדשים וגו׳ כן יעמוד
זרעכם ושמכם ואומר ובא לציון גואל וגו׳ ואומר
ואני זאת בריתי אותם אמר יי רוחי אשר עליך ודברי

99—100 זכריה ז׳, ט׳.   100 שם ח׳, ט״ז.   101 נ״ו, א׳.   104—106 דברים ו׳, ב׳.
107—106 שם י״א, י״ט.   107 שם י״א, כ״א.   108—107 ישעיה ס״ה, כ״ב.   109—108 שם
ס״ה, כ״ג.   110 שם מ״ח, י״ט.   111—110 דברים ה׳, כ״ו.   113—112 ישעיה ס״ו, כ״ב.
116—113 שם נ״ט, כ׳—כ״א.

95 ולא יתומים] ד. אין יתומין אלא.   96 למכור] ד. < א׳׳א. לירד / בנכסי] א. מנכסי
/ בחזקת שהן] ד. מפני שהן בחזקת.   98—97 קל וחומר—ובניכם יתומים] א. <.
97 כשלא תענון] מ. ט״כ. כשתענון.   99—98 קל וחומר—וכן הוא אומר] ד. כשתעשון
את הדין על אחת כמה וכמה שכתב.   100 אמת ומשפט שלום] ד. אמת ושלום.
104—106 את כל חקותיו—יאריכון ימיך] הוספת: א. מ. וגו׳.   107 כי] א. < / כימי]
ק. ג. ימי.   111—110 ואומר מי יתן—ולבניהם לעולם] ד. <.

and My words which I have put in thy mouth, shall not depart out of thy mouth, nor out of the mouth of thy seed, nor out of the mouth of thy seed's seed, saith the Lord, from henceforth and for ever" (ibid. 59.20–21). All the more is it to be expected that in this world your days will be prolonged and you will live to see children and grandchildren and that you will also merit the life in the world to come.

115 אשר שמתי בפיך לא ימושו מפיך ומפי זרעך ומפי

זרע זרעך אמר יי מעתה ועד עולם על אחת כמה

וכמה שתאריכון ימים בעולם הזה ותראו לכם

בנים ובני בנים ותזכו לחיי העולם הבא.

סילק.

TRACTATE KASPA

If Thou Lend Money to Any of My People. R. Ishmael says: Every "if" in the Torah refers to a voluntary act except this and two others. "And if thou bring a meal-offering of first-fruits" (Lev. 2.14) refers to an obligatory act. You interpret it to be obligatory. Perhaps this is not so, but it is merely voluntary? Scripture, however, says: "Thou shalt bring for the meal-offering of thy first-fruits" (ibid.)—it is obligatory and not voluntary. Similarly, "And if thou make Me an altar of stone" (Ex. 20.22) refers to an obligatory act. You interpret it to be obligatory. Perhaps this is not so, but it is merely voluntary? Scripture however says: "Thou shalt build . . . of unhewn stones" (Deut. 27.6)—it is obligatory and not voluntary. And so also here you interpret: "If thou lend money" as referring to an obligatory act. You interpret it to be obligatory. Perhaps this is not so, but it is merely voluntary? Scripture however says: "Thou shalt surely lend him" (Deut. 15.8)—it is obligatory and not voluntary.

If Thou Lend Money. You may lend him money on condition that he repay money, but you may not lend him produce on condition that he return produce to you.[1] Another Interpretation: You may lend him money on condition that he repay you money, but you may neither lend him money on condition that he repay you in produce, nor produce on condition that he repay you in money.

---

1. The price of the produce at the time when it is returned may be higher. The lender would thus receive more than he actually loaned.

מסכתא דכספא

פרשה א (שמות כ״ב, כ״ד—כ״ט.)

אם כסף תלוה את עמי רבי ישמעאל
אומר כל אם שבתורה רשות חוץ מזה ועוד
שנים ואם תקריב מנחת בכורים חובה אתה אומר
חובה או אינו אלא רשות תלמוד לומר תקריב את
מנחת בכוריך חובה ולא רשות כיוצא בו ואם מזבח
אבנים תעשה לי חובה אתה אומר חובה או אינו
אלא רשות ת״ל אבנים שלמות תבנה חובה ולא
רשות ואף כאן אתה אומר אם כסף תלוה חובה
אתה אומר או אינו אלא רשות ת״ל העבט
תעביטנו חובה ולא רשות.

אם כסף תלוה כסף בכסף אתה מלוהו
ואין אתה מלוהו פירות בפירות דבר אחר כסף
בכסף אתה מלוהו ואין אתה מלוהו כסף בפירות
ופירות בכסף.

---

10 — 1 לעיל בחודש י״א. ש. 151.   3 ויקרא ב׳, י״ד.   6—5 שמות כ׳, כ״ה.   7 דברים
כ״ז, ו׳.   10—9 שם ט״ו, ח׳. מ״ת 82.   12—11 ב״מ ע״ה, א׳.   14—12 שם ע״ג, ב׳.
ת״כ בהר ה׳ (109א).

מסכת דכספא] הוספתי: א. מ. ד. .ר.   3 שנים] ק. שנינו / ואם] א. מ. אם.
5—4 תקריב את מנחת בכוריך] ק. נ. תקריב מנחת מ. תקריב את מנחת בכורים.
5 ואם] א. ד. אם.   7 ת״ל] ד. כשהוא אומר.   8 חובה] ד. ~ ולא רשות.   9 ת״ל] ד.
כשהוא אומר / העבט] במקרא שלפנינו והעבט.   13—12 ואין אתה מלוהו—בכסף אתה
מלוהו] א. .ר.   12 דבר אחר] מ. ט. ש״י. .ר.   14—12 כסף בכסף—ופירות בכסף] מ.
אם כסף וכל (טעות מן וכו׳ ?) כסף בכסף אתה מלוהו חוץ (טעות מן ואין ?) את מלוהו
כסף ופירות בכסף.   14 ופירות בכסף] ד. ~ וכסף בפירות.

To Any of My People. If an Israelite and a Gentile stand before you to borrow, "any of My people" should be given preference; if it be a poor man and a rich man, the poor man should be given preference; if it be your own[2] poor and the poor of your city, your own poor should be given preference over the poor of your city; if it be the poor of your city and the poor of another city, the poor of your city should be given preference, for it is said: "Even to the poor with thee."[3]

Even to the Poor with Thee, Thou Shalt Not Be to Him as a Dunner. "To the poor with thee" you may not be like a dunner, but you may be like a dunner to the rich.

Thou Shalt Not Be to Him as a Dunner. You shall not allow yourself to be seen by him too frequently.

Neither Shall Ye Lay upon Him Interest. What purpose is there in saying this? Since it says: "Thou shalt not give him thy money upon interest" (Lev. 25.37) there is a warning to the lender that he should not lend on interest. You interpret it as being a warning to the lender that he should not lend on interest. Perhaps it is a warning to the borrower? When it says: "Take thou not of him" (ibid. 25.36), behold the warning to the borrower is there stated.[4] Why then does Scripture say here: "Thou shalt not give him thy money upon interest"? It is a warning to the lender that he should not lend upon interest. So far I know only of a warning to the lender and to the borrower. But how would I know of a warning to the guarantor, to the witnesses, and to the notary? Therefore it says here: "Neither shall ye lay upon him interest"—in any capacity at all. In this connection the sages said: He who lends on interest transgresses five commandments, namely: "Not to give" (ibid. v. 37), "and not to take" (ibid. v. 36), "Thou shalt not be to him as a dunner" (Ex. 22.24), "Neither shall ye

2. I.e., your relatives.
3. The one nearer to thee should be given preference.
4. "Take thou not of him" is interpreted to mean, take not a loan on interest (see Introduction and cf. Commentaries, esp. *Beer Abraham,* Warsaw, 1927).

את עמי ישראל וגוי עומדים לפניך ללוות
עמי קודם עני ועשיר עני קודם ענייך ועניי עירך
ענייך קודמין לעניי עניי עירך ועניי עיר
אחרת עניי עירך קודמין שנאמר את העני עמך.
את העני עמך לא תהיה לו כנושה
לעני שעמך לא תהיה לו כנושה אבל הווה את
לעשיר כנושה.
לא תהיה לו כנושה לא תראה לו בכל
זמן.
לא תשימון עליו נשך מה ת״ל לפי שהוא
אומר את כספך לא תתן לו בנשך הרי זה אזהרה
למלוה שלא ילוה ברבית אתה אומר הרי זה אזהרה
למלוה שלא ילוה ברבית או הרי זה אזהרה ללוה
כשהוא אומר אל תקח מאתו הרי זה אזהרה ללוה
אמור ומה ת״ל את כספך לא תתן לו בנשך הרי
זה אזהרה למלוה שלא ילוה ברבית אין לי אלא
אזהרה למלוה וללוה אזהרה לערב ולעדים
וללבלר מניין ת״ל לא תשימון עליו נשך מכל מקום
מכאן אמרו המלוה ברבית עובר משום חמשה
דברים משום בל תתן ובל תקח לא תהיה לו כנושה

15—18 ב״מ ע״א, א׳.　38—22 שם ס״א, א׳; ע״ה, ב׳.　24—30 ספרי דברים רס״ב.
25 ויקרא כ״ה, ל״ז.　28 שם כ״ה, ל״ו.

---

15 את עמי] מ. <.　16 קודם] א. מ. <.　18—17 ענייך קודמין—עניי עירך קודמין].
א. מ. וגו׳.　18 שנאמר] א. מ. ת״ל.　19 את העני עמך] הוספתי.　20 לעני שעמך]
מ. לעם שעמך.　21—20 לא תהיה לו כנושה—לעשיר כנושה] ד. <. / אבל הוה את
לעשיר כנושה]=מ. ט״ב: א. ט. <.　22 לא תהיה לו כנושה] מ. לא תראה לו נפשך
/ לא תראה] מ. שלא תראה.　26 למלוה] מ״ח. ז״ר. ומא״ש. ללוה / ילוה] ד. ~
לו.　27—26 אתה אומר—שלא ילוה ברבית] א. < ד. אתה אומר למלוה.　27 או הרי
זה אזהרה ללוה] ד. או אינו אלא ללוה / ללוה] מ״ח. ז״ר. ומא״ש למלוה.　28 אל
תקח מאתו] א. מ. לא תקח מאתו (א. ~ נשך ותרבית) וגו׳ / ללוה] מ״ח. ז״ר. ומא״ש.
למלוה.　29—30 ומה ת״ל—שלא ילוה ברבית] ד. <.　31 לערב] מ. <.　34 משום]
ד. על.

lay upon him interest" (ibid.), and "nor put a stumbling-block before the blind"[5] (Lev. 19.14). And just as the lender and the borrower transgress five commandments, so also do the guarantor and the witnesses and the notary. R. Judah would exempt the notary. R. Meir says: He who lends on interest, saying to the scribe: "Come and write," and to the witnesses: "Come and sign," has no share in Him who decreed against taking interest.

If Thou At All Take to Pledge, etc. R. Ishmael says: Scripture comes to teach you that you should do your duty, but you may take what is yours.[6]

Thou Shalt Restore It unto Him Up to the Time of the Setting of the Sun. This refers to a garment worn during the day which you must restore to him for the whole day. I thus know only about the garment worn during the day that you must restore it to him for the whole day. How do I know about the garment worn during the night that you must restore it to him for the whole night? Scripture says: "Thou shalt surely restore to him the pledge when the sun goeth down" (Deut. 24.13). On the basis of this the sages said: During the night one may take as a pledge a garment worn by day, and during the day one may take as a pledge a garment worn by night. And one must return the garment worn by day for the day and the garment worn by night for the night.

For that Is His Only Covering. This refers to the cloak. *It Is the Garment for His Skin.* This refers to the shirt. *Wherein Shall He Sleep?* This refers to the skin sheet on his mattress.

And It Shall Come to Pass When He Crieth unto Me. R. Nathan says: Suppose one who left the court, adjudged to owe his neighbor one hundred shekels, has on a garment worth two hundred shekels. His creditor may not say to him: Sell your garment for two hundred

5. This verse is interpreted to mean, not to mislead the ignorant, causing him to sin (*Sifra, Kedoshim* 3, Weiss 88d).

6. I. e., you may take a pledge as security for your loan.

לא תשימון עליו נשך ולפני עור לא תתן מכשול
וכשם שהמלוה והלוה עוברים משום חמשה דברים
כך הערב והעדים והלבלר עוברים רבי יהודה
מתיר בלבלר רבי מאיר אומר המלוה ברבית
ואומר לסופר בא וכתוב ולעדים באו וחתמו אין
לו חלק במי שפקד על הרבית.

אם חבול תחבול וגו' רבי ישמעאל אומר
בא הכתוב ללמדך שתהא עושה מצוה ותהא נוטל
את שלך.

עד בא השמש תשיבנו לו זה כסות יום
שאתה מחזיר לו כל היום אין לי אלא כסות יום
שאתה מחזיר לו כל היום כסות לילה שאתה מחזיר
לו כל הלילה מנין ת"ל השב תשיב לו את העבוט
כבוא השמש מכאן אמרו ממשכנין כסות יום בלילה
וכסות לילה ביום ומחזירין כסות יום וכסות
לילה בלילה.

כי היא כסותה לבדה זו טלית היא שמלתו
לעורו זו חלוק במה ישכב להביא עוד מצע.

והיה כי יצעק אלי רבי נתן אומר הרי
שיצא חייב לחבירו מנה בבית דין ועליו כסות
במאתים לא יאמר לו מכור כסותך והתכסה במנה

40—38 ת"כ שם; ב"מ ע"א, א'; תוס' שם ו', ט"ז—י"ז. י' שם ה', י"א (10d).   48—47 דברים
כ"ד, י"ג.   52—48 ספרי דברים רע"ז. ב"מ קי"ג א'—קי"ד, ב'. י' שם ט', ט"ו (12b). מ"ת
158.   58—53 ב"מ קי"ג, ב'.

36 משום חמשה דברים] א"צ. ש"י. <.   37 עוברים] א. מ. < / רבי יהודה] ד. רבי
א"צ. רבי מאיר.   38 מתיר בלבלר] מ"ח. פוטר את הלבלר א"צ. מוציא את הלבלר
/ מאיר] א"צ. יוסי.   40 שפקד] מ. שסוגר.   42 עושה] א. <.   44 תשיבנו לו] א. וגו'
מה ת"ל מ. ת"ל.   47 כל הלילה] מ. ט. ט"ב. ~ וכל היום.   53 והיה כי יצעק אלי]
א. ~ ושמעתי וגו' ד. ~ ושמעתי כי חנן אני א"צ. ז"י. <.

shekels and get yourself a garment for one hundred and pay me one hundred. In this sense it is said: "For that is his only covering."—You may not deprive him of a garment which is becoming to him.

That I Will Hear; For I Am Gracious. For with mercy have I created the world.

Thou Shalt Not Curse Elohim. Why is this said? Since it says: "And he that blasphemeth the name of the Lord he shall surely be put to death" (Lev. 24.16), we have heard the penalty for it, but we have not heard the warning against it. Therefore it says here: "Thou shalt not curse *Elohim*"—whoever it may be.[7]—These are the words of R. Akiba. R. Ishmael says: This passage speaks of judges, as when it says: "The cause of both parties shall come before the judges"[8] (Ex. 22.8).

Thou Shalt Not Curse the Judge. I thus know only about a judge. How about a ruler? It says: "Neither shalt thou curse a ruler of thy people." It could have read merely: "A ruler of thy people thou shalt not curse," meaning both a ruler and a judge. Why then does it say: "Thou shalt not curse the judge"? To declare that one becomes guilty by cursing either of them. In this connection the sages said: There is a case when through a single utterance one becomes guilty on four counts. A son of a ruler who curses his father becomes thereby guilty on four counts, on the count of "the father" (Ex. 21.17), on the count of "judge" (ibid. 22.27), on the count of "ruler" (ibid.), and on the count of "Thy people thou shalt not curse" (ibid.). R. Judah b. Bathyra says: *Thou Shalt Not Curse Judges nor Curse a Ruler of Thy People.* I might understand this to mean that a person can become guilty only by cursing one who is both a judge and a ruler. Therefore it says: "Thou shalt not curse the judge," thus declaring one guilty on the count of "judge" separately, and on the count of "ruler" separately. But a "ruler" might be such as Ahab and his associates? It says how-

----

7. *Elohim* means God, but it also means judge. The prohibition against cursing *Elohim* is taken by R. Akiba to mean both, not to curse God or the judge.

8. The Hebrew for "judges" in this verse is *Elohim.*

ותן לי מנה לכך נאמר כי היא כסותה לבדה אי
אתה רשאי למנוע הימנו כסות שהיא נופלת לשארו.
ושמעתי כי חנון אני שברחמים בראתי
את עולמי.

60   **אלהים לא תקלל** למה נאמר לפי שהוא
אומר ונוקב שם יי מות יומת עונש שמענו אזהרה
לא שמענו תלמוד לומר אלהים לא תקלל מכל
מקום דברי רבי עקיבא רבי ישמעאל אומר בדיינין
הכתוב מדבר שנאמר עד אלהים יבא דבר שניהם.

65   **אלהים לא תקלל** אין לי אלא דיין נשיא
מנין ת״ל ונשיא בעמך לא תאור אני אקרא נשיא
בעמך לא תאור אחד דיין ואחד נשיא במשמע ומה
ת״ל אלהים לא תקלל לחייב על כל אחד ואחד
בפני עצמו מכאן אמרו יש מדבר דבר אחד וחייב

70   עליו משום ארבעה דברים בן נשיא שקלל את האב
חייב עליו משום ארבעה דברים משום האב ומשום
דיין ומשום נשיא ומשום בעמך לא תאור רבי יהודה
בן בתירה אומר אלהים לא תקלל ונשיא בעמך
לא תאור שומע אני לא יהא חייב עד שיהא דיין

75   ונשיא ת״ל אלהים לא תקלל לחייב עליו משום דיין
ומשום נשיא אי נשיא כאהאב וחביריו ת״ל בעמך

---

61 ויקרא כ״ד, ט״ז.   64 שמות כ״ב, ח׳.   64—68 סנהדרין נ״ו, א׳; ס״ו, א׳.   י׳ שם ז׳,
י׳ (ᵃ25). מס׳ סופרים ד׳, ה׳.   69—79 לעיל נזיקין ה׳.   76—79 ב״ב ד׳, א׳. ש. 152.

---

56 כי היא כסותה לבדה] מ״ח. היא שמלתו לעורו.   63 עקיבא] ד. ישמעאל / ישמעאל]
ד. עקיבא.   64 שנאמר] מ. <.   66 נשיא] מ. ד. ונשיא.   67—68 ומה ת״ל אלהים
לא תקלל] ק. ומה ת״ל ונשיא בעמך לא תאור.   72—71 חייב עליו—ומשום נשיא] ד.
חייב בארבעה דברים משום נשיא ואב ודיין.   73 בן בתירא] מ. <.   75 משום דיין] נ.
ל. ~ ונשיא בעמך לחייב עליו.   76 ומשום נשיא] ד. משום נשיא א. ונשיא / אי
נשיא—וחביריו] ד. ומה / כאהאב וחביריו] מ. כאהז וחביריו.

ever: "Of thy people." I can interpret it to mean only such as conduct themselves in the manner of thy people.

Thou Shalt Not Curse the Judge. I thus know about a judge and a ruler. How about all other people? It says: "Of thy people thou shalt not curse"—in any case.

Thou Shalt Not Delay to Offer of the Fulness of Thy Harvest and of the Outflow of Thy Presses. "The fulness of thy harvest," that is, the first-fruits that are taken from the full crop; and "the outflow of thy presses"[9] means, the heave-offering. "Thou shalt not delay," let not the second tithe precede the first, nor the first the heave-offering, nor the heave-offering the offering of the first-fruits. But I do not know whether the heave-offering should precede the offering of first-fruits or vice versa. You must reason: The offering of the first-fruits, designated by four names—"choicest" *(Reshit)*, "the first-fruits" *(Bikkurim)*, "the heave-offering" *(Terumah)*, and "the fulness of thy harvest" *(Meleah)* —should precede the heave-offering which is designated only by three names. Likewise the heave-offering, designated by three names —"choicest" *(Reshit)*, "the heave-offering" *(Terumah)* and "outflow of thy presses" *(Dema')*—should precede the first tithe which is designated by two names only. Likewise the first tithe, designated by two names—"heave-offering" *(Terumah)* and "tithe" *(ma'aser)*—should precede the second tithe which is designated by one name only. In this connection the sages said: One who gives the heave-offering before the first-fruits, or the first tithe before the heave-offering, or the second tithe before the first tithe, though he violates a prohibition, his act is valid.

Thou Shalt Not Delay to Offer of the Fulness of Thy Harvest and of the Outflow of Thy Presses. The First-Born of Thy Sons Shalt Thou Give unto

9. The Hebrew word רמע rendered in the Bible translations by "the outflow of the press" was understood by the Rabbis to be a designation for the heave-offering or *Terumah* (see Commentaries, and comp. Geiger, op. cit., pp. 466–67, and Strack, *Einleitung in Talmud u. Midrasch*, Munich, 1921, p. 34, note 2; Eng. transl. (1931), p. 255, note 2).

לא אמרתי אלא בזמן שהן נוהגין כמנהג עמך.

אלהים לא תקלל אין לי אלא דיין ונשיא

שאר כל אדם מנין ת״ל בעמך לא תאור מכל מקום.

80   **מלאתך ודמעך לא תאחר** מלאתך אלו

הביכורים הניטלין מן המלא ודמעך זו תרומה

לא תאחר שלא תקדים מעשר שני לראשון ולא

ראשון לתרומה ולא תרומה לביכורים אבל איני

יודע אי זה מהם יקדים אם תרומה לביכורים ואם

85   ביכורים לתרומה אמרת יקדמו הביכורים שהם

קרויין ארבעה שמות ראשית ביכורים תרומה

ומלאה לתרומה שאינה קרויה אלא שלשה שמות

תקדים תרומה שהיא קרויה שלשה שמות ראשית

תרומה ודמע למעשר ראשון שאינו קרוי אלא שני

90   שמות יקדים מעשר ראשון שהוא קרוי שני שמות

תרומה ומעשר למעשר שני שאינו קרוי אלא שם

אחד בלבד מכאן אמרו המקדים תרומה לביכורים

ומעשר ראשון לתרומה ומעשר שני לראשון אף

על פי שהוא עובר בלא תעשה מה שעשה עשוי.

95   **מלאתך ודמעך לא תאחר בכור**

79—78 ת״כ קדושים ב׳ (88ᶜ). שבועות ל״ו, א׳.   94—80 תרומות ג׳, ו׳—ז׳. תרומה ד׳,
א׳. ש. 152.   95—117 לעיל פסחא ט״ז.   127—95 ש. 153.

77 לא אמרתי אלא] ד. < / נוהגין כמנהג] ד.   81 מן המלא] ד. מהמלאה
/ ודמעך זו תרומה] ד. <.   85 אמרת] א. מ. אמרתי.   87 ומלאה] הגהתי=ג. ט. א״א.
ז״י. ומא״ש: א. מ. ק. נ. מ״ח. ודמע ל. ורבעי.   88 תקדים תרומה—שמות] ד.
<. 89 ודמע]=ג. ט. ז״י. א״א. ש״י: א. מ. ד. ומעשר.   94 עשוי] א. מ. ד. ~
ת״ל מ״ח. ~ שנאמר. וליתא ביילקוט ומוחקו בא״א. ועפ״ז השמטתיו.   96—95 בכור
בניך תתן לי] הוספתי=מ״ח: א. מ. וגו׳ ד. <.

Me. Likewise Shalt Thou Do with Thine Oxen. The first-born of human beings are compared to the first-born of beasts, and the first-born of beasts are compared to the first-born of human beings. Just as in the case of beasts a premature birth frees the one born after it from the law about the first-born, so also in the case of human beings a miscarriage frees the one born after it from the law about the first-born. And just as in the case of the first-born of human beings one may give its redemption money to the priest wherever one pleases, so also in the case of the first-born of beasts one may give it to the priest wherever one pleases. Since it says: "And thither ye shall bring your burnt-offerings and your sacrifices . . . and the firstlings of your herd and of your flock" (Deut. 12.6), I might understand that one is obliged to bring them to the Temple. Scripture however says: "Both of man and of beast" (Ex. 13.2), thus declaring the first-born of beasts to be like the first-born of human beings and the first-born of human beings to be like the first-born of beasts. Furthermore, just as one must tend the first-born of human beings for thirty days so also one must tend the first-born of beasts for thirty days.

Seven Days It Shall Be with Its Dam. Why is this said? Because of this. It says: "Then it shall be seven days under the dam" (Lev. 22.27), meaning with its dam. You interpret "under the dam" to mean with its dam. Perhaps this is not so, but it rather means under the dam literally? Scripture however says here: "Seven days it shall be with its dam." Now, just as here it means with its dam, so also there it means with its dam. R. Nathan says: Scripture uses the expression "under," but "under the dam" is only to be interpreted, as meaning after its dam.[10] Perhaps it rather means under the dam literally?[11] You must reason: Here "its dam" is mentioned and there "its dam" is men-

10. I. e., after it came out of the womb, even if its mother died immediately after giving birth to it.

11. I. e., that it must suck from its mother seven days. This would exclude the case of one whose mother died at the moment of giving birth.

בניך תתן לי כן תעשה לשורך הקיש
בכור אדם לבכור בהמה ובכור בהמה לבכור
אדם מה בהמה הנפלים פוטרין בה את הבכורה
אף באדם הנפלים פוטרין בו את הבכורה מה
100 בכור אדם אתה רשאי ליתן פדיונו לכהן בכל מקום
שתרצה אף בכור בהמה אתה רשאי ליתן לכהן
בכל מקום שתרצה לפי שהוא אומר והבאתם שמה
עולותיכם וזבחיכם וגו' ובכרת בקרכם וצאנכם
שומע אני יהיה בחובה להביאו לבית הבחירה ת"ל
105 באדם ובבהמה הקיש בכור בהמה לבכור אדם
ובכור אדם לבכור בהמה מה בכור אדם אתה
מטפל בו שלשים יום אף בכור בהמה תהא מטפל
בו שלשים יום.

שבעת ימים יהיה עם אמו למה נאמר
110 לפי שהוא אומר והיה שבעת ימים תחת אמו עם
אמו אתה אומר תחת אמו עם אמו או אינו אלא
תחת אמו כמשמעו ת"ל שבעת ימים יהיה עם אמו
מה כאן עם אמו אף להלן עם אמו רבי נתן אומר
לא בא הכתוב תחת אלא להדרש תחת אמו אחר
115 אמו או תחת אמו כשמועו הרי אתה דן נאמר כאן

---

102 — 103 דברים י"ב, ו'.   105 שמות י"ג, ב'.   109 — 117 לעיל פסחא י"ח. ת"כ אמור
ח' (99ª).   110 ויקרא כ"ב, כ"ז.

---

98 מה בהמה] ד. מה בכור בהמה.   99 באדם] ד. בכור אדם / בו] ד. בה / מה] א.
מ. <. ט. ומה.   100 ליתן פדיונו] א. מ. ליתנו / לכהן] ד. לכל כהן.   101 שתרצה]=מ"ח:
א. מ. ד. שירצה.   102 — 101 אף בכור בהמה—שתרצה] א. מ. <.   102 שתרצה]
ל. מא"ש. שירצה.   103 ובכרת בקרכם וצאנכם] הוספתי.   104 בחובה] א. ~ עליו
ד. חובה.   106 לבכור בהמה] מא"ש. ~ וכו'.   114 הכתוב] מ. / תחת] א. <.
116 — 114 תחת אמו—להלן אמו] א"צ. <.   115 כשמועו] ד. ממש.

tioned; just as there it is meant that she should be close to it, so also here it can only mean she should be close to it.[12]

Seven Days It Shall Be with Its Dam. Just as the first-born, being holy, sucks from a non-consecrated animal, so also all consecrated animals should suck only from non-consecrated animals. In this connection the sages said: The consecrated animals should not give suck to their young. Nor should the young dam set aside as tithe give suck to her young. All these cases are derived from the case of the first-born. Just as the first-born, being holy, sucks only from a non-consecrated animal, so also in the case of all the other consecrated animals. Their young shall be given suck only by non-consecrated animals. How is it done? Animals which are not consecrated are bought with the money of the sanctuary. These take kindly to the young and give them suck—although they also said: Some people when dedicating animals would make special provision for such cases.[13]

On the Eighth Day Thou Shalt Give It to Me. I thus know only about the eighth day. How about any day after the eighth? You must reason: Here it is said "the eighth" and there it is said "the eighth" (Lev. 22.27). Just as there when it says: "the eighth," it means to allow it on the eighth day and thenceforth, so also here when it says: "the eighth," it means to allow it on the eighth day and thenceforth. And just as here it is considered eight days old on the eighth day itself, so also there it means that on the eighth day itself it is already considered eight days old.[14]

On the Eighth Day Thou Shalt Give It to Me. This is to exclude the young animal wanting in the required time.

---

12. I. e., even if only for a short while (see Commentaries).
13. See Introduction and cf. Commentaries.
14. See Commentaries.

אמו ונאמר להלן אמו מה להלן בסמוך לו אף כאן
בסמוך לו.

שבעת ימים יהיה עם אמו מה בכור
קדש אינו יונה אלא מן החולין אף כולן לא ינקו
אלא מן החולין מכאן אמרו כל הקדשים לא יניקו
את בניהן ומעשרת קלה לא תניק את בנה וכולן
אינן למדין אלא מן הבכור מה בכור קודש אינו
יונק אלא מן החולין אף כולן לא יניקו את בניהן
אלא מן החולין כיצד עושין נוטלין מעות מן הקדש
ולוקחין בהמה מן החולין ומתרחמות עליהן
ומיניקות אותן אף על פי שאמרו אחרים מתנדבין
היו על מנת כן.

ביום השמיני תתנו לי אין לי אלא שמיני
משמיני ולהלן מנין הרי אתה דן נאמר כאן שמיני
ונאמר להלן שמיני מה שמיני שנאמר להלן להכשיר
בו שמיני ומשמיני ולהלן אף שמיני שנאמר כאן
להכשיר בו שמיני ומשמיני ולהלן מה כאן ביום
השמיני שמיני אף להלן ביום השמיני שמיני.

וביום השמיני תתנו לי להוציא מחוסר
זמן.

118—127 מעילה י"ג, א'.　127—125 ת"כ שם (99ל). ספרי במדבר כ"ט. מעילה י"ג:

116 להלן] א"צ. כאן / כאן] א"צ. להלן.　117 בסמוך לו] ד. ~ מהו.　119 כולן] א.
מ. כולהון.　123 את בניהן] ד. ◇.　125 ומתרחמות] ד. ומרחמת.　126 אחרים] א.
מ. ט. ◇.　131 בו] א. ד. בן / שמיני ומשמיני] מ. שמיני א"צ. מ"ח. משמיני.
132 בו] ד. בן / שמיני ומשמיני] מ. שמונה משמיני א"צ. מ"ח. משמיני.　133 ביום
השמיני שמיני] ד. כמו כן.

CHAPTER II
(Ex. 22.30–23.5)

And Ye Shall Be Holy Men unto Me. R. Ishmael says: If you are holy then you are Mine. Issi b. Akiba says: With every new commandment which God issues to Israel He adds holiness to them. Issi b. Gur Aryeh says: "holiness" is mentioned here (Deut. 14.21) and "holiness" is mentioned there[1] (Ex. 22.30). Just as the "holiness" mentioned there implies a prohibition against eating, so also the "holiness" mentioned here implies a prohibition against eating.

Therefore Any Flesh That is Torn of Beasts in the Field. I thus know only about the field. How about the house? Scripture says: "That which dieth of itself or that which is torn of beasts" (Lev. 17.15), thus declaring an animal torn of beasts to be like an animal dying of itself. Just as in the case of an animal dying of itself, it makes no difference whether it dies in the house or in the field, so also in the case of an animal torn of beasts there is no difference whether it is torn in the house or in the field. Why then does it say: "Therefore any flesh that is torn of beasts in the field"? Scripture simply speaks of the usual case. Similarly: "For he found her in the field" (Deut. 22.27). I thus know only about the field. How about the house? Scripture simply speaks of the usual case. Similarly: "If there be among you any man, that is not clean by reason of that which chanceth him by night" (ibid. 23.11). I thus know only about that which chanceth him by night. How about that which chanceth him by day? Scripture simply speaks of the usual case. Similarly: "What man is there that hath planted a vineyard" (ibid. 20.6). I thus know only about a vineyard. How about all other trees? Scripture simply speaks of the usual case. Similarly: "Thou shalt not seethe a kid in its mother's milk" (Ex.

1. The interpretation of Issi the son of Gur Aryeh was originally given to Deut. 14.21. Hence the verse in Ex. 22.30 is referred to in it by the expression "there."

פרשה ב   (שמות כ״ב, ל׳—כ״ג, ה׳.)

ואנשי קדש תהיון לי רבי ישמעאל אומר כשאתם
קדושים הרי אתם שלי איסי בן עקיבא אומר
כשהמקום מחדש מצוה לישראל הוא מוסיף להם
קדושה איסי בן גור אריה אומר נאמר כאן קדושה
5 ונאמר להלן קדושה מה קדושה האמורה להלן
אסורה באכילה אף קדושה האמורה כאן תהא
אסורה באכילה.

ובשר בשדה טרפה אין לי אלא בשדה
בית מנין ת״ל נבלה וטרפה הקיש טרפה לנבלה
10 מה נבלה לא חלק בה בין בבית ובין בשדה אף
טרפה לא נחלוק בה בין בבית ובין בשדה הא מה
ת״ל ובשר בשדה טרפה דבר הכתוב בהוה כיוצא
בו כי בשדה מצאה אין לי אלא בשדה בבית מנין
דבר הכתוב בהוה בו כי יהיה בך איש אשר
15 לא יהיה טהור מקרה לילה אין לי אלא מקרה
לילה מקרה יום מנין דבר הכתוב בהוה כיוצא
בו מי האיש אשר נטע כרם אין לי אלא כרם שאר
כל האילנות מנין דבר הכתוב בהוה כיוצא בו

4—1 ש. שם.   9 ויקרא י״ז, ט״ו.   11—10 ש. שם.   13 דברים כ״ב, כ״ז.   14—13 ספרי
דברים רמ״ג. מ״ת 143.   15—14 דברים כ״ג, י״א.   17 דברים כ׳, ו׳; ספרי דברים קצ״ה.
סוטה מ״ג, ב׳.

---

2 עקיבא] מ. עקביא ד. יהודה.   4 גור אריה] ד. יהודה.   5 קדושה האמורה] ד. >
/ להלן] א״צ. ז״י. ש״י. כאן.   6 אסורה באכילה] א״א. (בשם מפרש) אסורה בהנאה
/ כאן] א״צ. ז״י. ש״י. להלן.   7 אסורה באכילה] א. מ. אסורה בהנאה.   9 נבלה
וטרפה] ד. טרפה ונבלה / טרפה לנבלה] א. נבלה לטרפה.   10 בה] ד. לה.
14—16 כיוצא בו כי יהיה—דבר הכתוב בהוה] ד. >.   17 מי האיש] במקרא שלפנינו,
ומי האיש.   20—18 כיוצא בו לא תבשל—הכתוב בהוה] ד. >.

23.19). I thus know only about the kid. How about any other animal? Scripture simply speaks of the usual case. And so also here in interpreting: "Therefore any flesh that is torn of beasts in the field," you say, Scripture, speaking of the usual case, mentions the place where animals are likely to be torn.

Ye Shall Cast It to the Dogs. "To the dogs" and to such as are like dogs. You interpret it to mean to the dogs and to such as are like dogs. But perhaps "to the dogs" is to be taken literally? Scripture says: "Ye shall not eat of anything that dieth of itself; thou mayest give it unto the stranger that is within thy gates, that he may eat it or thou mayest sell it unto a foreigner" (Deut. 14.21). Now, by using the method of *kal vaḥomer,* we may reason: If an animal dying of itself, which makes its carrier unclean, is nevertheless permitted to be made use of, is it not logical that an animal torn of beasts,[2] which does not make its carrier unclean, should surely be permitted to be made use of? Hence, what must Scripture mean by saying: "Ye shall cast it to the dogs"? To the dogs and to such as are like dogs.—This would suggest to you that the dog was shown more honor than the foreigner: since the animal torn of beasts was assigned to the dog and the animal dying of itself was assigned to the foreigner.[3]—This is to teach you that the Holy One, blessed be He, does not withhold the reward of any creature. It is said: "But against any of the children of Israel shall not a dog whet his tongue" (Ex. 11.7). Said the Holy One, blessed be He: Give him his reward. Now, by using the method of *kal vaḥomer,* we may reason: If God did not withhold the reward due an animal, all the more will He not withhold the reward due a man. And

---

2. The Hebrew term for "torn of beast," טרפה, according to the Rabbis, applies to any injured or diseased animal that could not have lived more than a year (see Ḥul. 42a and 57b) whether as a result of an attack by a wild beast or of any other cause. Such an animal, even if ritually slaughtered, is not permitted to be eaten. If, however, an animal is "torn by a beast" and thereby killed—not ritually slaughtered—it is classed as נבלה, as something that dieth of itself.

3. See Commentaries.

לא תבשל גדי בחלב אמו אין לי אלא גדי שאר כל

20 בהמה מנין דבר הכתוב בהווה ואף כאן אתה אומר

ובשר בשדה טרפה דבר הכתוב בהווה מקום

שדרך בהמות להטרף.

לכלב תשליכון אותו לכלב וככלב אתה

אומר לכלב וככלב או לכלב כשמועו ת״ל לא

25 תאכלו כל נבלה לגר אשר בשעריך תתננה ואכלה

או מכור לנכרי והרי דברים קל וחומר ומה אם

נבלה שהיא מטמאה במשא הרי היא מותרת בהנאה

טרפה שאינה מטמאה במשא אינו דין שתהא מותרת

בהנאה הא מה ת״ל לכלב תשליכון אותו לכלב

30 וככלב ללמדך שהכלב מכובד מן הגוי שהטרפה

לכלב ונבלה לגוי ללמדך שאין הקב״ה מקפח

שכר כל בריה שנאמר ולכל בני ישראל לא יחרץ

כלב לשונו אמר הקב״ה תנו לו שכרו והרי דברים

קל וחומר ומה אם שכר חיה לא קפח המקום קל

19 שמות כ״ג, י״ט.   26—24 דברים י״ד, כ״א.   33—32 שמות י״א, ז׳. / שמו״ר ל״א,
ט׳.

21—20 אתה אומר ובשר] ד. <.   23 לכלב וככלב] ד. לכלב ככלב.   24—23 אתה
אומר לכלב וככלב] ד. <.   24 או] ד. ~ אינו אלא.   25—26 לגר—לנכרי] הוספתי: א.
מ. וגו׳.   26 והרי] ד. והלא.   29—30 אותו לכלב וככלב] ד. <.   30 הגוי] ד. העבד.
31—30 ללמדך—ונבלה לגוי] מ. מ״ח.   31 לגוי] ד. לעבד.   35—34 אם שכר
חיה—שכר אדם] ד. אם חיה כך אדם לא כל שכן שאינו מקפח שכרו.

thus it says: "Even to give every man according to his ways, according to the fruit of his doings. As the partridge that broodeth over young which she hath not brought forth, so is he that getteth riches, and not by right; in the midst of his days he shall leave them, and at his end he shall be a fool" (Jer. 17.10–11). And it continues to say: "Thou throne of glory, on high from the beginning, Thou place of our sanctuary" (ibid. v. 12).[4]

Thou Shalt Not Raise a False Report. Behold this is a warning to one who listens to the slanderous tongue. Another Interpretation: This is a warning to the judge that he should not listen to one litigant unless the other litigant is with him. For it is said: "The cause of both parties shall come before the judges" (Ex. 22.8). Another Interpretation: This is a warning to the litigant that he should not present his case to the judge unless the other litigant is with him. For it is said: "Then both the men shall stand," etc. (Deut. 19.17). Abba Ḥanin says in the name of R. Eliezer: This is to include the oath administered by the judge—that it must be responded to with "Amen." For, if it is not responded to with "Amen," it becomes a vain oath.[5]

Put Not Thy Hand with the Wicked. Suppose one should say to you: So-and-so owes me two hundred dinars, but I have only one witness. Come now and join him in testifying in my favor; you can take one hundred and I shall take one hundred. It is against such conduct that it is said: "Put not thy hand with the wicked," etc. Suppose one is told by his teacher: You know that even if a man should give me all the money in the world I would not prevaricate. But so-and-so does owe me a *manah* and I have only one witness. Come now and join him in testifying in my favor so that I may recover what is due me. It is against just such conduct that it is said: "Put not thy hand," etc.— Such a one would be an unrighteous witness. Such was the conduct of the pure-minded people in Jerusalem: None of them would ever

4. Vv. 11–12 are quoted here gratuitously (see, however, Commentaries).
5. See Commentaries.

35 וחומר שכר אדם וכן הוא אומר ולתת לאיש כדרכיו
כפרי מעלליו קורא דגר ולא ילד עושה עושר
ולא במשפט בחצי ימיו יעזבנו ובאחריתו יהיה
נבל ואומר כסא כבוד מרום מראשון מקום
מקדשנו.

40 **לא תשא שמע שוא** הרי זה אזהרה למקבל
לשון הרע דבר אחר הרי זה אזהרה לדיין שלא
ישמע מבעל דין עד שיהא בעל דינו עמו שנאמר
עד האלהים יבא דבר שניהם דבר אחר הרי זה
אזהרה לבעל דין שלא ישמיע דבריו לדיין עד
45 שיהא בעל דינו עמו שנאמר ועמדו שני האנשים
וגו' אבא חנין אומר משום רבי אליעזר להביא
שבועת הדיין שתהא באמן שאם אין עונה אחריו
אמן עושה אותה שבועת שוא.

אל תשת ידך עם רשע אמר לך איש פלוני
50 חייב לי מאתים דינרין ולי עד אחד בא והצטרף
לי עמו וטול אתה מנה ואני מנה לכך נאמר אל
תשת ידך עם רשע וגו' אמר לו רבו יודע אתה
שאפילו אדם נותן לי כל ממון שבעולם איני מבדא
אלא איש פלוני חייב לי מנה ולי עד אחד בוא
55 והצטרף לי עמו על מנת שאקח את שלי לכך נאמר
אל תשת ידך וגו' עד חמס הוא זה. כך היו נקיי
הדעת שבירושלים עושין לא היה אחד מהם הולך

39—35 ירמיה י"ז, י'—י"ב.   41—40 פסחים קי"ח, א'.   45—40 שבועות ל"א, א', ש.
154.   43 שמות כ"ב, ח'.   43—48 ספרי דברים ק"צ.   45 דברים י"ט, י"ז.   56—49 שבועות
שם.   59—56 סנהדרין כ"ג, א'. איכ"ר ד', ג'.

---

35 וכן הוא אומר] ד. שנאמר.   36—35 ולתת לאיש כדרכיו כפרי מעלליו] הוספתי.
38 מרום מראשון] א. > מ. מרום מראה.   46 אליעזר] ד. אלעזר.   47 אין] א. ~ אתה.
48 עושה אותה] ד. עושה אותו א. עושה אתה / שבועת שוא] א. שבועתו שוא מ"ח
שמע שוא.   50 בא] א. בו.   51 לי עמו] ד. עליו.   52 רבו] מ. רבי / אתה] ד. ~ בי.
53 שאפילו אדם נותן לי] ד. שאלו נותנין / מבדא] ד. מבדה מ. מבזה.   54 אלא איש
פלוני חייב לי מנה] ד. מנה לי אצל פלוני / ולי] ד. עמו / על
מנת שאקח] ד. כדי שאטול.

go to a banquet unless he knew who would be there with him, and none of them would ever sign a document unless he knew who would sign with him. R. Nathan says: "Put not thy hand"—do not let the wicked be a witness, and do not let the robber[6] be a witness, thus excluding violent men and robbers. For they are disqualified as witnesses, as it is said: "There shall not rise up . . . an unrighteous witness against any man" (Deut. 19.15–16). What does it say? "Then shall ye do unto him as he had purposed to do" (ibid. v. 19).

Thou Shalt Not Follow a Multitude to Do Evil. Interpreted simply, this means that you should not follow the majority for evil, but you may follow them for good. How so? If twelve are for acquittal and eleven are for conviction, the accused is acquitted. Suppose thirteen are for conviction and ten are for acquittal, then he is convicted. Well, then, if eleven are for acquittal and twelve are for conviction, I might understand that he should also be convicted. It says however: "Neither shalt thou bear witness in a cause."[7] Now then, the Torah says: You may sentence to death by the testimony of witnesses. And it also says: You may sentence to death on a majority vote. Just as there must be at least two witnesses, so there must be a majority vote of at least two.[8] Suppose eleven are for acquittal and eleven are for conviction and one says: I do not know. Behold, there is a warning to the judge not to swing the vote except for acquittal. For Scripture says: "Neither shalt thou speak up[9] in a cause to turn aside after a multitude to pervert justice."

6. The Hebrew word חמס is interpreted as if it read חמס or חמס.
7. This is understood to mean that one judge—the singular "thou" is used—cannot speak up to turn the decision unfavorably.
8. The expression לא תענה is ordinarily used in addressing the witness and means, "Do not bear false witness." It is used here in addressing the judges in the sense of "Do not speak up," to suggest that the judges must be like witnesses, in that no less than two should determine the decision by swinging the majority.
9. Here the expression לא תענה is rendered as in the Authorized Version, not as above. For here the *Mekilta* wishes to give it another turn, especially appropriate when addressed to the judge.

לבית המשתה עד שיודע מי הולך עמו ולא היה

חותם בגט עד שיודע מי חותם עמו. רבי נתן אומר

אל תשת ידך אל תשת רשע עד ואל תשת חמס עד

להוציא את הגזלנין ואת החמסנין שהן פסולין מן

העדות שנאמר לא יקום עד חמס באיש מה הוא

אומר ועשיתם לו כאשר זמם.

לא תהיה אחרי רבים לרעות ממשמע

שאין אתה הווה עמהם לרעה אבל אתה הווה עמהם

לטובה כיצד שנים עשר מזכין ואחד עשר מחייבין

זכאי שלשה עשר מחייבין ועשרה מזכין חייב או

אחד עשר מזכין ושנים עשר מחייבין שומע אני

יהא חייב ת"ל לא תענה על ריב אמרה תורה הרוג

על פי עדים הרוג על פי מטין מה עדים בשנים

אף מטין בשנים או אחד עשר מזכין ואחד עשר

מחייבין ואחד אומר איני יודע הרי זו אזהרה לדיין

שלא יטה אלא לכף זכות תלמוד לומר לא תענה

על ריב לנטות אחרי רבים להטות.

---

59 — 62 ספרי דברים קפ"ט.   59 — 63 סנהדרין כ"ז, א'. ש. שם.   62 דברים י"ט, ט"ו
(ט"ז?).   63 שם י"ט, י"ט.   64 — 71 סנהדרין ב', א'. י"ז, א'. תוס' שם ג', ז'.   69 — 71 ר'
שם א', א' (18ª).   72 — 74 סנהדרין מ"ב, א'.

---

60 אל תשת ידך] מ. < / אל תשת רשע עד] ד. >.   61 — 62 מן העדות] ד. לעדות.
62 לא יקום עד חמס] לא נמצא במקרא כן: ש"י. כי יקום עד חמס באיש מה הוא (דברים י"ט,
ט"ז) מא"ש. לא יקום וגו' עד חמס וגו' (שם י"ט, ט"ו, — ט"ז).   62 — 63 מה הוא אומר]
ד. מהו.   66 — 67 או אחד עשר — יהא חייב] א. < ק. או אחד עשר מחייבין שומע אני יהא
יהא חייב מ. או אחד עשר מזכין ואחד עשר מחייבין זכאי שלשה עשר שומע אני יהא
חייב.   68 ושנים עשר מחייבין] נ. ל. ~ אחד עשר מחייבין וליתא בט. וא"צ. וש"י.
מחקוהו.   69 לא תענה על ריב] א"צ. ש"י. לא תהיה אחרי רבים לרעות.   70 מטין]
א. ממון (?).   71 או] ד. >.   73 ת"ל] ד. >. ד. שנאמר.

Neither Shalt Thou Favour a Poor Man in His Cause. Why is this said? Because of this: It says: "Thou shalt not respect the person of the poor nor favour the person of the mighty" (Lev. 19.15). From this I know only these prohibitions in their exact form. But how about reversing them? It says here: "Neither shalt thou favour a poor man in his cause." Abba Ḥanin says in the name of R. Eliezer: Scripture here refers to the "gleaning," the "forgotten sheaf" and the "corner."[10]

If Thou Meet. I might understand this in its literal sense, but it says: "If thou see" (v. 50).—Then, I might understand: "If thou see" to mean, even at a distance of a mile. But it says: "If thou meet." How then can these two passages be maintained? The sages fixed the distance at two fifteenths of a mile, that is to say, a *ris.* We thus can learn that by failing to render assistance one violates a positive commandment (Ex. 23.5) and a negative commandment (Deut. 22.4).

The Ox of Thine Enemy. R. Josiah says: This means of a heathen worshiping idols. For thus we find everywhere that the heathen are designated as enemies of Israel, as it is said: "When thou goest forth in camp against thine enemies" (Deut. 23.10), "When thou goest forth to battle against thine enemies" (ibid. 21.10). R. Eliezer says: This passage refers to a proselyte who has relapsed into his former evil predilection. R. Isaac says: This passage refers to an apostate Israelite. R. Jonathan says: This passage actually refers to an Israelite. How then can Scripture say: "Thine enemy"? It is simply this: If one has beaten his son or has had a quarrel with him, he becomes his enemy for the time being.

The Ox of Thine Enemy or His Ass. This is to declare one liable in either case.

Going Astray. "Going astray" can mean only, beyond the Sabbath limits.[11] And although there is no explicit proof for this, there is a

10. One is not to favor one poor man more than the other in the matter of allowing them to gather these gifts (see Lev. 19.9–10).

11. I. e., beyond the territory within which the animals are usually kept (see Commentaries).

ודל לא תהדר בריבו למה נאמר לפי 75
שהוא אומר לא תשא פני דל ולא תהדר פני גדול
אין לי אלא אלו חלופיהן מנין ת"ל ודל לא תהדר
בריבו אבא חנין אומר משום רבי אליעזר בלקט
ושכחה ופיאה הכתוב מדבר.

כי תפגע שומע אני כשמועו ת"ל כי תראה 80
אי כי תראה שומע אני אפילו רחוק הימנו מלא
מיל ת"ל כי תפגע כיצד יתקיימו שני כתובים הללו
שיערו חכמים אחד משבעה ומחצה במיל הוי
אומר ריס נמצאינו למדין שהוא עובר על מצות עשה
ועל מצות לא תעשה. 85

שור אויבך רבי יאשיה אומר זה הוא גוי
עובד אלילים וכן מצינו שהגוים קרוים לישראל
אויבים בכל מקום שנאמר כי תצא מחנה על אויבך
כי תצא למלחמה על אויבך רבי אליעזר אומר
בגר שחזר לסורו הכתוב מדבר רבי יצחק אומר 90
בישראל משומד הכתוב מדבר רבי יונתן אומר
בישראל עצמו הכתוב מדבר ומה ת"ל אויבך אלא
אם הכה את בנו או שעשה עמו מריבה ונמצא אויבו
לשעה.

שור אויבך או חמורו לחייב על זה בפני 95
עצמו ועל זה בפני עצמו.

תועה אין תועה בכל מקום אלא חוץ לתחום
ואף על פי שאין ראיה לדבר זכר לדבר וימצאהו

---

76 ויקרא י"ט, ט"ו.   85—80 ספרי דברים רכ"ב. ב"מ ל"ג, א'. תוס' שם ב', כ"ה. י' שם
ב', י"א (8^d). מ"ת 132. ש. 155.   86—87 ב"ק קי"ג, ב'. סנהדרין ע"ו, ב'. ב"מ ל"ב, ב'.
תוס' שם ג', כ"ו. פסחים קי"ג, ב'.   94—86 מ"ת 118.   88 דברים כ"א, י'.   89 שם כ',
א'.   90—89 ע"ז כ"ו, ב'.   98—97 ספרי דברים רכ"ב. ב"מ ל', ב'. מ"ת 133.
99—98 בראשית ל"ז, ט"ו.

---

77 אלו חלופיהן מנין] ק. חילופיהן חלופי חלופיהן מנין.   83 ומחצה] א. מ. <.
84 נמצאינו למדין] מ"ח. נאמר כאן כי תפגע ונאמר להלן לא תראה נמצאינו למדים.
87 עובד אלילים] א. מ. <. / וכן] נ. ל. מכאן / שהגוים] ד. שעובדי אלילים.
88—87 לישראל אויבים] ד. אויבים לישראל.   88 בכל מקום] ק. נ. מכל מקום.
90 לסורו] מ. לסיאורו.   91—92 רבי יונתן אומר בישראל עצמו הכתוב מדבר] ד. <.
92 ומה] ד. אלא מה / אויבך] ד. על אויבך.   93—92 אלא אם הכה] ד. אלא אם כן
הכה.   93 ונמצא] מ. תמצא ד. נעשה.   100—98 ואף על פי—למה נאמר] א. <.

suggestion of it in the passage: "And a certain man found him and behold, he was wandering in the field" (Gen. 37.15).

Thou Shalt Surely Bring It Back to Him Again. Why is this said? Because it is said: "And if thy brother be not nigh," etc. (Deut. 22.2). I thus know only that the law applies both when he is near and when he is far. But how about when he is not known at all? It says: "And thou know him not"[12] (ibid.).

Then Thou Shalt Bring It Home (Deut. 22.2). The animal found must be such as is usually brought home. This excludes an injured one. *And It Shall Be with Thee,* that is, in your possession. *Until Thy Brother's Inquiry,* that is, until you inquired after your brother. Another Interpretation : *Until Thy Brother's Inquiry,* about it. You must find out whether your brother is a deceiver or not. Another Interpretation: *Until Thy Brother's Inquiry.* Until public announcement has been made about his loss. *And Thou Shalt Restore It to Him.* The animal found must be such as pays for its keep by its work, and not one the keep of which would entail a loss.

If Thou See. I might understand this to mean, even at a distance of a mile. But it says: "If thou meet." Then, I might understand: "If thou meet" in its literal sense. But it says: "If thou see." How then can these two passages be maintained? The sages fixed the distance at two fifteenths of a mile, i. e. a *ris.*

And Wouldest Forbear to Help Him, Thou Shalt Surely Help with Him. We thus find that by failing to render assistance one violates a positive commandment (Ex. 23.5) and a negative commandment (Deut. 22.4).

Lying. But not one which is in the habit of lying down.

Under Its Burden. But not under an overload. Another Interpretation: *Under Its Burden.* But not if the load is by its side.

---

12. There is something missing here in the text (See Introduction and cf. Commentaries).

אי והנה תועה בשדה.

‎100 **השב תשיבנו לו** למה נאמר לפי שהוא
אומר ואם לא קרוב אחיך וגו׳ אין לי אלא בזמן
שהוא קרוב ורחוק אם אינו מכירו מנין ת״ל ולא
ידעתו.

ואספתו מציאה שדרכה להאסף להוציא
‎105 את השבורה. **והיה עמך** ברשותך. **עד דרוש
אחיך** עד שתדרוש את אחיך דבר אחר עד דרוש
אחיך אותו אתה צריך לבדוק את אחיך אם רמאי
הוא אם אינו רמאי דבר אחר עד דרוש אחיך עד
שיצא עליו כרוז. **והשיבותו לו** מציאה שהיא
‎110 עושה ואוכלת ולא מציאה שיש עמה הפסד.

כי תראה שומע אני אפילו רחוק הימנו מלא
מיל ת״ל כי תפגע או כי תפגע שומע אני כשמועו
ת״ל כי תראה כיצד יתקיימו שני כתובים הללו
שיערו חכמים אחד משבעה ומחצה במיל הוי אומר
‎115 ריס.

וחדלת מעזוב לו עזוב תעזוב עמו
נמצינו למדין שהוא עובר על מצות עשה ועל מצות
לא תעשה.

רובץ ולא רבצן. **תחת משאו** ולא יתר על
‎120 משאו דבר אחר תחת משאו ולא שיהא משאו בצדו.

And Wouldest Forbear to Help Him. There are cases where you may forbear from helping and there are cases where you must help. How so? If the ass belongs to an Israelite and the load to a Gentile, then: "Thou shalt surely help with him." If the ass belongs to a Gentile and the load to an Israelite, "Thou wouldest forbear to help him." Thus, there are cases where you may forbear from helping and there are cases where you must help. If the animal is in a cemetery, the finder, if he is a priest, shall not defile himself on its account. Suppose his father says to him: Defile yourself, I might think that he should defile himself because a positive commandment takes precedence over a negative commandment?[13] But: "And wouldest forbear to help him" is said in this sense: There are cases where you may forbear from helping and there are cases where you may not forbear from helping. Suppose his father says to him: Do not help him unload, do not help him load, do not return his lost animal to him—in all these cases he should not listen to his father, because both he and his father are obliged to obey the commandments.

Thou Shalt Surely Help with Him. Why is this said? Because of this: It is said: "Thou shalt surely help him to lift them up again" (Deut. 22.4). From this I know only as regards loading. How about unloading? It says here: "Thou shalt surely help with him." R. Josiah says: Both in this passage (Ex. 23.5) and in that passage (Deut. 22.4) Scripture deals with unloading. I thus know only about unloading. How about loading? It is but logical: If you are commanded about helping in unloading, which one can do by oneself, is it not logical that you surely are commanded about helping in loading, which one cannot do by oneself? For Scripture mentions that which is lighter so that you learn from it about that which is more difficult. R. Judah b. Bathyra says: "Thou shalt surely help with him," means unloading.

13. I. e., he is to disregard the negative commandment which forbids the priest to defile himself in favor of the positive commandment to honor his father and do his bidding.

וחדלת מעזוב לו פעמים שאתה חדל
פעמים שאתה עוזב כיצד חמור של ישראל ומשאוי
של גוי עזוב תעזוב עמו חמור של גוי ומשאוי של
ישראל וחדלת מעזוב לו פעמים שאתה חדל
125 פעמים שאתה עוזב היה בין הקברות לא יטמא לו
אמר לו אביו הטמא יכול יטמא מפני שמצות עשה
קודמת למצות לא תעשה לכך נאמר וחדלת מעזוב
לו פעמים שאתה חדל ופעמים שאין אתה חדל אמר
לו אביו אל תפרוק עמו אל תטעון עמו אל תחזיר
130 לו אבדתו הרי זה לא ישמע לו מפני שהוא ואביו
חייבין במצות.

עזוב תעזוב עמו למה נאמר לפי שהוא
אומר הקם תקים עמו אין לי אלא טעינה פריקה
מנין ת״ל עזוב תעזוב עמו רבי יאשיה אומר אחד
135 זה ואחד זה בפריקה הכתוב מדבר אין לי אלא
פריקה טעינה מנין דין הוא ומה אם פריקה שהוא
יכול לפרוק בפני עצמו הרי את מוזהר עליה טעינה
שאינו יכול לטעון בפני עצמו אינו דין שתהא מוזהר
עליה מפני שדבר הכתוב בקל ללמוד ממנו את
140 החמור רבי יהודה בת בתירה אומר עזוב תעזוב

---

125 — 121 ב״מ ל״ב, ב׳. מ״ת 134. ש. 155.   125 — 124 ספרי דברים רכ״ה. ב״מ ל״ב, א׳.
131 — 125 ב״מ שם.   133 דברים כ״ב, ד׳.   141 — 140 ספרי דברים רכ״ב.

---

122 כיצד] א. מ. >.   126 אמר לו] מ. אם אמר לו / הטמא] א. מ. יטמא / יכול] א.
מ. ק. ט. >.   128 שאין אתה חדל] מ. שאתה עוזב.   130 שהוא ואביו] ד. שאביו
ואמו.   132 למה נאמר] ד. לכך נאמר.   136 דין] א. ודין מ. בדין.   137 הרי את] ד.
הרי זה / עליה] ק. עליו.   138 שתהא] ד. שיהא.   139 מפני שדבר] ג. לכך דבר /
בקל] ד. בהווה בקל.

"Thou shalt surely help him to lift them up again," means loading.
On the basis of this interpretation R. Simon b. Yoḥai used to say: Just
as it is a biblical commandment to help in unloading, so also is it a
biblical commandment to help in loading. *Thou Shalt Surely Help with
Him.* Why is this said? Because it says: "Thou shalt surely help him to
lift them up again"[14] (Deut. 22.4). So far I know only about helping
in unloading and in loading. How about helping the animal itself? It
says: "Thou shalt surely help him to lift them up again" (ibid.).

Thou Shalt Surely Help Him to Lift Them Up Again. Provided that
you are like him.[15]

CHAPTER III
(Ex. 23.6–12)

Thou Shalt Not Pervert the Judgment for Thy Needy in His Cause.[1]
Why is this said? Because it says: "Neither shalt thou favour a poor
man in his cause" (v. 3), from which I know only about the poor. But
how about the needy poor? It says here: "Thou shalt not pervert the
judgment for thy needy in his cause." Abba Ḥanin says in the name
of R. Eliezer: Scripture here refers to "gleaning," the "forgotten sheaf,"
and the "corner." If you have in a trial before you a wicked man and a
pious man, do not say: Since this man is wicked I will turn the judgment against him. It is with reference to this that it is said: "Thou

---

14. There is something missing in our text here. The equivalent of the following sentence: "From which I know only as regards loading. How about
unloading? It says here: 'Thou shalt surely help him,' " was probably omitted by a
mistake of the copyists (cf. Commentaries).

15. I. e., able to do that kind of work (see Commentaries).

1. This rendering is required by the *Mekilta*, which takes this verse to be a
prohibition against perverting the judgment in favor of the needy (see Yer. Peah
4.8 (18c) and cf. Commentaries).

עמו פריקה הקם תקים עמו טעינה מכאן היה רבי

שמעון בן יוחאי אומר כשם שהפריקה מן התורה

כך טעינה מן התורה. עזוב תעזוב עמו למה נאמר

לפי שהוא אומר הקם תקים עמו אין לי אלא פריקה

וטעינה בהמה עצמה מנין ת"ל הקם תקים עמו. 145

הקם תקים עמו בזמן שאתה שוה לו.

פרשה ג   (שמות כ"ג, ו'—י"ב.)

לא   תטה   משפט   אביונך   בריבו   למה

נאמר לפי שהוא אומר ודל לא תהדר בריבו אין

לי אלא דל עני תאב מנין ת"ל לא תטה משפט

אביונך בריבו אבא חנין אומר משום רבי אליעזר

בלקט שכחה ופאה הכתוב מדבר. רשע וכשר   5

עומדין לפניך בדין שלא תאמר הואיל ורשע הוא

141—143 ב"מ ל"ב, א'.   146 שם. ספרי דברים רכ"ה.
5—4 ר' פיאה ד', ח' (18c).   8—5 ש. 155.

141—142 ר' שמעון בן יוחאי] ד. ר' ישמעאל.   143—144 עזוב תעזוב עמו—תקים עמו]
ג. > ועיין א"צ.   145 ת"ל הקם תקים עמו] ש"י.   ת"ל עזוב תעזוב עמו ועיין מא"ש.
146 הקם תקים עמו] ש"י.   עזוב תעזוב עמו.
4 חנין] ד. חנן.

shalt not pervert the judgment of thy needy in his cause"—of one who is poor in good deeds.

Keep Thee Far from a False Matter. This is a warning to those who indulge in slanderous talk. Another Interpretation: *Keep Thee Far from a False Matter.* This is a warning to the judge not to allow an uncultivated person to sit with him in judgment. Another Interpretation: He should not allow advocates to function by his side. For it is said: "The cause of both parties shall come before the judges" (Ex. 22.8).

R. Nathan says: *Keep Thee Far from a False Matter.* Behold, here is a warning to keep away from heresy. And thus it says: "And I find more bitter than death," etc.[2] (Eccl. 7.26). And it also says: "But the king shall rejoice in God; every one that sweareth by Him shall glory; for the mouth of them that speak lies shall be stopped" (Ps. 63.12). Another Interpretation: *Keep Thee Far from a False Matter.* Suppose a scholar is sitting and stating a *halakah* correctly and a fellow scholar who is listening to it says to himself: I am going first to refute and disprove it and then I will reconstruct it—all for the purpose of being called learned. Against such conduct it is said: "Keep thee far from a false matter." Such a one is a speaker of falsehoods.

And the Innocent and Righteous Slay Thou Not. Suppose one witness testifies that a certain person worships the sun and another witness testifies that he worships the moon. I might understand that these two witnesses shall be considered joined together and that person be declared guilty. But it says: "And the innocent and righteous slay thou not."[3] Suppose they see him pursuing his fellow-man to kill him with a sword in his hand. They say to him: Know you that the man you are after is a son of the Covenant, and the Torah has said: "Whoso sheddeth man's blood, by man shall his blood be shed" (Gen. 9.6)?

2. "The woman" mentioned in the continuation of the verse is understood to be a personification of heresy, just as the woman against whom Prov. 5.8 warns was understood to be heresy (see 'Ab. Zarah 17a).

3. He has not been proved guilty, since there has been only one witness against him on each count.

הרי אני מטה עליו את הדין לכך נאמר לא תטה
משפט אביונך בריבו אביון הוא במצות.

מדבר שקר תרחק הרי זה אזהרה למדבר
לשון הרע דבר אחר מדבר שקר תרחק הרי זה
אזהרה לדיין שלא ישב אצלו דיין בור דבר אחר
שלא יעמיד אצלו סניגורין שנאמר עד האלהים
יבא דבר שניהם רבי נתן אומר מדבר שקר תרחק
הרי זה אזהרה לפרוש מן המינות וכן הוא אומר
ומוצא אני מר ממות וגו' ואומר והמלך ישמח
באלהים יתהלל כל הנשבע בו כי יסכר פי דוברי
שקר דבר אחר מדבר שקר תרחק היה חבר יושב
ומדבר הלכה כראוי ושמע חברו ואמר הרי אני
פורכה וסותרה מידו וחוזר ובונה אותה בשביל
שיקרא חכם לכך נאמר מדבר שקר תרחק דובר
שקרים הוא זה.

ונקי וצדיק אל תהרוג היה אחד מעידו
שהוא עובד לחמה ואחד מעידו שהוא עובד ללבנה
שומע אני שיצטרפו זה עם זה ויהא חייב ת"ל ונקי
וצדיק אל תהרוג ראוהו רודף אחר חברו להרגו
והסייף בידו אמרו לו הוי יודע שהוא בן ברית
והתורה אמרה שופך דם האדם באדם דמו ישפך

---

13 — 9 שבועות ל', ב'.   13 — 12 שמות כ"ב, ח'.   17 — 13 ספרי במדבר קט"ו.   15 קהלת
ז', כ"ו.   17 — 15 תהלים ס"ג, י"ב.   21 — 17 שבועות ל"א, א'.   31 — 25 סנהדרין ל"ז,
ב'. תוס' שם ח', ג', י' שם ד', י"א (22b).   27 בראשית ט', ו'.

---

7 לכך נאמר] ד. תלמוד לומר.   8 אביון] מ. עני.   10 — 9 מדבר שקר—דבר אחר] א.
<.   21 — 9 הרי זה אזהרה—דובר שקרים הוא זה] ד. וגומר כדכתיב. ועיין מא"ש.
12 סניגורין] א. ט. סנגרון.   15 והמלך] מ. המלך.   17 — 16 יתהלל כל—פי דוברי שקר
הוספתי: א. מ. ט. וגו'.   21 — 17 דבר אחר—דובר שקרים הוא זה] ט. <.   19 פורכה]
ל"ט. פורצה.   20 שיקרא] ל"ט. שאקרא.   22 היה אחד ד. כי אלו היה אחד.   23 ואחד
מעידו שהוא] ד. ואחד.   27 והתורה אמרה] מ. ד. ~ ונקי וצדיק אל תהרוג ואומר.

But he says to them: I know all about that. The witnesses then lose sight
of him. After a while, however, they find the one who had been pursued slain but still writhing, and blood dripping from the sword in the
hand of the pursuer. I might understand that he should be declared
guilty. But it says: "And the innocent and righteous slay thou not."[4]

Once Simon the son of Shetaḥ sentenced to death one false witness against whom an alibi had been established.[5] Judah b. Tabbai
then said to him: May I not live to see the Consolation[6] if you did not
shed innocent blood. For the Torah said: You may sentence to death
on the evidence of witnesses, and also, you may sentence witnesses to
death on the basis of an alibi. Just as there must be two witnesses giving evidence, so also must there be two against whom an alibi is established.[7] And once Judah b. Tabbai entered a ruin and found a slain
man still writhing, and a sword still dripping blood was in the hand of
the apparent slayer. Said Judah b. Tabbai to him. May[8]—come upon
me if it be not true that either I or you killed him. However what can
I do since the Torah has said: "At the mouth of two witnesses . . .
shall a matter be established" (Deut. 19.15)? But He who knows all,
even the thoughts of man, will exact punishment of that man. Hardly
had he come out when a serpent bit that man and he died.

4. There is only circumstantial evidence for his having committed the crime.
In Jewish law this is not considered sufficient.

5. Such a witness is subject to the same punishment that he had purposed to
bring upon his victim. See Deut. 19.19–21 and M. Sanh. 11.1,6 and Mak. 1.4.
The witness in question testified in a case of capital punishment. Comp. also Geiger, op. cit., p. 140–141.

6. "May I live to see," אראה, in our text is a euphemism for "may I not live to
see," לא אראה. To utter the evil is usually avoided because of the fear that uttering
it would bring it about.

7. An alibi established against only one of the witnesses does not subject him
to the law of Deut. 19.19. For his evidence alone as one witness would have been
considered insufficient to effect the harm which "he had purposed to do unto his
brother."

8. The punishment which he invoked upon himself is omitted from our text
for fear of bad luck (see above, note 6).

ואמר להם יודע אני על מנת כן והעלימו העדים

את עיניהם לאחר זמן מצאו הרוג מפרפר והסייף

מנטף דם מיד ההורג שומע אני יהא חייב ת״ל ונקי

וצדיק אל תהרוג. כבר הרג שמעון בן שטח עד

זוםם אמר לו יהודה בן טבאי אראה בנחמה אם

לא שפכת דם נקי ואמרה תורה הרוג על פי עדים

הרוג על פי זוממים מה עדים בשנים אף זוממים

בשנים וכבר נכנס יהודה בן טבאי לחורבה ומצא

שם הרוג מפרפר והסייף מנטף דם מיד ההורג

אמר לו יהודה בן טבאי תבא עלי אם לא אני או

אתה הרגנוהו אבל מה אעשה שהרי אמרה תורה

על פי שנים עדים יקום דבר אבל היודע ובעל

המחשבות הוא יפרע מאותו האיש לא הספיק

לצאת משם עד שהכישו נחש ומת.

31—35 מכות ה׳, ב׳. תוס׳ סנהדרין ו׳, ו׳.   41—35 סנהדרין ל״ז, ב׳. תוס׳ שם ח׳, ג׳.
ר׳ שם ד׳, י״א (22ᵇ).   39 דברים י״ט, ט״ו.

28 על מנת] מ״ח. ועל מנת נ. ל. עלמות.   29 לאחר זמן] ד. ואם כן א״צ. ואחר כך
/ מצאו] ד. מצאנוהו.   31 שמעון בן שטח] ט. ש״י. יהודה בן טבאי.   32 יהודה בן
טבאי] ט. ש״י. שמעון בן שטח.   37 יהודה בן טבאי תבא עלי אם לא] א״צ. >.
37—38 אני או אתה] ק. אני ואתה ט. אני אומר שאתה.   38 הרגנוהו] ט. הרגתו.
39 עפ״י שנים עדים יקום דבר] עפ״י שני עדים שלפנינו, על פי שני עדים או על פי שלשה עדים
יקום דבר.   41 לצאת משם] ד. לומר.

And the Innocent and Righteous Slay Thou Not. Suppose one comes out from court declared guilty but after a while they find evidence of his innocence. I might think that he should still be considered guilty. But it says: "And the innocent slay thou not." Has he come out from My court the same as he came out from your court? It is to teach you this that Scripture says: "For I will not justify the wicked."[9] *And the Righteous Slay Thou Not.* Suppose one comes out from court acquitted and after a while they find evidence of his guilt. I might understand that they should bring him back for a new trial. But it says: "And the righteous slay thou not." You might think that just as he came out acquitted from your court, he also came out acquitted from My court. It says however: "For I will not justify the wicked."[10] Now, by using the method of *kal vaḥomer,* you can reason thus: If with regard to meting out evil, which is of less importance, the Torah says: "For I will not justify the wicked," how much more should it be so with regard to meting out good, which is of great importance!

And Thou Shalt Take No Gift. Lest you say: I will receive money but will not pervert the judgment, Scripture says: "For a gift doth blind the eyes of the wise" (Deut. 16.19). Now, by using the method of *kal vaḥomer,* you can reason: If of him who takes a gift with the understanding not to pervert the judgment the Torah says: "For a gift doth blind," how much more does this apply to one who accepts a gift with the understanding that he is to pervert the judgment! *For a Gift Doth Blind the Eyes of the Wise.* That is, of those learned in the law. You interpret it to mean the eyes of those who are learned in the law. Perhaps it means the eyes of those who are wise, literally? It says however: "For a gift blindeth them that have sight" (Ex. 23.8), which

9. It was but a human court, liable to make a mistake, that declared him guilty, and its verdict should be revoked when evidence of his innocence is found. Not to give him a new trial would be wickedness which God would not justify (see Introduction and cf. Commentaries).

10. The human court, having once declared him innocent, cannot slay him. Before God, however, this man is wicked, and will not be justified.

ונקי וצדיק אל תהרוג והרי שיצא

מבית דין חייב ואחר כך מצאו לו זכות שומע אני

יהא חייב ת״ל ונקי אל תהרוג כשם שיצא מבית

דינך כך יצא מבית דיני ת״ל כי לא אצדיק רשע.

45 וצדיק אל תהרוג הרי שיצא מבית דין זכאי ואחר

כך מצאו לו חובה שומע אני יחזירוהו ת״ל וצדיק

אל תהרוג יכול כשם שיצא במית דינך זכאי כך

יצא מבית דיני ת״ל כי לא אצדיק רשע והרי דברים

50 קל וחומר ומה אם מדת הפורענות מעוטה אמרה

תורה כי לא אצדיק רשע קל וחומר למדת הטובה

מרובה.

ושוחד לא תקח שמא תאמר הריני נוטל

ממון ואיני מטה את הדין ת״ל כי השוחד יעור עיני

55 חכמים והרי דברים קל וחומר ומה אם הנוטל על

מנת שלא להטות אמרה תורה כי השוחד יעור קל

וחומר הנוטל על מנת להטות. **כי השוחד יעור**

עיני חכמים בתורה אתה אומר בתורה או עיני

חכמים כשמועו ת״ל כי השוחד יעור פקחים אלו

52 — 42 סנהדרין ל״ג, ב׳. י׳ שם ד׳, ג׳ (22ab).‏ ספרי דברים קמ״ד. ש. 156.‏ 66 — 53 כתובות
ק״ה, א׳ — ב׳. ספרי דברים שם. מ״ת 98.‏ 55 — 45 דברים ט״ז, י״ט.

────────────

44 ונקי] ד. ~ וצדיק.‏ 44 — 45 כשם שיצא—לא אצדיק רשע] א״צ. ז״ר. > ט. א״א.
ש״י. יכול כשם שיצא מבית דינך זכאי כך יצא מבית דיני (ט. א״א. דינו של מעלה)
ת״ל כי לא אצדיק רשע.‏ 47 יחזירוהו] ד. יהא חייב.‏ 48 אל] מ. לא / יכול] הוספתי=ט.
א״א. ש״י.‏ 49 דיני] מ. דינו.‏ 53 שמא תאמר] א. מ. ק. > ט. ג. שלא תאמר.
54 ת״ל] מ. שנאמר.‏ 55 — 54 עיני חכמים] ק. <.‏ 58 — 55 והרי דברים ק״ו — כי השוחד
יעור עיני חכמים] ד. <.‏ 58 עיני חכמים] א. וגו׳ / בתורה] ד. < / או עיני] ד. / או אינו
אלא.‏ 59 פקחים] ק. נ. עיני פקחים.

must mean such as are bright of mind, who on the basis of their own knowledge can decide what is unclean and what is clean.[11] In this connection the sages said: Whosoever takes money and perverts judgment will not leave this world before the light of his eyes will be diminished. R. Nathan says: Before one of these three things will happen to him: Either his mind will become confused with respect to the knowledge of the Torah so that he will declare unclean what is clean and clean what is unclean, or he will become dependent upon charity, or his eyesight will be diminished.

And Perverteth the Words of the Righteous. He changes the words of righteousness which were commanded on Sinai.

Six Years Thou Shalt Sow Thy Field[12] (Lev. 25.2). R. Ishmael says: When the Israelites do the will of God, they have to observe only one year of release in a septennate, as it is said: "Six years thou shalt sow thy field." But when the Israelites do not do the will of God, they are forced to have four years of release in a septennate. How so? One plows one year but cannot sow until the next year, again one plows one year but cannot sow until the next year. Thus they practically have four years of release in a septennate.

And Gather In the Increase Thereof and the Seventh Year (Ex. 23.10–11). This includes the produce of the year preceding the sabbatical year which continued growing for part of the seventh year. I thus know that the produce of the year preceding the sabbatical year which continued growing for part of the seventh year is regarded as produce of the year preceding the sabbatical year. And how do we know that the produce of the sabbatical year which continued growing for part of the year after the sabbatical year is to be regarded as produce of the sabbatical year? It says: "In like manner thou shalt

11. See Introduction and cf. Commentaries.
12. The verse here in Ex. 23.10 reads: "And six years thou shalt sow thy land." It is possible that the comment of R. Ishmael was originally made in connection with the verse in Leviticus, unless we assume that a copyist has by mistake here quoted the verse from Leviticus instead of the one in Exodus.

60 פקחי הדעת שהן מטמאין ומטהרין מדעת עצמן
מכאן אמרו כל הנוטל ממון ומטה את הדין אינו
נפטר מן העולם עד שיחסר מאור עיניו רבי נתן
אומר עד שיהיה בו אחד משלשה דברים הללו
או שדעתו מטורפת בתורה ומטמא את הטהור
65 ומטהר את הטמא או שיצטרך לבריות או שיחסר
מאור עיניו.

וַיִּסְלַף דברי צדיקים שונא דברים
המצודקים שנאמרו בסיני.

שש שנים תזרע שדך רבי ישמעאל אומר
70 כשישראל עושין רצונו של מקום הם עושין שמטה
אחת בשבוע אחד שנאמר שש שנים תזרע שדך
וכשאין ישראל עושין רצונו של מקום הם עושין
ארבעה שמיטין בשבוע אחד הא כיצד נרה שנה
וזורעה שנה נרה שנה וזורעה נמצאו שהן עושין
75 ארבעה שמיטין בשבוע אחד.

ואספת את תבואתה והשביעית להביא
פירות ערב שביעית שנכנסו לשביעית אין לי אלא
פירות ערב שביעית שנכנסו לשביעית שהן כפירות
ערב שביעית ומנין לפירות שביעית שיצאו למוצאי
80 שביעית שהן כפירות שביעית ת"ל כן תעשה לכרמך

---

77 — 76 ת"כ בהר א' (105cd). שביעית ב', ז'. י' שם (82a).

---

65 — 64 שדעתו מטורפת—את הטמא] ד. טירוף דעת בתורה שיטהר טמא או שיטמא
טהור.   67 ויסלף] ד. רבי נתן אומר ויסלף / שונא] רא"ם. ש"י. ומא"ש. משנה.
69 ישמעאל] ד. אליעזר.   75 — 73 הא כיצד—בשבוע אחד] א. מ. >.   74 נרה שנה
וזורעה נמצאו] הגהתי=ט. א"א. ומא"ש ד. נרה וזורעה נמצאו.   76 והשביעית] א.
>.   79 — 78 שהן כפירות ערב שביעית] ד. ט. >.   80 שהן] מ. ד. > / כפירות שביעית]
ד. >.

deal with thy vineyard and with thy oliveyard." Behold then, you reason and establish a general rule on the basis of what is common to these two: The peculiar aspect of the oliveyard is not like the peculiar aspect of the vineyard. Neither is the peculiar aspect of the vineyard like the peculiar aspect of the oliveyard. What is common to both of them is that since their fruit has been grown by the rain of the sabbatical year it is therefore regarded as fruit of the sabbatical year. So also any other produce that has been grown by the rain of the sabbatical year is to be regarded as produce of the sabbatical year.—These are the words of R. Josiah. R. Jonathan says: There is no need of this proof. Has it not already been said: "And what they leave the beast of the field shall eat"? This is to include fruit of the sabbatical year that continued growing for part of the year after the sabbatical year. And what then does it mean to teach by saying: "In like manner thou shalt deal with thy vineyard and with thy oliveyard"? This passage comes merely to set a separate time for the removal of the olives and a separate time for the removal of the fruit of the vineyard.[13]

And the Seventh Thou Shalt Let It Rest and Thou Shalt Abandon It. "Thou shalt let it rest," with respect to working it. "And thou shalt abandon it," with respect to eating its fruit. I thus know only about fruit. How about vegetables? It says: "And thou shalt abandon it"— altogether. Another Interpretation: *And the Seventh Year Thou Shalt Let It Rest and Thou Shalt Abandon It.* This tells that he is to make breaches in the fences of his field in the sabbatical year. The teachers however allowed him to keep it fenced in for the sake of a better social order.[14] One might say: And why did the Torah say this? Was it not in order that the poor people may eat it? Well then, I am going to gather in the fruit and distribute it among the poor. But Scripture says: "And the seventh year thou shalt let it rest and thou shalt abandon it," telling us thereby that he ought even to make breaches in the

13. See Introduction and cf. Commentaries, esp. *Shebut Yehudah.*
14. See Introduction and cf. Commentaries.

לזיתך הרי אתה דן בנין אב מבין שניהם לא הרי הזית

כהרי הכרם ולא הרי הכרם כהרי הזית הצד השוה

שבהן שגדלים על מי שביעית הרי הן כפירות שביעית

אף כל שהוא גדל על מי שביעית הרי הן כפירות

85   שביעית דברי רבי יאשיה רבי יונתן אומר אינו צריך

והלא כבר נאמר ויתרם תאכל חית השדה להביא

פירות שביעית שיצאו למוצאי שביעית שהן כפירות

שביעית ומה ת"ל כן תעשה לכרמך ולזיתך בא

הכתוב ליתן ביעור לזית בפני עצמו ולכרם בפני

90   עצמו.

והשביעית   תשמטנה   ונטשתה   תשמטנה

בעבודתה ונטשתה באכילתה ואין לי אלא פירות

עשבים מנין ת"ל ונטשתה מכל מקום. דבר אחר

והשביעית תשמטנה ונטשתה מגיד שהוא פורץ בה

95   פרצות אלא שגדרו חכמים מפני תיקון העולם

ואומר וכי מפני מה אמרה תורה לא שיאכלו

אותה עניים הרי אני מכניסה ומחלקה לעניים ת"ל

והשביעית תשמטנה ונטשתה מגיד שהוא פורץ בה

85—82 ר"ה י"ד, א'.   90—89 פסחים נ"ג, א'.

81 בנין אב] ד. < / שניהם] ד. ~ כאחד.   82 הצד השוה] א. מ. ט. מה להצד השוה.
86 והלא כבר] מ"ח. שהרי כבר / להביא] מ"ח. להוציא.   88 ומה] א. מ. >.   89 ביעור
לזית] מ. ביאור לזית ק. ביעור מאור.   91 והשביעית תשמטנה] ד. שנאמר והשביעית
תשמטנה א"צ. דבר אחר והשביעית תשמטנה.   93—92 ואין לי אלא פירות עשבים
מנין] ט. ואין לי אלא כרמים וזיתים פירות ועשבים מנין א"צ. ואין לי אלא פירות
האילן פירות הארץ מנין.   96—94 תשמטנה ונטשתה—ואומר וכי מפני] ד. וגומ' מפני
א"א. א"צ. ג. וגו' שלא תאמר מפני.

fences of his field. The teachers however allowed him to keep it fenced in.

That the Poor of Thy People May Eat. One passage says: "That the poor of thy people may eat," and another passage says: "For thee and for thy servant and for thy maid" (Lev. 25.6). How can both these passages be maintained? When the fruit is plentiful, all may eat of it. But when there is little fruit, then it should be: "For thee and for thy servant and for thy maid." R. Judah b. Bathyra says: One passage says: "That the poor of thy people may eat," and another passage says: "For thee and for thy servant and for thy maid" (ibid.). How can both these passages be maintained? Before the time for the removal has come, poor as well as rich may consume it. But after the time for removal has come, only the poor people may consume it, but not the rich.[15]

And What They Leave the Beast of the Field Shall Eat. Why is this said? Because of this: It says: "Thou shalt surely tithe all the increase of thy seed, that which is brought forth in the field year by year" (Deut. 14.22). I might understand that the fruit of the sabbatical year is also meant. But when it says: "For thee, etc. and for thy cattle"[16] (Lev. 25.6–7), it compares man to cattle—just as cattle in the sabbatical year eat what is fit for them, untithed, so also man in the sabbatical year may eat what is fit for him, untithed. You say it comes for this: Perhaps however it comes rather to compare cattle to man—just as man may eat only what has been tithed, so also the cattle should not be given to eat except what has been tithed? It says however: "And what they leave the beast of the field shall eat."[17] Now that you have learned that the beast in the sabbatical year eats what is fit for it untithed, you cannot compare cattle to man, but you must compare

15. See Commentaries.
16. It continues to say in verse 7: "And for thy cattle and for the beast that are in thy land," etc.
17. Here it must mean, "untithed."

פרצות אלא שגדרו חכמים מפני תיקון העולם.

ואכלו אביוני עמך כתוב אחד אומר 100
ואכלו אביוני עמך וכתוב אחד אומר לך ולעבדך
ולאמתך כיצד יתקיימו שני כתובים הללו כשהפירות
מרובין הכל אוכלין וכשהפירות מועטין לך
ולעבדך ולאמתך רבי יהודה בן בתירה אומר
כתוב אחד אומר ואכלו אביוני עמך וכתוב אחד 105
אומר לך ולעבדך ולאמתך כיצד יתקיימו שני
כתובין עד שלא הגיעה שעת הביעור מבערין אותה
עניים ועשירים משתגיע שעת הביעור מבערין אותה
עניים ולא עשירים.

ויתרם תאכל חית השדה למה נאמר 110
לפי שהוא אומר עשר תעשר את כל תבואת זרעך
היוצא השדה שנה שנה שומע אני אף פירות שביעית
במשמע כשהוא אומר לך וגו׳ ולבהמתך הקיש
אדם לבהמה מה בהמה אוכלת מן הראוי לה
בשביעית שלא מעושר אף אדם אוכל מן הראוי 115
לו בשביעית שלא מעושר אתה אומר לכך בא או
לא בא אלא להקיש בהמה לאדם מה אדם אינו
אוכל אלא מן המעושר אף בהמה לא תאכל אלא
מן המעושר ת״ל ויתרם תאכל חית השדה אחר
שלמדת שהחיה אוכלת מן הראוי לה בשביעית 120
שלא מעושר הא להקיש בהמה לאדם אין אתה

---

102 — 101 ויקרא כ״ה, ו׳.   104 — 109 ת״כ שם (106[bc]). שביעית ט׳, ח׳; י׳ שם (39[a]).
125 — 110 ספרי במדבר קי׳. ביצה ל״ד, ב׳. שביעית ט׳, ט׳. בכורות י״ב, ב׳.
112 — 111 דברים י״ד, כ״ב.   113 ויקרא כ״ה, ו׳—ז׳.

---

107 — 105 כתוב אחד אומר—יתקיימו שני כתובים] ד. <.   107 מבערין] ד. היו הכל
מבערין א״צ. היו הכל אוכלים.   108 מבערין] א״צ. אוכלין.   112 — 111 את כל תבואת
זרעך היוצא השדה שנה שנה] הוספתי: מ. וגו׳.   113 — 111 עשר תעשר את כל—כשהוא
אומר] א. <.   113 לך וגו׳ ולבהמתך] הוספתי תיבת וגו׳. א. מ. לך ולבהמתך ד. לך
ולעבדך ולאמתך.   123 — 121 הא להקיש—בשביעית שלא מעושר] מ. ד. <.

man to cattle. Just as the cattle in the sabbatical year eat what is fit for them, untithed, so also man in the sabbatical year eats what is fit for him, untithed.—Hence, what does Scripture mean by saying: "In like manner thou shalt deal with thy vineyard and with thy oliveyard"? What we have interpreted it to mean.[18]

Six Days Thou Shalt Do Thy Work. The Sabbath commemorative of creation is mentioned here in connection with the subject of the sabbatical year, to intimate that the Sabbath commemorative of creation should never be removed from its position.

That Thine Ox and Thine Ass May Have Rest. This passage gives an additional rest to the animal, intimating that it should be allowed to pluck food from the ground and eat it. You say it comes for this. Perhaps however it only means that one should lock it up in the house? You must admit however that this would be no rest but suffering. And when Scripture says: "That thine ox and thine ass may have rest," it must mean to give an additional rest to the animal that it be allowed to pluck food from the ground and eat.

And the Son of Thy Handmaid . . . May Be Refreshed. This refers to an uncircumcised slave. You say it refers to the uncircumcised slave. Perhaps however it only refers to a son of the Covenant?[19] When it says: "Nor thy manservant nor thy maid-servant" (Ex. 20.10), behold, the son of the Covenant is there spoken of. Hence, what does Scripture mean by saying here: "And the son of thy handmaid . . . may be refreshed"? It refers to the uncircumcised slave.

And the Stranger. Meaning the resident alien. You interpret it to mean the resident alien. Perhaps this is not so, but it means, the righteous proselyte? When it says: "Nor thy stranger that is within thy gate" (ibid.), behold, the righteous proselyte is there spoken of. Hence, what does Scripture mean by saying here: "And the stranger"? It refers to the resident alien. His status on the Sabbath is like the sta-

18. See Commentaries.
19. I. e., one who is circumcised.

יכול אלא אדם לבהמה מה בהמה אוכלת מן הראוי
לה בשביעית שלא מעושר אף אדם אוכל מן הראוי
לו בשביעית שלא מעושר הא מה ת"ל כן תעשה
לכרמך לזיתיך לענין שאמרנו.

125

ששת ימים תעשה מעשיך נאמר כאן
שבת בראשית לענין שביעית שלא תסתרס ענין
שבת בראשית ממקומה.

למען ינוח שורך וחמורך הוסיף לו
הכתוב נייח אחד להיות תולש מן הקרקע ואוכל
אתה אומר לכך בא או אינו אלא יחבשנו בתוך
ביתו אמרת אין זה נייח אלא צער ת"ל למען ינוח
וגו' הוסיף לו הכתוב נייח אחד להיות תולש מן
הקרקע ואוכל.

130

וינפש בן אמתך זהו עבד ערל אתה אומר
זה עבד ערל או אינו אלא בן ברית כשהוא אומר
עבדך ואמתך הרי בן ברית אמור הא מה ת"ל וינפש
בן אמתך זהו עבד ערל.

135

והגר זה גר תושב אתה אומר זה גר תושב או
אינו אלא גר צדק כשהוא אומר וגרך אשר בשעריך
הרי גר צדק אמור הא מה ת"ל והגר זה גר תושב

140

---

134 — 129 שבת קכ"ב, א'.   141 — 135 לעיל בחודש ז'. יבמות מ"ח, ב'.   137 שמות כ',
י'.   141 ש. 157.

---

125 לענין] ד. כעניין.   127 תסתרס] א. תסתרם (?) / ענין] א. מ. <.   132 — 129 למען
ינוח—אמרת אין זה נייח] ראבי"ה שבת סי' רנ"ז (הוצאת אפטוביצר צד 338) יכול לא
יניחנו תולש תלמוד לומר למען ינוח שורך וגו' הא אין זה נייח.   135 אמתך] ד. ~
והגר.

tus of an Israelite on a holiday.[20] If one buys uncircumcised slaves from the heathen, their status on the Sabbath is like that of an Israelite on the intervening days of the festival.—These are the words of R. Jose, the Galilean. R. Akiba says it is the other way. In what case does the wine handled by such slaves become forbidden? When they still recall the idol with their mouth. And what would constitute "recalling the idol with their mouth"? Making vows by it.

CHAPTER IV
(Ex. 23.13–18)

And In All Things That I Have Said unto You Take Ye Heed. Why is this said? Because of this: It says: "And thou shalt set the table," etc. (Ex. 26.35). So, if he changes them around, he transgresses a negative commandment. For it is in this sense that it is said: "And in all things that I have said unto you take ye heed." R. Meir says: It is to make the words of the Torah obligatory upon you. R. Eliezer says: It is to make the positive commandments have the force of the negative commandments.[1] R. Eliezer son of Jacob says: Thus far I would know only what the text explicitly states. How about the subtleties of the scriptural section?[2] Scripture says: "And in all things that I have said unto you," etc. Another Interpretation: *And in All Things That I Have Said,* etc. Why is this said? Because it says: "Thou shalt not do any manner of work" (Ex. 20.10), from which I know only about activities that can be regarded as labor. But how about such activities as can be regarded as merely detracting from the restfulness of the day?

20. He is allowed to do on the Sabbath the kind of work which the Israelite is allowed to do on a holiday, i. e., work in connection with the preparation of food.

1. "Take ye heed," תשמרו, means, "do not fail to do." Hence, it has the force of a negative commandment לא תעשה (see above *Baḥodesh*, III, note 7).

2. See Commentaries.

הרי הוא בשבת כישראל ביום טוב הלוקח עבדים
ערלים מן הגוים הרי הן בשבת כישראל בחולו
של מועד דברי רבי יוסי הגלילי ורבי עקיבא
145 מחליף אימתי עושין יין נסך בשעה שמזכירין
עבודה זרה על פיהם ואימתי מזכירין עבודה זרה
על פיהם בשעה שנודרין בהם.

פרשה ד (שמות כ״ג, י״ג—י״ח.)

ובכל אשר אמרתי אליכם תשמרו

למה נאמר לפי שהוא אומר ושמת את השלחן וגו׳
אם שינן עובר בלא תעשה לכך נאמר ובכל אשר
אמרתי וגו׳ רבי מאיר אומר לעשות דברי תורה
עליך חובה רבי אליעזר אומר לעשות מצות עשה
5 ומצות לא תעשה רבי אליעזר בן יעקב אומר אין
לי אלא מה שפרט הכתוב שאר דיקדוקי פרשה
מנין ת״ל ובכל אשר אמרתי אליכם וגו׳ דבר אחר
ובכל אשר אמרתי וגו׳ למה נאמר לפי שהוא אומר
לא תעשה כל מלאכה אין לי אלא דברים שהן
10 משום מלאכה דברים שהן משום שבות מנין ת״ל

147 — 142 ע״ז נ״ז, א׳. תוס׳ שם ג׳, י״א. י׳ שם ד׳, ח׳ (44b).
2 שמות כ״ג, ל״ה. 13 — 8 לעיל פסחא ט׳. לקמן שבתא א׳. שבת י״ח, א׳. 10 שמות
כ׳, י׳.

142 הרי הוא] ד. הרי הן. 142 — 142 כישראל ביום טוב—הרי הן בשבת] א. <. 144 ר׳
יוסי הגלילי] ד. רבי יאשיה. 145 מחליף] מ. אומר מחליף שמזכירין] א. שמכריזין.
פרשה ד׳] ד. <. 8 — 1 ובכל אשר אמרתי—דבר אחר] ד. <. 3 שינן] ט. שנה.
14 — 10 דברים שהן משום מלאכה] ט. < ובהוצאות מאוחרות, דברים שהן אבות מלאכות.

Scripture says here: "And in all things that I have said," etc., to include activities that can be regarded as merely detracting from the restfulness of the day.[3]

And Make No Mention of the Name of Other Gods. This means that you may not cause the Gentile to swear[4] by his deity. *Neither Let It Be Heard Out of Thy Mouth.* This means that you may not swear to him by his deity.

Another Interpretation: *And Make No Mention of the Name of Other Gods.* This means that you may not make the temple of idolatry a meeting place. Do not say to anyone: Where do you live? In the place of such-and-such an idol? Nor say: Wait for me at the place of such-and-such an idol. R. Nathan says: Behold it says: "And they said: 'Come, let us build us a city, and a tower, with its top in heaven, and let us make us a name' " (Gen. 11.4). We would not know what is meant by this "name." But the expression "name" is used here (ibid.) and the expression "name" is used there (Ex. 23.13). Hence, just as there it refers to idolatry, so also here it refers to idolatry.[5] Another Interpretation: *And Make No Mention of the Name of Other Gods*—in praise. But as regards mentioning in reproach, Scripture says: "Thou shalt utterly detest it, and thou shalt utterly abhor it,"[6] etc. (Deut. 7.26). Idols are designated by terms of opprobrium, such as, "ban," "abhorrence," "abomination," "graven," "molten," "stump," "worthlessness," "pains,"[7] "obscenities,"[8] "contaminations," "detestations,"

3. On the terms "labor," מלאכה, and "activities detracting from the restfulness of the day," שבות, see above *Pisḥa,* IX, note 7.

4. The *Hif'il* form תזכירו has causative force; hence, it means not to cause others to mention.

5. R. Nathan's comment was originally made in connection with the passage in Gen. 11.4. Hence that passage is referred to by the expression "here" while the passage here in Exodus is referred to by the expression "there."

6. I.e., declare it to be more detestable by mentioning it in reproach.

7. This is a play on the word עצבים, which is taken as the plural of עצב, "pain."

8. See on "Terafim" I. Löw in *MGWJ,* 1929, p. 314 and 488.

ובכל אשר אמרתי וגו' להביא דברים שהן משום
שבות.

ושם אלהים אחרים לא תזכירו שלא

15 תשביע לגוי ביראתו ולא ישמע על פיך שלא תשבע
לו ביראתו דבר אחר ושם אלהים אחרים לא
תזכירו שלא תעשנו בית ועד ולא תאמר לו היכן
אתה שרוי במקום עבודה זרה פלונית אתה ממתין
לי אצל עבודה זרה פלונית רבי נתן אומר הרי
20 הוא אומר ויאמרו הבה נבנה לנו עיר ומגדל וראשו
בשמים ונעשה לו שם השם הזה אין אנו יודעין מה
הוא נאמר כאן שם ונאמר להלן שם מה להלן
בעבודה זרה אף כאן בעבודה זרה. דבר אחר
ושם אלהים אחרים לא תזכירו לשבח אבל לגנאי
25 ת"ל שקץ תשקצנו. עבודה זרה קרואה לשון פגמה
חרם שקץ תועבה פסל מסכה מצבה אלילים

14—19 סנהדרין ס"ג, ב'. ש. 58—157.   16—19 תוס' ע"ז ו', י"א.   19—23 סנהדרין
ק"ט, א'. ב"ר ל"ח, ח'.   21—20 בראשית י"א, ד'.   25—23 סנהדרין ס"ג, ב'. ע"ז ג',
ח' (43ᵃ).   25 דברים ז', כ"ו.   27—25 ת"כ קדושים א' (87ᵃ).   31—25 אדר"נ ל"ד.

12—13 משום שבות] ט. ~ דבר אחר ובכל אשר אמרתי אליכם תשמרו להביא שביתת
כלים.   14—15 שלא תשביע—ולא ישמע על פיך] ד. ט. <.   16 דבר אחר] א. ד. <.
17 ולא תאמרן] ד. לא יאמר.   20—21 ומגדל וראשו בשמים ונעשה לנו שם] הוספתי:
א. וגו'.   21—22 השם הזה—מה הוא] ד. <.   22 נאמר כאן שם ונאמר להלן שם] ד.
ונאמר להלן שם ונאמר כאן שם, ועיין מא"ש.   23 דבר אחר] ד. רבי אומר.   24 אבל]
א. ~ לא מ. אלא.   25 לשון] א. לשם.

and "provocations."[9] The Holy One, blessed be He, however, is designated by terms of praise, such as, "God," "Judge," "Almighty," "(Lord of) Hosts," "I am that I am," "Gracious and Merciful," "Long-suffering and of great kindness and true," and "Mighty Lord" (Ps. 89.9). Thus it says: "To declare that the Lord is upright, my Rock in whom there is no unrighteousness" (Ps. 92.16).

Three Times Thou Shalt Keep a Feast unto Me, etc. Why is this said? Because of this: It says: "Three times in the year," etc. (Ex. 23.17). I might understand this to mean, at any time one may desire. But it says: "On the feast of unleavened bread, and on the feast of weeks, and on the feast of tabernacles" (Deut. 15.16). This again might mean, on the feast of unleavened bread three times, and on the feast of weeks three times, and on the feast of tabernacles three times. Therefore it says here: "Three times thou shalt keep a feast unto Me in the year."

Three Times. This applies only to such as can travel on foot.[10] *Shall Be Seen.* This excludes the blind.[11] *Thy Males.* This excludes women. *All Thy Males.* This means to exclude the strangers, the *tumtum* and the hermaphrodite.[12] *Thou Shalt Read This Law before All Israel* (Deut. 31.11). This excludes strangers and slaves. *In Their Hearing* (ibid.). This excludes the deaf ones. *Thou Shalt Rejoice* (ibid. 16.11). This excludes the sick one and the minor. *Before the Lord Thy God* (ibid.). This excludes any person who has become defiled. In this connection the sages said: All are under obligation to appear in the Temple

9. The word חמנים is taken to be derived from חמה "anger," "provocation," instead of from חמה, "sun."

10. This interpretation is based upon a play on the Hebrew word for "times," רגלים, which is taken as the plural of רגל, "foot."

11. The Hebrew word for "shall be seen," יראה, is interpreted as if it read יראה, "shall see." Hence the blind are excluded (see Geiger, *Urschrift,* p. 337).

12. "All males" is taken to suggest that they must be completely male. Comp. Geiger in קבוצת מאמרים, edited by Poznanski, Warsaw, 1910, p. 4 ff. and A. Epstein in החוקר, I, Krakau, 1893, p. 179 ff.

עצבים תרפים גילולים שיקוצים חמנים אבל
הקדוש ברוך הוא קרוי לשון שבח אל אלהים שדי
צבאות אהיה אשר אהיה חנון ורחום ארך אפים

30 ורב חסד ואמת חסין יה ואומר להגיד כי ישר יי
צורי ולא עולתה בו.

שלש רגלים תחג לי וגו׳ למה נאמר לפי
שהוא אומר שלש פעמים בשנה וגו׳ שומע אני בכל
זמן שירצה ת״ל בחג המצות ובחג השבועות ובחג

35 הסוכות אי בחג המצות שלש פעמים ובחג השבועות
שלש פעמים ובחג הסוכות שלש פעמים ת״ל שלש
רגלים תחג לי בשנה.

שלש רגלים המהלכין ברגליהם. **יראה**
להוציא את הסומין. **זכורך** להוציא את הנשים.

40 **כל זכורך** להוציא את הגרים טומטום
ואנדרוגינוס. **תקרא את התורה הזאת נגד
כל ישראל** להוציא גרים ועבדים **באזניהם**
להוציא חרשים ושמחת להוציא את החולה ואת
הקטן **לפני יי אלהיך** להוציא את הטמא מכאן

31—30 תהלים צ״ב, ט״ז. 37—32 ספרי דברים קמ״ג. 42—32 מ״ת 95. 35—34 דברים
ט״ז, ט״ז. 46—38 חגיגה ב׳, א׳; ד׳, א׳—ב׳. י׳ שם א׳, א׳ (76ᵃ). ספרי דברים שם.
42—41 דברים ל״א, י״א.

---

28 לשון] א. לשם מ. לשום / אל אלהים] א. אל אלים אלהיך. 30 יה ואומר] ד. >.
33—34 בכל זמן שירצה] ק. בכל מקום ועת שירצה נ. ל. בכל מקום ובכל עת שירצה.
35—36 אי בחג—הסוכות שלש פעמים] הגהתי=ט: א״צ. יכול ג״פ בכל רגל א. מ.
הסוכות שלש פעמים ד. >. 37—36 ת״ל שלש—בשנה] נ. ל. >. 38 שלש רגלים
המהלכין ברגליהם] ד. > מ״ח. להוציא את החגרין. 40 הגרים] ק. נ. חגרים. 42 להוציא
גרים ועבדים] ד. > מ״ח. להוציא עבדים שאינן משוחררין.

except the deaf and dumb, the insane, the minor, the *tumtum,* the hermaphrodite, the lame, the blind, the sick, and the aged.

The Feast of Unleavened Bread Shalt Thou Keep. Commenting on this passage, R. Judah b. Bathyra used to say: "As I commanded thee" means, that you should bring the offering only in the month of Abib.

And None Shall Appear before Me Empty. That is, without sacrifices. You interpret it to mean without sacrifices. Perhaps this is not so, but it means without money? Behold, you must reason thus: Rejoicing is mentioned with reference to man and rejoicing is also implied with reference to God.[13] Just as in the former it means with sacrifices, so also in the latter it means with sacrifices. Another Interpretation: *And None Shall Appear before Me Empty.* That is, without burnt-offerings. But perhaps it only means without peace-offerings? Behold, you must reason thus: Rejoicing is mentioned with reference to man and rejoicing is also implied with reference to God. Just as the rejoicing mentioned with reference to man means with something fit to be brought to the hands of man, so also the rejoicing implied with reference to God must mean with something fit to be brought to God. It is not right that your own table be full while your Master's table be empty.

And the Feast of Harvest, the First Fruit of Thy Labours. The three festivals are mentioned in connection with the subject of the sabbatical year to intimate that the three festivals must not be removed from their place.[14]

Three Times in the Year (Ex. 34.23). Why is this[15] said? Has it not already been said: "Before the Lord God"? And what does Scripture mean to teach by saying: "The God of Israel"? Simply this: He conferred His name particularly on Israel. Similarly: "Hear, O Israel, the Lord our God, the Lord is One" (Deut. 6.5). Why is this said? Has it not already been said: "The Lord our God"? And what does Scripture

13. See Deut. 27.7.
14. I. e., even during the sabbatical year.
15. "This" refers to the last part of the verse: "The God of Israel."

45 אמרו הכל חייבין בראייה חוץ מחרש שוטה וקטן
טומטום ואנדרוגינוס החגר והסומא החולה והזקן.

את חג המצות תשמור מכאן היה רבי
יהודה בן בתירה אומר כאשר צויתיך כדי שלא
תהא מביא אלא אלא בחודש האביב.

50 **לא יראו פני ריקם** בזבחים אתה אומר
בזבחים או אינו אלא בכספים הרי אתה דן נאמרה
שמחה באדם ונאמרה שמחה בשמים מה להלן
בזבחים אף כאן בזבחים. דבר אחר לא יראו פני
ריקם בעולות או אינו אלא בשלמים הרי אתה דן
55 נאמרה שמחה באדם ונאמרה שמחה בשמים מה שמחה
האמורה באדם בדבר הראוי לבא בידי אדם אף
שמחה האמורה בשמים בדבר הראוי לבא בידי
שמים אינו דין שיהא שלחנך מלא ושלחן קונך ריקם.

וחג הקציר ביכורי מעשיך נאמרו
60 שלשה רגלים לענין שביעית שלא יסתרסו שלשה
רגלים ממקומן.

שלש פעמים בשנה וגו' למה נאמר והלא
כבר נאמר אל פני האדון יי ומה ת"ל אלהי ישראל
אלא על ישראל ייחד שמו ביותר. כיוצא בו שמע
65 ישראל יי אלהינו יי אחד למה נאמר והלא כבר

---

47 — 49 לעיל פסחא ב'. ספרי דברים קכ"ז. ר"ה כ"א, א'. ש. 158.   58 — 50 חגיגה ז',
א'.   62 — 73 ספרי דברים ל"א. מ"ת 25.   65 — 64 דברים ו', ד'.

46 והזקן] ד. והקטן.   47 מכאן] ט. <.   48 כאשר צויתיך] הגהתי=ט. ומא"ש: א. מ.
ד. כל אשר צויתיך ג. מ"ח.   ~ למועד חדש האביב שמרהו שיהא אביב בזמנו הא כיצד
עבר את אדר (ג. ~ כדי) שיבא אביב בזמנו.   49 — 48 כדי שלא תהא—האביב] ג. מ"ח.
<.   50 לא יראו] במקרא שלפנינו ולא יראו.   51 בכספים] ט. א"א. בנסכים.
54 — 51 נאמרה שמחה—בעולות או אינו אלא] מ"ח. ש"י. נאמרה חגיגה האמורה
להדיוט ונאמרה ראיה לגבוה מה להלן (ש"י. מה חגיגה האמורה להדיוט) זבחים אף
כאן בזבחים (ש"י. אף ראיה האמורה לגבוה זבחים) ומה הן זבחים עולות (ש"י ~ אתה
אומר עולות) או אינו אלא.   52 בשמים] ד. ט. בשלמים.   55 בשמים] ד. בשלמים.
58 — 55 נאמרה שמחה—לבא בידי שמים] מ"ח. ש"י. נאמרה חגיגה להדיוט ונאמרה
ראיה לגבוה מה חגיגה האמורה להדיוט בראוי לו אף ראיה האמורה לגבוה בראוי לו.
60 יסתרסו] ט. יסתרו מ. יסתרמו.   63 אל פני האדון יי] ד. את פני האדון יי אלהיך.
64 על ישראל] מ. אלהיו של ישראל.

mean to teach by saying: "The Lord is One"? Simply this: He conferred His name particularly on Israel. Similarly: "Therefore, thus saith the Lord, the God of Israel" (II Kings 21.12). But has it not already been said: "The Lord, the God of all flesh" (Jer. 32.27)? And what does Scripture mean to teach by saying: "The God of Israel"? Simply this: He conferred His name particularly on Israel. Similarly: "Hear, O My people, and I will speak; O Israel, and I will testify against thee: God, thy God, am I. I will not reprove thee for thy sacrifices; and thy burnt-offerings are continually before Me" (Ps. 50.7–8). I am God for all those who come into the world, nevertheless I have conferred My name particularly on My people Israel.[16]

Thou Shalt Not Offer the Blood of My Sacrifice with Leavened Bread. Thou shalt not slaughter the paschal lamb while the leavened bread is still there.—These are the words of R. Ishmael. I thus far know only about the slaughtering. How about the sprinkling of the blood? It says: "The blood of My sacrifice." R. Judah says: It means the sacrifice which is entirely Mine. And which one is this? It is the daily burnt-offering *(tamid)*.

Neither Shall the Fat of My Feast Remain All Night until the Morning. This passage comes to teach that the pieces of fat become unfit for use by being kept overnight on the pavement of the Temple floor. And I can then successfully argue this about the limbs of the sacrifice by reasoning thus: Since the pieces of fat are a gift to be wholly burnt on the fire and the limbs of the sacrifice are likewise a gift to be wholly burnt on the fire, it follows that, inasmuch as you have learned that the pieces of fat become unfit for use by being kept overnight on the pavement of the Temple floor, the limbs of the sacrifice should likewise become unfit for use by being kept overnight on the pavement of the Temple floor. One might think that the limbs should become unfit for use even by being kept overnight upon the pile of wood on the altar. But Scripture says: "On its firewood upon the altar

16. See Introduction.

נאמר יי אלהינו ומה ת"ל יי אחד אלא אלא עלינו ייחד
שמו ביותר כיוצא בו לכן כה אמר יי אלהי ישראל
והלא כבר נאמר אלהי כל בשר ומה ת"ל אלהי
ישראל אלא על ישראל ייחד שמו ביותר. כיוצא

70 בו שמעה עמי ואדברה ישראל ואעידה בך אלהים
אלהיך אנכי לא על זבחיך אוכיחך ועולותיך לנגדי
תמיד אלהים אני לכל באי עולם אף על פי כן לא
ייחדתי שמי אלא על עמי ישראל.

לא תזבח על חמץ דם זבחי לא תשחט

75 את הפסח ועדיין חמץ קיים דברי רבי ישמעאל
אין לי אלא אלא זביחה זריקה מנין ת"ל דם זבחי רבי
יהודה אומר הזבח שכלו שלי ואי זה זה תמיד.

לא ילין חלב חגי עד בקר בא הכתוב
ללמד על החלבים שיהו נפסלין בלינה על גבי
80 הרצפה וזכיתי לדון על האיברים הואיל והחלבים
מתנה לאישים ואיברים מתנה לאישים אם למדת
על חלבים שהם נפסלין בלינה על גבי הרצפה
אף איברים נפסלין בלינה על גבי הרצפה יכול
איברים יהו נפסלין בלינה על גבי המערכה ת"ל

67 מלכים ב. כ"א, י"ב.   68 ירמיה ל"ב, כ"ז.   70—72 תהלים נ', ז'—ח'.   74—76 לעיל
פסחא ח'. י' פסחים ה', ד' (32ל). ש. 159. פסחים ס"ד, א'.

72—70 ואעידה בך—לנגדי תמיד] א. מ. וגו'.   71 לנגדי] ד. נגדי.   75 ישמעאל] ד.
~ ר' עקיבא אומר.   76 זבחי] ד. זבחין] (ק. ~ ישפך).   80 הרצפה] מ. המערכה הרצפה.
83 אף איברים—הרצפה] הוספתי=ט. א"א. ש"י. ז"י. א"צ. ומא"ש / יכול] א. מ.
~ אף.

all night unto the morning" (Lev. 6.2), declaring that they may be kept upon the pile of wood on the altar. Now inasmuch as you have learned that the limbs do not become unfit for use by being kept overnight upon the pile of wood on tire altar, I can successfully argue this about the pieces of fat by reasoning thus: Since the limbs are a gift to be wholly burnt on the fire and the pieces of fat are likewise a gift to be wholly burnt on the fire, it follows that, inasmuch as you have learned that the limbs do not become unfit for use by being kept overnight upon the pile of wood on the altar, the pieces of fat should likewise not become unfit for use by being kept overnight upon the pile of wood on the altar. Hence, what must Scripture mean by saying: "Neither shall the fat of My feast remain all night until the morning"? As we have interpreted it.[17]

CHAPTER V
(Ex. 23.19)

The Choicest First Fruit of Thy Land, etc. Why is this section set forth? Because it says: "That thou shalt take of the first of all the fruit of the ground" (Deut. 26.2), from which I know only that fruits are to be brought as the first-fruit offering. But how about liquids? It says here: "Thou shalt bring into the house of the Lord thy God"—in any form. And what is the difference between fruits and liquids? Those who bring the former recite the prescribed section,[1] but those who bring the latter do not. *Which Thou Shalt Bring In from Thy Land.* (Deut. 26.2). This is to exclude tenants on shares, tenants on fixed rents, the holder of confiscated fields, and the robber. *That the Lord Thy God.* This excludes foreigners and slaves. *Giveth Thee.* This excludes women, a *tumtum* and an hermaphrodite. This might mean to exclude

17. Cf. L. Ginzberg in גנזי שעכטער, I, New York, 1928, p. 69.
1. I. e., Deut. 26.5–10.

85 על מוקדה על המזבח כל הלילה עד הבקר על
גבי המערכה אחר שלמדת על האיברים שאינם
נפסלין בלינה על גבי המערכה וזכיתי לדון על
החלבים הואיל ואיברים מתנה לאישים וחלבים
מתנה לאישים אם למדת על איברים שאינם נפסלין
90 בלינה על גבי המערכה אף החלבים לא יהיו
נפסלין בלינה על גבי המערכה הא מה ת״ל לא
ילין חלב חגי עד בקר לענין שאמרנו.

פרשה ה   (שמות כ״ג, י״ט.)

ראשית ביכורי אדמתך וגו׳ למה נאמרה
פרשה זו לפי שהוא אומר ולקחת מראשית כל פרי
האדמה אין לי אלא פירות דרך ביכורים משקין
מנין ת״ל תביא בית יי אלהיך מכל מקום ומה הפרש
5 בין אלו לאלו אלא אלו מביאין וקורין ואלו מביאין
ואין קורין. אשר תביא מארצך להוציא אריסין
וחכורות והסיקריקון והגזלן. אשר יי אלהיך להוציא
גרים ועבדים. נתן לך להוציא נשים טומטום

---

85 ויקרא ו׳, ב׳.

6—1 ספרי דברים רצ״ז.   3—2 דברים כ״ו, ב׳.   8—6 ספרי דברים רצ״ט.

---

85 על מוקדה על המזבח] הוספתי / כל הלילה עד הבקר] נ. ל. לא ילין חלב חגי עד
בקר.   90 אף החלבים] מ. ד. יכול אף החלבים.   91 המערכה] א. ד. הרצפה / הא
מה] ד. >.

פרשה ה׳] ד. >.   7 אלהיך] א. ד. אלהינו.   8 נתן] א. מ. נ. ל. נותן / לך]
הגהתי=ט. א״א: א. מ. ד. לנו.

them from bringing the offering as well as from reciting the prescribed section. But it says: "Thou shalt bring"—in every case. And what is the difference between the one group and the other? The one brings the offerings and recites the prescribed section, while the other brings the offering but does not recite the prescribed section.

Thou Shalt Not Seethe a Kid in Its Mother's Milk. R. Ishmael says: Why is this law stated in three places?[2] To correspond to the three covenants which the Holy One, blessed be He, made with Israel: One at Horeb (Ex. 24.7–8), one in the plains of Moab (Deut. 29.11), and one on Mount Gerizim and Mount Ebal (ibid. 28.69). R. Josiah says: As regards the first of these passages—it is the very first statement of the subject. And first statements cannot be employed for any special interpretation. The second one was said in order to meet the following argument: A clean animal, if it died a natural death, makes one who carries it unclean, and an unclean animal after its death likewise makes the one who carries it unclean. Now, inasmuch as you have learned about the clean animal that its flesh is forbidden to be cooked with its milk, I might think that as regards the unclean animal its flesh should likewise be forbidden to be cooked with its milk. Therefore it says: "In its mother's milk"—excluding the milk of an unclean animal. The third one was said to intimate that it does not apply to human milk. R. Jonathan says: Why is this law stated in three places? Once to apply to domestic animals, once to apply to the beast of chase, and once to apply to fowl. Abba Ḥanin in the name of R. Eliezer says: Why is this law stated in three places? Once to apply to large cattle, once to apply to goats, and once to apply to sheep. R. Simon b. Eleazar says: Why is this law stated in three places? Once to apply to large cattle, once to apply to small cattle, and once to apply to wild animals. R. Simon b. Yoḥai says: Why is this law stated in three places? One is a prohibition against eating it, one is a prohibition against deriving any benefit from it, and one is a prohibition

2. Ex. 23.19; 34.26 and Deut. 14.21.

ואנדרוגינס משמע מוציאין שלא יקראו ומוציאין שלא

10   יביאו ת"ל תביא מכל מקום ומה הפרש בין אלו

לאלו אלו מביאין וקורין ואלו מביאין ואין קורין.

לא תבשל גדי בחלב אמו רבי ישמעאל

אומר מפני מה נאמר בשלשה מקומות כנגד שלש

בריתות שכרת הקב"ה עם ישראל אחת בחורב

15   ואחת בערבות מואב ואחת על הר גריזים ועל הר

עיבל רבי יאשיה אומר תחלה נאמר ואין

דורשין תחלות שני לו מפני הדין בהמה טהורה

מטמאה במשא וטמאה מטמאה במשא אם למדת

על הטהורה שבשרה אסור להתבשל בחלבה

20   יכול אף טמאה יהיה בשרה אסור להתבשל

בחלבה ת"ל בחלב אמו ולא בחלב טמאה שלישית

ולא בחלב אדם רבי יונתן אומר מפני מה נאמרה

בשלשה מקומות אחת לבהמה ואחת לחיה ואחת

לעוף אבא חנין אומר משום רבי אליעזר מפני מה

25   נאמר בשלשה מקומות אחת לבהמה גסה ואחת

לעזים ואחת לרחלים רבי שמעון בן אלעזר אומר

מפני מה נאמר בשלשה מקומות אחת לבהמה גסה

ואחת לבהמה דקה ואחת לחיה רבי שמעון בן

יוחאי אומר מפני מה נאמר בשלשה מקומות אחת

30   איסור אכילה ואחת איסור הנאה ואחת איסור

13—16 שם ק"ד. מ"ת 56.   16—17 לעיל נזיקין ט"ז.

___

12 ישמעאל] ד. שמען.   16 יאשיה] מ"ח. יונתן.   17 שני] ט. ושני מ. שנית / לו
מפני הדין] א. לו מן הדין ד. לו מה דין א"צ. למה נאמר שיכול.   21 שלישית]
הגהה=ט. ש"י: ז"י: א"צ. שלישי בחלב אמו.   22 יונתן] מ"ח. יאשיה.   24 חנין]
ד. חנן.   26 אלעזר] א. אליעזר.   29—28 רשב"י אומר] ד. דבר אחר.   29 מפני מה
נאמר בשלשה מקומות] ד. >.

against the mere cooking of it. Another Interpretation: Once to make
it obtain both in the land of Israel as well as outside of the land of
Israel, once to make it obtain in times when there is a temple, and
once to make it obtain in times when there is no temple. Since it
says: "The choicest first fruit of thy land," etc.,[3] we have heard only
that in times when the practice of bringing the first-fruits offering
obtains and in the places where the practice of bringing the first-
fruits offering obtains, there the law about meat with milk obtains.
But as to the times when the practice of bringing the first-fruits offering does not obtain and as to the places where the practice of bringing the first-fruits offering does not obtain, we have not heard. It says
however: "Ye shall not eat anything that dieth of itself" (Deut. 14.21),
and there it is also said: "Thou shalt not seethe a kid in its mother's
milk," to intimate that just as the law not to eat anything that dies of
itself obtains both in the land of Israel and outside of the land of
Israel; in times when there is a temple as well as in times when there
is no temple; so also the law about meat with milk is to obtain both
in the land of Israel and outside of the land of Israel; in times when
there is a temple as well as in times when there is no temple.[4] R.
Akiba says: Why is this law stated in three places? One is to exclude
cattle, one is to exclude wild animals, and one is to exclude fowl.[5] R.
Jose the Galilean says: It is said: "Ye shall not eat anything that dieth
of itself" (ibid.), and in the same passage it is said: "Thou shalt not
seethe a kid in its mother's milk"—the flesh of any animal which
would become forbidden to eat if the animal died of itself is also for-

3. The rest of the verse reads: "Thou shalt not seethe a kid in its mother's
milk." The two laws are thus mentioned together in one verse.

4. See Introduction.

5. According to Akiba, the term נדי, "kid," can mean a young lamb as well as
a kid, but it cannot include the young of cattle, or a calf. It is, however, possible
that פרט in the saying of Akiba means not "to exclude" but "to specify." In this
sense, then, Akiba's opinion as expressed here would be different from the opinion ascribed to him in the Talmud (Ḥul. 113a) (see Introduction and cf. Commentaries).

בישול דבר אחר אחת בין בארץ בין בחוצה לארץ

ואחת בפני הבית ואחת שלא בפני הבית לפי שהוא

אומר ראשית ביכורי אדמתך וגו׳ ולא שמענו אלא

בזמן שהביכורים נוהגים מקום שהביכורים נוהגים

35   שם בשר בחלב נוהג בזמן שאין הביכורים נוהגין

מקום שאין הביכורים נוהגין לא שמענו ת״ל לא

תאכלו כל נבלה ונאמר לא תבשל גדי בחלב אמו

מה נבלה נוהגת בין בארץ בין בחוצה לארץ בפני

הבית ושלא בפני הבית אף בשר בחלב יהיה נוהג

40   בארץ ובחוצה לארץ בפני הבית ושלא בפני הבית

רבי עקיבא אומר מפני מה נאמר בשלשה מקומות

פרט לבהמה פרט לחיה פרט לעוף רבי יוסי הגלילי

אומר נאמר לא תאכלו כל נבלה ונאמר לא תבשל

גדי בחלב אמו את שהוא אסור משום נבלה אסור

36—37 דברים י״ד, כ״א.   40—39 תוס׳ חולין ח׳, א׳.   49—43 ספרי דברים ק״ד. חולין קי״ג, א׳. ש. 159.

---

34 מקום שהביכורים נוהגים] ד. >.   39—38 בפני הבית ושלא] ד. בין בפני הבית ובין שלא.   40—39 נוהג בארץ—ושלא בפני הבית] ד. נוהג כן.   42 לבהמה] ט. ש״י. ~ טמאה.   43 לא תאכלו] ד. לא תאכל.   44 את שהוא אסור משום נבלה] א. ~ יכול יהיה מ״ח. יכול את שהוא אסור משום נבלה.

bidden to be cooked with milk. One might think then that fowl, since it becomes forbidden to eat if it dies of itself, should also be forbidden to be cooked with milk. It says however: "in its mother's milk." Thus, fowl is excluded because it has no mother's milk. The unclean animal is excluded since it is forbidden to be eaten whether it be ritually slaughtered or died of itself.

Thou Shalt Not Seethe a Kid in Its Mother's Milk. I thus know only that it is forbidden to be cooked. How do we know that it is forbidden to be eaten? You must reason by using the method of *kal vahomer:* If in the case of the paschal lamb, where there is no express law not to cook it, there is a prohibition against eating it if cooked, it is but logical that in the case of meat with milk, where there is an express law not to cook it, it should surely be prohibited to be eaten if so cooked. No! If you cite the case of the paschal lamb—that is different, for there it is forbidden to be cooked with anything at all. Therefore it is forbidden to be eaten if cooked. But will you argue the same about meat cooked with milk? It is not forbidden to be cooked in any other way. Therefore it should not be forbidden to be eaten even if cooked with milk. R. Akiba says: There is no need of this argument: If the sinew of the thigh-vein, about which there is no law not to cook it, is nevertheless forbidden to be eaten, it is but logical that meat cooked with milk, about which there is an express law not to cook it, should surely be forbidden to be eaten. No! If you cite the case of the sinew of the thigh-vein—that is different, for the prohibition against it dates from the time prior to the giving of the Torah.[6] Therefore it is forbidden to be eaten. But will you argue the same about meat with milk? The prohibition against it does not date from the time prior to the giving of the Torah. Therefore it should not be forbidden to be eaten. But behold the law about the carcass would disprove this. For the prohibition against it likewise does not date from the time prior to the giving of the Torah. And yet the carcass is

6. See Gen. 32.33.

45 לבשל בחלב עוף שהוא אסור משום נבלה יכול
יהא אסור לבשל בחלב ת"ל בחלב אמו יצא עוף
שאין לו חלב אם יצאת בהמה טמאה אחת
בשחיטתה ואחת במיתתה.

לא תבשל גדי בחלב אמו אין לי אלא
50 שהוא אסור בבישול ומנין שהוא אסור באכילה
אמרת קל וחומר ומה אם הפסח שאין בו בל תבשל
יש בו בל תאכל בשר בחלב שיש בו בל תבשל דין
הוא שיהיה בו בל תאכל לא אם אמרת בפסח
שאיסורו בכל דבר לפיכך הוא אסור באכילה
55 תאמר בבשר בחלב שאין איסורו בכל דבר לפיכך
לא יהיה אסור באכילה רבי עקיבא אומר אינו
צריך אם גיד הנשה שאין בו בל תבשל יש בו בל
תאכל בשר בחלב שיש בו בל תבשל דין הוא שיהא
בו בל תאכל לא אם אמרת בגיד הנשה שאיסורו
60 קודם למתן תורה לפיכך הוא אסור באכילה
תאמר בבשר בחלב שאין איסורו קודם למתן תורה
לפיכך לא יהא אסור באכילה והרי נבלה תוכיח
שאין אסורה קודם למתן תורה ואסורה באכילה

45 יכול] ד. ‹.   55 איסורו בכל דבר] ד. איסורו באכילה בכל דבר.   59—58 שיהא בו]
ד. שיש בו.   62 אסור באכילה] א. מ. ד. ~ ת"ל לא תאכלנו. והשמטתיו=ט. א"א.
ז"י. א"צ. ומא"ש.

forbidden to be eaten. This should prove concerning meat with milk that although the prohibition against it does not date from the time prior to the giving of the Torah, it should nevertheless be forbidden to be eaten. No! If you cite the law about the carcass—that is different, for the carcass makes one who carries it unclean. Therefore it is forbidden to be eaten. But will you argue the same about meat cooked with milk? It does not make one who carries it unclean. Therefore it should not be forbidden to be eaten. But behold the law about tallow and blood would disprove this. For the tallow and the blood likewise do not make one who carries them unclean. And yet they are forbidden to be eaten. This would prove concerning meat cooked with milk that although it does not make the one who carries it unclean it should nevertheless be forbidden to be eaten. No! If you cite the law about tallow and blood—that is different, for the prohibition against them carries with it the penalty of extermination. But will you argue the same about meat cooked with milk? It cannot make one incur the penalty of extermination. Therefore it should not be forbidden to be eaten. It says however: "Thou shalt not eat it" (Deut. 12.24), which is to include meat cooked with milk—it should be forbidden to be eaten. Issi says: "Thou shalt not eat the life with the flesh" (ibid. 12.23) means to include meat cooked with milk—it should be forbidden to be eaten. Issi b. Gur Aryeh says: "holiness" is mentioned here (ibid. 14.21) and "holiness" is mentioned there (Ex. 22.30). Just as there it implies a prohibition against eating, so also here it implies a prohibition against eating. I thus far know only that it is forbidden to be eaten. How do we know that it is also forbidden to be made use of? You must reason by using the method of *kal vaho-mer:* If the fruit of the trees of the first three years, in the production of which no law was violated, is forbidden both to be eaten and to be made use of, it is but logical that meat cooked with milk, in the preparation of which a law has been violated, should surely be forbidden both to be eaten and to be made use of. No! If you cite the case of the

היא תוכיח על בשר בחלב אף על פי שאין איסורו

65 קודם למתן תורה יהיה אסור באכילה לא אם

אמרת בנבלה שהיא מטמאה במשא לפיכך אסורה

באכילה תאמר בבשר בחלב שאינו מטמא במשא

לפיכך לא יהיה אסור באכילה והרי חלב ודם

יוכיחו שאינן מטמאין במשא ואסורין באכילה הם

70 יוכיחו על בשר בחלב אף על פי שאינו מטמא

במשא יהיה אסור באכילה לא אם אמרת בחלב

ודם שחייבין עליהם כרת תאמר בבשר בחלב

שאין חייבין עליהן כרת לפיכך לא יהיה אסור

באכילה ת״ל לא תאכלנו להביא בשר בחלב

75 שיהיה אסור באכילה איסי אומר לא תאכל הנפש

עם הבשר להביא בשר בחלב שיהיה אסור

באכילה איסי בן גור אריה אומר נאמר כאן קדושה

ונאמר להלן קדושה מה להלן אסור באכילה אף

כאן אסור באכילה אין לי אלא שהוא אסור

80 באכילה בהנאה מנין אמרת קל וחומר ומה אם

ערלה שלא נעבדה בה עבירה אסורה באכילה

ובהנאה בשר בחלב שנעבדה בו עבירה דין הוא

שיהיה אסור באכילה ובהנאה לא אם אמרת

74 דברים י״ב, כ״ה.   76—75 שם י״ב, כ״ג.   77—75 ספרי דברים ע״ו.   97—75 חולין קט״ו, ב׳.

---

65 —64 על בשר בחלב—אסור באכילה] ד. <.   67 —66 לפיכך אסורה באכילה] ד. <.
68 לפיכך לא—באכילה] ד. < / והרי] ד. <.   73 שאין חייבין עליהן כרת] ד. שאין
איסורו משום כרת.   73—74 לפיכך—באכילה] ד. <.   75 איסי אומר] א. מ. > ק.
איסי אומר / לא תאכל] במקרא שלפנינו, ולא תאכל.   77 גור אריה] ד. גוריא.

fruit of the trees of the first three years—that is different, for it never had a time when it was permitted. Therefore it is forbidden to be made use of. But will you argue the same about meat cooked with milk? It had a time when it was permitted.[7] Therefore it should be permitted to be made use of. But behold the law about leaven during the Passover would disprove this. For the leaven certainly had a time when it was permitted. And yet during the Passover it is forbidden to be made use of. This should prove concerning meat cooked with milk that although it had a time when it was permitted, it should nevertheless be forbidden to be made use of. No! If you cite the case of leaven during the Passover—that is different, for the prohibition against it carries with it the penalty of extermination. Therefore it is forbidden to be made use of. But will you argue the same about meat cooked with milk? It cannot make one incur the penalty of extermination. Therefore it should not be forbidden to be made use of. But behold the law about mixed seeds in the vineyard[8] would disprove this. The prohibition against them likewise does not carry with it the penalty of extermination, and yet they are forbidden to be made use of. This should prove concerning meat cooked with milk that even though it cannot make one incur the penalty of extermination, it should nevertheless be forbidden to be made use of. Rabbi says: "Or thou mayest sell it unto a foreigner . . . Thou shalt not seethe a kid" (Deut. 14.21). The Torah thus says: When you sell it you may not cook it first and then sell it. Behold then you thus learn that it is forbidden to make any use of it.

Thou Shalt Not Seethe a Kid in Its Mother's Milk. I thus know only about cooking it with the milk of its mother. How about cooking it with the milk of a sister species? You must reason by using the method of *kal vaḥomer:* If it is forbidden to be cooked with the milk

---

7. Before having been cooked together, both the meat and the milk were permitted to be eaten.

8. See Deut. 22.9.

בערלה שלא היתה לה שעת היתר לפיכך אסורה

בהנאה תאמר בבשר בחלב שהיתה לו שעת היתר 85

לפיכך לא יהיה אסור בהנאה והרי חמץ בפסח

יוכיח שהיתה לו שעת היתר ואסור בהנאה הוא

יוכיח על בשר בחלב אף על פי שהיתה לו שעת

היתר יהא אסור בהנאה לא אם אמרת בחמץ בפסח

שחייבין עליו כרת לפיכך אסור בהנאה תאמר 90

בבשר בחלב שאין חייבין עליו כרת לפיכך לא

יהיה אסור בהנאה והרי כלאי הכרם יוכיחו שאין

חייבין עליו כרת ואסורין בהנאה הם יוכיחו על

בשר בחלב אף על פי שאין חייבין עליו כרת יהא

אסור בהנאה רבי אומר או מכור לנכרי לא תבשל 95

גדי אמרה תורה כשתמכרנו לא תבשלנו ותמכרנו

הא למדת שהוא אסור בהנאה.

לא תבשל גדי בחלב אמו אין לי אלא

חלב אמו חלב אחותו מנין אמרת קל וחומר הוא

95 שם י״ד, כ״א.   110—98 חולין קי״ד, א׳—ב׳. מ״ת 75.

85 שהיתה לו] ד. שהיה לה.   86 והרי] ד. <.   89—87 הוא יוכיח—יהא אסור בהנאה]
ד. <.   92 והרי] ד. <.   96 כשתמכרנו] א. מ. בשעת שאת מוכרה (מ. מוכרו).   97 הוא]
ד. מכאן / למדת] מ. למדנו.   99 אחותו] ד. ~ גדולה.

of its mother, although the species of the latter comes in with it to the shed to be tithed, it is but logical that it should be forbidden to be cooked with the milk of any other species with which it cannot come in together to the shed to be tithed.[9] How about cooking it in its own milk? You must reason by using the method of *kal vaḥomer*: If where the law permits product with product, as with respect to slaughtering them on the same day, it forbids product with parent together,[10] it is but logical that here where the law forbids product with product[11] we should surely forbid product with parent. How about using goat's milk to cook lamb in? You must reason by using the method of *kal vaḥomer*: If where the law permits product with product, as with respect to coupling, it forbids the product to be used with the parent,[12] here where the law forbids product with product, even with regard to coupling,[13] we should surely forbid the use of the product with the parent.—The same argument applies to using goat's milk to cook beef in.[14] Why then does Scripture speak of the kid? Because its mother is rich in milk. Rabbi says: Here it is said "its mother," and there (Lev. 22.27) it is also said "its mother." Just as there when it says "its mother" Scripture deals with the mother of an ox or a sheep or a goat,[15] so also here when it says "its mother" Scripture deals with the mother of an ox or a sheep or a goat.

Thou Shalt Not Seethe a Kid in Its Mother's Milk. Only meat and milk are forbidden to be cooked together, but all other prohibited things mentioned in the Torah are not. For the following argument

9. See M. Bek. 9.1.

10. See Lev. 22.28.

11. The kid and its mother's milk are both the products of the mother. The animal, so to speak, is the parent of its own milk.

12. The animal may be coupled with another animal of its own species, but its flesh may not be cooked with the milk of its own species.

13. It is forbidden to couple sheep with goats (see M. Bek. l.c.).

14. See Introduction and cf. Commentaries.

15. It expressly says there: "When a bullock, or a sheep or a goat is brought forth then it shall be seven days under its mother."

100 ומה אם שנכנסת עמו לדיר להתעשר אסור

להתבשל בחלבה אחותו שאינה נכנסת עמו לדיר

להתעשר דין הוא שיהא אסור להתבשל בחלבה

חלב עצמה בבשרה מנין אמרת קל וחומר ומה אם

במקום שהתיר פרי עם פרי בשחיטה אסר פרי

105 עם האם כאן שאסר פרי עם פרי דין הוא שנאסור פרי

עם האם חלב עזים ברחלים מנין אמרת קל וחומר

מה אם במקום שהתיר פרי עם פרי ברביעה אסר

פרי עם האם כאן שאסר פרי עם פרי ברביעה דין

הוא שנאסר פרי עם האם הוא הדין אף לבקר מפני

110 מה דיבר הכתוב בגדי מפני שהחלב מרובה באמו

רבי אומר נאמר כאן אמו ונאמר להלן אמו מה אמו

האמורה להלן בשור וכשב ועז הכתוב מדבר אף

אמו האמורה כאן בשור וכשב ועז הכתוב מדבר.

לא תבשל גדי בחלב אמו בשר בחלב

115 את אסור לבשל ולא כל שאר האיסורין שבתורה

could be advanced: If it is forbidden to cook together meat with milk, although each one by itself is permitted to be cooked and eaten, is it not logical that prohibited things mentioned in the Torah, each of which by itself is forbidden,[16] should surely be forbidden to be cooked together? Therefore it says: "Thou shalt not seethe the kid," etc.—only meat and milk are forbidden to be cooked together, but all other prohibited things mentioned in the Torah are not.

Thou Shalt Not Seethe a Kid in Its Mother's Milk. I thus know only about non-consecrated animals. How about animals consecrated for sacrifices? You must reason: If it is forbidden in the case of non-consecrated animals, shall it not be forbidden in the case of consecrated animals? No! If you cite the case of non-consecrated animals—that is different, for the law also forbids pinching off the head in the case of non-consecrated animals. But will you argue the same of consecrated animals? The law does not forbid pinchings either,[17] in the case of consecrated animals. It says however: "In the house of the Lord thy God thou shalt not seethe a kid in its mother's milk."

16. I. e., to be eaten.
17. See Lev. 1.15. The law prescribes pinching off the head for the sacrificial animal, a mode of slaughtering which is forbidden in the case of fowl used for ordinary food.

והדין נותן ומה אם בשר בחלב שזה מותר בפני

עצמו וזה מותר בפני עצמו הרי הן אסורין בבישול

שאר כל האסורין שבתורה שזה אסור בפני עצמו

וזה אסור בפני עצמו אינו דין שיהו אסורין בבישול

120 ת״ל לא תבשל גדי וגו׳ בשר בחלב את אסור לבשל

ולא שאר כל האיסורין שבתורה.

לא תבשל גדי בחלב אמו אין לי אלא

בחולין במוקדשין מנין אמרת אם נאסר בחולין

לא נאסר במוקדשין לא אם אמרת בחולין שכן

125 אסר מליקה בחולין תאמר במוקדשין שלא אסר

מליקה במוקדשין ת״ל בית יי אלהיך לא תבשל

גדי בחלב אמו.

חסלת מסכתא דכספא

122—120 וגו׳ בשר בחלב—לא תבשל גדי] ד. <. ‏ 128 חסלת מסכת דכספא] א. מ. <
מא״ש. ~ וסליקא פרשת משפטים ק. נ. עד כאן פרשת דינין ל. חסלת פרשת משפטים.
The Arrangement and the Divisions of the Mekilta, Hebrew Union College עיין מאמרי
Annual, I, pp. 444-445.

TRACTATE SHABBATA

And the Lord Spoke unto Moses. Directly and not through the medium of an angel or a messenger.

Verily, Ye Shall Keep My Sabbaths. Why is this said? Because it says: "Thou shalt not do any manner of work" (Ex. 20.10), from which I know only about activities that can be regarded as labor. But how about activities that can be regarded as merely detracting from the restfulness of the Sabbath?[1] Scripture says here: "Verily, ye shall keep My sabbaths," thus prohibiting even such activities as only detract from the restfulness of the day.

Once R. Ishmael, R. Eleazar b. Azariah and R. Akiba were walking along the road followed by Levi the netmaker and Ishmael the son of R. Eleazar b. Azariah. And the following question was discussed by them: Whence do we know that the duty of saving life supersedes the Sabbath laws? R. Ishmael, answering the question, said: Behold it says: "If a thief be found breaking in," etc. (Ex. 22.1). Now of what case does the law speak? Of a case when there is a doubt whether the burglar came merely to steal or even to kill. Now, by using the method of *kal vaḥomer,* it is to be reasoned: Even shedding of blood, which defiles the land and causes the Shekinah to remove, is to supersede the laws of the Sabbath if it is to be done in protection of one's life.[2] How much more should the duty of saving life supersede

1. See above *Kaspa,* IV, note 3.
2. Cf. above *Nezikin,* XIII. The law in Ex. 22.1 does not make any distinction

מסכתא דשבתא

פרשה א   (שמות ל׳, י״ב, — י״ז.)

ויאמר יי אל משה לא על ידי מלאך ולא
על ידי השליח.

אך את שבתותי תשמורו למה נאמר לפי
שהוא אומר לא תעשה כל מלאכה אין לי אלא
דברים שהם משום מלאכה דברים שהן משום שבות
מנין ת״ל אך את שבתותי תשמורו להביא דברים
שהן משום שבות. כבר היה רבי ישמעאל ורבי
אלעזר בן עזריה ורבי עקיבא מהלכין בדרך ולוי
הסדר וישמעאל בנו של רבי אלעזר בן עזריה
מהלכין אחריהם ונשאלה שאלה זו לפניהם מנין
לפיקוח נפש שידחה את השבת נענה רבי ישמעאל
ואמר הרי הוא אומר אם במחתרת ימצא הגנב
וגו׳ ומה זה ספק שהוא בא לגנוב ספק שהוא בא
להרוג והרי דברים קל וחומר ומה אם שפיכות
דמים שמטמא את הארץ ומסלקת את השכינה
הרי היא דוחה את השבת קל וחומר לפיקוח נפש

44 — 1 ש. 161 — 160.   7 — 3 לעיל כספא ד׳.   4 שמות כ׳, י׳.   30 — 7 יומא פ״ה,
א׳ — ב׳.   12 שמות כ״ב, א׳.

מסכתא דשבתא] א. מ. < ד. פרשת כי תשא. עיין מאמרי הנ״ל שם צד 446 / פרשה
א׳] א. מ. ~ דשבת ד. >.   4 תעשה] מ. ק. נ. תעשו.   9 וישמעאל] ד. ורבי ישמעאל.
12 הרי הוא אומר] ד. >.

the Sabbath laws! R. Eleazar b. Azariah, answering the question, said: If in performing the ceremony of circumcision, which affects only one member of the body, one is to disregard the Sabbath laws, how much more should one do so for the whole body when it is in danger! The sages however said to him: From the instance cited by you it would also follow that just as there the Sabbath is to be disregarded only in a case of certainty,[3] so also here the Sabbath is to be disregarded only in a case of certainty.[4] R. Akiba says: If punishment for murder sets aside even the Temple service,[5] which in turn supersedes the Sabbath, how much more should the duty of saving life supersede the Sabbath laws! R. Jose the Galilean says: When it says: "But My sabbath ye shall keep," the word "but" (ak) implies a distinction. There are Sabbaths on which you must rest and there are Sabbaths on which you should not rest. R. Simon b. Menasiah says: Behold it says: "And ye shall keep the sabbath for it is holy unto you" (v. 14). This means: The Sabbath is given to you but you are not surrendered to the Sabbath. R. Nathan says: Behold it says: "Wherefore the children of Israel shall keep the sabbath to observe the sabbath throughout their generations" (v. 16). This implies that we should disregard one Sabbath for the sake of saving the life of a person so that that person may be able to observe many Sabbaths.

For It Is a Sign between Me and You. But not between Me and the nations of the world.

Throughout Their Generations. This law should obtain throughout the generations.

---

as to whether the burglar breaks in on a Sabbath or on a week-day.

3. If the child is born at twilight of Friday evening or of Saturday evening, in which case it is not certain that the following Sabbath is the eighth day after birth, the circumcision may not be performed on that Sabbath day (see M. Shab. 19.5 and Shab. 134b–135a).

4. I. e., that life will be saved by the work done in violation of the Sabbath (cf. *Nesikin,* XIII, note 1).

5. See above *Nezikin,* IV; Ex. 21.14 and *Mekilta* ad loc.

שידחה את השבת נענה רבי אלעזר בן עזריה ואמר

ומה אם מילה שאינה אלא אחד מאיבריו של אדם

דוחה את השבת קל וחומר לשאר כל הגוף אמרו

20   לו ממקום שבאת מה להלן בודאי אף כאן בודאי

רבי עקיבא אומר אם דוחה רציחה את העבודה

שהיא דוחה שבת קל וחומר לפיקוח נפש שידחה

את השבת רבי יוסי הגלילי אומר כשהוא אומר

אך את שבתותי תשמרו אך חלק יש שבתות שאתה

25   שובת ויש שבתות שאין אתה שובת רבי שמעון בן

מנסיא אומר הרי הוא אומר ושמרתם את השבת

כי קדש היא לכם לכם שבת מסורה ואין אתם

מסורין לשבת רבי נתן אומר הרי הוא אומר ושמרו

בני ישראל את השבת לעשות את השבת לדורותם

30   חלל עליו שבת אחת וישמור שבתות הרבה.

כי   אות   היא   ביני   וביניכם   ולא   ביני

ובין אומות העולם.

לדורותיכם שינהוג הדבר לדורות.

23—21 לעיל נזיקין ד'.   30—28 י' יומא ח', ה' (45[b]).   32—31 סנהדרין נ"ח, ב'. ד"ר א', כ"א.

23 כשהוא] ד. כשם שהוא.   25—24 יש שבתות—שאין אתה שובת] ד. ויש שבתות שאתה דוחה ויש שבתות שאתה שובת.   30 חלל] א. מ. פקוח / עליו] ד. < / וישמור] ד. כדי שתשמור.   33 לדורותיכם—לדורות] מ. <.

That Ye May Know. Why is this said? Because it says: "Wherefore the children of Israel shall keep the sabbath" (ibid.), from which I might understand that the deaf and dumb, the insane and the minor are also included in this commandment. Therefore it says here: "That ye may know." So I must interpret it as speaking only of such persons as have understanding.

That I Am the Lord Who Sanctifies You. In the future world, which is characterized by the kind of holiness possessed by the Sabbath of this world. We thus learn that the Sabbath possesses a holiness like that of the future world. And thus it says: "A Psalm; a Song of the sabbath day" (Ps. 92.1), referring to the world in which there is Sabbath all the time.

And Ye Shall Keep the Sabbath for It Is Holy unto You. This is the verse which R. Simon the son of Menasiah interpreted as saying: The Sabbath is given to you but you are not surrendered to the Sabbath.

For It Is Holy unto You. This tells that the Sabbath adds holiness to Israel. Why is the shop of so-and-so closed? Because he keeps the Sabbath. Why does so-and-so abstain from work? Because he keeps the Sabbath. He thus bears witness to Him by whose word the world came into being that He created His world in six days and rested on the seventh. And thus it says: "Therefore ye are my witnesses, saith the Lord, and I am God" (Isa. 43.12).

Everyone That Profaneth It Shall Surely Be Put to Death. Why is this said? Because it says: "Whosoever doeth any work in the sabbath day, he shall surely be put to death" (v. 15). We have thus heard the penalty. But we have not heard the warning. Therefore it says: "But the seventh day is a sabbath unto the Lord thy God, in it thou shalt not do any manner of work" (Ex. 20.10). I thus know only the penalty for and the warning against work on Sabbath during the daytime. How do I know that there is also a penalty for and a warning against work during the nighttime of the Sabbath? It says here: "Everyone that profaneth it shall surely be put to death." From this however we

לדעת למה נאמר לפי שהוא אומר ושמרו

35 בני ישראל את השבת שומע אני אפילו חרש שוטה

וקטן במשמע ת״ל לדעת לא אמרתי אלא במי שיש

בו דעת.

כי **אני** **יי** **מקדשכם** לעולם הבא כגון

קדושת שבת בעולם הזה נמצינו למדין שהוא מעין

40 קדושת העולם הבא וכן הוא אומר מזמור שיר ליום

השבת לעולם שכולו שבת.

ושמרתם **את** **השבת** **כי** **קדש** **היא** **לכם**

זה הוא שהיה רבי שמעון בן מנסיא אומר שבת

מסורה לכם ואין אתם מסורין לשבת.

45 **כי** **קדש** **היא** **לכם** מגיד שהשבת מוספת

קדושה על ישראל מה לפלוני חנותו נעולה שהוא

משמר את השבת מה לפלוני בטל ממלאכתו שהוא

משמר את השבת מעיד למי שאמר והיה העולם

שברא עולמו בששה ימים ונח בשביעי וכן הוא אומר

50 ואתם עדי נאם יי ואני אל.

מחלליה **מות** **יומת** למה נאמר לפי שהוא

אומר כל העושה מלאכה ביום השבת מות יומת

עונש שמענו אזהרה לא שמענו ת״ל ויום השביעי

שבת ליי אלהיך לא תעשה כל מלאכה אין לי אלא

55 עונש ואזהרה על מלאכת היום עונש ואזהרה על

מלאכת הלילה מנין ת״ל מחלליה מות יומת עונש

37—34 לעיל בחודש ז׳.   41—38 ר״ה ל״א, א׳.   41—40 תהלים צ״ב, א׳.   50 ישעיה

מ״ג, י״ב.   70—51 לעיל בחודש ז׳.   54—53 שמות כ׳, י׳.

---

39 קדושת] מ. ‹.   42 כי קדש היא לכם] הוספתי: א. וגו׳.   48 מעיד] א. ולא עוד

אלא מעיד כ. (ישעיה מ״ג, א׳) מגיד / למי] א. מ. כ. מ״ח. לפני מי.   52 העושה

מלאכה] ד. העושה בו מלאכה.   55—56 על מלאכת הלילה] ק. ‹.

only learn about the penalty. But we have not heard any warning.[6]
Scripture says: "But the seventh day is a sabbath unto the Lord thy
God." Now, there would be no purpose in saying "a sabbath" except
to include the nighttime in the warning.—These are the words of R.
Aḥai the son of Josiah. R. Judah b. Bathyra says: Suppose the Gentiles
surrounded Israelitish cities and the Israelites in self-defence had to
profane the Sabbath. The Israelites should not in such a case say:
Since we had to profane part of the Sabbath, we might as well continue to profane the rest of the day. For it says: "Everyone that profaneth it shall surely be put to death," meaning: Everyone that
profaneth it even for one moment shall be put to death.

For Whosoever Doeth Any Work Therein. Provided that he does a
complete act of work. But suppose he writes one letter on Sabbath
morning and the other letter late in the afternoon, or he spins one
thread in the morning and another thread late in the afternoon, I
might understand that he should also be guilty. But it says: "For whosoever doeth any work therein"—that is, provided he does a complete act of work at one time.

That Soul Shall Be Cut Off from among His People. Why is this said?
Since it says: "Everyone that profaneth it shall surely be put to
death," I know only that one who does it presumptuously, despite
the warning of witnesses, incurs the penalty. But how about one who
acts presumptuously but privately? Scripture says here: "Shall be cut
off"—to include even one who profanes the Sabbath presumptuously
even though only privately.

Shall Be Cut Off. To be cut off merely means to cease to exist. *That
Soul.* This means the soul acting presumptuously.—These are the
words of R. Akiba. *From among His People.* And his people is left in
peace.

Six Days Shall Work Be Done. One passage says: "Six days shall
work be done," and another passage says: "Six days shalt thou labour

6. I.e., against work during the nighttime of the Sabbath.

שמענו אזהרה לא שמענו ת"ל ויום השביעי שבת
ליי אלהיך שאין תלמוד לומר שבת אלא להביא
את הלילה בכלל אזהרה דברי רבי אחי ברבי
יאשיה רבי יהודה בן בתירה אומר והרי הגוים
שהקיפו את ערי ישראל וחללו ישראל את השבת
שלא יהו ישראל אומרין הואיל וחללנו מקצתה
נחלל את כולה ת"ל מחלליה מות יומת אפילו
כהרף עין מחלליה מות יומת.

כי כל העושה בה מלאכה עד שיעשה
בה מלאכה גמורה הרי שכתב אות אחת בשחרית
ואות אחת בין הערבים או שארג חוט אחד בשחרית
וחוט אחד בין הערבים שומע אני יהא חייב ת"ל
כי כל העושה בה מלאכה עד שיעשה מלאכה
גמורה.

ונכרתה הנפש ההיא מקרב עמיה
למה נאמר לפי שהוא אומר מחלליה מות יומת
אין לי אלא המזיד בהתראת עדים המזיד בינו לבין
עצמו מנין ת"ל ונכרתה להביא את המזיד בינו
לבין עצמו.

ונכרתה אין הכרתה אלא הפסקה **הנפש**
ההיא מזידה דברי רבי עקיבא **מקרב עמה**
ועמה שלום.

ששת ימים יעשה מלאכה כתוב אחד
אומר ששת ימים יעשה מלאכה וכתוב אחד אומר

65—70 י' ברכות א', א' (ב2).   76—78 לעיל פסחא ח'. ספרי במדבר י"ד.   79—89 ספרי
דברים מ"ב. ברכות ל"ה, ב'.

58 שבת] ד. ~ מה תלמוד לומר.   59 אחי] ד. יוסי.   61 ערי] ד. ארץ.   65 העושה
בה] ק. נ. העושה בו.   70—66 הרי שכתב—מלאכה גמורה] מ. <.   69 בה] ק. נ. בו.
71 מקרב עמיה] הגהתי כמו במקרא: א. מ. ט. מקרב עמה ד. מעמיה.   79 יעשה] א.
ד. תעשה.   80—79 כתוב אחד אומר—יעשה מלאכה] ד. <.

and do all thy work" (Ex. 20.9). How can both these passages be
maintained? When the Israelites do the will of God, then: "Six days
shall work be done." Their work is done for them by others. And
thus it says: "And strangers shall stand and feed your flocks, and
aliens shall be your plowmen and your vinedressers" (Isa. 61.5). But
when the Israelites do not do the will of God, then: "Six days shalt
thou labour and do all thy work." They themselves must do their
work. And not only this but even the work of others is done by them,
as it is said: "Thou shalt serve thine enemy," etc. (Deut. 28.48).

But on the Seventh Day Is a Sabbath of Solemn Rest Holy to the Lord.
Why is this said? Because it says: "These are the appointed seasons of
the Lord, even holy convocations, which ye shall proclaim in their
appointed season" (Lev. 23.4). One might think that just as the holiness of the festival depends on the *bet din*[7] that fixes their dates, so
also shall the holiness of the Sabbath depend on the proclamation of
the *bet din*. Therefore it says: "But on the seventh day is a sabbath of
solemn rest holy to the Lord," meaning that the Sabbath is in the
charge of God who definitely fixed the day, and it does not depend
on the *bet din*. And thus is says: "Ye shall keep the sabbath," etc.

*Wherefore the Children of Israel Shall Keep the Sabbath to Observe the
Sabbath.* This is the verse that R. Nathan interpreted as implying that
we should profane one Sabbath for the sake of saving the life of a person in order that he may be able to observe many Sabbaths. R. Eliezer
says: *To Observe the Sabbath Throughout Their Generations for a Perpet-
ual Covenant*—to do on the Sabbath that for which a covenant has
been made. And what is this? It is circumcision. R. Eleazar b. Perata
says: How can you prove that if one keeps the Sabbath it is accounted
to him as if he had made the Sabbath? It says: "Wherefore the children of Israel shall keep the sabbath to make the sabbath." Rabbi
says: How can you prove that if one keeps but one Sabbath properly,

7. I. e., the tribunal which proclaims the new moon and thus determines on
which day the festival should fall (see M. R. H. 2.7–9 and 3.1).

ששת ימים תעבוד ועשית כל מלאכתך כיצד
יתקיימו שני כתובים הללו כשישראל עושין רצונו
של מקום ששת ימים יעשה מלאכה מלאכתן נעשית
על ידי אחרים וכן הוא אומר ועמדו זרים ורעו
85 צאנכם ובני נכר אכריכם וכרמיכם וכשישראל
אין עושין רצונו של מקום ששת ימים תעבוד ועשית
כל מלאכתך מלאכתן נעשית על ידי עצמן ולא
עוד אלא אפילו מלאכת אחרים נעשית על ידן
שנאמר ועבדת את אויביך וגו'.

90 **וביום השביעי שבת שבתון קדש ליי**
למה נאמר לפי שהוא אומר אלה מועדי יי מקראי
קדש אשר תקראו אותם במועדם יכול כשם
שקדושת מועדות מסורה לבית דין כך תהא קדושת
שבת מסורה לבית דין ת"ל וביום השביעי שבת
95 שבתון קדש ליי לשם שבת מסורה ואינה מסורה
לבית דין וכן הוא אומר ושמרתם את השבת וגו'.

**ושמרו בני ישראל את השבת לעשות
את השבת** זה הוא שהיה רבי נתן אומר חלל
עליו שבת אחת כדי שישמור שבתות הרבה
100 רבי אליעזר אומר לעשות את השבת לדורותם
ברית עולם דבר שהברית כרותה לו ואיזו זו מילה
רבי אלעזר בן פרטא אומר מנין אתה אומר כל
מי שהוא שומר את השבת מעלין עליו כאלו עשה
השבת שנאמר ושמרו בני ישראל את השבת לעשות
105 את השבת רבי אומר מנין אתה אומר שכל מי שהוא

81 שמות כ', ט'.   84 ישעיה ס"א, ה'.   89 דברים כ"ח, מ"ח.   90—96 ב"ב קכ"א, א'.
91—92 ויקרא כ"ג, ד'.

82 כשישראל] ד. אלא בזמן שישראל.   83 ששת ימים יעשה מלאכה] ד. >.   84 אחרים]
ד. ~ שנאמר תעשה מלאכה.   86—87 ששת ימים—כל מלאכתך] ד. >.   87 עצמן]
ד. ~ שנאמר ועשית כל מלאכתך.   88—89 אפילו מלאכת—שנאמר] ד. >.   90 וביום]
מ. ד. ויום / שבת שבתון קדש ליי] ד. שבת ליי אלהיך.   91 אלה] א. אלא.   92 אשר
תקראו אותם במועדם] הוספתי: א. מ. וגו' / יכול] א. מ. ק. >.   94 וביום] מ. ד.
ויום.   95 קדש ליי לשם] א. קדש לכם מ. קדש וגו' לשום ק. קדש לשום.   99—98 חלל
עליו] א. מ. פקוה עליו.   99 שישמור] מ. שיעשה.   100 רבי אליעזר] מ"ח. לעשות
את השבת לדורותם ברית עולם רבי אליעור.   101—100 לעשות את השבת—ברית
עולם] ד. > מ"ח. לעשות בשבת / לדורותם ברית עולם] הוספתי: א. וגו'.   102 מנין
אתה אומר] ד. >.

it is accounted to him as if he had observed all the Sabbaths from the day that God created His world to the time of the resurrection of the dead? It is said: "Wherefore the children of Israel shall keep the sabbath to observe the sabbath throughout their generations."

Between Me and the Children of Israel. But not between Me and the nations of the world.

It Is a Sign for Ever. This tells that the Sabbath will never be abolished in Israel. And so you find that anything to which the Israelites were devoted with their whole souls has been preserved among them. But anything to which the Israelites were not devoted with their whole souls has not been retained by them. Thus the Sabbath, circumcision, the study of the Torah, and the ritual of immersion,[8] for which the Israelites laid down their lives, have been retained by them. But such institutions as the Temple, civil courts, the sabbatical and jubilee years, to which the Israelites were not whole-heartedly devoted, have not been preserved among them.

For in Six Days . . . And on the Seventh Day He Ceased from Work and Rested. He ceased from the thought of work. Perhaps also from administering justice? It says: "and rested."[9] This tells that His administration of justice never stops. And thus it says: "Righteousness and justice are the foundation of Thy throne" (Ps. 89.15), "Clouds and darkness are round about Him, righteousness and justice," etc. (Ps. 97.2), "The Rock, His work is perfect, for all His ways are justice," etc. (Deut. 32.4).

---

8. I. e., the ritual bath which the Jewish woman takes after the completion of each period of menstruation.

9. "Resting" means merely ceasing from the work of creation, but not from administering justice (see Commentaries, esp. *Shebut Yehudah*).

משמר שבת אחת כתקנה מעלים עליו כאלו שימר
כל השבתות מיום שברא הקב"ה עולמו עד שיחיו
המתים שנאמר ושמרו בני ישראל את השבת לעשות
את השבת לדורותם.

ביני ובין בני ישראל ולא ביני ובין אומות   110
העולם.

אות היא לעולם מגיד שאין השבת בטלה
מישראל לעולם וכן את מוצא שכל דבר ודבר
שנתנו ישראל נפשן עליהן נתקיימו בידן וכל דבר
ודבר שלא נתנו ישראל נפשן עליהן לא נתקיימו   115
בידן כגון שבת והמילה ותלמוד תורה וטבילה
שנתנו נפשן עליהן נתקיימו בידן וכגון בית המקדש
והדינין והשמיטין ויובלות שלא נתנו ישראל נפשן
עליהן לא נתקיימו בידן.

כי ששת ימים וגו' **וביום השביעי שבת**   120
וינפש שבת ממחשבת עבודה או אף מן הדין
ת"ל וינפש מגיד שאין הדין בטל מלפניו לעולם
וכן הוא אומר צדק ומשפט מכון כסאך וגו' ענן
וערפל סביביו צדק ומשפט וגו' הצור תמים פעלו
כי כל דרכיו משפט וגו'.   125

---

125 — 120 ב"ר י"א, י'. ת. כי תשא ל"ג.   123 תהלים פ"ט, ט"ו.   124 — 123 שם צ"ז,
ב'.   125 — 124 דברים ל"ב, ד'.

---

107 — 106 שימר כל השבתות] הגהתי=ט. כ. (ישעיה נ"ו, ב') מ"ח: א. מ. ד. שומר
שבתות.   113 מישראל לעולם] ד. מישראל.   114 עליהן] ד. עליו כגון שבת ומילה
ותלמוד תורה וטבילה / נתקיימו בידן] ד. ~ ואין ניטלין כ. ~ ואין בטילין.   117 — 116 כגון
שבת — נתקיימו בידן] ד. <.   120 כי ששת — וביום השביעי] ד. <.   121 שבת ממחשבת
עבודה] ד. ממה שבת מן העבודה.   125 משפט וגו'] ק. נ. ~ חסלת מסכת נזיקין והיא
פרשת ואלה המשפטים עיין מאמרי הנ"ל צד 445.

CHAPTER II
(Ex. 35.1–3)

And Moses Gathered, etc. Why is this section set forth? Because it says: "And let them make Me a sanctuary." I might understand it to mean either on week-days or on the Sabbath. And to what am I to apply: "Everyone that profaneth it shall surely be put to death" (Ex. 31.14)? To all other kinds of work except work on the sanctuary. Perhaps however it applies even to work on the sanctuary. And how am I to maintain: "And let them make Me a sanctuary"? On all other days but on the Sabbath. Perhaps however it means even on the Sabbath. For the following argument might be advanced: If the Temple service, which can be carried out only by means of the preparations, sets aside the laws of the Sabbath, is it not logical that the preparations for the service, without which no service is possible, should set aside the laws of the Sabbath? I might therefore think that if the horn of the altar has broken off or if the knife became defective, it is permissible to repair these on the Sabbath. In setting forth in this section: "And Moses gathered," etc., Scripture teaches that even such work is to be done only on week-days but not on the Sabbath. *And Said unto Them: These Are the Words,* etc. Rabbi says: This includes the laws about the thirty-nine categories of work prohibited on the Sabbath which Moses gave them orally.[1]

Six Days Shall Work Be Done. One passage says: "Six days shall work be done," and another passage says: "Six days shalt thou labour and do all thy work" (Ex. 20.9). How can both these passages be maintained? When the Israelites do the will of God, then: "Six days shall work be done." Their work is done for them by others. And thus it says: "And strangers shall stand and feed your flocks, and aliens shall be your plowmen and your vinedressers" (Isa. 61.5). But when the Israelites do not do the will of God, then: "Six days shalt

1. See M. Shab. 7.2, and cf. Shab. 97b.

פרשה ב (שמות ל"ה, א'–ג'.)

ויקהל משה וגו' למה נאמרה פרשה זו לפי
שהוא אומר ועשו לי מקדש שומע אני בין בחול
בין בשבת ומה אני מקיים מחלליה מות יומת בשאר
כל מלאכות חוץ ממלאכת המשכן או אפילו
במלאכת המשכן ומה אני מקיים ועשו לי מקדש
בשאר כל הימים חוץ מן השבת או אף בשבת והדין
נותן ומה עבודה שאינה באה אלא מכח המכשירין
הרי היא דוחה את השבת מכשירי עבודה שאין עבודה
באה אלא אלא מכוחן דין הוא שידחו את השבת כגון
שנטלה קרנו של מזבח או שנפגמה הסכין שומע אני
יתקנם בשבת ת"ל ויקהל משה בחול ולא בשבת.
ויאמר אליהם אלה הדברים וגו' רבי
אומר להביא שלשים ותשע אבות המלאכות שאמר
להם משה על פה.

ששת ימים תעשה מלאכה כתוב אחד
אומר ששת ימים תעשה מלאכה וכתוב אחד אומר
ששת ימים תעבד וגו' כיצד יתקיימו שני כתובים
כשישראל עושין רצונו של מקום ששת ימים תעשה
מלאכה מלאכתן נעשית על ידי אחרים וכן הוא
אומר ובני נכר אכריכם וכרמיכם וכשאין ישראל
עושין רצונו של מקום ששת ימים תעבד וגו' מלאכתן

1–40 ש. 166–165. 2 שמות ב"ה, י'. 3 שם ל"א, י"ד. 14–12 שבת צ"ז, ב'. י' שם ז', ב' (9b). 23–15 לעיל א'. 17 שמות כ', ט'. 20 ישעיה ס"א, ה'.

פרשה ב'] ד. פרשת ויקהל. 1 פרשה זו] א. >. 5–4 או אפילו במלאכת המשכן]
הגהתי=ש"י. ט. (הוצאות מאוחרות) ומ"א: א"צ. או אינו אפילו בעשיית המשכן
א. במלאכת המשכן. 6 או אף בשבת] מ. והשבת. 9–8 שאין עבודה באה] ק. שאין
להם נ. ל. שאין באה. 10 שנטלה קרנו של מזבח] מ"ח. אם ניטלה אבן מן המזבח.
11 ת"ל] ק. שנאמר מ"ח. לכך נאמר. 13 אבות] ד. >. 17 כיצד יתקיימו שני כתובים]
ד. >. 19–18 ששת–מלאכה] ד. >. 20–19 וכן הוא אומר–וכרמיכם] ד. >.
21 ששת ימים תעבד וגו'] ד. >.

thou labour and do all thy work." They themselves must do their work. And not only this but even the work of others is done by them, as it is said: "Thou shalt serve thine enemy," etc. (Deut. 28.48).

But on the Seventh Day There Shall Be to You a Holy Day. Lest the Israelites say: Since work is permitted to be done on the Sabbath within the Sanctuary it should also be permitted outside of the Sanctuary. Therefore Scripture says: "But on the seventh day there shall be to you a holy day." To you it shall be a holy day. To God[2] however it is like a profane day.

Whosoever Doeth Any Work on It Shall Be Put to Death. If he does the work "on it," but not if he does it on it and on its neighboring day.[3] But suppose the Day of Atonement happens to fall on Friday[4] and one does work on Friday at twilight. I might understand that in this case one should be guilty. Therefore Scripture says: "Whosoever doeth any work on it shall be put to death"—for work done "on it," but not for work done on it and on its neighboring day.

Ye Shall Kindle No Fire, etc. Since it says: "In plowing time and in harvest thou shalt rest" (Ex. 34.21), which means: Refrain from plowing in the harvest time, that is, that one must refrain from plowing in the sixth year for the sabbatical year, I only know that already on the sixth year one must rest from work which is done for the sabbatical year. But one might think that in like manner a person should rest on Friday from work done for the Sabbath. And the following argument might be advanced: The sabbatical year is observed in the name of God, and the Sabbath day is also observed in the name of God. Now, since you have proved that one must rest during the sixth year from work for the seventh, it follows also that one should rest on Friday from work for the Sabbath. And furthermore, by using the

2. I. e., as regards the service of God in the Temple.
3. I. e., at twilight of the evening of Friday or of Saturday.
4. In the fixed calendar of later times the Day of Atonement never falls on a Friday, or a Sunday.

נעשית על ידי עצמן ולא עוד אלא ועבדת את
אויביך וגו'.

וביום השביעי יהיה לכם קדש וגו'
25 שלא יהו ישראל אומרים הואיל ומותרים בעשיית
מלאכה בבית המקדש נהא מותרין לעשות מלאכה
בגבולין ת״ל וביום השביעי יהיה לכם קדש לכם
קדש ולמקום חול.

כל העושה בו מלאכה יומת בו ולא בו
30 ובחברו והרי שחל יום הכפורים להיות בערב
שבת ועשה מלאכה בין השמשות שומע אני יהא
חייב ת״ל כל העושה בו מלאכה יומת בו ולא בו
ובחברו.

לא תבערו אש וגו' לפי שהוא אומר בחריש
35 ובקציר תשבות שבות מן החריש בשעת הקציר
שישבות מערב שביעית לשביעית אין לי אלא שהוא
שובת מערב שביעית לשביעית יכול כן ישבות
מערב שבת לשבת והדין נותן הואיל ושביעית לשום
השם ושבת לשום השם אם למדת שהוא שובת מערב
40 שביעית לשביעית כך ישבות מערב שבת לשבת

35—34 שמות ל״ד, כ״א.   49—34 ר״ה ט', א'.

23—22 ולא עוד אלא—וגו'] ד. ‹.   25 ומותרים] א. מ. ט. ואנו מותרים.   26 לעשות
מלאכה] ד. ‹.   27 יהיה לכם קדש] א. וגו' ד. יהיה.   29 בו ולא בו] ד. ולא בו.
37—38 יכול כן—לשבת] ד. יכול כן ישבות מערב שבת לערב שבת מ״ח. ר' אברהם
בן הרמב״ם ספר מעשה נסים (הוצאת ב״ג. פאריש תרכ״ז) צד 89, מערב שבת לשבת
מנין.   40—38 והדין נותן—מערב שבת לשבת] ד. ‹.

method of *kal vahomer,* one could reason: If in the case of the sabbatical year, for the disregard of which one does not incur the penalty of extinction or of death at the hands of the human court, one must begin already on the sixth year to rest from work for the seventh, it is but logical that in the case of the Sabbath, for the disregard of which one incurs the penalty of extinction or of death at the hands of the human court,[5] one should already on Friday rest from work done for the Sabbath. In other words, or to be specific,[6] one should not be permitted on Friday to light a candle, or to put away things to be kept warm, or to make a fire, for the Sabbath. Therefore Scripture says: "Ye shall kindle no fire in your dwelling-places on the sabbath day." On the sabbath day itself you may not kindle a fire, but you may on Friday kindle a fire for the Sabbath. Another Interpretation: *Ye Shall Kindle No Fire in Your Dwelling-Place on the Sabbath Day.* Since it is said: "Fire shall be kept burning upon the altar continually" (Lev. 6.6), I understand this to mean both on week-days and on the Sabbath. And how am I to maintain: "Everyone that profaneth it shall surely be put to death" (Ex. 31.14)? By applying it to all other works except the arrangement for the fire on the altar. But it could be argued that it applies also to the arrangement for the fire on the altar. And how am I to maintain: "It shall not go out" (Lev. 6.6)? On all other days except the Sabbath. Scripture therefore says: "Ye shall kindle no fire in your dwelling-places." In your dwelling-places you may not kindle a fire, but you may kindle it in the Sanctuary. Said one of the disciples of R. Ishmael: Behold it says: *Ye Shall Kindle No Fire,* etc. Why is this said? Because it says: "And if a man have committed a sin worthy of death," etc.[7] (Deut. 21.22–23). I might understand that

5. I. e., if the violation of the Sabbath is committed presumptuously and in despite of the warning of witnesses.

6. The term אוֹ, "or," is here used in this sense.

7. The law there prescribes that the sinner be put to death and then be hung upon a tree. The execution involves work which would constitute a violation of the Sabbath.

ועוד קל וחומר מה אם שביעית שאין חייבין
עליה לא כרת ולא מיתת בית דין הרי הוא
שובת מערב שביעית לשביעית שבת שחייבין עליה
כרת ומיתת בית דין דין הוא שישבות מערב
שבת לשבת או לא יהיה רשאי להדליק לו את
הנר ולהטמין לו את החמין ולעשות לו מדורה
ת"ל לא תבערו אש בכל מושבותיכם ביום השבת
ביום השבת אין אתה מבעיר אבל אתה מבעיר
מערב שבת לשבת דבר אחר לא תבערו אש בכל
מושבותיכם ביום השבת לפי שנאמר אש תמיד
תוקד וגומר שומע אני בין בחול בין בשבת ומה
אני מקיים מחלליה מות יומת בשאר כל המלאכות
חוץ מן המערכה או אף במערכה ומה אני מקיים
לא תכבה בשאר כל הימים חוץ מן השבת ת"ל
לא תבערו אש בכל מושבותיכם במושבות אין אתה
מבער אבל מבער אתה בבית המקדש. אמר אחד
מתלמידי רבי ישמעאל הרי הוא אומר לא תבערו
אש וגו' למה נאמר לפי שהוא אומר וכי יהיה באיש

49—56 שבת כ', א'.   50—51 ויקרא ו', ו'.   52 שמות ל"א, י"ד.   66—56 יבמות ו',
ב'. סנהדרין ל"ה, ב'.   59—58 דברים כ"א, כ"ב.

45 או לא יהיה] הגהתי=ט. ז"י. ש"י. ומא"ש: מ"ח. ולא יהיה א. מ. ד. או יהיה.
49 לשבת] א. לערב שבת.   53 או אף במערכה] הגהתי=ש"י: א. מ. ובמערכה ד. >
ט. א"א. מ"ח. או אינו אלא אף (מ"ח. אפילו) במערכה.   55 במושבות] ד. >.
56 בבית המקדש] מ"ח. ~ במערכה.

this applies both to week-days and to the Sabbath. And how am I to maintain: "Everyone that profaneth it shall surely be put to death" (Ex. 31.14)? By applying it to all other cases of death[8] except that decreed by the court. Perhaps it is not so, but it applies even to deaths decreed by court? And I am to interpret: "And thou hang him on a tree," to mean only on all other days but the Sabbath? Perhaps however it means even on the Sabbath? Therefore Scripture says: "Ye shall kindle no fire," etc. And you reason: Burning was included in the general category of work prohibited on the Sabbath and it has been singled out for special mention to teach that just as in the case of "burning," specifically mentioned, which is one of the modes of death decreed by the court, the Sabbath laws are not to be superseded, so also in the case of all the other modes of death decreed by the court, the Sabbath laws are not to be superseded.

R. Jonathan says: *Ye Shall Kindle No Fire.* Why is this said? Since it says: "And Moses gathered," etc. (Ex. 35.1), I might understand that one can become guilty only by transgressing all the laws against the thirty-nine categories of work prohibited on the Sabbath. But Scripture says: "In plowing time and in harvest thou shalt rest"[9] (Ex. 34.21). But I might still say that one becomes guilty only by transgressing at least two laws,[10] but by transgressing less than two one is not guilty. Therefore it says: "Ye shall not kindle any fire." And you reason: "Kindling" has been included in the general category of work prohibited on the Sabbath. And it has been singled out for special mention merely to teach: Just as in the case of the specifically mentioned kindling, which is one of the thirty-nine categories of prohibited work, one becomes guilty by doing it by itself, so also in the case

8. See Commentaries. The reading מלאכות, "kinds of work," instead of מיתות, "kinds of death," would seem preferable.

9. This is interpreted to mean, thou shalt rest from plowing and harvesting, thus showing that by doing these kinds of work alone one already violates the commandment to rest.

10. Like "plowing" and "harvesting."

חטא משפט מות וגו' שומע אני בין בחול בין בשבת

60 ומה אני מקיים מחלליה מות יומת בשאר כל המיתות

חוץ ממיתת בית דין או אינו אפילו במיתת בית דין

ומה אני מקיים ותלית אותו על עץ בשאר כל הימים

חוץ מן השבת או אף בשבת ת"ל לא תבערו אש

וגו' שריפה היתה בכלל ויצאת ללמד מה שריפה

65 שהיא אחת ממיתות בית דין אינה דוחה את השבת

אף כל שאר מיתות בית דין לא ידחו את השבת

רבי יונתן אומר לא תבערו אש למה נאמר לפי

שהוא אומר ויקהל משה וגו' שומע אני לא יהא חייב

עד שיעבור על שלשים ותשע אבות המלאכות ת"ל

70 בחריש ובקציר תשבות ועדיין אני אומר עד

שיעבור על שתים ואם לאו אינו חייב ת"ל לא

תבערו הבערה היתה בכלל ויצאת ללמד אלא

מה הבערה מיוחדת שהיא אחת משלשים ותשע

אבות המלאכות חייבין עליה בפני עצמה אף כל

62 שם.   76—67 שבת ע', א'.   70 שמות ל"ד, כ"א.

___

60 כל המיתות] מ"ח. מלאכות א"צ. כל המלאכות.   61 או אינו אפילו] א. מ. ק. >
/ במיתת בית דין] א. ובמיתת בית דין שאינו דין.   63 או אף בשבת] הגהתי=ט: ד.
< א. מ. ובשבת מ"ח. או אינו אלא אפילו בשבת.   64 וגו'—ללמד] מ"ח. בכל
מושבותיכם ולהלן הוא אומר והיו אלה לחקת משפט בכל מושבותיכם מה להלן
בבית דין אף כאן כאן בבית דין / מה שריפה] א. מ. אלא מה שריפה מ"ח. ומה שריפה.
65 שהיא] מ. מ"ח. מיוחדת שהיא.   67 יונתן] מ"ח. נתן.   70 ועדיין אני אומר]
הוספתי=ט. מ"ח. א"א.

of all the other thirty-nine categories of work it is but logical that one should become guilty by doing each one of them by itself. R. Nathan says: *Ye Shall Kindle No Fire,* etc. Why is this said? Because it says: "And Moses gathered the whole congregation of Israel," etc. I might understand this to mean that one should not be allowed even on Friday to light a candle, or to put away the things to be kept warm, or to make a fire, for the Sabbath. Therefore it says: "Ye shall kindle no fire in your dwelling-places on the sabbath day."[11] Only on the Sabbath day you shall not kindle any fire. You may however kindle a fire on the day of a festival.

11. There is something missing here. Possibly the words: "On the Sabbath day," forming a caption for the following comment, have been omitted by the mistake of a copyist (see Commentaries).

75 שאר שלשים ותשע אבות המלאכות דין הוא שיהא

חייב על כל אחת ואחת בפני עצמה רבי נתן אומר

לא תבערו אש וגו' למה נאמר לפי שהוא אומר

ויקהל משה את כל עדת בני ישראל וגו' שומע אני

לא יהא רשאי להדליק לו את הנר ולהטמין לו

80 את החמין ולעשות לו מדורה ת"ל לא תבערו אש

בכל מושבותיכם ביום השבת ביום השבת אין אתה

מבעיר אבל אתה מבעיר ביום טוב.

חסלת מכילתא לאלהא שמיא תושבחתא

ואית בה מסכתות תשעה ואילן אינון סימניהון

85 **ואמר פרעה למשה ונטל עמלק בירחא**

למידן כספא דשבתא ואית בה פרשיות

שמונים ושתים.

---

82 — 81 י' ביצה ה', ב' (63[b]).

76 — 75 דין הוא—בפני עצמה] ד. חייב עליה בפני עצמה.   76 נתן] א"צ. יונתן.
78 ויקהל משה—וגו'] א"צ. מועדי יי וגומר.   79 לא יהא רשאי] הגהתי=א"א. א"צ:
ט. אינו רשאי א. מ. ד. יהיה רשאי. עיין ש"י.   87 — 84 עיין מאמרי הנ"ל.

INDICES

INDEX I

Lists scriptural passages cited or referred to in the text and in the apparatus criticus.

Opposite the reference to each verse is given the tractate, chapter and line of the Hebrew text of the *Mekhilta* in which the verse is cited or referred to. The roman numerals refer to the chapter of the tractate, the arabic numerals to the line within the chapter. A little circle like this ° alongside the reference to the verse indicates that the verse is cited not in the text proper but in the apparatus criticus. An asterisk * alongside the numeral referring to the line indicates that in the quotation of the verse by the *Mekhilta,* or in at least one of the variants given in the apparatus criticus, the reading is slightly different from that of the masoretic text.

Numbers

Joshua

Judges

INDEX II

This is a list of the teachers and other persons or groups of persons who were the authors of the sayings or participated in the discussions and contributed to the teachings contained in the *Mekhilta*. These persons are mentioned in the *Mekhilta* either by their respective proper names or by some characterizing designation, such as "Disciple" or "Philosopher," or are referred to as a class, like "Elders," זקנים; Allegorists; "Our teachers," רבותינו; or "Wise men," חכמים. Sometimes they are left in utter obscurity as far as their persons are concerned, and their teachings or sayings are recorded merely as "Another Interpretation," thus indicating that the teachings originated in sources or with persons other than those previously mentioned in the context. Sometimes they are referred to anonymously as "Others say," אחרים אומרים, or "Some say," יש אומרים, or simply "They say," or "They said," אמרו. The latter phrase may in some instances mean simply "People say" and refer to a popular legend or tradition. But in most cases it is merely the short form for אמרו חכמים, "The wise men said," and refers to the teachers. Among the sayings thus ascribed to the wise men, or teachers, there is a large group introduced by the formula, "In connection with this" or "On the basis of this, they," i.e. the teachers, "said," or "Hence they said," מכאן אמרו. Some of the sayings thus cited in the *Mekhilta* are indeed found in the Mishna or *Tosefta* (comp. Bacher, *Tradition und Tradenten,* Leipzig 1914, pp. 171–192), and those not found in any other tannaitic work preserved to us may have been, or most likely were, found in some older tannaitic work known to the redactor of the *Mekhilta* though no longer extant. This group of sayings may thus be regarded as a group of quotations by the *Mekhilta* from other works. Therefore these sayings have been singled out as a special class and arranged in this index under the heading: "Hence they said."

This index also lists all the stories and incidents or events related in the *Mekhilta*, whether told without any introductory formula or introduced by the heading מעשה "an event," or כבר היה, "It happened once," as well as all the parables found in the *Mekhilta*, whether introduced by the heading משל, "a parable," or merely by the phrase: "To what is [was] this comparable."

Since the purpose of this index is to group together the references to the different authors, originators or sources of the various sayings and teachings found scattered throughout the *Mekhilta,* the variants of the names of these authors and sources, as given in the apparatus criticus, also had to be included in the list. However, to distinguish the latter from the names found in the text proper, a little circle like this ° is added to the number of the line to which the apparatus criticus citing the variant refers.

In listing those teachers who are mentioned by more than one name or whose names occur in different forms, the following rules have been observed. Of course, when the different names or different forms of the name do or may designate different persons, as in the case of Eliezer and Eleazar, each name or form is listed separately. But where there can be no doubt as to the identity of the person designated by both names, the different forms of the name being merely different ways of spelling it, then the name is listed under the form more frequently found in the *Mekhilta* and the other form of the name is merely cited, with a cross reference to the one adopted for the listing, as in the case of Ḥananiah and Ḥanina, or Issi b. Akiba and Issi b. Akabyah, and the like. The same is also done in the case of those teachers who are sometimes mentioned by their names alone and sometimes by their names together with their fathers' names, like Jose b. Ḥalafta, Judah b. Il'ai and Simon b. Yoḥai; the form of the name more frequently used in the *Mekhilta* is adopted in this list and the other merely mentioned with a cross reference to the one adopted. In the case of Judah Ha-Nasi and Rabbi; Judah b. Bathyra and Ben Bathyra; and Simon b. Azzai and Ben Azzai, the different forms of the names are listed separately, but in each case reference is also given to the instances grouped under the other form in the list.

Roman numerals refer to chapters, arabic numerals to lines.

Judah b. Bathyra: Pisḥa V, 55; VIII,
79°; XIII, 4; XVI, 129; XVII, 78;
Beshallaḥ IV, 23; VIII, 9; Nezikin
X, 80; XI, 49; XVII, 63; Kaspa I,
72; II, 140; III, 104; IV, 48;
Shabbata I, 60.
Judah b. Il'ai: see Judah.
Judah b. Lakish: Baḥodesh I, 61.
Judah b. Tabbai: Kaspa III,
32, 35, 37.
Judah Ha-Nasi: Amalek I, 26; IV,
171; see also Rabbi.
Judah of Kefar Akko: Amalek IV, 16.

LEVI HA-SADOR: Shabbata I, 8.

MATIAH B. ḤERESH: Pisḥa V, 3;
Baḥodesh VII, 18.
Meir: Pisḥa II, 44; Beshallaḥ III, 138,
140°; IV, 9, 50°; VI, 1, 2; Shirata I,
148; Baḥodesh X, 32; Nezikin II,
73, 74, 81°; X, 115, 117°; 127,
129°; XII, 25, 67; XIV, 62; XV,
87°; Kaspa I, 37°, 38; IV, 4.
Men of the Great Synagogue: Pisḥa
VI, 37.

NATHAN: Pisḥa I, 103; II, 28, 48°,
59°; IV, 29°; V, 23, 98°, 121; VI,
11°; VII, 55; XIII, 51, 118, 138;
XIV, 34°; XV, 10°, 124; XVI, 102,
119, 160°, 164; XVII, 26°, 134;
Beshallaḥ I, 102, 153; IV, 64; V,
31; VII, 25, 39°; Vayassa' I, 112;
Amalek I, 29; II, 160; IV, 114,
125; Baḥodesh V, 33; VI, 127,
136; VII, 69°; IX, 22, 125; X, 4;
XI, 4, 67; Nezikin II, 12; III,

138°, 164; VI, 28; VII, 59; XIV,
17; XV, 7; XVI, 35; XVIII, 8;
Kaspa I, 53, 113; II, 59; III, 13,
62, 67°; IV, 19; Shabbata I, 28, 98;
II, 67°, 78.
Nehemiah: Pisḥa XIV, 21; Beshallaḥ
VI, 132; VII, 46, 134; Shirata I,
87; Vayassa' VII, 34; Amalek III,
113; Baḥodesh X, 52.
Nehorai: Pisḥa XII, 81;
Beshallaḥ I, 76.

OSHAYA: Pisḥa I, 125°;
Vayassa' VII, 19°.
Others say: Beshallaḥ IV, 82; Vayassa'
I, 69, 129, 183; IV, 29; VI, 40;
Amalek I, 13, 31, 55, 175; II, 70;
Nezikin XVI, 94.

PAPPIAS: Beshallaḥ VII, 58, 63, 67, 70,
73, 74, 78, 80; Amalek III, 192.
Pappius: Beshallaḥ VII, 58°.
Pappus: Beshallaḥ VII, 58°.
Parable: Pisḥa I, 82; XVI, 65, 68;
Beshallaḥ II, 110, 143, 149; III,
86; IV, 36; V, 16, 60; VI, 8; VII, 28;
Shirata II, 130; III, 32, 65, 80; VII,
57; IX, 20; X, 43; Amalek II, 22;
Baḥodesh II, 31; V, 2, 83; VI, 2,
113; VII, 65; Nezikin XIII, 81.
Philosopher: Baḥodesh VI, 103.
Phinehas: Beshallaḥ VII, 58°.
Pius: Beshallaḥ VII, 58°.

RABBENU HA-GADOL: Vayassa' I, 58.
Rabbenu ha-Kadosh:
Shirata II, 127; VI, 100.
Rabbi: Pisḥa I, 17; IV, 54; V, 117; VI,

---

1. Here mentioned merely as R. Simon, without his father's name.

INDEX III

This contains proper names of persons and places mentioned in the *Mekhilta*. The list of the names of persons contains both names of biblical persons—when mentioned in the comments of the *Mekhilta*, but not when they form part of a biblical quotation—as well as of non-biblical persons. The latter are marked by a little circle like this °. The list of the names of places contains only such names as are not found in the Bible. An asterisk * alongside the number of the line indicates that the reference is not to the text proper but to the apparatus criticus referring to that line.

Roman numerals refer to chapters, arabic numerals to lines.